For Reference

Not to be taken from this room

Date: 11/14/13

REF 737.4973 USC 2014
U.S. coin digest : the complete guide to current market values

2014

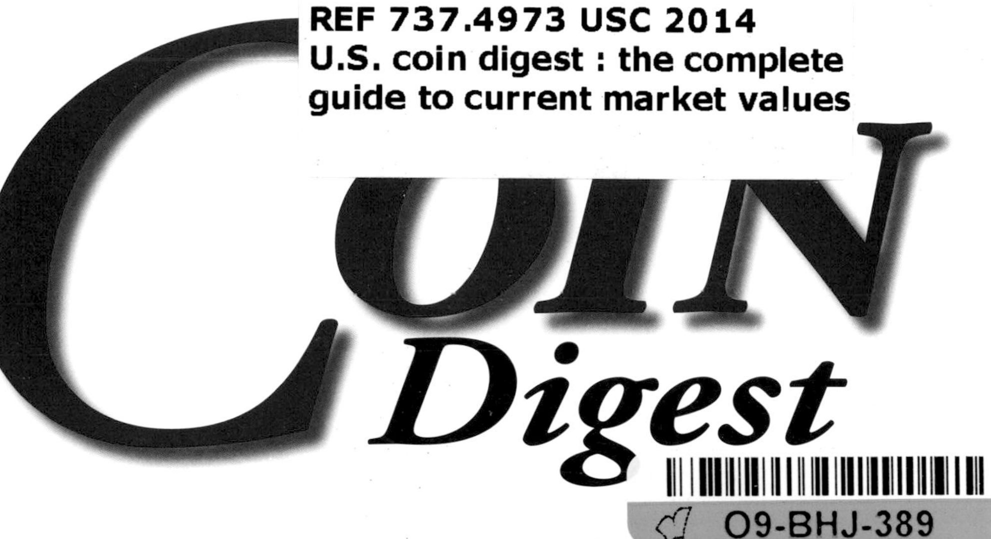

O9-BHJ-389

The Complete Guide to Current Market Values

PALM BEACH COUNTY
LIBRARY SYSTEM
3650 Summit Boulevard
West Palm Beach, FL 33406-4198

David C. Harper, Editor
Harry Miller, Market Analyst

Copyright ©2013 F+W Media, Inc.

All rights reserved. No portion of this publication may be reproduced or transmitted in any form or by any means, electronic or mechanical, including photocopy, recording, or any information storage and retrieval system, without permission in writing from the publisher, except by a reviewer who may quote brief passages in a critical article or review to be printed in a magazine or newspaper, or electronically transmitted on radio, television, or the Internet.

Published by

Krause Publications, a division of F+W Media, Inc.
700 East State Street • Iola, WI 54990-0001
715-445-2214 • 888-457-2873
www.krausebooks.com

To order books or other products call toll-free 1-800-258-0929
or visit us online at www.shopnumismaster.com

ISSN 1544-8517
ISBN-13: 978-1-4402-3569-6
ISBN-10: 1-4402-3569-4

Cover Design by Kevin Ulrich
Designed by Sandi Carpenter
Edited by George Cuhaj

Printed in China

Contents

Preface

Since 1952, Krause Publications has built its business and reputation by serving the needs of coin collectors. Three questions dominate every collector's thinking.

The first is: "What is it?" We hope the photographs in this price guide will help you identify the coins you own.

The second question is: "What's it worth?" The prices contained in this volume are intended to serve as a retail guide. That means if you want to buy a specific coin in a specific grade, the price listed will be approximately what you would have to pay at the time this book was compiled. The prices listed are neither an offer to buy nor an offer to sell the coins listed. They are simply a guide assembled for your convenience by the authors. Remember that prices fluctuate. What dealers will pay to buy coins from you is a question beyond the scope of this book.

The third question is: "How do I buy a specific coin?" There are several thousand coin dealers across America who are ready, willing and able to serve your needs. To find them, you can consult the phone book in your local area, but beyond that, there is a whole hobby world out there and newspapers and magazines that feature advertisements by dealers who want to fill your needs. For more information on numismatic products and pricing go to www.numismaster.com.

Photo Credits

We wish to thank the following auction houses and individuals for the fabulous color images contained within these pages.

Mike Locke **Jay M. Galst, M.D.** **Chester L. Krause**

Heritage Numismatic Auctions, Inc.
www.HeritageCoins.com

Stack's
www.stacks.com

Ken Potter
www.koinpro.com

Professional Coin Grading Service
www.pcgs.com

Introduction

The authors have organized this book in a manner that we hope you will find both logical and useful.

Value listings

Values listed in the price guide are average retail prices. These are the approximate prices collectors can expect to pay when purchasing coins from dealers. They are not offers to buy or sell. The pricing section should be considered a guide only; actual selling prices will vary.

The values were compiled by Krause Publications' independent staff of market analysts. They derived the values listed by monitoring auction results, business on electronic dealer trading networks and at major shows, and in consultation with a panel of dealers. For rare coins, when only a few specimens of a particular date and mintmark are known, a confirmed transaction may occur only once every several years. In those instances, the most recent auction result is listed.

Grading

Values are listed for coins in various states of preservation, or grades. Standards used in determining grade for U.S. coins are those set by the American Numismatic Association (www.money.org). See Chapter 3 for more on grading.

Precious metal content

Throughout this book precious metal content is indicated in troy ounces. One troy ounce equals 480 grains, or 31.103 grams. This is followed by ASW or AGW, which stand for Actual Silver (Gold) Weight.

Dates and mintmarks

The dates listed are the individual dates that appear on each coin. The letter that follows the date is the mintmark and indicates where the coin was struck: "C" – Charlotte, N.C. (1838-1861); "CC" – Carson City, Nev. (1870-1893); "D" – Dahlonega, Ga. (1838-1861), and Denver (1906-present); "O" – New Orleans (1838-1909); "P" – Philadelphia (1793-present), coins without mintmarks also were struck at Philadelphia; "S" – San Francisco (1854-present); and "W" – West Point, N.Y. (1984-present).

A slash mark in a date indicates an overdate. This means a new date was engraved on a die over an old date. For example, if the date is listed as "1899/8," an 1898 die had a 9 engraved over the last 8 in the date. Portions of the old numeral are still visible on the coin.

A slash mark in a mintmark listing indicates an overmintmark (example: "1922-P/D"). The same process as above occurred, but this time a new mintmark was engraved over an old.

See Chapter 8, "U.S. Minting Varieties and Errors," for more information on overdates and overmintmarks.

1 Type Identification Guide

United States coins are often given nicknames based on their obverse design. This Type Identification Guide is a start for coin identification. It also shows the changes in the sizes of various denominations over time.

Half Cent

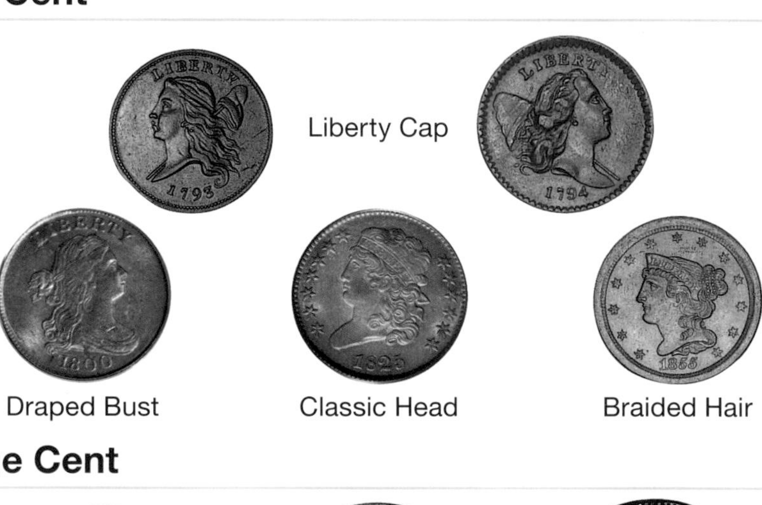

Liberty Cap

Draped Bust Classic Head Braided Hair

Large Cent

Liberty Cap Draped Bust Classic Head

Coronet Braided Hair Flowing Hair

Small Cent

Flying Eagle

Indian Head

Lincoln

Shield

Silver 3 Cents

Coronet

Half Dime

Flowing Hair

Draped Bust

Liberty Cap

Seated Liberty

Nickel

Shield

Liberty

Buffalo

Jefferson

Jefferson
large profile

Jefferson
large facing portrait

Dime

Draped Bust

Liberty Cap

Seated Liberty

Barber

Mercury

Roosevelt

Twenty Cents

Seated Liberty within circle of stars

Quarter

Draped Bust

Liberty Cap

Seated Liberty

Barber

Standing Liberty

Washington

50 State

Half Dollar

Flowing Hair

Draped Bust

Capped Bust

Seated Liberty

Barber

Walking Liberty

Franklin

Kennedy

Dollar

Flowing Hair

Gobrecht

Draped Bust

Seated Liberty

Morgan

Trade

Peace

Eisenhower

Dollar

Susan B. Anthony

Sacagawea

Liberty Head - Type 1

Indian Head - Type 2

Indian Head - Type 3

$2.50 Gold Quarter Eagle

Liberty Cap

Turban Head

Coronet Head

Indian Head

$3.00 Gold

Indian Head with headress

$5.00 Gold Half Eagle

Liberty Cap

Turban Head

Indian Head

Classic Head

Coronet Head

$10.00 Gold Eagle

Liberty Cap

Coronet Head

Indian Head

$20.00 Gold Double Eagle

Coronet Head

Saint-Gaudens

2 Care and Storage of Your Coins

Use caution to retain coin's value

Once you find a coin you love, or begin to build a collection that you are dedicating time and money to, you really need to consider proper care and storage methods. Careless handling of your coins can quickly lead to loss of value.

Here is some quick and simple advice, which you should always follow when handling your coins:

- Always hold your coin by the edge.
- Never touch your coin on its large surfaces.

You leave fingerprints on surfaces that you touch and fingerprints on coins cause long-term damage which degrades the quality of your coin. If you are not comfortable handling your coins, it is best to wear special gloves available through coin supply dealers and to do your work over a jeweler's tray for your coins safety.

Another quick and simple bit of advice regarding cleaning your coins:

- Don't clean coins.

Some coins you acquire may seem dirty to you and an early impulse may be to clean them. Many inexperienced collectors degrade or even destroy their coins value through cleaning. Most cleaning methods are abrasive and remove not only the dirt, but also the metal surface of the coin. In most instances you will damage your coins value by attempting to clean them, so don't.

Most collectors enjoy examining the coins they have acquired and some collectors concentrate on finding varieties. Close examination requires magnification. The following instruments are commonly used to examine coins more closely:

- Magnifying glass
- Jeweler's loupe
- Microscope

Magnifiers come in different strengths and all shapes and sizes. Most coin collectors find a 5x magnifying glass quite versatile for checking out a coin's surface for wear. When looking for varieties, a 10x loupe works pretty well. For a closer look, many specialists use a 10x to 60x adjustable microscope. Each of these tools has its proper use and appropriate cost. Start simple with a nice 5x magnifier and see how it works for you.

Spend a little time at a coin show or in a coin shop and you will see that there are many different methods of storing your coins. The simplest are coin envelopes, which are produced in various colors of paper and are usually 2-inch by 2-inch in size. Information can be written on these holders, the coin inserted and the flap tucked in so that the coin does not easily fall out if the envelope is tipped or dropped. If you use coin envelopes, it is best to stick with plain white paper, as colored paper will tone your coin over time. When writing information on the envelope, do so before you insert the coin and use a ball-point pen or pencil, as a felt-tip marker may bleed through and harm your coin.

For standard sized U.S. coins, coin boards have been used for many years as a simple cataloging and storage method for beginning collectors. Coin boards provide several useful services. Coin boards:

- Organize your collection.
- Focus your attention on a single type of coin.
- Offer a cheap method of storage.

Sounds pretty good? Yes, for common circulating coins, the coin board is a great way to get started. However, there are drawbacks to this system that you may notice over time. You may find that it is difficult to insert your coins in the board and to get them to stay put. Because of this, you may find that you are handling your coins too much. If you don't place a soft cloth over the coin before you push it into the board, you will leave a fingerprint on the coin's surface. Over time you will notice that material from which the board was manufactured may have added a color tint to your coins. This is called toning. Some collectors like toning and some do not, so toning may hamper or help in your collection's appreciation over time.

If you like the display feature of boards, but do not care for some of these drawbacks, you can consider using any number of the vast array of containment storage methods available. There are hard plastic holders, tight plastic capsules, plastic envelopes called flips, and die-cut cardboard holders with Mylar lining. The last three of these can be inserted in pocket sheets for three ring binder display or simply placed into special coin boxes for storage.

The simplest and most widely used of these individual storage methods is the die cut cardboard holder with Mylar lining. These holders come in different size die cuts. To use this type of holder, follow these simple steps:

- Choose a die cut that is slightly larger than your coin.
- Place your coin on the Mylar over the die cut hole.
- Carefully fold the top over your coin.
- Grasp the holder and coin between your thumb and forefinger.
- Carefully staple the three open sides of the holder to secure your coin.
- Flatten the staples with a set of pliers.

Once this process is complete, you can write information on the outer edges of the cardboard to catalog, value and grade or otherwise identify the attributes of your coin.

Plastic flip envelopes are made from different materials. There are soft plastic types and hard plastic types. The soft plastic should only be used for short term storage. Soft plastic flips contain polyvinylchloride or PVC which, over time, can cause serious damage to your coins in the form of a green corrosive slime which eats away at the coin's surface. The hard plastic is normally made from Mylar, which does not contain PVC, but does get brittle and can crack as it ages. Both types of flips are constructed with two pockets, one for your coin and one for a small, square piece of paper or thin cardboard on which you can write your coin's catalog information.

The storage methods mentioned above are good for low to medium value coins. If your collecting advances into coins of higher value, you may want to consider a third party grading service. These services will grade and encapsulate your coin in an airtight hard plastic holder containing both your coin and coin information.

Use your common sense in choosing appropriate methods of care and storage for maintaining your coins. Here are a few more basic rules to remember:

- Keep you coins in a cool, dry place.
- Make sure your coins are secure from tampering or theft.
- Do not store your coins in a leather pouch or bag.
- Do not allow you coins to knock or slide against each other.
- Put your coins in some sort of holder that protects them.
- Be sure that your choice of holder does not cause damage to your coins.
- Examine your coins regularly and check for any changes.

Your collection can provide you with both an enjoyable hobby and a valuable investment, but it is your responsibility to organize, store, care for and maintain your coins properly.

How to Grade

Better condition equals better value

Grading is one of the most important factors in buying and selling coins as collectibles. Unfortunately, it's also one of the most controversial. Since the early days of coin collecting in the United States, buying through the mail has been a convenient way for collectors to acquire coins. As a result, there has always been a need in numismatics for a concise way to classify the amount of wear on a coin and its condition in general.

A look back

In September 1888, Dr. George Heath, a physician in Monroe, Mich., published a four-page pamphlet titled *The American Numismatist*. Publication of subsequent issues led to the founding of the American Numismatic Association, and *The Numismatist*, as it's known today, is the association's official journal. Heath's first issues were largely devoted to selling world coins from his collection. There were no formal grades listed with the coins and their prices, but the following statement by Heath indicates that condition was a consideration for early collectors:

"The coins are in above average condition," Heath wrote, "and so confident am I that they will give satisfaction, that I agree to refund the money in any unsatisfactory sales on the return of the coins."

As coin collecting became more popular and *The Numismatist* started accepting paid advertising from others, grading became more formal. The February 1892 issue listed seven "classes" for the condition of coins (from worst to best): mutilated, poor, fair, good, fine, uncirculated, and proof. Through the years, the hobby has struggled with developing a grading system that would be accepted by all and could apply to all coins. The hobby's growth was accompanied by a desire for more grades, or classifications, to more precisely define a coin's condition. The desire for more precision, however, was at odds with the basic concept of grading: to provide a concise method for classifying a coin's condition.

For example, even the conservatively few classifications of 1892 included fudge factors.

"To give flexibility to this classification," *The Numismatist* said, "such modification of find, good and fair, as 'extremely,' 'very,' 'almost,' etc., are used to express slight variations from the general condition."

The debate over grading continued for decades in *The Numismatist*. A number of articles and letters prodded the ANA to write grading guidelines and endorse them as the association's official standards. Some submitted specific suggestions for terminology and accompanying standards for each grade. But grading remained a process of "instinct" gained through years of collecting or dealing experience.

A formal grading guide in book form finally appeared in 1958, but it was the work of two individuals rather than the ANA. *A Guide to the Grading of United States Coins* by Martin R. Brown and John W. Dunn was a break-through in the great grading debate. Now collectors had a reference that gave them specific guidelines for specific coins and could be studied and restudied at home.

The first editions of Brown and Dunn carried text only, no illustrations. For the fourth edition, in 1964, publication was assumed by Whitman Publishing Co. of Racine, Wis., and line drawings were added to illustrate the text.

The fourth edition listed six principal categories for circulated coins (from worst to best): good, very good, fine, very fine, extremely fine, and about uncirculated. But again, the desire for more precise categories was evidenced. In the book's introduction, Brown and Dunn wrote, "Dealers will sometimes advertise coins that are graded G-VG, VG-F, F-VF, VF-XF. Or the description may be ABT. G. or VG plus, etc. This means that the coin in question more than meets minimum standards for the lower grade but is not quite good enough for the higher grade."

When the fifth edition appeared, in 1969, the "New B & D Grading System" was introduced. The six principal categories for circulated coins were still intact, but variances within those categories were now designated by up to four letters: "A," "B," "C" or "D." For example, an EF-A coin was "almost about uncirculated." An EF-B was "normal extra fine" within the B & D standards. EF-C had a "normal extra fine" obverse, but the reverse was "obviously not as nice as obverse due to poor strike or excessive wear." EF-D had a "normal extra fine" reverse but a problem obverse.

But that wasn't the end. Brown and Dunn further listed 29 problem points that could appear on a coin – from No. 1 for an "edge bump" to No. 29 for "attempted re-engraving outside of the Mint." The number could be followed by the letter "O" or "R" to designate whether the problem appeared on the obverse or reverse and a Roman numeral corresponding to a clock face to designate where the problem appears on the obverse or reverse. For example, a coin described as "VG-B-9-O-X" would grade "VG-B"; the "9" designated a "single rim nick"; the "O" indicated the nick was on the obverse; and the "X" indicated it appeared at the 10 o'clock position, or upper left, of the obverse.

The authors' goal was noble – to create the perfect grading system. They again, however, fell victim to the age-old grading-system problem: Precision comes at the expense of brevity. Dealer Kurt Krueger wrote in the January 1976 issues of *The Numismatist*, "Under the new B & D system, the numismatist must contend with a minimum of 43,152 different grading combinations! Accuracy is apparent, but simplicity has been lost." As a result, the "New B & D Grading System" never caught on in the marketplace.

The 1970s saw two important grading guides make their debut. The first was *Photograde* by James F. Ruddy. As the title implies, Ruddy uses photographs instead of line drawings to show how coins look in the various circulated grades. Simplicity is also a virtue of Ruddy's book. Only seven circulated grades are listed (about good, good, very good, fine, very fine, extremely fine, and about uncirculated), and the designations stop there.

In 1977 the longtime call for the ANA to issue grading standards was met with the release of *Official A.N.A. Grading Standards for United States Coins*. Like Brown and Dunn, the first edition of the ANA guide used line drawings to illustrate coins in various states of wear. But instead of using adjectival descriptions, the ANA guide adopted a numerical system for designating grades.

The numerical designations were based on a system used by Dr. William H. Sheldon in his book *Early American Cents*, first published in 1949. He used a scale of 1 to 70 to designate the grades of large cents.

"On this scale," Sheldon wrote, "1 means that the coin is identifiable and not mutilated – no more than that. A 70-coin is one in flawless Mint State, exactly as it left the dies, with perfect mint color and without a blemish or nick."

(Sheldon's scale also had its pragmatic side. At the time, a No. 2 large cent was worth about twice a No. 1 coin; a No. 4 was worth about twice a No. 2, and so on up the scale.)

With the first edition of its grading guide, the ANA adopted the 70-point scale for grading all U.S. coins. It designated 10 categories of circulated grades: AG-3, G-4, VG-8, F-12, VF-20, VF-30, EF-40, EF-45, AU-50, and AU-55. The third edition, released in 1987, replaced the line drawings with photographs, and another circulated grade was added: AU-58. A fourth edition was released in 1991.

Grading circulated U.S. coins

Dealers today generally use either the ANA guide or *Photograde* when grading circulated coins for their inventories. (Brown and Dunn is now out of print.) Many local coin shops sell both books. Advertisers in *Numismatic News*, *Coins* magazine, and *Coin Prices* must indicate which standards they are using in grading their coins. If the standards are not listed, they must conform to ANA standards.

Following are some general guidelines, accompanied by photos, for grading circulated U.S. coins. Grading even circulated pieces can be subjective, particularly when attempting to draw the fine line between, for example, AU-55 and AU-58. Two longtime collectors or dealers can disagree in such a case.

But by studying some combination of the following guidelines, the ANA guide, and *Photograde*, and by looking at a lot of coins at shops and shows, collectors can gain enough grading knowledge to buy circulated coins confidently from dealers and other collectors. The more you study, the more knowledge and confidence you will gain. When you decide which series of coins you want to collect, focus on the guidelines for that particular series. Read them, reread them, and then refer back to them again and again.

AU-50

AU-50 (about uncirculated): Just a slight trace of wear, result of brief exposure to circulation or light rubbing from mishandling, may be evident on elevated design areas. These imperfections may appear as scratches or dull spots, along with bag marks or edge nicks. At least half of the original mint luster generally is still evident.

Indian cent **Lincoln cent**

Buffalo nickel **Jefferson nickel**

Mercury dime

Standing Liberty quarter

Washington quarter

Walking Liberty half dollar

Morgan dollar

Barber coins

XF-40

XF-40 (extremely fine): The coin must show only slight evidence of wear on the highest points of the design, particularly in the hair lines of the portrait on the obverse. The same may be said for the eagle's feathers and wreath leaves on the reverse of most U.S. coins. A trace of mint luster may still show in protected areas of the coin's surface.

Indian cent

Lincoln cent

Buffalo nickel

Jefferson nickel

Mercury dime

Standing Liberty quarter

Washington quarter

Walking Liberty half dollar

Morgan dollar

Barber coins

VF-20

VF-20 (very fine): The coin will show light wear at the fine points in the design, though they may remain sharp overall. Although the details may be slightly smoothed, all lettering and major features must remain sharp.

Indian cent: All letters in "Liberty" are complete but worn. Headdress shows considerable flatness, with flat spots on the tips of the feathers.

Lincoln cent: Hair, cheek, jaw, and bow-tie details will be worn but clearly separated, and wheat stalks on the reverse will be full with no weak spots.

Buffalo nickel: High spots on hair braid and cheek will be flat but show some detail, and a full horn will remain on the buffalo.

Jefferson nickel: Well over half of the major hair detail will remain, and the pillars on Monticello will remain well defined, with the triangular roof partially visible.

Mercury dime: Hair braid will show some detail, and three-quarters of the detail will remain in the feathers. The two diagonal bands on the fasces will show completely but will be worn smooth at the middle, with the vertical lines sharp.

Standing Liberty quarter: Rounded contour of Liberty's right leg will be flattened, as will the high point of the shield.

Washington quarter: There will be considerable wear on the hair curls, with feathers on the right and left of the eagle's breast showing clearly.

Indian cent

Lincoln cent

Buffalo nickel

Jefferson nickel

VF-20

Walking Liberty half dollar: All lines of the skirt will show but will be worn on the high points. Over half the feathers on the eagle will show.

Morgan dollar: Two-thirds of the hair lines from the forehead to the ear must show. Ear should be well defined. Feathers on the eagle's breast may be worn smooth.

Barber coins: All seven letters of "Liberty" on the headband must stand out sharply. Head wreath will be well outlined from top to bottom.

Mercury dime | **Standing Liberty quarter**

Washington quarter | **Walking Liberty half dollar**

Morgan dollar | **Barber coins**

F-12

F-12 (fine): Coins show evidence of moderate to considerable but generally even wear on all high points, though all elements of the design and lettering remain bold. Where the word "Liberty" appears in a headband, it must be fully visible. On 20th century coins, the rim must be fully raised and sharp.

Indian cent

Lincoln cent

Buffalo nickel

Jefferson nickel

Mercury dime

Standing Liberty quarter

Washington quarter

Walking Liberty half dollar

Morgan dollar

Barber coins

VG-8

VG-8 (very good): The coin will show considerable wear, with most detail points worn nearly smooth. Where the word "Liberty" appears in a headband, at least three letters must show. On 20th century coins, the rim will start to merge with the lettering.

Indian cent

Lincoln cent

Buffalo nickel

Jefferson nickel

Mercury dime

Standing Liberty quarter

Washington quarter

Walking Liberty half dollar

Morgan dollar

Barber coins

G-4

G-4 (good): Only the basic design remains distinguishable in outline form, will all points of detail worn smooth. The word "Liberty" has disappeared, and the rims are almost merging with the lettering.

About good or fair: The coin will be identifiable by date and mint but otherwise badly worn, with only parts of the lettering showing. Such coins are of value only as fillers in a collection until a better example of the date and mintmark can be obtained. The only exceptions would be rare coins.

Indian cent

Lincoln cent

Buffalo nickel

Jefferson nickel

Mercury dime

Standing Liberty quarter

Washington quarter

Walking Liberty half dollar

Morgan dollar

Barber coins

Grading uncirculated U.S. coins

The subjectivity of grading and the trend toward more classifications becomes more acute when venturing into uncirculated, or mint-state, coins. A minute difference between one or two grade points can mean a difference in value of hundreds or even thousands of dollars. In addition, the standards are more difficult to articulate in writing and illustrate through drawings or photographs. Thus, the possibilities for differences of opinion on one or two grade points increase in uncirculated coins.

Back in Dr. George Heath's day and continuing through the 1960s, a coin was either uncirculated or it wasn't. Little distinction was made between uncirculated coins of varying condition, largely because there was little if any difference in value. When *Numismatic News* introduced its value guide in 1962 (the forerunner of today's Coin Market section in the *News*), it listed only one grade of uncirculated for Morgan dollars.

But as collectible coins increased in value and buyers of uncirculated coins became more picky, distinctions within uncirculated grade started to surface. In 1975 *Numismatic News* still listed only one uncirculated grade in Coin Market, but added this note: "Uncirculated and proof specimens in especially choice condition will also command proportionately higher premiums than these listed."

The first edition of the ANA guide listed two grades of uncirculated, MS-60 and MS-65, in addition to the theoretical but non-existent MS-70 (a flawless coin). MS-60 was described as "typical uncirculated" and MS-65 as "choice uncirculated." *Numismatic News* adopted both designations for Coin Market. In 1981, when the second edition of the ANA grading guide was released, MS-67 and MS-63 were added. In 1985 *Numismatic News* started listing six grades of uncirculated for Morgan dollars: MS-60, MS-63, MS-65, MS-65+, and MS-63 prooflike.

Then in 1986, a new entity appeared that has changed the nature of grading and trading uncirculated coins ever since. A group of dealers led by David Hall of Newport Beach, Calif., formed the Professional Coin Grading Service. For a fee, collectors could submit a coin through an authorized PCGS dealer and receive back a professional opinion of its grade.

The concept was not new; the ANA had operated an authentication service

Collectors have a variety of grading services to choose from. This set of Arkansas half dollars that appeared in an Early American History Auctions sale used two of the services.

since 1972 and a grading service since 1979. A collector or dealer could submit a coin directly to the service and receive a certificate giving the service's opinion on authenticity and grade. The grading service was the source of near constant debate among dealers and ANA officials. Dealers charged that ANA graders were too young and inexperienced, and that their grading was inconsistent.

Grading stability was a problem throughout the coin business in the early 1980s, not just with the ANA service. Standards among uncirculated grades would tighten during a bear market and loosen during a bull market. As a result, a coin graded MS-65 in a bull market may have commanded only MS-63 during a bear market.

PCGS created several innovations in the grading business in response to these problems:

1. Coins could be submitted through PCGS-authorized dealers only.

2. Each coin would be graded by at least three members of a panel of "top graders," all prominent dealers in the business. (Since then, however, PCGS does not allow its graders to also deal in coins.)

3. After grading, the coin would be encapsulated in an inert, hard-plastic holder with a serial number and the grade indicated on the holder.

4. PCGS-member dealers pledged to make a market in PCGS-graded coins and honor the grades assigned.

5. In one of the most far-reaching moves, PCGS said it would use all 11 increments of uncirculated on the 70-point numerical scale: MS-60, MS-61, MS-62, MS-63, MS-64, MS-65, MS-66, MS-67, MS-68, MS-69, and MS-70.

Numerous other commercial grading services followed in the steps of PCGS and third-party grading is an accepted part of the hobby.

How should a collector approach the buying and grading of uncirculated coins? Collecting uncirculated coins worth thousands of dollars implies a higher level of numismatic expertise by the buyer. Those buyers without that level of expertise should cut their teeth on more inexpensive coins, just as today's experienced collectors did. Inexperienced collectors can start toward that level by studying the guidelines for mint-state coins in the ANA grading guide and looking at lots of coins at shows and shops.

Study the condition and eye appeal of a coin and compare it to other coins of the same series. Then compare prices. Do the more expensive coins look better? If so, why? Start to make your own judgments concerning relationships between condition and value. Experience remains the best teacher in the field of grading.

Grading U.S. proof coins

Because proof coins are struck by a special process using polished blanks, they receive their own grading designation. A coin does not start out being a proof and then become mint state if it becomes worn. Once a proof coin, always a proof coin.

In the ANA system, proof grades use the same numbers as circulated and uncirculated grades, and the amount of wear on the coin corresponds to those grades. But the number is preceded by the word "proof." For example, Proof-65, Proof-55, Proof-45, and so on. In addition, the ANA says a proof coin with many marks, scratches or other defects should be called an "impaired proof."

4 Organization is Key

Sets worth more than accumulations

There are two major ways to organize a collection: by type, and by date and mintmark. By following either method, you will create a logically organized set that other collectors perceive as having a value greater than a random group of similar coins

Let's take collecting by type first. Look at a jar of coins, or take the change out of your pocket. You find Abraham Lincoln and the Lincoln Memorial on current cents. You find Thomas Jefferson and his home, Monticello, on the nickel. Franklin D. Roosevelt and a torch share the dime. George Washington and the eagle, or the more recent state, territories and park designs, appear on the quarter. John F. Kennedy and the presidential seal are featured on the half dollar. Sacagawea and Presidents adorn the dollar coins.

Each design is called a "type." If you took one of each and put the five coins in a holder, you would have a type set of the coins that are currently being produced for circulation by the U.S. Mint.

With just these five coins, you can study various metallic compositions. You can evaluate their states of preservation and assign a grade to each. You can learn about the artists who designed the coins, and you can learn of the times in which these designs were created.

As you might have guessed, many different coin types have been used in the United States over the years. You may remember seeing some of them circulating. These designs reflect the hopes and aspirations of people over time. Putting all of them together forms a wonderful numismatic mosaic of American history.

George Washington did not mandate that his image appear on the quarter. Quite the contrary. He would have been horrified. When he was president, he headed off those individuals in Congress who thought the leader of the country should have his image on its coins. Washington said it smacked of monarchy and would have nothing to do with it.

Almost a century and a half later, during the bicentennial of Washington's birth in 1932, a nation searching for its roots during troubled economic times decided that it needed his portrait on its coins as a reminder of his great accomplishments and as reassurances that this nation was the same place it had been in prosperous days.

In its broadest definition, collecting coins by type requires that you obtain an example of every design that was struck by the U.S. Mint since it was founded in 1792. That's a tall order. You would be looking for denominations like the half cent, two-cent piece, three-cent piece, and 20-cent piece, which have not been produced in over a century. You would be looking for gold coins ranging in face value from $1 to $50.

But even more important than odd-sounding denominations or high face values is the question of rarity. Some of the pieces in this two-century type set are rare and expensive. That's why type collectors often divide the challenge into more digestible units.

Type collecting can be divided into 18th, 19th, 20th and 21st century units. Starting type collectors can focus on 20th century coin designs, which are easily obtainable. The fun and satisfaction of putting the 20th or 21st century set together then creates the momentum to continue backward in time. In the process of putting a 20th century type set together, one is also learning how to grade, learning hobby jargon, and discovering how to obtain coins from dealers, the U.S. Mint, and other collectors. All of this knowledge is then refined as the collector increases the challenge to himself.

This book is designed to help. How many dollar types were struck in the 20th century? Turn to the price-guide section and check it out. We see the Morgan dollar, Peace dollar, Eisenhower dollar, and Anthony dollar. The Sacagawea dollar arrived in 2000 and the Presidential dollars in 2007. Hobbyists could also add the Ike dollar with the Bicentennial design of 1976 and the silver American Eagle bullion coin struck since 1986. One can also find out their approximate retail prices from the listings. The beauty of type collecting is that one can choose the most inexpensive example of each type. There is no need to select a 1903-O Morgan when the 1921 will do just as well. With the 20th century type set, hobbyists can dodge some truly big-league prices.

As a collector's hobby confidence grows, he can tailor goals to fit his desires. He can take the road less traveled if that is what suits him. Type sets can be divided by denomination. You can choose two centuries of one-cent coins. You can take just obsolete denominations or copper, silver or gold denominations.

You can even collect by size. Perhaps you would like to collect all coin types larger than 30 millimeters or all coins smaller than 20 millimeters. Many find this freedom of choice stimulating.

Type collecting has proven itself to be enduringly popular over the years. It provides a maximum amount of design variety while allowing collectors to set their own level of challenge.

The second popular method of collecting is by date and mintmark. What this means, quite simply, is that a collector picks a given type – Jefferson nickels, for example – and then goes after an example of every year, every mintmark, and every type of manufacture that was used with the Jefferson design.

Looking at this method of collecting brings up the subject of mintmarks. The "U.S. Mint" is about as specific as most non-collectors get in describing the government agency that provides everyday coins. Behind that label are the various production facilities that actually do the work.

In two centuries of U.S. coinage, there have been eight such facilities. Four are still in operation. Those eight in alphabetical order are Carson City, Nev., which used a "CC" mintmark to identify its work; Charlotte, N.C. ("C"); Dahlonega, Ga. ("D"); Denver (also uses a "D," but it opened long after the Dahlonega Mint closed, so there was never any confusion); New Orleans ("O"); Philadelphia (because it was the primary mint, it used no mintmark for much of its history, but currently uses a "P"); San Francisco ("S"); and West Point, N.Y. ("W").

A person contemplating the collecting of Jefferson nickels by date and mintmark will find that three mints produced them: San Francisco, Denver and Philadelphia. Because the first two are branch mints serving smaller populations, their output has tended over time to be smaller than that of Philadelphia. This fact, repeated in other series, has helped give mintmarks quite an allure to collectors. It provides one of the major attractions in collecting coins by date and mintmark.

The key date for Jeffersons is the 1950-D when using mintages as a guide. In that year, production was just 2.6 million pieces. Because collectors of the time were aware of the coin's low mintage, many examples were saved. As a result, prices are reasonable.

The Depression-era 1939-D comes in as the most valuable regular-issue Jefferson nickel despite a mintage of 3.5 million – almost 1 million more than the 1950-D. The reason: Fewer were saved for later generations of coin collectors.

Date and mintmark collecting teaches hobbyists to use mintage figures as a guide but to take them with a grain of salt. Rarity, after all, is determined by the number of surviving coins, not the number initially created.

The Jefferson series is a good one to collect by date and mintmark, because the mintmarks have moved around, grown in size, and expanded in number.

When the series was first introduced, the Jefferson nickel was produced at the three mints previously mentioned. In 1942, because of a diversion of certain metals to wartime use, the coin's alloy of 75 percent copper and 25 percent nickel was changed. The new alloy was 35 percent silver, 56 percent copper, and 9 percent manganese.

To denote the change, the mintmarks were moved and greatly enlarged. The pre-1942 mintmarks were small and located to the right of Monticello; the wartime mintmarks were enlarged and placed over the dome. What's more, for the first time in American history, the Philadelphia Mint used a mintmark ("P").

The war's end restored the alloy and mintmarks to their previous status. The "P" disappeared. This lasted until the 1960s, when a national coin shortage saw all mintmarks removed for three years (1965-1967) and then returned, but in a different location. Mintmarks were placed on the obverse, to the right of Jefferson's portrait near the date in 1968. In 1980 the "P" came back in a smaller form and is still used.

Another consideration arises with date and mintmark collecting: Should the hobbyist include proof coins in the set? This can be argued both ways. Suffice to say that anyone who has the desire to add proof coins to the set will have a larger one. It is not necessary nor is it discouraged.

Some of the first proof coins to carry mintmarks were Jefferson nickels. When proof coins were made in 1968 after lapsing from 1965 to 1967, production occurred at San Francisco instead of Philadelphia. The "S" mintmark was placed on the proof coins of that year, including the Jefferson nickel, to denote the change. Since that time, mintmarks used on proof examples of various denominations have included the "P," "D," "S," and "W."

For all of the mintmark history that is embodied in the Jefferson series, prices are reasonable. For a first attempt at collecting coins by date and mintmark, it provides excellent background for going on to the more expensive and difficult types. After all, if you are ever going to get used to the proper handling of a coin, it is far better to experiment on a low-cost coin than a high-value rarity.

As one progresses in date and mintmark collecting and type collecting, it is important to remember that all of the coins should be of similar states of preservation. Sets look slapdash if one coin is VG and another is MS-65 and still another is VF. Take a look at the prices of all the coins in the series before you get too far, figure out what you can afford, and then stick to that grade or range of grades.

Sure, there is a time-honored practice of filling a spot with any old example until a better one comes along. That is how we got the term "filler." But if you get a few placeholders, don't stop there. By assembling a set of uniform quality, you end up with a more aesthetically pleasing and more valuable collection.

The date and mintmark method used to be the overwhelmingly dominant form of collecting. It still has many adherents. Give it a try if you think it sounds right for you.

Before we leave the discussion of collecting U.S. coins, it should be pointed out that the two major methods of organizing a collection are simply guidelines. They are not hard-and-fast rules that must be followed without questions. Collecting should be satisfying to the hobbyist. It should never be just one more item in the daily grind. Take the elements of these aproaches that you like and ignore the rest.

It should also be pointed out that U.S. coinage history does not start with 1792 nor do all of the coins struck since that time conform precisely to the two major organizational approaches. But these two areas are good places to start.

There are coins and tokens from the American Colonial period (1607-1776) that are just as fascinating and collectible as regular U.S. Mint issues. There are federal issues struck before the Mint was actually established. See the Colonial price-guide section in this book.

There are special coins called commemoratives, which have been struck by the U.S. Mint since 1892 to celebrate some aspect of American history or a contemporary event. They are not intended for circulation. There was a long interruption between 1954 and 1982, but currently numerous commemoratives are being offered for sale directly to collectors by the Mint.

Collecting commemoratives has always been considered something separate from collecting regular U.S. coinage. It is, however, organized the same way. Commemoratives can be collected by date and mintmark or by type.

Current commemoratives can be purchased from the U.S. Mint. Check the Web site at www.usmint.gov or telephone (800) USA-MINT.

Buying coins from the Mint can be considered a hobby pursuit in its own right. Some collectors let the Mint organize their holdings for them. They buy complete sets and put them away. They never buy anything from anywhere else.

Admittedly, this is a passive form of collecting, but there are individuals around the world who enjoy collecting at this level without ever really going any deeper. They like acquiring every new issue as it comes off the Mint's presses.

Once done, there is a certain knowledge that one has all the examples of the current year. Obviously, too, collectors by date and mintmark of the current types would have to buy the new coins each year, but, of course, they do not stop there.

5 Don't be Fooled by High Grades

It is a settled expectation among collectors that high grade coins should be valuable.

This is certainly true when you consider coins that are 50 or 100 years old and the survivors had to run the many risks of circulation and mishandling before being carefully tucked away in a collection.

High grade in cases like these coins mean rarity, or at least scarcity, and that usually means higher value.

However, since the U.S. Mint began producing collector-only coins in large quantities in the 1980s, simply finding one in a top grade like MS-69 or MS-70 has gotten far easier. Something that is easy to find, or even just easier to find, means that even when the top grade requirement might be met, the rarity requirement that bestows value is not.

Potential buyers blinded by the label of MS-70 might blunder into paying drastically more than what a coin is worth over the long term.

We saw evidence of this as the state quarter program progressed from 1999 to 2008. Coins would go from the Mint, to collectors, to a grading service and then to the secondary market. In the early stages of the process, the simple act of getting a coin slabbed by the grading service would elevate the value so much that the trade was extremely profitable.

But as the years passed and the graded quantities increased, top graded coins aren't what they used to be. There are just too many of them in certain series.

The U.S. Mint has gotten very good in the production process of collector-only coins. This means most of the output if sent to a grading service would attain very high grades. So why would anyone bother?

Collectors are a bit funny. They often put a premium price on coins when they can be the first to own them. The first slabbed examples of new coins can bring what many dealers call "stupid money." But the buyers are beguiled or they like to brag to their friends when they are the first to own one. They pay a high premium for the privilege.

There is nothing wrong with that, but you should know that a coin potentially will be vastly more valuable 18 days after the first release than at 18 months. Will you be a disappointed owner at 18 months? Act with knowledge and you can avoid that fate.

Nevertheless, the notion of high grades, or ulta-grades as they are sometimes called, is here to stay. Sometimes, it can be to a collector's great benefit to know about them.

But to get this benefit it takes work. It won't simply just happen.

Consider a 1946-S Washington quarter. It MS-65, it catalogs for $35, or thereabouts. That's a bit better than ordinary.

But in early 2011, an MS-68 1946-S quarter as graded by the Professional Coin Grading Service's Secure service and verified with a Certified Acceptance Corporation sticker sold for $14,950 at a Bowers and Merena Auction.

Now the difference in price between a $14,950 coin and a $35 coin is worth a little time and trouble spent to find it and have it certified by two grading services, don't you think?

This is obviously the case where the ultra-grade means a lot in terms of value and scarcity. At the present time, no finer 1946-S quarter is known. That doesn't mean a finer one won't be found. It might be. It is certainly worth looking for one among any unslabbed coins you might run across.

A recent Numismatic Guaranty Corp. Census report shows that this grading firm has seen 4,306 1946-S Washington quarters. There were 1,705 called MS-65. That perhaps explains why it is a $35 coin in that grade. In MS-66 there were 2,078 and 347 in MS-67. In MS-68, there were just 3, with none graded MS-69 or MS-70.

For comparison, a silver 1999-S Delaware proof quarter sold originally only to collectors, has been examined by NGC 7,940 times. Of that number, 7,440 were graded MS-69 and 324 were graded MS-70.

Now do you see why the 1946-S Washington quarter in the lower MS-68 grade is so much more valuable? In that grade it is truly rare.

The lesson is clear: a high grade alone is not sufficient to make a coin valuable. It must be scarce also.

To be fair to collectors, ultra-grades have not been used in numismatics very long. What really got them into the headlines and noticed was an auction that occurred in 2003 at the Florida United Numismatists Convention.

A Proof-70 Deep Cameo 1963 cent went on the block. What do you think it sold for? A Proof-65 lists for $8. You can buy all you want.

The gavel came down on the Proof-70 at $39,100. That's not a typo.

You can imagine how collectors reacted. There are 3 million proof 1963 cents to look through. Another Proof-70 might be found someday. Auction results like this helped form the hobby myth that all coins that get an ultra-grade of -69 or -70 are valuable.

If you know how to watch your step, you can treat the special ultra-grade pieces like the prizes in a treasurer hunt.

It will be a challenge to find one. You might never succeed. But if you are a collector of these fairly modern coins, the product of different times and a different collector mindset, you might just be rewarded by finding the next $10,000, $20,000 or $30,000 auction winner.

What have you got to lose? More importantly, you will know not to get carried away when offered the opportunity to buy the collector-only issues of the past 30 years for prices that can most charitably be called inflated when there are numbers like -69 or -70 attached to them. In most cases, they just aren't rare.

10 Ways to Buy Coins

But not all are smart

Coin collecting is not a complicated concept. Collectors want to know what something is. They want to know what it is worth and they want to know how to buy one if it appeals to them.

What could be simpler?

Coin Digest is compiled to tell readers the answers to the first two questions. This book helps identify the many coin issues of the United States and it will tell you what each coin is worth on the retail market in many states of preservation by the terms of the official American Numismatic Association grading system that uses a 1-70 scale in ranking quality. Coins that show no wear are at the top end in the Mint State grades MS-60 to MS-70.

It is the final question of how to buy something that will set the average collector off on a lifetime of acquisitions. It also sets off discussions among collectors as to whether there might be other ways of making purchases, or better ways.

Let's look at 10 purchase methods and see what you think. Most are good. Some are not. Most collectors will use multiple methods to reach their goals.

1. Coin shops

The first method of buying coins is to walk into a traditional coin shop and talk to the person behind the counter about what it is you are interested in purchasing.

That person would then direct you to a specific tray in the display case, a three-ring binder of coins in 2x2 holders, or a display of slabs (coins graded by a third-party grading firm and then encapsulated in plastic) that the business might have on hand. You might even get a kick out of going through their junk box from time to time, if they have one.

Shops generally have a good working inventory of the popularly collected coin series, but they cannot own everything. If you don't see what you are looking for, you can ask about it. Sometimes they can get it for you. Sometimes they can't.

But let's say you find a few items you want to add to your collection. What then? How do you make a purchase?

Shops generally are the most retail oriented numismatic businesses. Prices are often marked and the purchase process is like checking out at the grocery store. However, depending on the size of the purchase, or whether you have become a regular customer, prices might be reduced a bit for you.

The advantages of buying at shops is that if you are near one, it is quick. You can see what you are buying and you get immediate satisfaction. You might also become a regular customer and that can provide you with valuable noncash benefits.

Knowledge is king in this hobby. The more you know, the better you get at buying right. If you become a regular shop customer, you open the door to many discussions with the owner/employees. These discussions can often be highly valuable educational tools. If a shop operator knows you are collecting a particular series, he very likely will not only sell you coins, but he will serve as a tutor so you can learn the ins and outs of specific sets. You want to know what "FBL" means? The shop owner can tell you all about full bell lines on the Liberty bell on the reverse of the Franklin half dollar.

You get the idea.

2. Coin shows

Another way of making purchases is to attend a coin show. Most localities have at least one coin show a year. These range in size from 20 dealers in a VFW Hall to hundreds of dealers in a downtown convention center.

No matter the show's size, the purpose is the same. The dealers who are paying for the privilege of sitting behind an 8-foot table would like to do business with you.

Coins are displayed in glass-topped display cases. You ask a dealer to show you things and he will do so. If you see something you like, know that prices are usually not marked.

You might say something like, "What can you do for me on this?"

The dealer will reply with a price. Because it is a show, some dickering is expected. But if you have never done business with the dealer before, keep your counterproposal reasonable. Valuable lasting relationships are made at coin shows because the larger ones offer the collector access to specialists in various coin series. If you like large cents, for example, you will be encountering a highly specialized community of collectors and dealers who will enrich your hobby experience.

You can find coins at flea markets and antique malls, but the people handling them often have no background in numismatics and may knowingly or unknowingly offer you coins. You have to learn your stuff to be able to spot the difference.

3. Online auctions

Online auctions sites, such as eBay, are another popular way to buy coins. You can look at as few, or as many of the listed coins as you want and you can participate in the bidding. You can set up alerts for coins posted in your area of interest.

Some people get hooked on the process and enjoy sniping at the last second of bidding before a sale closes.

The advantage of online auctions is you might get a better price on the coin you are looking for. The disadvantage is you can't see the coin, hold it closely and examine it. You must depend on the accuracy of the description and the quality of the posted images.

Not being able to see a coin first-hand brings up the necessity of return privileges. Don't do business with someone who won't let you send a coin back. Even the best descriptions and photos might miss something that you consider important.

eBay has PayPal, which as a convenient payment mechanism also provides an important consumer protection. If a transaction does not go appropriately PayPal can retrieve payments from sellers and get your money back for you.

Online auctions have the benefit of being available to you from the comfort of your own home.

There are pitfalls, but with *Coin Digest* in your hands, you will likely not fall for sales that pop up from time to time of the rare 1804 dollar of which there are just 15 known. Naturally, the whereabouts of the 15 are known, so the seller is not likely to have a real one.

4. Traditional auctions

Owners of the great rarities are likely to sell them by the traditional auction method. These bring the highest prices of any sales method on average for top quality coins.

Traditional auctions where buyers gather in a ballroom to bid on lots are still quite popular for this reason, though all but the smallest usually have an online component.

For bidders in the room, it is expected that you have examined the lots beforehand during the lot viewing hours and any bids you then win generally are not refundable. However, if you bid online and you did not see anything more than a lot description, you will have a return privilege.

Traditional auctions are conducted by the very largest numismatic firms to the very smallest estate sales.

5. Mail order

Advertisements in newspapers and magazines are another way to buy coins. Care must be taken. Compare grades in the description with those in this book. Compare prices.

If nonstandard grading terminology is employed in an advertisement, say brilliant uncirculated instead of MS-63, you might want to keep up your guard. If prices of all listed coins are well below price guide prices, you might be on your guard as well. After all, if the retail market enables the dealer to get guide book prices, why would he be offering his coins for much less?

In that case, something is likely wrong. The coin might not be what average collectors would presume it is supposed to be. It might be called a grade that is far higher than what it turns out to be.

To protect yourself, look for the return privilege in all ads. Buying a coin you cannot personally examine before the sale makes it extremely important that you can send it back if you are not satisfied when you get the chance to examine it closely.

There are specialty coin publications like the weekly *Numismatic News* hobby newspaper that make the process of buying by mail easier, but even here it is important to assure yourself of a return privilege before sending in your money.

All terms usually are spelled out. The ads will tell you what the postage and handling charges are, what a minimum order size needs to be if any, how coins are graded, the details of the return privilege, sales tax applicability and what forms of payment are accepted. It is expected that coins must stay in the holders in which they were sent to you in order to get a refund.

The ad will also tell you where to send mail orders, or what number to telephone to reach the firm.

6. Online retail advertisements

Online versions of ads have links to coin retailing Web sites that should also spell out sales terms just like an ad in a newspaper. Treat them as you would a newspaper or magazine ad. Look for the sales terms before you do anything else.

Purchases can be completed online, but depending on your payment method, it doesn't hurt to see if the firm is part of the regular numismatic industry, or is actually operated by someone hiding in Kazakhstan.

The Web site for *Numismatic News* is www.numismaticnews.com. It is a good portal to learn about coins in the online numismatic world.

7. TV coin shows

Another way of buying coins, especially if you like to stay up into the wee hours of the morning, is through television coin programs.

Watch yourself here. The sales pitches are so perfectly made that you can hardly contain your excitement and you will want to telephone the number immediately to get your very rare and unusual coin that will only be available for the next half hour at a very special price.

If you are going to buy through programs like this, keep *Coin Digest* handy and see how the TV price compares to the retail prices listed in the book.

If you discover that the TV prices are higher, you will at least be aware that there are cheaper coins available elsewhere, but you will just have to wait until you can go online, or to a coin show to get those better deals.

Sometimes higher prices are justified. It is up to you to make that determination. TV time is costly. The coins they are selling might be hard to find otherwise. Know your alternatives before you pick up the phone.

8. Phone solicitations

Sometimes the telephone can be your enemy. If you get a telephone call out of the blue and the caller wants to sell you coins, hang up. Don't talk. Hang up. Telephone solicitations that you haven't asked for are dangerous to the health of your checkbook balance. The caller could just as easily be trying to sell you oil leases in Patagonia. The sales pressure starts immediately and the end result of any purchase is not usually good.

9. Coin club meetings

An old-fashioned way to buy coins is at a meeting of a local coin club. There are fewer clubs nowadays, but they are still out there. One of the primary aspects of club meetings is providing a time for members to trade coins among themselves.

Each club is different. Find out what their rules and habits are.

The learning aspect to the social occasions provided by clubs is invaluable. You also might find that you will become a better collector by learning what the other members can teach you for free.

Coin collectors love to share what they know. If you enjoy coins as much as they do, the benefits to you can be large.

10. The U.S. Mint

The final method to purchase coins is to go right to the United States Mint. It produces coins every year for use in your change and it sells collector versions of these coins directly to collectors.

Visit the Web site at www.usmint.gov to see what is available, or telephone (800) USA-MINT.

Just remember that the Mint sells new coins for the most part. The older ones you have to find out there yourself.

Beware of firms that put the word "mint" in their title. There is only one official government mint in the United States. It operates minting facilities in Philadelphia, Pa., West Point, N.Y., Denver, Colo., and San Francisco, Calif. These minting plants do not sell coins directly to collectors, unless you happen to stop by the gift shops in Philadelphia and Denver.

Private firms with "mint" in their names might offer you something you want to buy, but don't mistake them for the U.S. government. There is only one United States Mint and that is its formal name.

Summary

There is no great mystery to coin buying for Americans who have been raised on shopping. The process is the same, but the hunt for specific coins might take just a bit longer than the hunt for a new car.

What makes coin collecting so interesting is the challenge that it presents. Some coins are easy to find. Some are not so easy. Some are downright hard and you may only get one or two chances in your lifetime to buy them.

If you get out there and try the various coin buying methods, you will not only find out which methods suit you best, you will also find out how to recognize the difference between contrived rarity and when those very rare coins have genuinely come your way.

Get out there and get started.

10 ways to buy coins

1. Coin shops
2. Coin shows
3. Online auctions
4. Traditional auctions
5. Mail order
6. Online retail ads
7. TV coin shows
8. Phone solicitations (Avoid)
9. Coin club meetings
10. United States Mint

Five Tips on Selling

And five ways to do it

Selling coins is more challenging than buying them. The first thing to remember is you cannot force anybody to buy your coins. There is no automatic process. You have to work at it.

The smarter you work at it, the better the result. There are do's and don'ts to follow.

There are five tips to keep in mind as you prepare to sell your coins and there are five popular methods of selling coins.

Tip 1: Know prices

When you want to sell coins, you usually cannot obtain retail coin prices listed in Coin Digest. Dealers have to make a profit on what they buy and you must expect them to offer less than the prices printed here in this book.

How much less?

The answer can be a shock. For accurately graded and described material, offers will come in depending on how long the dealer expects that he will have to hold the material in inventory before he can in turn sell it to someone else.

For coins that might hang around for awhile, you are likely to get no more than 60 percent of retail. Coins that contain precious metals trade at far less of a discount to retail. Because metals were hot as this is written, many U.S. coins that trade close to bullion prices were actually trading at premium prices. These include many of the common circulated U.S. gold coin dates

Knowing what is easily traded will help you accurately determine what has the higher values. Lincoln cents are expected to be hot in 2009, but to sell a Lincoln cent set that is anything less than Mint State, a dealer will look for the keys, the 1909-S, 1909-S VDB, 1910-S, 1914-D, 1922 and 1931-S. He might pass altogether if they are not there.

Series like Jefferson nickels are very hard to sell at premium prices. Most circulated dates are just returned to the bank. Even the Mint State grade coins are not in particularly high demand.

If your collection contains classically rare coins, the prices you will get for them will be closer to retail value. Age does not automatically translate to value, but it has given the hobby time to establish pricing relationships that hold up year after year. Learn what these are and profit from them.

Tip 2. Complete inventory

It is crucial to have an accurate inventory of what you are trying to sell, whether it is two coins you want to get rid of because you have others, or whether it is a lifetime collection.

A buyer needs solid information on which to base his calculations of what he will pay. An inventory is usually a starting point for discussion. It doesn't mean the dealer doesn't want to see what you have. He will ask if and when he is ready for the next step. A look at an inventory list will give him the opportunity to say that even if the coins are as you represent them, he just doesn't have a need for them. That saves you the trouble of hauling them around.

Specialists in Seated Liberty coinage, for example, are less likely to spend time analyzing the value of coins outside of their area, but a generalist, which coin shop proprietors usually are, might be interested in everything.

Tip 3. Complete sets are better

It is far easier to sell complete sets of various American coins for better prices than hodgepodge accumulations. Accumulations can have some good values hidden in them, but it is harder for a would-be buyer to make that judgment.

A complete set of large cents speaks volumes in a few words. The same is true of Morgan dollars or Standing Liberty quarters or almost any other set.

These are easier to evaluate and to sell to others. Thus, prices offered to sellers will tend to be higher.

Tip 4. Be up-front and honest

If you don't know something, the would-be buyer will figure this out in a hurry. If your lack of knowledge paints you as an unreasonable person, say trying to pass off AU-58 coins as MS-65, the buyer will not want to do business with you, or he will lowball you to protect himself.

Just being honest won't make a deal happen, but it is a critical foundation to eventually making a satisfactory deal happen.

Tip 5. Don't ship coins without permission

Shipping coins to someone without being asked is a frequent mistake and it is a stupid one. Make sure that the recipient knows something is coming to him, that he knows precisely what is coming and that he wants them to come.

Nothing is so irritating as getting coins in the mail that are unexpected and perhaps unneeded.

Think about this for your own protection. A dealer who doesn't need something is going to offer you less money if he makes an offer at all. A dealer for whom you've made things difficult is going to discount his prices to pay for the trouble that is caused.

A would-be buyer might not want your coins at all and you are on the hook for the return shipping costs.

Five ways to sell

You have educated yourself about prices, you have a full and accurate inventory and you are ready to courteously contact would-be buyers

What's next?

Method 1. Sell to a shop

Walking into a coin shop can be the best way to sell your coins. This is especially true if this shop is where you purchased many of your prize pieces and the owner helped you along the way.

If the owner knows you, not only will that facilitate the negotiating process, but it is to be expected that he will also know your coins. After all, he handled many of them. Coin dealers as a group have remarkable memories. They can discourse, if you let them, on the salient details of the XF-45 1909-S VDB cent that you bought from them a decade ago.

A dealer who helped you build a set will know the quality of your coins and if there are any problems. He will know how to make you feel most comfortable with the whole selling process.

And from the perspective of the seller, knowing the buyer can make all the difference. Who would you rather deal with, someone you know or someone you don't know?

If you don't happen to know the person in the shop doing the buying, your complete inventory and straight-forward manner will keep the process on track on a businesslike basis.

If there is anything in a shop scenario that makes you uncomfortable, you are best able to make the changes necessary face to face with the other party. If it turns into a high-pressure session, something has gone wrong and it might be best to go somewhere else, or try some other sales method.

Method 2. Sell in traditional auction

Since the turn of the 21st century, public auctions have been doing better and better at getting the maximum value for coins.

If your collection is of a certain size and quality, it might be in your best interest to consider consigning the coins to an auction firm. Naturally, the larger your collection and the higher the expected values, the bigger the firm that you might choose to deal with.

Auction firms usually charge the seller fees. These vary and can even be waived entirely for desirable material. The auctioneer calculates the public relations value of having your coins in his sale. You can even negotiate the option to buy back a piece that appears to be going too cheaply.

Almost anything that is mutually agreeable is possible, but you have to negotiate the terms ahead of time.

What if your collection won't be making headlines in the next Heritage or Stack's auction? Don't give up. Most collections don't.

Smaller auction firms might want to handle your coins. Here again, your accurate inventory will help these firms in making a decision quickly in determining whether they will sell your coins. They can quickly determine whether you make their financial threshold.

And, as is the case with shops, if you were a regular buyer at the auctions conducted by these firms, they will remember you and be just as delighted to help you sell your coins as they were to help you buy them.

For successful collectors, personal relationships between them and their dealers are as close or closer than a collector and his doctor.

Method 3. Sell in online auction

The arrival of eBay in the 1990s opened a new door for collectors interested in selling their coins themselves. You can sell one coin at a time at any pace you choose. You can sell a whole collection this way or any part of one. The choice is yours.

You simply need to prepare yourself to write accurate descriptions and post high-quality photos. Once again, that inventory that you prepared will serve you well.

Selling online has the advantage that you can get the highest possible price for individual coins. There are many retail buyers online who will be willing to pay higher prices than a dealer who is watching his profit margin. This is to your benefit.

The downside is the time element and your comfort level with computers and dealing with many persons otherwise unknown to you. Your commitment to being up-front and honest in your approach will serve you well here.

Method 4. Sell at a show

Sometimes the dealer or dealers you know best do business at shows and it is at a show that you would like to sell your coins.

This works well for portable quantities of coins. However, the larger the quantities, the more you will have to consider the logistics.

If you want to sell your Proof-65 1895 Morgan dollar to your favorite Morgan dollar specialist at a coin show, go for it. This is quick and convenient and you probably will maximize the value you receive.

However, if you are going to show up unannounced with bag quantities of medium value circulated Mercury dimes, unless you know the dealer is prepared to handle them, you might be handicapping your effort to get the best value for your coins.

The show dealer you sell them to will be mentally figuring in his shipping and insurance costs to get them back to his base of operation. It might be better to sell this kind of thing in a shop or in a pre-arranged deal.

Nevertheless, shows in the United States do billions of dollars' worth of deals in the course of a year and logistical issues are built right into everybody's plans.

Method 5. Sell at a club

This is selling as a social activity. Many coin collectors who are longtime club members might remember their favorite collector.

"Old Joe" has attended all the meetings you have ever been at, and he just always happens to have a few nice pieces in his pocket that he is getting rid of for the benefit of younger collectors.

You might discover someday that it is you who are Old Joe. You can enjoy the society of fellow collectors. You can educate the newcomers, and you can get a fair but not an incredible price for the pieces you choose to sell this way.

This, of course, depends on the rules of each club, but if you already know Old Joe, you already know the rules.

Summary

It is your choice which way you choose to sell your coins. There is no right or wrong way. It is a matter of getting the best prices possible.

You can choose to sell in multiple ways over time. You can break collections up and sell your best Morgans to the specialist, your bulk circulated silver coin sets to a shop owner and put a few medals online to see what they will bring.

But remember one final bit of advice. As a collector, it is up to you to be ready to sell when the time comes. This means test your sales skills from time to time.

Even when you are most interested in buying, plan to sell a piece here and there just to see who treats you the best and who gives you the best prices.

Desirable outcomes aren't always a given, but if you practice, the odds tilt in your favor. People change over the years as old-timers leave the business and newcomers enter. A bitter divorce might change the nature of a dealer's business dealings. He might become less pleasant to deal with.

You might hate dealing with online buyers, but you won't find this out if you don't do a little advance preparation.

It is up to the collector to be ready to sell his collection when the time comes. A part of this process is to do some test runs with a few pieces over the years.

If you do that when the time comes, you will be ready to get the best prices for the collection that you have built. That is the name of the game. We collectors are merely custodians of our collections. Sooner or later, we have to give them up. A properly prepared collector will achieve the most satisfactory result.

Good luck. Now get out there and mix it up a little.

10 Tips and ways to sell coins

1. Know prices
2. Complete inventory
3. Complete sets are better
4. Be up-front and honest
5. Don't ship coins without permission
6. Sell to a shop
7. Sell at traditional auction
8. Sell at a online auction
9. Sell at a show
10. Sell at a club

8 U.S. Minting Varieties and Errors

Most are common, some are rare

Introduction

The P.D.S. cataloging system used here to list minting varieties was originally compiled by Alan Herbert in 1971. PDS stands for the three main divisions of the minting process, "planchet," "die" and "striking." Two more divisions cover collectible modifications after the strike, as well as non-collectible alterations, counterfeits and damaged coins.

This listing includes 445 classes, each a distinct part of the minting process or from a specific non-mint change in the coin. Classes from like causes are grouped together. The PDS system applies to coins of the world, but is based on U.S. coinage with added classes for certain foreign minting practices.

Price ranges are based on a U.S. coin in MS-60 grade (uncirculated.) The ranges may be applied in general to foreign coins of similar size or value although collector values are not usually as high as for U.S. coins. Prices are only a guide as the ultimate price is determined by a willing buyer and seller.

To define minting varieties, "A coin which exhibits a variation of any kind from the normal, as a result of any portion of the minting process, whether at the planchet stage, as a result of a change or modification of the die, or during the striking process. It includes those classes considered to be intentional changes, as well as those caused by normal wear and tear on the dies or other minting equipment and classes deemed to be "errors."

The three causes are represented as follows:

1. (I) = Intentional Changes
2. (W) = Wear and Tear
3. (E) = Errors

Note: A class may show more than one cause and could be listed as (IWE).

Rarity level

The rarity ratings are based on the following scale:

1 - Very Common. Ranges from every coin struck down to 1,000,000.

2 - Common. From 1,000,000 down to 100,000.

3 - Scarce. From 100,000 down to 10,000.

4 - Very Scarce. From 10,000 down to 1,000.

5 - Rare. From 1,000 down to 100.

6 - Very Rare. From 100 down to 10.

7 - Extremely Rare. From 10 down to 1.

Unknown: If there is no confirmed report of a piece fitting a particular class, it is listed as Unknown. Reports of finds by readers would be appreciated in order to update future presentations.

An Unknown does not mean that your piece automatically is very valuable. Even a Rarity 7 piece, extremely rare, even unique, may have a very low collector value because of a lack of demand or interest in that particular class.

Classes, definitions and price ranges are based on material previously offered in Alan Herbert's book, The Official Price Guide to Minting Varieties and Errors and in Coin Prices Magazine.

Pricing information has also been provided by John A. Wexler and Ken Potter, with special pricing and technical advice from Del Romines.

Also recommended is the Cherrypicker's Guide to Rare Die Varieties by Bill Fivaz and J.T. Stanton. Check your favorite coin shop, numismatic library or book seller for availability of the latest edition.

For help with your coin questions, to report significant new finds and for authentication of your minting varieties, include a loose first class stamp and write to Alan Herbert, 700 E. State St., Iola, WI 54990-0001. Don't include any numismatic material until you have received specific mailing instructions from me.

Quick check index

If you have a coin and are not sure where to look for the possible variety:

If your coin shows doubling, first check V-B-I.

Then try II-A, II-B, II-C, II-I (4 & 5), III-J, III-L, or IV-C.

If part of the coin is missing, check III-B, III-C, or III-D.

If there is a raised line of coin metal, check II-D, II-G.

If there is a raised area of coin metal, check II-E, II-F, or III-F.

If the coin is out of round, and too thin, check III-G.

If coin appears to be the wrong metal, check III-A, III-E, III-F-3 and III-G.

If the die appears to have been damaged, check II-E, II-G. (Damage to the coin itself usually is not a minting variety.)

If the coin shows incomplete or missing design, check II-A, II-E, III-B-3, III-B-5 or III-D.

If only part of the planchet was struck, check III-M.

If something was struck into the coin, check III-J and III-K.

If something has happened to the edge of the coin, check II-D-6, II-E-10, III-I, III-M and III-O.

If your coin shows other than the normal design, check II-A or II-C.

If a layer of the coin metal is missing, or a clad layer is missing, check III-B and III-D.

If you have an unstruck blank, or planchet, check I-G.

If your coin may be a restrike, check IV-C.

If your coin has a counterstamp, countermark, additional engraving or apparent official modifications, check IV-B and V-A-8.

Do not depend on the naked eye to examine your coins. Use a magnifying lens whenever possible, as circulation damage, wear and alterations frequently can be mistaken for legitimate minting varieties.

The planchet varieties

DIVISION I

The first division of the PDS System includes those minting varieties that occur in the manufacture of the planchet upon which the coins will ultimately be struck and includes classes resulting from faulty metallurgy, mechanical damage, faulty processing, or equipment or human malfunction prior to the actual coin striking.

•PLANCHET ALLOY MIX (I-A)

This section includes those classes pertaining to mixing and processing the various metals which will be used to make a coin alloy.

I-A-1 Improper Alloy Mix (WE), Rarity Level: 3-4, Values: $5 to $10.

I-A-2 Slag Inclusion Planchet (WE), Rarity Level: 5-6, Values: $25 up.

•DAMAGED AND DEFECTIVE PLANCHETS (I-B)

To be a class in this section the blank, or planchet, must for some reason not meet the normal standards or must have been damaged in processing. The classes cover the areas of defects in the melting, rolling, punching and processing of the planchets up to the point where they are sent to the coin presses to be struck.

I-B-1 Defective Planchet (WE), Rarity Level: 6, Values: $25 up.

I-B-2 Mechanically Damaged Planchet (WE), Rarity Level: –, Values: No Value. (See values for the coin struck on a mechanically damaged planchet.)

I-B-3 Rolled Thin Planchet (WE), Rarity Level: 6 - (Less rare on half cents of 1795, 1797 and restrikes of 1831-52.) Values: $10 up.

I-B-4 Rolled Thick Planchet (WE), Rarity Level: 7 - (Less rare in Colonial copper coins. Notable examples occur on the restrike half cents of 1840-52.) Values: $125 up.

I-B-5 Tapered Planchet (WE), Rarity Level: 7, Values: $25 up.

I-B-6 Partially Unplated Planchet (WE), Rarity Level: 6, Values: $15 up.

I-B-7 Unplated Planchet (WE), Rarity Level: 6-7, Values: $50 up.

I-B-8 Bubbled Plating Planchet (WE), Rarity Level: 1, Values: No Value.

I-B-9 Included Gas Bubble Planchet (WE), Rarity Level: 6-7, Values: $50 up.

I-B-10 Partially Unclad Planchet (WE), Rarity Level: 6, Values: $20 up.

I-B-11 Unclad Planchet (WE), Rarity Level: 6-7, Values: $50 up.

I-B-12 Undersize Planchet (WE), Rarity Level: 7, Values: $250 up.

I-B-13 Oversize Planchet (WE), Rarity Level: 7, Values: $250 up.

I-B-14 Improperly Prepared Proof Planchet (WE), Rarity Level: 7, Values: $100 up.

I-B-15 Improperly Annealed Planchet (WE), Rarity Level: - , Values: No Value.

I-B-16 Faulty Upset Edge Planchet (WE), Rarity Level: 5-6, Values: $10 up.

I-B-17 Rolled-In Metal Planchet (WE), Rarity Level: 6-7, Values: $50 up.

I-B-18 Weld Area Planchet (WE), Rarity Level: Unknown, Values: No Value Established. (See values for the coins struck on weld area planchets.)

I-B-19 Strike Clip Planchet (WE), Rarity Level: 7, Values: $150 up.

I-B-20 Unpunched Center-Hole Planchet (WE), Rarity Level: 5-7, Values: $5 and up.

I-B-21 Incompletely Punched Center-Hole Planchet (WE), Rarity Level: 6-7, Values: $15 up.

I-B-22 Uncentered Center-Hole Planchet (WE), Rarity Level: 6-7, Values: $10 up.

I-B-23 Multiple Punched Center-Hole Planchet (WE), Rarity Level: 7, Values: $35 up.

I-B-24 Unintended Center-Hole Planchet (WE), Rarity Level: Unknown, Values: -.

I-B-25 Wrong Size or Shape Center-Hole Planchet (IWE), Rarity Level: 5-7, Values: $10 up.

•CLIPPED PLANCHETS (I-C)

Clipped blanks, or planchets, occur when the strip of coin metal fails to move forward between successive strokes of the gang punch to clear the previously punched holes, in the same manner as a cookie cutter overlapping a previously cut hole in the dough. The size of the clip is a function of the amount of overlap of the next punch.

The overlapping round punches produce a missing arc with curve matching the outside circumference of the blanking punch. Straight clips occur when the punch overlaps the beginning or end of a strip which has had the end sheared or sawed off. Ragged clips occur in the same manner when the ends of the strip have been left as they were rolled out.

The term "clip" as used here should not be confused with the practice of clipping or shaving small pieces of metal from a bullion coin after it is in circulation.

I-C-1 Disc Clip Planchet (WE), Rarity Level: 3-5, Values: $5 up.
I-C-2 Curved Clip Planchet - (To 5%) (WE), Rarity Level: 5-6, Values: $5 up.
I-C-3 Curved Clip Planchet - (6 to 10%) (WE), Rarity Level: 6, Values: $10 up.
I-C-4 Curved Clip Planchet - (11 to 25%) (WE), Rarity Level: 5-6, Values: $15 up.
I-C-5 Curved Clip Planchet - (26 to 60%) (WE), Rarity Level: 6-7, Values: $25 up.
I-C-6 Double Curved Clip Planchet (WE), Rarity Level: 6, Values: $10 up.
I-C-7 Triple Curved Clip Planchet (WE), Rarity Level: 5-6, Values: $25 up.
I-C-8 Multiple Curved Clip Planchet (WE), Rarity Level: 6-7, Values: $35 up.
I-C-9 Overlapping Curved Clipped Planchet (WE), Rarity Level: 6-7, Values: $50 up.
I-C-10 Incompletely Punched Curved Clip Planchet (WE), Rarity Level: 6, Values: $35 up.
I-C-11 Oval Curved Clip Planchet (WE), Rarity Level: 6-7, Values: $50 up.
I-C-12 Crescent Clip Planchet - (61% or more) (WE), Rarity Level: 7, Values: $200 up.
I-C-13 Straight Clip Planchet (WE), Rarity Level: 6, Values: $30 up.
I-C-14 Incompletely Sheared Straight Clip Planchet (WE), Rarity Level: 6, Values: $50 up.
I-C-15 Ragged Clip Planchet (WE), Rarity Level: 6-7, Values: $35 up.
I-C-16 Outside Corner Clip Planchet (E), Rarity Level: -, Values: No Value.
I-C-17 Inside Corner Clip Planchet (E), Rarity Level: -, Values: No Value.
I-C-18 Irregularly Clipped Planchet (E) Rarity Level: -, Values: Value not established.
I-C-19 Incompletely Punched Scalloped or Multi-Sided Planchet (E), Rarity Level: 7, Values: $25 up.

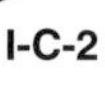
I-C-2

•Laminated, split, or broken planchet (I-D)

For a variety of reasons the coin metal may split into thin layers (delaminate) and either split completely off the coin, or be retained. Common causes are included gas or alloy mix problems. Lamination cracks usually enter the surface of the planchet at a very shallow angle or are at right angles to the edge. The resulting layers differ from slag in that they appear as normal metal.

Lamination cracks and missing metal of any size below a split planchet are too common in the 35 percent silver 1942-1945 nickels to be collectible or have any significant value.

I-D-1 Small Lamination Crack Planchet (W), Rarity Level: 4-5, Values: $1 up.
I-D-2 Large Lamination Crack Planchet (W), Rarity Level: 3-4, Values: $5 up.
I-D-3 Split Planchet (W), Rarity Level: 5-6, Values: $15 up.
I-D-4 Hinged Split Planchet (W), Rarity Level: 6-7, Values: $75 up.
I-D-5 Clad Planchet With a Clad Layer Missing (W), Rarity Level: 5-6, Values: $35 up.
I-D-6 Clad Planchet With Both Clad Layers Missing (W), Rarity Level: 6-7, Values: $75 up.
I-D-7 Separated Clad Layer (W), Rarity Level: 5, Values: $25 up.
I-D-8 Broken Planchet (WE), Rarity Level: 3-4, Values: $5 up.

•Wrong stock planchet (I-E)

The following classes cover those cases where the wrong coin metal stock was run through the blanking press, making blanks of the correct diameter, but of the wrong thickness, alloy or metal or a combination of the wrong thickness and the wrong metal.

I-E-1 Half Cent Stock Planchet (IE), Rarity Level: Unknown, Values: No Value Established.
I-E-2 Cent Stock Planchet (IE), Rarity Level: Unknown, Values: No Value Established.
I-E-3 Two Cent Stock Planchet (E), Rarity Level: Unknown, Values: No Value Established.
I-E-4 Three Cent Silver Stock Planchet (E), Rarity Level: Unknown, Values: No Value Established.
I-E-5 Three Cent Nickel Stock Planchet (E), Rarity Level: Unknown, Values: No Value Established.

I-E-6 Half Dime Stock Planchet (E), Rarity Level: Unknown, Values: No Value Established.

I-E-7 Dime Stock Planchet (E), Rarity Level: 7, Values: $200 up.

I-E-8 Twenty Cent Stock Planchet (E), Rarity Level: Unknown, Values: No Value Established.

I-E-9 Quarter Stock Planchet (E), Rarity Level: Unknown, Values: No Value Established.

I-E-10 Half Dollar Stock Planchet (E), Rarity Level: Unknown, Values: No Value Established.

I-E-11 Dollar Stock Planchet (E), Rarity Level: 7, Values: $300 up.

I-E-12 Token or Medal Stock Planchet (E), Rarity Level: Unknown, Values: No Value Established.

I-E-13 Wrong Thickness Spoiled Planchet (IWE), Rarity Level: Unknown, Values: No Value Established.

I-E-14 Correct Thickness Spoiled Planchet (IWE), Rarity Level: Unknown, Values: No Value Established.

I-E-15 Cut Down Struck Token Planchet (IWE), Rarity Level: Unknown, Values: No Value Established.

I-E-16 Experimental or Pattern Stock Planchet (IE), Rarity Level: Unknown, Values: No Value Established.

I-E-17 Proof Stock Planchet (IE), Rarity Level: Unknown, Values: No Value Established.

I-E-18 Adjusted Specification Stock Planchet (IE), Rarity Level: 7, Values: $25 up.

I-E-19 Trial Strike Stock Planchet (IE), Rarity Level: Unknown, Values: No Value Established.

I-E-20 U.S. Punched Foreign Stock Planchet (E), Rarity Level: 7, Values: $75 up.

I-E-21 Foreign Punched Foreign Stock Planchet (E), Rarity Level: 7, Values: $75 up.

I-E-22 Non-Standard Coin Alloy Planchet (IE), Rarity Level: 7, Values: Unknown.

•Extra metal on a blank, or planchet (I-F)

True extra metal is only added to the blank during the blanking operation. This occurs as metal is scraped off the sides of the blanks as they are driven down through the thimble, or lower die in the blanking press. The metal is eventually picked up by a blank passing through, welded to it by the heat of friction.

A second form of extra metal has been moved to this section, the sintered coating planchet, the metal deposited on the planchet in the form of dust during the annealing operation.

I-F-1 Extra Metal on a Type 1 Blank (W), Rarity Level: 7, Values: $50 up.

I-F-2 Extra Metal on a Type 2 Planchet (W), Rarity Level: 6-7, Values: $75 up.

I-F-3 Sintered Coating Planchet (W), Rarity Level: 7, Values: $75 up.

•Normal or abnormal planchets (I-G)

This section consists of the two principal forms – the blank as it comes from the blanking press – and in the form of a planchet after it has passed through the upsetting mill. It also includes a class for purchased planchets and one for planchets produced by the mint.

I-G-1 Type I Blank (IWE), Rarity Level: 3-5, Values: $2 up.

I-G-2 Type II Planchet (IWE), Rarity Level: 3-4, Values: 50 up.

I-G-3 Purchased Planchet (I), Rarity Level: 1, Values: No Value.

I-G-4 Mint Made Planchet (I), Rarity Level: 1, Values: No Value.

I-G-5 Adjustment-Marked Planchet (I), Rarity Level: Unknown, Values: No Value.

I-G-6 Hardness Test-Marked Planchet (I), Rarity Level: -, Values: No Value Established.

Note: There are no classes between I-G-6 and I-G-23

I-G-23 Proof Planchet (IE), Rarity Level: 6-7, Values: $1 up.

•Coin metal strip (I-H)

When the coin metal strip passes through the blanking press it goes directly to a chopper. This cuts the remaining web into small pieces to be sent back to the melting furnace. Pieces of the web or the chopped up web may escape into the hands of collectors.

I-H-1 Punched Coin Metal Strip (IWE), Rarity Level: 4-6, Values: $5 up, depending on size, denomination and number of holes showing.

I-H-2 Chopped Coin Metal Strip (IE), Rarity Level: 3-5, Values: $5 up.

The die varieties

DIVISION II

Die varieties may be unique to a given die, but will repeat for the full life of the die unless a further change occurs. Anything that happens to the die will affect the appearance of the struck coin. This includes all the steps of the die making:

- Cutting a die blank from a tool steel bar.
- Making the design.
- Transferring it to a model.
- Transferring it to the master die or hub.
- The hubbing process of making the die.
- Punching in the mintmark.
- Heat treating of the die.

The completed dies are also subject to damage in numerous forms, plus wear and tear during the striking process and repair work done with abrasives. All of these factors can affect how the struck coin looks.

•ENGRAVING VARIETIES (II-A)

In all cases in this section where a master die, or master hub is affected by the class, the class will affect all the working hubs and all working dies descending from it.

Identification as being on a master die or hub depends on it being traced to two or more of the working hubs descended from the same master tools.

II-A-1 Overdate (IE), Rarity Level: 1-7, Values: $1 up.

II-A-2 Doubled Date (IE), Rarity Level: 1-7, Values: $1 up.

II-A-3 Small Date (IE), Rarity Level: 2-5, Values: $1 up.

II-A-4 Large Date (IE), Rarity Level: 2-5, Values: $1 up.

II-A-5 Small Over Large Date (IE), Rarity Level: 4-6, Values: $15 up.

II-A-6 Large Over Small Date (IE), Rarity Level: 3-5, Values: $10 up.

II-A-7 Blundered Date (E), Rarity Level: 6-7, Values: $50 up.

II-A-8 Corrected Blundered Date (IE), Rarity Level: 3-5, Values: $5 up.

II-A-9 Wrong Font Date Digit (IE), Rarity Level: 5-6, Values: Minimal.

II-A-10 Worn, Broken or Damaged Punch (IWE), Rarity Level: 5-6, Values: $5 up.

II-A-11 Expedient Punch (IWE), Rarity Level: 5-6, Values: $10 up.

II-A-12 Blundered Digit (E), Rarity Level: 4-5, Values: $50 up.

II-A-13 Corrected Blundered Digit (IE), Rarity Level: 3-6, Values: $10 up.

II-A-14 Doubled Digit (IWE), Rarity Level: 2-6, Values: $2 up.

II-A-15 Wrong Style or Font Letter or Digit (IE), Rarity Level: 3-5, Values: Minimal.

II-A-1

II-A-2

II-A-2

II-A-16 One Style or Font Over Another (IE), Rarity Level: 4-6, Values: $10 up.

II-A-17 Letter Over Digit (E), Rarity Level: 6-7, Values: $25 up.

II-A-18 Digit Over Letter (E), Rarity Level: 6-7, Values: $25 up.

II-A-19 Omitted Letter or Digit (IWE), Rarity Level: 4-6, Values: $5 up.

II-A-20 Blundered Letter (E), Rarity Level: 6-7, Values: $50 up.

II-A-21 Corrected Blundered Letter (IE), Rarity Level: 1-3, Values: $10 up.

II-A-22 Doubled Letter (IWE), Rarity Level: 2-6, Values: $2 up.

II-A-23 Blundered Design Element (IE), Rarity Level: 6-7, Values: $50 up.

II-A-24 Corrected Blundered Design Element (IE), Rarity Level: 3-5, Values: $10 up.

II-A-25 Large Over Small Design Element (IE), Rarity Level: 4-6, Values: $2 up.

II-A-26 Omitted Design Element (IWE), Rarity Level: 5-7, Values: $10 up.

II-A-27 Doubled Design Element (IWE), Rarity Level: 2-6, Values: $2 up.

II-A-28 One Design Element Over Another (IE), Rarity Level: 3-6, Values: $5 up.

II-A-29 Reducing Lathe Doubling (WE), Rarity Level: 6-7, Values: $50 up.

II-A-30 Extra Design Element (IE), Rarity Level: 3-5, Values: $10 up.

II-A-31 Modified Design (IWE), Rarity Level: 1-5, Values: No Value up.

II-A-32 Normal Design (I), Rarity Level: 1, Values: No Extra Value.

II-A-33 Design Mistake (IE), Rarity Level: 2-6, Values: $1 up.

II-A-34 Defective Die Design (IWE), Rarity Level: 1, Values: No Value.

II-A-35 Pattern (I), Rarity Level: 6-7, Values: $100 up.

II-A-36 Trial Design (I), Rarity Level: 5-7, Values: $100 up.

II-A-37 Omitted Designer's Initial (IWE), Rarity Level: 3-7, Values: $1 up.

II-A-38 Layout Mark (IE), Rarity Level: 5-7, Values: Minimal.

II-A-39 Abnormal Reeding (IWE), Rarity Level: 2-5, Values: $1 up.

II-A-40 Modified Die or Hub (IWE), Rarity Level: 1-5, Values: No Value up.

II-A-41 Numbered Die (I), Rarity Level: 3-5, Values: $5 up.

II-A-42 Plugged Die (IW), Rarity Level: 5-6, Values: Minimal.

II-A-43 Cancelled Die (IE), Rarity Level: 3-6, Values: No Value up.

II-A-44 Hardness Test Marked Die (IE), Rarity Level: 7, Values: $100 up.

II-A-45 Coin Simulation (IE), Rarity Level: 6-7, Values: $100 up, but may be illegal to own.

II-A-46 Punching Mistake (IE), Rarity Level: 2-6, Values: $1 up.

II-A-47 Small Over Large Design (IE), Rarity Level: 4-6, Values: $5 up.

II-A-48 Doubled Punch (IE), Rarity Level: 5-7, Values: $5 up.

II-A-49 Mint Display Sample (I) Rarity Level: 7, Values not established.

II-A-50 Center Dot, Stud or Circle (IE) Rarity Level: 7, much more common on early cents, Values not established

•Hub doubling varieties (II-B)

This section includes eight classes of hub doubling. Each class is from a different cause, described by the title of the class. At the latest count over 2,500 doubled dies have been reported in the U.S. coinage, the most famous being examples of the 1955, 1969-S and 1972 cent dies.

II-B-I Rotated Hub Doubling (WE), Rarity Level: 3-6, Values: $1 up

II-B-II Distorted Hub Doubling (WE), Rarity Level: 3-6, Values: $1 up.

II-B-III Design Hub Doubling (IWE), Rarity Level: 3-6, Values: $1 up to five figure amounts.

II-B-IV Offset Hub Doubling (WE), Rarity Level: 4-6, Values: $15 up.

II-B-V Pivoted Hub Doubling (WE), Rarity Level: 3-6, Values: $10 up.

II-B-VI Distended Hub Doubling (WE), Rarity Level: 2-5, Values: $1 up.

II-B-VII Modified Hub Doubling (IWE), Rarity Level: 2-5, Values: $1 up.

II-B-VIII Tilted Hub Doubling (WE), Rarity Level: 4-6, Values: $5 up.

•Mintmark varieties (II-C)

Mintmarks are punched into U.S. coin dies by hand (Up to 1985 for proof coins, to 1990 for cents and nickels and 1991 for other denominations). Variations resulting from mistakes in the punching are listed in this section. Unless exceptionally mispunched, values are usually estimated at 150 percent of numismatic value. Slightly tilted or displaced mintmarks have no value.

II-C-1 Doubled Mintmark (IE), Rarity Level: 2-6, Values: 50 cents up.

II-C-2 Separated Doubled Mintmark (IE), Rarity Level: 5-6, Values: $15 up.

II-C-3 Over Mintmark (IE), Rarity Level: 3-6, Values: $2 up.

II-C-4 Tripled Mintmark (IE), Rarity Level: 3-5, Values: 50 up.

II-C-5 Quadrupled Mintmark (IE), Rarity Level: 4-6, Values: $1 up.

II C 6 Small Mintmark (IE), Rarity Level: 2-5, Values: No Extra Value up.

II-C-7 Large Mintmark (IE), Rarity Level: 2-5, Values: No Extra Value up.

II-C-8 Large Over Small Mintmark (IE), Rarity Level: 2-5, Values: $2 up.

II-C-9 Small Over Large Mintmark (IE), Rarity Level: 3-6, Values: $5 up.

II-C-10 Broken Mintmark Punch (W), Rarity Level: 5-6, Values: $5 up.

II-C-11 Omitted Mintmark (IWE), Rarity Level: 4-7, Values: $125 up.

II-C-12 Tilted Mintmark (IE), Rarity Level: 5-7, Values: $5 up.

II-C-13 Blundered Mintmark (E), Rarity Level: 4-6, Values: $5 up.

II-C-14 Corrected Horizontal Mintmark (IE), Rarity Level: 4-6, Values: $5 up.

II-C-15 Corrected Upside Down Mintmark (IE), Rarity Level: 4-6, Values: $5 up.

II-C-16 Displaced Mintmark (IE), Rarity Level: 4-6, Values: $5 to $10.

II-C-17 Modified Mintmark (IWE), Rarity Level: 1-4, Values: No Extra Value up.

II-C-18 Normal Mintmark (I), Rarity Level: 1, Values: No Extra Value.

II-C-19 Doubled Mintmark Punch (I), Rarity Level: 6-7, Values: No Extra Value up.

II-C-20 Upside Down Mintmark (E) Rarity Level 6-7, Values: $5 up.

II-C-21 Horizontal Mintmark (E) Rarity Level 6-7, Values: $5 up.

II-C-22 Wrong Mintmark (E) Rarity Level 6-7, Values $15 up. (Example has a D mintmark in the date, but was used at Philadelphia.)

II-C-3

II-C-3

II-C-1

II-C-4

•Die, collar and hub cracks (II-D)

Cracks in the surface of the die allow coin metal to be forced into the crack during the strike, resulting in raised irregular lines of coin metal above the normal surface of the coin. These are one of the commonest forms of die damage and wear, making them easily collectible.

Collar cracks and hub cracks are added to this section because the causes and effects are similar or closely associated.

Die cracks, collar cracks and hub cracks are the result of wear and tear on the tools, with intentional use assumed for all classes.

II-D-1 Die Crack (W), Rarity Level: 1-3, Values: 10 to $1, $25 up on a proof coin with a rarity level of 6-7.

II-D-2 Multiple Die Cracks (W), Rarity Level: 1-3, Values: 25 cents to $2.

II-D-3 Head-To-Rim Die Crack (Lincoln Cent) (W), Rarity Level: 2-6, Values: 25 to $10 for multiple die cracks.

II-D-4 Split Die (W), Rarity Level: 5-6, Values: $10 up.

II-D-5 Rim-To-Rim Die Crack (W), Rarity Level: 2-5, Values: $1 up.

II-D-6 Collar Crack (W), Rarity Level: 4-6, Values: $10 up.

II-D-7 Hub Crack (W), Rarity Level: 3-5, Values: $1-$2.

•Die breaks (II-E)

Breaks in the surface of the die allow coin metal to squeeze into the resulting holes, causing raised irregular areas above the normal surface of the coin. Die chips and small die breaks are nearly as common as the die cracks, but major die breaks, which extend in from the edge of the coin, are quite rare on the larger coins.

If the broken piece of the die is retained, the resulting design will be above or below the level of the rest of the surface.

II-E-1 Die Chip (W), Rarity Level: 1-2, Values: 10 to $1.

II-E-2 Small Die Break (W), Rarity Level: 1-3, Values: 10 to $2.

II-E-3 Large Die Break (W), Rarity Level: 3-5, Values: $1 to $50 and up.

II-E-4 Rim Die Break (W), Rarity Level: 2-3, Values: 25 cents to $5.

II-E-5 Major Die Break (WE), Rarity Level: 3-6, Values: $5 to $100 and up.

II-E-6 Retained Broken Die (W), Rarity Level: 3-5, Values: $1 to $10 and up.

II-E-7 Retained Broken Center of the Die (W), Rarity Level: 6-7, Values: $100 up.

II-E-8 Laminated Die (W), Rarity Level: 3-5, Values: 10 cents to $5.

II-E-9 Chipped Chrome Plating (W), Rarity Level: 4-5, Values: $10 to $25 on proofs.

II-E-10 Collar Break (W), Rarity Level: 4-6, Values: $5 to $25 and up.

II-E-11 Broken Letter or Digit on an Edge Die (W), Rarity Level: 4-6, Values: Minimal.

II-E-12 "Bar" Die Break (W), Rarity Level: 3-5, Values: 25 to $20.

II-E-13 Hub Break (W), Rarity Level: 4-6, Values: 50 to $10 and up.

•"BIE" varieties (II-F)

A series of small die breaks or die chips in the letters of "LIBERTY" mostly on the wheat-reverse Lincoln cent are actively collected. The name results from the resemblance to an "I" between the "B" and "E" on many of the dies, but they are found between all of the letters in different cases. Well over 1,500 dies are known and cataloged. Numerous more recent examples are known.

II-F-1 ILI Die Variety (W), Rarity Level: 4-5, Values: 25 cents to $10.

II-F-2 LII Die Variety (W), Rarity Level: 3-5, Values: 50 cents to $15.

II-F-3 IIB Die Variety (W), Rarity Level: 3-5, Values: 50 cents to $15.

II-F-4 BIE Die Variety (W), Rarity Level: 3-5, Values: $1 to $20.

II-F-5 EIR Die Variety (W), Rarity Level: 3-5, Values: 50 to $15.

II-F-6 RIT Die Variety (W), Rarity Level: 4-5, Values: $2 to $25.

II-F-7 TIY Die Variety (W), Rarity Level: 4-5, Values: $5 to $30.

II-F-8 TYI Die Variety (W), Rarity Level: 4-5, Values: $2 to $25.

•Worn and damaged dies, collars and hubs (II-G)

Many dies are continued deliberately in service after they have been damaged, dented, clashed or show design transfer, since none of these classes actually affect anything but the appearance ofthe coin. The root cause is wear, but intent or mistakes may enter the picture.

II-G-1 Dented Die, Collar or Hub (IWE), Rarity Level: 3-5, Values: 25 to $5.

II-G-2 Damaged Die, Collar or Hub (IWE), Rarity Level: 3-5, Values: 25 to $5.

II-G-3 Worn Die, Collar or Hub (IWE), Rarity Level: 2-3, Values: No Extra Value to Minimal Value.

II-G-4 Pitted or Rusted Die, Collar or Hub (IWE), Rarity Level: 3-4, Values:No Extra Value, marker only.

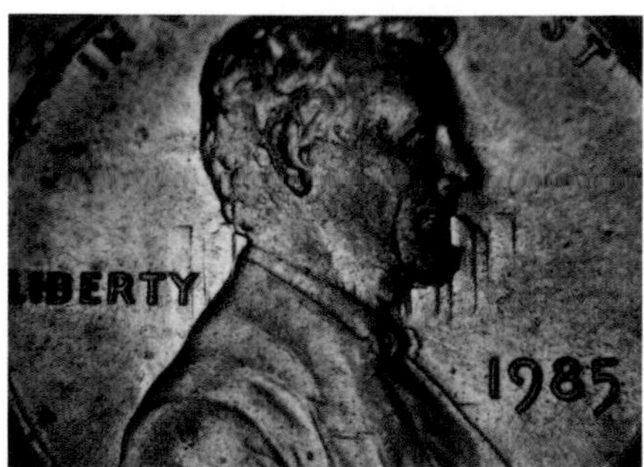

II-G-5

II-G-5 Heavy Die Clash (IWE), Rarity Level: 4-5, Values: $1 to $10 and up.

II-G-6 Heavy Collar Clash (IWE), Rarity Level: 3-4, Values: $1 to $5 and up.

II-G-7 Heavy Design Transfer (IWE), Rarity Level: 3-4, Values: 10 cents to $1.

•Die progressions (II-H)

The progression section consists of three classes. These are useful as cataloging tools for many different die varieties, but especially the die cracks and die breaks which may enlarge, lengthen or increase in number.

II-H-1 Progression (W), Rarity Level: 3-5, Values: $1 up.

II-H-2 Die Substitution (IW), Rarity Level: 2-4, Values: No Extra Value to Minimal Value.

II-H-3 Die Repeat (I), Rarity Level: 2-4, Values: No Extra Value to Minimal Value.

•Die scratches, polished and abraded dies (II-I)

This section consists of those classes having to do with the use of an abrasive in some form to intentionally polish proof dies, or repair the circulating die surface. Several classes which previously were referred to as "polished" now are listed as "abraded."

II-I-1 Die Scratch (IW), Rarity Level: 1-2, Values: No Extra Value to 10 cents to 25 cents, as a marker.

II-I-2 Polished (proof) Die (IW), Rarity Level: 1, Values: No Extra Value.

II-I-3 Abraded (Circulation) Die (IW), Rarity Level: 1-2, Values: No Extra Value up to $10.

II-I-4 Inside Abraded Die Doubling (IW), Rarity Level: 1-3, Values: No Extra Value to $1.

II-I-5 Outside Abraded Die Doubling (IW), Rarity Level: 1-3, Values: No Extra Value to $1.

II-I-6 Lathe Marks (IW), Rarity Level: 5-7, Values: No Extra Value, marker only.

Striking varieties

DIVISION III

Once the dies are made and the planchets have been prepared, they are struck by a pair of dies and become a coin. In this division, we list the misstrikes resulting from human or mechanical malfunction in the striking process. These are one-of-a-kind varieties, but there may be many similar coins that fall in a given class.

Multiples and combinations of classes must be considered on a case by case basis. The first several sections match the planchet sections indicated in the title.

•Struck on defective alloy mix planchets (III-A)

This section includes those classes of coins struck on planchets that were made from a defective alloy.

III-A-1 Struck on an Improper Alloy Mix Planchet (IE), Rarity Level: 2-3, Values: 10 cents to $2.

III-A-2 Struck on a Planchet With Slag Inclusions(IE), Rarity Level: 5-6, Values: $10 up.

•Struck on damaged, defective or abnormal planchet (III-B)

Coins get struck on many strange objects. The more common of course are planchets which have been damaged in some way in the production process. In most of the classes in this section intent is at least presumed, if not specifically listed as a cause.

III-B-1 Struck on a Defective Planchet (IWE), Rarity Level: 4-6, Values: $5 to $10 and up.

III-B-2 Struck on a Mechanically Damaged Planchet (IWE), Rarity Level: 5-6, Values: $10 to $20 and up.

III-B-3 Struck on a Rolled Thin Planchet (IWE), Rarity Level: 5-6, Values: $2 to $5 and up.

III-B-4 Struck on a Rolled Thick Planchet (IWE), Rarity Level: 5-6, Values: $35 to $50 and up.

III-B-5 Struck on a Tapered Planchet (WE), Rarity Level: 4-6, Values: $2 to $5 and up.

III-B-6 Struck on a Partially Unplated Planchet (WE), Rarity Level: 5, Values: $10 up.

III-B-7 Struck on an Unplated Planchet (WE), Rarity Level: 6-7, Values: $100 up.

III-B-11

III-B-19

III-B-29

III-B-8 Struck on a Bubbled Plating Planchet (IWE), Rarity Level: 1, Values: No Value.

III-B-9 Struck on an Included Gas Bubble Planchet (WE), Rarity Level: 5-6, Values: $5 up.

III-B-10 Struck on a Partially Unclad Planchet (WE), Rarity Level: 5-6, Values: $5 up.

III-B-11 Struck on an Unclad Planchet (WE), Rarity Level: 4-5, Values: $5 and up.

III-B-12 Struck on an Undersize Planchet (WE), Rarity Level: 4-6, Values: Minimal.

III-B-13 Struck on an Oversize Planchet (WE), Rarity Level: 6-7, Values: Minimal.

III-B-14 Struck on an Improperly Prepared Proof Planchet (IWE), Rarity Level: 3-5, Values: $5 up.

III-B-15 Struck on an Improperly Annealed Planchet (IWE), Rarity Level: 4-5, Values: $5 up.

III-B-16 Struck on a Faulty Upset Edge Planchet (IWE), Rarity Level: 4-5, Values: $1 to $2.

III-B-17 Struck on a Rolled In Metal Planchet (WE), Rarity Level: 4-6, Values: $2 up.

III-B-18 Struck on a Weld Area Planchet (WE), Rarity Level: 6, Values: $25 to $50.

III-B-19 Struck on a Strike Clip Planchet (W), Rarity Level: 6-7, Values: $25 up.

III-B-20 Struck on an Unpunched Center Hole Planchet (WE), Rarity Level: 4-6, Values: $1 and up.

III-B-21 Struck on an Incompletely Punched Center Hole Planchet (WE), Rarity Level: 6-7, Values: $5 up.

III-B-22 Struck on an Uncentered Center Hole Planchet (WE), Rarity Level: 6-7, Values: $10 up.

III-B-23 Struck on a Multiple Punched Center Hole Planchet (WE), Rarity Level: 7, Values: $25 up.

III-B-24 Struck on an Unintended Center Hole Planchet (WE), Rarity Level: 6-7, Values: $25 and up.

III-B-25 Struck on a Wrong Size or Shape Center Hole Planchet (WE), Rarity Level: 5-7, Values: $5 up.

III-B-26 Struck on Scrap Coin Metal (E), Rarity Level: 4-6, Values: $10 up.

III-B-27 Struck on Junk Non Coin Metal (E), Rarity Level: 4-6, Values: $15 up.

III-B-28 Struck on a False Planchet (E), Rarity Level: 3-5, Values: $35 up.

III-B-29 Struck on Bonded Planchets (E), Rarity Level: 6-7, Values: $50 up.

•Struck on a clipped planchet (III-C)

Coins struck on clipped blanks, or planchets, exhibit the same missing areas as they did before striking, modified by the metal flow from the strike which rounds the edges and tends to move metal into the missing areas. Values for blanks will run higher than planchets with similar clips.

III-C-1 Struck on a Disc Clip Planchet (WE), Rarity Level: 4-5, Values: $1 on regular coins, $20 and up for clad coins.

III-C-2 Struck on a Curved Clip Planchet - to 5% (WE), Rarity Level: 3-5, Values: 50 cents up.

III-C-3 Struck on a Curved Clip Planchet - (6 to 10%) (WE), Rarity Level: 4-5, Values: $1 up.

III-C-4 Struck on a Curved Clip Planchet - (11 to 25%) (WE), Rarity Level: 4-5, Values: $2 up.

III-C-5 Struck on a Curved Clip Planchet - (26 to 60%) (WE), Rarity Level: 4-6, Values: $10 up.

III-C-6 Struck on a Double Curved Clip Planchet (WE), Rarity Level: 3-4, Values: $2 up.

III-C-7 Struck on a Triple Curved Clip Planchet (WE), Rarity Level: 4-5, Values: $5 up.

III-C-8 Struck on a Multiple Curved Clip Planchet (WE), Rarity Level: 4-6, Values: $5 up.

III-C-9 Struck on an Overlapping Curved Clipped Planchet (WE), Rarity Level: 5-6, Values: $15 up.

III-C-10 Struck on an Incomplete Curved Clip Planchet (WE), Rarity Level: 4-5, Values: $10 up.

III-C-11 Struck on an Oval Clip Planchet (WE), Rarity Level: 5-6, Values: $20 up.

III-C-12 Struck on a Crescent Clip Planchet - (61% or more) (WE), Rarity Level: 6-7, Values: $100 up.

III-C-13 Struck on a Straight Clip Planchet (E), Rarity Level: 4-6, Values: $10 up.

III-C-14 Struck on an Incomplete Straight Clip Planchet (WE), Rarity Level: 5-6, Values: $20 up.

III-C-15 Struck on a Ragged Clip Planchet (E), Rarity Level: 4-6, Values: $15 up.

III-C-16 Struck on an Outside Corner Clip Planchet (E), Rarity Level: 7, Values: $100 up.

III-C-17 Struck on an Inside Corner Clip Planchet (E), Rarity Level: Unknown outside mint., Values: -.

III-C-18 Struck on an Irregularly Clipped Planchet (E), Rarity Level: 6-7, Values: $20 up.

III-C-19 Struck on an Incompletely Punched Scalloped or Multi-Sided Planchet (E), Rarity Level: 7, Values: $20 up.

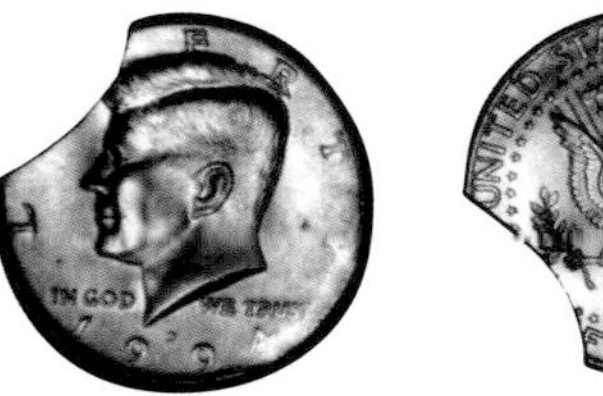

III-C-3

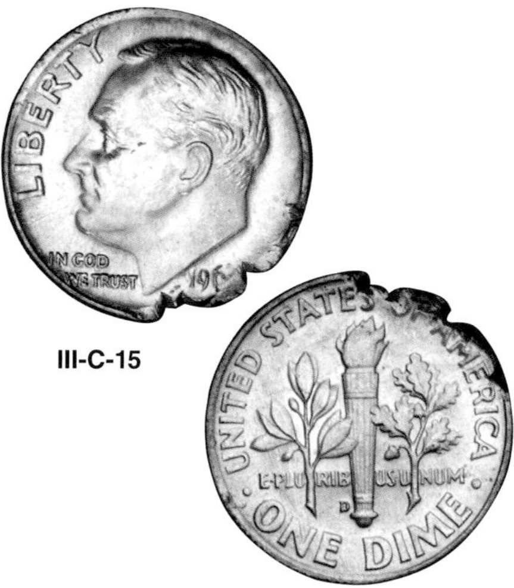

III-C-15

•Struck on a laminated, split or broken planchet (III-D)

This section has to do with the splitting, cracking or breaking of a coin parallel to the faces of the coin, or at least very nearly parallel, or breaks at right angles to the faces of the coin.

Lamination cracks and missing metal of any size below a split planchet are too common in the 35-percent silver 1942-1945 nickels to be collectible or have any significant value.

III-D-1 Struck on a Small Lamination Crack Planchet (W), Rarity Level: 3-4, Values: 10 up.

III-D-2 Struck on a Large Lamination Crack Planchet (W), Rarity Level: 3-6, Values: $1 up.

III-D-3 Struck on a Split Planchet (W), Rarity Level: 4-6, Values: $5 up.

III-D-4 Struck on a Hinged Split Planchet (W), Rarity Level: 5-6, Values: $35 up.

III-D-5 Struck on a Planchet With a Clad Layer Missing (W), Rarity Level: 4-5, Values: $15 up.

III-D-6 Struck on a Planchet With Both Clad Layers Missing (W), Rarity Level: 4-5, Values: $25 up.

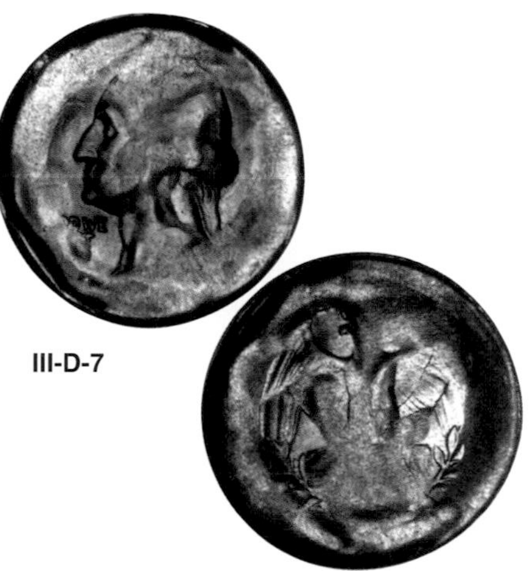

III-D-7

III-E-2

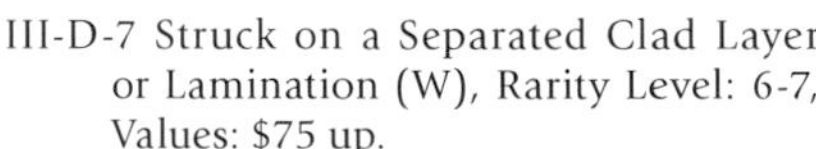

III-D-7 Struck on a Separated Clad Layer or Lamination (W), Rarity Level: 6-7, Values: $75 up.

III-D-8 Struck on a Broken Planchet Before the Strike (W), Rarity Level: 3-5, Values: $10 up.

III-D-9 Broken Coin During or After the Strike (W), Rarity Level: 4-6, Values: $20 up.

III-D-10 Struck Coin Fragment Split or Broken During or After the Strike (W), Rarity Level: 3-5, Values: $5 up.

III-D-11 Reedless Coin Broken During or After the Strike (W), Rarity Level: Unknown, Values: -.

•Struck on Wrong Stock Planchets (III-E)

These classes cover those cases where the wrong stock was run through the blanking press, making planchets of the correct diameter, but of the wrong thickness, alloy or metal or a combination of incorrect thickness and metal.

III-E-1 Struck on a Half Cent-Stock Planchet (IE), Rarity Level: Unknown, Values: No Value Established.

III-E-2 Struck on a Cent-Stock Planchet (IE), Rarity Level: Unknown, Values: No Value Established.

III-E-3 Struck on a Two-Cent-Stock Planchet (E), Rarity Level: Unknown, Values: -.

III-E-4 Struck on a Three-Cent-Silver Stock Planchet (E), Rarity Level: Unknown, Values: -.

III-E-5 Struck on a Three-Cent-Nickel Stock Planchet (E), Rarity Level: Unknown, Values: -.

III-E-6 Struck on a Half Dime-Stock Planchet (E), Rarity Level: Unknown, Values: -.

III-E-7 Struck on a Dime-Stock Planchet (E), Rarity Level: 5-6, Values: $20 up.

III-E-8 Struck on a Twenty-Cent-Stock Planchet (E), Rarity Level: Unknown, Values: -.

III-E-9 Struck on a Quarter-Stock Planchet (E), Rarity Level: 6, Values: $50 up.

III-E-10 Struck on a Half Dollar-Stock Planchet (E), Rarity Level: 6-7, Values: $100 up.

III-E-11 Struck on a Dollar-Stock Planchet (E), Rarity Level: 6-7, Values: $300 up.

III-E-12 Struck on a Token/Medal-Stock Planchet (E), Rarity Level: 7, Values: No Value Established.

III-E-13 Struck on a Wrong Thickness Spoiled Planchet (IWE), Rarity Level: 7, Values: $50 up.

III-E-14 Struck on a Correct Thickness Spoiled Planchet (IWE), Rarity Level: Unknown, Values: No Value Established.

III-E-15 Struck on a Cut Down Struck Token (IWE), Rarity Level: 6-7, Values: $50 up.

III-E-16 Struck on an Experimental or Pattern-Stock Planchet (IE), Rarity Level: 7, Values: $50 up.

III-E-17 Struck on a Proof-Stock Planchet (IE), Rarity Level: 7, Values: $100 up.

III-E-18 Struck on an Adjusted Specification-Stock Planchet (IE), Rarity Level: 3-7, Values: No Value to $5 and up.

III-E-19 Struck on a Trial Strike-Stock Planchet (IE), Rarity Level: Unknown, Values: No Value Established.

III-E-20 U.S. Coin Struck on a Foreign-Stock Planchet. (E), Rarity Level: 5, Values: $35 up.

III-E-7

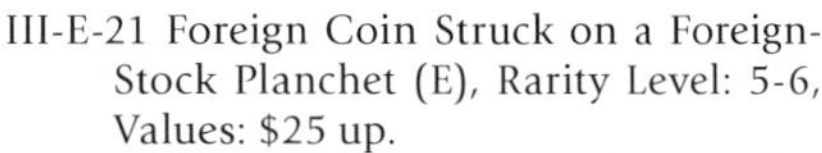

III-G-18

III-E-21 Foreign Coin Struck on a Foreign-Stock Planchet (E), Rarity Level: 5-6, Values: $25 up.

III-E-22 Struck on a Non-Standard Coin Alloy (IE), Rarity Level: 4-7, Values: $20 up.

•Extra metal (III-F)

The term "extra metal" for the purpose of this section includes both extra metal added to the blank during the blanking operation and metal powder added to the planchet during the annealing operation.

III-F-1 Struck on a Type 1 Blank With Extra Metal (W), Rarity Level: Unknown, Values: -.

III-F-2 Struck on a Type 2 Planchet With Extra Metal (W), Rarity Level: 4-5, Values: $10 up.

III-F-3 Struck on a Sintered Coating Planchet (W), Rarity Level: 6-7, Values: $35 up.

•Struck on normal or abnormal blanks, or planchets (III-G)

This section includes coins struck on either a blank, as it comes from the blanking press, or as a planchet that has passed through the upsetting mill. Added to this section are those planchets which are normal until they are struck by the wrong dies. These differ from the wrong stock planchets because the wrong stock planchets are already a variety before they are struck.

III-G-1 Struck on a Type 1 Blank (IWE), Rarity Level: 4-6, Values: $10 up.

III-G-2 Struck on a Type 2 Planchet (I), Rarity Level: 1, Values: No Extra Value.

III-G-3 Struck on a Purchased Planchet (I), Rarity Level: 1, Values: No Extra Value.

III-G-4 Struck on a Mint-Made Planchet (I), Rarity Level: 1, Values: No Extra Value.

III-G-5 Struck on an Adjustment-Marked Planchet (I), Rarity Level: 4-7, Values: Minimal, and may reduce value of coin in some cases.

III-G-6 Struck on a Hardness Test-Marked Planchet (I), Rarity Level: 6-7, Values: $10 up.

III-G-7 Wrong Planchet or Metal on a Half Cent Planchet (IE), Rarity Level: 5-7, Values: $100 up.

III-G-8 Wrong Planchet or Metal on a Cent Planchet (IE), Rarity Level: 3-6, Values: $25 up.

III-G-9 Wrong Planchet or Metal on a Nickel Planchet (E), Rarity Level: 4-6, Values: $35 up

III-G-10 Wrong Planchet or Metal on a Dime Planchet (E), Rarity Level: 4-6, Values: $50 up.

III-G-11 Wrong Planchet or Metal on a Quarter Planchet (E), Rarity Level: 4-6. Values: $100 up.

III-G-12 Wrong Planchet or Metal on a Half Dollar Planchet (E), Rarity Level: 6-7, Values: $500 up.

III-G-13 Wrong Planchet or Metal on a Dollar Planchet (E), Rarity Level: 7, Values: $500 up.

III-G-14 Wrong Planchet or Metal on a Gold Planchet (E), Rarity Level: 7, Values: $1000 up.

III-G-15 Struck on a Wrong Series Planchet (IE), Rarity Level: 6-7, Values: $1500 up.

III-G-16 U.S. Coin Struck on a Foreign Planchet (E), Rarity Level: 5-7, Values: $35 up.

III-G-17 Foreign Coin Struck on a U.S. Planchet (E), Rarity Level: 6-7, Values: $50 up.

III-G-18 Foreign Coin Struck on a Wrong Foreign Planchet (E), Rarity Level: 6-7, Values: $50 up.

III-G-19 Struck on a Medal Planchet (E), Rarity Level: 6-7, Values: $100 up.

III-G-20 Medal Struck on a Coin Planchet (IE), Rarity Level: 3-5, Values: $10 up.

III-G-21 Struck on an Official Sample Planchet (IE), Rarity Level: Unknown, Values: No Value Established.

III-G-22 Struck Intentionally on a Wrong Planchet (I), Rarity Level: 6-7, Values: Mainly struck as Presentation Pieces, full numismatic value.

III-G-23 Non-Proof Struck on a Proof Planchet (IE), Rarity Level: 6-7, Values: $500 up.

•Struck on Coin Metal Strip (III-H)

Pieces of the coin metal strip do manage at times to escape into the coin press.

III-H-1 (See I-H-1 Punched Coin Metal Strip), Rarity Level: Impossible, Values: -.

III-H-2 Struck on Chopped Coin Metal Strip (E), Rarity Level: 6-7, Values: $25 up.

•Die Adjustment Strikes (III-I)

As the dies are set up and adjusted in the coin press, variations in the strike occur until the dies are properly set. Test strikes are normally scrapped, but on occasion reach circulation.

III-I-1 Die Adjustment Strike (IE), Rarity Level: 5-6, Values: $35 up.

III-I-2 Edge Strike (E), Rarity Level: 5-6, Values: $10 to $20 and up.

III-I-3 Weak Strike (W), Rarity Level: 1, Values: No Extra Value.

III-I-4 Strong Strike (IWE), Rarity Level: 1, Values: No value except for the premium that might be paid for a well struck coin.

III-I-5 Jam Strike (IE), Rarity Level: 7, Values: $50 up.

III-I-6 Trial Piece Strike (I), Rarity Level: 6-7, Values: $100 up.

III-I-7 Edge-Die Adjustment Strike (I), Rarity Level: 5-7, Values: $5 up.

III-I-8 Uniface Strike (I), Rarity Level 7, Values: $50 up.

III-I-3

•Indented, Brockage and Counter-Brockage Strikes (III-J)

Indented and uniface strikes involve an extra unstruck planchet between one of the dies and the planchet being struck. Brockage strikes involve a struck coin between one of the dies and the planchet and a counter-brockage requires a brockage coin between one of the dies and the planchet.

A cap, or capped die strike results when a coin sticks to the die and is squeezed around it in the shape of a bottle cap.

III-J-1 Indented Strike (W), Rarity Level: 3-6, Values: $5 up.

III-J-2 Uniface Strike (W), Rarity Level: 3-5, Values: $15 up.

III-J-3 Indented Strike By a Smaller Planchet (WE), Rarity Level: 5-7, Values: $100 up.

III-J-4 Indented Second Strike (W), Rarity Level: 3-5, Values: $10 up, about the same as a regular double strike of comparable size.

III-J-5 Partial Brockage Strike (W), Rarity Level: 3-6, Values: $15 up.

III-J-6 Full Brockage Strike (W), Rarity Level: 3-6, Values: $5 up.

III-J-7 Brockage Strike of a Smaller Coin (WE), Rarity Level: 6-7, Values: $200 up.

III-J-8 Brockage Strike of a Struck Coin Fragment (WE), Rarity Level: 4-6, Values: $5 up.

III-J-9 Brockage Second Strike (WE), Rarity Level: 3-5, Values: $5 up.

III-J-10 Partial Counter-Brockage Strike (WE), Rarity Level: 3-5, Values: $10 up.

III-J-11 Full Counter-Brockage Strike (WE), Rarity Level: 5-7, Values: $100 up.

III-J-12 Counter-Brockage Second Strike (WE), Rarity Level: 4-6, Values: $10 up.

III-J-13 Full Brockage-Counter-Brockage Strike (WE), Rarity Level: 6-7, Values: $150 up.

III-J-14 Multiple Brockage or Counter-Brockage Strike (WE), Rarity Level: 5-7, Values: $100 up.

III-J-15 Capped Die Strike (WE), Rarity Level: 6-7, Values: $500 up.

III-J-16 Reversed Capped Die Strike (WE), Rarity Level: 7, Values: $1,000 up.

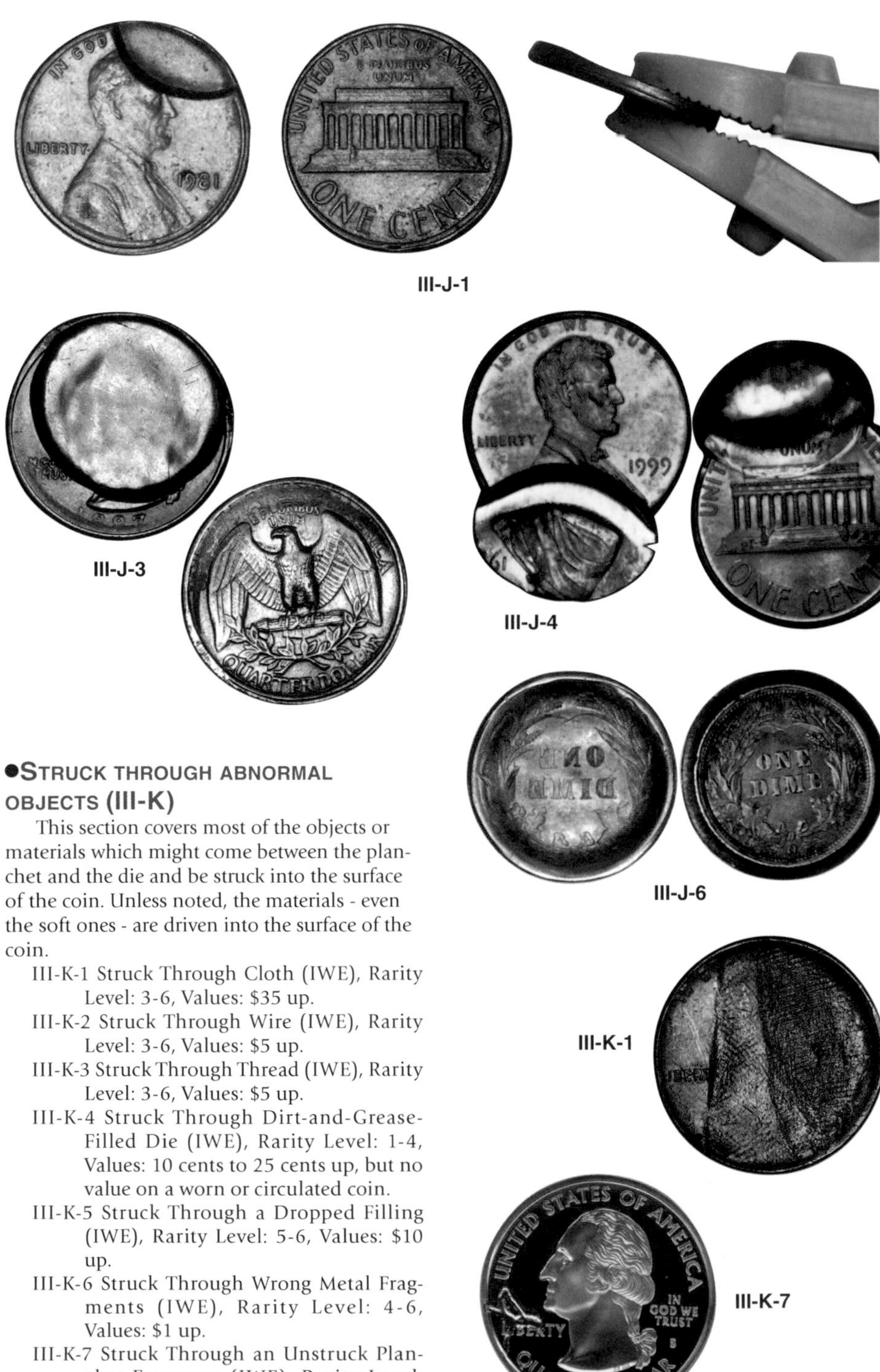
III-J-1

III-J-3

III-J-4

III-J-6

III-K-1

III-K-7

●Struck through abnormal objects (III-K)

This section covers most of the objects or materials which might come between the planchet and the die and be struck into the surface of the coin. Unless noted, the materials - even the soft ones - are driven into the surface of the coin.

III-K-1 Struck Through Cloth (IWE), Rarity Level: 3-6, Values: $35 up.

III-K-2 Struck Through Wire (IWE), Rarity Level: 3-6, Values: $5 up.

III-K-3 Struck Through Thread (IWE), Rarity Level: 3-6, Values: $5 up.

III-K-4 Struck Through Dirt-and-Grease-Filled Die (IWE), Rarity Level: 1-4, Values: 10 cents to 25 cents up, but no value on a worn or circulated coin.

III-K-5 Struck Through a Dropped Filling (IWE), Rarity Level: 5-6, Values: $10 up.

III-K-6 Struck Through Wrong Metal Fragments (IWE), Rarity Level: 4-6, Values: $1 up.

III-K-7 Struck Through an Unstruck Planchet Fragment (IWE), Rarity Level: 3-5, Values: $1 up.

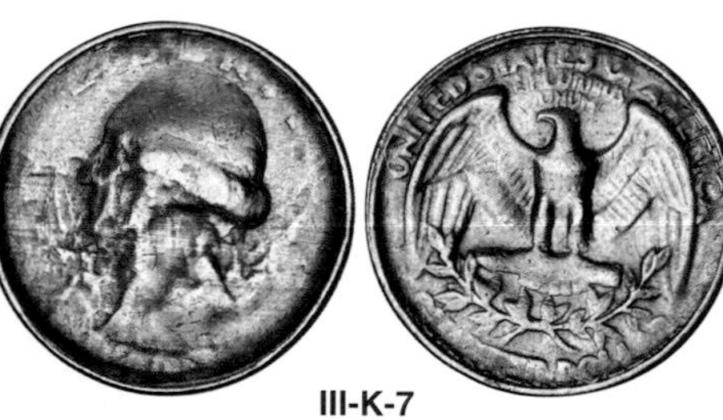

III-K-7

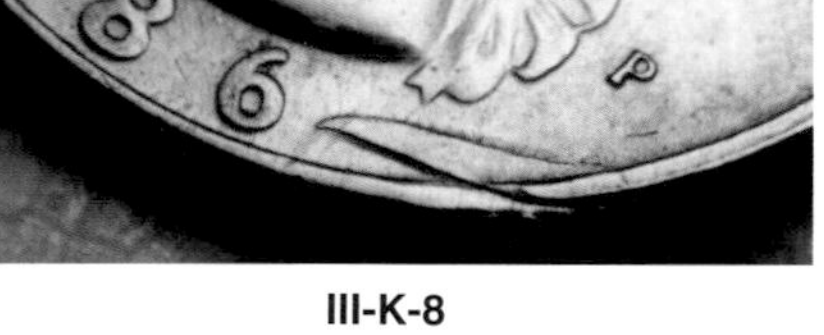

III-K-8

III-K-8

III-K-8 Struck Through a Rim Burr (IWE), Rarity Level: 3-5, Values: $1 to $2 and up.

III-K-9 Struck Through plit-Off Reeding (IWE), Rarity Level: 5-6, Values: $25 up.

III-K-10 Struck Through a Feed Finger (IWE), Rarity Level: 5-7, Values: $25 to $50 and up.

III-K-11 Struck Through Miscellaneous Objects (IWE), Rarity Level: 4-6, Values: $1 up.

III-K-12 Struck Through Progression (IWE), Rarity Level: 4-6, Values: $1 up.

Note: Some 1987 through 1994 quarters are found without mintmarks, classed as III-K-4, a Filled Die. Values depend on market conditions. Filled dies have value ONLY on current, uncirculated grade coins.

•Double strikes (III-L)

Only coins which receive two or more strikes by the die pair fall in this section and are identified by the fact that both sides of the coin are affected. Unless some object interferes, an equal area of both sides of the coin will be equally doubled.

The exception is the second strike with a loose die, which will double only one side of a coin, but is a rare form usually occurring only on proofs. A similar effect is flat field doubling from die chatter.

III-L-1 Close Centered Double Strike (WE), Rarity Level: 4-6, Values: $15 up.

III-L-2 Rotated Second Strike Over a Centered First Strike (WE), Rarity Level: 4-6, Values: $15 up.

III-L-3 Off-Center Second Strike Over a Centered First Strike (WE), Rarity Level: 4-6, Values: $15 up.

III-L-4 Off-Center Second Strike Over an Off-Center First Strike (WE), Rarity Level: 4-6, Values: $10 up.

III-L-5 Off-Center Second Strike Over a Broadstrike (WE), Rarity Level: 5-6, Values: $20 up.

III-L-6 Centered Second Strike Over an Off Center First Strike (WE), Rarity Level: 5-6, Values: $50 up.

III-L-7 Obverse Struck Over Reverse (WE), Rarity Level: 5-6, Values: $25 up.

III-L-8 Nonoverlapping Double Strike (WE), Rarity Level: 5-6 Values: $20 up.

III-L-9 Struck Over a Different Denomination or Series (WE), Rarity Level: 6, Values: $300 and up.

III-L-10 Chain Strike (WE), Rarity Level: 6, Values: $300 up for the pair of coins that were struck together.

III-L-11 Second-Strike Doubling From a Loose Die (W), Rarity Level: 6-7, Values: $200 up.

III-L-12 Second-Strike Doubling From a Loose Screw Press Die (W), Rarity Level: 5-6, Values: $100 up.

III-L-13 Second Strike on an Edge Strike (WE), Rarity Level: 5-6, Values: $20 up.

III-L-14 Folded Planchet Strike (WE), Rarity Level: 5-7, Values: $100 up.
III-L-15 Triple Strike (WE), Rarity Level: 6-7, Values: $100 up.
III-L-16 Multiple Strike (WE), Rarity Level: 6-7, Values: $200 up.
III-L-17 U.S. Coin Struck Over a Struck Foreign Coin (WE), Rarity Level: 6-7, Values: $300 up.
III-L-18 Foreign Coin Struck Over a Struck U.S. Coin (WE), Rarity Level: 6-7, Values: $400 up.
III-L-19 Foreign Coin Struck Over a Struck Foreign Coin (WE), Rarity Level: 7, Values: $500 up.
III-L-20 Double Strike on Scrap or Junk (E), Rarity Level: 6, Values: $50 up.
III-L-21 Struck on a Struck Token or Medal (E), Rarity Level: 5-6, Values: $100 up.
III-L-22 Double-Struck Edge Motto or Design (E), Rarity Level: 6-7, Values: $200 up.
III-L-23 One Edge Motto or Design Struck Over Another (E), Rarity Level: 7, Values: $300 up.
III-L-24 Flat Field Doubling (W), Rarity Level: 2-3, Values: $1 to $5.
III-L-25 Territorial Struck over Struck U.S. Coin: (I) Rarity Level: 6-7, Values: $200 up.
III-L-26 Pattern Struck over Struck U.S. Coin: (I) Rarity Level: 6-7, Values: $200 up.
III-L-27 Pattern Struck over Struck Pattern:(I) Rarity Level 6-7, Values: $200 up.
III-L-28 Pattern Struck Over Foreign Coin:(I) Rarity Level 6-7, Values - $200 up.

•COLLAR STRIKING VARIETIES (III-M)

The collar is often referred to as the "Third Die," and is involved in a number of forms of misstrikes. The collar normally rises around the planchet, preventing it from squeezing sideways between the dies and at the same time forming the reeding on reeded coins.

If the collar is out of position or tilted, a partial collar strike results; if completely missing, it causes a broadstrike; if the planchet is not entirely between the dies, an off-center strike.

III-M-1 Flanged Partial Collar Strike (WE), Rarity Level: 5-6, Values: $20 up.
III-M-2 Reversed Flanged Partial Collar Strike (WE), Rarity Level: 6-7, Values: $35 up.
III-M-3 Tilted Partial Collar Strike (WE), Rarity Level: 5-6, Values: $20 up.
III-M-4 Centered Broadstrike (WE), Rarity Level: 5-6, Values: $5 up.

III-L-3

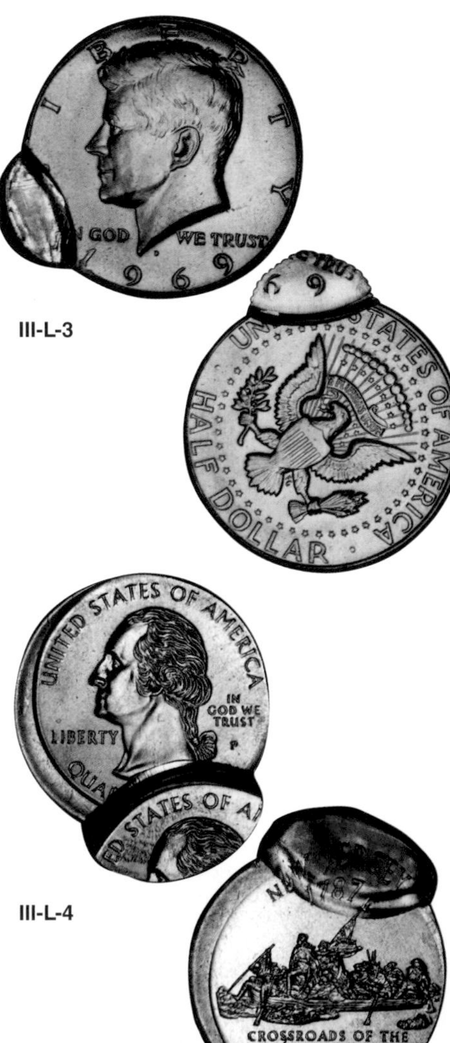

III-L-3

III-L-4

III-M-5

III-M-8

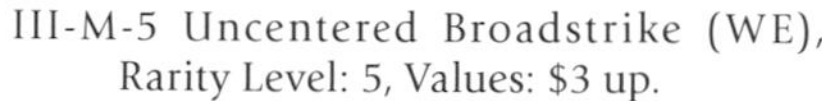

III-M-5 Uncentered Broadstrike (WE), Rarity Level: 5, Values: $3 up.

III-M-6 Reversed Broadstrike (WE), Rarity Level: 6, Values: $10 up.

III-M-7 Struck Off-Center 10-30% (W), Rarity Level: 3-6, Values: $3 up.

III-M-8 Struck Off-Center 31-70% (W), Rarity Level: 4-6, Values: $5 up.

III-M-9 Struck Off-Center 71% or More (W), Rarity Level: 3-5, Values: $2 up.

III-M-10 Rotated Multi-sided Planchet Strike (W), Rarity Level: 5-6, Values: $10 up.

III-M-11 Wire Edge Strike (IWE), Rarity Level: 1-2, Values: No Extra Value.

III-M-12 Struck With the Collar Too High (WE), Rarity Level: 6-7, Values: $20 up.

III-M-13 Off-Center Slide Strike (W), Rarity Level:3-6 $4 up.

•Misaligned and Rotated (Die) Strike Varieties (III-N)

One (rarely both) of the dies may be Offset Misaligned, off to one side, or may be tilted (Vertically Misaligned). One die may either have been installed so that it is turned in relation to the other die, or may turn in the holder, or the shank may break allowing the die face to rotate in relation to the opposing die.

Vertical misaligned dies are rarely found, and like rotated dies, find only limited collector interest. Ninety and 180 degree rotations are the most popular. Rotations of 14 degrees or less have no value. The 1989-D Congress dollar is found with a nearly 180 degree rotated reverse, currently retailing for around $2,000. Only about 30 have been reported to date.

III-N-1 Offset Die Misalignment Strike (WE), Rarity Level: 3-5, Values: $2 up.

III-N-2 Vertical Die Misalignment Strike (WE), Rarity Level: 4-6, Values: $1 up.

III-N-3 Rotated Die Strike - 15 to 45 Degrees (IWE), Rarity Level: 4-6, Values: $2 up.

III-N-4 Rotated Die Strike - 46 to 135 Degrees (IWE), Rarity Level: 5-6, Values: $10 up.

III-N-5 Rotated Die Strike - 136 to 180 Degrees (IWE), Rarity Level: 5-6, Values: $25 up.

•Lettered and Design Edge Strike Varieties (III-O)

Early U.S. coins and a number of foreign coins have either lettered edges, or designs on the edge of the coin. Malfunctions of the application of the motto or design to the edge fall in this section.

III-O-1 Overlapping Edge Motto or Design (WE), Rarity Level: 3-4, Values: $5 to $10 and up.

III-O-2 Wrong Edge Motto or Design (WE), Rarity Level: 5-6-7, Values: $50 up.

III-O-3 Missing Edge Motto, Design or Security Edge (IWE), Rarity Level: 5-6-7, Values: $50 up.

III-O-4 Jammed Edge Die Strike (W), Rarity Level: 6, Values: $10 up.

III-O-5 Misplaced Segment of an Edge Die (E), Rarity Level: 4-7, Values: $25 up.

III-O-6 Reeded Edge Struck Over a Lettered Edge (IE), Rarity Level: 3-6, Values: No Extra Value up.

•Defective Strikes and Mismatched Dies (III-P)

The final section of the Striking Division covers coins which are not properly struck for reasons other than those in previous classes, such as coins struck with mismatched (muled) dies. The mismatched die varieties must be taken on a case by case basis, while the otherclasses presently have little collector demand or premium.

III-P-1 Defective Strike (WE), Rarity Level: 1, Values: No Extra Value.

III-P-2 Mismatched Die Strike (E), Rarity Level: 4-7, Values: $25 up.

III-P-3 Single-Strike Proof (WE), Rarity Level: 4-5, Values: Minimal.

III-P-4 Single Die-Proof Strike (IE), Rarity Level: 5-6, Values: $100 up.

III-P-5 Reversed Die Strike (I), Rarity Level: 4-5, Values: No Extra Value to Minimal.

Official Mint modifications

DIVISION IV

Several mint produced varieties occur after the coin has been struck, resulting in the addition of the fourth division to my PDS System. Since most of these coins are either unique or are special varieties, each one must be taken on a case by case basis. All classes listed here are by definition intentional.

I have not listed values as the coins falling in these classes which are sold through regular numismatic channels, are cataloged with the regular issues or are covered in specialized catalogs in their particular area.

•Matte proofs (IV-A)

Matte proofs as a section include several of the forms of proof coins which have the striking characteristics of a mirror proof but have been treated AFTER striking to give them a grainy, non-reflective surface.

IV-A-1 Matte Proof (I), Rarity Level: 3-5, Values: Normal Numismatic Value.

IV-A-2 Matte Proof on One Side (I), Rarity Level: 7, Values: Normal Numismatic Value.

IV-A-3 Sandblast Proof (I), Rarity Level: 4-6, Values: Normal Numismatic Value.

•Additional engraving (IV-B)

This section includes any added markings which are placed on the struck coin and struck coins which later were cut into pieces for various purposes. The warning is repeated: Anything done to a coin after the strike is extremely difficult to authenticate and is much easier to fake than a die struck coin.

IV-B-1 Counterstamp and Countermark (I), Rarity Level: 3-6, Values: Normal Numismatic Value.

IV-B-2 Perforated and Cut Coins (I), Rarity Level: 4-6, Values: Normal Numismatic Value.

•Restrikes (IV-C)

Restrikes cover a complicated mixture of official use of dies from a variety of sources. Whether or not some were officially sanctioned is always a problem for the collector.

IV-C-1 Restrike on the Same Denomination Planchet (I), Rarity Level: 4-6, Values: Normal Numismatic Value.

IV-C-2 Restrike on a Different Denomination or Series Planchet (I), Rarity Level: 4-6, Values: Normal Numismatic Value.

IV-C-3 Restrike on a Foreign Coin (I), Rarity Level: 6-7, Values: Normal Numismatic Value.

IV-C-4 Restrike on a Token or Medal (I), Rarity Level: 5-6, Values: Normal Numismatic Value.

IV-C-5 Restruck With the Original Dies (I), Rarity Level: 4-6, Values: Normal Numismatic Value.

IV-C-6 Restruck With Mismatched Dies (I), Rarity Level: 4-6, Values: Normal Numismatic Value.

IV-C-7 Copy Strike With New Dies (I), Rarity Level: 3-5, Values: Normal Numismatic Value.

IV-C-8 Fantasy Strike (I), Rarity Level: 4-6, Values: Normal Numismatic Value.

After strike modifications

DIVISION V

This division includes both modifications that have value to collectors – and those that don't. I needed a couple of divisions to cover other things that happen to coins to aid in cataloging them. This avoids the false conclusion that an unlisted coin is quite rare, when the exact opposite is more likely to be the case.

•Collectible modifications after strike (V-A)

This section includes those classes having to do with deliberate modifications of the coin done with a specific purpose or intent which makes them of some value to collectors. Quite often these pieces were made specifically to sell to collectors, or at least to the public under the guise of being collectible.

V-A-1 Screw Thaler, Rarity Level: 5-6, Values: Normal Numismatic Value.

V-A-2 Love Token, Rarity Level: 3-6, Values: $10 up.

V-A-3 Satirical or Primitive Engraving, Rarity Level: 6-7, Values: $5 up.

V-A-4 Elongated Coin, Rarity Level: 2-7, Values: 50 cents to $1 and up.

V-A-5 Coin Jewelry, Rarity Level: 2-5, Values: $1 up.

V-A-6 Novelty Coin, Rarity Level: 1-3, Values: No Value up to $5 to $10.

V-A-7 Toning, Rarity Level: 3-6, Values: No value up, depending on coloration. Easily faked.

V-A-8 Mint Modification, Rarity Level: 4-7, Values: $5 up. Easily faked.

V-A-9 Mint Packaging Mistake, Rarity Level: 5-7, Values: Nominal $1. Very easily faked.

•ALTERATIONS AND DAMAGE AFTER THE STRIKE(V-B)

This section includes those changes in a coin which have no collector value. In most cases their effect on the coin is to reduce or entirely eliminate any collector value - and in the case of counterfeits they are actually illegal to even own.

V-B-1 Machine Doubling Damage: NOTE: Machine doubling damage is defined as: "Damage to a coin after the strike, due to die bounce or chatter or die displacement, showing on the struck coin as scrapes on the sides of the design elements, with portions of the coin metal in the relief elements either displaced sideways or downward, depending on the direction of movement of the loose die." Machine doubling damage, or MDD, is by far the most common form of doubling found on almost any coin in the world. Rarity Level: 0, Values: Reduces the coin's value.

V-B-2 Accidental or Deliberate Damage, Rarity Level: 0, Values: Reduces the coin's value.

V-B-3 Test Cut or Mark, Rarity Level: 0, Values: Reduces value of coin to face or bullion value.

V-B-4 Alteration, Rarity Level: 0, Values: Reduces value to face or bullion value.

V-B-5 Whizzing, Rarity Level: 0, Values: Reduces value sharply and may reduce it to face or bullion value.

V-B-6 Counterfeit, Copy, Facsimile, Forgery or Fake, Rarity Level: 0, Values: No Value and may be illegal to own.

V-B-7 Planchet Deterioration. Very common on copper-plated zinc cents. Rarity level: 0, Values: No Value.

9 American Coin History

U.S. Mint founded in 1792

At peak production, the U.S. Mint strikes nearly 30 billion coins a year. Who would have thought it possible at its founding? In July 1792, a site for the new U.S. Mint not yet having been secured, 1,500 silver half dismes were struck on a small screw press in the cellar of a Philadelphia building owned by sawmaker John Harper. Though some have since categorized these early emissions of the fledgling U.S. Mint as patterns, it is clear that first President George Washington – who is said to have deposited the silver from which the coins were struck – considered this small batch of half dismes to be the first official U.S. coins.

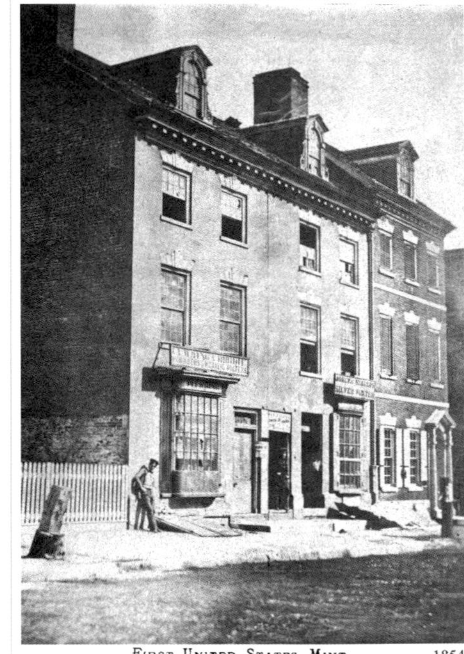

First United States Mint, Philadelphia Pa. 1854

The law establishing the Mint dates to April 2, 1792. From that early legislative birth has flowed the coins that have underpinned the workings of U.S. commerce for over two centuries. It must be remembered that the Mint was born in chaos. It was a time shortly after the Revolutionary War and as hard as it was to win independence from Great Britain, setting up American government finances on a sound basis was to prove almost as daunting.

At first a cumbersome system was proposed by Robert Morris, a Revolutionary War financier and first superintendent of finance. Refinements tendered by Thomas Jefferson and Alexander Hamilton then firmly placed the nation on an easily understood decimal system of coinage. They were working with a hodgepodge system that grew up in the Colonial period.

Despite a dire need for coinage in the Colonies, Great Britain considered it a royal right and granted franchises sparingly. Much of the Colonial economy, therefore, revolved around barter, with food staples, crops, and goods serving as currency. Indian wampum or bead money also was used, first in the fur trade and later as a form of money for Colonial use.

Copper pieces were produced around 1616 for Sommer Islands (now Bermuda), but coinage within the American Colonies apparently didn't begin until 1652, when John Hull struck silver threepence, sixpence and shillings under authority of the General Court of Massachusetts. This coinage continued, with design changes (willow, oak, and pine trees), through 1682. Most of the coins were dated 1652, apparently to avoid legal problems with England.

In 1658 Cecil Calvert, second Lord Baltimore, commissioned coins to be struck in England for use in Maryland. Other authorized and unauthorized coinages – including those of Mark Newby, John Holt, William Wood, and Dr. Samuel Higley – all became part of the landscape of circulating coins. In the 1780s there were influxes of counterfeit British halfpence and various state coinages.

The Articles of Confederation had granted individual states the right to produce copper coins. Many states found this to be appealing, and merchants in the mid-1780s traded copper coins of Vermont, Connecticut, Massachusetts, New Jersey, and New York. Not all were legal issues; various entrepreneurs used this as an invitation to strike imitation state coppers and British halfpence. Mutilated and worn foreign coins also circulated in abundance. Included among these were coins of Portugal, Great Britain, and France, with the large majority of the silver arriving from Spain.

The accounting system used by the states was derived from the British system of pounds, shillings, and pence. Each state was allowed to set its own rates at which foreign gold and silver coins would trade in relation to the British pound.

In 1782 Robert Morris, newly named superintendent of finance, was appointed to head a committee to determine the values and weights of the gold and silver coins in circulation. Asked simply to draw up a table of values, Morris took the opportunity to propose the establishment of a federal mint. In his Jan. 15, 1782, report (largely prepared by his assistant, Gouverneur Morris), Morris noted that the exchange rates between the states were complicated.

He observed that a farmer in New Hampshire would be hard-pressed if asked to determine the value of a bushel of wheat in South Carolina. Morris recorded that an amount of wheat worth four shillings in his home state of New Hampshire would be worth 21 shillings and eightpence under the accounting system used in South Carolina.

Morris claimed these difficulties plagued not only farmers, but that "they are perplexing to most Men and troublesome to all." Morris further pressed for the adoption of an American coin to solve the problems of the need for small change and debased foreign coinages in circulation.

In essence, what he was advocating was a monometallic system based on silver.

He said that gold and silver had fluctuated throughout history. Because these fluctuations resulted in the more valuable metal leaving the country, any nation that adopted a bimetallic coinage was doomed to have its gold or silver coins disappear from circulation.

Gouverneur Morris calculated the rate at which the Spanish dollar traded to the British pound in the various states. Leaving out South Carolina, because it threw off his calculations, Gouverneur Morris arrived at a common denominator of 1,440. Robert Morris, therefore, recommended a unit of value of 1/1,440, equivalent to a quarter grain of silver. He suggested the striking of a silver 100-unit coin, or cent; a silver 500-unit coin, or quint; a silver 1,000-unit coin, or mark; and two copper coins, one of eight units and the other of five units.

On Feb. 21, 1782, the Grand Committee of Congress approved the proposal and directed Morris to press forward and report with a plan to establish a mint. Morris had already done so. Apparently feeling confident that Congress would like his coinage ideas, Morris (as shown by his diary) began efforts at the physical establishment prior to his January 1782 report. He had already engaged Benjamin Dudley to acquire necessary equipment for the mint and hoped to have sample coins available to submit with his original report to Congress.

It wasn't until April 23, 1783, that Morris was able to send his Nova Constellatio patterns to Congress and suggest that he was ready to report on establishing a mint. Apparently nothing came of Morris' efforts. Several committees looked into the matter, but nothing was accomplished. Dudley was eventually discharged as Morris' hopes dimmed.

Thomas Jefferson was the next to offer a major plan. Jefferson liked the idea of a decimal system of coinage, but disliked Morris' basic unit of value. As chairman of the Currency Committee, Jefferson reviewed Morris' plan and formulated his own ideas.

To test public reaction, Jefferson gave his "Notes on Coinage" to The Providence Gazette, and Country Journal, which published his plan in its July 24, 1784, issue. Jefferson disagreed with Morris' suggestion for a 1/1,440 unit of value and instead proposed a decimal coinage based on the dollar, with the lowest unit of account being the mil, or 1/1,000.

"The most easy ratio of multiplication and division is that by ten," Jefferson wrote. "Every one knows the facility of Decimal Arithmetic."

Jefferson argued that although Morris' unit would have eliminated the unwanted fraction that occurred when merchants converted British farthings to dollars, this was of little significance. After all, the original idea of establishing a mint was to get rid of foreign currencies.

Morris' unit, Jefferson said, was too cumbersome for use in normal business transactions. According to Jefferson, under Morris' plan a horse valued at 80 Spanish dollars would require a notation of six figures and would be shown as 115,200 units.

Jefferson' coinage plan suggested the striking of a dollar, or unit; half dollar, or five-tenths; a double tenth, or fifth of a dollar, equivalent to a pistareen; a tenth, equivalent to a Spanish bit; and a one-fifth copper coin, relating to the British farthing. He also wanted a gold coin of $10, corresponding to the British double guinea; and a copper one-hundredth coin, relating to the British halfpence.

In reference to his coinage denominations, Jefferson said, it was important that the coins "coincide in value with some of the known coins so nearly, that the people may by quick reference in the mind, estimate their value." The Spanish dollar was the most commonly used coin in trade, so it was natural basis for the new U.S. silver dollar. In the Spanish system, the coin was called an eight reales, or piece of eight.

More than a year, however, passed without any further action on his plan or that proposed by Morris. In a letter to William Grayson, a member of the Continental Congress, Washington expressed concern for the establishment of a national coinage system, terming it "indispensably necessary." Washington also complained of the coinage in circulation: "A man must travel with a pair of scales in his pocket, or run the risk of receiving gold at one-fourth less than it counts."

On May 13, 1785, the 13-member Grand Committee, to whom Jefferson's plan had been submitted, filed its report, generally favoring Jefferson's coinage system. The committee did, however, make slight alterations, including the elimination of the gold $10 coin, the addition of a gold $5 coin, and the dropping of Jefferson's double tenth, which it replaced with a quarter dollar. The committee also added a coin equal to 1/200 of a dollar (half cent). On July 6, 1785, Congress unanimously approved the Grand Committee's plan. It failed, however, to set a standard weight for the silver dollar or to order plans drawn up for a mint.

Several proposals were offered for a contract coinage. On April 21, 1787, the board accepted a proposal by James Jarvis to strike 300 tons of copper coin at the federal standard. Jarvis, however, delivered slightly less than 9,000 pounds of his contract. The contract was voided the following year for his failure to meet scheduled delivery times, but helped to delay further action on a mint. Concerted action on a coinage system and a mint would wait until the formation of the new government.

Alexander Hamilton, named in September 1789 to head the new Treasury, offered three different methods by which the new nation could achieve economic stability, including the funding of the national debt, establishment of the Bank of North America and the founding of the U.S. Mint. On Jan. 21, 1791, Hamilton submitted to Congress a "Report on the Establishment of a Mint."

Hamilton agreed with Jefferson that the dollar seemed to be best suited to serve as the basic unit, but believed it necessary to establish a proper weight and fineness for the new coin. To do so, Hamilton had several Spanish coins assayed to determine the fine weight of the Spanish dollar. He also watched the rate at which Spanish dollars traded for fine gold (24 3/4 grains per dollar) on the world market.

From his assays and observations he determined that the Spanish dollar contained 371 grains of silver. He then multiplied 24 3/4 by 15 (the gold value of silver times his suggested bimetallic ratio) and arrived at 371 1/4 as the proper fine silver weight for the new silver dollar.

The Spanish dollar actually contained 376 grains of pure silver when new, 4 3/4 grains more than Hamilton's proposed silver dollar.

Hamilton also wanted a bimetallic ratio of 15-to-1. Hamilton said his ratio was closer to Great Britain's, which would be important for trade, and Holland's, which would be important for repaying loans from that country.

His report suggested the striking of a gold $10; gold dollar; silver dollar; silver tenth, or disme; and copper one-hundredth and half-hundredth. Hamilton felt the last of these, the half cent, was necessary because it would enable merchants to lower their prices, which would help the poor.

Congress passed the act establishing the U.S. Mint April 2, 1792. It reinstated several coin denominations left out by Hamilton and dropped his gold dollar. In gold, the act authorized at $10 coin, or "eagle"; a $5 coin, or "half eagle"; and a $2.50 coin, or "quarter eagle." In silver were to be a dollar, half dollar, quarter dollar, disme, and half disme, and in copper a cent and half cent.

Though it established a sound system of U.S. coinage, the act failed to address the problem of foreign coins in circulation. It was amended in February 1793 to cancel their legal-tender status within three years of the mint's opening.

Coinage totals at the first mint in Philadelphia were understandably low. Skilled coiners, assayers and others who could handle the mint's daily operations were in short supply in the United States. Also in want were adequate equipment and supplies of metal for coinage. Much of the former had to be built or imported. Much of the latter was also imported or salvaged from various domestic sources, including previously struck tokens and coins, and scrap metal.

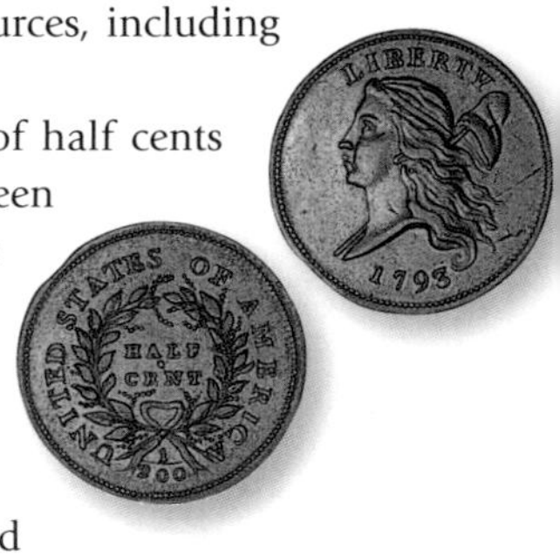

Coinage began in earnest in 1793 with the striking of half cents and cents at the new mint located at Seventh Street between Market and Arch streets in Philadelphia. Silver coinage followed in 1794, with half dimes, half dollars, and dollars. Gold coinage did not begin until 1795 with the minting of the first $5 and $10 coins. Silver dimes and quarters and gold $2.50 coins did not appear until 1796.

Under the bimetallic system of coinage by which gold and silver served as equal representations of the unit of value, much of the success and failure of the nation's coinage to enter and remain in circulation revolved around the supply and valuation of precious metals. From the Mint's beginning, slight miscalculations in the proper weight for the silver dollar and a proper bimetallic ratio led gold and silver to disappear from circulation. The U.S. silver dollar traded at par with Spanish and Mexican dollars, but because the U.S. coin was lighter, it was doomed to be exported.

A depositor at the first mint could make a profit at the mint's expense by sending the coins to the West Indies. There they could be traded at par for the heavier Spanish or Mexican eight reales, which were then shipped back to the United States for recoinage. As a result, few early silver dollars entered domestic circulation; most failed to escape the melting pots.

Gold fared no better. Calculations of the bimetallic ratio by which silver traded for gold on the world market were also askew at first and were always subject to fluctuations. Gold coins either disappeared quickly after minting or never entered circulation, languishing in bank vaults. These problems led President Jefferson to halt coinage of the gold $10 and the silver dollar in 1804.

The gold $10 reappeared in 1838 at a new, lower weight standard. The silver dollar, not coined for circulation since 1803, returned in 1836 with a limited mintage. Full-scale coinage waited until 1840.

Nor was the coinage of copper an easy matter for the first mint. Severe shortages of the metal led the mint to explore various avenues of obtaining sufficient supplies for striking cents and half cents.

Witness, for example, the half-cent issues of 1795 and 1797 struck over privately issued tokens of the New York firm of Talbot, Allum & Lee because of a shortage of copper for the federal issue. Rising copper prices and continued shortages forced the mint to lower the cent's weight from 208 grains to 168 grains in 1795.

In 1798, because of the coinage shortage, the legal-tender status of foreign coins was restored. Several more extensions were given during the 1800s, ending with the withdrawal of legal-tender status for Spanish coins in 1857.

A new law made the mint lower the standard weight of all gold coins in 1834. This reflected market conditions and in effect recognized a higher gold price when bought with silver coins. For example, $5 in silver coins bought a new, lighter $5 gold piece, meaning the buyer got less gold. This led to the melting of great numbers of the older, heavier gold coins as speculators grabbed a 4.7 percent profit.

By the 1850s discovery of gold in California made silver more expensive in terms of gold. All silver quickly disappeared from circulation. Congress reacted in 1853 by lowering the weight of the silver half dime, dime, quarter, and half dollar, hoping to keep silver in circulation. A new gold coin of $20 value, the "double eagle," was introduced to absorb a great amount of the gold from Western mines.

Not long after, silver was discovered in Nevada. By the mid-1870s the various mines that made up what was known as the Comstock Lode (named after its colorful early proprietor, Henry P. Comstock) had hit the mother lode. Large supplies of silver from the Comstock, combined with European demonetization, caused a severe drop in its value. Silver coins were made heavier as a result in 1873.

Also, it was believed that the introduction of a heavier, 420-grain silver dollar in 1873, known as the Trade dollar, would create a market for much of the Comstock silver, bolster its price, and at the same time wrest control from Great Britain of lucrative trade with the Orient. It didn't. Large numbers of Trade dollars eventually flooded back into the United States. They were demonetized in 1887.

Morgan dollars were introduced in 1878 as a panacea to the severe economic problems following the Civil War. Those who proudly carried the banner of free silver contended that by taking the rich output of the Comstock mines and turning it into silver dollars, a cheaper, more plentiful form of money would become available. This was supposed to give the economy a boost.

The Free Silver Movement reached its peak in 1896 when William Jennings Bryan attempted to gain the White House on a plank largely based on restoration of the free and unlimited coinage of the standard 412.5-grain silver dollar. He failed. Silver failed. In 1900 the United States officially adopted a gold standard.

Silver continued to be a primary coinage metal until 1964, when rising prices led the Mint to remove it from the dime and quarter. Mintage of the silver dollar had ended in 1935. The half dollar continued to be coined through 1970 with a 40 percent silver composition. It, too, was then made of copper-nickel clad metal.

Gold coinage ended in 1933 and exists today only in commemorative issues and American Eagle bullion coins with fictive face values. A clad composition of copper and nickel is now the primary coinage metal. Even the cent is no longer all copper; a copper-coated zinc composition has been used since 1982.

Precious-metal supplies were also linked to the opening of additional mints, which served the parent facility in Philadelphia. The impact of gold discoveries in the 1820s in the southern Appalachian Mountains was directly tied to the construction of branch mints in Dahlonega, Ga., and Charlotte, N.C., in 1838. These new mints struck only gold coins. New Orleans also became the site of a branch mint in the same year as Dahlonega and Charlotte. It took in some of the outflow of gold from Southern mines, but also struck silver coins.

Discovery of gold in California in the late 1840s created a gold rush, and from it sprang a great western migration. Private issues of gold coinage, often of debased quality, were prevalent, and the cost of shipping the metal eastward for coinage at Philadelphia was high. A call for an official branch mint was soon heard and heeded in 1852 with the authorization of the San Francisco Mint, which began taking deposits in 1854.

The discovery of silver in the Comstock Lode led to yet another mint. Located only a short distance via Virginia & Truckee Railroad from the fabulous Comstock Lode, the Carson City mint began receiving bullion in early 1870.

Denver, also located in a mineral-rich region, became the site of an assay office in 1863 when the government purchased the Clark, Gruber & Co. private mint. It became a U.S. branch mint in 1906. Now four mints exist. They are in Denver, Philadelphia, San Francisco and West Point, N.Y. The latter strikes current precious metal coinage for collectors and investors.

10 How are Coins Made?

Mints are really factories

Copper, nickel, silver, and gold are pretty much the basic coin metals for the United States. When mixed with tin, copper becomes bronze, and this alloy was used in cents. Current cents have a pure zinc core. There have been patterns made of aluminum, but these never were issued for use in circulation. Platinum joined gold and silver as a precious metal used in U.S. coinage starting in 1997.

There are three basic parts of the minting process: (1) the making of the planchet, which is divided into the selection and processing of the metal and the preparation of the planchets, (2) the making of the dies, and (3) the use of the dies to strike the planchets. To help you remember these three parts, think of "P," "D," and "S" for planchet, die, and striking.

Making the 'blanks'

The piece of metal that becomes a coin is known as a "blank." This is a usually round, flat piece that has been punched or cut from a sheet or strip of coin metal.

Before a blank can become a coin it has to be processed, cleaned, softened, and given what is known as an "upset edge" – a raised ridge or rim around both sides. The blank then becomes a "planchet" and is ready to be struck into a coin by the dies. First they go through what looks like a monstrous cement mixer. A huge cylinder revolves slowly as the planchets are fed in at one end and spiral their way through. This is an annealing oven, which heats the planchets to soften them. When they come out the end, they fall into a bath where they are cleaned with a diluted acid or soap solution. As the final step, they go through the upsetting mill, the machine that puts the raised rim on the blank and turns it into a planchet, ready to be struck. In a different department the process of making the dies used to strike the coins has already begun.

Preparing the dies

For those who haven't studied metallurgy, the concept of hard metal flowing about is pretty hard to swallow, but this is actually what happens. It is basically the same process as the one used in an auto plant to turn a flat sheet of steel into a fender with multiple curves and sharp bends. The cold metal is moved about by the pressure applied.

To make the metal move into the desired design, there has to be a die. Actually, there have to be two dies, because one of the laws of physics is that for every action there has to be an equal and opposite reaction. You cannot hold a piece of metal in midair and strike one side of it. Instead you make two dies, fix one, and drive the other one against it – with a piece of metal in between to accept the design from each die.

A die is a piece of hard metal, like steel, with a design on its face that helps to form a mirror image on the struck coin. Early dies were made by hand. Engravers used hand tools, laboriously cutting each letter, each digit, and each owl or eagle or whatever design was being used into the face of the die. Notice that this is "into" the surface of the die. Each part of the die design is a hole or cavity of varying shape and depth.

This is because we want a mirror image on the coin, but we want it raised, or in "relief." To make a relief image on a coin, the image on the die has to be recessed into the face of the die, or "incuse." Of course, if we want an incuse image on the coin, such as the gold $2.50 and $5 coins of 1908-1929, the design on the die face would have to be in relief.

To fully understand this, take a coin from your pocket and a piece of aluminum foil. Press the foil down over the coin design and rub it with an eraser. When you take the foil off and look at the side that was in contact with the coin, you have a perfect copy of a die. Everywhere there is a relief design on the coin there is an incuse design on your foil "die."

From sketchbook to coin

The design process begins with an artist's sketch. This is translated into a three-dimensional relief design that is hand-carved from plaster or, in recent years, from a form of plastic.

The plaster or plastic design is then transformed into a "galvano," which is an exact copy of the design that has been plated with a thin layer of copper. This is used as a template or pattern in a reducing lathe, which cuts the design into a die blank.

This die becomes the master die, from which all of the following steps descend. The process can be reversed so that the designs will be cut in relief, forming a tool called a "hub," which is simply a piece of steel with the design in relief, exactly the same as the relief design on the intended coin.

To make working dies, pieces of special steel are prepared, with one end shaped with a slight cone. The die blank is softened by heating it. Then the hub is forced into the face of the die, forming the incuse, mirror-image design in the face of the die.

The process usually has to be repeated because the die metal will harden from the

A galvano of the 1976 half dollar goes on the reducing lathe.

pressure. The die is removed, softened, and returned to the hubbing press for a second impression from the hub. As you can imagine, it takes several hundred tons per square inch to force the hub into the die. Logically, this process is called "hubbing" a die.

The advantage of hubbing a die is that thousands of working dies can be made from a single hub, each one for all practical purposes as identical as the proverbial peas in a pod. This enables, for example, U.S. mints to strike billions of one-cent coins each year, each with the identical design.

Die making has come a long way from the early days. Philadelphia used to make all dies and then shipped them to the branch mints. Now Denver has its own die shop and creates dies of its own.

Striking the coin

Yesterday's die might strike only a few hundred coins. Today it is not unusual for a die to strike well over a million coins.

The coin press used to strike modern coins is a complicated piece of equipment that consists basically of a feed system to place the planchets in position for the stroke of the hammer die to form a coin. This process takes only a fraction of a second, so the press has to operate precisely to spew out the hundreds of coins that are struck every minute.

The end of the early hammered coinage came with the introduction of the collar, which often is called the "third" die. The collar is nothing more than a steel plate with a hole in it. This hole is the exact diameter of the intended coin and often is lined with carbide to prolong its life. It surrounds the lower, or fixed, die. Its sole purpose is to contain the coin metal to keep it from spreading too far sideways under the force of the strike.

If the intended coin has serrations, or "reeds," on the edge, then the collar has the matching design. The strike forces the coin metal against the serrations in the collar, forming the reeded edge at the same time that the two dies form the front and back, or obverse and reverse, of the coin.

Lettered-edge coins are produced usually by running the planchets through an edge-lettering die, or by using a segmented collar that is forced against the edge of the planchet during the strike by hydraulic pressure.

A binful of blanks are ready for the coin press.

Several hundred tons were required to drive a hub into a die. Not as much but still significant amounts of force are needed to strike coins. A cent requires about 30 tons per square inch. A silver dollar took 150 tons. Other denominations fall between.

Modern coin presses apply pressure in a variety of ways. A ram, carrying the moving or "hammer" die, is forced against the planchet. Most commonly this is with the mechanical advantage of a "knuckle" or connected pieces to which pressure is applied from the side. When the joint straightens – like straightening your finger – the ram at the end of the piece is driven into the planchet. Once the strike is complete, at the final impact of the die pair, the coin has been produced. It is officially a coin now, and it's complete and ready to be spent.

Making proof coins

Proof coins started out as special presentation pieces. They were and still are struck on specially prepared planchets with specially prepared dies. Today the definition of a proof coin also requires that it be struck two or more times.

Currently all proof versions of circulating U.S. coins are struck at the San Francisco Mint, but some of the proof commemorative coins have been struck at the other mints. West Point currently strikes proof American Eagles of silver, gold, and platinum, and they carry a "W" mintmark.

After the proof blanks are punched from the strip, they go through the annealing oven, but on a conveyor belt rather than being tumbled in the revolving drum. After cleaning and upsetting they go into a huge vibrating machine where they are mixed with steel pellets that look like tiny footballs. The movement of the steel pellets against the planchets burnishes, or smooths, the surface so any scratches and gouges the planchets pick up during processing are smoothed over.

Proof dies get an extra polishing before the hubbing process. They are made at Philadelphia and shipped to the branch mints. When the proof dies arrive at San Francisco, they are worked on by a team of specialists who use diamond dust and other polishing agents to turn the fields of the proof dies into mirrorlike surfaces. The incuse design is sandblasted to make the surface rough, producing what is known as a "frosted" design. Because collectors like the frosted proofs, the design is periodically swabbed with acid to keep the surface rough and increase the number of frosted proofs from each die. This process has been around about a quarter century, so frosted examples of earlier proofs are considerably scarcer.

The presses that strike proof coins usually are hand-operated rather than automatic. Some of the newer presses use equipment such as vacuum suction devices to pick up the planchets, place them in the coining chamber, and then remove the struck coins. This avoids handling the pieces any more than necessary.

On a hand-operated press, the operator takes a freshly washed and dried planchet and, using tongs, places it in the collar. The ram with the die descends two or more times before the finished coin is removed from the collar and carefully stored in a box for transport to storage or the packaging line. After each strike the operator wipes the dies to make sure that lint or other particles don't stick to the dies and damage the coins as they are struck.

Proof dies are used for only a short time. Maximum die life is usually less than 10,000 coins, varying with the size of the coin and the alloy being struck.

UNITED STATES
CIRCULATION COINAGE

HALF CENT

Liberty Cap Half Cent.

Head facing left.

KM# 10 Designer: Henry Voigt. **Diameter:** 22 **Weight:** 6.7400 g. **Composition:** Copper

Date	Mintage	G-4	VG-8	F-12	VF-20	XF-40	MS-60
1793	35,334	3,250	5,350	8,500	15,000	27,000	61,000

Head facing right.

KM# 14 Designer: Robert Scot (1794) and John Smith Gardner (1795). **Diameter:** 23.5 **Composition:** Copper **Weight:** 6.74 g. (1794-95) and 5.44 g. (1795-97) **Notes:** The "lettered edge" varieties have TWO HUNDRED FOR A DOLLAR inscribed around the edge. The "pole" varieties have a pole upon which the cap is hanging, resting on Liberty's shoulder. The "punctuated date" varieties have a comma after the 1 in the date. The 1797 "1 above 1" variety has a second 1 above the 1 in the date.

Date	Mintage	G-4	VG-8	F-12	VF-20	XF-40	MS-60
1794 Normal Relief Head	81,600	440	650	975	1,675	3,750	17,000
1794 High Relief Head	Inc. above	—	—	—	—	—	—
1795 lettered edge, pole	25,600	450	700	950	1,500	4,550	17,500
1795 plain edge, no pole	109,000	375	475	800	1,400	3,500	16,000
1795 lettered edge, punctuated date	Inc. above	475	700	1,000	1,600	3,750	50,000
1795 plain edge, punctuated date	Inc. above	350	450	750	1,500	3,000	57,500
1796 pole	5,090	16,000	50,000	53,500	30,000	35,000	—
1796 no pole	1,390	27,000	35,500	47,500	90,000	—	—
1797 plain edge	119,215	400	575	950	1,900	6,000	57,500
1797 lettered edge	Inc. above	1,700	5,700	4,000	8,000	55,000	—
1797 1 above 1	Inc. above	375	475	950	1,600	3,550	50,000
1797 gripped edge	Inc. above	16,000	37,500	48,000	60,000	70,000	—

Draped Bust Half Cent.

Draped bust right, date at angle below. Value within thin wreath.

KM# 33 Designer: Robert Scot. **Diameter:** 23.5 **Weight:** 5.4400 g. **Composition:** Copper **Notes:** The wreath on the reverse was redesigned slightly in 1802, resulting in "reverse of 1800" and "reverse of 1802" varieties. The "stems" varieties have stems extending from the wreath above and on both sides of the fraction on the reverse. On the 1804 "crosslet 4" variety, a serif appears at the far right of the crossbar on the 4 in the date. The "spiked chin" variety appears to have a spike extending from Liberty's chin, the result of a damaged die. Varieties of the 1805 strikes are distinguished by the size of the 5 in the date. Varieties of the 1806 strikes are distinguished by the size of the 6 in the date.

Stemless Stems

Date	Mintage	G-4	VG-8	F-12	VF-20	XF-40	MS-60
1800	211,530	65.00	90.00	125	205	500	5,500
1802/0 rev. 1800	14,366	15,000	55,000	30,000	—	—	—
1802/0 rev. 1802	Inc. above	800	1,400	5,750	6,500	17,000	—
1803	97,900	75.00	95.00	105	575	950	7,000
1804 plain 4, stemless wreath	1,055,312	60.00	80.00	90.00	170	550	1,400
1804 plain 4, stems	Inc. above	60.00	90.00	155	550	1,500	15,000
1804 crosslet 4, stemless	Inc. above	65.00	90.00	100.00	195	550	1,350
1804 crosslet 4, stems	Inc. above	62.00	90.00	125	215	300	1,500
1804 spiked chin	Inc. above	75.00	105	155	215	355	1,500

Date	Mintage	G-4	VG-8	F-12	VF-20	XF-40	MS-60
1805 small 5, stemless	814,464	65.00	90.00	105	195	400	3,500
1805 small 5, stems	Inc. above	800	1,500	5,400	4,500	8,000	—
1805 large 5, stems	Inc. above	65.00	85.00	100.00	180	400	3,000
1806 small 6, stems	356,000	500	355	600	1,000	5,750	—
1806 small 6, stemless	Inc. above	65.00	85.00	100.00	215	535	1,350
1806 large 6, stems	Inc. above	65.00	85.00	100.00	215	550	1,500
1807	476,000	65.00	95.00	155	220	300	1,400
1808/7	400,000	300	400	600	1,500	6,000	57,500
1808	Inc. above	65.00	85.00	105	215	350	5,000

Classic Head Half Cent.

Classic head left, flanked by stars, date below. Value within wreath.

KM# 41 **Designer:** John Reich. **Diameter:** 23.5 **Weight:** 5.4400 g. **Composition:** Copper **Notes:** Restrikes listed were produced privately in the mid-1800s. The 1831 restrikes have two varieties with different sized berries in the wreath on the reverse. The 1828 strikes have either 12 or 13 stars on the obverse.

Date	Mintage	G-4	VG-8	F-12	VF-20	XF-40	MS-60
1809/6	1,154,572	60.00	80.00	110	150	515	1,000
1809	Inc. above	59.00	78.00	90.00	110	515	800
1809 circle in 0	—	66.00	93.00	90.00	150	550	5,100
1810	215,000	66.00	103	150	500	600	3,550
1811 Close Date	63,140	255	375	750	1,800	4,000	—
1811 Wide Date Inc. Above	—	290	725	1,550	2,550	4,750	—
1811 restrike, reverse of 1802, uncirculated	—	—	—	—	—	—	57,500
1825	63,000	56.00	73.00	85.00	110	500	950
1826	234,000	51.00	68.00	82.00	90.00	500	750
1828 13 stars	606,000	51.00	68.00	75.00	85.00	95.00	225
1828 12 stars	Inc. above	61.00	78.00	125	175	550	850
1829	487,000	51.00	71.00	82.00	100.00	150	500
1831 original	2,200	—	—	—	—	65,000	—
1831 1st restrike, lg. berries, reverse of 1836	—	—	—	—	—	—	6,500
1831 2nd restrike, sm. berries, reverse of 1840, proof	—	—	—	—	—	—	55,000
1832	154,000	51.00	68.00	75.00	85.00	95.00	225
1833	120,000	51.00	68.00	75.00	85.00	95.00	225
1834	141,000	51.00	68.00	75.00	85.00	95.00	225
1835	398,000	51.00	68.00	75.00	85.00	95.00	225
1836 original, proof	—	—	—	—	—	—	6,000
1836 restrike, reverse of 1840, proof	—	—	—	—	—	—	50,000

Braided Hair Half Cent.

Head left, braided hair, within circle of stars, date below. Value within wreath.

KM# 70 **Designer:** Christian Gobrecht. **Diameter:** 23 **Weight:** 5.4400 g. **Composition:** Copper **Notes:** 1840-1849 and 1852 strikes, both originals and restrikes, are known in proof only; mintages are unknown. The small-date varieties of 1849, both originals and restrikes are known in proof only. The restrikes were produced clandestinely by Philadelphia Mint personnel in the mid-1800s.

Date	Mintage	G-4	VG-8	F-12	VF-20	XF-40	MS-60	Prf-60
1840 original	—	—	—	—	—	3,000	—	3,250
1840 1st restrike	—	—	—	—	—	3,000	—	3,250
1840 2nd restrike	—	—	—	—	—	3,000	—	5,500
1841 original	—	—	—	—	—	3,000	—	3,250
1841 1st restrike	—	—	—	—	—	3,000	—	3,250
1841 2nd restrike	—	—	—	—	—	3,000	—	6,000
1842 original	—	—	—	—	—	3,000	—	3,250
1842 1st restrike	—	—	—	—	—	3,000	—	3,250
1842 2nd restrike	—	—	—	—	—	3,000	—	6,000
1843 original	—	—	—	—	—	3,000	—	3,250
1843 1st restrike	—	—	—	—	—	3,000	—	3,250
1843 2nd restrike	—	—	—	—	—	3,000	—	6,500
1844 original	—	—	—	—	—	3,000	—	3,250
1844 1st restrike	—	—	—	—	—	3,000	—	3,250
1844 2nd restrike	—	—	—	—	—	3,000	—	6,000

Date	Mintage	G-4	VG-8	F-12	VF-20	XF-40	MS-60	Prf-60
1845 original	—	—	—	—	—	3,000	—	6,000
1845 1st restrike	—	—	—	—	—	3,000	—	3,250
1845 2nd restrike	—	—	—	—	—	3,000	—	6,000
1846 original	—	—	—	—	—	3,000	—	3,250
1846 1st restrike	—	—	—	—	—	3,000	—	3,250
1846 2nd restrike	—	—	—	—	—	3,000	—	6,000
1847 original	—	—	—	—	—	3,000	—	3,250
1847 1st restrike	—	—	—	—	—	5,500	—	3,250
1847 2nd restrike	—	—	—	—	—	3,000	—	6,000
1848 original	—	—	—	—	—	3,000	—	6,000
1848 1st restrike	—	—	—	—	—	3,000	—	3,250
1848 2nd restrike	—	—	—	—	—	3,000	—	6,000
1849 original, small date	—	—	—	—	—	3,000	—	3,250
1849 1st restrike small date	—	—	—	—	—	3,000	—	3,250
1849 large date	39,864	58.00	76.00	82.00	92.00	110	300	—
1850	39,812	58.00	76.00	82.00	92.00	110	340	—
1851	147,672	54.00	71.00	77.00	84.00	96.00	195	—
1852 original	—	15,000	55,000	30,000	35,000	40,000	—	90,000
1852 1st restrike	—	1,000	1,500	1,850	2,600	3,000	—	5,000
1852 2nd restrike	—	1,000	1,500	1,850	2,600	3,000	—	7,000
1853	129,694	54.00	71.00	77.00	84.00	96.00	195	—
1854	55,358	54.00	71.00	77.00	84.00	96.00	195	—
1855	56,500	54.00	71.00	77.00	84.00	96.00	195	3,250
1856	40,430	54.00	71.00	77.00	84.00	96.00	195	3,250
1857	35,180	59.00	78.00	87.00	102	126	270	3,250

CENT

Flowing Hair Cent.

Chain.

KM# 11 Designer: Henry Voigt. **Diameter:** 26-27
Weight: 13.4800 g. **Composition:** Copper

Date	Mintage	G-4	VG-8	F-12	VF-20	XF-40	MS-60
1793 "AMERI"	36,103	9,950	14,750	25,500	45,500	96,000	245,000
1793 "AMERICA"	Inc. above	6,950	10,500	17,750	36,500	71,500	140,000
1793 periods after "LIBERTY"	Inc. above	7,850	12,250	19,850	38,500	73,500	147,000

Flowing Hair Cent.

Wreath.

KM# 12 Designer: Henry Voigt. **Diameter:** 26-28
Weight: 13.4800 g. **Composition:** Copper

Date	Mintage	G-4	VG-8	F-12	VF-20	XF-40	MS-60
1793 vine and bars edge	63,353	2,900	3,500	7,000	12,000	22,500	48,500
1793 lettered edge	Inc. above	3,200	4,200	8,100	14,000	25,500	56,000
1793 strawberry leaf; 4 known	—	350,000	550,000	875,000	—	—	—

Liberty Cap Cent.

KM# 13 Designer: Joseph Wright (1793-1795) and John Smith Gardner (1795-1796). **Diameter:** 29 **Composition:** Copper **Weight:** 13.48 g. (1793-95) and 10.89 g. (1795-96) **Notes:** The heavier pieces were struck on a thicker planchet. The Liberty design on the obverse was revised slightly in 1794, but the 1793 design was used on some 1794 strikes. A 1795 "lettered edge" variety has ONE HUNDRED FOR A DOLLAR and a leaf inscribed on the edge.

Date	Mintage	G-4	VG-8	F-12	VF-20	XF-40	MS-60
1793 cap	11,056	5,500	12,500	23,500	45,000	98,500	—
1794 NO FRACTION BAR	Inc. above	500	800	1,350	3,000	8,000	40,000
1794 head '93	918,521	1,550	2,600	4,250	9,850	21,500	85,000
1794 head '94	Inc. above	445	650	1,025	2,175	4,500	16,500
1794 head '95	Inc. above	525	715	1,090	2,525	5,000	20,000
1794 starred rev.	Inc. above	13,500	23,500	44,500	115,000	275,000	—
1795 Lettered Edge	Inc. above	510	650	1,200	3,200	4,500	16,500
1795 plain edge	501,500	370	550	875	1,525	3,800	12,500
1795 reeded edge	Inc. above	350,000	700,000	—	—	—	—
1795 Jefferson head plain edge	Inc. above	24,500	49,500	95,000	150,000	—	—
1795 Jefferson head lettered edge	Inc. above	75,000	95,000	155,000	250,000	—	—

Liberty Cap Cent.

KM# 13a Designer: Joseph Wright (1793-1795) and John Smith Gardner (1795-1796). **Diameter:** 29 **Weight:** 10.8900 g. **Composition:** Copper

Date	Mintage	G-4	VG-8	F-12	VF-20	XF-40	MS-60
1795 lettered edge, "One Cent" high in wreath	37,000	440	675	925	1,925	4,800	15,000
1796	109,825	420	550	1,475	3,850	9,500	36,500

Draped Bust Cent.

Draped bust right, date at angle below. Value within wreath.

KM# 22 Designer: Robert Scot. **Diameter:** 29 **Weight:** 10.9800 g. **Composition:** Copper **Notes:** The 1801 "3 errors" variety has the fraction on the reverse reading "1/000," has only one stem extending from the wreath above and on both sides of the fraction on the reverse, and UNITED in UNITED STATES OF AMERICA appears as "Iinited."

Stemless

Stems

Date	Mintage	G-4	VG-8	F-12	VF-20	XF-40	MS-60
1796 Rev. of 1794	363,375	300	450	1,050	2,800	6,850	36,500
1796 Rev. of 1795	Inc. above	260	375	850	3,250	9,500	11,000
1796 Rev. of 1797	Inc. above	240	350	1,050	2,150	4,250	75,000
1796 Liherty error	Inc. above	450	850	1,800	5,500	13,500	38,500
1797 reverse of 1795plain edge	897,510	165	300	600	3,450	5,500	—
1797 reverse of 1795 gripped edge	Inc. above	185	425	850	1,450	4,750	—
1797 stems	Inc. above	165	325	450	1,275	2,650	9,000
1797 stemless	Inc. above	300	495	750	1,850	4,750	38,500
1798/7	1,841,745	200	325	650	2,100	5,100	22,000
1798 reverse of 1796	Inc. above	150	250	600	1,750	3,600	9,500
1798 1st hair style	Inc. above	90.00	130	325	800	4,450	9,850
1798 2nd hair style	Inc. above	85.00	125	310	750	2,850	8,000
1799	42,540	2,750	4,650	11,500	24,500	85,000	650,000
1799/98	Inc. above	2,600	4,300	11,000	34,000	110,000	—
1800	2,822,175	100.00	165	375	1,850	3,000	12,500
1800/798	Inc. above	85.00	225	550	1,550	4,000	—

Date	Mintage	G-4	VG-8	F-12	VF-20	XF-40	MS-60
1800/79	Inc. above	80.00	200	375	1,500	3,300	16,500
1801	1,362,837	75.00	100.00	250	700	1,725	7,750
1801 3 errors	Inc. above	225	500	1,150	2,400	6,850	35,000
1801 1/000	Inc. above	80.00	175	475	1,350	2,650	9,850
1801 100/000	Inc. above	150	325	850	1,650	4,200	12,500
1802	3,435,100	65.00	100.00	250	485	1,200	4,500
1802 stemless	Inc. above	68.00	95.00	200	465	1,500	5,000
1802 fraction 1/000	Inc. above	80.00	135	325	700	1,750	7,500
1803 small date, small fraction	2,471,353	65.00	100.00	225	375	900	32,500
1803 small date, large fraction	Inc. above	65.00	100.00	225	385	950	3,350
1803 large date, small fraction	Inc. above	4,600	11,500	14,500	42,000	75,000	—
1803 large date, large fraction	Inc. above	80.00	135	450	1,550	3,150	—
1803 1/100 over 1/1000	—	95.00	165	360	900	2,600	10,000
1803 Stemless wreath	—	80.00	150	350	650	2,100	6,950
1804	96,500	1,650	2,650	4,000	8,950	16,500	80,000
1804 Restrike of 1860	—	—	—	650	750	875	1,750
1805	941,116	60.00	90.00	245	375	1,300	4,650
1806	348,000	70.00	110	305	550	1,775	7,500
1807 small fraction	727,221	65.00	100.00	265	575	2,200	4,600
1807 large fraction	Inc. above	65.00	100.00	225	460	1,100	3,150
1807/6 large 7/6	Inc. above	65.00	175	225	575	1,400	—
1807/6 small 7/6	Inc. above	1,900	4,250	9,500	24,500	49,500	—
1807 Comet Variety	Inc. above	95.00	175	345	1,100	3,200	16,500

CENT

Classic Head Cent.

Classic head left, flanked by stars, date below. Value within wreath.

KM# 39 **Designer:** John Reich. **Diameter:** 29
Weight: 10.8900 g. **Composition:** Copper

Date	Mintage	G-4	VG-8	F-12	VF-20	XF-40	MS-60
1808	1,109,000	106	160	440	700	1,850	9,500
1809	222,867	135	285	450	1,050	3,350	13,500
1810/09	1,458,500	90.00	160	420	675	1,850	10,500
1810	Inc. above	75.00	110	320	675	1,550	9,500
1811/10	218,025	175	300	700	1,950	4,650	60,000
1811	Inc. above	110	225	575	1,300	3,350	11,000
1812 small date	1,075,500	75.00	115	345	650	1,650	8,000
1812 large date	—	75.00	115	345	660	1,700	8,500
1813	418,000	60.00	175	400	800	1,950	9,000
1814 Plain 4	357,830	75.00	120	305	675	1,450	5,750
1814 Crosslet 4	Inc. above	75.00	115	295	650	1,350	5,600

Coronet Cent.

Coronet head left, within circle of stars, date below. Value within wreath.

KM# 45 **Designer:** Robert Scot. **Diameter:** 28-29
Weight: 10.8900 g. **Composition:** Copper

Date	Mintage	G-4	VG-8	F-12	VF-20	XF-40	MS-60
1816	2,820,982	31.00	42.00	60.00	117	245	1,350
1817 13 obverse stars	3,948,400	29.00	33.00	44.00	74.00	155	650
1817 15 obverse stars	Inc. above	35.00	56.00	90.00	225	675	2,650
1818	3,167,000	29.00	35.00	42.00	74.00	150	450
1819 Large date, 9/8	2,671,000	—	—	—	—	—	—
1819	—	31.00	38.00	46.00	116	315	1,000
1819/8	—	—	—	—	—	—	—
1819 Large date	Inc. above	29.00	33.00	42.00	78.00	183	600
1819 Small date	Inc. above	30.00	35.00	45.00	82.00	203	675
1820 Large date, 20/19	4,407,550	31.00	38.00	50.00	88.00	250	950
1820 Large date	—	33.00	39.00	60.00	117	335	1,600
1820 Small date	—	29.00	36.00	46.00	78.00	188	450
1821	389,000	45.00	72.00	200	525	1,375	7,500
1822	2,072,339	31.00	45.00	45.00	150	365	1,500
1823 Included in 1824 mintage	—	90.00	200	450	1,350	3,950	30,000

Date	Mintage	G-4	VG-8	F-12	VF-20	XF-40	MS-60
1823/22 Included in 1824 mintage	—	80.00	165	425	975	3,250	—
1823 Restrike	—	600	650	700	800	900	1,850
1824	1,262,000	31.00	35.00	46.00	210	450	1,950
1824/22	Inc. above	40.00	49.00	110	440	1,000	5,500
1825	1,461,100	30.00	35.00	45.00	125	400	2,150
1826	1,517,425	30.00	35.00	45.00	87.00	265	950
1826/25	Inc. above	40.00	55.00	95.00	275	1,200	4,250
1827	2,357,732	29.00	33.00	42.00	92.00	260	800
1828 Large date	2,260,624	29.00	33.00	44.00	87.00	225	900
1828 Small date	—	32.00	37.00	49.00	110	265	1,650
1829 Large letters	1,414,500	29.00	33.00	40.00	93.00	208	1,100
1829 Medium letters	Inc. above	32.00	45.00	90.00	275	675	5,250
1830 Large letters	1,711,500	25.00	29.00	36.00	70.00	188	650
1830 Medium letters	Inc. above	45.00	90.00	265	650	1,650	7,500
1831 Large letters	3,359,260	25.00	31.00	36.00	70.00	193	500
1831 Medium letters	—	29.00	34.00	41.00	76.00	225	950
1832 Large letters	2,362,000	25.00	31.00	36.00	70.00	158	525
1832 Medium letters	—	27.00	32.00	39.00	74.00	178	850
1833	2,739,000	25.00	31.00	36.00	70.00	158	475
1834 Large 8, stars and letters	1,855,100	75.00	120	145	250	625	2,350
1834 Large 8 & stars, medium letters	Inc. above	190	275	600	1,100	3,250	6,200
1834 Large 8, small stars, medium letters	Inc. above	25.00	29.00	36.00	70.00	158	650
1834 Small 8 & stars	Inc. above	25.00	29.00	36.00	70.00	145	750
1835 Large 8 & stars	3,878,400	25.00	31.00	39.00	74.00	168	1,000
1835 Head '36	—	25.00	31.00	39.00	74.00	158	550
1835 Small 8 & stars	—	25.00	29.00	36.00	70.00	158	650
1836	2,111,000	25.00	29.00	36.00	70.00	125	290
1837 Plain hair cords, medium letters	5,558,300	25.00	29.00	36.00	70.00	125	290
1837 Plain hair cords, small letters	Inc. above	25.00	31.00	39.00	74.00	133	485
1837 Head '38	Inc. above	25.00	31.00	39.00	74.00	125	250
1838	6,370,200	25.00	29.00	36.00	70.00	125	250
1839 Head '38, beaded hair cords	3,128,661	29.00	33.00	40.00	74.00	130	450
1839/36 Plain hair cords	Inc. above	300	600	1,250	2,450	6,800	75,000
1839 Silly head	Inc. above	35.00	40.00	50.00	90.00	165	900
1839 Booby head	Inc. above	34.00	38.00	47.00	85.00	153	875

Braided Hair Cent.

Head left, braided hair, within circle of stars, date below. Value within wreath.

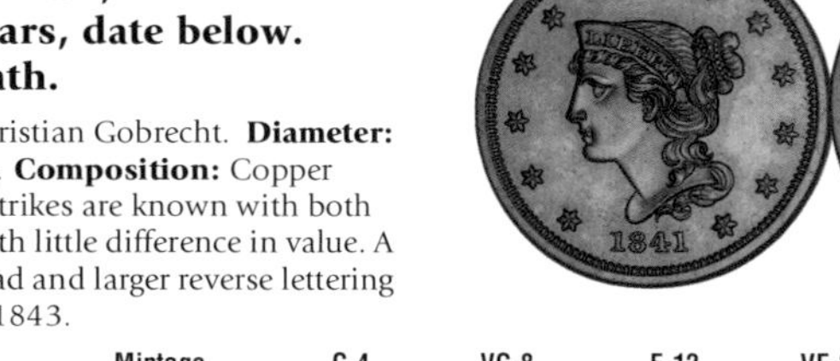

KM# 67 **Designer:** Christian Gobrecht. **Diameter:** 27.5 **Weight:** 10.8900 g. **Composition:** Copper **Notes:** 1840 and 1842 strikes are known with both small and large dates, with little difference in value. A slightly larger Liberty head and larger reverse lettering were used beginning in 1843.

Date	Mintage	G-4	VG-8	F-12	VF-20	XF-40	MS-60
1839 Petite Head	3,128,661	29.00	33.00	47.00	62.50	100.00	825
1840 Large date	2,462,700	25.00	28.00	36.00	51.50	80.00	1,250
1840 Small date	Inc. above	30.00	35.00	42.00	53.50	90.00	550
1840 Small date over large 18	Inc. above	40.00	50.00	75.00	125	210	1,150
1841	1,597,367	25.00	28.00	36.00	51.50	79.00	450
1842 Small date	2,383,390	25.00	28.00	36.00	51.50	69.00	400
1842 Large date	Inc. above	28.00	32.00	42.00	57.50	100.00	365
1843 Petite Head, small date	2,425,342	25.00	28.00	35.00	51.50	69.00	360
1843 Petite Head, (rev '44)	Inc. above	27.00	30.00	37.00	51.50	79.00	550
1843 Mature Head	—	28.00	32.00	50.00	140	260	600
1844	2,398,752	25.00	28.00	36.00	51.50	69.00	375
1844/81	Inc. above	40.00	60.00	80.00	100.00	225	1,900
1845	3,894,804	25.00	28.00	33.00	51.50	69.00	300
1846 Small date	4,120,800	23.00	27.00	31.00	51.50	69.00	225
1846 MD	Inc. above	25.00	28.00	35.00	53.50	72.00	375
1846 TD	Inc. above	36.00	45.00	80.00	125	260	1,650
1847	6,183,669	23.00	27.00	31.00	47.50	65.00	250
1847/7	Inc. above	37.00	50.00	90.00	150	385	1,350
1848	6,415,799	25.00	28.00	33.00	47.50	61.00	185
1849	4,178,500	25.00	28.00	33.00	47.50	61.00	225
1850	4,426,844	25.00	28.00	33.00	39.50	61.00	195
1851	9,889,707	23.00	26.00	31.00	37.50	59.00	165
1851/81	Inc. above	36.00	45.00	60.00	90.00	175	700
1852	5,063,094	23.00	26.00	31.00	37.50	59.00	165
1853	6,641,131	23.00	26.00	31.00	37.50	59.00	165
1854	4,236,156	23.00	26.00	31.00	37.50	59.00	165
1855 Slanted 5's	1,574,829	43.00	56.00	65.00	74.50	95.00	215
1855 Upright 5's	Inc. above	23.00	26.00	33.00	37.50	59.00	165

Date	Mintage	G-4	VG-8	F-12	VF-20	XF-40	MS-60
1855 Slanted 5's Knob on Ear	Inc. above	27.00	34.00	46.00	70.00	99.00	450
1856 Slanted 5	2,690,463	23.00	26.00	31.00	37.50	59.00	165
1856 Upright 5	Inc. above	30.00	40.00	52.00	63.50	80.00	220
1857 Large date	333,456	90.00	125	175	235	310	600
1857 Small date	Inc. above	75.00	100.00	160	195	265	550

Flying Eagle Cent.

Flying eagle above date. Value within wreath.

KM# 85 **Designer:** James B. Longacre. **Diameter:** 19 **Weight:** 4.6700 g. **Composition:** Copper-Nickel **Notes:** On the large-letter variety of 1858, the "A" and "M" in AMERICA are connected at their bases; on the small-letter variety, the two letters are separated.

Large letters – AM touch at bottom

Small letters – Space between AM

Date	Mintage	G-4	VG-8	F-12	VF-20	XF-40	AU-50	MS-60	MS-65	Prf-65
1856	Est. 2,500	6,250	7,250	9,000	10,750	12,850	13,500	16,500	65,000	28,500
1857	17,450,000	27.50	39.00	40.00	47.00	125	165	320	3,500	29,000
1858/7	Inc. below	65.00	92.50	175	380	760	1,500	3,300	60,000	—
1858 large letters	24,600,000	27.50	41.00	43.50	56.00	150	220	340	3,850	24,500
1858 small letters	Inc. above	26.00	39.00	42.00	47.00	135	175	320	3,650	30,000

Indian Head Cent.

Indian head with headdress left above date. Value within wreath.

KM# 87 **Designer:** James B. Longacre. **Diameter:** 19 **Weight:** 4.6700 g. **Composition:** Copper-Nickel

Date	Mintage	G-4	VG-8	F-12	VF-20	XF-40	AU-50	MS-60	MS-65	Prf-65
1859	36,400,000	13.00	16.00	22.50	48.00	100.00	175	230	3,650	5,200

Indian Head Cent.

Indian head with headdress left above date. Value within wreath, shield above.

KM# 90 **Designer:** James B. Longacre. **Diameter:** 19 **Weight:** 4.6700 g. **Composition:** Copper-Nickel

Date	Mintage	G-4	VG-8	F-12	VF-20	XF-40	AU-50	MS-60	MS-65	Prf-65
1860 Rounded Bust	20,566,000	11.00	15.00	22.00	46.00	68.00	110	190	965	3,600
1860	(1,000)	—	—	—	—	—	—	—	—	—
1860 Pointed Bust	Inc. above	20.00	30.00	42.00	60.00	100.00	160	300	6,000	—
1861	10,100,000	20.00	30.00	42.00	58.00	95.00	160	180	975	7,250
1862	28,075,000	11.00	11.50	12.50	15.00	28.00	60.00	80.00	1,050	2,350
1863	49,840,000	7.50	9.25	11.00	12.50	25.00	58.00	75.00	1,050	3,100
1864	13,740,000	16.50	28.50	35.00	72.00	125	175	220	1,350	3,200

Indian Head Cent.

Indian head with headdress left above date. Value within wreath, shield above.

KM# 90a **Designer:** James B. Longacre. **Diameter:** 19 **Weight:** 3.1100 g. **Composition:** Bronze **Notes:** The 1864 "L" variety has the designer's initial in Liberty's hair to the right of her neck.

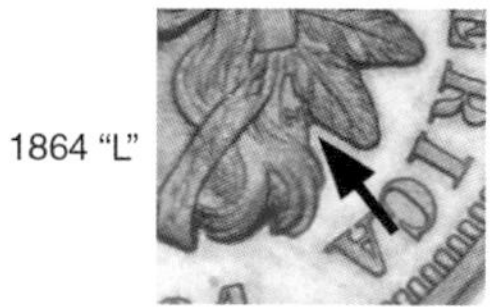
1864 "L"

CENT

Date	Mintage	G-4	VG-8	F-12	VF-20	XF-40	AU-50	MS-60	MS-65	Prf-65
1864	39,233,714	8.00	20.00	25.00	45.00	70.00	80.00	110	335	10,500
1864 L pointed bust	Inc. above	52.50	72.50	139	185	275	325	410	1,700	200,000
1865 plain 5	35,429,286	7.00	11.00	20.00	25.00	45.00	60.00	90.00	485	6,750
1865 fancy 5	Inc. above	6.00	10.50	18.50	23.00	40.00	55.00	85.00	465	—
1866	9,826,500	46.00	66.00	80.00	115	195	240	280	1,350	4,500
1867	9,821,000	52.00	72.00	110	120	195	240	285	1,350	6,100
1867/1867	Inc. above	60.00	85.00	130	190	275	385	565	1,950	—
1868	10,266,500	37.50	50.00	77.00	120	180	245	265	985	5,750
1869/9	6,420,000	145	280	495	660	825	1,000	1,250	2,350	—
1869	Inc. above	90.00	125	230	335	450	560	625	1,750	3,100
1870	5,275,000	62.00	118	225	285	410	510	600	1,400	2,650
1871	3,929,500	88.00	125	280	310	420	510	610	2,400	2,500
1872	4,042,000	90.00	180	390	425	625	750	840	3,850	4,250
1873 closed 3	11,676,500	30.00	52.00	95.00	135	235	300	400	2,850	2,950
1873 open 3	Inc. above	20.00	34.00	65.00	82.00	175	215	250	1,300	—
1873 Double Liberty die 1	Inc. above	275	450	950	1,500	2,400	4,250	7,500	—	—
1873 Double Liberty die 2	Inc. above	—	—	450	900	1,650	2,800	4,500	—	—
1874	14,187,500	15.00	22.50	46.00	65.00	112	150	225	700	2,850
1875	13,528,000	16.00	29.00	56.00	72.00	120	165	215	800	8,500
1876	7,944,000	27.00	38.50	74.00	130	230	295	335	975	2,600
1877	852,500	985	1,190	1,600	2,050	2,650	3,000	3,450	13,000	12,500
1878	5,799,850	26.00	35.00	68.00	135	245	290	350	875	1,375
1879	16,231,200	7.00	10.00	16.50	33.00	75.00	90.00	100.00	365	1,250
1880	38,964,955	3.50	5.50	6.50	11.00	28.00	48.00	66.00	360	1,250
1881	39,211,575	3.50	4.25	6.50	8.00	22.00	30.00	43.00	325	1,250
1882	38,581,100	3.50	4.25	5.00	10.00	22.00	30.00	40.00	325	1,450
1883	45,589,109	3.00	4.00	4.50	7.50	17.50	30.00	42.00	325	1,600
1884	23,261,742	3.50	4.50	7.00	12.50	29.00	40.00	60.00	460	1,250
1885	11,765,384	6.75	8.00	12.00	27.00	62.00	82.00	105	725	1,500
1886 Type 1 obverse	17,654,290	3.75	6.60	19.80	56.00	148	170	190	1,250	2,650
1886 Type 2 obverse	Inc. above	7.00	10.00	35.00	90.00	200	250	325	2,500	7,500
1887	45,226,483	2.50	3.00	4.00	7.00	19.00	28.00	50.00	400	6,200
1888	37,494,414	2.75	3.25	5.00	8.00	21.00	28.00	48.00	900	5,400
1889	48,869,361	2.25	2.75	3.50	6.00	12.00	26.00	40.00	400	1,900
1890	57,182,854	2.10	2.50	3.00	5.50	10.00	23.00	37.50	400	1,800
1891	47,072,350	2.25	2.75	3.25	5.50	13.00	23.00	37.00	400	2,150
1892	37,649,832	2.40	3.25	4.40	6.00	18.50	25.00	35.00	400	1,325
1893	46,642,195	2.10	2.75	3.25	5.50	10.00	22.00	30.00	340	1,250
1894	16,752,132	5.00	6.00	13.00	20.00	50.00	65.00	85.00	375	1,350
1894/94	Inc. above	24.00	34.00	80.00	150	275	440	800	8,000	—
1895	38,343,636	2.10	2.40	3.50	4.50	11.00	22.00	32.00	200	1,275
1896	39,057,293	1.95	2.50	3.25	4.75	13.00	26.00	34.00	225	1,900
1897	50,466,330	1.95	2.40	2.75	4.00	10.00	22.00	30.00	195	1,600
1898	49,823,079	1.95	2.40	2.75	4.00	10.00	22.00	30.00	195	1,275
1899	53,600,031	1.95	2.20	2.60	4.00	10.00	22.00	30.00	165	1,275
1900	66,833,764	1.95	2.20	2.50	4.00	12.00	23.00	30.00	175	1,275
1901	79,611,143	1.85	2.20	2.50	4.00	11.00	22.00	29.00	165	1,275
1902	87,376,722	1.85	2.20	2.50	4.00	10.00	22.00	28.00	165	1,325
1903	85,094,493	1.85	2.20	2.50	4.00	10.00	21.00	28.00	165	1,275
1904	61,328,015	1.75	2.20	2.50	4.00	10.00	21.00	28.00	165	1,275
1905	80,719,163	1.75	2.20	2.50	3.50	9.00	20.00	28.00	165	1,350
1906	96,022,255	1.75	2.20	2.50	3.50	9.00	21.00	28.00	165	1,275
1907	108,138,618	1.75	2.20	2.50	3.50	8.50	20.00	28.00	165	1,950
1908	32,327,987	1.75	2.30	2.50	3.50	9.00	20.00	28.00	165	1,275
1908S	1,115,000	77.00	82.00	105	122	166	195	285	2,650	—
1909	14,370,645	14.00	14.80	15.50	15.90	18.50	30.00	38.00	155	1,275
1909S	309,000	590	655	720	825	900	950	1,000	2,250	—

Lincoln Cent.

Wheat Ears.

KM# 132 Designer: Victor D. Brenner. **Diameter:** 19 **Weight:** 3.1100 g. **Composition:** Bronze **Notes:** The 1909 "VDB" varieties have the designer's initials inscribed at the 6 o'clock position on the reverse. The initials were removed until 1918, when they were restored on the obverse • MS60 and MS63 prices are for brown coins and MS65 prices are for coins that are at least 90% original red.

1922 Plain

Date	Mintage	G-4	VG-8	F-12	VF-20	XF-40	AU-50	MS-60	MS-65	Prf-65
1909 VDB	27,995,000	12.50	13.00	13.25	13.50	14.00	16.50	24.00	50.00	2,750
1909 VDB Doubled Die Obverse	Inc. above	—	—	55.00	75.00	100.00	120	200	1,500	—

Date	Mintage	G-4	VG-8	F-12	VF-20	XF-40	AU-50	MS-60	MS-65	Prf-65
1909S VDB	484,000	750	935	1,000	1,175	1,450	1,575	1,825	4,150	—
1909	72,702,618	3.65	3.50	4.35	4.75	5.50	12.50	14.50	85.00	625
1909S	1,825,000	105	110	122	165	245	265	340	750	—
1909S/S S over horizontal S	Inc. above	115	135	148	200	275	290	365	850	—
1910	146,801,218	.50	.60	.75	1.00	4.25	10.00	17.50	120	610
1910S	6,045,000	16.50	21.00	21.00	28.00	47.50	72.00	98.00	425	—
1911	101,177,787	.45	.60	1.60	2.35	6.75	11.00	18.50	175	525
1911D	12,672,000	4.75	5.75	9.00	22.50	50.00	75.00	90.00	750	—
1911S	4,026,000	49.00	53.00	55.00	59.00	75.00	105	175	1,100	—
1912	68,153,060	1.60	1.75	2.35	5.50	13.50	20.00	33.00	235	625
1912D	10,411,000	6.50	9.25	10.00	26.00	70.00	110	165	800	—
1912S	4,431,000	24.00	26.00	29.00	42.00	78.00	118	175	1,250	—
1913	76,532,352	.80	1.00	1.45	3.25	18.50	28.50	34.50	240	625
1913D	15,804,000	2.75	3.25	3.60	11.00	49.00	62.00	105	875	—
1913S	6,101,000	13.50	16.50	21.00	31.00	57.00	110	195	2,100	—
1914	75,238,432	.60	.95	2.10	6.00	18.50	40.00	52.00	240	625
1914D	1,193,000	205	235	320	450	945	1,500	2,100	9,500	—
1914S	4,137,000	25.00	27.50	30.00	40.00	85.00	175	310	3,250	—
1915	29,092,120	2.25	2.90	4.00	18.00	60.00	70.00	82.00	375	625
1915D	22,050,000	2.25	2.85	4.50	6.85	24.00	44.00	72.00	350	—
1915S	4,833,000	21.00	24.50	28.50	32.00	70.00	96.00	190	2,600	—
1916	131,833,677	.45	.55	.85	2.40	8.00	14.50	19.00	135	650
1916D	35,956,000	1.35	2.00	3.10	6.50	17.50	38.00	88.00	850	—
1916S	22,510,000	1.65	3.25	4.40	9.50	27.50	48.00	105	1,100	—
1917	196,429,785	.30	.40	.55	1.85	4.75	14.50	18.50	150	—
1917 Doubled Die Obverse	Inc. above	175	225	2.75	350	1,350	2,000	3,200	15,000	—
1917D	55,120,000	1.00	1.50	2.85	5.00	36.50	44.00	72.00	850	—
1917S	32,620,000	.55	.90	1.40	2.60	11.50	26.00	74.00	1,350	—
1918	288,104,634	.30	.40	.50	1.00	4.40	10.00	13.50	185	—
1918D	47,830,000	.95	1.45	2.45	5.50	15.50	36.00	76.00	1,200	—
1918S	34,680,000	.40	.90	1.45	3.65	11.00	33.00	70.00	1,750	—
1919	392,021,000	.30	.40	.50	.80	1.60	5.75	8.00	85.00	—
1919D	57,154,000	.80	1.20	1.60	4.85	12.75	35.00	60.00	775	—
1919S	139,760,000	.40	.60	1.50	2.45	5.75	17.50	48.00	1,175	—
1920	310,165,000	.25	.35	.75	1.25	2.80	7.50	15.50	225	—
1920D	49,280,000	1.00	1.65	2.90	6.85	18.50	37.00	70.00	650	—
1920S	46,220,000	.60	.80	1.50	2.75	13.00	34.50	105	2,150	—
1921	39,157,000	.55	.80	1.15	3.00	10.75	22.50	42.00	175	—
1921S	15,274,000	1.50	2.00	3.50	6.25	36.50	68.00	110	1,100	—
1922D	7,160,000	23.50	24.50	25.50	27.00	37.50	75.00	105	475	—
1922D Weak Rev	Inc. above	22.00	23.00	24.00	25.50	34.00	65.00	95.00	400	—
1922D Weak D	Inc. above	30.00	44.00	48.00	60.00	135	190	285	7,500	—
1922 No D Die 2 Strong Rev	Inc. above	700	775	975	1,175	2,450	4,750	10,500	85,000	—
1922 No D Die 3 Weak Rev	Inc. above	275	325	375	475	950	3,000	8,500	45,000	—
1923	74,723,000	.40	.60	.85	1.50	5.75	10.50	13.50	160	—
1923S	8,700,000	5.85	7.00	8.50	12.50	42.00	105	190	2,850	—
1924	75,178,000	.25	.35	.45	1.00	5.25	11.00	17.50	120	—
1924D	2,520,000	37.50	45.00	50.00	62.00	118	170	255	1,800	—
1924S	11,696,000	1.25	1.50	2.75	5.35	34.50	68.00	110	2,350	—
1925	139,949,000	.25	.35	.45	.70	3.00	6.50	9.50	65.00	—
1925D	22,580,000	1.00	1.65	3.10	6.25	15.50	30.00	62.00	625	—
1925S	26,380,000	.80	1.20	1.85	2.75	11.75	31.50	85.00	3,650	—
1926	157,088,000	.25	.35	.45	.60	1.65	5.25	7.50	70.00	—
1926D	28,020,000	1.50	1.70	3.40	5.25	15.50	34.00	82.00	800	—
1926S	4,550,000	9.00	10.00	11.75	16.50	35.00	72.00	140	5,500	—
1927	144,440,000	.20	.25	.35	.60	1.60	5.25	7.50	60.00	—
1927D	27,170,000	1.15	1.70	2.25	3.35	7.50	25.00	60.00	525	—
1927S	14,276,000	1.40	1.85	2.65	5.25	14.50	42.00	65.00	2,550	—
1928	134,116,000	.20	.25	.35	.60	1.45	4.00	7.50	82.00	—
1928D	31,170,000	.90	1.40	2.15	3.65	6.75	19.00	37.50	300	—
1928S Small S	17,266,000	1.00	1.65	2.60	4.00	9.50	31.00	71.50	800	—
1928S Large S	Inc. above	1.65	2.85	4.25	7.50	16.50	55.00	135	1,250	—
1929	185,262,000	.20	.25	.35	.55	2.75	5.25	7.00	55.00	—
1929D	41,730,000	.50	1.00	1.40	2.75	5.85	13.50	25.00	145	—
1929S	50,148,000	.60	1.10	1.85	2.80	6.75	14.75	20.00	100.00	—
1930	157,415,000	.20	.25	.35	.60	1.25	2.75	4.00	45.00	—
1930D	40,100,000	.25	.35	.60	.90	2.00	5.50	11.00	55.00	—
1930S	24,286,000	.25	.35	.55	.80	1.50	6.50	9.50	48.00	—
1931	19,396,000	.65	.75	1.10	2.00	4.00	9.50	19.00	85.00	—
1931D	4,480,000	5.00	5.85	6.50	8.00	13.00	33.50	48.50	375	—
1931S	866,000	105	110	125	125	138	150	160	350	—
1932	9,062,000	1.60	1.95	2.85	3.50	6.75	13.00	17.50	65.00	—
1932D	10,500,000	1.50	1.90	2.50	2.85	4.15	11.00	18.50	65.00	—
1933	14,360,000	1.50	1.80	2.65	2.85	6.50	11.50	16.50	65.00	—
1933D	6,200,000	3.50	4.25	5.65	7.50	13.50	19.00	24.00	60.00	—
1934	219,080,000	.15	.25	.30	.45	1.25	4.00	9.00	25.00	—
1934D	28,446,000	.35	.50	.80	1.25	5.50	9.00	20.00	30.00	—
1935	245,338,000	.15	.20	.25	.40	.90	1.50	5.00	20.00	—
1935D	47,000,000	.20	.30	.40	.55	.95	2.50	5.50	20.00	—

Date	Mintage	G-4	VG-8	F-12	VF-20	XF-40	AU-50	MS-60	MS-65	Prf-65
1935S	38,702,000	.25	.35	.60	1.75	3.00	5.00	11.00	44.00	—
1936 (Proof in Satin Finish)	309,637,569	.15	.20	.30	.40	.85	1.40	1.90	10.00	600
1936 Brilliant Proof	Inc. above	—	—	—	—	—	—	—	—	800
1936 DDO	Inc. above	—	—	25.00	50.00	80.00	125	175	1,000	—
1936D	40,620,000	.20	.30	.40	.55	.90	1.50	4.00	15.00	—
1936S	29,130,000	.20	.30	.45	.60	1.50	2.25	5.00	18.00	—
1937	309,179,320	.15	.20	.30	.40	.50	.75	1.75	13.50	110
1937D	50,430,000	.20	.30	.40	.60	.80	1.20	2.65	15.00	—
1937S	34,500,000	.20	.30	.40	.55	.00	1.25	2.75	10.50	—
1938	156,696,734	.15	.20	.30	.40	.50	1.20	2.25	18.00	90.00
1938D	20,010,000	.20	.30	.45	.60	1.00	1.50	3.50	20.00	—
1938S	15,180,000	.30	.40	.50	.70	1.00	1.75	3.00	15.00	—
1939	316,479,520	.15	.20	.30	.40	.45	.75	1.00	16.00	60.00
1939D	15,160,000	.35	.45	.50	.60	.95	1.75	3.00	18.00	—
1939S	52,070,000	.30	.40	.50	.60	.80	1.20	2.50	16.00	—
1940	586,825,872	.10	.20	.30	.35	.45	.75	1.00	12.00	65.00
1940D	81,390,000	.20	.30	.40	.55	.75	1.10	2.00	11.00	—
1940S	112,940,000	.20	.30	.40	.55	.70	1.25	2.50	12.50	—
1941	887,039,100	.10	.20	.30	.35	.45	.60	1.25	10.00	60.00
1941 Doubled Die Obv	Inc. above	35.00	50.00	70.00	80.00	95.00	135	200	1,000	—
1941D	128,700,000	.20	.30	.40	.55	.90	1.35	2.20	12.50	—
1941S	92,360,000	.20	.30	.40	.55	.95	1.75	2.50	15.00	—
1942	657,828,600	.10	.20	.30	.35	.40	.55	.85	11.00	65.00
1942D	206,698,000	.20	.25	.30	.35	.45	.60	1.00	12.00	—
1942S	85,590,000	.25	.35	.45	.85	1.25	2.50	5.00	18.00	—
1943S Copper	—	—	—	125,000	150,000	185,000	275,000	—	—	—
1943 Copper	—	—	—	35,000	42,000	45,000	80,000	155,000	—	—

Lincoln Cent.

Wheat Ears.

KM# 132a Designer: Victor D. Brenner. **Diameter:** 19 **Weight:** 2.7000 g. **Composition:** Zinc Coated Steel

Date	Mintage	G-4	VG-8	F-12	VF-20	XF-40	AU-50	MS-60	MS-65	Prf-65
1943	684,628,670	.20	.30	.35	.45	.60	.85	1.25	18.00	—
1943D	217,660,000	.35	.40	.45	.50	.70	1.00	1.50	—	—
1943D/D RPM	Inc. above	30.00	38.00	50.00	65.00	90.00	125	200	—	—
1943S	191,550,000	.40	.45	.50	.65	.90	1.40	4.00	28.00	—

Lincoln Cent.

Wheat Ears.

KM# A132 Designer: Victor D. Brenner. **Diameter:** 19 **Weight:** 3.1100 g. **Composition:** Brass **Notes:** KM#132 design and composition resumed • MS60 prices are for brown coins and MS65 prices are for coins that are at least 90% original red.

1955 Double die

Date	Mintage	XF-40	MS-65	Prf-65
1944	1,435,400,000	.30	8.00	—
1944D	430,578,000	.40	14.00	—
1944D/S Type 1	Inc. above	220	3,750	—
1944D/S Type 2	Inc. above	175	1,600	—
1944S	282,760,000	.35	8.00	—
1945	1,040,515,000	.40	13.50	—
1945D	226,268,000	.40	8.00	—
1945S	181,770,000	.40	7.50	—
1946	991,655,000	.25	13.50	—
1946D	315,690,000	.30	10.00	—
1946S	198,100,000	.30	13.50	—
1946S/D	—	70.00	650	—
1947	190,555,000	.45	18.50	—
1947D	194,750,000	.35	7.50	—
1947S	99,000,000	.35	8.00	—
1948	317,570,000	.35	18.50	—
1948D	172,637,000	.40	12.00	—
1948S	81,735,000	.40	12.00	—
1949	217,775,000	.40	18.00	—
1949D	153,132,000	.40	15.00	—
1949S	64,290,000	.50	10.00	—
1950	272,686,386	.35	16.50	65.00
1950D	334,950,000	.35	12.50	—
1950S	118,505,000	.30	9.00	—
1951	295,633,500	.40	16.50	62.00
1951D	625,355,000	.30	8.50	—
1951S	136,010,000	.40	9.00	—
1952	186,856,980	.40	16.00	36.00
1952D	746,130,000	.30	8.50	—
1952S	137,800,004	.60	12.00	—
1953	256,883,800	.25	18.00	37.00
1953D	700,515,000	.25	8.50	—
1953S	181,835,000	.40	8.00	—
1954	71,873,350	.25	20.00	19.00
1954D	251,552,500	.25	8.50	—
1954S	96,190,000	.25	10.00	—
1955	330,958,000	.25	9.00	14.00
1955 Doubled Die	Inc. above	1,900	37,500	—

Note: The 1955 "doubled die" has distinct doubling of the date and lettering on the obverse.

Date	Mintage	XF-40	MS-65	Prf-65
1955D	563,257,500	.20	8.00	—
1955S	44,610,000	.35	7.50	—
1956	421,414,384	.20	12.00	5.00
1956D	1,098,201,100	.20	7.00	—
1957	283,787,952	.20	7.50	4.00
1957D	1,051,342,000	.20	6.00	—
1958	253,400,652	.20	9.00	6.50
1958D	800,953,300	.20	7.00	—

Lincoln Cent.

Lincoln Memorial.

KM# 201 **Rev. Designer:** Frank Gasparro. **Diameter:** 19 **Weight:** 3.1100 g. **Composition:** Brass **Notes:** MS60 prices are for brown coins and MS65 prices are for coins that are at least 90% original red. The dates were modified in 1960, 1970 and 1982, resulting in large-date and small date varieties for those years. The 1972 "doubled die" shows doubling of IN GOD WE TRUST. The 1979-S and 1981-S Type II proofs have a clearer mint mark than the Type I proofs of those years. Some 1982 cents have the predominantly copper composition; others have the predominantly zinc composition. They can be distinguished by weight.

Small date | Large date

Small date | Large date

Date	Mintage	XF-40	MS-65	Prf-65
1959	610,864,291	—	15.00	10.00
1959D	1,279,760,000	—	12.00	—
1960 small date, low 9	588,096,602	1.85	12.00	16.00
1960 large date, high 9	Inc. above	—	8.00	7.50
1960D small date, low 9	1,580,884,000	—	10.00	—
1960D large date, high 9	Inc. above	—	8.00	—
1960D/D small over large date	Inc. above	—	300	—
1961	756,373,244	—	8.50	9.00
1961D	1,753,266,700	—	18.00	—
1962	609,263,019	—	8.00	8.00
1962D	1,793,148,400	—	14.00	—
1963	757,185,645	—	10.00	6.00
1963D	1,774,020,400	—	12.00	—
1964	2,652,525,762	—	8.50	6.00
1964D	3,799,071,500	—	10.00	—
1965	1,497,224,900	—	10.00	—
1965 SMS	Inc. above	—	7.50	—
1966	2,188,147,783	—	10.00	—
1966 SMS	Inc. above	—	8.00	—
1967	3,048,667,100	—	12.00	—
1967 SMS	Inc. above	—	8.00	—
1968	1,707,880,970	—	12.00	—
1968D	2,886,269,600	—	12.50	—
1968S	261,311,510	—	10.00	4.50
1969	1,136,910,000	—	7.00	—
1969D	4,002,832,200	—	10.00	—
1969S	547,309,631	—	15.00	5.50
1969S Doubled Die Obverse	Inc. above	10,000	125,000	100,000
1970	1,898,315,000	—	8.00	—
1970D	2,891,438,900	—	6.00	—
1970S small date, level 7	Inc. above	30.00	65.00	60.00
1970S large date, low 7	Inc. above	—	15.00	5.00
1970S Doubled Die Obverse	Inc. above	—	20,000	15,000
1971	1,919,490,000	—	20.00	—
1971D	2,911,045,000	—	6.50	
1971S	528,354,192	—	7.50	5.50
1971S Doubled Die Obverse	Inc. above	—	—	400
1972	2,933,255,000	—	6.00	—
1972 Doubled Die Obverse	Inc. above	290	785	—
1972D	2,665,071,400	—	12.00	—
1972S	380,200,104	—	26.50	5.50
1973	3,728,245,000	—	8.00	—
1973D	3,549,576,588	—	11.00	—
1973S	319,937,634	—	10.00	5.50
1974	4,232,140,523	—	12.00	—
1974D	4,235,098,000	—	9.00	—
1974S	412,039,228	—	12.00	5.00
1975	5,451,476,142	—	8.00	—
1975D	4,505,245,300	—	13.50	—
1975S	2,845,450	—	—	5.00
1976	4,674,292,426	—	14.00	—
1976D	4,221,592,455	—	16.00	—
1976S	4,149,730	—	—	6.00
1977	4,469,930,000	—	16.00	—
1977D	4,149,062,300	—	16.00	—
1977S	3,251,152	—	—	5.00
1978	5,558,605,000	—	16.00	—
1978D	4,280,233,400	—	14.00	—
1978S	3,127,781	—	—	5.00
1979	6,018,515,000	—	12.00	—
1979D	4,139,357,254	—	8.00	—
1979S type I, proof	3,677,175	—	—	5.00
1979S type II, proof	Inc. above	—	—	10.00
1980	7,414,705,000	—	6.50	—
1980D	5,140,098,660	—	12.00	—
1980S	3,554,806	—	—	5.00
1981	7,491,750,000	—	8.50	—
1981D	5,373,235,677	—	9.00	—
1981S type I, proof	4,063,083	—	—	5.00
1981S type II, proof	Inc. above	—	—	42.00
1982 large date	10,712,525,000	—	7.00	—
1982 small date	Inc. above	—	9.00	—
1982D large date	6,012,979,368	—	7.50	—
1982S	3,857,479	—	—	5.00

Lincoln Cent.

Lincoln Memorial.

KM# 201a **Diameter:** 19 **Weight:** 2.5000 g. **Composition:** Copper Plated Zinc **Notes:** MS60 prices are for brown coins and MS65 prices are for coins that are at least 90% original red.

Date	Mintage	XF-40	MS-65	Prf-65
1982 large date	—	—	6.00	—
1982 small date	—	—	9.00	—
1982D large date	—	—	8.00	—
1982D small date	—	—	6.00	—

Lincoln Cent.

Lincoln Memorial.

KM# 201b **Diameter:** 19 **Composition:** Copper Plated Zinc **Notes:** MS60 prices are for brown coins and MS65 prices are for coins that are at least 90% original red.

Date	Mintage	XF-40	MS-65	Prf-65
1983	7,752,355,000	—	7.00	—
1983 Doubled Die	Inc. above	135	450	—
1983D	6,467,199,428	—	5.50	—
1983S	3,279,126	—	—	3.50
1984	8,151,079,000	—	7.50	—
1984 Doubled Die	Inc. above	100.00	325	—
1984D	5,569,238,906	—	6.50	—
1984S	3,065,110	—	—	3.50
1985	5,648,489,887	—	4.50	—
1985D	5,287,399,926	—	4.50	—
1985S	3,362,821	—	—	3.50
1986	4,491,395,493	—	5.00	—
1986D	4,442,866,698	—	8.00	—
1986S	3,010,497	—	—	3.50
1987	4,682,466,931	—	7.50	—
1987D	4,879,389,514	—	5.50	—
1987S	4,227,728	—	—	3.50
1988	6,092,810,000	—	10.00	—
1988D	5,253,740,443	—	6.00	—
1988S	3,262,948	—	—	3.50
1989	7,261,535,000	—	6.50	—
1989D	5,345,467,111	—	6.50	—
1989S	3,220,194	—	—	5.00
1990	6,851,765,000	—	5.00	—
1990D	4,922,894,533	—	5.50	—
1990S	3,299,559	—	—	3.50
1990 no S, Proof only	Inc. above	—	—	4,650
1991	5,165,940,000	—	6.50	—
1991D	4,158,442,076	—	5.50	—
1991S	2,867,787	—	—	3.50
1992	4,648,905,000	—	5.50	—
1992D	4,448,673,300	—	5.50	—
1992D Close AM, Proof Reverse Die	Inc. above	—	—	—
1992S	4,176,560	—	—	3.50
1993	5,684,705,000	—	5.00	—
1993D	6,426,650,571	—	4.50	—
1993S	3,394,792	—	—	3.50
1994	6,500,850,000	—	6.00	—
1994D	7,131,765,000	—	4.50	—
1994S	3,269,923	—	—	3.50
1995	6,411,440,000	—	5.00	—
1995 Doubled Die Obverse	Inc. above	20.00	60.00	—
1995D	7,128,560,000	—	4.50	—
1995S	2,707,481	—	—	3.50
1996	6,612,465,000	—	4.50	—
1996D	6,510,795,000	—	4.50	—
1996S	2,915,212	—	—	3.50
1997	4,622,800,000	—	3.00	—
1997D	4,576,555,000	—	3.50	—
1997S	2,796,678	—	—	4.00
1998	5,032,155,000	—	3.00	—
1998 Wide AM, reverse from proof die	Inc. above	—	110	—
1998D	5,255,353,500	—	3.00	—
1998S	2,957,286	—	—	4.00
1999	5,237,600,000	—	3.00	—
1999 Wide AM, reverse from proof die	Inc. above	—	450	—
1999D	6,360,065,000	—	3.00	—
1999S	3,362,462	—	—	3.50
2000 Wide AM, reverse from proof die	Inc. above	—	45.00	—
2000	5,503,200,000	—	3.00	—
2000D	8,774,220,000	—	3.00	—
2000S	4,063,361	—	—	3.50
2001	4,959,600,000	—	3.00	—
2001D	5,374,990,000	—	3.00	—
2001S	3,099,096	—	—	3.50
2002	3,260,800,000	—	3.00	—
2002D	4,028,055,000	—	3.00	—
2002S	3,157,739	—	—	3.50
2003	3,300,000,000	—	3.50	—
2003D	3,548,000,000	—	3.50	—
2003S	3,116,590	—	—	3.50
2004	3,379,600,000	—	3.50	—
2004D	3,456,400,000	—	3.50	—
2004S	2,992,069	—	—	3.50
2005	3,935,600,000	—	2.50	—
2005 Satin Finish	Inc. above	—	4.00	—
2005D	3,764,450,000	—	2.50	—
2005D Satin Finish	Inc. above	—	4.00	—
2005S	3,273,000	—	—	3.50
2006	4,290,000,000	—	2.00	—
2006 Satin Finish	Inc. above	—	4.00	—
2006D	3,944,000,000	—	2.50	—
2006 Satin Finish	Inc. above	—	4.00	—
2006S	2,923,105	—	—	3.50
2007	—	—	2.00	—
2007 Satin Finish	—	—	4.00	—
2007D	—	—	2.00	—
2007 Satin Finish	—	—	4.00	—
2007S	—	—	—	3.50
2008	—	—	2.25	—
2008 Satin Finish	—	—	4.00	—
2008D	—	—	2.25	—
2008 Satin Finish	—	—	4.00	—
2008S	—	—	—	4.50

Lincoln Bicentennial.

Bust right. Log cabin.

KM# 441 **Rev. Designer:** Richard Masters and James Licaretz. **Diameter:** 19 **Weight:** 2.5000 g. **Composition:** Copper Plated Zinc

Date	Mintage	XF-40	MS-65	Prf-65
2009P	284,400,000	—	1.50	—
2009D	350,400,000	—	1.50	—

KM# 441a **Rev. Designer:** Richard Masters and James Licaretz. **Weight:** 3.3100 g. **Composition:** Brass

Date	Mintage	XF-40	MS-65	Prf-65
2009S	—	—	—	4.00

Lincoln seated on log.

KM# 442 **Rev. Designer:** Charles Vickers. **Diameter:** 19 **Weight:** 2.5000 g. **Composition:** Copper Plated Zinc

Date	Mintage	XF-40	MS-65	Prf-65
2009P	376,000,000	—	1.50	—
2009D	363,600,000	—	1.50	—

KM# 442a **Rev. Designer:** Charles Vickers. **Diameter:** 19 **Weight:** 3.1100 g. **Composition:** Brass

Date	Mintage	XF-40	MS-65	Prf-65
2009S	—	—	—	4.00

Lincoln standing before Illinois Statehouse.

KM# 443 **Rev. Designer:** Joel Ishowitz and Don Everhart. **Diameter:** 19 **Weight:** 2.5000 g. **Composition:** Copper Plated Zinc

Date	Mintage	XF-40	MS-65	Prf-65
2009P	316,000,000	—	1.50	—
2009D	336,000,000	—	1.50	—

KM# 443a **Rev. Designer:** Joel Iskowitz and Don Everhart. **Diameter:** 19 **Weight:** 3.1100 g. **Composition:** Brass

Date	Mintage	XF-40	MS-65	Prf-65
2009S	—	—	—	4.00

Capitol Building.

KM# 444 **Rev. Designer:** Susan Gamble and Joseph Menna. **Weight:** 2.5000 g. **Composition:** Copper Plated Zinc

Date	Mintage	XF-40	MS-65	Prf-65
2009P	129,600,000	—	1.50	—
2009D	198,000,000	—	1.50	—

KM# 444a **Rev. Designer:** Susan Ganmble and Joseph Menna. **Diameter:** 19 **Weight:** 3.1100 g. **Composition:** Brass

Date	Mintage	XF-40	MS-65	Prf-65
2009S	—	—	—	4.00

Lincoln - Shield Reverse.

Lincoln bust right. Shield.

KM# 468 **Obv. Designer:** Victor D. Brenner. **Rev. Designer:** Lyndall Bass and Joseph Menna. **Diameter:** 19 **Weight:** 2.5000 g. **Composition:** Copper Plated Zinc

Date	Mintage	XF-40	MS-65	Prf-65
2010P	—	—	1.50	—
2010D	—	—	1.50	—
2010S	—	—	—	4.00
2011P	—	—	1.50	—
2011D	—	—	1.50	—
2011S	—	—	—	4.00
2012P	—	—	1.50	—
2012D	—	—	1.50	—
2012S	—	—	—	4.00
2013P	—	—	1.50	—
2013D	—	—	1.50	—
2013S	—	—	—	4.00

2 CENTS

2 CENTS

Shield in front of crossed arrows, banner above, date below. Value within wheat wreath.

KM# 94 **Designer:** James B. Longacre. **Diameter:** 23 **Weight:** 6.2200 g. **Composition:** Copper-Tin-Zinc
Notes: The motto IN GOD WE TRUST was modified in 1864, resulting in small-motto and large-motto varieties for that year.

Small motto

Large motto

Date	Mintage	G-4	VG-8	F-12	VF-20	XF-40	AU-50	MS-60	MS-65	Prf-65
1864 small motto	19,847,500	140	210	285	425	650	725	1,125	3,000	45,000
1864 large motto	Inc. above	16.50	18.50	20.00	27.50	42.50	72.00	88.00	375	1,100

Date	Mintage	G-4	VG-8	F-12	VF-20	XF-40	AU-50	MS-60	MS-65	Prf-65
1865 fancy 5	13,640,000	16.50	18.50	20.00	27.50	42.50	72.00	88.00	375	—
1865 plain 5	Inc. above	16.50	18.50	21.00	29.00	45.00	75.00	92.00	400	650
1866	3,177,000	17.00	20.00	21.50	29.00	46.00	77.00	98.00	395	650
1867	2,938,750	18.00	21.00	36.00	46.00	60.00	96.00	125	395	650
1867 double die obverse	Inc. above	—	80.00	165	250	350	500	650	4,750	—
1868	2,803,750	18.00	22.00	37.50	47.50	65.00	105	135	465	650
1869	1,546,000	20.00	23.00	40.00	50.00	79.00	125	165	550	650
1869 repunched 18	Inc. above	35.00	45.00	75.00	150	325	550	—	—	—
1869/9 die crack	Inc. above	150	185	375	435	650	900	—	—	—
1870	861,250	31.00	42.00	60.00	82.00	135	190	280	550	650
1871	721,250	43.50	49.00	70.00	110	150	215	285	650	650
1872	65,000	400	550	700	900	1,200	1,800	3,150	5,500	850
1873 closed 3 proof only	Est. 600	1,250	1,400	1,535	1,650	1,750	2,000	—	—	3,850
1873 open 3 proof only	Est. 500	1,275	1,400	1,575	1,700	1,875	2,150	—	—	4,200

SILVER 3 CENTS

Silver 3 Cents - Type 1.

Shield within star, no outlines in star. Roman numeral in designed C, within circle of stars.

KM# 75 **Designer:** James B. Longacre. **Diameter:** 14 **Weight:** 0.8000 g. **Composition:** 0.7500 Silver, 0.0193 oz. ASW.

Date	Mintage	G-4	VG-8	F-12	VF-20	XF-40	AU-50	MS-60	MS-65	Prf-65
1851	5,447,400	32.00	48.50	51.00	58.50	68.00	145	180	825	—
1851O	720,000	38.50	58.50	61.00	95.00	160	275	500	3,100	—
1852	18,663,500	32.00	48.50	51.00	58.50	68.00	145	180	825	—
1853	11,400,000	32.00	48.50	51.00	58.50	68.00	145	180	825	—

Silver 3 Cents - Type 2.

Shield within star, three outlines in star. Roman numeral in designed C, within circle of stars.

KM# 80 **Designer:** James B. Longacre. **Diameter:** 14 **Weight:** 0.7500 g. **Composition:** 0.9000 Silver, 0.0217 oz. ASW.

Date	Mintage	G-4	VG-8	F-12	VF-20	XF-40	AU-50	MS-60	MS-65	Prf-65
1854	671,000	32.00	48.50	51.00	59.50	112	205	340	2,700	33,500
1855	139,000	44.00	57.50	75.00	125	200	325	520	7,400	15,000
1856	1,458,000	34.00	50.50	54.00	67.00	119.5	205	260	3,250	15,500
1857	1,042,000	34.00	50.50	54.00	67.00	112	223	285	2,375	13,500
1858	1,604,000	33.00	49.50	52.00	62.00	122	205	230	2,350	6,400

Silver 3 Cents - Type 3.

Shield within star, two outlines in star. Roman numeral in designed C, within circle of stars.

KM# 88 **Designer:** James B. Longacre. **Diameter:** 14 **Weight:** 0.7500 g. **Composition:** 0.9000 Silver, 0.0217 oz. ASW.

Date	Mintage	G-4	VG-8	F-12	VF-20	XF-40	AU-50	MS-60	MS-65	Prf-65
1859	365,000	40.00	53.50	56.00	64.00	87.00	160	195	975	2,150
1860	287,000	40.00	53.50	56.00	64.00	83.00	160	195	1,050	4,000
1861	498,000	40.00	53.50	56.00	64.00	83.00	160	195	1,050	1,800
1862	343,550	46.00	55.50	58.00	66.00	88.00	180	235	935	1,400
1862/1	Inc. above	43.00	57.50	62.00	71.00	94.00	177	210	865	—
1863	21,460	375	420	450	485	520	725	825	2,250	1,350
1863/62 proof only; Rare	Inc. above	—	—	—	—	—	—	—	—	5,400
1864	12,470	375	420	450	485	520	725	850	1,675	1,350
1865	8,500	475	525	550	620	665	700	875	1,650	1,350
1866	22,725	375	420	450	485	520	675	775	1,950	1,325
1867	4,625	475	525	575	625	675	725	850	2,750	1,300
1868	4,100	475	535	585	640	690	750	875	5,750	1,400
1869	5,100	475	535	585	640	690	750	875	2,450	1,400
1869/68 proof only; Rare	Inc. above	—	—	—	—	—	—	—	—	—
1870	4,000	450	460	525	600	665	750	950	5,650	1,350
1871	4,360	440	450	535	625	670	710	835	1,800	1,450

Date	Mintage	G-4	VG-8	F-12	VF-20	XF-40	AU-50	MS-60	MS-65	Prf-65
1872	1,950	465	485	550	645	690	750	875	5,500	1,350
1873 proof only	600	—	—	—	—	950	1,050	—	—	2,950

NICKEL 3 CENTS

Coronet head left, date below. Roman numeral value within wreath.

KM# 95 Designer: James B. Longacre. **Diameter:** 17.9 **Weight:** 1.9400 g. **Composition:** Copper-Nickel

Date	Mintage	G-4	VG-8	F-12	VF-20	XF-40	AU-50	MS-60	MS-65	Prf-65
1865	11,382,000	15.50	16.50	17.50	22.50	37.50	60.00	100.00	550	6,500
1866	4,801,000	15.50	16.50	17.50	22.50	37.50	60.00	100.00	550	1,725
1867	3,915,000	15.50	16.50	17.50	22.50	37.50	60.00	100.00	670	1,575
1868	3,252,000	15.50	16.50	17.50	22.50	37.50	60.00	100.00	550	1,450
1869	1,604,000	16.50	17.50	19.50	25.50	40.50	61.00	120	730	1,050
1870	1,335,000	17.50	18.50	20.50	26.50	41.50	62.00	135	725	2,250
1871	604,000	17.50	19.00	22.50	27.50	42.50	64.00	155	740	1,200
1872	862,000	19.00	22.50	24.50	29.00	43.50	68.00	175	995	910
1873 Cl 3	1,173,000	16.50	18.50	22.50	25.50	40.50	62.00	145	1,050	1,125
1873 Op 3	Inc. above	16.50	18.50	22.50	26.00	41.50	68.00	180	4,500	—
1874	790,000	17.50	20.50	22.50	27.50	42.50	66.00	160	950	950
1875	228,000	19.00	22.50	27.50	30.50	45.50	82.00	190	750	1,500
1876	162,000	20.50	23.50	26.50	34.50	49.50	97.00	225	1,290	1,025
1877 proof	Est. 900	1,100	1,150	1,175	1,250	1,275	1,350	—	—	3,750
1878 proof	2,350	615	645	720	770	795	830	—	—	1,200
1879	41,200	70.00	80.00	96.00	110	122	180	320	750	690
1880	24,955	100.00	115	130	165	185	235	375	730	700
1881	1,080,575	15.50	16.50	19.00	23.50	39.50	60.00	100.00	585	680
1882	25,300	130	150	180	225	300	325	425	1,025	700
1883	10,609	200	225	265	305	375	425	480	4,850	690
1884	5,642	400	445	550	600	645	730	800	6,250	700
1885	4,790	470	520	645	700	745	775	900	12,000	720
1886 proof	4,290	320	330	345	385	385	420	—	—	715
1887/6 proof	7,961	350	390	415	450	460	515	—	—	940
1887	Inc. above	305	355	395	440	455	500	540	1,200	1,125
1888	41,083	54.00	63.00	70.00	80.00	100.00	170	315	650	690
1889	21,561	90.00	115	145	180	230	260	320	775	690

HALF DIME

Flowing Hair Half Dime.

KM# 15 Designer: Robert Scot. **Diameter:** 16.5 **Weight:** 1.3500 g. **Composition:** 0.8920 Silver, 0.0387 oz. ASW.

Date	Mintage	G-4	VG-8	F-12	VF-20	XF-40	MS-60
1794	86,416	1,325	1,625	2,150	3,125	7,325	19,000
1795	Inc. above	1,050	1,350	1,875	2,900	5,800	13,000

Draped Bust Half Dime.

Draped bust right. Small eagle.

KM# 23 Designer: Robert Scot. **Diameter:** 16.5 **Weight:** 1.3500 g. **Composition:** 0.8920 Silver, 0.0387 oz. ASW.

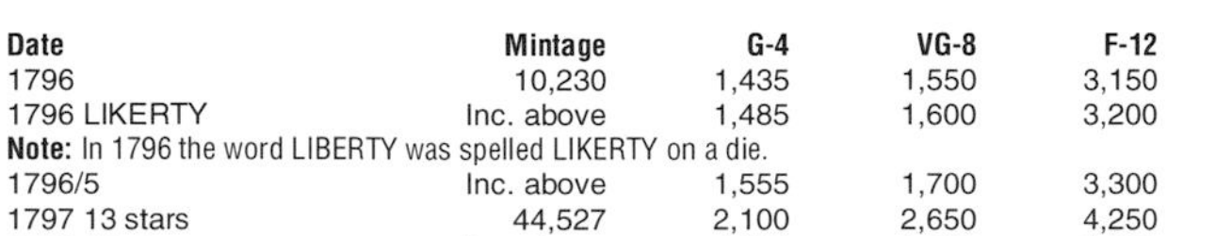

Date	Mintage	G-4	VG-8	F-12	VF-20	XF-40	MS-60
1796	10,230	1,435	1,550	3,150	4,850	8,650	17,550
1796 LIKERTY	Inc. above	1,485	1,600	3,200	4,900	8,700	17,600

Note: In 1796 the word LIBERTY was spelled LIKERTY on a die.

Date	Mintage	G-4	VG-8	F-12	VF-20	XF-40	MS-60
1796/5	Inc. above	1,555	1,700	3,300	5,000	8,800	17,700
1797 13 stars	44,527	2,100	2,650	4,250	5,950	9,750	30,750
1797 15 stars	Inc. above	1,385	1,500	3,100	4,800	8,600	17,500
1797 16 stars	Inc. above	1,535	1,750	3,350	5,050	8,850	17,750

Draped Bust Half Dime.

Draped bust right, flanked by stars, date at angle below. Heraldic eagle.

KM# 34 Designer: Robert Scot. **Diameter:** 16.5 **Weight:** 1.3500 g. **Composition:** 0.8920 Silver, 0.0387 oz. ASW.

Date	Mintage	G-4	VG-8	F-12	VF-20	XF-40	MS-60
1800	24,000	1,000	1,250	1,875	2,550	6,500	13,500
1800 LIBEKTY	Inc. above	1,000	1,250	1,875	2,550	7,000	15,050
1801	33,910	1,225	1,500	2,125	2,800	6,750	17,750
1802	3,060	44,500	65,000	95,000	135,000	300,000	—
1803 Large 8	37,850	1,100	1,375	2,000	2,675	6,625	13,625
1803 Small 8	Inc. above	1,325	1,625	2,250	2,925	6,875	15,850
1805	15,600	1,225	1,525	2,350	3,025	9,900	31,000

Liberty Cap Half Dime.

Classic head left, flanked by stars, date below. Eagle with arrows in talons, banner above.

KM# 47 Designer: William Kneass. **Diameter:** 15.5 **Weight:** 1.3500 g. **Composition:** 0.8920 Silver, 0.0387 oz. ASW.

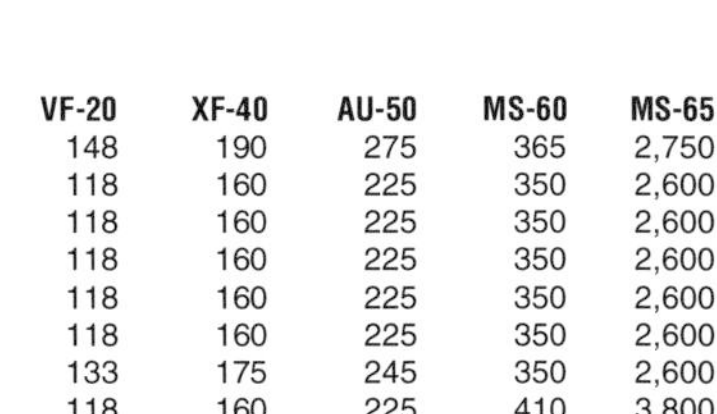

Date	Mintage	G-4	VG-8	F-12	VF-20	XF-40	AU-50	MS-60	MS-65
1829	1,230,000	60.00	75.00	85.00	148	190	275	365	2,750
1830	1,240,000	52.50	67.50	75.00	118	160	225	350	2,600
1831	1,242,700	52.50	67.50	75.00	118	160	225	350	2,600
1832	965,000	52.50	67.50	75.00	118	160	225	350	2,600
1833	1,370,000	52.50	67.50	75.00	118	160	225	350	2,600
1834	1,480,000	52.50	67.50	75.00	118	160	225	350	2,600
1835 large date and 5C.	2,760,000	52.50	75.00	87.00	133	175	245	350	2,600
1835 large date, small 5C.	Inc. above	52.50	67.50	75.00	118	160	225	410	3,800
1835 small date, large 5C.	Inc. above	52.50	67.50	75.00	118	160	225	375	3,500
1835 small date and 5C.	Inc. above	52.50	67.50	75.00	118	160	225	350	2,600
1836 large 5C.	1,900,000	52.50	67.50	75.00	118	160	225	350	2,600
1836 small 5C.	Inc. above	54.50	70.50	79.00	128	172	237	362	3,100
1837 large 5C.	2,276,000	52.50	67.50	83.00	136	175	245	395	3,800
1837 small 5C.	Inc. above	59.50	77.50	90.00	148	240	465	950	11,000

HALF DIME

Seated Liberty Half Dime.

Seated Liberty, no stars around border, date below. Value within wreath.

KM# 60 Designer: Christian Gobrecht. **Diameter:** 15.5 **Weight:** 1.3400 g. **Composition:** 0.9000 Silver, 0.0388 oz. ASW. **Notes:** A design modification in 1837 resulted in small-date and large-date varieties for that year.

Date	Mintage	G-4	VG-8	F-12	VF-20	XF-40	AU-50	MS-60	MS-65
1837 small date	Inc. above	35.00	46.50	75.00	135	220	495	750	4,450
1837 large date	Inc. above	39.00	49.50	82.00	150	235	445	620	3,650
1838O	70,000	110	130	250	475	975	1,450	2,500	29,500

Seated Liberty Half Dime.

Seated Liberty, stars around top 1/2 of border, date below. Value within wreath.

KM# 62.1 Designer: Christian Gobrecht. **Diameter:** 15.5 **Weight:** 1.3400 g. **Composition:** 0.9000 Silver, 0.0388 oz. ASW. **Notes:** The two varieties of 1838 are distinguished by the size of the stars on the obverse. The 1839-O with reverse of 1838-O was struck from rusted reverse dies. The result is a bumpy surface on this variety's reverse.

Date	Mintage	G-4	VG-8	F-12	VF-20	XF-40	AU-50	MS-60	MS-65
1838 large stars	2,255,000	22.50	25.50	29.00	36.00	88.00	198	265	2,475
1838 small stars	Inc. above	26.50	31.50	46.00	115	189	299	595	3,950

Date	Mintage	G-4	VG-8	F-12	VF-20	XF-40	AU-50	MS-60	MS-65
1839	1,069,150	23.50	26.50	30.00	37.00	93.00	203	265	2,000
1839O	1,034,039	27.50	30.50	34.00	41.00	88.00	198	715	6,850
1839O reverse 1838O	Inc. above	500	700	1,200	1,750	3,000	—	—	—
1840	1,344,085	24.50	27.50	31.00	38.00	80.00	190	255	2,275
1840O	935,000	29.50	32.50	38.00	48.00	138	368	1,235	—

Seated Liberty Half Dime.

Seated Liberty, stars around top 1/2 of border, date below.

KM# 62.2 **Designer:** Christian Gobrecht. **Diameter:** 15.5 **Weight:** 1.3400 g. **Composition:** 0.9000 Silver, 0.0388 oz. ASW. **Notes:** In 1840 drapery was added to Liberty's left elbow. Varieties for the 1848 Philadelphia strikes are distinguished by the size of the numerals in the date.

Date	Mintage	G-4	VG-8	F-12	VF-20	XF-40	AU-50	MS-60	MS-65
1840	Inc. above	21.50	18.00	75.00	135	210	350	490	3,850
1840O	Inc. above	52.50	60.00	115	225	650	1,350	6,500	—
1841	1,150,000	18.50	21.50	23.50	31.00	60.50	127	180	1,325
1841O	815,000	21.50	24.50	30.00	50.00	125	300	650	6,750
1842	815,000	18.50	21.50	23.50	28.00	57.50	127	175	1,750
1842O	350,000	39.50	45.00	75.00	225	550	1,050	2,250	16,500
1843	1,165,000	18.50	21.50	23.50	28.00	57.50	122	175	1,365
1844	430,000	20.50	24.50	26.50	34.00	60.50	127	180	1,150
1844O	220,000	80.00	110	210	600	1,300	2,650	5,400	27,500
1845	1,564,000	18.50	21.50	23.50	35.00	60.50	122	175	1,150
1845/1845	Inc. above	20.50	24.50	26.50	38.00	85.00	132	190	1,200
1846	27,000	410	550	850	1,250	2,475	3,600	11,500	—
1847	1,274,000	18.50	21.50	23.50	28.00	57.50	127	175	1,150
1848 medium date	668,000	20.50	24.50	26.50	34.00	67.50	137	215	3,150
1848 large date	Inc. above	24.00	28.00	48.00	65.00	145	275	635	4,250
1848O	600,000	21.50	25.50	33.00	62.00	135	265	450	2,350
1849/8	1,309,000	28.50	35.00	47.50	67.50	140	250	785	2,950
1849/6	Inc. above	24.00	26.00	30.00	56.50	110	200	425	2,800
1849	Inc. above	20.50	18.50	27.50	52.50	67.50	137	190	1,825
1849O	140,000	29.00	40.00	95.00	225	540	1,100	2,350	—
1850	955,000	20.50	24.50	26.50	34.00	62.50	127	190	1,300
1850O	690,000	21.50	24.50	35.00	65.00	125	280	685	4,450
1851	781,000	17.50	21.50	23.50	28.00	59.90	122	175	1,350
1851O	860,000	20.50	24.50	26.50	41.50	110	220	500	4,350
1852	1,000,500	17.50	21.50	23.50	28.00	59.50	122	175	1,150
1852O	260,000	26.50	44.50	79.00	135	275	475	885	11,500
1853	135,000	40.00	60.00	90.00	175	300	525	850	2,850
1853O	160,000	285	325	450	850	1,800	3,500	6,450	27,500

Seated Liberty Half Dime.

Seated Liberty, stars around top 1/2 of border, arrows at date. Value within wreath.

KM# 76 **Designer:** Christian Gobrecht. **Weight:** 1.2400 g. **Composition:** 0.9000 Silver, 0.0359 oz. ASW.

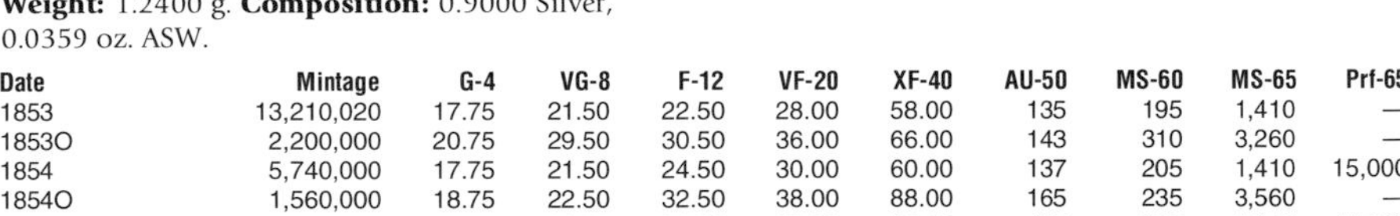

Date	Mintage	G-4	VG-8	F-12	VF-20	XF-40	AU-50	MS-60	MS-65	Prf-65
1853	13,210,020	17.75	21.50	22.50	28.00	58.00	135	195	1,410	—
1853O	2,200,000	20.75	29.50	30.50	36.00	66.00	143	310	3,260	—
1854	5,740,000	17.75	21.50	24.50	30.00	60.00	137	205	1,410	15,000
1854O	1,560,000	18.75	22.50	32.50	38.00	88.00	165	235	3,560	—
1855	1,750,000	18.75	22.50	24.50	30.00	60.00	137	200	1,810	15,000
1855O	600,000	22.75	27.50	38.50	54.00	140	220	540	4,260	—

HALF DIME

Seated Liberty Half Dime.

Seated Liberty, stars around top 1/2 of border, date below. Value within wreath.

KM# A62.2 **Designer:** Christian Gobrecht. **Weight:** 1.2400 g. **Composition:** 0.9000 Silver, 0.0359 oz. ASW. **Notes:** On the 1858/inverted date variety, the date was engraved into the die upside down and then re-engraved right side up. Another 1858 variety has the date doubled.

Date	Mintage	G-4	VG-8	F-12	VF-20	XF-40	AU-50	MS-60	MS-65	Prf-65
1856	4,880,000	17.50	21.00	23.00	27.00	52.50	115	175	1,200	15,000
1856O	1,100,000	18.50	22.00	26.00	28.00	97.50	260	470	2,150	—
1857	7,280,000	17.50	21.00	23.00	27.00	52.50	115	175	1,050	5,600
1857O	1,380,000	18.50	22.00	24.00	28.00	62.50	185	320	1,750	—
1858	3,500,000	17.50	21.00	23.00	27.00	52.50	115	175	1,150	5,500
1858 inverted date	Inc. above	30.00	43.50	62.50	100.00	225	300	675	3,950	—
1858 double date	Inc. above	45.00	60.00	90.00	175	285	425	800	—	—
1858O	1,660,000	18.50	22.00	24.00	28.00	71.50	137	245	1,650	—
1859	340,000	19.50	23.00	25.00	29.00	54.50	117	225	1,350	4,000
1859O	560,000	20.50	24.00	26.00	42.00	128.5	200	285	1,850	—

Seated Liberty Half Dime.

Seated Liberty, date below. Value within wreath.

KM# 91 **Designer:** Christian Gobrecht. **Weight:** 1.2400 g. **Composition:** 0.9000 Silver, 0.0359 oz. ASW.

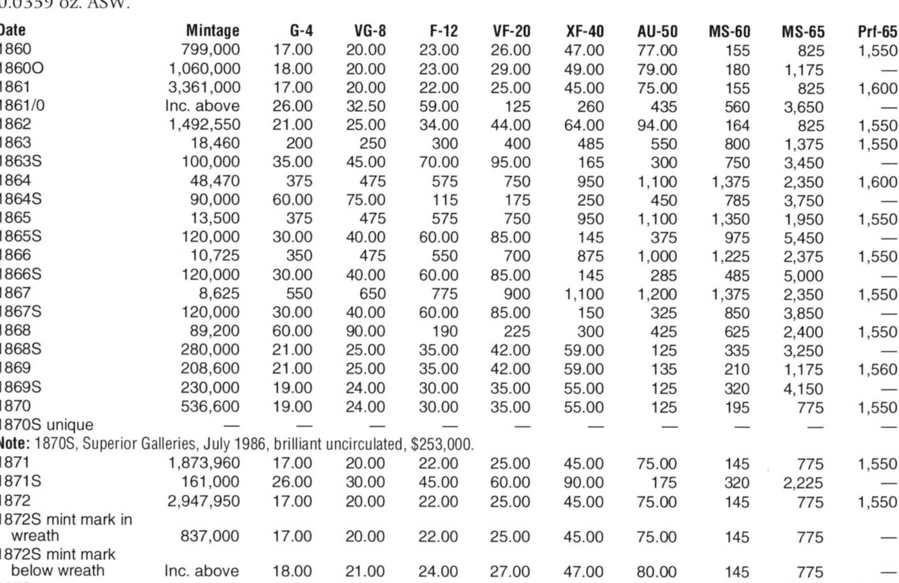

Date	Mintage	G-4	VG-8	F-12	VF-20	XF-40	AU-50	MS-60	MS-65	Prf-65
1860	799,000	17.00	20.00	23.00	26.00	47.00	77.00	155	825	1,550
1860O	1,060,000	18.00	20.00	23.00	29.00	49.00	79.00	180	1,175	—
1861	3,361,000	17.00	20.00	22.00	25.00	45.00	75.00	155	825	1,600
1861/0	Inc. above	26.00	32.50	59.00	125	260	435	560	3,650	—
1862	1,492,550	21.00	25.00	34.00	44.00	64.00	94.00	164	825	1,550
1863	18,460	200	250	300	400	485	550	800	1,375	1,550
1863S	100,000	35.00	45.00	70.00	95.00	165	300	750	3,450	—
1864	48,470	375	475	575	750	950	1,100	1,375	2,350	1,600
1864S	90,000	60.00	75.00	115	175	250	450	785	3,750	—
1865	13,500	375	475	575	750	950	1,100	1,350	1,950	1,550
1865S	120,000	30.00	40.00	60.00	85.00	145	375	975	5,450	—
1866	10,725	350	475	550	700	875	1,000	1,225	2,375	1,550
1866S	120,000	30.00	40.00	60.00	85.00	145	285	485	5,000	—
1867	8,625	550	650	775	900	1,100	1,200	1,375	2,350	1,550
1867S	120,000	30.00	40.00	60.00	85.00	150	325	850	3,850	—
1868	89,200	60.00	90.00	190	225	300	425	625	2,400	1,550
1868S	280,000	21.00	25.00	35.00	42.00	59.00	125	335	3,250	—
1869	208,600	21.00	25.00	35.00	42.00	59.00	135	210	1,175	1,560
1869S	230,000	19.00	24.00	30.00	35.00	55.00	125	320	4,150	—
1870	536,600	19.00	24.00	30.00	35.00	55.00	125	195	775	1,550
1870S unique	—	—	—	—	—	—	—	—	—	—
Note: 1870S, Superior Galleries, July 1986, brilliant uncirculated, $253,000.										
1871	1,873,960	17.00	20.00	22.00	25.00	45.00	75.00	145	775	1,550
1871S	161,000	26.00	30.00	45.00	60.00	90.00	175	320	2,225	—
1872	2,947,950	17.00	20.00	22.00	25.00	45.00	75.00	145	775	1,550
1872S mint mark in wreath	837,000	17.00	20.00	22.00	25.00	45.00	75.00	145	775	—
1872S mint mark below wreath	Inc. above	18.00	21.00	24.00	27.00	47.00	80.00	145	775	—
1873	712,600	17.00	20.00	22.00	25.00	45.00	75.00	145	1,175	1,550
1873S	324,000	21.00	25.00	30.00	42.00	62.00	90.00	160	775	—

HALF DIME

5 CENTS

Shield Nickel.

Draped garland above shield, date below. Value within center of rays between stars.

KM# 96 **Designer:** James B. Longacre.
Diameter: 20.5 **Weight:** 5.0000 g.
Composition: Copper-Nickel

Date	Mintage	G-4	VG-8	F-12	VF-20	XF-40	AU-50	MS-60	MS-65	Prf-65
1866	14,742,500	29.00	38.00	55.00	80.00	150	250	280	2,050	3,450
1867	2,019,000	37.00	45.50	63.50	90.00	180	280	330	3,850	75,000

Shield Nickel.

Draped garland above shield, date below. Value within circle of stars.

KM# 97 **Weight:** 5.0000 g.
Composition: Copper-Nickel

Date	Mintage	G-4	VG-8	F-12	VF-20	XF-40	AU-50	MS-60	MS-65	Prf-65
1867	28,890,500	18.50	28.00	30.00	37.50	64.00	115	150	825	2,500
1868 Rev'67	28,817,000	18.50	28.00	30.00	37.50	64.00	115	150	675	1,325
1868 Rev'68	Inc. above	22.00	34.00	36.00	45.00	77.00	144	188	—	—
Note: Star points to center of A in STATES.										
1869	16,395,000	18.50	28.00	30.00	37.50	64.00	115	150	700	900
1870	4,806,000	27.00	35.00	54.00	69.00	100.00	150	210	1,600	1,060
1871	561,000	72.00	95.00	140	210	310	365	415	2,100	910
1872	6,036,000	39.00	48.00	85.00	96.00	135	180	235	1,350	715
1873 Open 3	4,550,000	29.00	39.00	54.00	68.00	80.00	135	230	1,950	—
1873 Closed 3	Inc. above	36.00	48.00	70.00	100.00	150	220	350	3,250	715
1874	3,538,000	31.00	45.00	74.00	94.00	120	165	245	1,400	800
1875	2,097,000	46.00	62.00	90.00	125	170	230	290	1,500	1,500
1876	2,530,000	40.00	54.00	84.00	125	165	200	255	1,350	825
1877 proof	Est. 900	—	—	—	2,100	2,150	2,300	—	—	4,850
1878 proof	2,350	—	—	—	1,100	1,250	1,450	—	—	2,100
1879	29,100	390	485	625	660	720	800	970	1,900	750
1879/8	Inc. above	—	—	—	—	—	—	—	—	825
1880	19,995	500	575	700	850	1,275	1,700	3,250	47,500	730
1881	72,375	260	340	430	500	600	675	735	1,800	700
1882	11,476,600	18.50	28.00	30.00	37.50	64.00	115	150	635	645
Note: Many exist with excess metal at numeral 2 & 3 these should not be confused with the following overdate.										
1883	1,456,919	18.50	28.00	32.00	39.50	67.00	135	160	750	645
Note: Many exist with excess metal at numeral 2 & 3 these should not be confused with the following overdate.										
1883/2	Inc. above	220	300	535	850	1,250	1,750	2,000	3,750	—

Liberty Nickel.

Liberty head left, within circle of stars, date below. Roman numeral value within wreath, without CENTS below.

KM# 111 **Designer:** Charles E. Barber.
Diameter: 21.2 **Weight:** 5.0000 g.
Composition: Copper-Nickel

Date	Mintage	G-4	VG-8	F-12	VF-20	XF-40	AU-50	MS-60	MS-65	Prf-65
1883	5,479,519	7.00	7.75	8.50	8.75	9.25	12.00	25.50	215	1,075

Liberty Nickel.

Liberty head left, within circle of stars, date below. Roman numeral value within wreath, CENTS below.

KM# 112 **Diameter:** 21.2 **Weight:** 5.0000 g.
Composition: Copper-Nickel

Date	Mintage	G-4	VG-8	F-12	VF-20	XF-40	AU-50	MS-60	MS-65	Prf-65
1883	16,032,983	19.00	29.50	39.50	55.00	85.00	120	160	625	610

Date	Mintage	G-4	VG-8	F-12	VF-20	XF-40	AU-50	MS-60	MS-65	Prf-65
1884	11,273,942	22.50	33.50	39.50	59.00	92.00	135	190	1,675	610
1885	1,476,490	585	635	875	1,050	1,350	1,650	1,950	8,650	3,150
1886	3,330,290	285	335	400	500	685	850	1,950	7,250	1,950
1887	15,263,652	16.00	25.00	31.00	44.00	78.00	115	150	1,025	585
1888	10,720,483	28.00	44.00	68.00	130	185	250	295	1,500	585
1889	15,881,361	14.50	19.50	30.00	52.50	77.00	125	155	850	585
1890	16,259,272	10.50	20.50	26.00	39.50	68.50	115	165	1,365	585
1891	16,834,350	5.75	11.00	22.00	37.50	60.00	120	160	1,050	585
1892	11,699,642	6.50	11.00	22.50	[illegible]	65.00	120	165	1,300	585
1893	13,370,195	5.50	11.00	24.00	37.50	60.00	120	155	1,050	585
1894	5,413,132	16.50	31.00	98.00	165	230	295	350	1,500	585
1895	9,979,884	5.75	7.50	24.00	45.00	66.00	120	145	2,200	585
1896	8,842,920	9.00	21.00	41.50	68.50	98.00	150	205	1,950	585
1897	20,428,735	3.25	4.50	12.50	27.50	46.00	69.50	95.00	925	585
1898	12,532,087	2.15	4.25	11.00	23.50	40.00	68.50	130	1,025	585
1899	26,029,031	1.80	3.00	8.50	19.50	34.00	62.50	89.00	560	585
1900	27,255,995	1.60	2.50	8.50	19.00	34.00	69.50	84.00	650	585
1901	26,480,213	1.60	2.50	7.00	14.50	34.00	65.00	100.00	550	585
1902	31,480,579	1.60	2.50	4.00	15.00	32.00	65.00	102	550	585
1903	28,006,725	1.80	2.50	4.75	14.50	32.00	60.00	77.00	500	585
1904	21,404,984	1.60	2.40	4.75	11.50	30.00	65.00	96.00	500	585
1905	29,827,276	1.60	2.40	4.00	12.00	30.00	65.00	96.00	550	585
1906	38,613,725	1.80	2.40	4.00	11.50	30.00	65.00	96.00	650	585
1907	39,214,800	1.50	2.20	4.00	12.00	30.00	65.00	96.00	1,000	585
1908	22,686,177	1.80	2.20	4.00	12.00	30.00	68.00	104	1,100	585
1909	11,590,526	2.50	2.80	4.35	13.00	33.00	80.00	112	1,075	585
1910	30,169,353	1.50	1.85	4.00	10.00	30.00	52.00	62.00	550	585
1911	39,559,372	1.50	1.85	4.00	10.00	30.00	52.00	62.00	500	585
1912	26,236,714	1.50	1.85	4.00	10.00	30.00	52.00	62.00	570	585
1912D	8,474,000	2.75	3.60	11.50	38.00	70.00	170	280	2,200	—
1912S	238,000	165	190	220	480	810	1,300	1,475	5,900	—
1913 5 known	—	—	—	—	—	—	—	—	—	—

Note: 1913, Heritage Sale, January 2010, Proof-64 (Olsen), $3,737,500. Private treaty, 2007, (Eliasburg) Proof-66 $5 million.

Buffalo Nickel.

American Bison standing on a mound.

KM# 133 **Designer:** James Earle Fraser. **Diameter:** 21.2 **Weight:** 5.0000 g. **Composition:** Copper-Nickel

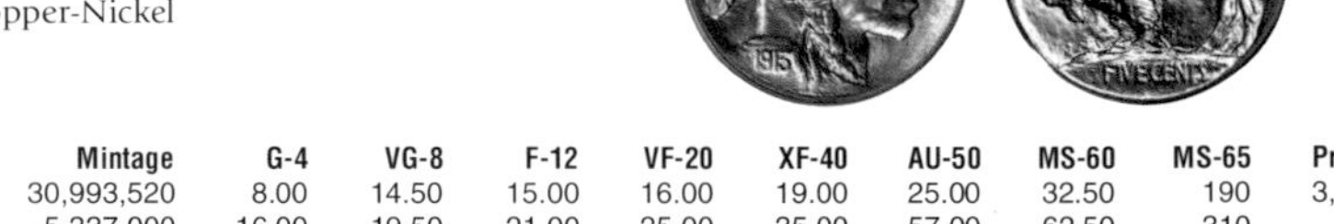

Date	Mintage	G-4	VG-8	F-12	VF-20	XF-40	AU-50	MS-60	MS-65	Prf-65
1913	30,993,520	8.00	14.50	15.00	16.00	19.00	25.00	32.50	190	3,150
1913D	5,337,000	16.00	19.50	21.00	25.00	35.00	57.00	62.50	310	—
1913S	2,105,000	43.00	47.00	50.00	60.00	75.00	100.00	125	690	—

Buffalo Nickel.

American Bison standing on a line.

KM# 134 **Designer:** James Earle Fraser. **Diameter:** 21.2 **Weight:** 5.0000 g. **Composition:** Copper-Nickel **Notes:** In 1913 the reverse design was modified so the ground under the buffalo was represented as a line rather than a mound. On the 1937D 3-legged variety, the buffalo's right front leg is missing, the result of a damaged die.

1918/17D

1937D 3-legged

Date	Mintage	G-4	VG-8	F-12	VF-20	XF-40	AU-50	MS-60	MS-65	Prf-65
1913	29,858,700	8.00	12.00	13.00	14.00	19.00	25.00	34.00	355	2,500
1913D	4,156,000	125	155	180	190	265	240	285	1,450	—
1913S	1,209,000	350	400	420	430	575	675	885	3,850	—
1914	20,665,738	18.00	21.00	22.00	23.00	27.50	37.50	47.00	420	2,250
1914/3	Inc. above	150	300	425	525	700	1,050	2,850	30,000	—
1914D	3,912,000	90.00	132	165	200	335	390	475	1,600	—
1914/3D	Inc. above	115	225	335	450	625	900	3,500	—	—
1914S	3,470,000	26.00	37.50	45.00	62.50	90.00	145	165	22,350	—
1914/3S	Inc. above	250	500	750	1,000	1,450	2,260	4,300	—	—

5 CENTS

Date	Mintage	G-4	VG-8	F-12	VF-20	XF-40	AU-50	MS-60	MS-65	Prf-65
1915	20,987,270	6.25	7.00	7.75	11.00	21.50	38.50	50.00	325	2,100
1915D	7,569,500	21.50	31.00	41.50	66.00	115	150	235	2,250	—
1915S	1,505,000	47.00	74.00	105	185	326	490	625	3,150	—
1916	63,498,066	5.50	6.40	7.00	8.00	13.50	24.00	43.50	315	3,250
1916 2 Feathers	Inc. above	35.00	—	45.00	—	—	—	—	150	—
1916/16	Inc. above	1,800	3,650	7,150	10,850	16,500	34,500	49,500	375,000	—
1916D	13,333,000	15.00	26.50	29.00	38.50	82.50	110	165	2,250	—
1916S	11,860,000	11.00	13.50	26.00	35.00	75.00	125	185	2,300	—
1917	51,424,029	7.50	8.00	8.75	10.00	16.00	32.50	59.00	535	—
1917 2 Feathers	Inc. above	40.00	—	50.00	—	—	—	—	165	—
1917D	9,910,800	26.00	31.00	55.00	80.00	135	255	345	3,250	—
1917S	4,193,000	23.00	42.00	80.00	110	180	285	395	4,850	—
1917S 2 Feathers	Inc. above	50.00	—	95.00	—	—	—	—	315	—
1918	32,086,314	5.25	6.75	8.00	15.00	31.00	48.50	105	1,550	—
1918/17D	8,362,314	1,000	1,475	2,600	4,950	7,950	10,750	36,500	350,000	—
1918D	Inc. above	22.50	39.00	66.00	135	226	330	430	4,650	—
1918 2 Feathers	Inc. above	50.00	—	95.00	—	—	—	—	315	—
1918S	4,882,000	14.00	27.50	55.00	100.00	175	300	495	25,500	—
1919	60,868,000	2.60	3.50	3.90	7.00	16.00	32.00	58.00	535	—
1919D	8,006,000	15.50	31.00	66.00	115	235	335	570	6,850	—
1919S	7,521,000	8.00	26.00	50.00	110	225	360	540	24,000	—
1920	63,093,000	1.50	2.75	3.25	8.00	16.00	30.00	59.00	700	—
1920D	9,418,000	8.50	19.00	35.00	125	275	340	575	6,850	—
1920S	9,689,000	4.50	12.75	30.00	100.00	260	300	525	25,500	—
1921	10,663,000	4.00	6.25	8.50	25.00	53.50	73.00	125	800	—
1921S	1,557,000	64.00	100.00	180	400	825	1,150	1,575	7,350	—
1923	35,715,000	1.70	3.25	4.25	7.00	14.00	37.50	59.00	575	—
1923S	6,142,000	8.00	11.00	27.00	125	275	335	625	11,500	—
1924	21,620,000	1.25	2.40	4.50	10.00	19.00	41.00	73.50	850	—
1924D	5,258,000	8.00	12.00	30.00	90.00	215	315	375	4,950	—
1924S	1,437,000	16.50	32.00	96.00	455	1,100	1,700	2,300	12,850	—
1925	35,565,100	2.50	3.00	3.75	8.50	16.50	32.00	42.00	490	—
1925D	4,450,000	10.00	26.00	38.00	80.00	160	240	375	5,650	—
1925S	6,256,000	4.50	9.00	17.50	77.50	170	250	425	28,500	—
1926	44,693,000	1.50	2.00	2.80	5.40	11.50	26.00	31.50	235	—
1926D	5,638,000	10.00	17.50	28.50	100.00	170	295	335	5,850	—
1926S	970,000	20.00	42.00	100.00	345	850	2,450	4,950	125,000	—
1927	37,981,000	1.40	1.75	2.50	4.50	12.50	26.00	35.00	290	—
1927D	5,730,000	3.00	6.00	7.00	27.50	75.00	115	155	7,950	—
1927S	3,430,000	2.00	3.00	6.00	31.00	80.00	160	490	18,500	—
1928	23,411,000	1.40	1.75	2.50	4.50	12.50	25.00	32.50	310	—
1928D	6,436,000	1.90	2.50	3.75	16.00	40.00	46.50	53.00	685	—
1928S	6,936,000	1.75	2.35	3.00	12.00	27.50	105	225	4,750	—
1929	36,446,000	1.40	1.75	2.50	4.50	13.00	21.00	35.00	325	—
1929D	8,370,000	1.50	1.85	3.00	6.75	32.50	42.50	60.00	1,850	—
1929S	7,754,000	1.50	1.85	2.25	4.00	12.50	25.00	49.50	485	—
1930	22,849,000	1.40	1.75	2.50	4.50	12.00	21.00	32.50	235	—
1930S	5,435,000	1.50	2.00	3.00	4.50	16.00	37.50	65.00	480	—
1931S	1,200,000	15.00	16.00	17.00	19.00	31.00	46.00	59.00	300	—
1934	20,213,003	1.40	1.75	2.50	4.50	11.00	19.00	47.50	355	—
1934D	7,480,000	2.00	3.00	4.75	9.60	22.00	50.00	79.50	800	—
1935	58,264,000	1.25	1.60	2.25	3.00	4.00	11.00	20.00	145	—
1935 Double Die Rev.	Inc. above	50.00	75.00	125	250	675	1,800	4,000	75,000	—
1935D	12,092,000	1.60	2.50	3.00	9.00	26.00	48.00	72.00	415	—
1935S	10,300,000	1.35	1.75	2.50	3.50	4.50	17.50	48.50	250	—
1936	119,001,420	1.25	1.60	2.25	3.00	4.00	6.75	14.50	105	1,650
1936 Brilliant	Inc. above	—	—	—	—	—	—	—	—	2,450
1936D	24,814,000	1.35	1.75	2.75	4.00	5.35	11.50	33.50	118	—
1936D 3-1/2 leg	Inc. above	750	1,250	2,000	3,500	6,000	10,500	17,500	—	—
1936D/S	Inc. above	1.35	—	10.00	16.00	25.00	—	—	—	—
1936S	14,930,000	1.35	1.75	2.50	3.50	4.50	11.00	33.50	115	—
1937	79,485,769	1.25	1.60	2.25	3.00	4.00	6.75	14.50	69.00	2,100
1937D	17,826,000	1.35	1.75	2.50	3.50	4.50	9.00	29.00	73.00	—
1937D 3-legged	Inc. above	535	660	725	775	965	1,225	2,375	37,000	—
1937S	5,635,000	1.35	1.75	2.50	3.50	4.50	10.00	27.50	72.00	—
1938D	7,020,000	3.50	3.75	3.90	4.00	4.50	8.00	26.00	66.00	—
1938D/D	Inc. above	4.00	4.50	6.00	8.00	10.00	17.00	32.00	125	—
1938D/S	Inc. above	4.50	6.75	9.00	12.50	19.00	32.50	50.00	185	—

Jefferson Nickel.

Monticello, mintmark to right side.

KM# 192 **Designer:** Felix Schlag. **Diameter:** 21.2 **Weight:** 5.0000 g. **Composition:** Copper-Nickel **Notes:** Some 1939 strikes have doubling of the word MONTICELLO on the reverse.

Date	Mintage	VG-8	F-12	VF-20	XF-40	MS-60	MS-65	-65FS	Prf-65
1938	19,515,365	.50	.75	1.00	2.25	7.50	18.00	125	—
1938D	5,376,000	1.00	1.25	1.50	2.00	4.00	15.00	95.00	—
1938S	4,105,000	1.75	2.00	2.50	3.00	5.25	12.00	165	—
1939 T I, wavy steps, Rev. of 1939	120,627,535	—	—	—	—	—	—	300	—
1939 T II, even steps, Rev. of 1940	Inc. above	—	.20	.25	.30	1.75	3.50	50.00	—
1939 doubled MONTICELLO T II	Inc. above	40.00	60.00	90.00	165	300	1,250	2,000	—
1939D T IT I, wavy steps, Rev. of 1939	3,514,000	—	—	10.00	17.50	75.00	160	275	—
1939D T IIT II, even steps, Rev. of 1940	Inc. above	4.00	5.00	8.00	14.00	55.00	105	400	—
1939S T IT I, wavy steps, Rev. of 1939	6,630,000	.45	.60	1.50	4.00	17.00	45.00	250	—
1939S T IIT II, even steps, Rev. of 1940	Inc. above	—	—	—	5.00	24.00	250	275	—
1940	176,499,158	—	—	—	.25	1.00	12.00	60.00	125
1940D	43,540,000	—	.20	.30	.40	1.50	2.75	25.00	—
1940S	39,690,000	.25	.40	.50	1.25	4.50	20.00	55.00	—
1941	203,283,720	—	—	—	.20	.75	20.00	55.00	—
1941D	53,432,000	—	.20	.30	.50	2.25	7.50	25.00	—
1941S	43,445,000	.25	.40	.50	1.35	5.00	14.00	60.00	—
1942	49,818,600	—	—	—	.40	5.00	22.00	75.00	—
1942D	13,938,000	1.00	1.75	3.00	5.00	38.00	65.00	85.00	—
1942D D over horizontal D	Inc. above	35.00	60.00	100.00	165	750	10,000	25,000	—

Note: Fully Struck Full Step nickels command higher prices. Bright, Fully Struck coins command even higher prices. 1938 thru 1989 - 5 Full Steps. 1990 to date - 6 Full Steps. Without bag marks or nicks on steps.

Jefferson Nickel.

Monticello, mint mark above.

KM# 192a **Designer:** Felix Schlag. **Diameter:** 21.2 **Composition:** 0.3500 Copper-Silver-Manganese **Notes:** War-time composition nickels have the mint mark above MONTICELLO on the reverse.

1943/2P

Date	Mintage	VG-8	F-12	VF-20	XF-40	MS-60	MS-65	-65FS	Prf-65
1942P	57,900,600	2.00	2.10	2.30	2.70	9.00	20.00	75.00	150
1942S	32,900,000	2.00	2.10	2.30	2.50	11.00	30.00	170	—
1943P	271,165,000	2.00	2.10	2.30	2.70	5.00	20.00	40.00	—
1943P	—	—	—	32.00	54.00	135	650	1,100	—
1943/2P	Inc. above	35.00	50.00	75.00	110	250	650	1,000	—
1943D	15,294,000	2.20	2.30	2.50	2.90	4.00	20.00	40.00	—
1943S	104,060,000	2.00	2.10	2.30	2.70	6.75	18.50	48.00	—
1944P	119,150,000	2.00	2.10	2.30	2.70	14.00	28.00	75.00	—
1944D	32,309,000	2.00	2.10	2.30	2.80	12.00	22.50	65.00	—
1944S	21,640,000	2.00	2.10	2.30	2.80	9.50	20.00	185	—
1945P	119,408,100	2.00	2.10	2.30	2.70	6.00	26.00	120	—
1945D	37,158,000	2.10	2.20	2.40	2.90	5.50	20.00	40.00	—
1945S	58,939,000	2.00	2.10	2.30	2.70	5.00	20.00	250	—

Note: Fully Struck Full Step nickels command higher prices. Bright, Fully Struck coins command even higher prices. 1938 thru 1989 - 5 Full Steps. 1990 to date - 6 Full Steps. Without bag marks or nicks on steps.

Jefferson Nickel.

Pre-war design resumed.

KM# A192 **Designer:** Felix Schlag. **Diameter:** 21.2 **Weight:** 5.0000 g. **Composition:** Copper-Nickel

Date	Mintage	XF-40	MS-65	Prf-65
1946	161,116,000	.25	20.00	—
1946D	45,292,200	.35	16.00	—
1946S	13,560,000	.40	17.00	—
1947	95,000,000	.25	18.00	—
1947D	37,822,000	.30	15.00	—
1947S	24,720,000	.25	15.00	—
1948	89,348,000	.25	16.00	—
1948D	44,734,000	.35	14.00	—
1948S	11,300,000	.50	14.00	—
1949	60,652,000	.30	18.00	—
1949D	36,498,000	.40	12.00	—
1949D/S	Inc. above	65.00	400	—
1949S	9,716,000	.90	10.00	—
1950	9,847,386	.75	12.00	75.00
1950D	2,630,030	10.00	20.00	—
1951	28,609,500	.50	18.00	70.00
1951D	20,460,000	.50	14.00	—
1951S	7,776,000	1.10	18.50	—
1952	64,069,980	.25	17.00	42.00
1952D	30,638,000	.45	18.00	—
1952S	20,572,000	.25	18.00	—
1953	46,772,800	.25	9.00	45.00
1953D	59,878,600	.25	16.00	—
1953S	19,210,900	.25	20.00	—
1954	47,917,350	—	9.00	20.00
1954D	117,136,560	—	10.00	—
1954S	29,384,000	.20	16.00	—
1954S/D	Inc. above	20.00	250	—
1955	8,266,200	.45	6.50	13.50
1955D	74,464,100	—	16.00	—
1955D/S	Inc. above	25.00	225	—
1956	35,885,384	—	16.00	3.00
1956D	67,222,940	—	16.00	—
1957	39,655,952	—	12.00	2.50
1957D	136,828,900	—	12.00	—
1958	17,963,652	.20	28.00	8.00
1958D	168,249,120	—	13.00	—

Note: Fully Struck Full Step nickels command higher prices. Bright, Fully Struck coins command even higher prices. 1938 thru 1989 - 5 Full Steps. 1990 to date - 6 Full Steps. Without bag marks or nicks on steps.

Date	Mintage	XF-40	MS-65	Prf-65
1959	28,397,291	—	8.00	1.40
1959D	160,738,240	—	5.50	—
1960	57,107,602	—	6.00	1.25
1960D	192,582,180	—	20.00	—
1961	76,668,244	—	6.00	1.00
1961D	229,342,760	—	20.00	—
1962	100,602,019	—	5.00	1.00
1962D	280,195,720	—	75.00	—
1963	178,851,645	—	.55	1.00
1963D	276,829,460	—	.55	—
1964	1,028,622,762	—	.55	1.00
1964D	1,787,297,160	—	.50	—
1965	136,131,380	—	.50	—
1965SMS	2,360,000	—	—	—
1966	156,208,283	—	.50	—
1967	107,325,800	—	.50	—
1968 none minted	—	—	—	—
1968D	91,227,880	—	4.50	—
1968S	103,437,510	—	.50	0.75
1969 none minted	—	—	—	—
1969D	202,807,500	—	.50	—
1969S	123,099,631	—	.50	4.00

Date	Mintage	XF-40	MS-65	Prf-65
1970 none minted	—	—	—	—
1970D	515,485,380	—	.50	—
1970S	241,464,814	—	8.00	3.00
1971	106,884,000	—	2.00	—
1971D	316,144,800	—	.50	—
1971S	3,220,733	—	—	2.00
1972	202,036,000	—	.50	—
1972D	351,694,600	—	.50	—
1972S	3,260,996	—	—	2.00
1973	384,396,000		.50	
1973D	261,405,000	—	.50	—
1973S	2,760,339	—	—	1.75
1974	601,752,000	—	.50	—
1974D	277,373,000	—	.50	—
1974S	2,612,568	—	—	2.00
1975	181,772,000	—	.75	—
1975D	401,875,300	—	.50	—
1975S	2,845,450	—	—	2.25
1976	367,124,000	—	.75	—
1976D	563,964,147	—	.60	—
1976S	4,149,730	—	—	3.00
1977	585,376,000	—	.40	—
1977D	297,313,460	—	.55	—
1977S	3,251,152	—	—	1.75
1978	391,308,000	—	.40	—
1978D	313,092,780	—	.40	—
1978S	3,127,781	—	—	1.75
1979	463,188,000	—	.40	—
1979D	325,867,672	—	.40	—
1979S type I, proof	3,677,175	—	—	1.50
1979S type II, proof	Inc. above	—	—	1.75
1980P	593,004,000	—	6.00	—
1980D	502,323,448	—	.40	—
1980S	3,554,806	—	—	1.50
1981P	657,504,000	—	.40	—
1981D	364,801,843	—	.40	—
1981S type I, proof	4,063,083	—	—	2.00
1981S type II, proof	Inc. above	—	—	2.50
1982P	292,355,000	—	12.50	—
1982D	373,726,544	—	3.50	—
1982S	3,857,479	—	—	3.50
1983P	561,615,000	—	4.00	—
1983D	536,726,276	—	2.50	—
1983S	3,279,126	—	—	4.00
1984P	746,769,000	—	3.00	—
1984D	517,675,146	—	.85	—
1984S	3,065,110	—	—	5.00
1985P	647,114,962	—	.75	—
1985D	459,747,446	—	.75	—
1985S	3,362,821	—	—	4.00
1986P	536,883,483	—	1.00	—
1986D	361,819,140	—	2.00	—
1986S	3,010,497	—	—	7.00
1987P	371,499,481	—	.75	—
1987D	410,590,604	—	.75	—
1987S	4,227,728	—	—	3.50
1988P	771,360,000	—	.75	—
1988D	663,771,652	—	.75	—
1988S	3,262,948	—	—	6.50
1989P	898,812,000	—	.75	—
1989D	570,842,474	—	.75	—
1989S	3,220,194	—	—	5.50
1990P	661,636,000	—	.75	—
1990D	663,938,503	—	.75	—
1990S	3,299,559	—	—	5.50
1991P	614,104,000	—	.75	—
1991D	436,496,678	—	.75	—
1991S	2,867,787	—	—	5.00
1992P	399,552,000	—	2.00	—
1992D	450,565,113	—	.75	—
1992S	4,176,560	—	—	4.00
1993P	412,076,000	—	.75	—
1993D	406,084,135	—	.75	—
1993S	3,394,792	—	—	4.50
1994P	722,160,000	—	.75	—
1994P Special Uncirculed matte finish	167,703	—	—	58.00

Date	Mintage	XF-40	MS-65	Prf-65
1994D	715,762,110	—	.75	—
1994S	3,269,923	—	—	4.00
1995P	774,156,000	—	.75	—
1995D	888,112,000	—	.85	—
1995S	2,707,481	—	—	4.00
1996P	829,332,000	—	.75	—
1996D	817,736,000	—	.75	—
1996S	2,915,212	—	—	4.00
1997P	470,972,000	—	.75	—
1997P Special Uncirculated matte finish	25,000	—	—	160
1997D	466,640,000	—	2.00	—
1997S	1,975,000	—	—	5.00
1998P	688,272,000	—	.80	—
1998D	635,360,000	—	.80	—
1998S	2,957,286	—	—	4.50
1999P	1,212,000,000	—	.80	—
1999D	1,066,720,000	—	.80	—
1999S	3,362,462	—	—	3.50
2000P	846,240,000	—	.80	—
2000D	1,509,520,000	—	.80	—
2000S	4,063,361	—	—	2.00
2001P	675,704,000	—	.50	—
2001D	627,680,000	—	.50	—
2001S	3,099,096	—	—	4.00
2002P	539,280,000	—	.50	—
2002D	691,200,000	—	.50	—
2002S	3,157,739	—	—	2.00
2003P	441,840,000	—	.50	—
2003D	383,040,000	—	.50	—
2003S	3,116,590	—	—	2.00

Jefferson - Westward Expansion - Lewis & Clark Bicentennial.

Jefferson era peace medal design: two clasped hands, pipe and hatchet.

KM# 360 **Obv. Designer:** Felix Schlag. **Rev. Designer:** Norman E. Nemeth. **Diameter:** 21.2 **Weight:** 5.0000 g. **Composition:** Copper-Nickel

Date	Mintage	MS-65	Prf-65
2004P	361,440,000	1.50	—
2004D	372,000,000	1.50	—
2004S	—	—	10.00

Lewis and Clark's Keelboat.

KM# 361 **Obv. Designer:** Felix Schlag. **Rev. Designer:** Al Maletsky. **Diameter:** 21.2 **Weight:** 5.0000 g. **Composition:** Copper-Nickel

Date	Mintage	MS-65	Prf-65
2004P	366,720,000	1.50	—
2004D	344,880,000	1.50	—
2004S	—	—	10.00

Thomas Jefferson large profile right. American Bison right.

KM# 368 **Obv. Designer:** Joe Fitzgerald and Don Everhart II. **Rev. Designer:** Jamie Franki and Norman E. Nemeth. **Diameter:** 21.2 **Weight:** 5.0000 g. **Composition:** Copper-Nickel

Date	Mintage	MS-65	Prf-65
2005P	448,320,000	1.50	—
2005D	487,680,000	1.50	—
2005S	—	—	6.50

Jefferson, large profile. Pacific coastline.

KM# 369 **Obv. Designer:** Joe Fitzgerald and Don Everhart. **Rev. Designer:** Joe Fitzgerald and Donna Weaver. **Diameter:** 21.2 **Weight:** 5.0000 g. **Composition:** Copper-Nickel

Date	Mintage	MS-65	Prf-65
2005P	394,080,000	1.25	—
2005D	411,120,000	1.25	—
2005S	—	—	5.50

Jefferson large facing portrait - Enhanced Monticello Reverse.

Jefferson head facing. Monticello, enhanced design.

KM# 381 **Obv. Designer:** Jamie N. Franki and Donna Weaver. **Rev. Designer:** Felix Schlag and John Mercanti. **Diameter:** 21.2 **Weight:** 5.0000 g. **Composition:** Copper-Nickel

Date	Mintage	MS-65	Prf-65
2006P	693,120,000	2.50	—
2006P Satin finish	—	4.00	—
2006D	809,280,000	2.50	—
2006D Satin finish	—	4.00	—
2006S	—	—	5.00
2007P	—	2.50	—
2007P Satin finish	—	4.00	—
2007D	—	2.50	—
2007D Satin finish	—	4.00	—
2007S	—	—	4.00
2008P	—	2.50	—
2008P Satin finish	—	4.00	—
2008D	—	2.50	—

Date	Mintage	MS-65	Prf-65
2008D Satin finish	—	4.00	—
2008S	—	—	4.00
2009P	—	2.50	—
2009P Satin finish	—	4.00	—
2009D	—	2.50	—
2009D Satin finish	—	4.00	—
2009S	—	—	3.00
2010P	—	2.50	—
2010P Satin finish	—	4.00	—
2010D		2.50	
2010D Satin finish	—	4.00	—
2010S	—	—	3.00
2011P	—	2.50	—
2011D	—	2.50	—
2011S	—	—	3.00
2012P	—	2.50	—
2012D	—	2.50	—
2012S	—	—	3.00
2013P	—	2.50	—
2013D	—	2.50	—
2013S	—	—	3.00

DIME

Draped Bust Dime.

Draped bust right. Small eagle.

KM# 24 Designer: Robert Scot. **Diameter:** 19 **Weight:** 2.7000 g. **Composition:** 0.8920 Silver, 0.0774 oz. ASW.

Date	Mintage	G-4	VG-8	F-12	VF-20	XF-40	MS-60
1796	22,135	2,850	3,600	5,500	7,000	12,350	24,500
1797 13 stars	25,261	3,100	3,950	6,050	8,000	13,150	70,000
1797 16 stars	Inc. above	3,000	3,850	5,800	7,150	13,650	36,500

Draped Bust Dime.

Draped bust right. Heraldic eagle.

KM# 31 Designer: Robert Scot. **Diameter:** 19 **Weight:** 2.7000 g. **Composition:** 0.8920 Silver, 0.0774 oz. ASW. **Notes:** The 1805 strikes have either 4 or 5 berries on the olive branch held by the eagle.

Date	Mintage	G-4	VG-8	F-12	VF-20	XF-40	MS-60
1798 large 8	27,550	725	1,250	1,550	2,100	3,625	8,850
1798 small 8	Inc. above	975	1,450	2,350	3,250	6,000	53,500
1798/97 13 stars	Inc. above	2,150	3,850	5,650	8,850	13,850	59,000
1798/97 16 stars	Inc. above	775	1,125	1,800	2,650	4,600	10,500
Note: The 1798 overdates have either 13 or 16 stars under the clouds on the reverse; Varieties of the regular 1798 strikes are distinguished by the size of the 8 in the date							
1800	21,760	700	1,075	1,400	2,700	4,350	37,500
1801	34,640	750	1,150	1,650	3,100	6,250	49,500
1802	10,975	1,750	2,650	3,500	4,750	10,000	37,500
1803	33,040	675	1,150	1,900	2,750	5,900	49,500
1804 13 stars	8,265	2,650	4,450	10,500	19,000	41,500	—
1804 14 stars	Inc. above	4,850	6,500	12,500	24,500	46,500	—
1805 5 berries	Inc. above	625	1,000	1,400	2,100	3,700	9,100
1805 4 berries	120,780	615	920	1,225	1,650	2,950	7,350
1807	165,000	575	900	1,200	1,650	2,950	6,850

Liberty Cap Dime.

Draped bust left, flanked by stars, date below. Eagle with arrows in talons, banner above, value below.

KM# 42 Designer: John Reich. **Diameter:** 18.8 **Weight:** 2.7000 g. **Composition:** 0.8920 Silver, 0.0774 oz. ASW. **Notes:** The 1820 varieties are distinguished by the size of the 0 in the date. The 1823 overdates have either large E's or small E's in UNITED STATES OF AMERICA on the reverse.

Date	Mintage	G-4	VG-8	F-12	VF-20	XF-40	AU-50	MS-60	MS-65
1809	51,065	140	220	450	700	1,500	2,850	4,500	24,500
1811/9	65,180	110	175	275	650	1,350	2,000	4,000	33,500
1814 small date	421,500	60.00	80.00	145	300	650	1,250	2,000	19,500
1814 large date	Inc. above	43.00	52.00	75.00	135	435	670	1,175	15,000
1814 STATESOF	Inc. above	70.00	88.00	160	335	750	1,400	2,350	24,500
1820 large O	942,587	42.00	50.00	71.00	122	430	665	1,160	12,750
1820 small O	Inc. above	43.00	52.00	75.00	137	450	750	1,425	15,250

Date	Mintage	G-4	VG-8	F-12	VF-20	XF-40	AU-50	MS-60	MS-65
1820 STATESOF	Inc. above	43.00	52.00	75.00	135	435	670	1,175	14,500
1821 large date	1,186,512	42.00	50.00	71.00	122	430	665	1,160	12,750
1821 small date	Inc. above	43.00	52.00	75.00	137	450	750	1,425	17,000
1822	100,000	1,000	1,850	3,250	4,500	6,250	7,850	13,500	70,000
1823/22 large E's	440,000	42.00	50.00	71.00	130	450	685	1,210	14,850
1823/22 small E's	Inc. above	42.00	50.00	71.00	130	450	685	1,210	13,600
1824/22	—	50.00	80.00	145	300	650	1,250	2,000	19,500
1825	510,000	39.00	46.00	65.00	112	410	625	1,100	12,850
1827	1,215,000	39.00	46.00	65.00	112	410	625	1,100	12,500
1827/7	Inc. above	250	—	—	750	1,100	1,500	—	—
1828 large date	125,000	70.00	110	175	375	750	1,250	2,850	6,850

Liberty Cap Dime.

Draped bust left, flanked by stars, date below. Eagle with arrows in talons, banner above, value below.

KM# 48 **Designer:** John Reich. **Diameter:** 18.5 **Composition:** Silver ASW. **Notes:** The three varieties of 1829 strikes and two varieties of 1830 strikes are distinguished by the size of "10C." on the reverse. On the 1833 "high 3" variety, the last 3 in the date is higher thatn the first 3. The two varieties of the 1834 strikes are distinguished by the size of the 4 in the date.

Date	Mintage	G-4	VG-8	F-12	VF-20	XF-40	AU-50	MS-60	MS-65
1828 small date	Inc. above	40.00	48.00	80.00	155	425	625	1,250	12,500
1829 very large 10C.	770,000	60.00	75.00	120	235	550	800	1,500	—
1829 large 10C.	Inc. above	54.00	65.00	110	200	400	600	1,150	9,250
1829 medium 10C.	Inc. above	36.00	42.00	54.00	85.00	255	375	775	6,850
1829 small 10C.	Inc. above	36.00	42.00	56.00	90.00	270	395	795	7,050
1829 curl base 2	Inc. above	7,750	10,500	16,500	27,500	38,500	44,000	—	—
1830 large 10C.	510,000	36.00	42.00	56.00	85.00	255	375	775	6,850
1830 small 10C.	Inc. above	36.00	42.00	54.00	90.00	270	400	825	8,850
1830/29	Inc. above	52.00	75.00	120	220	430	750	1,500	—
1831	771,350	36.00	42.00	54.00	85.00	255	375	775	6,850
1832	522,500	36.00	42.00	54.00	85.00	255	375	775	6,850
1833	485,000	36.00	42.00	54.00	85.00	260	390	790	6,850
1833 last 3 high	Inc. above	36.00	42.00	54.00	85.00	260	390	820	9,350
1834 small 4	635,000	36.00	42.00	54.00	85.00	255	375	775	7,000
1834 large 4	Inc. above	36.00	42.00	54.00	85.00	255	375	775	6,850
1835	1,410,000	36.00	42.00	54.00	85.00	255	375	775	6,850
1836	1,190,000	36.00	42.00	54.00	85.00	255	375	775	6,850
1837	1,042,000	36.00	42.00	56.00	90.00	270	395	795	7,000

Seated Liberty Dime.

Seated Liberty, date below. Value within wreath.

KM# 61 **Designer:** Christian Gobrecht. **Diameter:** 17.9 **Weight:** 2.6700 g. **Composition:** 0.9000 Silver, 0.0773 oz. ASW.

Date	Mintage	G-4	VG-8	F-12	VF-20	XF-40	AU-50	MS-60	MS-65
1837 flat top	Inc. above	44.00	58.00	110	285	515	700	1,050	6,500
1837 curly top	Inc. above	40.00	52.00	95.00	250	465	750	1,000	6,500
1838O	406,034	47.50	70.00	125	375	725	1,250	3,500	21,000

Seated Liberty Dime.

Seated Liberty, stars around top 1/2 of border, date below. Value within wreath.

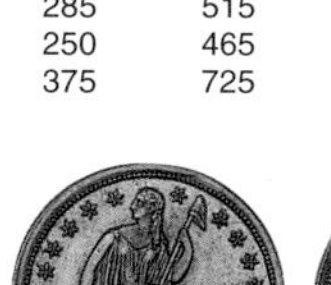

KM# 63.1 **Obv. Designer:** Christian Gobrecht. **Diameter:** 17.9 **Weight:** 2.6700 g. **Composition:** 0.9000 Silver, 0.0773 oz. ASW. **Notes:** The 1839-O with reverse of 1838-O variety was struck from rusted dies, it has a bumpy reverse surface.

No drapery at elbow

Date	Mintage	G-4	VG-8	F-12	VF-20	XF-40	AU-50	MS-60	MS-65
1838 small stars	1,992,500	27.00	38.00	55.00	85.00	175	400	625	—

Date	Mintage	G-4	VG-8	F-12	VF-20	XF-40	AU-50	MS-60	MS-65
1838 large stars	Inc. above	22.00	25.50	34.50	45.00	135	260	375	8,500
1838 partial drapery	Inc. above	35.00	50.00	85.00	150	225	350	550	—
1839	1,053,115	19.00	23.50	28.50	40.00	125	245	315	3,000
1839O	1,323,000	23.50	30.00	47.00	140	150	280	650	6,000
1839O reverse 1838O	Inc. above	165	225	375	550	1,150	—	—	—
1840	1,358,580	19.00	24.50	28.50	40.00	125	245	315	4,000
1840O	1,175,000	23.00	28.50	36.50	60.00	165	325	2,750	6,500

Seated Liberty Dime.

Seated Liberty, stars around top 1/2 of border, date below. Value within wreath.

KM# 63.2 **Designer:** Christian Gobrecht. **Diameter:** 17.9 **Weight:** 2.6700 g. **Composition:** 0.9000 Silver, 0.0773 oz. ASW. **Notes:** Drapery added to Liberty's left elbow

Drapery at elbow

Date	Mintage	G-4	VG-8	F-12	VF-20	XF-40	AU-50	MS-60	MS-65
1840	Inc. above	32.00	50.00	90.00	175	300	400	2,400	—
1841	1,622,500	17.50	20.00	22.50	29.00	50.00	150	310	2,700
1841O	2,007,500	23.50	28.50	33.00	41.50	90.00	250	1,500	5,000
1841O large O	Inc. above	600	900	1,200	2,500	—	—	—	—
1842	1,887,500	16.50	18.00	22.00	28.50	47.00	150	280	2,700
1842O	2,020,000	25.00	30.00	37.50	75.00	225	1,350	2,900	—
1843	1,370,000	16.50	18.00	22.00	28.50	47.00	150	280	3,000
1843/1843	Inc. above	16.00	18.50	22.50	30.00	75.00	200	295	—
1843O	150,000	50.00	75.00	135	300	1,100	3,450	—	—
1844	72,500	200	300	375	600	1,350	1,850	3,000	—
1845	1,755,000	17.50	18.00	22.00	28.50	47.00	150	280	2,600
1845/1845	Inc. above	17.00	20.00	35.00	55.00	100.00	175	—	—
1845O	230,000	32.00	48.00	90.00	225	650	1,350	—	—
1846	31,300	150	250	365	575	1,600	9,000	5,500	—
1847	245,000	19.50	30.00	40.00	70.00	125	350	950	9,000
1848	451,500	19.50	25.00	28.50	52.50	95.00	175	750	7,000
1849	839,000	19.50	21.50	25.00	37.50	55.00	150	500	4,000
1849O	300,000	26.00	33.00	50.00	125	275	750	2,200	—
1850	1,931,500	19.50	21.50	24.50	34.50	50.00	150	280	5,900
1850O	510,000	25.00	32.00	40.00	75.00	135	300	1,250	—
1851	1,026,500	19.50	21.50	24.50	32.50	50.00	150	335	5,000
1851O	400,000	25.00	34.00	42.50	85.00	175	475	1,850	—
1852	1,535,500	16.50	18.00	20.00	26.50	45.00	150	280	2,550
1852O	430,000	28.50	34.00	53.50	145	250	400	1,800	—
1853	95,000	95.00	145	220	300	425	575	750	—

Seated Liberty Dime.

Seated Liberty, stars around top 1/2 of border, arrows at date. Value within wreath.

KM# 77 **Designer:** Christian Gobrecht. **Weight:** 2.4900 g. **Composition:** 0.9000 Silver, 0.0720 oz. ASW.

Date	Mintage	G-4	VG-8	F-12	VF-20	XF-40	AU-50	MS-60	MS-65	Prf-65
1853	12,078,010	16.00	18.00	19.00	25.00	44.00	145	260	2,500	31,500
1853O	1,100,000	18.00	20.00	24.00	45.00	125	285	900	—	—
1854	4,470,000	16.00	18.00	19.00	22.00	44.00	145	260	2,500	31,500
1854O	1,770,000	17.00	20.00	22.00	26.00	60.00	160	600	—	—
1855	2,075,000	16.00	18.00	19.00	22.00	48.00	150	350	3,800	31,500

Seated Liberty Dime.

Seated Liberty, stars around top 1/2 of border, date below. Value within wreath.

KM# A63.2 **Designer:** Christian Gobrecht. **Weight:** 2.4900 g. **Composition:** 0.9000 Silver, 0.0720 oz. ASW.

Date	Mintage	G-4	VG-8	F-12	VF-20	XF-40	AU-50	MS-60	MS-65	Prf-65
1856 small date	5,780,000	15.50	17.00	18.50	21.00	42.00	138	250	7,050	38,000

Date	Mintage	G-4	VG-8	F-12	VF-20	XF-40	AU-50	MS-60	MS-65	Prf-65
1856 large date	Inc. above	20.00	23.50	27.00	34.00	65.00	175	475	—	—
1856O	1,180,000	19.00	22.00	23.50	32.00	70.00	225	625	5,250	—
1856S	70,000	135	185	360	575	1,150	1,750	—	—	—
1857	5,580,000	15.50	17.00	18.50	21.00	42.00	138	250	2,600	3,400
1857O	1,540,000	16.50	18.00	19.50	26.00	55.00	175	375	2,600	—
1858	1,540,000	15.50	17.00	18.50	21.00	42.00	138	260	2,600	3,400
1858O	290,000	16.50	25.00	36.00	85.00	120	280	800	5,000	—
1858S	60,000	135	200	265	475	1,000	1,650	—	—	—
1859	430,000	16.00	20.00	23.50	38.00	55.00	138	350	—	3,400
1859O	480,000	16.00	20.00	25.00	40.00	80.00	240	550	—	—
1859S	60,000	100.00	175	350	600	1,350	2,750	—	—	—
1860S	140,000	37.50	55.00	70.00	145	325	625	—	—	—

Seated Liberty Dime.

UNITED STATES OF AMERICA replaced stars. Value within wreath.

KM# 92 Obv. Designer: Christian Gobrecht. **Weight:** 2.4900 g. **Composition:** 0.9000 Silver, 0.0720 oz. ASW. **Notes:** The 1873 "closed-3" and "open-3" varieties are distinguished by the amount of space between the upper left and lower left serifs of the 3 in the date.

Date	Mintage	G-4	VG-8	F-12	VF-20	XF-40	AU-50	MS-60	MS-65	Prf-65
1860	607,000	17.50	19.00	29.00	32.00	44.00	115	275	1,350	1,400
1860O	40,000	400	600	900	1,950	3,650	6,500	8,500	—	—
1861	1,884,000	16.50	18.00	20.00	23.00	32.00	85.00	150	1,250	1,400
1861S	172,500	55.00	90.00	150	200	400	650	1,400	—	—
1862	847,550	17.50	19.00	21.00	24.00	45.00	75.00	165	1,250	1,400
1862S	180,750	45.00	60.00	95.00	175	300	675	1,000	—	—
1863	14,460	425	500	650	900	1,050	1,100	1,300	—	1,400
1863S	157,500	45.00	55.00	75.00	145	250	500	1,200	—	—
1864	11,470	425	500	650	800	1,000	1,150	1,200	—	1,400
1864S	230,000	35.00	45.00	75.00	120	225	375	1,200	—	—
1865	10,500	475	575	700	875	1,250	1,200	1,350	—	1,400
1865S	175,000	45.00	55.00	85.00	200	350	775	—	—	—
1866	8,725	500	600	775	950	1,300	1,200	1,800	—	1,750
1866S	135,000	50.00	65.00	100.00	150	275	400	1,900	—	—
1867	6,625	600	700	950	1,100	1,450	1,600	1,800	—	1,750
1867S	140,000	45.00	80.00	135	200	365	675	1,200	—	—
1868	464,000	25.00	30.00	36.00	50.00	90.00	175	300	—	1,400
1868S	260,000	32.00	38.00	50.00	115	175	275	600	—	—
1869	256,600	30.00	35.00	45.00	110	145	250	600	—	1,400
1869S	450,000	25.00	30.00	40.00	55.00	90.00	160	400	—	—
1870	471,000	17.50	22.00	30.00	40.00	50.00	85.00	150	—	1,400
1870S	50,000	300	375	500	650	850	1,050	2,000	—	—
1871	907,710	16.50	18.00	20.00	30.00	45.00	160	300	—	1,400
1871CC	20,100	2,000	3,500	4,500	9,500	12,500	25,000	—	—	—
1871S	320,000	35.00	55.00	85.00	135	195	325	900	—	—
1872	2,396,450	15.00	16.50	18.50	21.50	30.00	85.00	175	—	1,400
1872CC	35,480	650	1,250	1,850	3,000	7,500	—	—	—	—
1872S	190,000	40.00	65.00	85.00	165	250	400	1,100	—	—
1873 closed 3	1,568,600	16.50	18.00	20.00	24.00	32.50	75.00	200	—	1,400
1873 open 3	Inc. above	28.00	35.00	60.00	90.00	140	220	650	—	—
1873CC	12,400	—	—	—	—	—	—	—	—	—

Note: 1873-CC, Heritage Sale, April 1999, MS-64, $632,500.

Seated Liberty Dime.

Seated Liberty, arrows at date. Value within wreath.

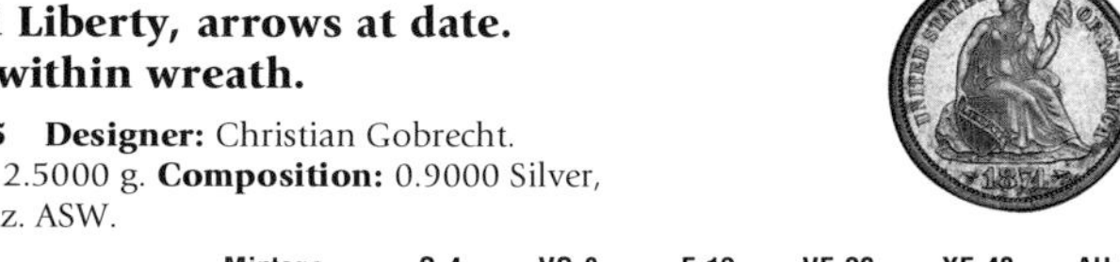

KM# 105 Designer: Christian Gobrecht. **Weight:** 2.5000 g. **Composition:** 0.9000 Silver, 0.0723 oz. ASW.

Date	Mintage	G-4	VG-8	F-12	VF-20	XF-40	AU-50	MS-60	MS-65	Prf-65
1873	2,378,500	17.00	20.00	27.50	60.00	118	280	500	4,500	4,500
1873CC	18,791	1,350	2,850	4,250	9,500	16,500	—	—	—	—
1873S	455,000	22.00	30.00	40.00	80.00	200	425	1,500	—	—
1874	2,940,700	16.00	19.00	26.00	60.00	118	280	500	4,500	4,500
1874CC	10,817	5,000	7,000	10,500	18,500	34,000	—	—	—	—
1874S	240,000	50.00	60.00	85.00	150	265	450	1,500	—	—

DIME

Seated Liberty Dime.

Seated Liberty, date below. Value within wreath.

KM# A92 **Designer:** Christian Gobrecht. **Weight:** 2.5000 g. **Composition:** 0.9000 Silver, 0.0723 oz. ASW. **Notes:** On the 1876-CC doubled-obverse variety, doubling appears in the words OF AMERICA in the legend.

Date	Mintage	G-4	VG-8	F-12	VF-20	XF-40	AU-50	MS-60	MS-65	Prf-65
1875	10,350,700	16.00	17.50	19.50	22.50	32.00	80.00	145	2,250	4,600
1875CC mint mark in wreath	4,645,000	29.00	32.00	36.00	52.00	68.00	130	190	2,700	—
1875CC mint mark under wreath	Inc. above	32.00	34.00	40.00	58.00	90.00	165	235	3,000	—
1875S mint mark in wreath	9,070,000	19.00	23.00	28.00	40.00	65.00	95.00	225	3,100	—
1875S mint mark under wreath	Inc. above	16.00	18.00	20.00	22.50	32.00	80.00	145	1,100	—
1876 Type 1 rev	11,461,150	15.00	17.00	19.00	22.50	30.00	75.00	145	1,100	1,200
1876 Type 2 rev	Inc. above	19.00	25.00	30.00	40.00	60.00	120	200	—	—
1876CC Type 1 rev	8,270,000	29.00	32.00	36.00	50.00	70.00	125	225	—	—
1876CC Type 2 rev	Inc. above	32.00	34.00	48.00	65.00	90.00	175	300	—	—
1876CC doubled die obverse	Inc. above	35.00	40.00	55.00	100.00	185	340	600	—	—
1876S Type 1 rev	10,420,000	15.00	16.50	18.50	22.50	30.00	75.00	145	1,750	—
1876S Type 2 rev	Inc. above	20.00	20.00	24.00	30.00	40.00	90.00	150	—	—
1877 Type 1 rev	7,310,510	15.00	16.50	18.50	22.50	30.00	75.00	145	1,100	1,200
1877 Type 2 rev	Inc. above	18.00	24.00	30.00	40.00	40.00	90.00	150	—	—
1877CC Type 1 rev	7,700,000	35.00	42.00	48.00	70.00	90.00	175	300	1,100	—
1877CC Type 2 rev	Inc. above	29.00	32.00	36.00	52.00	70.00	125	225	—	—
1877S Type 1 rev	2,340,000	—	—	—	—	—	—	—	—	—
1877S Type 2 rev	Inc. above	15.00	16.50	18.50	22.50	30.00	85.00	225	—	—
1878 Type 1 rev	1,678,800	28.00	35.00	50.00	65.00	100.00	175	—	—	—
1878 Type 2 rev	Inc. above	15.00	16.50	18.50	22.50	33.00	75.00	145	1,500	1,200
1878CC Type 1 rev	200,000	100.00	135	175	285	450	600	—	—	—
1878CC Type 2 rev	Inc. above	65.00	90.00	135	225	370	500	900	3,500	—
1879	15,100	275	310	375	500	625	700	800	1,750	1,500
1880	37,335	225	275	330	425	475	585	675	1,750	1,500
1881	24,975	240	300	350	450	500	610	700	2,500	1,600
1882	3,911,100	15.00	16.50	18.50	21.50	30.00	75.00	145	1,100	1,200
1883	7,675,712	15.00	16.50	18.50	21.50	30.00	75.00	145	1,100	1,200
1884	3,366,380	15.00	16.50	18.50	21.50	30.00	75.00	145	1,100	1,200
1884S	564,969	26.00	33.00	42.00	55.00	125	280	650	—	—
1885	2,533,427	15.00	16.50	18.50	21.50	30.00	75.00	145	1,100	1,200
1885S	43,690	475	575	850	1,400	2,400	3,350	5,000	—	—
1886	6,377,570	15.00	16.50	18.50	21.50	30.00	75.00	145	1,100	1,200
1886S	206,524	30.00	45.00	65.00	125	150	175	600	—	—
1887	11,283,939	15.00	16.50	18.50	21.50	30.00	75.00	145	1,100	1,200
1887S	4,454,450	15.00	16.50	18.50	21.50	30.00	75.00	145	1,100	—
1888	5,496,487	15.00	16.50	18.50	21.50	30.00	75.00	145	1,100	1,200
1888S	1,720,000	15.00	16.50	18.50	25.50	35.00	90.00	200	—	—
1889	7,380,711	15.00	16.50	18.50	21.50	30.00	75.00	145	1,100	1,200
1889S	972,678	15.00	18.50	25.00	45.00	70.00	150	475	4,500	—
1890	9,911,541	15.00	16.50	18.50	21.50	30.00	75.00	145	1,100	1,200
1890S	1,423,076	15.00	16.50	24.00	44.00	85.00	145	400	4,900	—
1891	15,310,600	15.00	16.50	18.50	21.50	30.00	75.00	145	1,100	1,200
1891O	4,540,000	16.00	17.50	20.50	25.50	35.00	90.00	175	1,750	—
1891O /horizontal O	Inc. above	65.00	95.00	125	175	225	400	—	—	—
1891S	3,196,116	15.00	17.00	19.00	21.50	30.00	75.00	175	1,650	—
1891S/S	Inc. above	25.00	30.00	40.00	85.00	135	250	—	—	—

Barber Dime.

Laureate head right, date at angle below. Value within wreath.

KM# 113 **Designer:** Charles E. Barber. **Diameter:** 17.9 **Weight:** 2.5000 g. **Composition:** 0.9000 Silver, 0.0723 oz. ASW.

Date	Mintage	G-4	VG-8	F-12	VF-20	XF-40	AU-50	MS-60	MS-65	Prf-65
1892	12,121,245	6.75	7.50	16.00	25.00	27.50	63.00	105	710	1,485
1892O	3,841,700	11.00	15.00	32.50	56.00	75.00	96.00	135	1,275	—
1892S	990,710	66.00	115	210	245	285	340	425	3,500	—
1893/2	3,340,792	135	155	175	225	300	325	450	4,850	—
1893	Inc. above	8.25	12.50	20.00	30.00	46.00	80.00	165	1,000	1,485
1893O	1,760,000	31.00	45.00	135	168	190	250	315	2,950	—
1893S	2,491,401	14.00	25.00	39.00	50.00	85.00	155	360	3,750	—

Date	Mintage	G-4	VG-8	F-12	VF-20	XF-40	AU-50	MS-60	MS-65	Prf-65
1894	1,330,972	25.00	45.00	122	165	190	235	310	1,150	1,485
1894O	720,000	70.00	105	215	280	425	650	1,550	15,500	—
1894S	24	—	—	—	—	—	—	—	1,900,000	—

Note: 1894S, Eliasberg Sale, May 1996, Prf-64, $451,000.

Date	Mintage	G-4	VG-8	F-12	VF-20	XF-40	AU-50	MS-60	MS-65	Prf-65
1895	690,880	85.00	180	355	480	565	650	750	2,650	1,485
1895O	440,000	385	575	900	1,285	2,500	3,650	6,000	19,500	—
1895S	1,120,000	43.50	60.00	135	190	240	320	500	7,500	—
1896	2,000,762	11.50	23.00	56.00	82.00	100.00	120	145	1,450	1,485
1896O	610,000	80.00	155	305	375	465	700	075	0,600	
1896S	575,056	85.00	160	310	335	385	525	770	4,650	—
1897	10,869,264	3.50	3.75	8.00	15.00	31.50	73.00	125	710	1,485
1897O	666,000	69.50	115	290	385	480	600	975	4,450	—
1897S	1,342,844	21.00	45.00	98.00	125	185	265	435	3,950	—
1898	16,320,735	3.50	3.75	7.50	15.00	28.00	68.00	125	710	1,485
1898O	2,130,000	13.50	27.50	88.00	145	200	285	450	3,850	—
1898S	1,702,507	8.50	15.00	33.00	48.00	78.00	160	370	3,750	—
1899	19,580,846	3.50	3.75	7.50	12.00	26.00	68.00	110	710	1,485
1899O	2,650,000	10.00	19.50	72.00	110	150	230	415	4,450	—
1899S	1,867,493	9.00	16.00	34.00	37.00	46.00	105	300	4,350	—
1900	17,600,912	4.00	5.00	7.00	11.00	26.00	63.00	105	740	1,485
1900O	2,010,000	19.50	38.50	115	165	225	355	595	5,750	—
1900S	5,168,270	5.00	6.25	12.50	19.50	31.50	75.00	155	1,850	—
1901	18,860,478	4.00	5.00	6.50	10.00	27.50	63.00	105	755	1,485
1901O	5,620,000	4.00	5.50	16.00	27.50	67.50	175	450	4,350	—
1901S	593,022	80.00	150	360	475	520	675	985	5,350	—
1902	21,380,777	4.00	5.00	6.25	8.00	23.00	63.00	105	755	1,485
1902O	4,500,000	4.00	5.50	15.00	32.50	62.50	145	350	4,500	—
1902S	2,070,000	8.00	21.00	58.00	90.00	135	195	375	3,950	—
1903	19,500,755	4.00	5.00	6.25	8.00	25.00	63.00	105	1,100	1,485
1903O	8,180,000	4.00	5.50	13.50	23.50	50.00	110	250	4,850	—
1903S	613,300	84.00	130	350	490	750	840	1,100	3,150	—
1904	14,601,027	4.00	5.00	7.00	9.75	25.00	63.00	110	1,850	1,485
1904S	800,000	45.00	75.00	165	245	335	465	725	4,500	—
1905	14,552,350	4.25	5.25	6.75	9.75	25.00	63.00	105	735	1,485
1905O	3,400,000	4.25	14.50	36.50	57.50	92.00	155	285	1,650	—
1905O micro O	Inc. above	35.00	50.00	75.00	140	235	375	1,750	12,500	—
1905S	6,855,199	3.50	5.00	9.00	18.50	43.50	96.00	210	775	—
1906	19,958,406	3.25	4.50	4.50	7.25	22.00	58.00	100.00	735	1,485
1906D	4,060,000	3.75	4.85	7.00	15.00	35.00	78.00	175	1,650	—
1906O	2,610,000	5.50	13.00	50.00	78.00	100.00	135	195	1,150	—
1906S	3,136,640	4.25	6.25	12.50	22.50	44.00	110	240	1,350	—
1907	22,220,575	3.25	3.50	4.25	7.25	22.00	58.00	100.00	700	1,485
1907D	4,080,000	3.75	5.00	8.75	17.50	43.50	115	275	3,950	—
1907O	5,058,000	4.25	6.75	33.50	50.00	62.50	110	210	1,350	—
1907S	3,178,470	4.25	5.50	16.00	27.50	67.50	150	410	2,450	—
1908	10,600,545	3.25	3.50	4.25	7.25	22.00	58.00	100.00	700	1,485
1908D	7,490,000	3.25	3.50	5.75	9.75	29.00	63.00	125	990	—
1908O	1,789,000	5.25	11.00	44.50	64.00	92.00	150	290	1,350	—
1908S	3,220,000	4.50	6.25	11.50	22.00	46.00	175	310	2,350	—
1909	10,240,650	3.25	3.50	4.25	7.25	22.00	58.00	100.00	700	1,485
1909D	954,000	7.25	18.50	60.00	100.00	135	225	485	3,150	—
1909O	2,287,000	4.00	7.25	12.50	22.00	50.00	92.50	185	1,650	—
1909S	1,000,000	8.75	19.50	88.00	130	182	315	525	3,150	—
1910	11,520,551	3.25	3.50	4.00	9.75	22.00	58.00	100.00	700	1,485
1910D	3,490,000	3.50	4.00	8.50	19.00	47.50	100.00	210	1,650	—
1910S	1,240,000	5.25	9.00	50.00	74.00	110	195	425	2,450	—
1911	18,870,543	3.25	3.50	4.00	7.00	22.00	58.00	100.00	700	1,485
1911D	11,209,000	3.25	3.50	4.00	7.00	22.00	58.00	100.00	700	—
1911S	3,520,000	4.00	4.75	8.50	18.50	39.50	105	195	1,050	—
1912	19,350,700	3.25	3.50	4.00	7.00	22.00	58.00	100.00	700	1,485
1912D	11,760,000	3.25	3.50	4.00	7.00	22.00	58.00	100.00	700	—
1912S	3,420,000	3.50	4.50	5.60	12.50	34.00	92.50	155	775	—
1913	19,760,622	3.25	3.50	4.00	7.00	22.00	58.00	100.00	700	1,485
1913S	510,000	35.00	50.00	120	190	240	325	480	1,375	—
1914	17,360,655	3.25	3.50	4.00	7.00	22.00	58.00	100.00	700	1,485
1914D	11,908,000	3.25	3.50	4.00	7.00	22.00	58.00	100.00	700	—
1914S	2,100,000	3.50	4.50	8.00	17.50	39.50	78.00	150	1,250	—
1915	5,620,450	3.25	3.50	4.00	7.00	22.00	58.00	100.00	700	1,485
1915S	960,000	7.50	11.50	34.50	49.50	66.50	135	250	1,550	—
1916	18,490,000	3.25	3.50	4.00	8.00	22.00	58.00	100.00	700	—
1916S	5,820,000	3.50	4.50	5.00	8.50	25.50	63.00	105	795	—

Mercury Dime.

KM# 140 **Designer:** Adolph A. Weinman. **Diameter:** 17.8 **Weight:** 2.5000 g. **Composition:** 0.9000 Silver, 0.0723 oz. ASW. **Notes:** All specimens listed as -65FSB are for fully struck MS-65 coins with fully split and rounded horizontal bands on the fasces.

Mint mark

Full split bands

Date	Mintage	G-4	VG-8	F-12	VF-20	XF-40	AU-50	MS-60	MS-63	MS-65	-65FSB
1916	22,180,080	3.80	4.75	6.00	7.00	12.00	22.50	29.00	43.00	110	165
1916D	264,000	850	1,500	2,750	3,950	5,750	9,250	13,200	18,400	26,500	48,500
1916S	10,450,000	4.00	5.00	9.25	15.00	25.00	28.00	44.00	60.00	210	800
1917	55,230,000	3.40	3.80	4.40	5.50	8.00	12.50	27.00	55.00	155	375
1917D	9,402,000	4.30	6.00	12.50	26.00	52.50	90.00	120	300	1,100	5,650
1917S	27,330,000	3.40	3.90	4.60	7.50	15.00	28.00	60.00	170	470	1,265
1918	26,680,000	3.40	4.60	5.75	12.00	34.00	42.00	67.00	95.00	420	1,325
1918D	22,674,800	3.40	4.50	6.50	13.00	32.00	46.00	100.00	210	600	27,500
1918S	19,300,000	3.40	3.90	4.40	11.00	24.00	38.50	92.00	230	660	7,450
1919	35,740,000	3.40	3.80	4.40	5.50	12.00	23.00	36.00	105	315	685
1919D	9,939,000	3.40	6.00	13.50	31.00	46.00	70.00	175	420	2,100	38,500
1919S	8,850,000	3.40	4.50	10.50	20.00	42.00	70.00	175	450	1,250	14,350
1920	59,030,000	3.40	3.80	4.40	4.50	8.50	14.00	28.00	67.00	235	540
1920D	19,171,000	3.40	4.50	4.75	9.00	24.00	43.00	110	310	750	4,750
1920S	13,820,000	3.40	3.90	7.00	9.00	21.00	39.00	110	300	1,300	8,250
1921	1,230,000	60.00	77.00	110	245	540	850	1,150	1,465	2,850	4,350
1921D	1,080,000	80.00	120	185	365	650	1,050	1,250	1,650	2,900	5,200
1923	50,130,000	3.40	3.80	4.40	4.50	7.00	15.00	28.00	42.00	115	340
1923S	6,440,000	3.40	4.50	8.25	19.00	75.00	100.00	155	375	1,150	7,450
1924	24,010,000	3.40	3.80	4.40	4.50	13.50	26.50	40.00	88.00	175	500
1924D	6,810,000	3.90	4.90	9.00	23.50	63.00	100.00	165	460	1,050	1,365
1924S	7,120,000	3.40	3.90	4.40	12.00	59.00	95.00	185	450	1,100	16,750
1925	25,610,000	3.40	3.80	4.40	5.50	11.00	16.00	28.00	75.00	210	990
1925D	5,117,000	4.90	5.00	12.75	46.50	135	185	335	725	1,750	3,500
1925S	5,850,000	3.40	3.90	7.75	18.50	85.00	100.00	180	475	1,400	4,650
1926	32,160,000	3.40	3.80	3.90	4.00	5.75	12.00	26.00	55.00	240	525
1926D	6,828,000	3.90	4.00	5.00	12.00	32.00	43.00	125	260	550	2,500
1926S	1,520,000	11.75	13.50	29.00	67.50	275	400	850	1,425	3,000	6,750
1927	28,080,000	3.40	3.80	4.40	4.50	6.00	11.00	26.00	48.00	138	350
1927D	4,812,000	3.90	5.00	7.75	25.50	88.00	95.00	165	360	1,285	8,500
1927S	4,770,000	3.40	3.90	5.50	11.00	30.00	46.00	270	550	1,400	7,600
1928	19,480,000	3.40	3.80	4.40	4.50	4.75	16.00	28.00	48.00	120	345
1928D	4,161,000	3.70	4.90	11.50	25.50	62.50	85.00	165	315	875	2,750
1928S Large S	7,400,000	4.40	5.40	7.50	12.00	40.00	85.00	225	385	750	6,500
1928S Small S	Inc. above	3.40	3.80	4.40	6.50	19.00	36.00	140	280	425	2,000
1929	25,970,000	3.40	3.80	4.40	4.50	4.50	10.00	21.00	28.00	60.00	175
1929D	5,034,000	3.40	3.90	4.40	8.00	15.00	21.00	28.00	30.00	75.00	225
1929S	4,730,000	3.40	3.80	4.40	5.00	7.50	20.00	32.50	42.00	90.00	560
1929S Doubled Die Obv	Inc. above	5.00	9.00	16.00	25.00	40.00	60.00	95.00	140	275	1,150
1930	6,770,000	3.40	3.80	2.40	2.60	7.00	13.00	26.00	48.00	120	575
1930S	1,843,000	3.40	3.90	4.80	6.50	19.00	45.00	80.00	122	200	685
1931	3,150,000	3.40	3.80	4.40	4.70	12.50	22.50	33.00	62.50	135	800
1931D	1,260,000	8.50	10.00	15.00	19.50	48.00	53.00	100.00	125	285	375
1931 Doubled Die Obv & Rev	Inc. above	—	—	—	50.00	70.00	90.00	135	200	485	650
1931S	1,800,000	4.00	5.00	5.50	11.00	23.50	42.50	100.00	135	275	2,500
1931S Doubled Die Obv	Inc. above	7.50	10.00	13.00	25.00	35.00	60.00	140	200	425	3,850
1934	24,080,000	2.10	2.20	2.30	2.40	6.50	10.00	28.00	33.00	42.00	130
1934D	6,772,000	2.80	2.90	3.90	7.50	14.00	27.50	48.00	60.00	78.00	320
1935	58,830,000	2.10	2.20	2.30	2.40	4.25	7.50	10.00	15.00	30.00	68.00
1935D	10,477,000	2.50	2.60	2.70	6.50	13.00	25.00	37.00	46.00	84.00	500
1935S	15,840,000	2.50	2.60	2.70	3.30	5.50	14.00	24.00	28.00	37.00	360

Date	Mintage	G-4	VG-8	F-12	VF-20	XF-40	AU-50	MS-60	MS-63	MS-65	-65FSB
1936	87,504,130	2.10	2.20	2.30	2.40	2.80	6.50	9.00	15.00	26.50	84.00
1936 Doubled Die Obv	Inc. above	—	—	8.00	15.00	25.00	35.00	50.00	100.00	165	—
1936D	16,132,000	2.50	2.60	2.70	4.30	8.50	17.00	28.00	36.00	53.00	290
1936S	9,210,000	—	2.60	2.70	3.00	6.00	12.50	20.00	30.00	33.00	88.00
1937	56,865,756	2.10	2.20	2.30	2.40	3.75	6.00	8.00	12.00	24.00	52.00
1937 Doubled Die Obv	Inc. above	—	—	—	6.00	9.00	12.00	20.00	40.00	60.00	175
1937D	14,146,000	2.50	2.60	2.70	3.00	6.00	12.50	22.50	30.00	43.00	105
1937S	9,740,000	2.50	2.60	2.70	3.00	5.50	10.00	22.00	27.00	36.00	190
1937S Doubled Die Obv	Inc. above	—	—	—	5.00	8.00	12.00	28.00	42.00	80.00	275
1938	22,198,728	2.10	2.20	2.30	2.40	3.75	7.50	13.50	15.00	25.00	80.00
1938D	5,537,000	2.50	2.60	2.70	5.00	6.00	12.00	18.50	24.00	34.00	62.00
1938S	8,090,000	2.50	2.60	2.70	3.00	5.00	12.00	21.50	27.50	37.00	160
1939	67,749,321	2.10	2.20	2.30	2.40	2.80	3.60	9.00	11.00	25.00	170
1939 Doubled Die Obv	Inc. above	—	—	—	4.00	6.00	8.00	14.00	20.00	35.00	450
1939D	24,394,000	2.30	2.40	2.50	2.70	3.50	5.50	7.50	10.00	26.00	49.00
1939S	10,540,000	2.60	2.70	2.80	3.10	6.75	14.00	25.00	32.00	50.00	765
1940	65,361,827	2.10	2.20	2.30	2.40	2.80	3.10	6.00	11.00	30.00	48.00
1940D	21,198,000	2.30	2.40	2.50	2.70	4.20	6.00	8.00	13.00	32.00	48.00
1940S	21,560,000	2.30	2.40	2.50	2.70	4.20	6.50	8.50	12.50	32.00	95.00
1941	175,106,557	2.10	2.20	2.30	2.40	2.80	3.10	6.00	9.50	30.00	46.00
1941 Doubled Die Obv	Inc. above	—	—	—	10.00	16.00	30.00	55.00	80.00	140	295
1941D	45,634,000	2.30	2.40	2.50	2.70	3.20	3.60	8.00	13.00	23.00	46.00
1941D Doubled Die Obv	Inc. above	—	—	—	9.00	14.00	20.00	30.00	60.00	90.00	250
1941S Small S	43,090,000	2.30	2.40	2.50	2.70	3.20	4.50	7.00	10.00	30.00	46.00
1941S Large S	Inc. above	4.00	5.00	8.00	15.00	25.00	60.00	110	145	250	425
1941S Doubled Die Rev	Inc. above	4.00	4.50	5.00	5.50	6.00	7.50	18.00	25.00	50.00	85.00
1942	205,432,329	2.10	2.20	2.30	2.40	2.80	3.10	6.00	9.50	24.00	46.00
1942/41	Inc. above	525	545	610	640	750	1,285	2,700	4,000	12,500	35,000
1942D	60,740,000	2.30	2.40	2.50	2.70	3.20	3.60	8.00	12.75	27.50	46.00
1942/41D	Inc. above	475	540	600	650	825	1,350	2,650	4,500	7,000	26,500
1942S	49,300,000	2.30	2.40	2.50	2.70	3.20	3.60	9.80	16.00	24.00	145
1943	191,710,000	2.10	2.20	2.30	2.40	2.80	3.10	6.00	9.50	31.00	50.00
1943D	71,949,000	2.30	2.40	2.50	2.70	3.20	3.40	7.80	12.00	30.00	47.00
1943S	60,400,000	2.30	2.40	2.50	2.70	3.20	3.60	9.50	13.00	26.50	66.00
1944	231,410,000	2.10	2.20	2.30	2.40	2.80	3.10	6.00	9.50	23.00	75.00
1944D	62,224,000	2.30	2.40	2.50	2.70	3.20	3.40	7.50	15.00	23.00	46.00
1944S	49,490,000	2.30	2.40	2.50	2.70	3.20	3.60	7.50	16.00	30.00	50.00
1945	159,130,000	2.10	2.20	2.30	2.40	2.80	3.10	6.00	9.50	23.00	97.50
1945D	40,245,000	2.30	2.40	2.50	2.70	3.20	3.60	6.50	10.00	24.00	46.50
1945S	41,920,000	2.30	2.40	2.50	2.70	3.20	3.60	7.00	10.00	24.00	105
1945S micro S	Inc. above	3.30	4.00	6.00	9.00	13.00	20.00	28.00	38.00	115	685

Roosevelt Dime.

KM# 195 **Designer:** John R. Sinnock. **Diameter:** 17.9 **Weight:** 2.5000 g. **Composition:** 0.9000 Silver, 0.0723 oz. ASW.

Mint mark 1946-64

Date	Mintage	G-4	VG-8	F-12	VF-20	XF-40	AU-50	MS-60	MS-65	Prf-65
1946	225,250,000	—	—	—	—	3.50	3.70	3.90	14.50	—
1946D	61,043,500	—	—	—	—	3.50	3.90	3.90	13.50	—
1946S	27,900,000	—	—	—	—	3.50	4.00	3.90	18.50	—
1947	121,520,000	—	—	—	—	3.50	3.60	3.70	15.00	—
1947D	46,835,000	—	—	—	—	3.50	3.60	4.50	16.00	—
1947S	34,840,000	—	—	—	—	3.50	3.60	3.70	15.00	—
1948	74,950,000	—	—	—	—	3.50	3.60	3.70	14.00	—
1948D	52,841,000	—	—	—	—	3.50	3.60	5.00	15.00	—
1948S	35,520,000	—	—	—	—	3.50	3.60	4.50	17.00	—
1949	30,940,000	—	—	3.30	3.30	3.50	8.50	16.00	65.00	—
1949D	26,034,000	—	—	3.30	3.30	3.50	5.50	9.00	25.00	—
1949S	13,510,000	—	—	3.30	3.50	8.00	15.00	35.00	65.00	—
1950	50,181,500	—	—	—	3.30	3.50	3.50	7.00	32.00	55.00
1950D	46,803,000	—	—	—	—	—	3.60	3.70	15.00	—
1950S	20,440,000	—	—	3.30	3.30	3.75	9.00	23.00	68.00	—
1951	102,937,602	—	—	—	—	—	3.80	3.90	11.00	60.00
1951D	56,529,000	—	—	—	—	—	3.70	3.90	11.00	—
1951S	31,630,000	—	—	—	3.30	3.50	4.00	10.00	34.00	—
1952	99,122,073	—	—	—	—	—	3.60	3.90	22.00	35.00

Date	Mintage	G-4	VG-8	F-12	VF-20	XF-40	AU-50	MS-60	MS-65	Prf-65
1952D	122,100,000	—	—	—	—	—	3.60	3.90	11.00	—
1952S	44,419,500	—	—	—	3.30	3.90	4.10	5.50	16.00	—
1953	53,618,920	—	—	—	—	—	3.60	3.90	12.00	42.00
1953D	136,433,000	—	—	—	—	—	3.60	4.20	11.00	—
1953S	39,180,000	—	—	—	—	—	4.00	5.50	12.50	—
1954	114,243,503	—	—	—	—	—	3.60	3.90	10.00	18.00
1954D	106,397,000	—	—	—	—	—	3.60	3.90	10.00	—
1954S	22,860,000	—	—	—	—	—	3.60	4.00	10.00	—
1955	12,828,381	—	—	—	3.30	3.50	3.60	3.90	8.50	17.00
1955D	13,959,000	—	—	—	3.30	3.50	3.60	3.90	8.50	
1955S	18,510,000	—	—	—	3.30	3.50	3.60	3.90	8.00	—
1956	109,309,384	—	—	—	—	—	3.60	3.90	9.50	8.00
1956D	108,015,100	—	—	—	—	—	3.60	4.00	9.00	—
1957	161,407,952	—	—	—	—	—	3.60	3.90	8.50	5.00
1957D	113,354,330	—	—	—	—	—	3.60	3.90	7.50	—
1958	32,785,652	—	—	—	—	—	3.60	3.90	11.00	6.00
1958D	136,564,600	—	—	—	—	—	3.60	3.90	10.00	—
1959	86,929,291	—	—	—	—	—	3.60	3.90	8.00	4.50
1959D	164,919,790	—	—	—	—	—	3.60	3.90	8.50	—
1960	72,081,602	—	—	—	—	—	3.60	3.20	8.50	4.50
1960D	200,160,400	—	—	—	—	—	3.60	3.90	7.50	—
1961	96,758,244	—	—	—	—	—	3.60	3.90	8.00	4.00
1961D	209,146,550	—	—	—	—	—	3.60	3.90	6.50	—
1962	75,668,019	—	—	—	—	—	3.60	3.90	6.50	4.00
1962D	334,948,380	—	—	—	—	—	3.60	3.90	7.00	—
1963	126,725,645	—	—	—	—	—	3.60	3.90	7.50	3.75
1963D	421,476,530	—	—	—	—	—	3.60	3.90	7.00	—
1964	933,310,762	—	—	—	—	—	3.60	3.90	7.50	3.75
1964D	1,357,517,180	—	—	—	—	—	3.60	3.90	7.00	—

Roosevelt Dime.

KM# 195a Designer: John R. Sinnock. **Diameter:** 17.91 **Weight:** 2.2680 g. **Composition:** Copper-Nickel Clad Copper **Notes:** The 1979-S and 1981-S Type II proofs have clearer mint marks than the Type I proofs of those years. On the 1982 no-mint-mark variety, the mint mark was inadvertently left off.

Mint mark 1968- present

1982 No mint mark

Date	Mintage	MS-65	Prf-65
1965	1,652,140,570	6.00	—
1965SMS	—	2.00	—
1966	1,382,734,540	6.50	—
1966SMS	—	2.25	—
1967	2,244,007,320	7.00	—
1967SMS	—	3.50	—
1968	424,470,000	6.50	—
1968D	480,748,280	6.50	—
1968S	3,041,506	—	4.00
1968 no S error	—	—	7,500
1969	145,790,000	7.00	—
1969D	563,323,870	6.00	—
1969S	2,934,631	—	4.00
1970	345,570,000	5.50	—
1970D	754,942,100	5.00	—
1970S	2,632,810	—	4.00
1970S No S	—	—	1,300
1971	162,690,000	10.00	—
1971D	377,914,240	8.00	—
1971S	3,220,733	—	4.00
1972	431,540,000	7.50	—
1972D	330,290,000	8.50	—
1972S	3,260,996	—	4.00
1973	315,670,000	6.00	—
1973D	455,032,426	5.50	—
1973S	2,760,339	—	4.00
1974	470,248,000	5.50	—
1974D	571,083,000	4.50	—
1974S	2,612,568	—	4.00
1975	585,673,900	4.50	—
1975D	313,705,300	4.50	—
1975S	2,845,450	—	4.00
1976	568,760,000	4.50	—
1976D	695,222,774	4.50	—
1976S	4,149,730	—	4.00
1977	796,930,000	4.50	—
1977D	376,607,228	8.00	—
1977S	3,251,152	—	4.00
1978	663,980,000	5.00	—
1978D	282,847,540	4.50	—
1978S	3,127,781	—	4.00
1979	315,440,000	5.50	—
1979D	390,921,184	5.00	—
1979S type I	3,677,175	—	5.00
1979S type II	Inc. above	—	2.00
1980P	735,170,000	6.00	—
1980D	719,354,321	5.00	—
1980S	3,554,806	—	4.00
1981P	676,650,000	4.00	—
1981D	712,284,143	4.00	—
1981S type I	—	—	4.00
1981S type II	—	—	6.50
1982P	519,475,000	8.50	—
1982 no mint mark	Inc. above	300	—
1982D	542,713,584	3.20	—
1982S	3,857,479	—	4.00
1983P	647,025,000	6.00	—
1983D	730,129,224	4.00	—
1983S	3,279,126	—	4.00
1984P	856,669,000	4.00	—
1984D	704,803,976	3.50	—
1984S	3,065,110	—	4.00
1985P	705,200,962	5.00	—
1985D	587,979,970	3.50	—
1985S	3,362,821	—	4.00
1986P	682,649,693	3.50	—
1986D	473,326,970	3.50	—
1986S	3,010,497	—	4.00
1987P	762,709,481	4.50	—
1987D	653,203,402	4.50	—

Date	Mintage	MS-65	Prf-65
1987S	4,227,728	—	4.00
1988P	1,030,550,000	5.50	—
1988D	962,385,488	5.50	—
1988S	3,262,948	—	3.00
1989P	1,298,400,000	4.00	—
1989D	896,535,597	5.00	—
1989S	3,220,194	—	4.00
1990P	1,034,340,000	4.50	—
1990D	839,995,824	5.50	—
1990S	3,299,559	—	4.00
1991P	927,220,000	5.00	—
1991D	601,241,114	5.00	—
1991S	2,867,787	—	3.00
1992P	593,500,000	4.50	—
1992D	616,273,932	4.50	—
1992S	2,858,981	—	4.00
1993P	766,180,000	3.50	—
1993D	750,110,166	4.50	—
1993S	2,633,439	—	7.00
1994P	1,189,000,000	4.00	—
1994D	1,303,268,110	5.50	—
1994S	2,484,594	—	5.00
1995P	1,125,500,000	4.00	—
1995D	1,274,890,000	4.50	—
1995S	2,010,384	—	20.00
1996P	1,421,163,000	3.00	—
1996D	1,400,300,000	5.00	—
1996W	1,457,949	24.00	—
1996S	2,085,191	—	3.50
1997P	991,640,000	4.00	—
1997D	979,810,000	3.00	—
1997S	1,975,000	—	14.00
1998P	1,163,000,000	2.75	—
1998D	1,172,250,000	2.75	—
1998S	2,078,494	—	4.00
1999P	2,164,000,000	2.75	—
1999D	1,397,750,000	2.75	—
1999S	2,557,897	—	4.00
2000P	1,842,500,000	2.75	—
2000D	1,818,700,000	2.75	—
2000S	3,097,440	—	1.00
2001P	1,369,590,000	2.75	—
2001D	1,412,800,000	2.75	—
2001S	2,249,496	—	3.75
2002P	1,187,500,000	2.75	—
2002D	1,379,500,000	3.00	—
2002S	2,268,913	—	2.50
2003P	1,085,500,000	3.00	—
2003D	986,500,000	3.00	—
2003S	2,076,165	—	2.60
2004P	1,328,000,000	3.00	—
2004D	1,159,500,000	3.00	—
2004S	1,804,396	—	4.75
2005P	1,412,000,000	2.75	—
2005P Satin Finish	—	4.00	—
2005D	1,423,500,000	2.75	—
2005D Satin Finish	—	4.00	—
2005S	—	—	2.60
2006P	1,381,000,000	2.50	—
2006P Satin Finish	—	4.00	—
2006D	1,447,000,000	2.50	—
2006D Satin Finish	—	4.00	—
2006S	—	—	2.50
2007P	—	2.00	—
2007P Satin Finish	—	3.00	—
2007D	—	2.00	—
2007D Satin Finish	—	3.00	—
2007S	—	—	2.50
2008P	—	1.25	—
2008 Satin Finish	—	2.50	—
2008D	—	1.25	—
2008 Satin Finish	—	2.50	—
2008S	—	—	2.50
2009P	—	1.25	—
2009 Satin Finish	—	1.00	—
2009D	—	1.25	—
2009 Satin Finish	—	1.00	—
2009S	—	—	2.50
2010P	—	4.00	—
2010P Satin Finish	—	2.00	—
2010D	—	4.00	—
2010D Satin Finish	—	2.00	—
2010S	—	—	2.50
2011P	—	4.00	—
2011D	—	4.00	—
2011S	—	—	2.50
2012P	—	4.00	—
2012D	—	4.00	—
2012S	—	—	2.50
2013P	—	4.00	—
2013D	—	4.00	—
2013S	—	—	2.50

Roosevelt Dime.

KM# 195b Designer: John R. Sinnock. **Diameter:** 17.9 **Weight:** 2.5000 g. **Composition:** 0.9000 Silver, 0.0723 oz. ASW.

Date	Mintage	Prf-65
1992S	1,317,579	5.00
1993S	761,353	9.00
1994S	785,329	9.00
1995S	838,953	12.00
1996S	830,021	8.00
1997S	821,678	14.00
1998S	878,792	8.00
1999S	804,565	8.00
2000S	965,921	5.50
2001S	849,600	5.00
2002S	888,826	5.00
2003S	1,090,425	4.75
2004S	—	5.00
2005S	—	5.00
2006S	—	4.50
2007S	—	6.00
2008S	—	6.50
2009S	—	6.75
2010S	—	6.75
2011S	—	6.75
2012S	—	6.75
2013S	—	6.75

DIME

20 CENTS

Seated Liberty within circle of stars, date below. Eagle with arrows in talons, value below.

KM# 109 Designer: William Barber. **Diameter:** 22 **Weight:** 5.0000 g. **Composition:** 0.9000 Silver, 0.1447 oz. ASW.

Date	Mintage	G-4	VG-8	F-12	VF-20	XF-40	AU-50	MS-60	MS-65	Prf-65
1875	39,700	165	210	270	325	415	550	835	5,500	9,500
1875S	1,155,000	100.00	110	120	175	210	320	500	4,900	—

Note: 1875-S exists as a branch mint proof

Date	Mintage	G-4	VG-8	F-12	VF-20	XF-40	AU-50	MS-60	MS-65	Prf-65
1875S Clear S	Inc. above	110	120	135	200	235	350	600	5,500	—
1875S over horizontal S	Inc. above	100.00	110	120	175	210	320	500	4,900	—
Note: Also known as filled S										
1875S as $	Inc. above	—	120	130	150	225	260	375	1,300	—
1875CC	133,290	335	385	475	600	775	1,150	1,650	10,000	—
1876	15,900	185	225	285	350	410	535	800	5,600	9,400
1876CC	10,000	—	—	—	—	—	60,000	—	—	175,000
Note: Only one circulated example known. Eliasberg Sale, April 1997, MS-65, $148,500. Heritage 1999 ANA, MS-63, $86,500.										
1877 proof only	510	—	—	2,700	2,900	3,300	3,500	—	—	10,000
1878 proof only	600	—	—	2,000	2,300	2,400	2,800	—	—	9,500

QUARTER

Draped Bust Quarter.

Draped bust right. Small eagle.

KM# 25 Designer: Robert Scot. **Diameter:** 27.5 **Weight:** 6.7400 g. **Composition:** 0.8920 Silver, 0.1933 oz. ASW.

Date	Mintage	G-4	VG-8	F-12	VF-20	XF-40	AU-50	MS-60	MS-65
1796	6,146	12,000	17,500	25,500	36,500	52,500	59,000	83,000	325,000

Draped Bust Quarter.

Draped bust right, flanked by stars, date at angle below. Heraldic eagle.

KM# 36 Designer: Robert Scot. **Diameter:** 27.5 **Weight:** 6.7400 g. **Composition:** 0.8920 Silver, 0.1933 oz. ASW.

Date	Mintage	G-4	VG-8	F-12	VF-20	XF-40	AU-50	MS-60	MS-65
1804	6,738	5,500	6,750	9,250	14,500	32,500	56,500	92,500	425,000
1805	121,394	555	675	1,075	1,750	3,900	6,000	11,500	95,000
1806/5	206,124	585	710	1,150	2,150	4,200	6,300	12,500	100,000
1806	Inc. above	525	635	975	1,650	3,950	5,850	11,000	93,500
1807	220,643	525	635	975	1,650	3,950	5,850	11,500	95,000

Liberty Cap Quarter.

Draped bust left, flanked by stars, date below. Eagle with arrows in talons, banner above, value below.

KM# 44 Designer: John Reich. **Diameter:** 27 **Weight:** 6.7400 g. **Composition:** 0.8920 Silver, 0.1933 oz. ASW. **Notes:** Varieties of the 1819 strikes are distinguished by the size of the 9 in the date. Varieties of the 1820 strikes are distinguished by the size of the 0 in the date. One 1822 variety and one 1828 variety have "25" engraved over "50" in the denomination. The 1827 restrikes were produced privately using dies sold as scrap by the U.S. Mint.

Date	Mintage	G-4	VG-8	F-12	VF-20	XF-40	AU-50	MS-60	MS-65
1815	89,235	120	160	215	435	1,550	2,250	3,800	39,000
1818/15	361,174	120	180	275	750	1,650	2,350	4,200	29,000
1818	Inc. above	110	135	180	400	1,500	2,150	3,750	28,000
1819 small 9	144,000	95.00	135	180	480	1,700	2,275	3,750	35,000
1819 large 9	Inc. above	95.00	145	190	540	1,800	2,350	4,750	42,500
1820 small 0	127,444	95.00	135	180	400	1,500	2,150	3,750	35,000
1820 large 0	Inc. above	95.00	140	185	800	1,950	3,150	5,500	42,500
1821	216,851	115	160	205	425	1,500	2,100	3,550	28,000
1822	64,080	150	240	350	850	1,800	3,000	4,250	38,500
1822 25/50C.	Inc. above	2,750	6,500	4,850	11,000	18,500	25,000	36,500	125,000

Date	Mintage	G-4	VG-8	F-12	VF-20	XF-40	AU-50	MS-60	MS-65
1823/22	17,800	35,000	35,000	48,500	70,000	85,000	110,000	150,000	—
Note: 1823/22, Superior, Aug. 1990, Proof, $62,500.									
1824/2	—	950	1,350	2,250	4,000	5,850	9,000	22,500	—
1825/22	168,000	170	275	400	2,250	5,500	8,800	18,500	38,000
1825/23	Inc. above	160	235	375	700	1,700	2,350	3,850	35,000
1825/24	Inc. above	140	225	350	650	1,650	2,250	3,750	32,500
1827 original curl base 2	4,000	—	—	—	70,000	75,000	80,000	—	—
Note: Eliasberg, April 1997, VF-20, $39,600.									
1827 restrike, square base 2	Inc. above	—	—	—	—	—	—	—	—
Note: 1827 restrike, Eliasberg, April 1997, Prf-65, $77,000.									
1828	102,000	95.00	135	180	400	1,400	2,050	3,550	28,000
1828 25/50C.	Inc. above	500	850	1,550	1,900	3,000	4,250	9,500	—

Liberty Cap Quarter.

Draped bust left, flanked by stars, date below. Eagle with arrows in talons, value below.

KM# 55 Designer: William Kneass. **Diameter:** 24.3 **Composition:** 0.8920 Silver ASW. **Notes:** Varieties of the 1831 strikes are distinguished by the size of the lettering on the reverse.

Date	Mintage	G-4	VG-8	F-12	VF-20	XF-40	AU-50	MS-60	MS-65
1831 small letter rev.	398,000	68.00	120	145	165	410	800	1,250	25,000
1831 large letter rev.	Inc. above	90.00	135	165	200	455	845	1,295	25,000
1832	320,000	68.00	110	135	150	385	775	1,225	27,000
1833	156,000	80.00	120	145	165	420	810	1,260	22,500
1834	286,000	68.00	110	135	150	385	775	1,225	25,000
1834 0 over O	Inc. above	—	—	—	—	—	—	—	—
1835	1,952,000	68.00	110	135	150	385	825	1,275	22,500
1836	472,000	68.00	110	135	150	385	775	1,225	25,000
1837	252,400	68.00	110	135	150	385	775	1,225	22,500
1838	832,000	68.00	110	135	150	385	775	1,225	25,000

Seated Liberty Quarter.

Seated Liberty, stars around top 1/2 of border, date below. Eagle with arrows in talons, value below.

KM# 64.1 Designer: Christian Gobrecht. **Diameter:** 24.3 **Weight:** 6.6800 g. **Composition:** 0.9000 Silver, 0.1933 oz. ASW.

Date	Mintage	G-4	VG-8	F-12	VF-20	XF-40	AU-50	MS-60	MS-65
1838	Inc. above	35.00	42.00	53.00	90.00	365	660	1,265	36,500
1839	491,146	37.00	46.00	58.00	96.00	380	685	1,340	38,000
1840O	425,200	40.00	54.00	75.00	135	425	700	1,650	48,500

Seated Liberty Quarter.

Drapery added to Liberty's left elbow, stars around top 1/2 of border. Eagle with arrows in talons, value below.

KM# 64.2 Designer: Christian Gobrecht. **Diameter:** 24.3 **Weight:** 6.6800 g. **Composition:** 0.9000 Silver, 0.1933 oz. ASW.

Date	Mintage	G-4	VG-8	F-12	VF-20	XF-40	AU-50	MS-60	MS-65
1840	188,127	31.00	36.50	55.00	100.00	225	350	800	14,500
1840O	Inc. above	34.00	55.00	90.00	200	350	525	1,100	17,500
1841	120,000	52.00	75.00	95.00	190	275	400	950	11,000
1841O	452,000	30.00	33.50	50.00	85.00	190	325	750	10,000
1842 small date	88,000	—	—	—	—	—	—	—	—
Note: 1842 small date, Eliasberg, April 1997, Prf-63, $66,000.									
1842 large date	Inc. above	80.00	140	235	325	390	750	1,750	14,500
1842O small date	769,000	500	1,000	1,750	2,650	4,500	9,000	25,000	—

Date	Mintage	G-4	VG-8	F-12	VF-20	XF-40	AU-50	MS-60	MS-65
1842O large date	Inc. above	31.00	44.50	55.00	95.00	275	400	1,500	—
1843	645,600	28.00	31.50	34.00	44.00	75.00	185	400	6,750
1843O	968,000	31.00	44.50	55.00	145	400	825	2,200	—
1844	421,200	28.00	31.50	34.00	44.00	95.00	215	450	8,250
1844O	740,000	31.00	44.50	52.00	90.00	200	375	1,250	8,000
1845	922,000	28.00	31.50	34.00	44.00	110	200	485	6,250
1846	510,000	30.00	33.50	36.00	46.00	200	275	510	10,000
1847	734,000	28.00	31.50	34.00	44.00	85.00	200	450	6,650
1847O	368,000	36.00	55.00	100.00	200	475	1,750	3,650	—
1848	146,000	38.00	52.00	90.00	175	275	465	1,075	—
1849	340,000	30.00	33.50	38.00	75.00	145	290	700	13,500
1849O	—	550	800	1,300	2,200	4,000	5,750	10,000	—
1850	190,800	31.00	350	75.00	135	180	360	850	10,500
1850O	412,000	31.00	44.50	85.00	150	245	575	1,550	15,000
1851	160,000	36.00	65.00	125	200	285	400	875	8,000
1851O	88,000	200	350	550	950	1,650	3,000	5,850	—
1852	177,060	42.00	62.00	85.00	185	285	400	750	6,200
1852O	96,000	210	300	600	1,250	2,850	4,250	12,500	—
1853 recut date	44,200	350	450	1,050	1,250	1,750	2,500	3,850	11,000

Seated Liberty Quarter.

Seated Liberty, arrows at date. Rays around eagle.

KM# 78 Designer: Christian Gobrecht. **Diameter:** 24.3 **Weight:** 6.2200 g. **Composition:** 0.9000 Silver, 0.1800 oz. ASW.

Date	Mintage	G-4	VG-8	F-12	VF-20	XF-40	AU-50	MS-60	MS-65	Prf-65
1853	15,210,020	27.50	31.00	34.00	44.00	150	320	900	17,000	175,000
1853/4	Inc. above	40.00	70.00	110	200	400	950	1,950	45,000	—
1853O	1,332,000	29.50	45.00	54.00	85.00	300	1,100	2,950	25,000	—

Seated Liberty Quarter.

Seated Liberty, arrows at date. Eagle with arrows in talons, value below.

KM# 81 Designer: Christian Gobrecht. **Diameter:** 24.3 **Weight:** 6.2200 g. **Composition:** 0.9000 Silver, 0.1800 oz. ASW.

Date	Mintage	G-4	VG-8	F-12	VF-20	XF-40	AU-50	MS-60	MS-65	Prf-65
1854	12,380,000	27.50	31.00	33.00	42.00	70.00	245	460	8,900	37,500
1854O	1,484,000	29.50	33.00	35.00	60.00	125	265	900	10,000	—
1854O huge O	Inc. above	800	1,400	2,650	4,350	7,500	11,500	—	—	—
1855	2,857,000	27.50	31.00	33.00	42.00	75.00	245	460	8,900	37,500
1855O	176,000	40.00	60.00	115	250	475	1,250	3,000	—	—
1855S	396,400	45.00	60.00	120	225	550	1,350	2,400	29,500	—

Seated Liberty Quarter.

Seated Liberty, date below. Eagle with arrows in talons, value below.

KM# A64.2 Designer: Christian Gobrecht. **Diameter:** 24.3 **Weight:** 6.2200 g. **Composition:** 0.9000 Silver, 0.1800 oz. ASW.

Date	Mintage	G-4	VG-8	F-12	VF-20	XF-40	AU-50	MS-60	MS-65	Prf-65
1856	7,264,000	28.00	31.50	34.00	44.00	75.00	185	280	4,150	18,500
1856O	968,000	30.00	33.50	40.00	60.00	110	300	925	9,000	—
1856S	286,000	60.00	120	200	350	1,600	2,250	5,000	—	—
1856S/S	Inc. above	150	275	500	1,250	2,450	3,500	—	—	—
1857	9,644,000	28.00	31.50	34.00	44.00	75.00	185	280	4,000	11,500
1857O	1,180,000	30.00	33.50	36.00	46.00	125	380	1,025	—	—
1857S	82,000	100.00	150	250	400	700	1,350	2,900	—	—
1858	7,368,000	28.00	31.50	34.00	44.00	75.00	185	280	4,000	8,500
1858O	520,000	32.00	35.50	40.00	60.00	135	425	1,450	24,000	—
1858S	121,000	75.00	120	250	800	2,850	3,750	13,500	—	—

Date	Mintage	G-4	VG-8	F-12	VF-20	XF-40	AU-50	MS-60	MS-65	Prf-65
1859	1,344,000	30.00	33.50	36.00	46.00	80.00	185	400	7,300	7,000
1859O	260,000	32.00	33.50	50.00	65.00	185	475	1,100	12,500	—
1859S	80,000	150	250	400	900	3,250	9,850	—	—	—
1860	805,400	32.00	35.50	38.00	48.00	85.00	195	444	4,500	5,650
1860O	388,000	32.00	44.00	52.00	70.00	120	360	950	13,000	—
1860S	56,000	450	1,000	2,200	3,700	14,500	24,500	—	—	—
1861	4,854,600	30.00	33.50	36.00	46.00	80.00	195	310	3,600	5,650
1861S	96,000	90.00	160	235	750	3,850	9,000	—	—	—
1862	932,550	32.00	36.50	42.00	52.00	90.00	190	350	4,350	5,650
1862S	67,000	65.00	130	250	475	880	1,650	3,500	—	—
1863	192,060	45.00	57.00	75.00	140	250	360	650	4,850	5,650
1864	94,070	80.00	100.00	130	225	360	440	775	5,000	5,650
1864S	20,000	450	650	1,150	2,150	3,450	4,850	12,500	—	—
1865	59,300	75.00	95.00	150	235	340	450	850	6,950	5,650
1865S	41,000	105	180	255	400	800	1,150	2,800	12,000	—
1866 unique	—	—	—	—	—	—	—	—	—	—

Seated Liberty Quarter.

Seated Liberty, date below. "In God We Trust" above eagle.

KM# 98 Designer: Christian Gobrecht. **Diameter:** 24.3 **Weight:** 6.2200 g. **Composition:** 0.9000 Silver, 0.1800 oz. ASW. **Notes:** The 1873 closed-3 and open-3 varieties are distinguished by the amount of space between the upper left and lower left serifs in the 3.

Date	Mintage	G-4	VG-8	F-12	VF-20	XF-40	AU-50	MS-60	MS-65	Prf-65
1866	17,525	450	600	750	1,050	1,400	1,700	2,350	6,800	2,750
1866S	28,000	295	390	750	1,400	1,950	2,500	3,850	17,500	—
1867	20,625	260	325	500	850	1,325	1,575	1,950	—	2,550
1867S	48,000	250	450	850	1,350	2,850	7,000	14,000	—	—
1868	30,000	150	200	275	385	500	550	900	7,350	2,650
1868S	96,000	90.00	185	325	450	775	1,500	3,300	15,000	—
1869	16,600	300	450	560	700	935	1,050	1,600	7,500	2,650
1869S	76,000	100.00	185	325	475	840	1,400	2,650	15,500	—
1870	87,400	55.00	65.00	130	190	275	400	850	6,500	2,650
1870CC	8,340	8,500	14,500	18,500	24,500	40,000	55,000	75,000	—	—
1871	119,160	30.00	47.50	60.00	125	225	350	725	7,500	2,500
1871CC	10,890	3,250	7,500	10,000	15,500	26,500	40,000	66,500	—	—
1871S	30,900	400	525	850	1,150	1,400	2,600	4,450	11,500	—
1872	182,950	30.00	55.00	75.00	110	185	300	600	7,350	2,550
1872CC	22,850	1,250	1,850	3,250	6,000	13,000	20,000	44,500	—	—
1872S	83,000	850	1,250	2,250	3,350	5,000	6,750	8,750	52,500	—
1873 closed 3	212,600	250	425	550	800	1,650	2,200	7,500	—	2,650
1873 open 3	Inc. above	32.00	4,750	62.00	130	175	250	450	5,850	—
1873CC 6 known	4,000	—	75,000	—	—	100,000	124,000	140,000	—	—

Note: 1873CC, Heritage, April 1999, MS-62, $106,375.

Seated Liberty Quarter.

Seated Liberty, arrows at date. "In God We Trust" above eagle.

KM# 106 Designer: Christian Gobrecht. **Diameter:** 24.3 **Weight:** 6.2500 g. **Composition:** 0.9000 Silver, 0.1808 oz. ASW.

Date	Mintage	G-4	VG-8	F-12	VF-20	XF-40	AU-50	MS-60	MS-65	Prf-65
1873	1,271,700	28.00	32.00	37.50	60.00	190	425	725	3,900	8,000
1873CC	12,462	2,950	5,750	10,500	16,500	26,500	47,500	93,500	—	—
1873S	156,000	35.00	45.00	85.00	175	325	525	1,450	20,000	—
1874	471,900	28.00	32.00	37.50	60.00	190	425	725	3,650	8,000
1874S	392,000	33.00	37.00	47.50	110	275	485	900	3,650	—

Seated Liberty Quarter.

Seated Liberty, date below. "In God We Trust" above eagle.

KM# A98 **Designer:** Christian Gobrecht. **Diameter:** 24.3 **Weight:** 6.2500 g. **Composition:** 0.9000 Silver, 0.1808 oz. ASW. **Notes:** The 1876-CC fine-reeding variety has a more finely reeded edge.

Date	Mintage	G-4	VG-8	F-12	VF-20	XF-40	AU-50	MS-60	MS-65	Prf-65
1875	4,293,500	27.50	31.50	33.50	40.00	62.50	150	255	1,775	2,350
1875CC	140,000	95.00	155	270	450	825	1,250	3,650	30,000	—
1875S	680,000	40.00	50.00	67.00	110	175	275	575	3,350	—
1876	17,817,150	27.50	31.50	33.50	40.00	62.50	150	255	1,850	2,350
1876CC Ty1 rev. sm wide CC	4,944,000	60.00	80.00	95.00	125	165	310	550	5,500	—
1876CC Ty1 rev. sm close CC	Inc. above	55.00	73.00	87.50	110	150	275	500	4,250	—
1876CC Ty1 rev. tall CC	Inc. above	50.00	68.00	80.00	100.00	135	235	450	4,000	—
1876CC Ty2 rev. sm CC	Inc. above	50.00	68.00	80.00	100.00	135	235	450	4,150	—
1876CC Ty2 rev tall CC	Inc. above	58.00	75.00	90.00	115	155	300	525	4,400	—
1876S	8,596,000	27.50	31.50	33.50	40.00	62.50	150	255	2,350	—
1877	10,911,710	27.50	31.50	33.50	40.00	62.50	150	255	1,775	2,350
1877CC	4,192,000	50.00	68.00	80.00	100.00	135	235	450	2,600	—
1877S	8,996,000	27.50	31.50	33.50	40.00	62.50	150	255	1,825	—
1877S over horizontal S	Inc. above	34.00	44.00	85.00	175	250	335	650	4,350	—
1878	2,260,800	27.50	31.50	33.50	40.00	62.50	160	275	2,750	2,350
1878CC	996,000	55.00	75.00	90.00	140	150	265	550	3,650	—
1878S	140,000	150	225	345	475	785	1,075	1,950	—	—
1879	14,700	180	235	255	325	375	440	575	1,875	2,350
1880	14,955	155	215	275	325	375	435	575	2,100	2,350
1881	12,975	200	250	280	350	400	455	550	2,250	2,350
1882	16,300	210	260	290	350	400	420	600	2,150	2,350
1883	15,439	200	240	280	365	400	465	585	2,650	2,350
1884	8,875	225	285	475	550	550	600	725	2,150	2,350
1885	14,530	165	225	340	280	400	475	610	2,800	2,350
1886	5,886	325	450	550	750	675	750	925	3,250	2,350
1887	10,710	225	300	385	450	500	550	700	2,500	2,350
1888	10,833	200	275	325	425	475	520	660	2,000	2,350
1888S	1,216,000	27.50	31.50	33.50	40.00	62.50	160	340	4,000	—
1889	12,711	185	275	300	350	425	475	600	1,850	2,350
1890	80,590	60.00	75.00	100.00	135	200	300	440	1,825	2,350
1891	3,920,600	27.50	31.50	33.50	40.00	62.50	150	255	1,775	2,350
1891O	68,000	185	325	500	750	2,350	1,250	4,650	26,500	—
1891S	2,216,000	28.50	32.50	35.50	43.00	68.00	160	295	2,100	—

Barber Quarter.

Laureate head right, flanked by stars, date below. Heraldic eagle.

KM# 114 **Designer:** Charles E. Barber. **Diameter:** 24.3 **Weight:** 6.2500 g. **Composition:** 0.9000 Silver, 0.1808 oz. ASW.

Date	Mintage	G-4	VG-8	F-12	VF-20	XF-40	AU-50	MS-60	MS-65	Prf-65
1892	8,237,245	11.00	14.50	30.00	65.00	100.00	167	285	—	2,450
1892 Type 2 Rev	Inc. above	10.50	12.00	26.00	46.00	72.00	122	220	1,350	2,450
1892O	2,640,000	22.00	30.00	55.00	90.00	155	245	400	—	—
1892O Type 2 Rev	Inc. above	15.00	22.50	44.50	64.00	100.00	160	290	1,600	—
1892S	964,079	50.00	75.00	135	200	300	480	650	—	—
1892S Type 2 Rev	Inc. above	35.00	59.00	95.00	145	205	320	475	4,500	—
1893	5,484,838	10.50	12.50	32.00	39.00	70.00	122	220	1,550	2,450
1893O	3,396,000	13.50	22.00	44.00	75.00	165	285	390	—	—
1893O MM far right	Inc. above	12.00	15.50	32.00	60.00	120	175	265	1,850	—
1893S	1,454,535	26.00	47.50	82.00	158	255	390	635	—	—
1893S MM far right	Inc. above	21.00	38.00	69.00	128	195	320	450	6,350	—
1894	3,432,972	11.00	12.00	32.50	48.00	93.50	140	235	1,300	2,450
1894O	2,852,000	12.50	24.00	50.00	95.00	165	285	415	—	—
1894O MM far right	Inc. above	12.50	18.50	44.00	82.00	142	220	325	2,000	—
1894S	2,648,821	12.00	17.00	50.00	95.00	180	265	410	—	—
1894S MM far right	Inc. above	11.00	13.50	37.50	72.00	130	195	295	2,650	—
1895	4,440,880	10.50	13.00	30.00	39.00	78.00	135	235	1,650	2,450
1895O	2,816,000	17.50	27.50	60.00	92.00	175	290	525	—	—
1895O MM far right	Inc. above	12.50	19.50	46.00	77.50	145	230	390	2,650	—
1895S	1,764,681	28.00	40.00	85.00	165	235	375	560	—	—
1895S MM far right	Inc. above	22.00	36.00	77.00	128	190	300	425	3,650	—

Date	Mintage	G-4	VG-8	F-12	VF-20	XF-40	AU-50	MS-60	MS-65	Prf-65
1896	3,874,762	10.50	12.00	25.00	41.50	82.00	135	225	1,150	2,450
1896O	1,484,000	62.00	95.00	200	365	625	775	815	6,950	—
1896S	188,039	845	1,625	2,550	4,000	5,350	6,250	9,750	50,000	—
1897	8,140,731	10.50	12.00	21.50	33.50	70.00	122	220	1,450	2,450
1897O	1,414,800	45.00	75.00	200	390	420	625	900	3,550	—
1897S	542,229	130	160	320	475	625	925	1,400	6,850	—
1898	11,100,735	10.50	12.00	22.50	35.00	75.00	122	220	1,150	2,450
1898O	1,868,000	16.00	28.50	75.00	165	300	430	665	8,950	—
1898S	1,020,592	12.50	19.00	50.00	74.00	100.00	220	385	7,950	—
1899	12,624,846	10.50	12.00	22.50	35.00	75.00	120	220	1,150	2,450
1899O	2,644,000	14.00	21.00	38.50	72.00	145	290	425	2,850	—
1899S	708,000	18.00	28.50	70.00	95.00	145	275	410	3,650	—
1900	10,016,912	10.50	12.00	23.50	36.00	71.50	130	220	1,550	2,450
1900O	3,416,000	16.00	29.00	69.50	120	175	345	575	3,750	—
1900S	1,858,585	10.50	15.00	38.00	50.00	80.00	135	375	4,950	—
1901	8,892,813	30.00	36.00	45.00	75.00	88.00	200	215	1,550	2,450
1901O	1,612,000	70.00	112	215	385	625	820	1,065	5,450	—
1901S	72,664	5,200	9,500	18,500	26,500	31,000	38,000	41,500	77,500	—
1902	12,197,744	8.70	9.40	19.50	32.50	65.00	121	220	1,100	2,450
1902O	4,748,000	10.50	16.00	52.50	89.00	150	245	485	4,000	—
1902S	1,524,612	14.50	22.00	55.00	92.00	170	260	525	3,600	—
1903	9,670,064	8.70	9.40	20.00	34.00	70.00	121	220	2,150	2,450
1903O	3,500,000	10.50	13.50	41.50	65.00	130	260	435	4,850	—
1903S	1,036,000	15.50	26.00	46.00	89.00	150	285	435	2,450	—
1904	9,588,813	8.70	9.80	20.00	35.00	69.00	120	230	1,200	2,450
1904O	2,456,000	32.00	45.00	90.00	165	235	460	850	2,650	—
1905	4,968,250	30.00	36.00	50.00	65.00	72.00	125	220	1,500	2,450
1905O	1,230,000	44.00	62.50	125	245	265	365	500	6,850	—
1905S	1,884,000	32.00	42.00	72.00	105	115	220	345	3,650	—
1906	3,656,435	8.70	9.40	18.50	32.50	95.00	121	215	1,100	2,450
1906D	3,280,000	8.70	9.70	25.00	42.50	69.00	155	230	1,675	—
1906O	2,056,000	10.50	13.50	40.00	60.00	112	200	290	1,150	—
1907	7,192,575	8.70	9.80	17.00	32.50	62.00	121	215	1,100	2,450
1907D	2,484,000	8.70	9.50	29.00	50.00	76.00	175	240	2,650	—
1907O	4,560,000	10.50	13.50	19.00	38.50	66.00	135	215	1,950	—
1907S	1,360,000	10.50	18.50	47.50	75.00	135	275	465	5,650	—
1908	4,232,545	8.70	9.40	18.50	33.50	66.00	121	215	1,100	2,450
1908D	5,788,000	8.70	9.40	17.50	35.00	66.00	117	250	1,100	—
1908O	6,244,000	8.70	12.50	17.50	38.50	72.00	120	215	1,100	—
1908S	784,000	18.50	40.00	90.00	165	295	500	775	4,750	—
1909	9,268,650	8.70	9.40	17.50	33.50	63.00	117	215	1,100	2,450
1909D	5,114,000	8.70	9.50	22.00	41.50	85.00	160	215	1,350	—
1909O	712,000	42.00	110	310	485	650	1,000	1,525	8,750	—
1909S	1,348,000	10.50	15.00	37.50	57.50	90.00	200	300	2,250	—
1910	2,244,551	8.70	10.00	30.00	46.00	78.00	140	215	1,100	2,450
1910D	1,500,000	8.90	11.00	47.50	72.00	130	260	375	1,875	—
1911	3,720,543	8.70	9.40	19.50	33.50	72.50	125	225	1,100	2,450
1911D	933,600	31.00	44.00	160	310	460	650	900	5,750	—
1911S	988,000	10.50	13.00	53.00	92.00	210	300	385	1,425	—
1912	4,400,700	8.70	9.40	17.50	33.50	55.00	117	215	1,100	2,485
1912S	708,000	10.50	13.00	46.00	84.00	130	230	400	1,675	—
1913	484,613	16.00	26.00	75.00	190	390	535	900	4,450	2,485
1913D	1,450,800	12.50	14.50	38.50	58.50	90.00	185	275	1,200	—
1913S	40,000	1,800	2,450	5,350	7,950	10,500	13,250	15,500	31,500	—
1914	6,244,610	8.70	9.40	17.00	32.00	55.00	117	215	1,100	2,550
1914D	3,046,000	8.70	9.40	17.00	28.00	55.00	117	215	1,100	—
1914S	264,000	125	210	425	610	885	1,025	1,400	3,450	—
1915	3,480,450	8.70	9.40	17.00	28.00	61.00	117	215	1,100	2,485
1915D	3,694,000	8.70	9.40	17.00	28.00	61.00	117	215	1,100	—
1915S	704,000	28.00	42.00	63.50	92.00	110	220	285	1,200	—
1916	1,788,000	8.70	9.40	17.00	28.00	55.00	117	215	1,100	—
1916D	6,540,800	8.70	9.40	17.00	28.00	55.00	117	215	1,100	—
1916D/D	Inc. above	12.00	15.00	26.00	50.00	100.00	150	400	—	—

Standing Liberty Quarter.

Right breast exposed; Type 1.

KM# 141 **Designer:** Hermon A. MacNeil. **Diameter:** 24.3 **Weight:** 6.2500 g. **Composition:** 0.9000 Silver, 0.1808 oz. ASW.

Right breast exposed

Date	Mintage	G-4	VG-8	F-12	VF-20	XF-40	AU-50	MS-60	MS-65	-65FH
1916	52,000	2,850	5,650	6,900	9,000	10,000	12,000	14,500	26,500	37,500
1917	8,792,000	—	50.00	66.50	89.00	118	170	205	685	1,500
1917D	1,509,200	28.00	67.50	98.00	130	200	255	310	900	2,550
1917S	1,952,000	30.00	75.00	110	155	220	280	340	1,150	4,100

Standing Liberty Quarter.

Right breast covered; Type 2. Three stars below eagle.

KM# 145 **Designer:** Hermon A. MacNeil. **Diameter:** 24.3 **Weight:** 6.2500 g. **Composition:** 0.9000 Silver, 0.1808 oz. ASW.

Mint mark

Right breast covered

Date	Mintage	G-4	VG-8	F-12	VF-20	XF-40	AU-50	MS-60	MS-65	-65FH
1917	13,880,000	25.00	35.00	52.00	72.00	96.50	145	200	610	900
1917D	6,224,400	40.00	45.00	88.00	120	160	210	265	1,550	3,350
1917S	5,522,000	40.00	45.00	63.00	75.00	108	155	215	1,100	3,650
1918	14,240,000	17.00	21.00	29.00	35.00	46.00	80.00	135	560	1,750
1918D	7,380,000	26.00	36.00	66.00	78.00	122	195	250	1,485	4,850
1918S	11,072,000	17.00	21.00	32.00	35.00	48.00	95.00	185	1,250	13,500
1918/17S	Inc. above	1,550	2,250	3,850	5,200	7,500	13,500	17,850	110,000	320,000
1919	11,324,000	33.00	44.00	55.00	74.00	80.00	118	175	600	1,650
1919D	1,944,000	85.00	110	195	345	565	695	825	2,950	28,500
1919S	1,836,000	80.00	105	185	285	510	585	750	4,200	30,000
1920	27,860,000	15.00	18.00	25.00	37.00	51.00	90.00	165	600	2,100
1920D	3,586,400	48.00	65.00	88.00	120	160	215	325	2,250	7,200
1920S	6,380,000	19.00	25.00	30.00	37.00	57.00	110	235	2,650	24,000
1921	1,916,000	165	210	450	635	825	1,125	1,625	3,850	5,500
1923	9,716,000	15.00	18.00	35.00	37.00	55.00	95.00	155	620	4,000
1923S	1,360,000	300	425	675	1,000	1,500	2,000	2,600	5,500	7,500
1924	10,920,000	15.00	18.00	25.00	34.00	45.00	90.00	170	585	1,650
1924D	3,112,000	56.00	68.00	108	135	185	220	300	610	5,750
1924S	2,860,000	27.00	32.00	43.00	57.00	105	220	315	1,850	6,500
1925	12,280,000	8.00	8.60	9.40	16.50	44.00	90.00	150	575	950
1926	11,316,000	8.00	8.20	8.70	12.80	28.00	72.50	135	535	2,250
1926D	1,716,000	6.50	10.00	20.00	40.00	75.00	118	170	485	22,500
1926S	2,700,000	8.30	8.50	11.00	30.00	110	225	325	2,175	28,000
1927	11,912,000	8.00	8.20	8.70	10.50	40.00	97.50	92.00	485	1,300
1927D	976,400	14.00	19.00	32.00	70.00	140	210	250	600	2,650
1927S	396,000	35.00	48.00	110	285	1,000	2,650	4,750	12,000	165,000
1928	6,336,000	8.00	8.20	8.70	11.50	28.00	72.50	92.00	485	2,150
1928D	1,627,600	8.50	8.70	9.60	20.00	42.50	90.00	135	485	5,650
1928S Large S	2,644,000	9.90	10.60	12.00	25.00	65.00	115	200	—	—
1928S Small S	Inc. above	8.30	8.50	9.30	16.50	38.00	75.00	125	525	900
1929	11,140,000	8.00	8.20	8.70	11.50	28.00	72.50	92.00	485	900
1929D	1,358,000	8.50	8.70	9.60	16.00	38.50	79.00	135	485	5,850

Date	Mintage	G-4	VG-8	F-12	VF-20	XF-40	AU-50	MS-60	MS-65	-65FH
1929S	1,764,000	8.30	8.50	9.20	15.00	34.00	75.00	120	485	875
1930	5,632,000	8.00	8.20	8.70	10.50	28.00	72.50	92.00	485	875
1930S	1,556,000	8.30	8.50	8.70	10.50	34.00	70.00	115	485	925

Washington Quarter.

KM# 164 Designer: John Flanagan. **Diameter:** 24.3 **Weight:** 6.2500 g. **Composition:** 0.9000 Silver, 0.1808 oz. ASW.

Mint mark 1932-64

Date	Mintage	G-4	VG-8	F-12	VF-20	XF-40	AU-50	MS-60	MS-65	Prf-65
1932	5,404,000	6.80	6.39	7.00	7.10	9.50	14.50	25.00	300	—
1932D	436,800	115	125	140	180	290	440	1,150	12,500	—
1932S	408,000	125	140	150	165	225	260	465	4,000	—
1934 Medium Motto	31,912,052	6.38	7.40	7.80	8.10	9.50	10.50	26.00	100.00	—
1934 Heavy Motto	Inc. above	6.60	6.70	9.00	12.50	18.00	30.00	50.00	265	—
1934 Light motto	Inc. above	7.20	8.00	10.00	12.00	15.00	26.00	45.00	340	—
1934 Doubled Die Obverse	Inc. above	75.00	100.00	165	200	320	450	850	4,250	—
1934D Medium Motto	3,527,200	6.60	6.70	11.50	18.50	29.00	85.00	235	825	—
1934D Heavy Motto	Inc. above	6.80	7.50	12.50	20.00	34.00	100.00	265	1,350	—
1935	32,484,000	6.60	6.80	7.10	7.60	9.31	10.00	20.00	110	—
1935D	5,780,000	7.30	7.60	8.30	16.50	33.50	125	245	595	—
1935S	5,660,000	6.80	7.00	8.10	9.20	15.50	36.50	95.00	310	—
1936	41,303,837	6.60	6.80	7.10	7.60	9.10	9.50	26.00	100.00	1,550
1936D	5,374,000	7.30	7.60	10.50	26.00	52.00	255	585	975	—
1936S	3,828,000	7.00	7.30	8.10	8.60	14.50	48.50	108	345	—
1937	19,701,542	6.60	6.80	7.10	9.00	10.00	16.50	22.00	90.00	475
1937 Double Die Obverse	Inc. above	75.00	100.00	235	340	450	850	1,850	11,500	—
1937D	7,189,600	6.80	7.00	8.10	8.40	16.50	38.00	67.50	150	—
1937S	1,652,000	7.30	7.60	8.40	22.00	34.00	95.00	160	430	—
1938	9,480,045	6.80	7.00	8.10	8.50	18.00	49.00	90.00	215	350
1938S	2,832,000	7.30	7.50	7.70	9.75	22.50	55.00	108	215	—
1939	33,548,795	6.60	6.80	7.10	7.60	8.70	7.00	15.50	55.00	250
1939D	7,092,000	6.80	7.00	7.60	9.10	12.00	19.50	42.00	122	—
1939S	2,628,000	7.30	7.60	8.10	12.00	26.00	60.00	105	275	—
1940	35,715,246	6.60	6.80	7.10	7.60	8.60	7.50	17.50	53.50	160
1940D	2,797,600	6.80	7.00	7.10	12.50	26.00	65.00	130	300	—
1940S	8,244,000	6.80	7.00	7.10	7.20	9.00	16.50	28.50	52.00	—
1941	79,047,287	—	—	—	—	6.90	7.10	9.50	36.00	175
1941 Double Die Obv.	Inc. above	—	—	—	20.00	40.00	50.00	65.00	120	—
1941D	16,714,800	—	—	—	7.40	8.50	15.00	33.00	66.00	—
1941S	16,080,000	—	—	—	7.60	7.70	12.50	30.00	65.00	—
1941 Lg S	Inc. above	—	7.60	12.00	20.00	30.00	50.00	100.00	350	—
1942	102,117,123	—	—	—	—	6.70	6.90	8.50	29.00	135
1942D	17,487,200	—	—	—	7.40	8.50	11.00	18.00	38.00	—
1942D Double Die Obv.	Inc. above	—	115	250	440	650	1,350	2,150	5,000	—
1942D Double Die Rev.	Inc. above	—	22.00	40.00	60.00	75.00	150	350	1,850	—
1942S	19,384,000	—	—	—	7.50	11.00	22.50	70.00	135	—
1943	99,700,000	—	—	—	—	6.70	6.90	8.50	39.00	—
1943 Double Die Obv.	Inc. above	—	12.00	20.00	35.00	50.00	90.00	175	450	—
1943D	16,095,600	—	—	—	7.60	8.70	16.50	29.00	50.00	—
1943S	21,700,000	—	—	7.30	7.60	8.00	14.50	27.00	51.50	—
1943S Double Die Obv.	Inc. above	30.00	60.00	80.00	110	150	265	400	1,200	—
1943 Trumpet tail S	Inc. above	10.00	15.00	25.00	40.00	60.00	100.00	175	675	—
1944	104,956,000	—	—	—	—	6.70	6.90	7.60	29.00	—
1944D	14,600,800	—	—	—	7.30	7.40	11.00	19.00	38.50	—
1944S	12,560,000	—	—	—	7.30	7.40	9.50	14.50	31.00	—
1945	74,372,000	—	—	—	—	6.70	6.90	7.60	34.00	—
1945D	12,341,600	—	—	—	7.40	7.50	11.00	18.00	37.00	—
1945S	17,004,001	—	—	—	7.10	7.30	7.50	8.50	32.00	—
1946	53,436,000	—	—	—	—	6.70	6.90	7.60	38.00	—
1946D	9,072,800	—	—	—	7.30	7.90	8.10	9.75	40.00	—
1946S	4,204,000	—	—	—	7.30	7.90	8.10	8.70	34.00	—
1947	22,556,000	—	—	—	—	7.90	8.10	11.50	39.00	—
1947D	15,338,400	—	—	—	7.30	7.80	8.00	11.00	39.00	—

QUARTER

Date	Mintage	G-4	VG-8	F-12	VF-20	XF-40	AU-50	MS-60	MS-65	Prf-65
1947S	5,532,000	—	—	—	7.30	7.80	8.00	9.25	28.00	—
1948	35,196,000	—	—	—	7.30	7.80	8.00	7.70	30.00	—
1948D	16,766,800	—	—	—	7.30	7.90	8.20	13.00	45.00	—
1948S	15,960,000	—	—	—	7.30	7.70	7.90	8.60	40.00	—
1949	9,312,000	—	—	—	7.40	6.50	15.00	36.00	62.00	—
1949D	10,068,400	—	—	—	7.20	7.90	9.50	16.50	48.00	—
1950	24,971,512	—	—	—	—	7.40	9.00	11.00	30.00	65.00
1950D	21,075,600	—	—	—	—	6.90	7.10	7.70	32.00	—
1950D/S	Inc. above	30.00	37.00	45.00	75.00	140	225	350	5,000	—
1950S	10,284,004	—	—	—	—	7.50	7.50	13.50	34.00	—
1950S/D	Inc. above	32.00	44.00	65.00	125	180	285	400	1,250	—
1950S/S	Inc. above	6.00	7.00	8.00	10.00	14.00	18.00	35.00	135	—
1951	43,505,602	—	—	—	—	6.70	6.90	9.00	27.00	60.00
1951D	35,354,800	—	—	—	—	7.00	7.50	8.50	26.00	—
1951S	9,048,000	—	—	6.50	7.50	7.50	11.00	21.00	40.00	—
1952	38,862,073	—	—	—	—	6.70	7.70	10.90	28.00	46.00
1952D	49,795,200	—	—	—	—	6.70	6.90	8.60	32.00	—
1952S	13,707,800	—	—	—	7.40	7.50	11.00	15.00	32.00	—
1953	18,664,920	—	—	—	—	7.40	8.20	10.00	25.00	44.00
1953D	56,112,400	—	—	—	—	6.70	6.90	8.10	22.00	—
1953S	14,016,000	—	—	—	—	6.70	6.90	8.30	28.00	—
1954	54,645,503	—	—	—	—	6.70	6.90	7.60	24.00	18.00
1954D	42,305,500	—	—	—	—	6.70	6.90	7.60	24.00	—
1954S	11,834,722	—	—	—	—	6.70	6.90	8.10	22.00	—
1955	18,558,381	—	—	—	—	6.70	6.90	7.60	26.00	22.00
1955D	3,182,400	—	—	—	—	7.50	7.80	8.60	24.00	—
1956	44,813,384	—	—	—	—	6.70	6.90	7.60	22.00	15.00
1956 Double Bar 5	Inc. above	—	7.40	7.50	7.60	8.00	9.00	20.00	125	—
1956 Type B rev, proof rev die	Inc. above	—	—	8.00	12.00	18.00	25.00	35.00	275	—
1956D	32,334,500	—	—	—	—	6.70	6.90	7.60	15.00	—
1957	47,779,952	—	—	—	—	6.70	6.90	7.60	14.00	12.00
1957 Type B rev, proof rev die	Inc. above	—	—	—	7.40	10.00	20.00	40.00	125	—
1957D	77,924,160	—	—	—	—	6.70	6.90	7.60	16.00	—
1958	7,235,652	—	—	—	—	6.70	6.90	7.60	12.00	12.00
1958 Type B rev, proof rev die	Inc. above	—	—	—	7.40	10.00	16.00	24.00	90.00	—
1958D	78,124,900	—	—	—	—	6.70	6.90	7.60	15.00	—
1959	25,533,291	—	—	—	—	6.70	6.90	7.60	12.00	12.00
1959 Type B rev, proof rev die	Inc. above	—	—	—	7.60	8.00	12.00	18.00	65.00	—
1959D	62,054,232	—	—	—	—	6.70	6.90	7.60	18.00	—
1960	30,855,602	—	—	—	—	6.70	6.90	7.60	14.00	12.00
1960 Type B rev, proof rev die	Inc. above	—	—	—	6.90	10.00	16.00	24.00	90.00	—
1960D	63,000,324	—	—	—	—	6.70	6.90	7.60	14.00	—
1961	40,064,244	—	—	—	—	6.70	6.90	7.60	15.00	12.00
1961 Type B rev, proof rev die	Inc. above	—	—	—	7.60	10.00	14.00	20.00	200	—
1961D	83,656,928	—	—	—	—	6.70	6.90	7.60	20.00	—
1962	39,374,019	—	—	—	—	6.70	6.90	7.60	15.00	12.00
1962 Type B rev, proof rev die	Inc. above	—	—	—	8.00	12.00	15.00	30.00	175	—
1962D	127,554,756	—	—	—	—	6.70	6.90	7.60	22.00	—
1963	77,391,645	—	—	—	—	6.70	6.90	7.60	12.00	12.00
1963 Type B rev, proof rev die	Inc. above	—	—	—	7.60	7.70	8.00	15.00	50.00	—
1963D	135,288,184	—	—	—	—	6.70	6.90	7.60	15.00	—
1964	564,341,347	—	—	—	—	6.70	6.90	7.60	12.00	12.00
1964 Type B rev, proof rev die	Inc. above	—	—	—	7.60	9.00	10.00	18.00	75.00	—
1964 SMS	Inc. above	—	—	—	—	—	250	750	1,400	—
1964D	704,135,528	—	—	—	—	6.70	6.90	7.60	12.00	—
1964D Type C rev, clad rev die	Inc. above	—	—	—	40.00	55.00	75.00	125	450	—

Washington Quarter.

KM# 164a Designer: John Flanagan. **Diameter:** 24.3 **Weight:** 5.6700 g. **Composition:** Copper-Nickel Clad Copper

Date	Mintage	MS-65	Prf-65
1965	1,819,717,540	12.00	—
1965 SMS	2,360,000	9.00	—
1966	821,101,500	7.50	—
1966 SMS	2,261,583	9.00	—
1967	1,524,031,848	12.00	—
1967 SMS	1,863,344	9.00	—
1968	220,731,500	15.00	—
1968D	101,534,000	8.00	—
1968S	3,041,506	—	2.00
1969	176,212,000	14.00	—
1969D	114,372,000	10.00	—
1969S	2,934,631	—	2.25
1970	136,420,000	12.00	—
1970D	417,341,364	6.00	—
1970S	2,632,810	—	2.00
1971	109,284,000	15.00	—
1971D	258,634,428	6.50	—
1971S	3,220,733	—	2.00
1972	215,048,000	7.50	—
1972D	311,067,732	10.00	—
1972S	3,260,996	—	2.00
1973	346,924,000	10.00	—
1973D	232,977,400	11.00	—
1973S	2,760,339	—	1.75
1974	801,456,000	8.00	—

Date	Mintage	MS-65	Prf-65
1974D	353,160,300	15.00	—
1974S	2,612,568	—	2.10
1975 none minted	—	—	—
1975D none minted	—	—	—
1975S none minted	—	—	—

Washington Quarter.

Bicentennial design, drummer boy.

KM# 204 **Rev. Designer:** Jack L. Ahr. **Diameter:** 24.3 **Weight:** 5.6700 g. **Composition:** Copper-Nickel Clad Copper

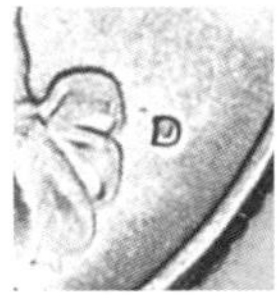

Mint mark
1968-present

Date	Mintage	MS-60	MS-65	Prf-65
1976	809,784,016	.50	8.00	—
1976D	860,118,839	.50	10.00	—
1976S	4,149,730	—	—	3.25

KM# 204a **Rev. Designer:** Jack L. Ahr. **Diameter:** 24.3 **Weight:** 5.7500 g. **Composition:** Silver Clad

Date	Mintage	MS-60	MS-65	Prf-65
1976S	4,908,319	1.50	6.00	—
1976S	3,998,621	1.50	6.00	4.50

Washington Quarter.

Regular design resumed.

KM# A164a **Diameter:** 24.3 **Weight:** 5.6700 g. **Composition:** Copper-Nickel Clad Copper **Notes:** KM#164 design and composition resumed. The 1979-S and 1981 Type II proofs have clearer mint marks than the Type I proofs for those years.

Date	Mintage	MS-65	Prf-65
1977	468,556,000	10.00	—
1977D	256,524,978	8.00	—
1977S	3,251,152	—	2.75
1978	521,452,000	9.00	—
1978D	287,373,152	11.00	—
1978S	3,127,781	—	2.75
1979	515,708,000	10.00	—
1979D	489,789,780	9.00	—
1979S T-I	3,677,175	—	2.50
1979S T-II	Inc. above	—	4.00
1980P	635,832,000	8.00	—
1980D	518,327,487	8.50	—
1980S	3,554,806	—	2.75
1981P	601,716,000	8.00	—
1981D	575,722,833	6.50	—
1981S T-I	4,063,083	—	2.75
1981S T-II	Inc. above	—	7.50
1982P	500,931,000	28.00	—
1982D	480,042,788	15.00	—
1982S	3,857,479	—	2.75
1983P	673,535,000	45.00	—
1983D	617,806,446	30.00	—
1983S	3,279,126	—	3.00
1984P	676,545,000	14.50	—
1984D	546,483,064	12.50	—
1984S	3,065,110	—	2.75
1985P	775,818,962	12.50	—
1985D	519,962,888	10.00	—
1985S	3,362,821	5.00	2.75
1986P	551,199,333	12.00	—
1986D	504,298,660	15.00	—
1986S	3,010,497	—	3.00
1987P	582,499,481	10.50	—
1987D	655,594,696	10.00	—
1987S	4,227,728	—	2.75
1988P	562,052,000	16.00	—
1988D	596,810,688	14.00	—
1988S	3,262,948	—	2.75
1989P	512,868,000	18.00	—
1989D	896,535,597	7.50	—
1989S	3,220,194	—	2.75
1990P	613,792,000	17.00	—
1990D	927,638,181	7.00	—
1990S	3,299,559	—	4.50
1991P	570,968,000	15.00	—
1991D	630,966,693	12.00	—
1991S	2,867,787	—	2.75
1992P	384,764,000	20.00	—
1992D	389,777,107	27.50	—
1992S	2,858,981	—	2.75
1993P	639,276,000	11.00	—
1993D	645,476,128	14.00	—
1993S	2,633,439	—	2.75
1994P	825,600,000	18.00	—
1994D	880,034,110	10.00	—
1994S	2,484,594	—	2.75
1995P	1,004,336,000	12.00	—
1995D	1,103,216,000	10.00	—
1995S	2,117,496	—	8.50
1996P	925,040,000	12.00	—
1996D	906,868,000	14.00	—
1996S	1,750,244	—	4.50
1997P	595,740,000	12.50	—
1997D	599,680,000	16.00	—
1997S	2,055,000	—	8.50
1998P	896,268,000	13.50	—
1998D	821,000,000	13.50	—
1998S	2,086,507	—	8.50

Washington Quarter.

KM# A164b **Diameter:** 24.3 **Weight:** 6.2500 g. **Composition:** 0.9000 Silver, 0.1808 oz. ASW.

Date	Mintage	Prf-65
1992S	1,317,579	6.80
1993S	761,353	6.80
1994S	785,329	8.00
1995S	838,953	8.00
1996S	775,021	8.00
1997S	741,678	8.00
1998S	878,792	6.80

50 State Quarters

Connecticut

KM# 297 **Diameter:** 24.3 **Weight:** 5.6700 g. **Composition:** Copper-Nickel Clad Copper

Date	Mintage	MS-63	MS-65	Prf-65
1999P	688,744,000	.80	6.00	—
1999D	657,480,000	.80	5.00	—
1999S	3,713,359	—	—	3.50

KM# 297a **Diameter:** 24.3 **Weight:** 6.2500 g. **Composition:** 0.9000 Silver, 0.1808 oz. ASW.

Date	Mintage	MS-63	MS-65	Prf-65
1999S	804,565	—	—	20.00

Delaware

KM# 293 **Diameter:** 24.3 **Weight:** 5.6700 g. **Composition:** Copper-Nickel Clad Copper

Date	Mintage	MS-63	MS-65	Prf-65
1999P	373,400,000	1.00	5.00	—
1999D	401,424,000	1.00	7.00	—
1999S	3,713,359	—	—	3.50

KM# 293a **Diameter:** 24.3 **Weight:** 6.2500 g. **Composition:** 0.9000 Silver, 0.1808 oz. ASW.

Date	Mintage	MS-63	MS-65	Prf-65
1999S	804,565	—	—	20.00

Georgia

KM# 296 **Diameter:** 24.3 **Weight:** 5.6700 g. **Composition:** Copper-Nickel Clad Copper

Date	Mintage	MS-63	MS-65	Prf-65
1999P	451,188,000	1.00	4.50	—
1999D	488,744,000	1.00	4.50	—
1999S	3,713,359	—	—	3.50

KM# 296a **Diameter:** 24.3 **Weight:** 6.2500 g. **Composition:** 0.9000 Silver, 0.1808 oz. ASW.

Date	Mintage	MS-63	MS-65	Prf-65
1999S	804,565	—	—	20.00

New Jersey

KM# 295 **Diameter:** 24.3 **Weight:** 5.6700 g. **Composition:** Copper-Nickel Clad Copper

Date	Mintage	MS-63	MS-65	Prf-65
1999P	363,200,000	1.00	5.00	—
1999D	299,028,000	1.00	4.00	—
1999S	3,713,359	—	—	3.50

KM# 295a **Diameter:** 24.3 **Weight:** 6.2500 g. **Composition:** 0.9000 Silver, 0.1808 oz. ASW.

Date	Mintage	MS-63	MS-65	Prf-65
1999S	804,565	—	—	20.00

Pennsylvania

KM# 294 **Diameter:** 24.3 **Weight:** 5.6700 g. **Composition:** Copper-Nickel Clad Copper

Date	Mintage	MS-63	MS-65	Prf-65
1999P	349,000,000	1.00	5.00	—
1999D	358,332,000	1.00	4.00	—
1999S	3,713,359	—	—	3.50

KM# 294a **Diameter:** 24.3 **Weight:** 6.2500 g. **Composition:** 0.9000 Silver, 0.1808 oz. ASW.

Date	Mintage	MS-63	MS-65	Prf-65
1999S	804,565	—	—	20.00

Maryland

KM# 306 **Diameter:** 24.3 **Weight:** 5.6700 g. **Composition:** Copper-Nickel Clad Copper

Date	Mintage	MS-63	MS-65	Prf-65
2000P	678,200,000	.80	6.00	—
2000D	556,526,000	.80	6.00	—
2000S	4,078,747	—	—	3.00

KM# 306a **Diameter:** 24.3 **Weight:** 6.2500 g. **Composition:** 0.9000 Silver, 0.1808 oz. ASW.

Date	Mintage	MS-63	MS-65	Prf-65
2000S	965,921	—	—	9.00

Massachusetts

KM# 305 **Diameter:** 24.3 **Weight:** 5.6700 g.
Composition: Copper-Nickel Clad Copper

Date	Mintage	MS-63	MS-65	Prf-65
2000P	629,800,000	.80	7.00	—
2000D	535,184,000	.80	8.00	—
2000S	4,078,747	—	—	3.00

KM# 305a **Diameter:** 24.3 **Weight:** 6.2500 g.
Composition: 0.9000 Silver, 0.1808 oz. ASW.

Date	Mintage	MS-63	MS-65	Prf-65
2000S	965,921	—	—	9.00

Virginia

KM# 309 **Diameter:** 24.3 **Weight:** 5.6700 g.
Composition: Copper-Nickel Clad Copper

Date	Mintage	MS-63	MS-65	Prf-65
2000P	943,000,000	.80	6.50	—
2000D	651,616,000	.80	6.50	—
2000S	4,078,747	—	—	3.00

KM# 309a **Diameter:** 24.3 **Weight:** 6.2500 g.
Composition: 0.9000 Silver, 0.1808 oz. ASW.

Date	Mintage	MS-63	MS-65	Prf-65
2000S	965,921	—	—	9.50

New Hampshire

KM# 308 **Diameter:** 24.3 **Weight:** 5.6700 g.
Composition: Copper-Nickel Clad Copper

Date	Mintage	MS-63	MS-65	Prf-65
2000P	673,040,000	.80	8.00	—
2000D	495,976,000	.80	9.00	—
2000S	4,078,747	—	—	3.00

KM# 308a **Diameter:** 24.3 **Weight:** 6.2500 g.
Composition: 0.9000 Silver, 0.1808 oz. ASW.

Date	Mintage	MS-63	MS-65	Prf-65
2000S	965,921	—	—	9.00

Kentucky

KM# 322 **Diameter:** 24.3 **Weight:** 5.6700 g.
Composition: Copper-Nickel Clad Copper

Date	Mintage	MS-63	MS-65	Prf-65
2001P	353,000,000	1.00	6.50	—
2001D	370,564,000	1.00	7.00	—
2001S	3,094,140	—	—	4.00

KM# 322a **Diameter:** 24.3 **Weight:** 6.2500 g.
Composition: 0.9000 Silver, 0.1808 oz. ASW.

Date	Mintage	MS-63	MS-65	Prf-65
2001S	889,697	—	—	9.50

South Carolina

KM# 307 **Diameter:** 24.3 **Weight:** 5.6700 g.
Composition: Copper-Nickel Clad Copper

Date	Mintage	MS-63	MS-65	Prf-65
2000P	742,756,000	.80	6.00	—
2000D	566,208,000	.80	9.00	—
2000S	4,078,747	—	—	3.00

KM# 307a **Diameter:** 24.3 **Weight:** 6.2500 g.
Composition: 0.9000 Silver, 0.1808 oz. ASW.

Date	Mintage	MS-63	MS-65	Prf-65
2000S	965,921	—	—	9.00

New York

KM# 318 **Diameter:** 24.3 **Weight:** 5.6700 g.
Composition: Copper-Nickel Clad Copper

Date	Mintage	MS-63	MS-65	Prf-65
2001P	655,400,000	.80	5.50	—
2001D	619,640,000	.80	5.50	—
2001S	3,094,140	—	—	4.00

KM# 318a **Diameter:** 24.3 **Weight:** 6.2500 g.
Composition: 0.9000 Silver, 0.1808 oz. ASW.

Date	Mintage	MS-63	MS-65	Prf-65
2001S	889,697	—	—	9.50

North Carolina

KM# 319 **Diameter:** 24.3 **Weight:** 5.6700 g.
Composition: Copper-Nickel Clad Copper

Date	Mintage	MS-63	MS-65	Prf-65
2001P	627,600,000	1.00	5.50	—
2001D	427,876,000	1.00	6.50	—
2001S	3,094,140	—	—	4.00

KM# 319a **Diameter:** 24.3 **Weight:** 6.2500 g.
Composition: 0.9000 Silver, 0.1808 oz. ASW.

Date	Mintage	MS-63	MS-65	Prf-65
2001S	889,697	—	—	9.50

Indiana

KM# 334 **Diameter:** 24.3 **Weight:** 5.6700 g.
Composition: Copper-Nickel Clad Copper

Date	Mintage	MS-63	MS-65	Prf-65
2002P	362,600,000	.80	5.00	—
2002D	327,200,000	.80	5.00	—
2002S	3,084,245	—	—	2.30

KM# 334a **Diameter:** 24.3 **Weight:** 6.2500 g.
Composition: 0.9000 Silver, 0.1808 oz. ASW.

Date	Mintage	MS-63	MS-65	Prf-65
2002S	892,229	—	—	8.50

Rhode Island

KM# 320 **Diameter:** 24.3 **Weight:** 5.6700 g.
Composition: Copper-Nickel Clad Copper

Date	Mintage	MS-63	MS-65	Prf-65
2001P	423,000,000	.80	5.50	—
2001D	447,100,000	.80	6.00	—
2001S	3,094,140	—	—	4.00

KM# 320a **Diameter:** 24.3 **Weight:** 6.2500 g.
Composition: 0.9000 Silver, 0.1808 oz. ASW.

Date	Mintage	MS-63	MS-65	Prf-65
2001S	889,697	—	—	9.50

Louisiana

KM# 333 **Diameter:** 24.3 **Weight:** 5.6700 g.
Composition: Copper-Nickel Clad Copper

Date	Mintage	MS-63	MS-65	Prf-65
2002P	362,000,000	.80	5.50	—
2002D	402,204,000	.80	6.00	—
2002S	3,084,245	—	—	2.30

KM# 333a **Diameter:** 24.3 **Weight:** 6.2500 g.
Composition: 0.9000 Silver, 0.1808 oz. ASW.

Date	Mintage	MS-63	MS-65	Prf-65
2002S	892,229	—	—	8.50

Vermont

KM# 321 **Diameter:** 24.3 **Weight:** 5.6700 g.
Composition: Copper-Nickel Clad Copper

Date	Mintage	MS-63	MS-65	Prf-65
2001P	423,400,000	.80	6.50	—
2001D	459,404,000	.80	6.50	—
2001S	3,094,140	—	—	4.00

KM# 321a **Diameter:** 24.3 **Weight:** 6.2500 g.
Composition: 0.9000 Silver, 0.1808 oz. ASW.

Date	Mintage	MS-63	MS-65	Prf-65
2001S	889,697	—	—	9.50

Mississippi

KM# 335 **Diameter:** 24.3 **Weight:** 5.6700 g.
Composition: Copper-Nickel Clad Copper

Date	Mintage	MS-63	MS-65	Prf-65
2002P	290,000,000	.80	5.00	—
2002D	289,600,000	.80	5.00	—
2002S	3,084,245	—	—	2.30

KM# 335a **Diameter:** 24.3 **Weight:** 6.2500 g.
Composition: 0.9000 Silver, 0.1808 oz. ASW.

Date	Mintage	MS-63	MS-65	Prf-65
2002S	892,229	—	—	8.50

Ohio

KM# 332 Diameter: 24.3 **Weight:** 5.6700 g.
Composition: Copper-Nickel Clad Copper

Date	Mintage	MS-63	MS-65	Prf-65
2002P	217,200,000	.80	5.50	—
2002D	414,832,000	.80	5.50	—
2002S	3,084,245	—	—	2.30

KM# 332a Diameter: 24.3 **Weight:** 6.2500 g.
Composition: 0.9000 Silver, 0.1808 oz. ASW.

Date	Mintage	MS-63	MS-65	Prf-65
2002S	892,229	—	—	8.50

Arkansas

KM# 347 Diameter: 24.3 **Weight:** 5.6700 g.
Composition: Copper-Nickel Clad Copper

Date	Mintage	MS-63	MS-65	Prf-65
2003P	228,000,000	.65	5.00	—
2003D	229,800,000	.65	5.00	—
2003S	3,408,516	—	—	2.30

KM# 347a Diameter: 24.3 **Weight:** 6.2500 g.
Composition: 0.9000 Silver, 0.1808 oz. ASW.

Date	Mintage	MS-63	MS-65	Prf-65
2003S	1,257,555	—	—	8.50

Tennessee

KM# 331 Diameter: 24.3 **Weight:** 5.6700 g.
Composition: Copper-Nickel Clad Copper

Date	Mintage	MS-63	MS-65	Prf-65
2002P	361,600,000	1.40	6.50	—
2002D	286,468,000	1.40	7.00	—
2002S	3,084,245	—	—	2.30

KM# 331a Diameter: 24.3 **Weight:** 6.2500 g.
Composition: 0.9000 Silver, 0.1808 oz. ASW.

Date	Mintage	MS-63	MS-65	Prf-65
2002S	892,229	—	—	8.50

Illinois

KM# 343 Diameter: 24.3 **Weight:** 5.6700 g.
Composition: Copper-Nickel Clad Copper

Date	Mintage	MS-63	MS-65	Prf-65
2003P	225,800,000	1.10	5.00	—
2003D	237,400,000	1.10	5.00	—
2003S	3,408,516	—	—	2.30

KM# 343a Diameter: 24.3 **Weight:** 6.2500 g.
Composition: 0.9000 Silver, 0.1808 oz. ASW.

Date	Mintage	MS-63	MS-65	Prf-65
2003S	1,257,555	—	—	8.50

Alabama

KM# 344 Diameter: 24.3 **Weight:** 5.6700 g.
Composition: Copper-Nickel Clad Copper

Date	Mintage	MS-63	MS-65	Prf-65
2003P	225,000,000	.65	5.00	—
2003D	232,400,000	.65	5.00	—
2003S	3,408,516	—	—	2.30

KM# 344a Diameter: 24.3 **Weight:** 6.2500 g.
Composition: 0.9000 Silver, 0.1808 oz. ASW.

Date	Mintage	MS-63	MS-65	Prf-65
2003S	1,257,555	—	—	8.50

Maine

KM# 345 Diameter: 24.3 **Weight:** 5.6700 g.
Composition: Copper-Nickel Clad Copper

Date	Mintage	MS-63	MS-65	Prf-65
2003P	217,400,000	.65	5.00	—
2003D	213,400,000	.65	5.00	—
2003S	3,408,516	—	—	2.30

KM# 345a Diameter: 24.3 **Weight:** 6.2500 g.
Composition: 0.9000 Silver, 0.1808 oz. ASW.

Date	Mintage	MS-63	MS-65	Prf-65
2003S	1,257,555	—	—	8.50

Missouri

KM# 346 **Diameter:** 24.3 **Weight:** 5.6700 g. **Composition:** Copper-Nickel Clad Copper

Date	Mintage	MS-63	MS-65	Prf-65
2003P	225,000,000	.65	5.00	—
2003D	228,200,000	.65	5.00	—
2003S	3,408,516	—	—	2.30

KM# 346a **Diameter:** 24.3 **Weight:** 6.2500 g. **Composition:** 0.9000 Silver, 0.1808 oz. ASW.

Date	Mintage	MS-63	MS-65	Prf-65
2003S	1,257,555	—	—	8.50

Michigan

KM# 355 **Diameter:** 24.3 **Weight:** 5.6700 g. **Composition:** Copper-Nickel Clad Copper

Date	Mintage	MS-63	MS-65	Prf-65
2004P	233,800,000	.65	5.00	—
2004D	225,800,000	.65	5.00	—
2004S	2,740,684	—	—	2.30

KM# 355a **Diameter:** 24.3 **Weight:** 6.2500 g. **Composition:** 0.9000 Silver, 0.1808 oz. ASW.

Date	Mintage	MS-63	MS-65	Prf-65
2004S	1,775,370	—	—	8.50

Florida

KM# 356 **Diameter:** 24.3 **Weight:** 5.6700 g. **Composition:** Copper-Nickel Clad Copper

Date	Mintage	MS-63	MS-65	Prf-65
2004P	240,200,000	.65	5.00	—
2004D	241,600,000	.65	5.00	—
2004S	2,740,684	—	—	2.30

KM# 356a **Diameter:** 24.3 **Weight:** 6.2500 g. **Composition:** 0.9000 Silver, 0.1808 oz. ASW.

Date	Mintage	MS-63	MS-65	Prf-65
2004S	1,775,370	—	—	8.50

Texas

KM# 357 **Diameter:** 24.3 **Weight:** 5.6700 g. **Composition:** Copper-Nickel Clad Copper

Date	Mintage	MS-63	MS-65	Prf-65
2004P	278,800,000	.65	5.00	—
2004D	263,000,000	.65	5.00	—
2004S	2,740,684	—	—	2.30

KM# 357a **Diameter:** 24.3 **Weight:** 6.2500 g. **Composition:** 0.9000 Silver, 0.1808 oz. ASW.

Date	Mintage	MS-63	MS-65	Prf-65
2004S	1,775,370	—	—	8.50

Iowa

KM# 358 **Diameter:** 24.3 **Weight:** 5.6700 g. **Composition:** Copper-Nickel Clad Copper

Date	Mintage	MS-63	MS-65	Prf-65
2004P	213,800,000	.65	5.00	—
2004D	251,800,000	.65	5.00	—
2004S	2,740,684	—	—	2.30

KM# 358a **Diameter:** 24.3 **Weight:** 6.2500 g. **Composition:** 0.9000 Silver, 0.1808 oz. ASW.

Date	Mintage	MS-63	MS-65	Prf-65
2004S	—	—	—	8.50

Wisconsin

KM# 359 **Diameter:** 24.3 **Weight:** 5.6700 g. **Composition:** Copper-Nickel Clad Copper

Date	Mintage	MS-63	MS-65	Prf-65
2004P	226,400,000	.65	5.00	—
2004D	226,800,000	.65	5.00	—
2004D Extra Leaf Low	Est. 9,000	135	190	—
2004D Extra Leaf High	Est. 3,000	175	285	—
2004S	—	—	—	2.30

KM# 359a **Diameter:** 24.3 **Weight:** 6.2500 g. **Composition:** 0.9000 Silver, 0.1808 oz. ASW.

Date	Mintage	MS-63	MS-65	Prf-65
2004S	1,775,370	—	—	8.50

California

KM# 370 **Diameter:** 24.3 **Weight:** 5.6700 g. **Composition:** Copper-Nickel Clad Copper

Date	Mintage	MS-63	MS-65	Prf-65
2005P	257,200,000	.65	5.00	—
2005P Satin Finish	Inc. above	1.50	4.50	—
2005D	263,200,000	.65	5.00	—
2005D Satin Finish	Inc. above	1.50	4.50	—
2005S	3,262,960	—	—	2.30

KM# 370a **Diameter:** 24.3 **Weight:** 6.2500 g. **Composition:** 0.9000 Silver, 0.1808 oz. ASW.

Date	Mintage	MS-63	MS-65	Prf-65
2005S	1,679,600	—	—	8.50

Kansas

KM# 373 **Diameter:** 24.3 **Weight:** 5.6700 g. **Composition:** Copper-Nickel Clad Copper

Date	Mintage	MS-63	MS-65	Prf-65
2005P	263,400,000	.65	5.00	—
2005P Satin Finish	Inc. above	1.50	4.50	—
2005D	300,000,000	.65	5.00	—
2005D Satin Finish	Inc. above	1.50	4.50	—
2005S	3,262,960	—	—	2.30

KM# 373a **Diameter:** 24.3 **Weight:** 6.2500 g. **Composition:** 0.9000 Silver, 0.1808 oz. ASW.

Date	Mintage	MS-63	MS-65	Prf-65
2005S	1,679,600	—	—	8.50

Minnesota

KM# 371 **Diameter:** 24.3 **Weight:** 5.6700 g. **Composition:** Copper-Nickel Clad Copper

Date	Mintage	MS-63	MS-65	Prf-65
2005P	226,400,000	.65	5.00	—
2005P Satin Finish	Inc. above	1.50	4.50	—
2005D	226,800,000	.65	5.00	—
2005D Satin Finish	Inc. above	1.50	4.50	—
2005S	3,262,960	—	—	2.30

KM# 371a **Diameter:** 24.3 **Weight:** 6.2500 g. **Composition:** 0.9000 Silver, 0.1808 oz. ASW.

Date	Mintage	MS-63	MS-65	Prf-65
2005S	1,679,600	—	—	8.50

Oregon

KM# 372 **Diameter:** 24.3 **Weight:** 5.6700 g. **Composition:** Copper-Nickel Clad Copper

Date	Mintage	MS-63	MS-65	Prf-65
2005P	316,200,000	.65	5.00	—
2005P Satin Finish	Inc. above	1.50	4.50	—
2005D	404,000,000	.65	5.00	—
2005D Satin Finish	Inc. above	1.50	4.50	—
2005S	3,262,960	—	—	2.30

KM# 372a **Diameter:** 24.3 **Weight:** 6.2500 g. **Composition:** 0.9000 Silver, 0.1808 oz. ASW.

Date	Mintage	MS-63	MS-65	Prf-65
2005S	1,679,600	—	—	8.50

West Virginia

KM# 374 **Diameter:** 24.3 **Weight:** 5.6700 g. **Composition:** Copper-Nickel Clad Copper

Date	Mintage	MS-63	MS-65	Prf-65
2005P	365,400,000	.65	5.00	—
2005P Satin Finish	Inc. above	1.50	4.50	—
2005D	356,200,000	.65	5.00	—
2005D Satin Finish	Inc. above	1.50	4.50	—
2005S	3,262,960	—	—	2.30

KM# 374a **Diameter:** 24.3 **Weight:** 6.2500 g. **Composition:** 0.9000 Silver, 0.1808 oz. ASW.

Date	Mintage	MS-63	MS-65	Prf-65
2005S	1,679,600	—	—	8.50

Colorado

KM# 384 **Diameter:** 24.3 **Weight:** 5.6700 g. **Composition:** Copper-Nickel Clad Copper

Date	Mintage	MS-63	MS-65	Prf-65
2006P	274,800,000	.65	5.00	—
2006P Satin Finish	Inc. above	1.50	4.50	—
2006D	294,200,000	.65	5.00	—
2006D Satin Finish	Inc. above	1.50	4.50	—
2006S	2,862,078	—	—	2.30

KM# 384a **Diameter:** 24.3 **Weight:** 6.2500 g. **Composition:** 0.9000 Silver, 0.1808 oz. ASW.

Date	Mintage	MS-63	MS-65	Prf-65
2006S	1,571,839	—	—	8.50

Nebraska

KM# 383 **Diameter:** 24.3 **Weight:** 5.6700 g. **Composition:** Copper-Nickel Clad Copper

Date	Mintage	MS-63	MS-65	Prf-65
2006P	318,000,000	.65	5.00	—
2006P Satin Finish	Inc. above	1.50	4.50	—
2006D	273,000,000	.65	5.00	—
2006D Satin Finish	Inc. above	1.50	4.50	—
2006S	2,862,078	—	—	2.30

KM# 383a **Diameter:** 24.3 **Weight:** 6.2500 g. **Composition:** 0.9000 Silver, 0.1808 oz. ASW.

Date	Mintage	MS-63	MS-65	Prf-65
2006S	1,571,839	—	—	8.50

Nevada

KM# 382 **Diameter:** 24.3 **Weight:** 5.6700 g. **Composition:** Copper-Nickel Clad Copper

Date	Mintage	MS-63	MS-65	Prf-65
2006P	277,000,000	.65	5.00	—
2006P Satin Finish	Inc. above	1.50	4.50	—
2006D	312,800,000	.65	5.00	—
2006D Satin Finish	Inc. above	1.50	4.50	—
2006S	2,862,078	—	—	2.30

KM# 382a **Diameter:** 24.3 **Weight:** 6.2500 g. **Composition:** 0.9000 Silver, 0.1808 oz. ASW.

Date	Mintage	MS-63	MS-65	Prf-65
2006S	1,571,839	—	—	8.50

North Dakota

KM# 385 **Diameter:** 24.3 **Weight:** 5.6700 g. **Composition:** Copper-Nickel Clad Copper

Date	Mintage	MS-63	MS-65	Prf-65
2006P	305,800,000	.65	5.00	—
2006P Satin Finish	Inc. above	1.50	4.50	—
2006D	359,000,000	.65	5.00	—
2006D Satin Finish	Inc. above	1.50	4.50	—
2006S	2,862,078	—	—	2.30

KM# 385a **Diameter:** 24.3 **Weight:** 6.2500 g. **Composition:** 0.9000 Silver, 0.1808 oz. ASW.

Date	Mintage	MS-63	MS-65	Prf-65
2006S	1,571,839	—	—	8.50

South Dakota

KM# 386 **Diameter:** 24.3 **Weight:** 5.6700 g. **Composition:** Copper-Nickel Clad Copper

Date	Mintage	MS-63	MS-65	Prf-65
2006P	245,000,000	.65	5.00	—
2006P Satin Finish	Inc. above	1.50	4.50	—
2006D	265,800,000	.65	5.00	—
2006D Satin Finish	Inc. above	1.50	4.50	—
2006S	2,862,078	—	—	2.30

KM# 386a **Diameter:** 24.3 **Weight:** 6.2500 g. **Composition:** 0.9000 Silver, 0.1808 oz. ASW.

Date	Mintage	MS-63	MS-65	Prf-65
2006S	1,571,839	—	—	8.50

Idaho

KM# 398 **Diameter:** 24.3 **Weight:** 5.6700 g. **Composition:** Copper-Nickel Clad Copper

Date	Mintage	MS-63	MS-65	Prf-65
2007P	294,600,000	.65	5.00	—
2007P Satin finish	—	1.50	4.50	—
2007D	286,800,000	.65	5.00	—
2007D Satin finish	—	1.50	4.50	—
2007S	2,374,778	—	—	2.30

KM# 398a **Diameter:** 24.3 **Weight:** 6.2500 g. **Composition:** 0.9000 Silver, 0.1808 oz. ASW.

Date	Mintage	MS-63	MS-65	Prf-65
2007S	1,299,878	—	—	8.50

Montana

KM# 396 **Diameter:** 24.3 **Weight:** 5.6700 g. **Composition:** Copper-Nickel Clad Copper

Date	Mintage	MS-63	MS-65	Prf-65
2007P	257,000,000	.65	5.00	—
2007 Satin Finish	—	1.50	4.50	—
2007 Satin Finish	—	1.50	4.50	—
2007D	256,240,000	.65	5.00	—
2007S	2,374,778	—	—	2.30

KM# 396a **Diameter:** 24.3 **Weight:** 6.2500 g. **Composition:** 0.9000 Silver, 0.1808 oz. ASW.

Date	Mintage	MS-63	MS-65	Prf-65
2007S	1,299,878	—	—	8.50

Utah

KM# 400 **Diameter:** 24.3 **Weight:** 5.6700 g. **Composition:** Copper-Nickel Clad Copper

Date	Mintage	MS-63	MS-65	Prf-65
2007P	255,000,000	.65	5.00	—
2007P Satin finish	—	1.50	4.50	—
2007D	253,200,000	.65	5.00	—
2007D Satin finish	—	1.50	4.50	—
2007S	2,374,778	—	—	2.30

KM# 400a **Weight:** 6.2500 g. **Composition:** 0.9000 Silver, 0.1808 oz. ASW.

Date	Mintage	MS-63	MS-65	Prf-65
2007S	1,299,878	—	—	8.50

Washington

KM# 397 **Diameter:** 24.3 **Weight:** 5.6700 g. **Composition:** Copper-Nickel Clad Copper

Date	Mintage	MS-63	MS-65	Prf-65
2007P	265,200,000	.65	5.00	—
2007P Satin Finish	—	1.50	4.50	—
2007D	280,000,000	.65	5.00	—
2007D Satin Finish	—	1.50	4.50	—
2007S	2,374,778	—	—	2.30

KM# 397a **Diameter:** 24.3 **Weight:** 6.2500 g. **Composition:** 0.9000 Silver, 0.1808 oz. ASW.

Date	Mintage	MS-63	MS-65	Prf-65
2007S	1,299,878	—	—	8.50

Wyoming

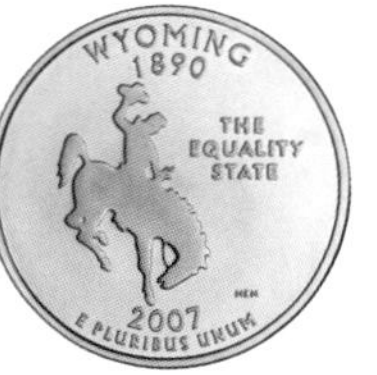

KM# 399 **Diameter:** 24.3 **Weight:** 5.6700 g. **Composition:** Copper-Nickel Clad Copper

Date	Mintage	MS-63	MS-65	Prf-65
2007P	243,600,000	.65	5.00	—
2007P Satin finish	—	1.50	4.50	—
2007D	320,800,000	.65	5.00	—
2007 Satin finish	—	1.50	4.50	—
2007S	2,374,778	—	—	2.30

KM# 399a **Diameter:** 24.3 **Weight:** 6.2500 g. **Composition:** 0.9000 Silver, 0.1808 oz. ASW.

Date	Mintage	MS-63	MS-65	Prf-65
2007S	1,299,878	—	—	8.50

Alaska

KM# 424 **Diameter:** 24.3 **Weight:** 5.6700 g. **Composition:** Copper-Nickel Clad Copper

Date	Mintage	MS-63	MS-65	Prf-65
2008P	251,800,000	.65	5.00	—
2008P Satin finish	—	1.50	4.50	—
2008D	254,000,000	.65	5.00	—
2008D Satin finish	—	1.50	4.50	—
2008S	2,100,000	—	—	2.30

KM# 424a **Diameter:** 24.3 **Weight:** 6.2500 g. **Composition:** 0.9000 Silver, 0.1808 oz. ASW.

Date	Mintage	MS-63	MS-65	Prf-65
2008S	1,200,000	—	—	8.50

Arizona

KM# 423 **Diameter:** 24.3 **Weight:** 5.6700 g. **Composition:** Copper-Nickel Clad Copper

Date	Mintage	MS-63	MS-65	Prf-65
2008P	244,600,000	.65	5.00	—
2008P Satin finish	—	1.50	4.50	—
2008D	265,000,000	.65	5.00	—
2008D Satin finish	—	1.50	4.50	—
2008S	2,100,000	—	—	2.30

KM# 423a **Diameter:** 24.3 **Weight:** 6.2500 g. **Composition:** 0.9000 Silver, 0.1808 oz. ASW.

Date	Mintage	MS-63	MS-65	Prf-65
2008S	1,200,000	—	—	8.50

Hawaii

KM# 425 **Diameter:** 24.3 **Weight:** 5.6700 g. **Composition:** Copper-Nickel Clad Copper

Date	Mintage	MS-63	MS-65	Prf-65
2008P	254,000,000	.65	5.00	—
2008P Satin finish	—	1.50	4.50	—
2008D	263,600,000	.65	5.00	—
2008D Satin finish	—	1.50	4.50	—
2008S	2,100,000	—	—	2.30

KM# 425a **Diameter:** 24.3 **Weight:** 6.2500 g. **Composition:** 0.9000 Silver, 0.1808 oz. ASW.

Date	Mintage	MS-63	MS-65	Prf-65
2008S	1,200,000	—	—	8.50

New Mexico

KM# 422 **Diameter:** 24.3 **Weight:** 5.6700 g. **Composition:** Copper-Nickel Clad Copper

Date	Mintage	MS-63	MS-65	Prf-65
2008P	244,200,000	.65	5.00	—
2008P Satin finish	—	1.50	4.50	—
2008D	244,400,000	.65	5.00	—
2008D Satin finish	—	1.50	4.50	—
2008S	2,100,000	—	—	2.30

KM# 422a **Diameter:** 24.3 **Weight:** 6.2500 g. **Composition:** 0.9000 Silver, 0.1808 oz. ASW.

Date	Mintage	MS-63	MS-65	Prf-65
2008S	1,200,000	—	—	8.50

Oklahoma

KM# 421 **Diameter:** 24.3 **Weight:** 5.6700 g. **Composition:** Copper-Nickel Clad Copper

Date	Mintage	MS-63	MS-65	Prf-65
2008P	222,000,000	.65	5.00	—
2008P Satin finish	—	1.50	4.50	—
2008D	194,600,000	.65	5.00	—
2008D Satin finish	—	1.50	4.50	—
2008S	2,100,000	—	—	2.30

KM# 421a **Diameter:** 24.3 **Weight:** 6.2500 g. **Composition:** 0.9000 Silver, 0.1808 oz. ASW.

Date	Mintage	MS-63	MS-65	Prf-65
2008S	1,200,000	—	—	8.50

DC and Territories

American Samoa

KM# 448 **Rev. Designer:** Charles Vickers. **Diameter:** 24.3 **Weight:** 5.6700 g. **Composition:** Copper-Nickel Clad Copper

Date	Mintage	MS-63	MS-65	Prf-65
2009P	42,600,000	.75	5.00	—
2009D	39,600,000	.75	5.00	—
2009S	—	—	—	3.75

KM# 448a **Diameter:** 24.3 **Weight:** 6.2500 g. **Composition:** 0.9000 Silver, 0.1808 oz. ASW.

Date	Mintage	MS-63	MS-65	Prf-65
2009S	—	—	—	7.75

District of Columbia

KM# 445 **Rev. Designer:** Don Everhart. **Diameter:** 24.3 **Weight:** 5.6700 g. **Composition:** Copper-Nickel Clad Copper

Date	Mintage	MS-63	MS-65	Prf-65
2009P	83,600,000	.75	5.00	—
2009D	88,800,000	.75	5.00	—
2009S	—	—	—	3.75

KM# 445a **Diameter:** 24.3 **Weight:** 6.2500 g. **Composition:** 0.9000 Silver, 0.1808 oz. ASW.

Date	Mintage	MS-63	MS-65	Prf-65
2009S	—	—	—	7.75

Guam

KM# 447 **Rev. Designer:** James Licaretz. **Diameter:** 24.3 **Weight:** 5.6700 g. **Composition:** Copper-Nickel Clad Copper

Date	Mintage	MS-63	MS-65	Prf-65
2009P	45,000,000	.75	5.00	—
2009D	42,600,000	.75	5.00	—
2009S	—	—	—	3.75

KM# 447a **Diameter:** 24.3 **Weight:** 6.2500 g. **Composition:** 0.9000 Silver, 0.1808 oz. ASW.

Date	Mintage	MS-63	MS-65	Prf-65
2009S	—	—	—	7.75

Northern Mariana Islands

KM# 466 **Rev. Designer:** Pheve Hemphill. **Weight:** 5.6700 g. **Composition:** Copper-Nickel Clad Copper

Date	Mintage	MS-63	MS-65	Prf-65
2009P	35,200,000	.75	5.00	—
2009D	37,600,000	.75	5.00	—
2009S	—	—	—	3.75

KM# 466a **Weight:** 6.2500 g. **Composition:** 0.9000 Silver, 0.1808 oz. ASW.

Date	Mintage	MS-63	MS-65	Prf-65
2009S	—	—	—	7.75

Puerto Rico

KM# 446 **Rev. Designer:** Joseph Menna. **Diameter:** 24.3 **Weight:** 5.6700 g. **Composition:** Copper-Nickel Clad Copper

Date	Mintage	MS-63	MS-65	Prf-65
2009P	53,200,000	.75	5.00	—
2009D	86,000,000	.75	5.00	—
2009S	—	—	—	3.75

KM# 446a **Diameter:** 24.3 **Weight:** 6.2500 g. **Composition:** 0.9000 Silver, 0.1808 oz. ASW.

Date	Mintage	MS-63	MS-65	Prf-65
2009S	—	—	—	7.75

US Virgin Islands

KM# 449 **Rev. Designer:** Joseph Menna. **Diameter:** 24.3 **Weight:** 5.6700 g. **Composition:** Copper-Nickel Clad Copper

Date	Mintage	MS-63	MS-65	Prf-65
2009P	41,000,000	.75	5.00	—
2009D	41,000,000	.75	5.00	—
2009S	—	—	—	3.75

KM# 449a **Diameter:** 24.3 **Weight:** 6.2500 g. **Composition:** 0.9000 Silver, 0.1808 oz. ASW.

Date	Mintage	MS-63	MS-65	Prf-65
2009S	—	—	—	7.75

America the Beautiful

Grand Canyon National Park

KM# 472 **Diameter:** 24.3 **Weight:** 5.6700 g. **Composition:** Copper-Nickel Clad Copper

Date	Mintage	MS-63	MS-65	Prf-65
2010P	—	.75	5.00	—
2010D	—	.75	5.00	—
2010S	—	—	—	3.75

KM# 472a **Weight:** 6.2500 g. **Composition:** 0.9000 Silver, 0.1808 oz. ASW.

Date	Mintage	MS-63	MS-65	Prf-65
2010	—	—	—	7.75

Hot Springs, Arkansas

KM# 469 **Diameter:** 24.3 **Weight:** 5.6700 g. **Composition:** Copper-Nickel Clad Copper

Date	Mintage	MS-63	MS-65	Prf-65
2010P	—	.75	5.00	—
2010D	—	.75	5.00	—
2010S	—	—	—	3.75

KM# 469a **Weight:** 6.2500 g. **Composition:** 0.9000 Silver, 0.1808 oz. ASW.

Date	Mintage	MS-63	MS-65	Prf-65
2010S	—	—	—	7.75

Mount Hood National Park

KM# 473 **Weight:** 5.6700 g. **Composition:** Copper-Nickel Clad Copper

Date	Mintage	MS-63	MS-65	Prf-65
2010P	—	.75	5.00	—
2010D	—	.75	5.00	—
2010S	—	—	—	3.75

KM# 473a **Weight:** 6.2500 g. **Composition:** 0.9000 Silver, 0.1808 oz. ASW.

Date	Mintage	MS-63	MS-65	Prf-65
2010	—	—	—	7.75

Yellowstone National Park

KM# 470 **Diameter:** 24.3 **Weight:** 5.6700 g. **Composition:** Copper-Nickel Clad Copper

Date	Mintage	MS-63	MS-65	Prf-65
2010P	—	.75	5.00	—
2010D	—	.75	5.00	—
2010S	—	—	—	3.75

KM# 470a **Weight:** 6.2500 g. **Composition:** 0.9000 Silver, 0.1808 oz. ASW.

Date	Mintage	MS-63	MS-65	Prf-65
2010	—	—	—	7.75

QUARTER

Yosemite National Park

KM# 471 **Diameter:** 24.3 **Weight:** 5.6700 g. **Composition:** Copper-Nickel Clad Copper

Date	Mintage	MS-63	MS-65	Prf-65
2010P	—	.75	5.00	—
2010D	—	.75	5.00	—
2010S	—	—	—	3.75

KM# 471a **Weight:** 6.2500 g. **Composition:** 0.9000 Silver, 0.1808 oz. ASW.

Date	Mintage	MS-63	MS-65	Prf-65
2010	—	—	—	7.75

Glacier National Park

KM# 495 **Diameter:** 24 **Weight:** 5.6700 g. **Composition:** Copper-Nickel Clad Copper

Date	Mintage	MS-63	MS-65	Prf-65
2011P	—	.75	5.00	—
2011D	—	.75	5.00	—
2011S	—	—	—	3.75

KM# 495a **Weight:** 6.2500 g. **Composition:** 0.9000 Silver, 0.1808 oz. ASW.

Date	Mintage	MS-63	MS-65	Prf-65
2011S	—	—	—	7.75

Chickasaw National Recreation Area

KM# 498 **Diameter:** 24 **Weight:** 5.6700 g. **Composition:** Copper-Nickel Clad Copper

Date	Mintage	MS-63	MS-65	Prf-65
2011P	—	.75	5.00	—
2011D	—	.75	5.00	—
2011S	—	—	—	3.75

KM# 498a **Weight:** 6.2500 g. **Composition:** 0.9000 Silver, 0.1808 oz. ASW.

Date	Mintage	MS-63	MS-65	Prf-65
2011S	—	—	—	7.75

Olympic National Park

KM# 496 **Diameter:** 24 **Weight:** 5.6700 g. **Composition:** Copper-Nickel Clad Copper

Date	Mintage	MS-63	MS-65	Prf-65
2011P	—	.75	5.00	—
2011D	—	.75	5.00	—
2011S	—	—	—	3.75

KM# 496a **Weight:** 6.2500 g. **Composition:** 0.9000 Silver, 0.1808 oz. ASW.

Date	Mintage	MS-63	MS-65	Prf-65
2011S	—	—	—	7.75

Gettysburg National Military Park

KM# 494 **Diameter:** 24 **Weight:** 5.6700 g. **Composition:** Copper-Nickel Clad Copper

Date	Mintage	MS-63	MS-65	Prf-65
2011P	—	.75	5.00	—
2011D	—	.75	5.00	—
2011S	—	—	—	3.75

KM# 494a **Weight:** 6.2500 g. **Composition:** 0.9000 Silver, 0.1808 oz. ASW.

Date	Mintage	MS-63	MS-65	Prf-65
2011S	—	—	—	7.75

Vicksburg National Military Park

KM# 497 **Diameter:** 24 **Weight:** 5.6700 g. **Composition:** Copper-Nickel Clad Copper

Date	Mintage	MS-63	MS-65	Prf-65
2011P	—	.75	5.00	—
2011D	—	.75	5.00	—
2011S	—	—	—	3.75

KM# 497a **Weight:** 6.2500 g. **Composition:** 0.9000 Silver, 0.1808 oz. ASW.

Date	Mintage	MS-63	MS-65	Prf-65
2011S	—	—	—	7.75

Acadia National Park

KM# 521 Diameter: 24.3 **Weight:** 5.6700 g. **Composition:** Copper-Nickel Clad Copper

Date	Mintage	MS-63	MS-65	Prf-65
2012P	—	.75	5.00	—
2012D	—	.75	5.00	—
2012S	—	—	—	3.75

KM# 521a Diameter: 24.3 **Weight:** 6.2500 g. **Composition:** 0.9000 Silver, 0.1808 oz. ASW.

Date	Mintage	MS-63	MS-65	Prf-65
2012S	—	—	—	7.75

Chaco Culture National Historic Park

KM# 520 Diameter: 24.3 **Weight:** 5.7100 g. **Composition:** Copper-Nickel Clad Copper

Date	Mintage	MS-63	MS-65	Prf-65
2012P	—	.75	8.00	—
2012D	—	.75	8.00	—
2012S	—	—	—	4.00

KM# 520a Diameter: 24.3 **Weight:** 6.2500 g. **Composition:** 0.9000 Silver, 0.1808 oz. ASW.

Date	Mintage	MS-63	MS-65	Prf-65
2012	—	—	—	7.75

Denali National Park

KM# 523 Diameter: 24.3 **Weight:** 5.6700 g. **Composition:** Copper-Nickel Clad Copper

Date	Mintage	MS-63	MS-65	Prf-65
2012P	—	.75	5.00	—
2012D	—	.75	5.00	—
2012S	—	—	—	3.75

KM# 523a Diameter: 24.3 **Weight:** 6.2500 g. **Composition:** 0.9000 Silver, 0.1808 oz. ASW.

Date	Mintage	MS-63	MS-65	Prf-65
2012	—	—	—	7.75

El Yunque National Forest

KM# 519 Diameter: 24.3 **Weight:** 5.6700 g. **Composition:** Copper-Nickel Clad Copper

Date	Mintage	MS-63	MS-65	Prf-65
2012P	—	.75	5.00	—
2012D	—	.75	5.00	—
2012S	—	—	—	3.75

KM# 519a Diameter: 24.3 **Weight:** 6.2500 g. **Composition:** 0.9000 Silver, 0.1808 oz. ASW.

Date	Mintage	MS-63	MS-65	Prf-65
2012S	—	—	—	7.75

Hawai'i Volcanoes National Park

KM# 522 Diameter: 24.3 **Weight:** 5.6700 g. **Composition:** Copper-Nickel Clad Copper

Date	Mintage	MS-63	MS-65	Prf-65
2012P	—	.75	5.00	—
2012D	—	.75	5.00	—
2012S	—	—	—	3.75

KM# 522a Diameter: 24.3 **Weight:** 6.2500 g. **Composition:** 0.9000 Silver, 0.1808 oz. ASW.

Date	Mintage	MS-63	MS-65	Prf-65
2012	—	—	—	7.75

HALF DOLLAR

Flowing Hair Half Dollar.

KM# 16 Designer: Robert Scot. **Diameter:** 32.5 **Weight:** 13.4800 g. **Composition:** 0.8920 Silver, 0.3866 oz. ASW. **Notes:** The 1795 "recut date" variety had the date cut into the dies twice, so both sets of numbers are visible on the coin. The 1795 "3 leaves" variety has three leaves under each of the eagle's wings on the reverse.

Date	Mintage	G-4	VG-8	F-12	VF-20	XF-40	MS-60
1794	23,464	2,850	5,750	8,850	19,500	37,500	225,000
1795	299,680	1,025	1,450	2,850	4,850	13,850	46,500
1795 recut date	Inc. above	1,040	1,470	2,895	5,200	14,250	46,500
1795 3 leaves	Inc. above	2,600	3,150	5,350	8,350	17,500	59,500

Draped Bust Half Dollar.

Draped bust right. Small eagle.

KM# 26 **Designer:** Robert Scot. **Diameter:** 32.5 **Weight:** 13.4800 g. **Composition:** 0.8920 Silver, 0.3866 oz. ASW.

Date	Mintage	G-4	VG-8	F-12	VF-20	XF-40	MS-60
1796 15 obverse stars	3,918	36,500	46,000	62,000	73,500	118,000	300,000
1796 16 obverse stars	Inc. above	39,500	50,000	67,000	79,500	128,000	320,000
1797	Inc. above	36,700	46,300	62,500	74,300	121,000	310,000

Draped Bust Half Dollar.

Draped bust right, flanked by stars, date at angle below. Heraldic eagle.

KM# 35 **Designer:** Robert Scot. **Diameter:** 32.5 **Weight:** 13.4800 g. **Composition:** 0.8920 Silver, 0.3866 oz. ASW. **Notes:** The two varieties of the 1803 strikes are distinguished by the size of the 3 in the date. The several varieties of the 1806 strikes are distinguished by the style of 6 in the date, size of the stars on the obverse, and whether the stem of the olive branch held by the reverse eagle extends through the claw.

Date	Mintage	G-4	VG-8	F-12	VF-20	XF-40	MS-60
1801	30,289	850	1,250	2,550	4,250	10,500	50,000
1802	29,890	900	1,350	2,750	4,500	11,000	52,000
1803 small 3	188,234	255	325	425	825	2,325	17,250
1803 large 3	Inc. above	195	235	295	715	1,925	14,750
1805	211,722	195	235	295	685	1,865	10,750
1805/4	Inc. above	270	385	570	1,515	3,325	30,000
1806 knobbed 6, large stars	839,576	195	235	295	665	1,825	—
1806 knobbed 6, small stars	Inc. above	195	235	295	680	2,025	13,500
1806 knobbed 6, stem not through claw	Inc. above	20,000	35,000	42,000	57,500	95,000	—
1806 pointed-top 6, stem not through claw	Inc. above	195	235	295	665	1,825	15,250
1806 pointed-top 6, stem through claw	Inc. above	195	235	295	665	1,825	9,750
1806/5	Inc. above	215	270	355	775	2,050	10,075
1806 /inverted 6	Inc. above	255	355	845	1,615	4,375	28,500
1807	301,076	195	235	295	665	1,825	9,750

Capped Bust.

Draped bust left, flanked by stars, date at angle below. "50 C." below eagle.

KM# 37 **Designer:** John Reich. **Diameter:** 32.5 **Weight:** 13.4800 g. **Composition:** 0.8920 Silver, 0.3866 oz. ASW. **Notes:** There are three varieties of the 1807 strikes. Two are distinguished by the size of the stars on the obverse. The third was struck from a reverse die that had a 5 cut over a 2 in the "50C" denomination. Two varieties of the 1811 are distinguished by the size of the 8 in the date. A third has a period between the 8 and second 1 in the date. One variety of the 1817 has a period between the 1 and 7 in the date. Two varieties of the 1820 are distinguished by the size of the date. On the 1823 varieties, the "broken 3" appears to be almost separated in the middle of the 3 in the date; the "patched 3" has the error reparied; the "ugly 3" has portions of its detail missing. The 1827 "curled-2" and "square-2" varieties are distinguished by the numeral's base -- either curled or square. Among the 1828 varieties, "knobbed 2" and "no knob" refers to whether the upper left serif of the digit is rounded. The 1830 varieties are distinguished by the size of the 0 in the date. The four 1834 varieties are distinguished by the sizes of the stars, date and letters in the inscriptions. The 1836 "50/00" variety was struck from a reverse die that has "50" recut over "00" in the denomination.

Date	Mintage	G-4	VG-8	F-12	VF-20	XF-40	AU-50	MS-60	MS-65
1807 small stars	750,500	125	175	350	750	1,900	6,500	9,850	54,000
1807 large stars	Inc. above	115	165	300	660	1,750	5,650	8,900	—
1807 50/20 C.	Inc. above	85.00	125	195	450	1,500	3,150	6,500	30,000
1807 bearded goddess	—	450	775	1,500	3,350	6,850	22,500	—	—
1808	1,368,600	67.00	84.00	97.00	145	350	550	1,800	20,000
1808/7	Inc. above	90.00	110	135	240	440	1,850	5,400	32,500
1809 XXXX edge	Inc. above	80.00	105	135	185	550	950	4,450	—
1809 IIIIII edge	Inc. above	85.00	110	140	210	450	850	4,000	—
1809 Normal edge	1,405,810	65.00	82.00	94.00	140	375	750	1,500	12,650
1810	1,276,276	64.00	81.00	91.00	135	265	650	1,950	19,500
1811 small 8	1,203,644	70.00	80.00	88.00	125	350	800	2,350	28,500
1811 large 8	Inc. above	80.00	107	119	175	425	1,000	2,400	28,500
1811 dated 18.11	Inc. above	78.00	100.00	110	165	650	1,250	3,500	28,500
1812	1,628,059	64.00	81.00	88.00	114	254	440	1,350	13,450
1812/1 small 8	Inc. above	80.00	97.00	119	200	500	1,350	2,500	—
1812/1 large 8	Inc. above	1,650	2,450	4,500	6,750	12,000	21,000	—	—
1812 Single leaf below wing	Inc. above	750	950	1,250	2,400	4,000	6,800	12,500	—
1813	1,241,903	64.00	81.00	88.00	114	184	480	1,400	12,650
1813 50/UNI reverse	1,241,903	74.00	101	124	179	650	1,350	3,650	27,500
1814	1,039,075	64.00	81.00	88.00	124	285	650	1,650	11,450
1814/3	Inc. above	100.00	165	245	300	850	1,650	3,250	—
1814 E/A in States	Inc. above	85.00	110	150	225	385	950	3,950	—
1814 Single leaf below wing	Inc. above	75.00	97.00	124	194	575	1,350	2,250	—
1815/2	47,150	1,100	1,550	2,250	3,650	5,500	7,950	14,500	85,000
1817	1,215,567	67.00	84.00	91.00	119	195	450	1,300	11,650
1817/3	Inc. above	115	175	280	525	1,150	2,350	4,850	—
1817/4	—	60,000	80,000	150,000	200,000	240,000	—	—	—
1817 dated 181.7	Inc. above	100.00	87.00	94.00	104	575	1,350	3,950	27,500
1817 Single leaf below wing	Inc. above	75.00	98.00	124	209	550	2,100	2,750	—
1818	1,960,322	64.00	81.00	88.00	119	225	440	1,350	11,250
1818/7 Large 8	Inc. above	100.00	115	145	190	325	950	1,850	17,500
1818/7 Small 8	Inc. above	98.00	110	130	150	250	850	1,650	16,500
1819	2,208,000	64.00	81.00	88.00	119	175	430	1,350	13,650
1819/8 small 9	Inc. above	75.00	92.00	109	184	290	650	1,900	11,650
1819/8 large 9	Inc. above	85.00	105	150	275	385	850	2,000	25,650
1820 Curl Base 2, small date	751,122	70.00	85.00	96.00	124	285	950	2,250	11,650
1820 Square Base 2 with knob, large date	Inc. above	72.00	90.00	104	139	400	800	2,400	13,150
1820 Square Base 2 without know, large date	Inc. above	72.00	90.00	104	154	475	1,100	2,500	26,500
1820 E's without Serifs	Inc. above	260	450	900	2,150	3,500	5,500	—	—
1820/19 Square Base 2	Inc. above	110	130	165	240	775	1,650	3,250	25,000
1820/19 Curled Base 2	Inc. above	95.00	115	140	200	650	1,450	2,900	24,500
1821	1,305,797	58.00	76.00	89.00	101	185	575	1,350	11,250
1822	1,559,573	58.00	76.00	89.00	101	180	450	1,250	10,950
1822/1	Inc. above	83.00	100.00	129	275	385	800	1,900	—
1823	1,694,200	58.00	76.00	89.00	101	175	425	1,150	11,150
1823 broken 3	Inc. above	68.00	88.00	104	139	500	1,500	3,200	—
1823 patched 3	Inc. above	73.00	94.00	119	159	550	950	2,000	15,150
1823 ugly 3	Inc. above	78.00	99.00	129	184	750	1,750	4,200	—
1824	3,504,954	58.00	76.00	89.00	101	175	360	1,075	10,150
1824/21	Inc. above	63.00	82.00	99.00	126	275	650	2,000	15,650
1824/4	Inc. above	61.00	80.00	91.00	114	225	500	1,350	—
1824 1824/various dates	Inc. above	60.00	79.00	91.00	104	300	875	2,000	15,150
1825	2,943,166	58.00	76.00	89.00	101	175	385	1,050	10,150
1826	4,004,180	58.00	76.00	89.00	101	175	385	1,050	10,150
1827 curled 2	5,493,400	61.00	81.00	99.00	134	185	485	1,400	12,650
1827 square 2	Inc. above	58.00	76.00	89.00	101	175	385	1,050	10,150
1827/6	Inc. above	85.00	95.00	120	155	265	650	1,450	11,650
1828 curled-base 2, no knob	3,075,200	58.00	76.00	89.00	101	175	385	1,150	11,150
1828 curled-base 2, knobbed 2	Inc. above	78.00	99.00	129	184	245	460	1,300	—

Date	Mintage	G-4	VG-8	F-12	VF-20	XF-40	AU-50	MS-60	MS-65
1828 small 8s, square-base 2, large letters	Inc. above	60.00	80.00	99.00	124	175	385	1,050	12,650
1828 small 8s, square-base 2, small letters	Inc. above	58.00	76.00	89.00	106	250	750	1,900	—
1828 large 8s, square-base 2	Inc. above	58.00	76.00	89.00	101	175	385	1,050	11,150
1829	3,712,156	55.00	72.00	79.00	89.00	159	350	1,000	10,150
1829 Large letters	Inc. above	59.00	79.00	89.00	104	180	420	1,250	12,650
1829/7	Inc. above	78.00	99.00	129	174	200	475	1,250	12,650
1830 Small O rev	4,764,800	55.00	72.00	79.00	89.00	159	350	1,000	10,150
1830 Large O	Inc. above	60.00	78.00	88.00	109	180	560	2,000	13,150
1830 Large letter rev	Inc. above	1,500	2,250	3,000	3,750	4,800	9,800	—	—
1831	5,873,660	55.00	72.00	79.00	89.00	159	350	1,000	10,150
1832 small letters	4,797,000	55.00	72.00	79.00	89.00	159	350	1,000	10,150
1832 large letters	Inc. above	58.00	75.00	85.00	99.00	175	410	1,350	12,650
1833	5,206,000	55.00	72.00	79.00	89.00	159	360	1,000	10,150
1834 small date, large stars, small letters	6,412,004	55.00	74.00	81.00	91.00	163	360	1,025	10,400
1834 small date, small stars, small letters	Inc. above	55.00	74.00	81.00	9.00	163	360	1,025	10,400
1834 large date, small letters	Inc. above	55.00	74.00	81.00	91.00	163	360	1,025	10,400
1834 large date, large letters	Inc. above	55.00	72.00	79.00	89.00	159	350	1,000	10,150
1835	5,352,006	55.00	72.00	79.00	89.00	159	350	1,000	10,150
1836	6,545,000	55.00	72.00	79.00	89.00	159	350	1,000	10,150
1836	Inc. above	80.00	95.00	120	265	450	1,000	2,500	—
1836 50/00	Inc. above	93.00	112	129	165	300	800	1,750	19,500

Bust Half Dollar.

Draped bust left, flanked by stars, date at angle below. "50 Cents" below eagle.

KM# 58 **Designer:** Christian Gobrecht. **Diameter:** 30 **Weight:** 13.4800 g. **Composition:** 0.8920 Silver, 0.3866 oz. ASW.

Date	Mintage	G-4	VG-8	F-12	VF-20	XF-40	AU-50	MS-60	MS-65
1836	1,200	850	1,075	1,600	2,000	3,350	4,400	8,850	66,500
1837	3,629,820	58.00	73.00	83.00	115	200	400	1,160	23,500

Bust Half Dollar.

Draped bust left, flanked by stars, date at angle below. "50 Cents" below eagle.

KM# 58a **Designer:** Christian Gobrecht. **Diameter:** 30 **Weight:** 13.3600 g. **Composition:** 0.9000 Silver, 0.3866 oz. ASW.

Date	Mintage	G-4	VG-8	F-12	VF-20	XF-40	AU-50	MS-60	MS-65
1837	3,629,820	58.00	73.00	80.00	115	200	345	1,100	24,500

Bust Half Dollar.

Draped bust left, flanked by stars, date below. HALF DOL. below eagle.

KM# 65 **Designer:** Christian Gobrecht. **Diameter:** 30 **Weight:** 13.3600 g. **Composition:** 0.9000 Silver, 0.3866 oz. ASW.

Date	Mintage	G-4	VG-8	F-12	VF-20	XF-40	AU-50	MS-60	MS-65
1838	3,546,000	58.00	70.00	82.00	120	205	420	1,200	17,500
1838O proof only	Est. 20	—	—	—	—	250,000	300,000	—	—
1839	1,392,976	60.00	76.00	92.00	130	245	410	1,350	39,500
1839O	116,000	240	325	425	650	1,350	2,350	4,500	46,500

HALF DOLLAR

Seated Liberty Half Dollar.

Seated Liberty, date below. "Half Dol." below eagle.

KM# 68 Designer: Christian Gobrecht. **Diameter:** 30.6 **Weight:** 13.3600 g. **Composition:** 0.9000 Silver, 0.3866 oz. ASW.

Date	Mintage	G-4	VG-8	F-12	VF-20	XF-40	AU-50	MS-60	MS-65
1839 no drapery from elbow	Inc. above	45.00	90.00	365	575	1,200	2,450	6,250	200,000
1839 drapery	Inc. above	50.00	57.00	75.50	110	185	2,550	1,000	25,000
1840 small letters	1,435,008	52.00	57.00	70.00	108	170	325	600	7,500
1840 reverse 1838	Inc. above	150	175	275	350	850	1,350	3,400	30,000
1840O	855,100	51.00	58.00	75.50	114	215	275	450	—
1841	310,000	52.00	65.00	110	165	235	325	1,200	6,850
1841O	401,000	50.00	65.00	75.00	106	265	2,515	600	7,000
1842 small date	2,012,764	48.00	55.00	80.00	135	200	325	1,300	13,500
1842 medium date	Inc. above	44.00	54.00	74.50	88.00	147	2,505	750	8,800
1842O small date	957,000	650	950	1,400	2,450	4,650	7,750	16,500	—
1842O medium date	Inc. above	42.00	58.00	75.50	85.00	175	500	1,250	10,500
1843	3,844,000	44.00	53.00	71.50	89.00	142	2,510	500	4,500
1843O	2,268,000	59.00	67.00	73.50	89.00	1,100	2,525	550	—
1844	1,766,000	49.00	55.00	71.50	65.00	160	210	440	4,500
1844O	2,005,000	46.00	55.00	71.50	70.00	165	225	550	—
1844/1844O	Inc. above	500	850	1,150	1,400	3,000	5,750	10,000	—
1845	589,000	49.00	57.00	79.50	125	220	325	850	12,000
1845O	2,094,000	46.00	55.00	71.50	70.00	165	240	550	9,400
1845O no drapery	Inc. above	45.00	70.00	100.00	165	350	375	750	—
1846 medium date	2,210,000	46.00	55.00	71.50	70.00	175	200	500	9,000
1846 tall date	Inc. above	47.00	61.00	90.50	135	350	250	650	12,000
1846 /horizontal 6	Inc. above	160	250	325	450	675	1,000	2,500	—
1846O medium date	2,304,000	49.00	57.00	79.50	70.00	220	225	550	12,000
1846O tall date	Inc. above	200	325	425	675	1,750	2,000	6,650	—
1847/1846	1,156,000	2,000	2,750	4,000	5,500	10,000	12,500	21,000	—
1847	Inc. above	44.00	59.00	74.50	91.00	137	2,500	480	9,000
1847O	2,584,000	46.00	55.00	71.50	89.00	152	2,560	640	7,000
1848	580,000	44.00	75.00	110	185	275	485	1,000	9,000
1848O	3,180,000	46.00	55.00	71.50	75.00	175	285	750	9,000
1849	1,252,000	49.00	59.00	75.50	91.00	140	365	1,250	15,000
1849O	2,310,000	46.00	55.00	71.50	70.00	175	250	650	9,000
1850	227,000	275	325	450	585	700	1,000	1,500	—
1850O	2,456,000	50.00	57.00	73.50	80.00	175	275	650	9,000
1851	200,750	335	475	550	850	1,350	1,200	2,250	—
1851O	402,000	49.00	55.00	67.50	120	225	300	700	9,000
1852	77,130	425	500	700	925	1,100	1,350	1,700	—
1852O	144,000	70.00	125	210	350	750	1,250	3,850	26,000
1853O mintage unrecorded	—	—	250,000	—	—	600,000	—	—	—

Note: 1853O, Eliasberg Sale, 1997, VG-8, $154,000.

Seated Liberty Half Dollar.

Seated Liberty, arrows at date. Rays around eagle.

KM# 79 Designer: Christian Gobrecht. **Weight:** 12.4400 g. **Composition:** 0.9000 Silver, 0.3599 oz. ASW.

Date	Mintage	G-4	VG-8	F-12	VF-20	XF-40	AU-50	MS-60	MS-65	Prf-65
1853	3,532,708	36.50	48.00	72.00	97.50	265	610	1,500	24,500	175,000
1853O	1,328,000	41.50	56.50	77.00	124.5	285	695	2,250	29,500	—

Seated Liberty Half Dollar.

Seated Liberty, arrows at date. HALF DOL. below eagle.

KM# 82 **Designer:** Christian Gobrecht. **Weight:** 12.4400 g. **Composition:** 0.9000 Silver, 0.3599 oz. ASW.

Date	Mintage	G-4	VG-8	F-12	VF-20	XF-40	AU-50	MS-60	MS-65	Prf-65
1854	2,982,000	36.50	48.00	60.00	73.50	135	270	675	8,000	37,500
1854O	5,240,000	36.50	48.00	60.00	73.50	135	270	600	8,000	—
1855	759,500	38.50	50.00	64.00	87.00	167	325	700	9,000	39,500
1855/4	Inc. above	65.00	75.00	135	195	400	600	2,000	17,500	37,000
1855O	3,688,000	39.50	55.00	60.00	73.50	135	270	650	8,000	—
1855S	129,950	350	575	800	1,600	3,650	6,850	19,500	—	—

Seated Liberty Half Dollar.

Seated Liberty, date below. HALF DOL. below eagle.

KM# A68 **Designer:** Christian Gobrecht. **Weight:** 12.4400 g. **Composition:** 0.9000 Silver, 0.3599 oz. ASW.

Date	Mintage	G-4	VG-8	F-12	VF-20	XF-40	AU-50	MS-60	MS-65	Prf-65
1856O	2,658,000	44.00	52.00	67.50	80.00	130	190	385	12,500	—
1856	938,000	44.00	52.00	67.50	80.00	130	215	425	6,500	12,500
1856S	211,000	85.00	110	165	275	750	1,250	3,500	19,000	—
1857	1,988,000	44.00	52.00	67.50	80.00	120	190	385	5,150	12,500
1857O	818,000	38.00	55.00	70.50	85.00	150	275	885	12,500	—
1857S	158,000	90.00	125	185	375	1,050	975	3,500	19,000	—
1858	4,226,000	44.00	52.00	67.50	80.00	120	215	385	6,500	12,500
1858O	7,294,000	44.00	52.00	67.50	80.00	120	215	385	12,500	—
1858S	476,000	50.00	65.00	85.00	140	365	400	950	12,500	—
1859	748,000	40.00	57.00	71.50	90.00	130	200	650	6,600	5,500
1859O	2,834,000	44.00	52.00	67.50	80.00	120	215	450	6,500	—
1859S	566,000	45.00	58.00	79.50	100.00	275	375	750	12,500	—
1860	303,700	48.00	56.00	71.50	100.00	150	350	1,000	6,500	5,500
1860O	1,290,000	44.00	52.00	67.50	80.00	125	230	450	5,150	—
1860S	472,000	49.00	57.00	72.50	88.00	215	245	850	12,500	—
1861	2,888,400	44.00	55.00	67.50	80.00	125	190	440	5,150	5,500
1861O	2,532,633	52.00	59.00	72.50	88.00	175	235	450	5,150	—
1861O CSA Obv, cracked die	Inc. above	150	350	500	750	1,200	1,750	—	—	—
1861S	939,500	49.00	60.00	74.50	93.00	165	195	975	9,500	—
1862	253,550	56.00	65.00	92.50	120	235	295	750	5,150	5,500
1862S	1,352,000	44.00	59.00	67.50	80.00	120	195	460	9,000	—
1863	503,660	59.00	73.00	92.50	110	190	250	750	5,150	5,500
1863S	916,000	52.00	69.00	82.50	90.00	220	195	460	9,000	—
1864	379,570	64.00	75.00	97.50	150	275	250	750	5,150	5,500
1864S	658,000	56.00	69.00	81.50	125	250	215	675	9,000	—
1865	511,900	48.00	71.00	90.50	100.00	265	275	750	5,150	5,500
1865S	675,000	56.00	63.00	82.50	100.00	250	235	500	9,000	—
1866 proof, unique	—	—	—	—	—	—	—	—	—	—
1866S	60,000	485	650	950	1,250	2,550	3,350	5,400	68,000	—

Seated Liberty Half Dollar.

Seated Liberty, date below. IN GOD WE TRUST above eagle.

KM# 99 **Designer:** Christian Gobrecht. **Weight:** 12.4400 g. **Composition:** 0.9000 Silver, 0.3599 oz. ASW.

HALF DOLLAR

Date	Mintage	G-4	VG-8	F-12	VF-20	XF-40	AU-50	MS-60	MS-65	Prf-65
1866	745,625	51.50	64.50	82.00	95.00	175	225	350	4,800	3,750
1866S	994,000	48.50	62.50	80.00	85.00	200	275	650	5,000	—
1867	449,925	53.50	67.50	88.00	130	275	250	350	4,800	3,750
1867S	1,196,000	47.50	61.50	70.00	70.00	200	250	350	7,000	—
1868	418,200	58.50	70.00	105	185	275	300	525	7,100	3,750
1868S	1,160,000	43.50	51.50	70.00	70.00	175	250	350	7,000	—
1869	795,900	48.50	64.50	78.00	85.00	165	190	385	4,600	3,750
1869S	656,000	50.50	66.50	80.00	95.00	210	265	600	7,000	—
1870	634,900	47.50	54.40	70.00	80.00	165	250	475	7,000	3,750
1870CC	54,617	1,200	1,850	4,500	7,250	16,000	30,000	100,000	—	—
1870S	1,004,000	43.50	54.50	72.00	95.00	200	275	575	7,000	—
1871	1,204,560	40.50	51.50	71.00	75.00	160	165	350	7,000	3,750
1871CC	153,950	325	400	600	1,275	2,850	10,000	15,000	—	—
1871S	2,178,000	42.50	50.50	68.00	70.00	175	215	400	7,000	—
1872	881,550	44.50	59.50	68.00	75.00	185	195	430	2,850	3,750
1872CC	272,000	110	175	325	750	2,100	4,000	8,000	50,000	—
1872S	580,000	48.50	60.50	86.00	135	300	375	975	7,000	—
1873 closed 3	801,800	43.50	57.50	83.00	115	165	250	545	4,500	3,750
1873 open 3	Inc. above	3,450	4,450	5,600	6,600	7,750	13,500	30,000	—	—
1873CC	122,500	225	325	550	950	2,350	6,500	12,000	80,000	—
1873S no arrows	5,000	—	—	—	—	—	—	—	—	—

Note: 1873S no arrows, no specimens known to survive.

Seated Liberty Half Dollar.

Seated Liberty, arrows at date. IN GOD WE TRUST above eagle.

KM# 107 **Designer:** Christian Gobrecht. **Weight:** 12.5000 g. **Composition:** 0.9000 Silver, 0.3617 oz. ASW.

Date	Mintage	G-4	VG-8	F-12	VF-20	XF-40	AU-50	MS-60	MS-65	Prf-65
1873	1,815,700	48.00	67.00	85.00	124	235	400	850	17,500	9,000
1873CC	214,560	150	400	650	1,100	2,350	2,400	5,700	42,000	—
1873S	233,000	55.00	110	150	245	475	675	2,200	40,000	—
1874	2,360,300	44.00	56.00	72.00	90.00	215	440	900	15,500	9,000
1874CC	59,000	500	1,000	2,200	3,250	5,400	5,600	10,500	—	—
1874S	394,000	43.00	65.00	85.00	185	365	685	1,850	20,000	—

Seated Liberty Half Dollar.

Seated Liberty, date below. IN GOD WE TRUST above eagle.

KM# A99 **Designer:** Christian Gobrecht. **Weight:** 12.5000 g. **Composition:** 0.9000 Silver, 0.3617 oz. ASW.

Date	Mintage	G-4	VG-8	F-12	VF-20	XF-40	AU-50	MS-60	MS-65	Prf-65
1875	6,027,500	38.50	47.50	66.00	88.00	128	2,465	6,310	3,500	3,375
1875CC	1,008,000	50.00	80.00	110	225	325	325	650	8,350	—
1875S	3,200,000	38.50	47.50	66.00	95.00	130	2,450	6,250	2,700	—
1876	8,419,150	36.50	47.50	66.00	88.00	118	2,450	6,250	5,300	3,775
1876S	4,528,000	36.50	47.50	66.00	88.00	118	2,450	6,250	2,700	—
1876CC	1,956,000	50.00	60.00	75.00	115	265	275	560	4,200	—
1877	8,304,510	36.50	47.50	66.00	88.00	118	2,450	6,250	2,700	3,825
1877CC	1,420,000	50.00	68.00	100.00	125	265	275	630	3,250	—
1877S	5,356,000	36.50	47.50	66.00	88.00	118	2,450	6,250	2,700	—
1878	1,378,400	38.50	55.50	86.00	112	150	2,450	425	3,650	3,900
1878CC	62,000	750	1,150	2,000	2,350	3,150	4,850	7,000	43,500	—
1878S	12,000	28,500	42,000	47,500	58,000	60,000	85,000	70,000	175,000	—
1879	5,900	275	310	375	450	525	575	700	3,650	3,150
1880	9,755	260	300	350	410	500	535	700	3,750	3,150
1881	10,975	270	325	345	400	455	565	700	4,000	3,150
1882	5,500	340	410	460	600	650	600	750	3,850	3,150
1883	9,039	325	390	480	560	625	575	775	3,950	3,150
1884	5,275	385	425	500	610	700	635	800	3,850	3,150

Date	Mintage	G-4	VG-8	F-12	VF-20	XF-40	AU-50	MS-60	MS-65	Prf-65
1885	6,130	390	450	485	575	660	700	825	3,850	3,150
1886	5,886	400	550	630	725	850	875	1,000	3,900	3,150
1887	5,710	475	600	700	800	875	950	1,100	3,900	3,150
1888	12,833	280	310	365	410	525	550	800	3,900	3,150
1889	12,711	275	315	400	465	510	550	800	3,900	3,150
1890	12,590	275	310	365	415	500	550	800	3,850	3,150
1891	200,600	55.00	75.00	94.00	125	155	240	480	3,850	3,150

HALF DOLLAR

Barber Half Dollar.

Laureate head right, flanked by stars, date below. Heraldic eagle.

KM# 116 **Designer:** Charles E. Barber. **Diameter:** 30.6 **Weight:** 12.5000 g. **Composition:** 0.9000 Silver, 0.3617 oz. ASW.

Date	Mintage	G-4	VG-8	F-12	VF-20	XF-40	AU-50	MS-60	MS-65	Prf-65
1892	935,245	29.50	44.00	73.50	120	195	385	505	3,150	3,750
1892O	390,000	310	420	515	600	630	690	850	4,350	—
1892O micro O	Inc. above	2,000	3,750	4,500	7,000	10,000	17,500	24,000	64,000	—
1892S	1,029,028	250	330	425	550	600	700	985	4,850	—
1893	1,826,792	20.00	36.00	78.00	150	205	385	540	5,250	3,750
1893O	1,389,000	36.00	70.00	130	230	360	435	635	9,650	—
1893S	740,000	165	240	325	525	595	675	1,275	25,000	—
1894	1,148,972	32.50	54.00	115	210	280	395	540	3,850	3,750
1894O	2,138,000	22.00	36.00	95.00	180	310	400	555	6,250	—
1894S	4,048,690	22.00	28.00	67.00	125	230	400	575	9,850	—
1895	1,835,218	22.00	28.00	72.00	165	225	400	595	3,650	3,750
1895O	1,766,000	23.00	43.00	110	195	285	425	650	6,950	—
1895S	1,108,086	32.00	56.00	130	235	315	440	635	8,250	—
1896	950,762	22.50	30.00	88.00	160	265	395	625	5,450	3,750
1896O	924,000	45.00	60.00	215	290	510	885	1,750	19,500	—
1896S	1,140,948	120	145	210	350	515	800	1,575	10,500	—
1897	2,480,731	19.80	21.00	47.50	105	195	385	520	3,950	3,750
1897O	632,000	170	230	485	835	1,050	1,350	1,850	9,650	—
1897S	933,900	155	230	385	560	840	1,050	1,650	7,350	—
1898	2,956,735	19.80	21.00	38.50	94.00	185	375	520	3,500	3,750
1898O	874,000	37.50	95.00	240	400	525	640	1,250	9,450	—
1898S	2,358,550	28.50	53.00	87.50	175	340	440	985	10,250	—
1899	5,538,846	19.00	21.00	39.50	98.00	185	405	525	3,950	3,750
1899O	1,724,000	26.00	38.00	85.00	180	300	410	700	8,150	—
1899S	1,686,411	25.00	45.00	92.00	155	220	395	660	6,900	—
1900	4,762,912	20.30	22.00	38.50	95.00	190	375	515	3,950	3,750
1900O	2,744,000	19.00	23.00	62.00	175	290	400	900	15,500	—
1900S	2,560,322	19.00	22.00	46.50	98.00	215	375	640	9,500	—
1901	4,268,813	19.00	23.00	38.50	94.00	195	385	550	4,250	3,750
1901O	1,124,000	19.00	30.00	85.00	235	365	500	1,350	14,850	—
1901S	847,044	34.00	55.00	175	375	675	1,050	1,950	16,500	—
1902	4,922,777	18.80	19.00	38.50	90.00	190	375	505	4,450	3,750
1902O	2,526,000	20.30	22.00	55.00	115	230	395	775	10,500	—
1902S	1,460,670	20.80	25.00	66.00	165	265	420	750	7,750	—
1903	2,278,755	20.30	22.00	47.50	105	205	375	500	7,650	3,750
1903O	2,100,000	19.80	20.00	55.00	135	215	385	665	9,500	—
1903S	1,920,772	20.00	22.00	60.00	145	265	400	675	5,350	—
1904	2,992,670	19.80	21.00	35.00	95.00	190	385	510	4,650	3,750
1904O	1,117,600	22.00	33.00	90.00	235	385	610	1,375	12,500	—
1904S	553,038	42.00	95.00	300	700	1,250	2,450	9,850	46,000	—
1905	662,727	23.50	34.00	95.00	195	270	410	625	6,600	3,750
1905O	505,000	30.00	45.00	130	235	340	460	760	5,200	—
1905S	2,494,000	20.00	24.00	50.00	130	230	410	615	9,350	—
1906	2,638,675	18.80	19.00	32.00	85.00	185	385	500	3,300	3,750
1906D	4,028,000	18.80	19.00	35.00	89.00	185	375	495	3,800	—
1906O	2,446,000	18.80	19.00	44.00	205	195	400	600	6,350	—
1906S	1,740,154	20.30	21.00	57.50	118	220	420	590	5,750	—
1907	2,598,575	18.80	19.00	30.00	83.00	185	375	495	3,250	3,750
1907D	3,856,000	18.80	19.00	30.00	75.00	185	375	495	3,000	—
1907O	3,946,000	18.80	19.00	32.00	89.00	190	375	535	3,100	—
1907S	1,250,000	22.00	25.00	85.00	170	365	665	1,275	12,500	—
1908	1,354,545	18.80	19.00	30.00	85.00	185	375	495	3,300	3,750
1908D	3,280,000	18.80	19.00	30.00	80.00	185	375	495	3,000	—
1908O	5,360,000	18.80	19.00	30.00	89.00	185	385	540	3,000	—
1908S	1,644,828	20.30	25.00	72.00	165	285	440	875	6,350	—
1909	2,368,650	19.80	21.00	32.00	83.00	185	375	565	3,000	3,750

Date	Mintage	G-4	VG-8	F-12	VF-20	XF-40	AU-50	MS-60	MS-65	Prf-65
1909O	925,400	23.10	24.00	56.00	150	315	525	775	3,950	—
1909S	1,764,000	19.10	20.00	37.50	100.00	195	395	600	3,750	—
1910	418,551	20.00	30.00	95.00	180	330	485	610	3,900	3,750
1910S	1,948,000	22.30	24.00	36.00	100.00	200	395	640	6,650	—
1911	1,406,543	18.80	19.00	30.00	83.00	185	375	495	3,000	3,750
1911D	695,080	19.80	21.00	40.00	91.00	195	385	565	3,950	—
1911S	1,272,000	20.30	21.00	42.00	98.00	185	385	580	5,950	—
1912	1,550,700	18.80	19.00	30.00	83.00	185	375	495	3,500	3,750
1912D	2,300,800	18.80	19.00	30.00	81.00	185	375	495	3,000	—
1912S	1,370,000	21.10	22.00	43.50	100.00	210	375	535	4,600	—
1913	188,627	77.00	88.00	235	435	615	875	1,225	4,950	3,900
1913D	534,000	19.00	22.00	44.00	100.00	200	395	515	4,850	—
1913S	604,000	21.00	25.00	53.50	110	235	425	755	4,450	—
1914	124,610	145	180	335	575	775	1,025	1,475	8,500	4,100
1914S	992,000	20.80	23.00	41.00	98.00	190	395	575	4,650	—
1915	138,450	112	168	285	380	575	920	1,350	6,350	4,100
1915D	1,170,400	18.80	19.00	30.00	80.00	185	375	495	3,000	—
1915S	1,604,000	22.30	23.00	43.50	94.00	200	390	510	3,000	—

HALF DOLLAR

Walking Liberty Half Dollar.

Liberty walking left wearing U.S. flag gown, sunrise at left. Eagle advancing left.

KM# 142 Designer: Adolph A. Weinman. **Diameter:** 30.6 **Weight:** 12.5000 g. **Composition:** 0.9000 Silver, 0.3617 oz. ASW. **Notes:** The mint mark appears on the obverse below the word "Trust" on 1916 and some 1917 issues. Starting with some 1917 issues and continuing through the remainder of the series, the mint mark was changed to the reverse, at about the 8 o'clock position near the rim.

Reverse mint mark
1917-1947

Obverse mint mark
1916-1917

Date	Mintage	G-4	VG-8	F-12	VF-20	XF-40	AU-50	MS-60	MS-65	Prf-65
1916	608,000	47.00	55.00	95.00	170	240	275	345	1,950	—
1916D	1,014,400	48.50	55.00	80.00	135	220	255	360	2,500	—
1916S	508,000	108	135	280	440	600	720	1,050	6,250	—
1917	12,292,000	14.20	14.50	15.20	19.50	42.00	72.00	130	1,050	—
1917D obv. mint mark	765,400	23.50	33.00	80.00	155	235	335	625	7,900	—
1917S obv. mint mark	952,000	27.00	44.00	135	365	700	1,200	2,300	22,500	—
1917D rev. mint mark	1,940,000	14.20	14.50	45.00	135	275	555	940	18,500	—
1917S rev. mint mark	5,554,000	14.20	14.50	16.50	32.00	65.00	155	330	13,850	—
1918	6,634,000	14.20	14.50	15.50	64.00	150	265	565	3,800	—
1918D	3,853,040	14.20	14.50	35.00	90.00	225	500	1,300	24,500	—
1918S	10,282,000	14.20	14.50	16.00	34.00	60.00	190	485	17,750	—
1919	962,000	26.00	32.50	78.50	265	535	885	1,325	7,750	—
1919D	1,165,000	25.00	38.50	95.00	320	765	1,750	5,950	130,000	—
1919S	1,552,000	17.50	28.50	72.00	310	825	1,750	3,300	20,000	—
1920	6,372,000	14.20	14.50	15.50	42.00	75.00	155	330	5,250	—
1920D	1,551,000	14.20	14.50	65.00	240	460	920	1,485	17,500	—
1920S	4,624,000	14.20	14.50	19.00	78.00	235	510	850	14,500	—
1921	246,000	165	210	350	750	1,575	2,650	4,500	19,500	—
1921D	208,000	310	370	550	950	2,200	3,150	5,650	29,500	—
1921S	548,000	45.00	65.00	210	750	4,850	7,950	12,950	130,000	—
1923S	2,178,000	14.20	14.50	27.50	110	295	650	1,375	16,500	—
1927S	2,392,000	14.50	14.80	16.50	46.00	165	425	990	9,750	—
1928S Large S	1,940,000	14.50	17.50	28.00	110	325	600	1,650	—	—
1928S Small S	Inc. above	14.20	14.50	18.50	66.00	195	450	985	10,750	—
1929D	1,001,200	14.20	14.50	17.50	32.00	98.00	195	390	3,350	—
1929S	1,902,000	14.20	14.50	15.50	28.50	115	220	400	3,750	—
1933S	1,786,000	14.20	14.50	17.60	20.00	58.00	240	590	4,500	—
1934	6,964,000	14.00	14.50	15.20	15.80	17.60	25.00	85.00	565	—
1934D	2,361,400	14.20	14.90	18.90	17.50	36.00	88.00	150	1,625	—
1934S	3,652,000	14.00	14.70	15.80	18.00	30.00	100.00	385	4,800	—
1935	9,162,000	14.00	14.50	15.20	15.80	17.76	21.50	45.00	365	—
1935D	3,003,800	14.00	14.70	15.80	16.20	33.00	66.00	140	2,450	—
1935S	3,854,000	14.00	14.70	15.60	13.50	32.00	95.00	285	2,850	—
1936	12,617,901	14.00	14.50	15.20	15.80	17.76	21.00	37.50	265	6,600
1936S	3,884,000	14.00	14.70	15.60	16.00	21.50	58.00	132	1,000	—
1936D	4,252,400	14.00	14.70	15.60	16.00	20.00	52.00	78.00	665	—
1937	9,527,728	14.00	14.50	15.20	15.80	17.76	22.00	38.00	285	1,700

Date	Mintage	G-4	VG-8	F-12	VF-20	XF-40	AU-50	MS-60	MS-65	Prf-65
1937D	1,676,000	14.00	14.70	17.20	17.60	33.50	105	220	965	—
1937S	2,090,000	14.00	14.70	15.80	17.20	25.50	62.00	168	785	—
1938	4,118,152	14.00	14.70	15.60	16.20	19.21	38.00	66.00	460	1,275
1938D	491,600	70.00	75.00	100.00	125	185	250	475	1,750	—
1939	6,820,808	14.00	14.30	15.00	15.80	17.76	22.00	41.00	210	1,150
1939D	4,267,800	14.00	14.50	15.20	16.80	18.51	26.00	45.00	225	—
1939S	2,552,000	14.00	14.70	15.60	16.00	25.00	76.00	145	375	—
1940	9,167,279	14.00	14.30	15.00	15.40	16.80	17.60	31.00	185	1,000
1940S	4,550,000	14.00	14.50	15.20	15.80	17.76	21.00	50.00	315	—
1941	24,207,412	14.00	14.30	15.00	15.36	16.10	17.60	30.00	155	850
1941D	11,248,400	14.00	14.50	15.20	15.80	16.20	18.00	37.50	180	—
1941S	8,098,000	14.00	14.50	15.20	15.80	19.60	27.50	70.00	925	—
1942	47,839,120	14.00	14.30	15.00	15.36	15.80	17.60	30.00	130	850
1942D	10,973,800	14.00	14.50	15.20	15.80	16.20	19.00	37.00	315	—
1942S	12,708,000	14.00	14.50	15.20	15.80	16.20	18.60	37.00	475	—
1943	53,190,000	14.00	14.30	15.00	15.36	16.10	17.60	30.00	140	—
1943D	11,346,000	14.00	14.50	15.20	15.80	16.20	25.00	42.00	240	—
1943D Double Die Obverse	—	14.20	15.00	17.00	19.00	22.00	30.00	55.00	450	—
1943S	13,450,000	14.00	14.50	15.20	15.80	16.20	18.50	42.00	290	—
1944	28,206,000	14.00	14.30	15.00	15.36	16.10	17.60	30.00	170	—
1944D	9,769,000	14.00	14.50	15.20	15.80	16.20	20.00	37.00	165	—
1944S	8,904,000	14.00	14.50	15.20	15.80	16.20	18.00	36.00	500	—
1945	31,502,000	14.00	14.30	15.00	15.36	16.10	17.60	30.00	130	—
1945D	9,966,800	14.00	14.50	15.20	15.80	16.20	19.00	36.00	130	—
1945S	10,156,000	14.00	14.50	15.20	15.80	16.20	17.50	36.00	135	—
1946	12,118,000	14.00	14.30	15.00	15.36	16.10	17.60	30.00	155	—
1946 Double Die Reverse	Inc. above	16.00	24.00	35.00	50.00	85.00	175	325	2,750	—
1946D	2,151,000	14.00	14.70	15.20	15.80	25.50	38.50	47.50	125	—
1946S	3,724,000	14.00	14.50	15.20	15.80	16.90	19.00	43.50	175	—
1947	4,094,000	14.00	14.30	15.00	15.80	16.20	22.00	50.00	220	—
1947D	3,900,600	14.00	14.70	15.20	15.80	16.20	31.50	52.50	145	—

Franklin Half Dollar.

Franklin bust right. Liberty Bell, small eagle at right.

KM# 199 **Designer:** John R. Sinnock. **Diameter:** 30.6 **Weight:** 12.5000 g. **Composition:** 0.9000 Silver, 0.3617 oz. ASW.

Mint mark

Date	Mintage	G-4	VG-8	F-12	VF-20	XF-40	AU-50	MS-60	MS-65	-65FBL	-65CAM
1948	3,006,814	—	13.80	13.90	14.50	15.10	15.30	17.00	75.00	190	—
1948D	4,028,600	—	13.80	13.90	14.50	14.60	15.00	16.00	125	260	—
1949	5,614,000	—	—	—	—	15.60	14.00	38.50	120	250	—
1949D	4,120,600	—	—	—	14.30	16.60	25.00	43.50	900	1,750	—
1949S	3,744,000	—	—	—	14.50	16.50	30.00	62.50	160	700	—
1950	7,793,509	—	—	—	—	13.90	13.00	26.00	110	285	2,000
1950D	8,031,600	—	—	—	—	14.90	15.10	22.00	425	900	—
1951	16,859,602	—	—	—	—	13.60	16.60	17.60	75.00	340	1,450
1951D	9,475,200	—	—	—	—	17.90	17.50	26.00	170	540	—
1951S	13,696,000	—	—	—	13.90	14.60	15.00	23.50	125	750	—
1952	21,274,073	—	—	—	—	13.80	16.60	17.00	70.00	210	775
1952D	25,395,600	—	—	—	—	13.80	16.60	17.00	130	450	—
1952S	5,526,000	—	—	13.90	16.50	16.00	32.00	52.00	140	1,500	—
1953	2,796,920	—	—	13.90	14.00	14.40	16.00	25.00	140	1,000	475
1953D	20,900,400	—	—	—	—	13.60	13.80	14.00	150	400	—
1953S	4,148,000	—	—	—	13.90	14.60	18.50	25.00	65.00	16,000	—
1954	13,421,503	—	—	—	—	13.60	14.60	14.80	75.00	225	175
1954D	25,445,580	—	—	—	—	13.60	14.60	14.80	110	235	—
1954S	4,993,400	—	—	—	—	14.00	14.60	15.10	42.00	440	—
1955	2,876,381	—	15.50	16.00	17.50	18.00	18.50	20.00	70.00	140	120
1955 Bugs Bunny	Inc. above	—	20.00	22.00	23.00	25.00	26.00	28.00	120	750	—
1956 Type 1 rev.	4,701,384	—	13.50	13.60	13.70	14.00	14.80	15.40	55.00	125	300
1956 Type 2 rev.	Inc. above	—	—	—	—	—	—	—	—	—	40.00
1957 Type 1 rev.	6,361,952	—	—	—	—	13.60	14.80	15.70	63.00	95.00	55.00
1957 Type 2 rev.	Inc. above	—	—	—	—	—	—	—	—	—	—
1957D	19,966,850	—	—	—	—	13.60	14.80	15.50	60.00	100.00	—

Date	Mintage	G-4	VG-8	F-12	VF-20	XF-40	AU-50	MS-60	MS-65	-65FBL	-65CAM
1958 Type 1 rev.	4,917,652	—	—	—	—	13.60	14.80	15.50	55.00	110	60.00
1958 Type 2 rev.	Inc. above	—	—	—	—	14.30	20.00	26.00	—	—	—
1958D	23,962,412	—	—	—	—	13.60	14.80	15.50	55.00	80.00	—
1959 Type 1 rev.	7,349,291	—	—	—	—	13.60	14.80	15.50	110	250	75.00
1959 Type 2 rev.	Inc. above	—	—	—	—	14.10	16.00	30.00	115	—	—
1959D	13,053,750	—	—	—	—	13.60	14.80	15.50	125	215	—
1960 Type 1 rev.	7,715,602	—	—	—	—	13.60	14.80	15.50	110	340	45.00
1960 Type 2 rev.	Inc. above	—	—	—	—	—	—	—	—	—	—
1960D	18,215,812	—	—	—	—	13.60	14.80	15.50	400	1,350	—
1961 Type 1 rev.	11,318,244	—	—	—	—	13.60	14.80	15.50	125	1,300	40.00
1961 Type 2 rev.	Inc. above	—	—	—	—	25.00	—	—	—	—	—
1961 Double die rev.	Inc. above	—	—	—	—	—	—	—	—	—	3,500
1961D	20,276,442	—	—	—	—	13.60	14.80	15.50	155	875	—
1962 Type 1 rev.	12,932,019	—	—	—	—	13.60	14.80	15.50	145	1,850	35.00
1962 Type 2 rev.	Inc. above	—	—	—	—	—	—	—	—	—	—
1962D	35,473,281	—	—	—	—	13.60	14.80	15.50	175	800	—
1963 Type 1 rev.	25,239,645	—	—	—	—	13.60	14.80	15.50	55.00	1,200	35.00
1963 Type 2 rev.	Inc. above	—	—	—	—	—	—	—	—	—	—
1963D	67,069,292	—	—	—	—	13.60	14.80	15.50	75.00	165	—

Kennedy Half Dollar.

KM# 202 Obv. Designer: Gilroy Roberts. **Rev. Designer:** Frank Gasparro. **Diameter:** 30.6 **Weight:** 12.5000 g. **Composition:** 0.9000 Silver, 0.3617 oz. ASW.

Mint mark 1964

Date	Mintage	XF-40	MS-60	MS-65	Prf-65
1964	277,254,766	10.10	10.30	22.00	15.00
1964 Accented Hair	Inc. above	—	—	—	40.00
1964D	156,205,446	10.20	10.50	24.00	—

Kennedy Half Dollar.

KM# 202a Obv. Designer: Gilroy Roberts. **Rev. Designer:** Frank Gasparro. **Diameter:** 30.6 **Weight:** 11.5000 g. **Composition:** 0.4000 Silver, 0.1479 oz. ASW.

Mint mark 1968 - present

Date	Mintage	MS-60	MS-65	Prf-65
1965	65,879,366	5.00	14.50	—
1965 SMS	2,360,000	—	15.00	—
1966	108,984,932	5.00	22.50	—
1966 SMS	2,261,583	—	17.00	—
1967	295,046,978	5.00	18.50	—
1967 SMS	1,863,344	—	18.00	—
1968D	246,951,930	5.00	16.50	—
1968S	3,041,506	—	—	7.49
1969D	129,881,800	5.00	20.00	—
1969S	2,934,631	—	—	7.49
1970D	2,150,000	8.50	40.00	—
1970S	2,632,810	—	—	12.00

Kennedy Half Dollar.

KM# 202b **Obv. Designer:** Gilroy Roberts. **Rev. Designer:** Frank Gasparro. **Diameter:** 30.6 **Weight:** 11.3400 g. **Composition:** Copper-Nickel Clad Copper

Date	Mintage	XF-40	MS-60	MS-65	Prf-65
1971	155,640,000	—	1.00	17.50	—
1971D	302,097,424	—	1.00	12.00	—
1971S	3,244,183	—	—	—	5.00
1972	153,180,000	—	1.00	15.50	—
1972D	141,890,000	—	1.00	14.50	—
1972S	3,267,667	—	—	—	5.00
1973	64,964,000	—	1.00	20.00	—
1973D	83,171,400	—	—	12.00	—
1973S	2,769,624	—	—	—	5.00
1974	201,596,000	—	1.00	25.00	—
1974D	79,066,300	—	1.00	17.00	—
1974D DDO	Inc. above	24.00	32.00	165	—
1974S	2,617,350	—	—	—	5.00
1975 none minted	—	—	—	—	—
1975D none minted	—	—	—	—	—
1975S none minted	—	—	—	—	—

Kennedy Half Dollar.

Bicentennial design, Independence Hall.

KM# 205 **Rev. Designer:** Seth Huntington. **Diameter:** 30.6 **Weight:** 11.2000 g. **Composition:** Copper-Nickel

Date	Mintage	MS-60	MS-65	Prf-65
1976	234,308,000	1.00	16.50	—
1976D	287,565,248	1.00	14.00	—
1976S	7,059,099	—	—	5.00

KM# 205a **Rev. Designer:** Seth Huntington. **Diameter:** 30.6 **Weight:** 11.5000 g. **Composition:** 0.4000 Silver, 0.1479 oz. ASW.

Date	Mintage	MS-60	MS-65	Prf-65
1976S	4,908,319	—	12.00	7.60
1976S	3,998,621	—	—	7.60

Kennedy Half Dollar.

Regular design resumed.

KM# A202b **Diameter:** 30.4 **Weight:** 11.1000 g. **Composition:** Copper-Nickel Clad Copper **Notes:** KM#202b design and composition resumed. The 1979-S and 1981-S Type II proofs have clearer mint marks than the Type I proofs of those years.

Date	Mintage	MS-65	Prf-65
1977	43,598,000	12.50	—
1977D	31,449,106	16.50	—
1977S	3,251,152	—	4.50
1978	14,350,000	12.00	—
1978D	13,765,799	15.00	—
1978S	3,127,788	—	5.00
1979	68,312,000	13.50	—
1979D	15,815,422	13.50	—
1979S Type I	3,677,175	—	5.00
1979S Type II	Inc. above	—	18.00
1980P	44,134,000	12.50	—
1980D	33,456,449	17.50	—
1980S	3,547,030	—	5.00
1981P	29,544,000	15.50	—
1981D	27,839,533	20.00	—
1981S Type I	4,063,083	—	5.00
1981S Type II	Inc. above	—	18.50
1982P	10,819,000	18.50	—
1982P no initials FG	Inc. above	110	—
1982D	13,140,102	20.00	—
1982S	38,957,479	—	5.00
1983P	34,139,000	22.50	—
1983D	32,472,244	12.50	—
1983S	3,279,126	—	5.00
1984P	26,029,000	12.00	—
1984D	26,262,158	18.00	—
1984S	3,065,110	—	6.00
1985P	18,706,962	16.50	—
1985D	19,814,034	12.50	—
1985S	3,962,138	—	5.00
1986P	13,107,633	17.50	—
1986D	15,336,145	14.00	—
1986S	2,411,180	—	6.00
1987P	2,890,758	16.50	—
1987D	2,890,758	12.50	—
1987S	4,407,728	—	5.00
1988P	13,626,000	16.50	—
1988D	12,000,096	10.00	—
1988S	3,262,948	—	5.00
1989P	24,542,000	13.00	—
1989S	3,220,194	—	5.00
1989D	23,000,216	13.00	—
1990P	22,780,000	17.50	—
1990D	20,096,242	20.00	—
1990S	3,299,559	—	5.00
1991P	14,874,000	12.50	—
1991D	15,054,678	16.00	—
1991S	2,867,787	—	5.00
1992P	17,628,000	10.00	—
1992D	17,000,106	10.00	—
1992S	2,858,981	—	5.00
1993P	15,510,000	12.00	—
1993D	15,000,006	10.00	—
1993S	2,633,439	—	5.00
1994P	23,718,000	12.00	—

Date	Mintage	MS-65	Prf-65
1994D	23,828,110	8.50	—
1994S	2,484,594	—	5.00
1995P	26,496,000	10.00	—
1995D	26,288,000	8.00	—
1995S	2,010,384	—	12.00
1996P	24,442,000	10.00	—
1996D	24,744,000	10.00	—
1996S	2,085,191	—	9.00
1997P	20,002,000	14.00	
1997D	19,876,000	13.50	—
1997S	1,975,000	—	10.00
1998P	15,646,000	12.50	—
1998D	15,064,000	12.50	—
1998S	2,078,494	—	7.00
1999P	8,900,000	11.00	—
1999D	10,682,000	10.00	—
1999S	2,557,897	—	8.00
2000P	22,600,000	12.00	—
2000D	19,466,000	12.00	—
2000S	3,082,944	—	5.00
2001P	21,200,000	10.00	—
2001D	19,504,000	9.00	—
2001S	2,235,000	—	5.00
2002P	3,100,000	10.00	—
2002D	2,500,000	10.50	—
2002S	2,268,913	—	5.00
2003P	2,500,000	6.00	—
2003D	2,500,000	6.00	—
2003S	2,076,165	—	5.00
2004P	2,900,000	4.50	—
2004D	2,900,000	4.50	—
2004S	1,789,488	—	6.00
2005P	3,800,000	6.00	—
2005P Satin finish	1,160,000	8.00	—
2005D	3,500,000	5.00	—
2005D Satin finish	1,160,000	10.00	—
2005S	2,275,000	—	5.00
2006P	2,400,000	4.50	—
2006P Satin finish	847,361	12.00	—
2006D	2,000,000	4.50	—
2006D Satin finish	847,361	14.00	—
2006S	1,934,965	—	6.00
2007P	—	4.50	—
2007P Satin finish	—	8.00	—
2007D	—	4.50	—
2007D Satin finish	—	8.00	—
2007S	—	—	6.00
2008P	—	4.50	—
2008P Satin finish	—	8.50	—
2008D	—	4.50	—
2008D Satin finish	—	8.50	—
2008S	—	—	9.00
2009P	—	4.50	—
2009P Satin finish	—	8.50	—
2009D	—	4.50	—
2009D Satin finish	—	8.50	—
2009S	—	—	6.00
2010P	—	4.50	—
2010P Satin finish	—	8.50	—
2010D	—	4.50	—
2010D Satin finish	—	8.50	—
2010S	—	—	13.00
2011P	—	4.50	—
2011D	—	4.50	—
2011S	—	—	9.00
2012P	—	4.50	—
2012D	—	4.50	—
2012S	—	—	9.00
2013P	—	4.50	—
2013D	—	4.50	—
2013S	—	—	9.00

Kennedy Half Dollar.

KM# A202c Designer: Gilroy Roberts. **Diameter:** 30.6 **Weight:** 12.5000 g. **Composition:** 0.9000 Silver, 0.3617 oz. ASW.

Date	Mintage	Prf-65
1992S	1,317,579	11.00
1993S	761,353	13.00
1994S	785,329	11.00
1995S	838,953	46.00
1996S	830,021	13.00
1997S	821,678	35.00
1998S	878,792	11.00
1998S Matte Proof	62,350	225
1999S	804,565	13.00
2000S	965,921	11.00
2001S	849,600	11.00
2002S	888,816	11.00
2003S	1,040,425	11.00
2004S	1,175,935	11.00
2005S	1,069,679	12.00
2006S	988,140	12.00
2007S	1,384,797	13.50
2008S	620,684	12.00
2009S	—	11.00
2010S	—	12.00
2011S	—	12.00
2012S	—	12.00
2013S	—	12.00

DOLLAR

Flowing Hair Dollar.

KM# 17 Designer: Robert Scot. **Diameter:** 39-40 **Weight:** 26.9600 g. **Composition:** 0.8920 Silver, 0.7731 oz. ASW. **Notes:** The two 1795 varieties have either two or three leaves under each of the eagle's wings on the reverse.

Date	Mintage	F-12	VF-20	XF-40	AU-50	MS-60	MS-63
1794	1,758	120,000	170,000	245,000	365,000	575,000	950,000
1795 2 leaves	203,033	4,450	7,800	16,150	25,500	80,500	196,500
1795 3 leaves	Inc. above	4,200	7,250	14,500	22,500	69,500	182,500
1795 Silver plug	Inc. above	9,850	13,950	28,500	48,500	115,000	235,000

Draped Bust Dollar.

Small eagle.

KM# 18 Designer: Robert Scot. **Diameter:** 39-40 **Weight:** 26.9600 g. **Composition:** 0.8920 Silver, 0.7731 oz. ASW.

Date	Mintage	F-12	VF-20	XF-40	AU-50	MS-60	MS-63
1795 Off-center bust	Inc. above	3,850	5,850	12,500	17,000	52,000	126,000
1795 Centered bust	—	3,900	5,950	12,700	17,250	52,500	126,000
1796 small date, small letters	72,920	4,100	6,300	13,750	18,500	70,000	—
1796 small date, large letters	Inc. above	3,875	6,400	13,700	19,400	—	—
1796 large date, small letters	Inc. above	4,250	6,750	14,350	19,200	57,000	136,000
1797 9 stars left, 7 stars right, small letters	7,776	5,200	9,000	18,850	36,500	—	—
1797 9 stars left, 7 stars right, large letters	Inc. above	4,250	6,850	13,950	20,300	55,500	—
1797 10 stars left, 6 stars right	Inc. above	4,050	6,350	13,600	18,500	53,500	125,000
1798 13 stars	327,536	4,150	6,300	13,750	21,000	85,000	—
1798 15 stars	Inc. above	4,700	7,450	16,150	25,500	95,000	—

Draped Bust Dollar.

Draped bust right, flanked by stars, date below. Heraldic eagle.

KM# 32 Designer: Robert Scot. **Diameter:** 39-40 **Weight:** 26.9600 g. **Composition:** 0.8920 Silver, 0.7731 oz. ASW. **Notes:** The 1798 "knob 9" variety has a serif on the lower left of the 9 in the date. The 1798 varieties are distinguished by the number of arrows held by the eagle on the reverse and the number of berries on the olive branch. On the 1798 "high-8" variety, the 8 in the date is higher than the other numberals. The 1799 varieties are distinguished by the number and positioning of the stars on the obverse and by the size of the berries in the olive branch on the reverse. On the 1700 "irregular date" variety, the first 9 in the date is smaller than the other numerals. Some varieties of the 1800 strikes had letters in the legend cut twice into the dies; as between the numerals in the date are wider than other varieties and the 8 is lower than the other numerals. The

1800 "small berries" variety refers to the size of the berries in the olive branch on the reverse. The 1800 "12 arrows" and "10 arrows" varieties refer to the number of arrows held by the eagle. The 1800 "Americai" variety appears to have the faint outline of an "I" after "America" in the reverse legend. The "close" and "wide" varieties of the 1802 refer to the amount of space between the numberals in the date. The 1800 large-3 and small-3 varieties are distinguished by the size of the 3 in the date.

Date	Mintage	F-12	VF-20	XF-40	AU-50	MS-60	MS-63
1798 knob 9, 4 stripes	423,515	1,785	2,735	5,550	9,850	21,750	95,000
1798 knob 9, 10 arrows	Inc. above	1,785	2,735	5,550	9,850	21,750	87,000
1798 knob 9, 5 stripes	Inc. above	—	—	—	—	—	124,500
1798 pointed 9, 4 berries	Inc. above	1,785	2,735	5,550	9,850	21,750	43,500
1798 5 berries, 12 arrows	Inc. above	1,785	2,735	5,550	9,850	21,750	43,500
1798 high 8	Inc. above	1,785	2,735	5,550	9,850	21,750	43,500
1798 13 arrows	Inc. above	1,785	2,735	5,550	9,850	21,750	45,000
1799/98 13-star reverse	Inc. above	2,000	2,950	4,300	8,600	23,500	45,000
1799/98 15-star reverse	Inc. above	1,875	2,850	4,000	8,300	24,500	47,500
1799 irregular date, 13-star reverse	Inc. above	1,825	3,000	3,900	8,200	23,500	45,000
1799 irregular date, 15-star reverse	Inc. above	1,825	3,200	5,550	9,850	21,500	42,500
1799 perfect date, 7- and 6-star obverse, no berries	Inc. above	1,750	2,700	3,850	8,150	18,500	42,500
1799 perfect date, 7- and 6-star obverse, small berries	Inc. above	1,750	2,700	3,850	8,150	18,500	42,500
1799 perfect date, 7- and 6-star obverse, medium large berries	Inc. above	1,750	2,700	3,850	8,150	18,500	42,500
1799 perfect date, 7- and 6-star obverse, extra large berries	Inc. above	1,750	2,700	3,850	8,150	18,500	51,500
1799 8 stars left, 5 stars right on obverse	Inc. above	1,825	2,800	3,900	8,200	24,000	45,000
1800 "R" in "Liberty" double cut	220,920	1,825	2,775	5,550	9,850	21,500	45,000
1800 first "T" in "States" double cut	Inc. above	1,800	2,750	5,550	9,850	21,500	45,000
1800 both letters double cut	Inc. above	1,800	2,750	5,550	9,850	21,500	45,000
1800 "T" in "United" double cut	Inc. above	1,800	2,750	5,550	9,850	21,500	45,000
1800 very wide date, low 8	Inc. above	1,800	2,750	5,550	9,850	21,500	—
1800 small berries	Inc. above	1,850	2,800	3,900	8,200	22,000	48,500
1800 dot date	Inc. above	2,000	3,000	4,300	8,600	21,500	45,000
1800 12 arrows	Inc. above	1,825	3,200	5,550	9,850	31,000	—
1800 10 arrows	Inc. above	1,825	3,200	5,550	9,850	—	—
1800 "Americai"	Inc. above	2,000	3,300	4,300	8,600	21,500	49,000
1801	54,454	2,050	3,200	4,000	8,300	25,000	—
1801 proof restrike	—	—	—	—	—	—	—
1802/1 close	Inc. above	2,000	3,300	4,300	8,600	20,500	—
1802/1 wide	Inc. above	2,000	3,300	4,300	8,600	20,500	—
1802 close, perfect date	Inc. above	1,850	2,800	3,900	8,200	20,500	—
1802 wide, perfect date	Inc. above	1,825	2,775	3,950	8,250	21,500	—
1802 proof restrike, mintage unrecorded	—	—	—	—	—	—	—
1803 large 3	85,634	1,875	3,000	4,000	8,300	20,500	47,500
1803 small 3	Inc. above	2,000	3,300	4,300	8,600	21,500	48,500
1803 proof restrike, mintage unrecorded	—	—	—	—	—	—	—
1804 15 known	—	—	—	—	3,000,000	—	—

Note: 1804, Childs Sale, Aug. 1999, Prf-68, $4,140,000.

Gobrecht Dollar.

"C Gobrecht F." in base. Eagle flying left amid stars.

KM# 59.1 **Obv. Designer:** Christian Gobrecht. **Diameter:** 38.1 **Weight:** 26.7300 g. **Composition:** 0.9000 Silver, 0.7734 oz. ASW.

Date	Mintage	VF-20	XF-40	AU-50	Prf-60
1836	1,000	11,500	14,850	—	25,500

"C. Gobrecht F." in base. Eagle flying in plain field.

KM# 59.2 **Obv. Designer:** Christian Gobrecht.. **Diameter:** 38.1 **Weight:** 26.7300 g. **Composition:** 0.9000 Silver, 0.7734 oz. ASW.

Date	Mintage	VF-20	XF-40	AU-50	Prf-60
1836 Restrike	—	—	—	—	24,000

"C. Gobrecht F." in base.

KM# 59a.1 **Diameter:** 38.1 **Weight:** 26.7300 g. **Composition:** 0.9000 Silver, 0.7734 oz. ASW.

Date	Mintage	VF-20	XF-40	AU-50	Prf-60
1836	600	—	—	—	—

"C. Gobrecht F." in base. Eagle flying left amid stars.

KM# 59a.2 **Diameter:** 38.1 **Weight:** 26.7300 g. **Composition:** 0.9000 Silver, 0.7734 oz. ASW.

Date	Mintage	VF-20	XF-40	AU-50	Prf-60
1836 Restrike	—	—	—	—	—

Designer's name omitted in base. Eagle in plain field.

KM# 59a.3 **Diameter:** 38.1 **Weight:** 26.7300 g. **Composition:** 0.9000 Silver, 0.7734 oz. ASW.

Date	Mintage	VF-20	XF-40	AU-50	Prf-60
1839	300	—	—	—	38,000

Designer's name omitted in base. Eagle in plain field.

KM# 59a.4 **Diameter:** 38.1 **Weight:** 26.7300 g. **Composition:** 0.9000 Silver, 0.7734 oz. ASW.

Date	Mintage	VF-20	XF-40	AU-50	Prf-60
1839 Restrike	—	—	—	—	36,500

Note: All other combinations are restrikes of the late 1850's.

DOLLAR

Seated Liberty Dollar.

Seated Liberty, date below. No motto above eagle.

KM# 71 Designer: Christian Gobrecht. **Diameter:** 38.1 **Weight:** 26.7300 g. **Composition:** 0.9000 Silver, 0.7734 oz. ASW.

Date	Mintage	G-4	VG-8	F-12	VF-20	XF-40	AU-50	MS-60	MS-63	MS-65	Prf-65
1840	61,005	290	320	340	420	680	1,075	4,000	21,500	—	—
1841	173,000	265	295	315	395	610	1,000	2,950	5,500	100,000	—
1842	184,618	265	295	315	395	630	925	2,650	4,700	—	—
1843	165,100	265	295	315	395	465	925	2,750	9,000	—	—
1844	20,000	280	313	360	455	785	1,250	6,450	15,000	100,000	—
1845	24,500	300	335	385	455	900	1,750	10,500	26,500	—	75,000
1846	110,600	275	313	345	490	650	1,100	2,750	5,200	98,000	125,000
1846O	59,000	285	330	370	480	775	1,325	8,750	20,000	—	—
1847	140,750	265	295	315	395	465	900	2,950	7,500	100,000	—
1848	15,000	325	385	515	795	1,250	1,700	4,100	12,500	100,000	—
1849	62,600	275	305	350	420	600	1,000	3,200	7,950	100,000	155,000
1850	7,500	465	545	380	845	1,750	2,650	7,850	15,000	—	80,000
1850O	40,000	335	400	515	750	1,550	3,950	12,850	34,500	—	—
1851	1,300	4,000	4,850	5,750	7,750	18,000	27,000	43,500	68,500	150,000	225,000
1851 Restrike	—	—	—	—	—	—	—	—	—	—	90,000
1852	1,100	3,500	4,150	5,200	7,000	15,000	26,000	38,500	60,000	150,000	200,000
1852 Restrike	—	—	—	—	—	—	—	—	—	—	70,000
1853	46,110	335	400	550	660	1,100	1,425	4,000	7,950	100,000	90,000
1853 Restrike	—	—	—	—	—	—	—	—	—	—	—
1854	33,140	1,100	1,450	2,000	2,850	4,500	5,750	8,500	13,500	100,000	80,000
1855	26,000	900	1,150	1,500	2,150	3,750	4,950	8,850	31,500	—	55,000
1856	63,500	400	450	650	775	1,650	2,850	4,350	11,500	—	39,500
1857	94,000	450	525	675	800	1,500	1,850	3,650	9,000	95,000	39,500
1858 proof only	Est. 800	3,200	3,600	4,000	4,800	7,250	8,850	—	—	—	42,500
Note: Later restrike.											
1859	256,500	285	335	400	515	655	1,000	2,850	5,850	95,000	17,500
1859O	360,000	265	295	315	395	465	800	2,250	4,150	56,000	—
1859S	20,000	330	390	515	750	1,550	3,500	15,000	36,500	—	—
1860	218,930	275	310	380	510	660	900	2,550	5,500	90,000	15,700
1860O	515,000	265	295	315	395	465	800	2,250	3,850	56,000	—
1861	78,500	600	750	900	985	1,750	1,975	2,950	5,650	90,000	15,700
1862	12,090	440	600	850	945	1,450	1,650	3,250	5,750	90,000	15,700
1863	27,660	375	525	575	660	985	1,400	3,250	6,000	90,000	18,000
1864	31,170	350	410	500	565	920	1,375	3,350	6,400	90,000	15,700
1865	47,000	300	350	420	585	1,050	1,750	3,250	6,250	90,000	15,700
1866 2 known without motto	—	—	—	—	—	—	—	—	—	—	—

Seated Liberty Dollar.

Seated Liberty, date below. IN GOD WE TRUST above eagle.

KM# 100 **Designer:** Christian Gobrecht. **Diameter:** 38.1 **Weight:** 26.7300 g. **Composition:** 0.9000 Silver, 0.7734 oz. ASW. **Notes:** In 1866 the motto IN GOD WE TRUST was added to the reverse above the eagle.

Date	Mintage	G-4	VG-8	F-12	VF-20	XF-40	AU-50	MS-60	MS-63	MS-65	Prf-65
1866	49,625	320	350	440	590	795	1,250	2,400	5,000	85,000	16,000
1867	47,525	315	345	405	565	670	895	2,435	5,050	85,000	16,000
1868	162,700	325	355	395	535	650	920	3,500	7,350	85,000	16,000
1869	424,300	290	320	370	490	640	985	2,400	5,000	85,000	16,000
1870	416,000	280	320	350	430	595	970	2,300	4,950	67,500	16,000
1870CC	12,462	475	600	825	1,375	3,650	8,250	27,500	44,500	—	—
1870S 12-15 known	—	150,000	235,000	350,000	600,000	850,000	1,350,000	1,850,000	2,500,000	—	—
Note: 1870S, Eliasberg Sale, April 1997, EF-45 to AU-50, $264,000.											
1871	1,074,760	270	300	330	410	545	970	2,300	4,950	67,500	16,000
1871CC	1,376	2,000	2,850	4,750	7,450	14,500	25,000	68,500	175,000	—	—
1872	1,106,450	270	300	330	410	495	820	2,300	4,850	67,500	16,000
1872CC	3,150	900	1,400	2,850	4,300	4,850	13,500	28,500	120,000	385,000	—
1872S	9,000	310	365	550	700	2,000	4,500	11,000	26,000	—	—
1873	293,600	275	310	340	420	510	840	2,350	4,900	67,500	16,000
1873CC	2,300	6,250	7,250	11,500	19,000	31,500	43,500	125,000	225,000	625,000	—
1873S none known	700	—	—	—	—	—	—	—	—	—	—

Trade Dollar.

Seated Liberty, IN GOD WE TRUST in base above date. TRADE DOLLAR below eagle.

KM# 108 **Designer:** William Barber. **Diameter:** 38.1 **Weight:** 27.2200 g. **Composition:** 0.9000 Silver, 0.7876 oz. ASW.

Date	Mintage	G-4	VG-8	F-12	VF-20	XF-40	AU-50	MS-60	MS-65	Prf-65
1873	397,500	115	155	165	185	280	360	1,200	15,500	10,250
1873CC	124,500	245	295	335	460	875	1,875	10,000	120,000	—
1873S	703,000	115	155	160	210	280	355	1,475	18,500	—
1874	987,800	125	155	160	185	280	365	1,100	18,250	10,250
1874CC	1,373,200	255	295	335	385	625	775	3,450	33,000	—
1874S	2,549,000	115	155	160	170	280	340	1,125	17,500	—
1875	218,900	145	185	350	425	550	800	2,450	18,000	15,000
1875CC	1,573,700	235	275	315	350	525	800	2,650	38,500	—
1875S	4,487,000	105	155	155	160	260	330	1,050	12,500	—
1875S/CC	Inc. above	210	285	365	560	925	1,450	4,650	59,000	—
1876	456,150	115	155	160	170	280	340	1,100	12,500	10,250

Date	Mintage	G-4	VG-8	F-12	VF-20	XF-40	AU-50	MS-60	MS-65	Prf-65
1876CC	509,000	245	285	310	365	585	985	8,000	76,500	—
1876CC	Inc. above	—	—	375	650	1,250	2,000	8,500	—	—
1876S	5,227,000	105	145	150	160	255	330	1,050	17,500	—
1877	3,039,710	115	155	160	170	265	340	1,150	23,500	10,250
1877CC	534,000	255	295	335	425	700	825	2,650	59,000	—
1877S	9,519,000	105	145	150	160	255	330	1,050	12,500	—
1878 proof only	900	—	—	—	1,200	1,300	1,500	—	—	11,000
1878CC	97,000	425	625	935	1,475	2,750	4,000	13,500	112,500	—
1878S	4,162,000	105	145	150	160	225	330	1,050	12,500	—
1879 proof only	1,541	—	—	—	1,175	1,275	1,400	—	—	10,250
1880 proof only	1,987	—	—	—	1,150	1,250	1,350	—	—	10,250
1881 proof only	960	—	—	—	1,200	1,300	1,400	—	—	10,250
1882 proof only	1,097	—	—	—	1,175	1,275	1,375	—	—	10,250
1883 proof only	979	—	—	—	1,200	1,300	1,400	—	—	10,250
1884 proof only	10	—	—	—	—	—	100,000	—	—	650,000
Note: 1884, Eliasberg Sale, April 1997, Prf-66, $396,000.										
1885 proof only	5	—	—	—	—	—	—	—	—	3,000,000
Note: 1885, Eliasberg Sale, April 1997, Prf-65, $907,500.										

Morgan Dollar.

Laureate head left, date below flanked by stars. Eagle within 1/2 wreath.

KM# 110 **Designer:** George T. Morgan. **Diameter:** 38.1 **Weight:** 26.7300 g. **Composition:** 0.9000 Silver, 0.7734 oz. ASW. **Notes:** "65DMPL" values are for coins grading MS-65 deep-mirror prooflike. The 1878 "8 tail feathers" and "7 tail feathers" varieties are distinguished by the number of feathers in the eagle's tail. On the "reverse of 1878" varieties, the top of the top feather in the arrows held by the eagle is straight across and the eagle's breast is concave. On the "reverse of 1879 varieties," the top feather in the arrows held by the eagle is slanted and the eagle's breast is convex. The 1890-CC "tail-bar" variety has a bar extending from the arrow feathers to the wreath on the reverse, the result of a die gouge. The Pittman Act of 1918 authorized the melting of 270 Million pieces of various dates. They were not indivudually recorded.

7 Tail feathers — 7/8 Tail feathers — 8 Tail feathers

Date	Mintage	VG-8	F-12	VF-20	XF-40	AU-50	MS-60	MS-63	MS-64	MS-65	65DMPL	Prf-65
1878 8 tail feathers	750,000	38.50	47.00	48.00	53.00	72.00	165	250	485	1,600	23,500	8,350
1878 7 over 8 tail feathers	9,759,550	38.00	47.00	48.00	52.00	68.00	165	275	485	2,400	17,000	—
1878 7 tail feathers, reverse of 1878	Inc. above	37.00	47.00	48.00	51.00	52.50	77.00	115	245	1,150	11,650	11,500
1878 7 tail feathers, reverse of 1879	Inc. above	37.00	47.00	48.00	50.00	51.00	86.00	195	495	2,650	24,500	185,000
1878CC	2,212,000	88.00	96.00	100.00	125	150	255	390	550	1,850	10,800	—
1878S	9,744,000	37.00	38.00	39.70	43.30	46.10	63.00	86.00	115	300	10,500	—
1879	14,807,100	35.00	36.00	37.70	39.30	43.60	58.00	83.50	145	875	17,250	7,550
1879CC	756,000	145	155	280	735	2,250	4,425	7,150	9,500	31,000	49,000	—
1879CC capped CC	Inc. above	145	182	250	640	1,850	4,100	6,175	9,350	43,000	63,500	—
1879O	2,887,000	35.00	36.00	37.70	39.30	49.10	84.00	225	530	4,150	28,500	—
1879S reverse of 1878	9,110,000	40.00	42.00	47.70	51.00	65.00	149	590	1,525	6,500	24,000	—

Date	Mintage	VG-8	F-12	VF-20	XF-40	AU-50	MS-60	MS-63	MS-64	MS-65	65DMPL	Prf-65
1879S reverse of 1879	9,110,000	35.00	36.00	37.70	39.30	43.60	56.00	76.00	90.00	165	1,300	—
1880	12,601,335	35.00	36.00	37.70	41.60	44.10	53.00	73.00	105	800	6,350	7,350
1880CC reverse of 1878	591,000	175	210	245	300	355	575	700	1,160	2,375	21,500	—
1880CC 80/79 reverse of 1878	Inc. above	190	230	270	335	410	640	850	1,750	4,000	—	—
1880CC 8/7 reverse of 1878	Inc. above	170	200	235	290	360	600	720	1,300	2,800	—	—
1880CC reverse of 1879	Inc. above	170	200	240	285	345	495	630	660	1,150	9,850	—
1880CC 8/7 high 7 reverse of 1879	Inc. above	175	205	245	290	355	525	655	775	1,800	—	—
1880CC 8/7 low 7 reverse of 1879	Inc. above	175	205	245	290	355	525	655	775	1,800	—	—
1880O	5,305,000	35.30	36.00	37.70	40.30	44.10	74.00	365	2,000	29,500	70,000	—
1880S	8,900,000	35.00	36.00	37.70	39.30	43.60	53.00	70.00	88.00	165	725	—
1880S 8/7 crossbar	—	39.00	41.00	44.70	45.00	75.00	90.00	265	335	450	—	—
1881	9,163,975	35.00	36.00	37.70	39.30	41.60	57.50	75.00	140	650	21,750	7,650
1881CC	296,000	375	385	410	425	460	540	585	605	880	3,050	—
1881O	5,708,000	35.00	36.00	37.70	39.60	42.30	51.00	71.50	190	1,375	35,000	—
1881S	12,760,000	35.00	36.00	37.70	39.60	43.60	53.00	70.00	90.00	165	850	—
1882	11,101,100	35.00	36.00	37.70	39.60	42.30	54.50	77.00	121	520	6,800	7,350
1882CC	1,133,000	92.00	96.00	110	130	155	220	265	280	495	1,950	—
1882O	6,090,000	35.30	36.00	37.70	40.30	43.60	57.00	71.50	119	1,175	4,950	—
1882O/S	Inc. above	46.00	47.00	55.00	67.50	99.50	245	765	2,325	61,500	65,000	—
1882S	9,250,000	35.00	36.00	37.70	39.30	43.60	52.00	74.50	88.00	177	4,000	—
1883	12,291,039	35.00	36.00	37.70	39.30	42.30	55.00	74.00	110	255	1,650	7,500
1883CC	1,204,000	92.00	96.00	110	125	148	210	248	260	455	1,450	—
1883O	8,725,000	35.00	36.00	37.70	39.30	41.60	48.50	70.00	88.00	177	1,400	—
1883S	6,250,000	35.00	37.00	41.20	44.30	145	665	2,650	5,350	51,500	94,500	—
1884	14,070,875	35.00	36.00	37.70	39.30	41.60	53.00	73.00	110	330	4,350	7,350
1884CC	1,136,000	125	135	140	145	160	210	248	260	430	1,450	—
1884O	9,730,000	35.00	36.00	37.70	39.30	41.60	51.00	72.00	88.00	197	1,000	—
1884S	3,200,000	35.00	36.50	39.70	43.00	310	7,500	35,500	110,000	235,000	220,000	—
1885	17,787,767	35.00	36.00	37.70	39.30	41.60	51.00	73.00	88.00	165	845	7,350
1885CC	228,000	550	565	580	585	595	620	695	755	1,100	2,400	—
1885O	9,185,000	35.00	36.00	37.70	39.30	41.60	50.00	70.00	88.00	177	1,000	—
1885S	1,497,000	39.00	39.50	40.00	64.00	110	265	355	710	2,225	42,500	—
1886	19,963,886	35.00	36.00	37.70	39.30	41.60	51.00	70.00	88.00	175	1,275	7,350
1886O	10,710,000	35.00	36.00	38.20	47.30	78.00	690	3,150	10,650	190,000	300,000	—
1886S	750,000	47.50	62.50	85.00	115	145	335	535	860	3,375	30,000	—
1887	20,290,710	35.00	36.00	37.70	39.30	41.60	51.00	70.00	88.00	165	1,200	7,350
1887/6	Inc. above	38.50	39.50	42.20	55.00	165	400	565	875	2,300	44,750	—
1887O	11,550,000	35.00	36.00	39.70	42.30	44.60	63.00	120	380	2,550	12,000	—
1887/6O	—	38.50	39.50	42.20	65.00	190	455	2,050	4,800	29,500	—	—
1887S	1,771,000	35.50	36.50	41.20	43.30	48.10	132	265	710	2,500	29,500	—
1888	19,183,833	35.00	36.00	37.70	39.30	41.60	53.00	70.00	92.00	240	3,000	7,500
1888O	12,150,000	35.00	36.00	37.70	41.30	44.10	53.00	74.00	99.00	655	2,850	—
1888O Hot Lips	Inc. above	55.00	125	250	600	3,000	—	—	—	—	—	—
1888S	657,000	115	190	210	225	235	335	495	915	3,400	16,500	—
1889	21,726,811	35.00	36.00	37.70	39.30	41.60	52.00	70.00	102	375	4,050	7,350
1889CC	350,000	635	940	1,300	3,150	6,900	25,500	43,500	66,000	320,000	—	—
1889O	11,875,000	35.30	36.00	39.70	41.30	43.60	180	390	960	7,750	14,500	—
1889S	700,000	51.00	60.00	65.00	82.00	125	265	390	675	2,150	38,500	—
1890	16,802,590	35.00	36.00	37.70	39.30	41.60	53.00	78.00	155	2,525	19,750	7,350
1890CC	2,309,041	85.00	96.00	105	140	235	455	825	1,425	5,250	15,500	—
1890CC tail bar	Inc. above	155	175	225	400	700	1,450	3,600	5,500	—	—	—
1890O	10,701,000	35.50	36.50	39.70	41.30	44.30	73.50	96.00	285	2,425	10,000	—
1890S	8,230,373	35.30	36.30	38.20	41.30	44.30	63.00	93.50	275	1,050	10,500	—
1891	8,694,206	35.50	37.00	38.70	41.30	44.30	64.00	165	775	9,000	27,500	7,350
1891CC	1,618,000	85.00	96.00	105	135	215	390	715	1,225	5,100	34,500	—
1891CC Spitting Eagle	Inc. above	105	115	135	185	260	425	900	1,600	6,000	—	—
1891O	7,954,529	35.50	36.40	38.20	41.30	44.10	175	350	770	8,550	37,500	—
1891S	5,296,000	35.50	36.50	38.70	41.30	45.10	63.00	135	310	1,725	21,500	—
1892	1,037,245	38.50	40.00	43.70	47.80	88.00	265	510	1,045	4,850	20,500	7,500
1892CC	1,352,000	190	210	290	485	725	1,375	2,275	2,650	8,900	39,500	—
1892O	2,744,000	38.50	40.00	43.70	42.50	67.50	265	420	1,225	7,750	52,500	—
1892S	1,200,000	38.70	43.50	136	315	1,650	44,500	66,500	112,500	205,000	225,000	—
1893	378,792	245	250	260	300	400	685	1,100	2,000	7,500	66,000	7,500
1893CC	677,000	245	310	660	1,500	2,500	4,200	7,050	11,400	70,000	90,000	—
1893O	300,000	205	250	380	620	850	2,650	6,650	16,500	210,000	215,000	—

Date	Mintage	VG-8	F-12	VF-20	XF-40	AU-50	MS-60	MS-63	MS-64	MS-65	65DMPL	Prf-65
1893S	100,000	3,000	4,150	5,750	9,500	21,000	130,000	205,000	365,000	715,000	735,000	—
1894	110,972	1,200	1,235	1,425	1,500	1,825	3,500	5,200	10,150	38,500	78,000	7,500
1894O	1,723,000	55.00	57.00	59.00	96.00	310	735	3,950	11,750	68,500	61,500	—
1894S	1,260,000	62.00	65.00	110	150	510	785	1,185	1,925	6,550	26,000	—
1895 proof only	12,880	21,500	29,500	36,500	38,000	40,000	—	—	—	—	—	75,000
1895O	450,000	315	350	480	595	1,225	15,500	57,500	85,000	165,000	—	—
1895S	400,000	465	525	900	1,325	1,865	3,850	6,350	8,550	28,000	42,500	—
1896	9,967,762	35.00	36.00	37.70	39.30	41.60	51.00	71.00	93.00	235	1,450	7,350
1896O	4,900,000	35.50	37.00	38.70	46.80	155	1,450	6,700	44,000	180,000	180,000	—
1896S	5,000,000	38.50	41.90	60.00	235	895	1,815	3,350	5,250	19,500	110,000	—
1897	2,822,731	35.00	36.00	37.70	41.30	44.10	50.00	66.00	99.00	355	3,950	7,350
1897O	4,004,000	35.50	37.00	39.70	55.30	110	735	4,400	15,900	70,000	72,500	—
1897S	5,825,000	35.50	37.00	38.70	41.30	47.10	77.00	122	165	610	3,250	—
1898	5,884,735	35.00	36.00	37.70	39.80	42.30	50.50	71.00	88.00	245	1,440	7,350
1898O	4,440,000	35.00	36.00	37.70	39.80	42.30	53.50	71.00	91.50	180	1,000	—
1898S	4,102,000	37.00	38.50	40.20	55.00	105	270	470	660	2,500	18,000	—
1899	330,846	170	182	195	205	245	265	290	390	935	2,850	7,350
1899O	12,290,000	35.00	36.00	37.70	39.30	41.60	53.50	70.00	95.00	178	1,550	—
1899S	2,562,000	37.50	38.50	42.20	58.50	145	410	495	825	2,275	26,000	—
1900	8,880,938	35.00	36.00	37.70	39.30	42.30	50.50	70.00	90.00	176	42,500	7,350
1900O	12,590,000	35.00	36.00	37.70	39.30	42.30	53.50	70.00	90.00	176	6,250	—
1900O/CC	Inc. above	37.50	47.50	62.50	100.00	190	285	770	935	1,800	19,000	—
1900S	3,540,000	37.00	41.50	43.20	46.80	85.00	320	400	660	1,800	38,500	—
1901	6,962,813	36.00	40.00	57.50	105	280	2,450	17,250	55,000	375,000	—	7,850
1901 doubled die reverse	Inc. above	275	450	900	2,000	3,850	—	—	—	—	—	—
1901O	13,320,000	32.80	38.00	39.70	41.30	45.30	53.50	71.00	84.00	192	10,000	—
1901S	2,284,000	32.80	38.50	37.50	51.00	200	510	745	1,000	3,150	24,500	—
1902	7,994,777	32.80	38.00	39.70	41.30	43.60	66.00	110	155	480	19,500	7,350
1902O	8,636,000	35.00	36.00	37.70	39.30	41.60	53.50	70.00	89.00	176	16,000	—
1902S	1,530,000	93.50	102	148	195	275	380	620	885	3,000	15,000	—
1903	4,652,755	47.00	48.00	49.00	50.00	52.00	66.00	82.50	116	320	36,850	7,350
1903O	4,450,000	325	350	375	390	398	412	455	480	635	5,950	—
1903S	1,241,000	95.00	130	210	365	1,725	3,950	6,500	7,150	11,750	40,000	—
1903S Micro S	Inc. above	135	225	450	1,150	3,000	—	—	—	—	—	—
1904	2,788,650	37.00	38.00	39.70	41.30	43.60	105	255	600	2,850	86,500	7,350
1904O	3,720,000	35.50	37.50	39.20	41.30	45.10	55.50	74.00	92.00	166	1,175	—
1904S	2,304,000	35.50	47.50	87.00	230	525	1,650	4,100	4,750	10,350	19,000	—
1921	44,690,000	33.60	34.20	36.20	37.70	39.90	45.00	52.00	80.00	185	11,500	—
1921D	20,345,000	34.00	34.60	36.50	38.10	41.00	53.50	71.00	122	420	10,000	—
1921S	21,695,000	34.00	34.60	36.50	38.10	41.00	53.50	69.00	155	1,525	31,000	—

Peace Dollar.

Liberty Head left. Eagle facing right perched on rock.

KM# 150 **Designer:** Anthony DeFrancisci. **Diameter:** 38.1 **Weight:** 26.7300 g. **Composition:** 0.9000 Silver, 0.7734 oz. ASW.

Mint mark

Date	Mintage	G-4	VG-8	F-12	VF-20	XF-40	AU-50	MS-60	MS-63	MS-64	MS-65
1921	1,006,473	95.00	120	126	133	143	165	265	420	715	1,925
1922	51,737,000	30.50	33.70	34.40	35.40	36.70	39.30	44.00	51.00	79.00	142
1922D	15,063,000	30.50	34.00	34.60	35.60	36.90	40.20	51.00	71.00	99.00	565
1922S	17,475,000	30.50	34.00	34.60	35.60	36.90	40.20	49.00	83.00	225	2,375
1923	30,800,000	30.50	33.70	34.40	35.40	36.70	39.30	44.00	51.00	79.00	142
1923D	6,811,000	30.50	34.00	34.60	35.60	36.90	43.30	63.00	139	320	1,155
1923S	19,020,000	30.50	34.00	34.60	35.60	36.90	40.20	50.00	83.00	330	6,600
1924	11,811,000	30.50	33.70	34.60	35.40	36.70	39.30	44.00	51.00	79.00	165
1924S	1,728,000	32.50	34.70	37.40	39.40	41.50	60.00	210	485	1,375	9,700
1925	10,198,000	30.50	33.70	34.40	35.40	36.70	39.30	46.00	51.00	79.00	154
1925S	1,610,000	30.50	33.70	35.30	39.40	36.70	46.00	90.00	215	935	25,000
1926	1,939,000	30.50	33.70	35.50	36.70	36.70	39.30	55.00	84.00	112	440
1926D	2,348,700	30.50	33.70	35.30	36.50	36.70	41.30	84.00	165	310	825

Date	Mintage	G-4	VG-8	F-12	VF-20	XF-40	AU-50	MS-60	MS-63	MS-64	MS-65
1926S	6,980,000	31.10	34.30	35.00	36.00	37.30	42.30	59.00	102	245	990
1927	848,000	32.50	36.70	39.40	41.40	42.70	50.00	79.00	180	485	2,850
1927D	1,268,900	31.10	34.70	35.40	38.40	40.70	80.00	187	355	950	4,950
1927S	866,000	31.10	34.70	35.40	38.40	40.70	80.00	187	450	1,150	9,900
1928	360,649	345	380	385	390	395	415	525	875	1,150	4,450
1928S	1,632,000	34.00	35.00	40.00	42.50	48.00	66.00	178	450	965	24,000
1934	954,057	35.00	44.00	45.00	46.00	47.50	50.00	115	215	360	750
1934D Large D	1,569,500	36.00	45.00	46.00	50.00	54.00	65.00	180	600	925	3,000
1934D Small D	Inc. above	35.00	44.00	45.00	46.00	47.50	50.00	155	385	500	1,765
1934S	1,011,000	38.00	45.00	53.00	80.00	172	475	1,900	3,150	4,450	8,150
1935	1,576,000	35.00	44.00	45.00	46.00	47.50	52.50	66.00	160	205	680
1935S 3 Rays	1,964,000	35.00	44.00	45.00	46.00	47.50	92.00	255	375	585	1,300
1935S 4 Rays	—	36.00	45.00	46.00	50.00	55.00	115	295	460	680	1,650

Eisenhower Dollar.

KM# 203 **Designer:** Frank Gasparro. **Diameter:** 38 **Weight:** 22.8000 g. **Composition:** Copper-Nickel Clad Copper

Date	Mintage	Proof	MS-63	Prf-65
1971	47,799,000	—	10.00	—
1971D	68,587,424	—	8.00	—
1972 Low Relief	75,890,000	—	18.00	—
1972 High Relief	Inc. above	—	175	—
1972 Modified High Relief	Inc. above	—	35.00	—
1972D	92,548,511	—	9.00	—
1973	2,000,056	—	12.00	—
1973D	2,000,000	—	12.00	—
1973S	—	2,769,624	—	12.00
1974	27,366,000	—	15.00	—
1974D	35,466,000	—	7.50	—
1974S	—	2,617,350	—	11.00

Eisenhower Dollar.

KM# 203a **Designer:** Frank Gasparro. **Diameter:** 38.1 **Weight:** 24.5900 g. **Composition:** 0.4000 Silver, 0.3162 oz. ASW.

Date	Mintage	Proof	MS-63	Prf-65
1971S	6,868,530	—	15.80	—
1971S	—	4,265,234	—	11.00
1971S Peg Leg "R" Variety	Inc. above	—	—	17.00
1971S Partial Peg Leg "R" Variety	Inc. above	—	—	18.00
1972S	2,193,056	—	15.80	—
1972S	—	1,811,631	—	9.00
1973S	1,833,140	—	15.80	—
1973S	—	1,005,617	—	45.00
1974S	1,720,000	—	15.80	—
1974S	—	1,306,579	—	11.00

Eisenhower Dollar.

Bicentennial design, moon behind Liberty Bell.

KM# 206 **Rev. Designer:** Dennis R. Williams. **Diameter:** 38.1 **Weight:** 22.6800 g. **Composition:** Copper-Nickel Clad Copper **Notes:** In 1976 the lettering on the reverse was changed to thinner letters, resulting in the Type II variety for that year. The Type I variety was minted 1975 and dated 1976.

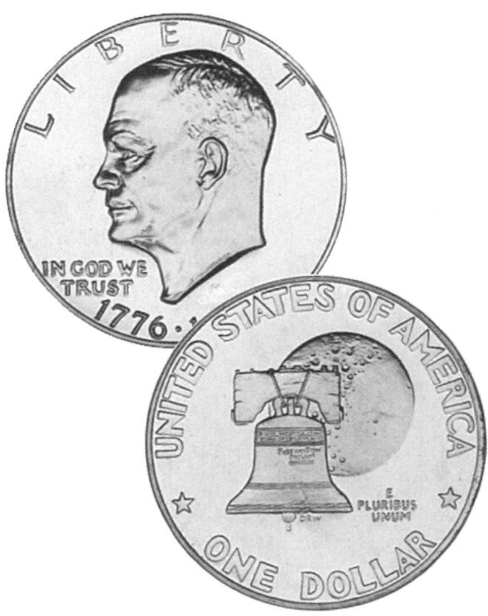

Type I
Squared "T"

Type II
Slant-top "T"

Date	Mintage	Proof	MS-63	Prf-65
1976 type I	117,337,000	—	12.00	—
1976 type II	Inc. above	—	8.00	—
1976D type I	103,228,274	—	7.50	—
1976D type II	Inc. above	—	6.00	—
1976S type I	—	2,909,369	—	10.00
1976S type II	—	4,149,730	—	9.00

KM# 206a **Rev. Designer:** Dennis R. Williams. **Weight:** 24.5900 g. **Composition:** 0.4000 Silver, 0.3162 oz. ASW.

Date	Mintage	Proof	MS-63	Prf-65
1976S	4,908,319	—	15.80	14.00
1976S	—	3,998,621	—	—

Eisenhower Dollar.

Regular design resumed.

KM# A203 **Diameter:** 38.1 **Composition:** Copper-Nickel Clad Copper

Date	Mintage	Proof	MS-63	Prf-65
1977	12,596,000	—	5.00	—
1977D	32,983,006	—	4.00	—
1977S	—	3,251,152	—	9.00
1978	25,702,000	—	4.00	—
1978D	33,012,890	—	4.75	—
1978S	—	3,127,788	—	9.00

Susan B. Anthony Dollar.

Susan B. Anthony bust right. Eagle landing on moon, symbolic of Apollo manned moon landing.

KM# 207 **Designer:** Frank Gasparro. **Diameter:** 26.5 **Weight:** 8.1000 g. **Composition:** Copper-Nickel Clad Copper **Notes:** The 1979-S and 1981-S Type II coins have a clearer mint mark than the Type I varieties for those years.

Date	Mintage	MS-63	Prf-65
1979P Near date	360,222,000	45.00	—
1979P	Inc. above	2.50	—
1979D	288,015,744	2.50	—
1979S Proof, Type I	3,677,175	—	—
1979S Proof, Type II	Inc. above	—	—
1979S	109,576,000	2.50	—
1980P	27,610,000	2.50	—
1980D	41,628,708	2.50	—
1980S	20,422,000	5.00	—
1980S Proof	3,547,030	—	—
1981P	3,000,000	5.00	—
1981D	3,250,000	5.00	—
1981S	3,492,000	5.00	—
1981S Proof, Type I	4,063,083	—	—
1981S Proof, Type II	Inc. above	—	—
1999P	29,592,000	3.00	—
1999P Proof	Est. 750,000	—	—
1999D	11,776,000	3.00	—

Sacagawea Dollar.

Sacagawea bust right, with baby on back. Eagle in flight left.

KM# 310 **Diameter:** 26.5 **Weight:** 8.0700 g. **Composition:** Copper-Zinc-Manganese-Nickel Clad Copper

Date	Mintage	MS-63	Prf-65
2000P	767,140,000	2.00	—
2000D	518,916,000	2.00	—
2000S	4,048,000	—	10.00
2001P	62,468,000	2.00	—
2001D	70,939,500	2.00	—
2001S	3,190,000	—	100.00
2002P	3,865,610	2.00	—
2002D	3,732,000	2.00	—
2002S	3,210,000	—	28.50
2003P	3,080,000	3.00	—
2003D	3,080,000	3.00	—
2003S	3,300,000	—	20.00
2004P	2,660,000	2.50	—
2004D	2,660,000	2.50	—
2004S	2,965,000	—	22.50
2005P	2,520,000	2.50	—
2005D	2,520,000	2.50	—
2005S	3,273,000	—	22.50
2006P	4,900,000	2.50	—
2006D	2,800,000	5.00	—
2006S	3,028,828	—	22.50
2007P	3,640,000	2.50	—
2007D	3,920,000	2.50	—
2007S	2,563,563	—	22.50
2008P	9,800,000	2.50	—
2008D	14,840,000	2.50	—
2008S	—	—	22.50

Native American Dollar - Planting crops reverse.

Sacagawea bust right with baby on back. Native American female planting corn, beans and squash.

KM# 467 **Diameter:** 26.5 **Weight:** 8.0700 g. **Composition:** Copper-Zinc-Manganese-Nickel Clad Copper **Notes:** Date and mint mark on edge

Date	Mintage	MS-63	Prf-65
2009P	37,380,000	2.00	—
2009D	33,880,000	2.00	—
2009S	—	—	22.50

Native American Dollar - Hiawatha belt reverse.

Sacagawea bust right with baby on back. Hiawatha belt and bundle of five arrows.

KM# 474 **Diameter:** 26.5 **Weight:** 8.0700 g. **Composition:** Copper-Zinc-Manganese-Nickel Clad Copper **Notes:** Date and mint mark on edge

Date	Mintage	MS-63	Prf-65
2010P	—	2.00	—
2010D	—	2.00	—
2010S	—	—	22.50

Native American Dollar - Peace Pipe reverse.

Sacagawea bust right with baby on back. Hands passing peace pipe.

KM# 503 **Obv. Designer:** Glenna Goodacre. **Rev. Designer:** Richard Masters and Joseph Menna. **Diameter:** 26.5 **Weight:** 8.0700 g. **Composition:** Copper-Zinc-Manganese-Nickel Clad Copper **Notes:** Date and mint mark on edge

Date	Mintage	MS-63	Prf-65
2011P	—	2.00	—
2011D	—	2.00	—
2011S	—	—	8.00

Native American Dollar - Horse reverse.

Sacagawea bust right with baby on back. Horse and Native American profile facing left.

KM# 528 **Diameter:** 26.5 **Weight:** 8.0700 g. **Composition:** Copper-Zinc-Manganese-Nickel Clad Copper **Notes:** Date and mint mark on edge

Date	Mintage	MS-63	Prf-65
2012P	—	2.00	—
2012D	—	2.00	—
2012S	—	—	8.00

Presidents

George Washington

KM# 401 **Diameter:** 26.5 **Weight:** 8.0700 g. **Composition:** Copper-Zinc-Manganese-Nickel Clad Copper **Notes:** Date and mint mark incuse on edge.

Date	Mintage	MS-63	MS-65	Prf-65
2007P	176,680,000	2.00	5.00	—
(2007) Plain edge error	Inc. above	75.00	—	—
2007D	163,680,000	2.00	5.00	—
2007S	3,883,103	—	—	5.00

James Madison

KM# 404 **Diameter:** 26.5 **Weight:** 8.0700 g. **Composition:** Copper-Zinc-Manganese-Nickel Clad Copper **Notes:** Date and mint mark incuse on edge.

Date	Mintage	MS-63	MS-65	Prf-65
2007P	84,560,000	2.00	5.00	—
2007D	87,780,000	2.00	5.00	—
2007S	3,876,829	—	—	5.00

John Adams

KM# 402 **Diameter:** 26.5 **Weight:** 8.0700 g. **Composition:** Copper-Zinc-Manganese-Nickel Clad Copper **Notes:** Date and mint mark incuse on edge.

Date	Mintage	MS-63	MS-65	Prf-65
2007P	112,420,000	2.00	5.00	—
2007P Double edge lettering	Inc. above	250	—	—
2007D	112,140,000	2.00	5.00	—
2007S	3,877,409	—	—	5.00

DOLLAR

Thomas Jefferson

KM# 403 **Diameter:** 26.5 **Weight:** 8.0700 g. **Composition:** Copper-Zinc-Manganese-Nickel Clad Copper **Notes:** Date and mint mark incuse on edge.

Date	Mintage	MS-63	MS-65	Prf-65
2007P	100,800,000	2.00	5.00	—
2007D	102,810,000	2.00	5.00	—
2007S	3,877,573	—	—	5.00

John Quincy Adams

KM# 427 **Diameter:** 26.5 **Weight:** 8.0700 g. **Composition:** Copper-Zinc-Manganese-Nickel Clad Copper **Notes:** Date and mint mark incuse on edge.

Date	Mintage	MS-63	MS-65	Prf-65
2008P	57,540,000	2.00	5.00	—
2008D	57,720,000	2.00	5.00	—
2008S	3,000,000	—	—	5.00

Andrew Jackson

KM# 428 **Diameter:** 26.5 **Weight:** 8.0700 g. **Composition:** Copper-Zinc-Manganese-Nickel Clad Copper **Notes:** Date and mint mark incuse on edge.

Date	Mintage	MS-63	MS-65	Prf-65
2008P	61,180,000	2.00	5.00	—
2008D	61,070,000	2.00	5.00	—
2008S	3,000,000	—	—	5.00

Martin van Buren

KM# 429 **Diameter:** 26.5 **Weight:** 8.0700 g. **Composition:** Copper-Zinc-Manganese-Nickel Clad Copper **Notes:** Date and mint mark incuse on edge.

Date	Mintage	MS-63	MS-65	Prf-65
2008P	51,520,000	2.00	5.00	—
2008D	50,960,000	2.00	5.00	—
2008S	3,000,000	—	—	5.00

James Monroe

KM# 426 **Diameter:** 26.5 **Weight:** 8.0700 g. **Composition:** Copper-Zinc-Manganese-Nickel Clad Copper **Weight:** Date and mint mark incuse on edge.

Date	Mintage	MS-63	MS-65	Prf-65
2008P	64,260,000	2.00	5.00	—
2008D	60,230,000	2.00	5.00	—
2008S	3,000,000	—	—	5.00

James K. Polk

KM# 452 **Diameter:** 26.5 **Weight:** 8.0700 g. **Composition:** Copper-Zinc-Manganese-Nickel Clad Copper **Notes:** Date and mint mark on edge

Date	Mintage	MS-63	MS-65	Prf-65
2009P	46,620,000	2.00	5.00	—
2009D	41,720,000	2.00	5.00	—
2009S	—	—	—	5.00

John Tyler

KM# 451 Diameter: 26.5 **Weight:** 8.0700 g. **Composition:** Copper-Zinc-Manganese-Nickel Clad Copper **Notes:** Date and mint mark on edge.

Date	Mintage	MS-63	MS-65	Prf-65
2009P	43,540,000	2.00	5.00	—
2009D	43,540,000	2.00	5.00	—
2009S	—	—	—	5.00

William Henry Harrison

KM# 450 Diameter: 26.5 **Weight:** 8.0700 g. **Composition:** Copper-Zinc-Manganese-Nickel Clad Copper **Notes:** Date and mint mark on edge

Date	Mintage	MS-63	MS-65	Prf-65
2009P	43,260,000	2.00	5.00	—
2009D	55,160,000	2.00	5.00	—
2009S	—	—	—	5.00

Zachary Taylor

KM# 453 Diameter: 26.5 **Weight:** 8.0700 g. **Composition:** Copper-Zinc-Manganese-Nickel Clad Copper **Notes:** Date and mint mark on edge.

Date	Mintage	MS-63	MS-65	Prf-65
2009P	41,580,000	2.00	5.00	—
2009D	36,680,000	2.00	5.00	—
2009S	—	—	—	5.00

Abraham Lincoln

KM# 478 Diameter: 26.5 **Weight:** 8.0700 g. **Composition:** Copper-Zinc-Manganese-Nickel Clad Copper **Notes:** Date and mint mark on edge.

Date	Mintage	MS-63	MS-65	Prf-65
2010P	—	2.00	5.00	—
2010D	—	2.00	5.00	—
2010S	—	—	—	5.00

Franklin Pierce

KM# 476 Diameter: 26.5 **Weight:** 8.0700 g. **Composition:** Copper-Zinc-Manganese-Nickel Clad Copper **Notes:** Date and mint mark on edge.

Date	Mintage	MS-63	MS-65	Prf-65
2010P	—	2.00	5.00	—
2010D	—	2.00	5.00	—
2010S	—	—	—	5.00

James Buchanan

KM# 477 Diameter: 26.5 **Weight:** 8.0700 g. **Composition:** Copper-Zinc-Manganese-Nickel Clad Copper **Notes:** Date and mint mark on edge.

Date	Mintage	MS-63	MS-65	Prf-65
2010P	—	2.00	5.00	—
2010D	—	2.00	5.00	—
2010S	—	—	—	5.00

DOLLAR

Millard Filmore

KM# 475 **Diameter:** 26.5 **Weight:** 8.0700 g. **Composition:** Copper-Zinc-Manganese-Nickel Clad Copper **Notes:** Date and mint mark on edge.

Date	Mintage	MS-63	MS-65	Prf-65
2010P	—	2.00	5.00	—
2010D	—	2.00	5.00	—
2010S	—	—	—	5.00

Rutherford B. Hayes

KM# 501 **Diameter:** 26.5 **Weight:** 8.0700 g. **Composition:** Copper-Zinc-Manganese-Nickel Clad Copper **Notes:** Date and mint mark on edge.

Date	Mintage	MS-63	MS-65	Prf-65
2011P	—	2.00	5.00	—
2011D	—	2.00	5.00	—
2011S	—	—	—	5.00

Andrew Johnson

KM# 499 **Diameter:** 26.5 **Weight:** 8.0700 g. **Composition:** Copper-Zinc-Manganese-Nickel Clad Copper **Notes:** Date and mint mark on edge.

Date	Mintage	MS-63	MS-65	Prf-65
2011P	—	2.00	5.00	—
2011D	—	2.00	5.00	—
2011S	—	—	—	5.00

Ulysses S. Grant

KM# 500 **Diameter:** 26.5 **Weight:** 8.0700 g. **Composition:** Copper-Zinc-Manganese-Nickel Clad Copper **Notes:** Date and mint mark on edge.

Date	Mintage	MS-63	MS-65	Prf-65
2011P	—	2.00	5.00	—
2011D	—	2.00	5.00	—
2011S	—	—	—	5.00

James Garfield

KM# 502 **Diameter:** 26.5 **Weight:** 8.0700 g. **Composition:** Copper-Zinc-Manganese-Nickel Clad Copper **Notes:** Date and mint mark on edge.

Date	Mintage	MS-63	MS-65	Prf-65
2011P	—	2.00	5.00	—
2011D	—	2.00	5.00	—
2011S	—	—	—	5.00

Benjamin Harrison

KM# 526 **Diameter:** 26.5 **Weight:** 8.0700 g. **Composition:** Copper-Zinc-Manganese-Nickel Clad Copper **Notes:** Date at mint mark on edge

Date	Mintage	MS-63	MS-65	Prf-65
2012P	—	2.00	5.00	—
2012D	—	2.00	5.00	—
2012S	—	—	—	5.00

Chester A. Arthur

KM# 524 **Diameter:** 26.5 **Weight:** 8.0700 g. **Composition:** Copper-Zinc-Manganese-Nickel Clad Copper **Notes:** Date and mintmark on edge

Date	Mintage	MS-63	MS-65	Prf-65
2012P	—	2.00	5.00	—
2012D	—	2.00	5.00	—
2012S	—	—	—	5.00

Grover Cleveland, first term

KM# 525 **Diameter:** 26.5 **Weight:** 8.0700 g. **Composition:** Copper-Zinc-Manganese-Nickel Clad Copper **Notes:** Date and mint mark on edge

Date	Mintage	MS-63	MS-65	Prf-65
2012P	—	2.00	5.00	—
2012D	—	2.00	5.00	—
2012S	—	—	—	5.00

Grover Cleveland, second term

KM# 527 **Diameter:** 26.5 **Weight:** 8.0700 g. **Composition:** Copper-Zinc-Manganese-Nickel Clad Copper **Notes:** Date and mint mark on edge

Date	Mintage	MS-63	MS-65	Prf-65
2012P	—	2.00	5.00	—
2012D	—	2.00	5.00	—
2012S	—	—	—	5.00

GOLD

Liberty Head - Type 1.

Liberty head left within circle of stars. Value, date within 3/4 wreath.

KM# 73 **Designer:** James B. Longacre. **Diameter:** 13 **Weight:** 1.6720 g. **Composition:** 0.9000 Gold, 0.0484 oz. AGW. **Notes:** On the "closed wreath" varieties of 1849, the wreath on the reverse extends closer to the numeral 1.

Date	Mintage	F-12	VF-20	XF-40	AU-50	MS-60
1849 open wreath	688,567	175	225	265	300	650
1849 small head, no L	—	—	—	—	—	—
1849 closed wreath	Inc. above	175	210	245	270	335
1849C closed wreath	11,634	800	950	1,450	2,400	8,850
1849C open wreath	Inc. above	135,000	240,000	320,000	475,000	600,000
1849D open wreath	21,588	1,050	1,300	1,875	2,600	6,000
1849O open wreath	215,000	195	235	310	390	800
1850	481,953	175	210	245	270	335
1850C	6,966	900	1,150	1,600	2,350	9,000
1850D	8,382	1,050	1,250	1,725	2,950	12,500
1850O	14,000	200	275	390	775	3,300
1851	3,317,671	175	210	245	270	335
1851C	41,267	840	1,150	1,500	1,700	3,150
1851D	9,882	1,000	1,250	1,675	2,500	5,650
1851O	290,000	160	195	240	265	775
1852	2,045,351	175	210	245	270	335
1852C	9,434	845	1,040	1,400	1,700	5,100
1852D	6,360	1,025	1,250	1,675	2,300	10,000
1852O	140,000	130	175	260	385	1,400
1853	4,076,051	175	210	245	270	335
1853C	11,515	900	1,100	1,400	2,000	5,600
1853D	6,583	1,040	1,250	1,700	2,650	9,700
1853O	290,000	135	160	235	270	665
1854	736,709	175	210	245	270	335
1854D	2,935	1,050	1,400	2,350	6,000	13,000
1854S	14,632	260	360	525	775	2,450

Indian Head - Type 2.

Indian head with headdress left. Value, date within wreath.

KM# 83 **Designer:** James B. Longacre. **Diameter:** 15 **Weight:** 1.6720 g. **Composition:** 0.9000 Gold, 0.0484 oz. AGW.

Date	Mintage	F-12	VF-20	XF-40	AU-50	MS-60
1854	902,736	250	280	410	535	1,680
1855	758,269	250	280	410	535	1,680
1855C	9,803	975	1,450	3,750	11,500	33,000
1855D	1,811	3,250	4,750	9,800	22,000	48,000
1855O	55,000	345	440	600	1,500	7,800
1856S	24,600	525	820	1,325	2,500	8,650

Indian Head - Type 3.

Indian head with headdress left. Value, date within wreath.

KM# 86 Designer: James B. Longacre. **Diameter:** 15 **Weight:** 1.6720 g. **Composition:** 0.9000 Gold, 0.0484 oz. AGW. **Notes:** The 1856 varieties are distinguished by whether the 5 in the date is slanted or upright. The 1873 varieties are distinguished by the amount of space between the upper left and lower left serifs in the 3.

DOLLAR GOLD

Date	Mintage	F-12	VF-20	XF-40	AU-50	MS-60	Prf-65
1856 upright 5	1,762,936	225	260	310	335	510	—
1856 slanted 5	Inc. above	220	250	285	300	360	55,000
1856D	1,460	2,350	3,650	5,800	8,000	32,000	—
1857	774,789	210	245	285	300	360	32,000
1857C	13,280	900	1,150	1,750	3,750	13,250	—
1857D	3,533	1,000	1,300	2,300	4,400	11,000	—
1857S	10,000	260	520	650	1,300	6,200	—
1858	117,995	210	245	285	300	360	28,500
1858D	3,477	1,025	1,250	1,600	2,850	10,000	—
1858S	10,000	300	400	575	1,450	5,350	—
1859	168,244	210	245	285	300	360	17,000
1859C	5,235	885	1,050	1,700	4,250	9,850	—
1859D	4,952	1,050	1,500	2,100	3,250	10,500	—
1859S	15,000	210	265	525	1,250	5,500	—
1860	36,668	210	245	285	300	360	16,500
1860D	1,566	2,150	2,500	4,200	7,000	19,500	—
1860S	13,000	300	380	500	750	2,900	—
1861	527,499	210	245	285	300	360	14,850
1861D mintage unrecorded	—	4,950	7,000	11,000	21,000	41,500	—
1862	1,361,390	210	245	285	300	360	15,000
1863	6,250	370	500	925	2,100	3,900	18,000
1864	5,950	290	370	475	825	1,050	18,000
1865	3,725	290	370	590	750	1,600	18,000
1866	7,130	300	385	470	685	1,025	18,000
1867	5,250	325	420	525	675	1,160	17,500
1868	10,525	265	290	415	500	1,025	19,000
1869	5,925	315	460	530	725	1,150	17,000
1870	6,335	255	290	410	500	875	16,000
1870S	3,000	300	475	785	1,250	2,650	—
1871	3,930	260	290	390	480	750	18,000
1872	3,530	260	295	400	480	975	18,500
1873 closed 3	125,125	325	425	825	950	1,650	—
1873 open 3	Inc. above	210	245	285	300	360	—
1874	198,820	210	245	285	300	360	30,000
1875	420	1,650	2,350	4,650	5,200	10,000	32,500
1876	3,245	240	300	360	475	725	16,750
1877	3,920	210	210	340	460	725	18,000
1878	3,020	195	250	365	480	675	15,500
1879	3,030	210	225	285	330	525	14,000
1880	1,636	235	180	300	300	475	14,000
1881	7,707	235	270	300	300	460	11,500
1882	5,125	245	275	300	300	460	10,500
1883	11,007	235	265	300	300	460	11,000
1884	6,236	235	265	—	300	460	10,000
1885	12,261	235	265	300	300	460	10,000
1886	6,016	235	265	300	300	460	10,000
1887	8,543	235	265	300	300	460	10,000
1888	16,580	235	265	300	300	460	10,000
1889	30,729	235	265	300	300	390	10,000

$2.50 (QUARTER EAGLE)

GOLD

Liberty Cap.

Liberty cap on head, right, flanked by stars. Heraldic eagle.

KM# 27 Designer: Robert Scot. **Diameter:** 20 **Weight:** 4.3700 g. **Composition:** 0.9160 Gold, 0.1287 oz. AGW. **Notes:** The 1796 "no stars" variety does not have stars on the obverse. The 1804 varieties are distinguished by the number of stars on the obverse.

Date	Mintage	F-12	VF-20	XF-40	MS-60
1796 no stars	963	55,000	71,500	100,000	245,000
1796 stars	432	26,500	32,500	65,000	185,000
1797	427	20,000	25,000	45,000	125,000
1798 close date	1,094	6,250	8,650	16,500	60,000
1798 wide date	Inc. above	5,250	7,650	15,500	57,500
1802/1	3,035	4,250	6,650	14,500	34,500
1804 13-star reverse	3,327	45,000	65,000	125,000	—
1804 14-star reverse	Inc. above	4,550	7,150	15,500	46,500
1805	1,781	4,250	6,650	14,500	37,000
1806/4	1,616	4,250	6,650	15,000	38,000
1806/5	Inc. above	6,250	8,650	21,500	95,000
1807	6,812	4,250	6,650	14,500	34,500

Turban Head.

Turban on head left flanked by stars. Banner above eagle.

KM# 40 Designer: John Reich. **Diameter:** 20 **Weight:** 4.3700 g. **Composition:** 0.9160 Gold, 0.1287 oz. AGW.

Date	Mintage	F-12	VF-20	XF-40	MS-60
1808	2,710	26,500	36,500	54,500	175,000

Turban Head.

Turban on head left within circle of stars. Banner above eagle.

KM# 46 Designer: John Reich. **Diameter:** 18.5 **Weight:** 4.3700 g. **Composition:** 0.9160 Gold, 0.1287 oz. AGW.

Date	Mintage	F-12	VF-20	XF-40	MS-60
1821	6,448	5,950	7,150	10,350	30,000
1824/21	2,600	5,950	7,150	10,250	29,500
1825	4,434	5,950	7,150	10,250	27,500
1826/25	760	6,450	7,900	11,000	100,000
1827	2,800	6,050	7,350	10,750	29,500

Turban Head.

Turban on head left within circle of stars. Banner above eagle.

KM# 49 Designer: John Reich. **Diameter:** 18.2 **Weight:** 4.3700 g. **Composition:** 0.9160 Gold, 0.1287 oz. AGW.

Date	Mintage	F-12	VF-20	XF-40	MS-60
1829	3,403	5,400	6,250	7,950	18,500
1830	4,540	5,400	6,250	7,950	18,500
1831	4,520	5,400	6,250	7,950	19,000
1832	4,400	5,400	6,250	7,950	18,500
1833	4,160	5,400	6,250	7,950	19,000
1834	4,000	8,900	11,750	15,450	48,500

Classic Head.

Classic head left within circle of stars. No motto above eagle.

KM# 56 **Designer:** William Kneass. **Diameter:** 18.2 **Weight:** 4.1800 g. **Composition:** 0.8990 Gold, 0.1208 oz. AGW.

Date	Mintage	VF-20	XF-40	AU-50	MS-60	MS-65
1834	112,234	475	675	965	3,300	27,000
1835	131,402	475	675	950	3,200	32,000
1836	547,986	475	675	940	3,100	29,000
1837	45,080	500	800	1,500	4,000	35,000
1838	47,030	500	625	1,100	3,200	30,000
1838C	7,880	1,700	3,000	8,000	27,000	55,000
1839	27,021	500	900	1,900	5,500	—
1839C	18,140	1,500	2,650	4,500	26,500	—
1839/8	Inc. above	—	—	—	—	—
1839D	13,674	1,750	3,450	8,000	24,000	—
1839O	17,781	700	1,100	2,500	7,250	—

KM# 72 **Designer:** Christian Gobrecht. **Diameter:** 18 **Weight:** 4.1800 g. **Composition:** 0.9000 Gold, 0.1209 oz. AGW.

1848 "Cal." reverse

Date	Mintage	F-12	VF-20	XF-40	AU-50	MS-60	Prf-65
1840	18,859	275	375	900	2,950	6,000	—
1840C	12,822	1,250	1,400	1,600	6,000	13,000	—
1840D	3,532	2,500	3,200	8,700	15,500	35,000	—
1840O	33,580	325	400	825	2,100	11,000	—
1841	—	—	48,000	100,000	—	—	—
1841C	10,281	1,100	1,500	2,000	3,500	18,500	—
1841D	4,164	1,350	2,100	4,750	11,000	25,000	—
1842	2,823	1,100	900	2,600	6,500	20,000	140,000
1842C	6,729	1,250	1,700	3,500	8,000	27,000	—
1842D	4,643	1,300	2,100	4,000	11,750	—	—
1842O	19,800	325	390	1,200	2,500	14,000	—
1843	100,546	275	345	450	915	3,000	140,000
1843C small date, Crosslet 4	26,064	1,500	2,400	5,500	9,000	29,000	—
1843C large date, Plain 4	Inc. above	1,200	1,600	2,200	3,500	8,800	—
1843D small date, Crosslet 4	36,209	1,350	1,800	2,350	3,250	10,500	—
1843O small date, Crosslet 4	288,002	285	315	375	400	1,700	—
1843O large date, Plain 4	76,000	295	370	465	1,600	8,000	—
1844	6,784	350	400	850	2,000	7,500	140,000
1844C	11,622	1,050	1,600	2,600	7,000	20,000	—
1844D	17,332	1,100	1,650	2,200	3,200	7,800	—
1845	91,051	325	395	360	600	1,275	140,000
1845D	19,460	1,100	1,900	2,600	3,900	15,000	—
1845O	4,000	575	1,050	2,300	9,000	20,000	—
1846	21,598	320	365	500	950	6,000	140,000
1846C	4,808	1,100	1,575	3,500	8,950	18,750	—
1846D	19,303	1,000	1,400	2,000	3,000	12,000	—
1846O	66,000	350	385	400	1,150	6,500	—
1847	29,814	275	350	360	825	3,800	—
1847C	23,226	900	1,800	2,300	3,500	7,250	—
1847D	15,784	950	1,650	2,250	3,250	10,500	—
1847O	124,000	275	365	400	1,000	4,000	—
1848	7,497	340	500	850	2,400	7,000	125,000
1848 "CAL."	1,389	35,000	40,000	45,000	50,000	55,000	—
1848C	16,788	950	1,600	2,100	3,800	13,750	—
1848D	13,771	1,100	2,000	2,500	4,500	12,000	—
1849	23,294	295	375	475	1,000	2,600	—
1849C	10,220	975	1,475	2,150	5,150	23,500	—
1849D	10,945	1,050	2,000	2,500	4,500	18,000	—
1850	252,923	265	310	360	385	1,100	—
1850C	9,148	800	1,500	2,000	3,600	13,500	—
1850D	12,148	950	1,700	2,350	3,450	1,600	—
1850O	84,000	300	345	485	1,300	4,500	—
1851	1,372,748	265	300	330	345	495	—
1851C	14,923	900	1,650	2,250	3,450	9,850	—
1851D	11,264	1,000	1,800	2,500	3,850	12,000	—
1851O	148,000	300	335	370	900	4,450	—
1852	1,159,681	265	300	330	345	495	—
1852C	9,772	975	1,500	2,050	4,250	16,500	—
1852D	4,078	1,100	1,650	2,950	7,000	17,500	—

Date	Mintage	F-12	VF-20	XF-40	AU-50	MS-60	Prf-65
1852O	140,000	300	335	365	1,000	5,000	—
1853	1,404,668	265	300	330	345	495	—
1853D	3,178	1,250	1,975	3,450	4,850	18,000	—
1854	596,258	265	300	330	345	495	—
1854C	7,295	1,100	1,450	2,450	4,750	13,500	—
1854D	1,760	2,100	3,350	6,950	11,500	27,500	—
1854O	153,000	300	335	365	420	1,600	—
1854S	246	95,000	175,000	300,000	—	—	—
1855	235,480	270	305	335	350	495	—
1855C	3,677	1,050	1,675	3,250	6,350	19,500	—
1855D	1,123	2,100	3,350	7,500	16,500	50,000	—
1856	384,240	270	305	335	350	515	75,000
1856C	7,913	985	1,600	2,500	4,000	14,500	—
1856D	874	3,850	6,500	12,850	30,000	72,500	—
1856O	21,100	300	345	750	1,350	7,500	—
1856S	71,120	300	335	425	950	4,350	—
1857	214,130	270	305	335	350	515	75,000
1857D	2,364	1,025	1,650	2,775	3,700	13,200	—
1857O	34,000	300	335	425	1,050	4,450	—
1857S	69,200	300	335	365	875	5,350	—
1858	47,377	275	310	340	395	1,250	59,000
1858C	9,056	965	1,500	2,100	3,350	9,250	—
1859	39,444	275	310	350	425	1,250	61,000
1859D	2,244	1,150	1,850	3,100	3,950	18,500	—
1859S	15,200	310	365	950	2,350	5,000	—
1860	22,675	275	310	340	450	1,150	58,000
1860C	7,469	985	1,475	2,175	3,100	20,000	—
1860S	35,600	310	365	625	1,150	3,850	—
1861	1,283,878	270	305	335	350	850	31,500
1861S	24,000	320	400	900	3,250	7,250	—
1862	98,543	310	340	600	1,950	5,150	32,500
1862/1	Inc. above	650	875	1,850	3,450	7,500	—
1862S	8,000	650	875	2,050	4,200	17,500	—
1863	30	—	—	—	—	—	95,000
1863S	10,800	465	475	1,475	3,150	13,500	—
1864	2,874	3,750	5,450	11,500	22,500	47,500	27,000
1865	1,545	2,950	4,750	7,750	18,000	37,500	30,000
1865S	23,376	320	335	595	1,450	4,400	—
1866	3,110	775	1,250	3,150	5,750	11,500	25,000
1866S	38,960	365	400	625	1,500	5,950	—
1867	3,250	350	395	850	1,150	4,750	27,000
1867S	28,000	300	335	575	1,600	4,100	—
1868	3,625	300	335	395	640	1,625	27,000
1868S	34,000	270	305	365	1,050	3,850	—
1869	4,345	300	335	435	685	2,750	24,500
1869S	29,500	300	365	445	800	4,000	—
1870	4,555	290	375	550	900	4,150	33,500
1870S	16,000	270	345	465	1,000	4,900	—
1871	5,350	295	360	385	850	3,100	36,500
1871S	22,000	270	345	415	550	2,350	—
1872	3,030	305	450	800	1,250	4,650	33,500
1872S	18,000	275	340	485	1,150	4,350	—
1873 closed 3	178,025	270	330	375	395	435	42,500
1873 open 3	Inc. above	270	325	355	375	405	—
1873S	27,000	280	345	395	900	2,800	—
1874	3,940	285	345	425	850	2,250	42,500
1875	420	1,950	3,500	5,500	11,000	24,000	70,000
1875S	11,600	270	330	375	850	3,950	—
1876	4,221	285	345	675	1,250	3,350	27,500
1876S	5,000	285	345	625	1,150	2,850	—
1877	1,652	310	395	875	1,250	3,250	35,000
1877S	35,400	265	325	355	415	750	—
1878	286,260	265	320	345	370	410	35,000
1878S	178,000	265	320	345	375	415	—
1879	88,990	270	325	355	385	435	26,000
1879S	43,500	270	340	365	765	2,500	—
1880	2,996	275	345	385	750	1,400	26,000
1881	691	950	2,150	3,150	5,250	9,850	26,500
1882	4,067	270	330	375	550	1,050	23,500
1883	2,002	280	395	750	1,350	3,350	23,500
1884	2,023	275	375	440	750	1,600	23,500
1885	887	400	750	1,850	2,650	4,850	22,500
1886	4,088	275	340	375	650	1,150	23,500
1887	6,282	275	340	365	500	850	17,500
1888	16,098	270	335	365	450	520	18,000
1889	17,648	270	335	365	450	535	20,500
1890	8,813	275	340	365	500	600	18,500
1891	11,040	—	—	—	—	—	17,500
1891 DDR	Inc. above	275	335	365	475	585	—

Date	Mintage	F-12	VF-20	XF-40	AU-50	MS-60	Prf-65
1892	2,545	275	330	365	500	950	15,500
1893	30,106	270	330	355	375	400	15,500
1894	4,122	275	330	365	440	800	18,000
1895	6,199	265	325	355	400	525	16,750
1896	19,202	265	325	350	370	400	16,750
1897	29,904	270	325	350	370	400	16,750
1898	24,165	265	325	345	365	385	15,000
1899	27,350	265	325	345	365	385	15,000
1900	67,205	265	325	345	365	385	15,000
1901	91,322	265	325	345	365	385	15,000
1902	133,733	265	320	345	365	385	15,000
1903	201,257	265	320	345	365	385	15,000
1904	160,960	265	320	345	365	385	15,000
1905	217,944	265	320	345	365	385	15,000
1906	176,490	265	320	345	365	385	15,000
1907	336,448	265	320	345	365	385	15,000

Indian Head.

KM# 128 Designer: Bela Lyon Pratt. **Diameter:** 18 **Weight:** 4.1800 g. **Composition:** 0.9000 Gold, 0.1209 oz. AGW.

Date	Mintage	VF-20	XF-40	AU-50	MS-60	MS-63	MS-65	Prf-65
1908	565,057	325	330	345	410	990	3,150	25,000
1909	441,899	325	330	345	420	1,650	6,540	53,000
1910	492,682	325	330	345	410	1,550	7,500	35,000
1911	704,191	325	330	345	410	1,005	8,500	25,000
1911D D strong D	55,680	2,750	3,850	4,750	8,750	20,500	77,500	—
1911 1D weak D	Inc. above	1,150	1,950	2,850	4,950	—	—	—
1912	616,197	325	330	350	435	1,750	11,850	25,000
1913	722,165	325	330	345	410	930	7,500	25,000
1914	240,117	330	355	405	595	4,950	34,500	30,000
1914D	448,000	325	330	355	425	1,500	36,500	—
1915	606,100	325	330	340	410	965	6,500	32,500
1925D	578,000	325	330	340	400	715	2,550	—
1926	446,000	325	330	340	400	715	2,550	—
1927	388,000	325	330	340	400	715	2,550	—
1928	416,000	325	330	340	400	715	2,550	—
1929	532,000	325	340	355	430	805	7,000	—

$2.50 GOLD

$3

GOLD

Indian head with headdress, left. Value, date within wreath.

KM# 84 Designer: James B. Longacre. **Diameter:** 20.5 **Weight:** 5.0150 g. **Composition:** 0.9000 Gold, 0.1451 oz. AGW. **Notes:** The 1873 "closed-3" and "open-3" varieties are distinguished by the amount of space between the upper left and lower left serifs of the 3 in the date.

Date	Mintage	VF-20	XF-40	AU-50	MS-60	MS-65	Prf-65
1854	138,618	860	1,150	1,290	2,650	19,500	175,000
1854D	1,120	8,300	16,500	35,000	77,500	—	—
1854O	24,000	1,150	2,650	5,000	50,000	—	—
1855	50,555	840	1,175	1,750	3,200	44,000	150,000
1855S	6,600	1,055	2,750	6,950	25,000	—	—
1856	26,010	830	1,125	1,650	3,250	45,000	115,000
1856S	34,500	930	1,600	2,650	12,500	—	—
1857	20,891	830	1,125	1,415	3,500	44,000	105,000
1857S	14,000	980	2,775	5,350	21,000	—	—
1858	2,133	980	1,900	3,650	9,300	50,000	95,000
1859	15,638	930	1,725	1,975	3,250	32,500	60,000
1860	7,155	930	1,625	2,150	3,600	33,000	60,000
1860S	7,000	980	2,450	8,650	26,000	—	—
1861	6,072	955	2,550	3,650	6,900	37,500	60,000
1862	5,785	955	2,350	3,650	6,900	44,500	60,000
1863	5,039	930	2,350	3,650	6,900	34,500	60,000
1864	2,680	980	2,350	3,650	6,900	39,500	60,000
1865	1,165	1,275	2,700	6,500	11,700	55,000	60,000
1866	4,030	1,000	1,500	2,250	3,500	38,500	60,000

Date	Mintage	VF-20	XF-40	AU-50	MS-60	MS-65	Prf-65
1867	2,650	1,025	1,550	2,650	3,600	39,500	60,000
1868	4,875	875	1,475	2,125	3,350	33,000	60,000
1869	2,525	1,150	1,550	2,350	4,300	50,000	60,000
1870	3,535	1,030	1,625	2,450	4,400	—	60,000
1870S unique	—	—	4,000,000	—	—	—	—
Note: H. W. Bass Collection. AU50, cleaned. Est. value, $1,250,000.							
1871	1,330	1,030	1,575	2,375	4,000	42,500	60,000
1872	2,030	930	1,525	2,250	3,850	4,500	60,000
1873 closed 3, mintage unknown	—	4,000	9,000	16,000	27,500	—	95,000
1873 open 3, proof only	25	—	—	—	—	—	90,000
1874	41,820	830	1,125	1,265	2,250	16,750	62,500
1875 proof only	20	20,000	28,000	47,500	—	—	225,000
1876	45	6,000	11,500	18,000	—	—	97,500
1877	1,488	1,350	3,150	7,500	23,000	—	65,000
1878	82,324	830	1,125	1,265	2,250	14,500	65,000
1879	3,030	880	1,325	2,000	3,200	22,500	50,000
1880	1,036	950	2,100	3,375	4,700	27,000	42,000
1881	554	1,400	3,350	6,750	12,000	38,500	36,500
1882	1,576	955	1,475	2,350	3,600	30,000	35,500
1883	989	1,000	1,625	2,950	3,800	34,500	35,500
1884	1,106	1,285	2,000	2,800	3,650	34,500	35,500
1885	910	1,300	2,050	3,450	5,200	38,500	34,500
1886	1,142	1,250	2,250	2,875	5,000	47,500	34,500
1887	6,160	930	1,550	2,175	3,250	22,500	34,500
1888	5,291	980	1,525	2,125	3,150	15,000	34,500
1889	2,429	955	1,475	2,000	3,200	22,500	34,500

$5 (HALF EAGLE)

$5 GOLD

GOLD

Liberty Cap.

Liberty Cap on head, right, flanked by stars. Small eagle.

KM# 19 **Weight:** 8.7500 g. **Composition:** 0.9160 Gold, 0.2577 oz. AGW.

Date	Mintage	F-12	VF-20	XF-40	MS-60
1795	8,707	19,500	25,000	31,000	79,500
1796/95	6,196	20,500	25,350	32,750	84,500
1797 15 obverse stars	Inc. above	23,000	27,500	42,250	—
1797 16 obverse stars	Inc. above	21,000	25,850	41,000	210,000
1798	—	112,000	185,000	350,000	—

Liberty Cap.

Liberty cap on head, right, flanked by stars. Large Heraldic eagle.

KM# 28 **Designer:** Robert Scot. **Diameter:** 25 **Weight:** 8.7500 g. **Composition:** 0.9160 Gold, 0.2577 oz. AGW.

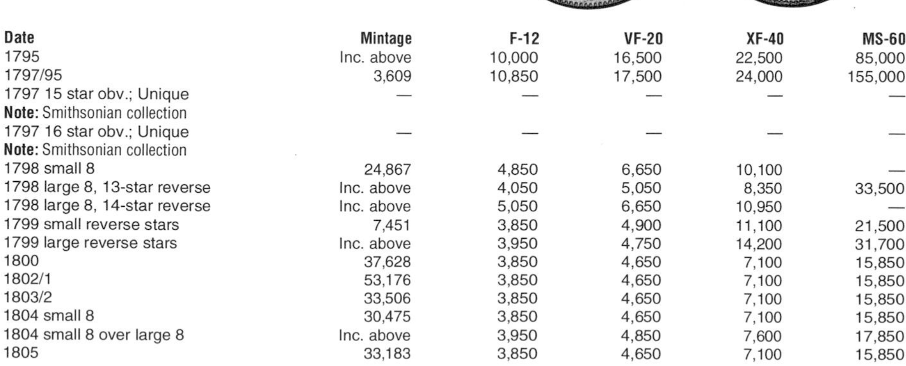

Date	Mintage	F-12	VF-20	XF-40	MS-60
1795	Inc. above	10,000	16,500	22,500	85,000
1797/95	3,609	10,850	17,500	24,000	155,000
1797 15 star obv.; Unique	—	—	—	—	—
Note: Smithsonian collection					
1797 16 star obv.; Unique	—	—	—	—	—
Note: Smithsonian collection					
1798 small 8	24,867	4,850	6,650	10,100	—
1798 large 8, 13-star reverse	Inc. above	4,050	5,050	8,350	33,500
1798 large 8, 14-star reverse	Inc. above	5,050	6,650	10,950	—
1799 small reverse stars	7,451	3,850	4,900	11,100	21,500
1799 large reverse stars	Inc. above	3,950	4,750	14,200	31,700
1800	37,628	3,850	4,650	7,100	15,850
1802/1	53,176	3,850	4,650	7,100	15,850
1803/2	33,506	3,850	4,650	7,100	15,850
1804 small 8	30,475	3,850	4,650	7,100	15,850
1804 small 8 over large 8	Inc. above	3,950	4,850	7,600	17,850
1805	33,183	3,850	4,650	7,100	15,850

Date	Mintage	F-12	VF-20	XF-40	MS-60
1806 pointed 6	64,093	3,850	4,650	7,100	17,750
1806 round 6	Inc. above	3,850	4,650	7,100	15,850
1807	32,488	3,850	4,650	7,100	15,850

Turban Head.

Capped draped bust, left, flanked by stars. Heraldic eagle.

KM# 38 **Designer:** John Reich. **Diameter:** 25 **Weight:** 8.7500 g. **Composition:** 0.9160 Gold, 0.2577 oz. AGW.

Date	Mintage	F-12	VF-20	XF-40	MS-60
1807	51,605	3,100	3,850	5,100	13,850
1808	55,578	3,600	4,500	5,950	18,850
1808/7	Inc. above	3,100	3,850	5,100	13,850
1809/8	33,875	3,100	3,850	5,100	13,850
1810 small date, small 5	100,287	17,500	32,500	48,500	125,000
1810 small date, large 5	Inc. above	3,100	3,850	5,100	16,250
1810 large date, small 5	Inc. above	17,500	37,500	60,000	135,000
1810 large date, large 5	Inc. above	3,100	3,850	5,100	13,850
1811 small 5	99,581	3,100	3,850	5,100	13,850
1811 tall 5	Inc. above	3,100	3,850	5,100	13,850
1812	58,087	3,100	3,850	5,100	13,850

Turban Head.

Capped head, left, within circle of stars. Heraldic eagle.

KM# 43 **Designer:** John Reich. **Diameter:** 25 **Weight:** 8.7500 g. **Composition:** 0.9160 Gold, 0.2577 oz. AGW.

Date	Mintage	F-12	VF-20	XF-40	MS-60
1813	95,428	3,100	3,850	5,500	13,250
1814/13	15,454	5,000	6,250	8,250	19,000
1815	635	32,500	50,000	200,000	250,000
Note: 1815, private sale, Jan. 1994, MS-61, $150,000					
1818	48,588	5,000	6,450	13,500	20,000
1818 5D over 50 Inc. Above	—	5,500	6,450	10,500	23,500
1819	51,723	8,800	16,500	50,000	64,000
1819 5D over 50 Inc. Above	—	5,500	11,000	35,000	64,000
1820 curved-base 2, small letters	263,806	5,250	6,600	12,850	22,500
1820 curved-base 2, large letters	Inc. above	5,100	6,400	12,000	20,000
1820 square-base 2	Inc. above	5,000	6,250	11,500	19,000
1821	34,641	12,000	22,000	43,000	115,000
1822 3 known	—	—	—	1,250,000	—
1823	14,485	5,500	6,250	11,500	19,000
1824	17,340	5,500	10,500	32,000	38,000
1825/21	29,060	5,750	9,500	25,000	39,500
1825/24	Inc. above	—	—	550,000	750,000
Note: 1825/4, Bowers & Merena, March 1989, XF, $148,500.					
1826	18,069	5,500	7,800	16,500	30,000
1827	24,913	6,000	10,000	23,500	34,500
1828/7	28,029	15,000	28,500	66,000	125,000
Note: 1828/7, Bowers & Merena, June 1989, XF, $20,900.					
1828	Inc. above	6,000	13,000	30,000	60,000
1829 large planchet	57,442	15,000	28,500	65,000	125,000
Note: 1829 large planchet, Superior, July 1985, MS-65, $104,500.					
1829 small planchet	Inc. above	37,500	54,000	86,500	140,000
Note: 1829 small planchet, private sale, 1992 (XF-45), $89,000.					
1830 small "5D."	126,351	16,500	27,500	44,650	70,000
1830 large "5D."	Inc. above	16,500	27,500	44,650	70,000
1831	140,594	16,500	27,500	44,650	70,000
1832 curved-base 2, 12 stars	157,487	50,000	80,000	175,000	—
1832 square-base 2, 13 stars	Inc. above	16,500	27,500	44,650	70,000
1833 small date	193,630	17,500	29,500	54,650	90,000
1833 large date	Inc. above	16,500	27,500	44,650	70,000
1834 plain 4	50,141	16,500	27,500	44,650	70,000
1834 crosslet 4	Inc. above	17,500	29,500	54,650	80,000

Classic Head.

Classic head, left, within circle of stars. No motto above eagle.

KM# 57 Designer: William Kneass. **Diameter:** 22.5 **Weight:** 8.3600 g. **Composition:** 0.8990 Gold, 0.2416 oz. AGW.

Date	Mintage	VF-20	XF-40	AU-50	MS-60	MS-65
1834 plain 4	658,028	550	790	1,400	3,000	48,000
1834 crosslet 4	Inc. above	1,650	2,900	6,000	20,000	—
1835	371,534	550	790	1,450	3,150	—
1836	553,147	550	790	1,450	2,950	70,000
1837	207,121	550	790	1,650	3,500	75,000
1838	286,588	550	890	1,450	3,700	58,000
1838C	17,179	2,550	5,500	13,000	42,500	—
1838D	20,583	2,100	4,650	9,750	31,000	—

Coronet Head.

Coronet head, left, within circle of stars. No motto above eagle.

KM# 69 Designer: Christian Gobrecht. **Diameter:** 21.6 **Weight:** 8.3590 g. **Composition:** 0.9000 Gold, 0.2419 oz. AGW. **Notes:** Varieties for 1843 are distinguished by the size of the numerals in the date. One 1848 variety has "Cal." incsribed on the reverse, indicating it was made from California gold. The 1873 "closed-3" and "open-3" varieties are distinguished by the amount of space between the upper left and lower left serifs in the 3 in the date.

Date	Mintage	F-12	VF-20	XF-40	MS-60	Prf-65
1839	118,143	532	562	591	4,000	—
1839/8 curved date	Inc. above	552	582	611	2,250	—
1839C	17,205	1,250	2,300	2,900	24,000	—
1839D	18,939	1,125	2,200	3,200	22,000	—
1840	137,382	522	552	570	3,700	—
1840C	18,992	1,200	2,200	3,000	26,000	—
1840D	22,896	1,200	2,200	3,000	16,000	—
1840O	38,700	532	582	611	11,000	—
1841	15,833	532	562	591	5,500	—
1841C	21,467	1,200	1,850	2,400	20,000	—
1841D	30,495	1,400	1,800	2,350	15,000	—
1841O 2 known	50	—	—	—	—	—
1842 small letters	27,578	200	345	1,100	—	—
1842 large letters	Inc. above	532	750	2,000	11,000	—
1842C small date	28,184	4,500	10,000	23,000	110,000	—
1842C large date	Inc. above	900	1,800	2,200	18,000	—
1842D small date	59,608	1,000	2,000	2,300	15,000	—
1842D large date	Inc. above	1,400	2,350	6,500	48,000	—
1842O	16,400	550	1,000	3,400	22,000	—
1843	611,205	522	552	581	1,850	—
1843C	44,201	1,250	1,850	2,500	14,000	—
1843D	98,452	1,250	1,950	2,600	13,000	—
1843O small letters	19,075	552	582	1,700	26,000	—
1843O large letters	82,000	532	586	1,175	12,000	—
1844	340,330	522	552	581	2,000	—
1844C	23,631	1,300	1,900	3,000	24,000	—
1844D	88,982	1,500	1,950	2,400	12,000	—
1844O	364,600	556	586	590	4,700	—
1845	417,099	522	552	581	2,000	—
1845D	90,629	1,300	1,900	2,400	12,500	—
1845O	41,000	556	415	800	9,900	—
1846	395,942	522	552	581	2,400	—
1846C	12,995	1,350	1,900	3,000	24,000	—
1846D	80,294	1,250	1,800	2,400	13,000	—
1846O	58,000	556	375	1,000	11,500	—
1847	915,981	522	552	581	1,650	—
1847C	84,151	1,350	1,800	2,400	13,000	—
1847D	64,405	1,400	2,000	2,000	10,000	—
1847O	12,000	550	2,200	6,750	28,000	—
1848	260,775	522	552	581	1,500	—
1848C	64,472	1,400	1,900	2,250	19,250	—
1848D	47,465	1,450	2,000	2,350	14,500	—
1849	133,070	522	552	581	2,800	—

Date	Mintage	F-12	VF-20	XF-40	MS-60	Prf-65
1849C	64,823	1,500	1,900	2,400	14,000	—
1849D	39,036	1,550	2,000	2,600	16,500	—
1850	64,491	522	552	581	4,250	—
1850C	63,591	1,350	1,850	2,300	14,000	—
1850D	43,984	1,450	1,950	2,500	33,000	—
1851	377,505	522	552	581	2,800	—
1851C	49,176	1,300	1,900	2,350	17,500	—
1851D	62,710	1,400	1,950	2,400	15,000	—
1851O	41,000	280	590	1,500	13,000	—
1852	573,901	522	552	581	1,400	—
1852C	72,574	1,350	1,900	2,450	7,750	—
1852D	91,584	1,450	2,000	2,450	13,000	—
1853	305,770	522	552	581	1,400	—
1853C	65,571	1,500	1,950	2,350	8.500	—
1853D	89,678	1,550	2,000	2,500	11,000	—
1854	160,675	522	552	581	2,000	—
1854C	39,283	1,400	1,900	2,300	14,000	—
1854D	56,413	1,400	1,875	2,200	11,500	—
1854O	46,000	552	582	611	8,250	—
1854S	268	—	—	—	—	—
Note: 1854S, Bowers & Merena, Oct. 1982, AU-55, $170,000.						
1855	117,098	522	552	581	1,800	—
1855C	39,788	1,400	1,900	2,300	16,000	—
1855D	22,432	1,500	1,950	2,400	19,000	—
1855O	11,100	315	675	2,100	20,000	—
1855S	61,000	552	390	1,000	15,500	—
1856	197,990	552	552	581	2,300	—
1856C	28,457	1,450	1,875	2,400	20,000	—
1856D	19,786	1,475	1,950	2,600	15,000	—
1856O	10,000	370	650	1,600	14,000	—
1856S	105,100	532	300	591	6,750	—
1857	98,188	522	552	581	1,600	123,500
1857C	31,360	1,400	1,900	2,500	9,500	—
1857D	17,046	1,500	2,000	2,650	14,500	—
1857O	13,000	340	640	1,400	15,000	—
1857S	87,000	532	562	591	11,000	—
1858	15,136	532	562	591	3,850	190,000
1858C	38,856	1,400	1,900	2,350	11,000	—
1858D	15,362	1,500	2,000	2,450	12,500	—
1858S	18,600	532	825	2,350	31,000	—
1859	16,814	532	562	591	7,000	—
1859C	31,847	1,400	1,900	2,450	16,000	—
1859D	10,366	1,600	2,150	2,600	16,000	—
1859S	13,220	615	1,800	4,150	30,000	—
1860	19,825	532	562	591	3,650	100,000
1860C	14,813	1,500	2,100	3,000	15,000	—
1860D	14,635	1,500	1,900	2,600	15,000	—
1860S	21,200	500	1,100	2,100	27,000	—
1861	688,150	522	552	591	1,450	100,000
1861C	6,879	1,500	2,400	3,900	25,000	—
1861D	1,597	3,000	4,700	7,000	50,000	—
1861S	18,000	500	1,100	4,500	36,500	—
1862	4,465	532	800	1,850	20,000	96,000
1862S	9,500	1,500	3,000	6,000	62,000	—
1863	2,472	532	1,200	3,750	27,500	90,000
1863S	17,000	600	1,450	4,100	35,500	—
1864	4,220	532	650	1,850	15,000	72,000
1864S	3,888	2,300	4,750	16,000	55,000	—
1865	1,295	500	1,450	4,100	20,000	82,500
1865S	27,612	475	1,400	2,400	20,000	—
1866S	9,000	750	1,750	4,000	40,000	—

Coronet Head.

Coronet head, left, within circle of stars. IN GOD WE TRUST above eagle.

KM# 101 **Designer:** Christian Gobrecht. **Diameter:** 21.6 **Weight:** 8.3590 g. **Composition:** 0.9000 Gold, 0.2419 oz. AGW.

Date	Mintage	VF-20	XF-40	AU-50	MS-60	MS-63	MS-65	Prf-65
1866	6,730	750	1,650	3,500	16,500	—	—	70,000
1866S	34,920	900	2,600	8,800	25,000	—	—	—
1867	6,920	500	1,500	3,300	11,500	—	—	70,000
1867S	29,000	1,400	2,900	8,000	34,500	—	—	—
1868	5,725	650	1,000	3,500	11,500	—	—	70,000
1868S	52,000	486	1,550	4,000	20,000	—	—	—

Date	Mintage	VF-20	XF-40	AU-50	MS-60	MS-63	MS-65	Prf-65
1869	1,785	925	2,400	3,500	17,500	34,000	—	65,000
1869S	31,000	500	1,750	4,000	26,000	—	—	—
1870	4,035	800	2,000	2,850	18,000	—	—	75,000
1870CC	7,675	5,250	15,000	30,000	110,000	137,500	200,000	—
1870S	17,000	950	2,600	8,250	29,000	—	—	—
1871	3,230	900	1,700	3,300	12,500	—	—	70,000
1871CC	20,770	1,250	3,000	12,000	60,000	—	—	—
1871S	25,000	500	950	2,950	13,000	—	—	—
1872	1,690	850	1,925	3,000	15,000	18,000	—	60,000
1872CC	16,980	1,250	5,000	20,000	60,000	—	—	—
1872S	36,400	537	800	3,400	13,500	—	—	—
1873 closed 3	49,305	472	486	500	1,200	6,500	24,000	70,000
1873 open 3	63,200	467	477	487	850	3,650	—	—
1873CC	7,416	2,600	12,500	27,500	60,000	—	—	—
1873S	31,000	525	1,400	3,250	21,000	—	—	—
1874	3,508	660	1,675	2,500	13,000	26,000	—	66,000
1874CC	21,198	850	1,700	9,500	36,000	—	—	—
1874S	16,000	640	2,100	4,800	22,500	—	—	—
1875	220	34,000	45,000	60,000	190,000	—	—	185,000
1875CC	11,828	1,400	4,500	11,500	52,000	—	—	—
1875S	9,000	715	2,250	5,000	16,500	32,500	—	—
1876	1,477	1,100	2,500	4,125	11,000	14,500	55,000	60,000
1876CC	6,887	1,450	5,000	14,000	46,500	82,500	165,000	—
1876S	4,000	2,000	3,600	9,500	30,000	—	—	—
1877	1,152	900	2,750	4,000	13,750	29,000	—	75,000
1877CC	8,680	1,000	3,300	11,000	52,500	—	—	—
1877S	26,700	499	650	1,400	9,200	—	—	—
1878	131,740	469	480	524	550	2,000	—	50,000
1878CC	9,054	3,100	7,200	20,000	60,000	—	—	—
1878S	144,700	467	475	3,000	675	4,250	—	—
1879	301,950	467	475	485	520	2,000	12,000	55,000
1879CC	17,281	1,000	1,500	3,150	22,000	—	—	—
1879S	426,200	469	480	524	950	3,300	—	—
1880	3,166,436	462	470	480	500	840	7,500	54,000
1880CC	51,017	625	815	1,375	9,900	—	—	—
1880S	1,348,900	462	470	480	490	800	5,750	—
1881	5,708,802	462	470	480	500	775	4,800	54,000
1881/80	Inc. above	465	600	750	1,500	4,500	—	—
1881CC	13,886	650	1,500	7,000	22,500	60,000	—	—
1881S	969,000	462	470	480	500	775	7,150	—
1882	2,514,568	462	470	480	500	800	6,150	54,000
1882CC	82,817	625	625	900	7,500	40,000	—	—
1882S	969,000	462	470	480	510	800	4,500	
1883	233,461	479	487	497	530	1,200	—	40,000
1883CC	12,958	625	1,100	3,200	18,000	—	—	—
1883S	83,200	479	478	490	1,000	2,950	—	—
1884	191,078	479	480	497	650	2,250	—	35,000
1884CC	16,402	625	975	3,000	17,000	—	—	—
1884S	177,000	479	487	497	490	2,000	—	—
1885	601,506	462	470	480	505	825	4,800	35,000
1885S	1,211,500	462	470	480	510	790	4,000	—
1886	388,432	462	470	480	510	1,125	5,600	44,000
1886S	3,268,000	462	470	480	510	815	4,500	—
1887	87	—	14,500	20,000	—	—	—	120,000
1887S	1,912,000	462	470	480	510	800	4,800	—
1888	18,296	477	485	497	550	1,500	—	29,000
1888S	293,900	467	475	547	1,200	4,000	—	—
1889	7,565	576	584	557	1,150	2,400	—	30,000
1890	4,328	499	507	550	2,200	6,500	—	27,000
1890CC	53,800	576	584	615	1,600	7,500	55,000	—
1891	61,413	469	480	524	640	2,000	5,400	29,000
1891CC	208,000	561	565	800	1,350	3,500	28,500	—
1892	753,572	462	470	480	530	1,350	7,000	30,000
1892CC	82,968	562	584	750	1,500	6,500	33,500	—
1892O	10,000	524	1,000	1,375	3,300	15,000	—	—
1892S	298,400	462	470	485	525	2,850	—	—
1893	1,528,197	462	470	480	510	1,150	3,900	34,000
1893CC	60,000	596	634	825	1,550	6,650	—	—
1893O	110,000	477	581	585	950	5,950	—	—
1893S	224,000	462	470	485	510	1,040	9,000	—
1894	957,955	462	470	480	500	905	2,600	35,000
1894O	16,600	479	487	570	1,300	5,500	—	—
1894S	55,900	489	487	575	2,900	10,000	—	—
1895	1,345,936	462	470	480	495	905	4,500	29,000
1895S	112,000	467	487	497	3,150	6,500	26,000	—
1896	59,063	462	470	485	510	1,650	4,500	30,000
1896S	155,400	469	480	524	1,150	6,000	24,500	—
1897	867,883	462	470	480	495	905	4,500	35,000
1897S	354,000	462	470	485	865	5,150	—	—

Date	Mintage	VF-20	XF-40	AU-50	MS-60	MS-63	MS-65	Prf-65
1898	633,495	462	470	480	500	905	6,000	30,000
1898S	1,397,400	462	470	480	495	1,310	—	—
1899	1,710,729	462	470	480	495	890	3,600	30,000
1899S	1,545,000	462	470	480	495	1,260	9,600	—
1900	1,405,730	462	470	480	495	890	3,600	30,000
1900S	329,000	462	470	480	500	1,260	14,000	—
1901	616,040	462	470	480	495	890	3,650	27,000
1901S	3,648,000	462	470	480	495	890	3,600	—
1902	172,562	462	470	480	495	890	4,100	27,000
1902S	939,000	462	470	480	495	890	3,600	—
1903	227,024	462	470	480	500	905	4,000	27,000
1903S	1,855,000	462	470	480	495	890	3,600	—
1904	392,136	462	470	480	495	890	3,600	27,000
1904S	97,000	469	480	524	885	4,000	9,600	—
1905	302,308	462	470	480	500	905	4,000	27,000
1905S	880,700	462	470	480	495	3,350	9,600	—
1906	348,820	462	470	480	495	890	3,600	26,000
1906D	320,000	462	470	480	495	905	3,200	—
1906S	598,000	462	470	480	500	1,190	4,400	—
1907	626,192	462	470	480	495	890	3,400	23,000
1907D	888,000	462	470	480	495	890	3,400	—
1908	421,874	462	470	485	510	905	3,400	—

Indian Head.

KM# 129 **Designer:** Bela Lyon Pratt. **Diameter:** 21.6 **Weight:** 8.3590 g. **Composition:** 0.9000 Gold, 0.2419 oz. AGW.

Date	Mintage	VF-20	XF-40	AU-50	MS-60	MS-63	MS-65	Prf-65
1908	578,012	463	475	489	585	1,850	12,500	25,500
1908D	148,000	463	475	489	585	2,000	36,500	—
1908S	82,000	538	600	1,150	2,350	7,000	21,500	—
1909	627,138	463	475	489	565	1,850	13,500	37,000
1909D	3,423,560	463	475	489	565	1,600	12,500	—
1909O	34,200	3,950	4,850	7,650	31,500	75,000	460,000	—
1909S	297,200	493	515	549	1,350	13,250	51,000	—
1910	604,250	463	475	489	565	1,650	13,750	28,500
1910D	193,600	463	475	489	585	4,175	38,500	—
1910S	770,200	503	530	559	975	8,500	49,500	—
1911	915,139	463	475	489	565	1,565	13,500	28,500
1911D	72,500	625	825	1,600	6,850	41,000	265,000	—
1911S	1,416,000	473	510	544	600	5,850	43,000	—
1912	790,144	463	475	489	565	1,565	13,500	28,500
1912S	392,000	508	540	634	1,675	14,500	142,500	—
1913	916,099	463	475	489	565	1,565	13,500	28,000
1913S	408,000	503	535	674	1,450	13,250	120,000	—
1914	247,125	463	475	489	585	2,250	15,500	28,500
1914D	247,000	463	475	489	585	2,550	23,500	—
1914S	263,000	508	530	584	1,375	14,350	105,000	—
1915	588,075	463	475	489	565	1,565	105,000	39,000
1915S	164,000	518	550	669	1,950	17,000	14,500	—
1916S	240,000	488	510	569	770	6,750	110,000	—
1929	662,000	11,500	14,750	18,000	27,500	45,000	88,500	—

$10 (EAGLE)

GOLD

Liberty Cap.

Small eagle.

KM# 21 **Designer:** Robert Scot. **Diameter:** 33 **Weight:** 17.5000 g. **Composition:** 0.9160 Gold, 0.5154 oz. AGW.

Date	Mintage	F-12	VF-20	XF-40	MS-60
1795 13 leaves	5,583	28,500	33,850	48,500	122,500
1795 9 leaves	Inc. above	30,000	45,000	73,500	250,000
1796	4,146	27,500	36,000	50,000	135,000
1797 small eagle	3,615	31,500	40,000	55,000	200,000

Liberty Cap.

Liberty cap on head, right, flanked by stars. Heraldic eagle.

KM# 30 **Designer:** Robert Scot. **Diameter:** 33 **Weight:** 17.5000 g. **Composition:** 0.9160 Gold, 0.5154 oz. AGW.

Date	Mintage	F-12	VF-20	XF-40	MS-60
1797 large eagle	10,940	9,800	12,850	21,400	58,500
1798/97 9 stars left, 4 right	900	13,500	19,000	34,500	127,500
1798/97 7 stars left, 6 right	842	28,500	38,500	87,500	235,000
1799 large star obv	37,449	9,350	10,750	18,200	37,500
1799 small star obv	Inc. above	9,350	10,750	18,200	37,500
1800	5,999	9,500	10,750	18,350	39,500
1801	44,344	9,250	10,900	17,400	37,500
1803 extra star	15,017	9,600	11,850	19,550	67,500
1803 large stars rev	Inc. above	9,250	11,400	17,800	37,500
1804 crosslet 4	3,757	16,500	22,750	31,500	92,500
1804 plain 4	—	—	—	—	400,000

Coronet Head.

Old-style head, left, within circle of stars. No motto above eagle.

KM# 66.1 **Designer:** Christian Gobrecht. **Diameter:** 27 **Weight:** 16.7180 g. **Composition:** 0.9000 Gold, 0.4837 oz. AGW.

Date	Mintage	F-12	VF-20	XF-40	MS-60	Prf-65
1838	7,200	1,750	2,650	6,850	43,500	1,500,000
1839/8 Type of 1838	25,801	1,100	1,450	5,850	28,500	1,500,000
1839 large letters	Inc. above	800	1,150	2,150	32,000	—

Coronet Head.

New-style head, left, within circle of stars. No motto above eagle.

KM# 66.2 **Designer:** Christian Gobrecht. **Diameter:** 27 **Weight:** 16.7180 g. **Composition:** 0.9000 Gold, 0.4837 oz. AGW.

Date	Mintage	F-12	VF-20	XF-40	MS-60	Prf-65
1839 small letters	12,447	975	1,550	6,850	75,000	—
1840	47,338	994	1,059	1,333	11,500	—
1841	63,131	974	1,049	1,233	9,000	—
1841O	2,500	1,750	3,450	6,950	—	—
1842 small date	81,507	974	1,049	1,158	15,000	—
1842 large date	Inc. above	974	1,049	1,148	9,500	—
1842O	27,400	974	1,059	1,463	22,500	—
1843	75,462	974	1,049	1,263	16,750	—
1843O	175,162	974	1,059	1,218	12,000	—
1844	6,361	800	1,350	3,200	16,750	—
1844O	118,700	974	1,059	1,403	15,000	—
1845	26,153	1,009	1,219	1,343	17,500	—
1845O	47,500	994	1,059	875	16,500	—
1845O repunched	Inc. above	1,069	1,419	3,850	—	—

$10 GOLD

Date	Mintage	F-12	VF-20	XF-40	MS-60	Prf-65
1846	20,095	1,019	1,289	1,250	—	—
1846O	81,780	974	1,059	1,150	—	—
1846/5	Inc. above	1,069	1,419	1,135	—	—
1847	862,258	974	1,049	1,093	3,450	—
1847O	571,500	974	1,049	1,093	6,500	—
1848	145,484	974	1,049	1,158	5,000	—
1848O	38,850	1,049	1,239	1,850	17,750	—
1849	653,618	974	1,049	1,093	3,400	—
1849O	20,900	1,049	1,239	2,450	27,500	—
1850 large date	291,451	974	1,049	1,093	4,500	—
1850 small date	Inc. above	1,049	1,239	1,150	8,500	—
1850O	57,500	994	1,074	1,275	19,500	—
1851	176,328	974	1,049	1,093	5,150	—
1851O	263,000	974	1,059	1,148	6,650	—
1852	263,106	974	1,049	1,093	5,250	—
1852O	18,000	1,049	1,219	1,650	27,500	—
1853	201,253	994	1,059	1,093	3,600	—
1853/2	Inc. above	994	1,074	1,428	14,950	—
1853O	51,000	974	1,074	1,158	14,500	—
1854	54,250	974	1,049	1,118	6,250	—
1854O small date	52,500	994	1,074	1,398	11,000	—
1854O large date	Inc. above	1,049	1,214	925	9,450	—
1854S	123,826	974	1,049	1,118	10,500	—
1855	121,701	974	1,049	1,093	4,750	—
1855O	18,000	994	1,074	2,100	28,000	—
1856	60,490	974	1,049	1,093	4,250	—
1856O	14,500	1,049	1,374	2,150	18,500	—
1856S	68,000	974	1,049	1,168	9,000	—
1857	16,606	994	1,074	1,050	13,500	—
1857O	5,500	1,149	1,800	3,650	—	—
1857S	26,000	994	1,059	1,050	11,500	—
1858	2,521	3,000	5,200	8,250	35,000	—
1858O	20,000	974	1,049	1,418	10,000	—
1858S	11,800	900	1,600	3,950	—	—
1859	16,093	994	1,074	1,278	10,500	—
1859O	2,300	2,000	4,250	10,500	—	—
1859S	7,000	1,450	2,600	5,250	—	—
1860	15,105	1,019	1,114	1,328	8,450	175,000
1860O	11,100	1,039	1,214	1,850	13,750	—
1860S	5,000	1,400	2,950	6,400	—	—
1861	113,233	974	1,049	1,093	6,250	170,000
1861S	15,500	690	1,600	3,750	—	—
1862	10,995	1,049	1,204	1,200	—	170,000
1862S	12,500	700	2,000	3,450	—	—
1863	1,248	2,400	4,000	10,000	52,500	165,000
1863S	10,000	700	1,600	3,750	29,500	—
1864	3,580	775	1,800	4,950	18,000	165,000
1864S	2,500	2,600	5,100	17,500	—	—
1865	4,005	900	1,950	4,850	34,500	165,000
1865S	16,700	1,700	4,850	12,500	—	—
1865S over inverted 186	Inc. above	1,300	3,450	8,750	50,000	—
1866S	8,500	1,000	2,650	5,950	—	—

$10 GOLD

Coronet Head.

New-style head, left, within circle of stars. IN GOD WE TRUST above eagle.

KM# 102 Designer: Christian Gobrecht. **Diameter:** 27 **Weight:** 16.7180 g. **Composition:** 0.9000 Gold, 0.4837 oz. AGW.

Date	Mintage	VF-20	XF-40	AU-50	MS-60	MS-63	MS-65	Prf-65
1866	3,780	850	2,450	5,000	—	—	—	110,000
1866S	11,500	1,550	3,850	8,000	—	—	—	—
1867	3,140	1,500	2,600	5,000	33,000	—	—	—
1867S	9,000	2,350	6,650	9,850	—	—	—	—
1868	10,655	1,008	1,100	2,250	19,000	—	—	110,000
1868S	13,500	1,350	2,400	3,900	—	—	—	—
1869	1,855	1,550	3,000	5,650	36,000	—	—	—
1869S	6,430	1,500	2,700	6,250	25,000	—	—	—
1870	4,025	985	1,650	3,950	—	—	—	—
1870CC	5,908	13,000	30,000	52,500	—	—	—	—
1870S	8,000	1,150	2,850	7,400	33,500	—	—	—
1871	1,820	1,500	3,000	5,000	20,000	—	—	110,000

Date	Mintage	VF-20	XF-40	AU-50	MS-60	MS-63	MS-65	Prf-65
1871CC	8,085	2,600	6,400	22,500	65,000	—	—	—
1871S	16,500	1,300	2,200	6,000	30,000	—	—	—
1872	1,650	2,400	5,500	8,700	15,000	34,000	—	90,000
1872CC	4,600	2,850	9,850	24,500	—	—	—	—
1872S	17,300	850	1,175	1,900	—	—	—	—
1873 closed 3	825	4,500	9,750	17,500	55,000	—	—	—
1873CC	4,543	6,000	13,500	31,000	—	—	—	—
1873S	12,000	1,150	2,850	5,100	27,500	—	—	—
1874	53,160	934	966	980	2,100	7,250	42,500	120,000
1874CC	16,767	1,150	3,050	11,000	52,500	75,000	—	—
1874S	10,000	1,275	3,400	7,250	—	—	—	—
1875	120	40,000	67,500	80,000	—	—	—	—

Note: 1875, Akers, Aug. 1990, Proof, $115,000.

Date	Mintage	VF-20	XF-40	AU-50	MS-60	MS-63	MS-65	Prf-65
1875CC	7,715	4,250	9,850	25,000	71,500	—	—	—
1876	732	3,000	8,500	18,500	—	—	—	—
1876CC	4,696	3,600	7,750	21,500	—	—	—	—
1876S	5,000	1,300	2,950	7,500	—	—	—	—
1877	817	3,350	6,350	9,850	37,500	—	—	—
1877CC	3,332	2,400	6,750	15,000	—	—	—	—
1877S	17,000	936	1,250	2,450	33,500	—	—	—
1878	73,800	924	966	980	975	6,750	29,000	—
1878CC	3,244	3,850	10,000	19,000	—	—	—	—
1878S	26,100	936	975	2,150	16,500	29,500	—	—
1879	384,770	927	966	980	1,117	5,000	15,750	83,000
1879/78	Inc. above	934	978	1,265	1,250	2,850	—	—
1879CC	1,762	6,650	12,500	26,000	—	—	—	—
1879O	1,500	2,150	5,450	10,250	—	—	—	—
1879S	224,000	927	966	980	1,150	6,500	49,500	—
1880	1,644,876	909	928	942	972	3,650	—	—
1880CC	11,190	900	1,000	1,950	15,500	—	—	—
1880O	9,200	1,029	1,450	1,850	20,000	—	—	—
1880S	506,250	909	928	942	992	4,850	25,000	—
1881	3,877,260	909	928	942	972	1,385	16,500	63,000
1881CC	24,015	1,055	1,200	1,800	6,850	36,500	—	—
1881O	8,350	1,009	1,150	1,500	6,950	—	—	—
1881S	970,000	909	928	942	982	1,385	—	—
1882	2,324,480	909	928	942	972	1,385	19,500	63,000
1882CC	6,764	985	1,750	3,250	—	—	—	—
1882O	10,820	937	1,115	1,250	6,350	18,500	—	—
1882S	132,000	937	966	980	1,054	3,650	—	—
1883	208,740	909	928	942	982	3,100	—	63,000
1883CC	12,000	1,109	1,250	2,600	22,500	—	—	—
1883O	800	3,000	7,950	10,500	—	—	—	—
1883S	38,000	937	966	980	1,275	10,500	23,500	—
1884	76,905	937	966	980	1,152	5,100	15,000	53,000
1884CC	9,925	1,129	1,450	2,350	12,850	55,000	—	—
1884S	124,250	909	928	942	1,067	6,500	—	—
1885	253,527	909	928	942	972	4,850	—	53,000
1885S	228,000	909	928	942	972	4,400	—	—
1886	236,160	909	928	942	972	5,100	—	53,000
1886S	826,000	909	928	942	982	1,500	—	—
1887	53,680	937	966	980	1,050	6,150	—	53,000
1887S	817,000	909	928	942	982	2,950	—	—
1888	132,996	937	966	980	1,212	6,600	—	—
1888O	21,335	937	966	980	1,152	5,750	—	—
1888S	648,700	909	928	942	972	2,700	—	—
1889	4,485	967	1,155	1,100	2,700	—	—	53,000
1889S	425,400	909	928	942	982	1,500	18,500	—
1890	58,043	947	966	1,000	1,015	5,500	16,000	46,000
1890CC	17,500	1,049	1,148	1,200	3,850	18,500	—	—
1891	91,868	967	1,006	1,020	1,050	4,500	—	48,000
1891CC	103,732	1,049	1,108	1,125	1,300	7,150	—	—
1892	797,552	909	928	942	972	1,385	9,100	48,000
1892CC	40,000	1,049	1,108	1,165	3,800	22,500	—	—
1892O	28,688	967	969	980	1,030	11,000	—	—
1892S	115,500	937	990	1,004	1,034	4,500	—	—
1893	1,840,895	909	928	942	972	1,385	16,500	46,000
1893CC	14,000	1,049	1,148	1,800	8,500	—	—	—
1893O	17,000	937	966	1,022	1,252	5,450	—	—
1893S	141,350	937	966	980	1,010	4,950	19,500	—
1894	2,470,778	909	928	942	972	1,510	—	46,000
1894O	107,500	937	966	975	1,000	6,350	—	—
1894S	25,000	937	990	1,100	3,950	—	—	—
1895	567,826	909	928	942	972	1,385	17,500	43,500
1895O	98,000	937	966	992	1,122	8,000	—	—
1895S	49,000	937	978	1,040	2,400	9,500	—	—
1896	76,348	909	928	942	982	2,550	30,000	43,500
1896S	123,750	937	961	1,002	2,500	12,000	28,500	—
1897	1,000,159	909	928	942	972	1,510	10,000	—

Date	Mintage	VF-20	XF-40	AU-50	MS-60	MS-63	MS-65	Prf-65
1897O	42,500	937	966	980	1,105	5,850	27,500	—
1897S	234,750	937	961	975	1,125	5,750	22,500	—
1898	812,197	909	928	942	972	1,510	9,000	43,500
1898S	473,600	937	861	975	1,042	5,100	18,500	—
1899	1,262,305	909	928	942	972	1,385	6,500	43,500
1899O	37,047	937	966	982	1,152	8,450	—	—
1899S	841,000	909	928	942	982	3,650	12,850	—
1900	293,960	909	928	942	982	1,385	9,500	43,500
1900O	81,000	937	966	980	1,205	6,750	—	—
1901	1,718,825	909	928	942	972	1,385	4,050	43,500
1901O	72,041	937	966	980	1,092	3,750	12,500	—
1901S	2,812,750	909	928	942	972	1,385	6,250	—
1902	82,513	909	928	942	982	2,800	11,750	43,500
1902S	469,500	909	928	942	972	1,385	6,250	—
1903	125,926	909	928	942	982	2,450	13,500	43,500
1903O	112,771	937	966	980	1,082	3,250	18,000	—
1903S	538,000	909	928	942	982	1,410	5,350	—
1904	162,038	909	928	942	982	2,000	9,500	46,000
1904O	108,950	937	966	980	1,082	3,700	16,500	—
1905	201,078	909	928	942	972	1,450	8,500	43,500
1905S	369,250	937	961	1,007	1,100	5,600	22,500	—
1906	165,497	909	928	942	982	2,450	10,000	43,500
1906D	981,000	909	928	942	972	1,385	7,000	—
1906O	86,895	937	966	980	1,122	4,900	14,500	—
1906S	457,000	937	961	980	1,132	5,000	15,500	—
1907	1,203,973	909	928	942	972	1,385	3,950	43,500
1907D	1,030,000	909	928	942	982	2,250	—	—
1907S	210,500	937	961	1,002	1,172	5,450	17,000	—

Indian Head.

No motto next to eagle.

KM# 125 **Designer:** Augustus Saint-Gaudens. **Diameter:** 27 **Weight:** 16.7180 g. **Composition:** 0.9000 Gold, 0.4837 oz. AGW. **Notes:** 1907 varieties are distinguished by whether the edge is rolled or wired, and whether the legend E PLURIBUS UNUM has periods between each word.

Date	Mintage	VF-20	XF-40	AU-50	MS-60	MS-63	MS-65	Prf-65
1907 wire edge, periods before and after legend	500	13,850	17,500	21,000	26,500	44,500	72,500	—
1907 same, without stars on edge, unique	—	—	—	—	—	—	—	—
1907 rolled edge, periods	42	26,000	38,500	49,000	66,500	113,000	265,000	—
1907 without periods	239,406	1,013	1,030	1,052	1,215	3,400	10,500	—
1908 without motto	33,500	998	1,015	1,037	1,200	4,650	15,500	—
1908D without motto	210,000	998	1,015	1,037	1,240	7,000	37,500	—

Indian Head.

IN GOD WE TRUST left of eagle.

KM# 130 **Designer:** Augustus Saint-Gaudens. **Diameter:** 27 **Weight:** 16.7180 g. **Composition:** 0.9000 Gold, 0.4837 oz. AGW.

Date	Mintage	VF-20	XF-40	AU-50	MS-60	MS-63	MS-65	Prf-65
1908	341,486	993	1,010	1,032	1,185	2,450	12,250	75,000
1908D	836,500	998	1,030	1,052	1,205	7,000	29,000	—
1908S	59,850	1,008	1,085	1,150	2,950	11,500	25,500	—
1909	184,863	993	1,010	1,032	1,165	3,950	18,500	80,000
1909D	121,540	998	1,015	1,037	1,230	6,100	36,500	—
1909S	292,350	998	1,015	1,037	1,375	6,350	19,000	—
1910	318,704	993	1,010	1,032	1,155	1,500	12,750	76,500

Date	Mintage	VF-20	XF-40	AU-50	MS-60	MS-63	MS-65	Prf-65
1910D	2,356,640	988	1,005	1,032	1,155	1,500	10,250	—
1910S	811,000	998	1,015	1,037	1,500	8,850	54,500	—
1911	505,595	988	1,005	1,027	1,170	1,550	10,000	75,000
1911D	30,100	1,200	1,400	1,700	9,000	31,000	140,000	—
1911S	51,000	1,028	1,150	1,200	2,050	10,000	21,500	—
1912	405,083	993	1,010	1,032	1,155	1,475	12,000	75,000
1912S	300,000	998	1,015	1,037	1,600	7,300	46,000	—
1913	442,071	993	1,010	1,032	1,155	1,500	11,000	75,000
1913S	66,000	1,043	1,200	1,300	4,650	31,500	125,000	—
1914	151,050	993	1,010	1,032	1,005	2,250	12,000	75,000
1914D	343,500	993	1,010	1,032	1,155	2,550	18,000	—
1914S	208,000	1,003	1,165	1,250	1,400	7,750	33,500	—
1915	351,075	993	1,010	1,032	155	2,000	12,000	75,000
1915S	59,000	1,043	1,075	1,200	3,150	15,500	58,500	—
1916S	138,500	1,028	1,045	1,100	1,425	6,350	26,500	—
1920S	126,500	12,500	16,850	19,750	37,000	88,500	275,000	—
1926	1,014,000	988	1,005	1,027	1,150	1,300	3,600	—
1930S	96,000	8,500	11,250	14,850	23,500	46,500	79,500	—
1932	4,463,000	988	1,005	1,027	1,150	1,300	3,600	—
1933	312,500	—	140,000	160,000	180,000	225,000	600,000	—

$20 (DOUBLE EAGLE)

GOLD

Liberty Head.

Coronet head, left, within circle of stars. TWENTY D. below eagle, no motto above eagle.

KM# 74.1 **Designer:** James B. Longacre. **Diameter:** 34 **Weight:** 33.4360 g. **Composition:** 0.9000 Gold, 0.9675 oz. AGW.

Date	Mintage	VF-20	XF-40	AU-50	MS-60	MS-63	MS-65	Prf-65
1849 unique, in Smithsonian collection	1	—	—	—	—	—	—	—
1850	1,170,261	1,946	2,026	3,000	8,500	43,500	175,000	—
1850O	141,000	1,880	3,500	9,800	45,000	—	—	—
1851	2,087,155	1,986	2,156	2,441	3,850	13,500	—	—
1851O	315,000	2,061	2,856	4,250	23,000	58,500	—	—
1852	2,053,026	1,986	2,156	2,341	3,950	17,500	—	—
1852O	190,000	2,016	2,650	3,800	22,500	—	—	—
1853	1,261,326	1,986	2,156	2,156	5,000	27,500	—	—
1853/2	Inc. above	2,066	2,250	6,850	33,500	—	—	—
1853O	71,000	2,076	3,650	4,850	32,500	65,000	—	—
1854	757,899	1,986	2,156	2,156	9,250	26,500	—	—
1854	Inc. above	2,226	2,350	6,000	—	—	—	—
1854O	3,250	95,000	225,000	365,000	—	—	—	—
1854S	141,468	2,066	2,146	3,000	6,000	15,500	52,500	—
1855	364,666	1,986	2,146	2,250	8,850	66,500	—	—
1855O	8,000	3,650	19,500	24,500	110,000	—	—	—
1855S	879,675	1,966	2,156	2,441	7,200	19,500	—	—
1856	329,878	1,986	2,156	2,241	8,400	24,500	—	—
1856O	2,250	97,500	165,000	300,000	525,000	750,000	—	—
1856S	1,189,750	1,966	2,156	2,241	5,900	15,000	30,000	—
1857	439,375	1,986	2,156	2,341	3,400	26,500	—	—
1857O	30,000	2,041	2,950	6,400	31,000	115,000	—	—
1857S	970,500	1,966	2,156	2,341	4,500	7,250	12,850	—
1858	211,714	2,041	2,146	2,241	5,500	34,500	—	—
1858O	35,250	2,250	3,850	7,500	42,000	—	—	—
1858S	846,710	1,966	2,176	2,531	8,500	—	—	—
1859	43,597	2,041	2,450	4,400	28,000	—	—	280,000

Date	Mintage	VF-20	XF-40	AU-50	MS-60	MS-63	MS-65	Prf-65
1859O	9,100	6,400	16,500	44,000	110,000	—	—	—
1859S	636,445	1,966	2,156	2,491	5,000	35,000	—	—
1860	577,670	1,966	2,156	2,341	3,950	18,000	63,500	—
1860O	6,600	3,650	14,500	24,000	100,000	—	—	—
1860S	544,950	1,986	2,446	2,531	7,350	18,500	48,000	—
1861	2,976,453	1,966	2,156	2,316	3,950	12,850	41,500	275,000
1861O	17,741	5,650	17,500	24,000	88,000	—	—	—
1861S	768,000	1,986	2,256	2,250	10,500	31,500	—	—

Liberty.

Coronet head, left, within circle of stars. Paquet design, TWENTY D. below eagle.

KM# 93 **Weight:** 33.4360 g. **Composition:** 0.9000 Gold, 0.9675 oz. AGW. **Notes:** In 1861 the reverse was redesigned by Anthony C. Paquet, but it was withdrawn soon after its release. The letters in the inscriptions on the Paquet-reverse variety are taller than on the regular reverse.

Date	Mintage	VF-20	XF-40	AU-50	MS-60	MS-63	MS-65	Prf-65
1861 2 Known	—	—	—	—	—	—	—	—
Note: 1861 Paquet reverse, Bowers & Merena, Nov. 1988, MS-67, $660,000.								
1861S	—	19,500	54,000	92,500	275,000	—	—	—
Note: Included in mintage of 1861S, KM#74.1								

Liberty.

Longacre design resumed.

KM# A74.1 **Weight:** 33.4360 g. **Composition:** 0.9000 Gold, 0.9675 oz. AGW.

Date	Mintage	VF-20	XF-40	AU-50	MS-60	MS-63	MS-65	Prf-65
1862	92,133	1,966	3,500	6,000	17,500	36,500	—	250,000
1862S	854,173	1,951	2,031	2,100	12,400	36,000	—	—
1863	142,790	1,966	2,650	3,950	19,500	39,500	—	250,000
1863S	966,570	1,951	2,111	2,196	7,350	28,500	—	—
1864	204,285	1,966	2,046	2,450	14,500	40,000	—	250,000
1864S	793,660	1,951	2,091	2,176	8,600	32,000	—	—
1865	351,200	1,966	2,111	2,281	6,200	26,000	—	250,000
1865S	1,042,500	1,951	2,111	2,191	4,200	9,000	19,500	—
1866S	Inc. below	2,750	11,500	37,500	—	—	—	—

Liberty.

Coronet head, left, within circle of stars. TWENTY D. below eagle. IN GOD WE TRUST above eagle.

KM# 74.2 Designer: James B. Longacre. **Diameter:** 34 **Weight:** 33.4360 g. **Composition:** 0.9000 Gold, 0.9675 oz. AGW.

Date	Mintage	VF-20	XF-40	AU-50	MS-60	MS-63	MS-65	Prf-65
1866	698,775	1,911	2,076	2,136	6,950	28,500	—	200,000
1866S	842,250	1,911	2,086	2,100	15,500	—	—	—
1867	251,065	1,911	2,096	2,136	3,250	30,000	—	200,000
1867S	920,750	1,911	2,086	2,100	15,000	—	—	—
1868	98,600	1,951	2,186	2,250	11,500	50,000	—	200,000
1868S	837,500	1,911	2,056	2,150	10,000	—	—	—
1869	175,155	1,921	2,046	2,100	6,800	22,750	—	210,000
1869S	686,750	1,911	2,076	2,100	7,000	45,000	—	—
1870	155,185	1,931	2,076	2,300	9,250	50,000	—	215,000
1870CC	3,789	200,000	275,000	400,000	—	—	—	—
1870S	982,000	1,911	2,031	2,091	5,450	34,000	—	—
1871	80,150	1,921	2,031	2,100	4,500	24,500	—	—
1871CC	17,387	9,500	19,500	45,000	97,500	300,000	650,000	—
1871S	928,000	1,911	2,046	2,131	4,750	22,000	—	—
1872	251,880	1,911	2,076	2,161	3,750	24,500	—	—
1872CC	26,900	2,550	5,450	8,950	38,500	—	—	—
1872S	780,000	1,911	2,076	2,136	3,250	23,500	—	—
1873 closed 3	Est. 208,925	1,911	2,136	2,196	3,350	—	—	200,000
1873 open 3	Est. 1,500,900	1,911	2,076	2,146	2,310	12,000	85,000	—
1873CC	22,410	2,900	4,750	11,750	37,500	115,000	—	—
1873S closed 3	1,040,600	1,911	2,046	2,139	2,150	20,000	—	—
1873S open 3	Inc. above	1,911	2,076	2,136	5,900	29,500	—	—
1874	366,800	1,911	2,076	2,136	2,300	19,500	—	—
1874CC	115,085	2,100	2,450	3,400	11,500	—	—	—
1874S	1,214,000	1,911	2,046	2,139	2,192	24,000	—	—
1875	295,740	1,911	2,076	2,136	2,222	13,500	—	—
1875CC	111,151	1,950	2,250	2,650	4,850	26,500	—	—
1875S	1,230,000	1,911	2,046	2,139	2,331	16,850	—	—
1876	583,905	1,911	2,066	2,139	2,350	13,500	78,500	—
1876CC	138,441	1,960	2,300	2,700	7,750	—	—	—
1876S	1,597,000	1,911	2,046	2,139	2,310	12,400	90,000	—

Liberty.

Coronet head, left, within circle of stars. TWENTY DOLLARS below eagle.

KM# 74.3 Weight: 33.4360 g. **Composition:** 0.9000 Gold, 0.9675 oz. AGW.

Date	Mintage	VF-20	XF-40	AU-50	MS-60	MS-63	MS-65	Prf-65
1877	397,670	1,831	1,971	2,005	2,096	11,500	—	—
1877CC	42,565	1,986	2,150	3,850	19,500	—	—	—
1877S	1,735,000	1,821	1,871	1,935	2,066	15,500	—	—

Date	Mintage	VF-20	XF-40	AU-50	MS-60	MS-63	MS-65	Prf-65
1878	543,645	1,841	1,971	2,015	2,186	12,500	—	—
1878CC	13,180	2,450	3,950	7,250	30,000	—	—	—
1878S	1,739,000	1,821	1,846	1,860	2,066	20,500	—	—
1879	207,630	1,901	1,971	1,965	2,066	16,500	—	—
1879CC	10,708	3,000	4,850	8,850	34,000	77,500	—	—
1879O	2,325	12,500	21,500	27,500	88,500	127,500	—	—
1879S	1,223,800	1,821	1,846	1,860	2,150	30,000	—	—
1880	51,456	1,931	2,001	2,040	3,150	25,000	—	110,000
1880S	836,000	1,821	1,846	1,870	2,050	17,500	—	—
1881	2,260	12,500	21,000	34,500	79,000	—	—	110,000
1881S	727,000	1,821	1,846	1,870	2,166	20,000	—	—
1882	630	13,500	39,500	88,000	130,000	225,000	—	130,000
1882CC	39,140	1,971	2,000	2,600	8,850	65,000	—	—
1882S	1,125,000	1,821	1,846	1,850	2,136	18,500	—	—
1883 proof only	92	—	—	27,500	—	—	—	195,000
1883CC	59,962	1,971	2,000	2,600	7,850	30,000	—	—
1883S	1,189,000	1,821	1,846	1,860	2,066	8,500	—	—
1884 proof only	71	—	—	35,000	—	—	—	225,000
1884CC	81,139	1,971	2,000	2,600	5,000	25,000	—	—
1884S	916,000	1,821	1,846	1,860	2,006	6,150	46,500	—
1885	828	8,450	13,850	18,500	60,000	100,000	—	115,000
1885CC	9,450	2,500	3,850	6,450	19,500	48,500	—	—
1885S	683,500	1,821	1,846	1,870	2,006	5,700	29,500	—
1886	1,106	10,500	18,500	37,500	70,000	140,000	—	105,000
1887	121	—	—	26,500	—	—	—	142,500
1887S	283,000	1,821	1,846	1,860	2,066	15,000	36,500	—
1888	226,266	1,821	1,846	1,880	2,116	7,900	36,500	93,500
1888S	859,600	1,821	1,846	1,860	2,006	4,650	—	—
1889	44,111	1,981	2,101	2,205	2,456	13,500	36,500	105,000
1889CC	30,945	1,971	2,150	3,000	7,950	25,500	—	—
1889S	774,700	1,821	1,846	1,860	2,016	5,400	—	—
1890	75,995	1,821	1,871	1,935	2,066	10,000	—	100,000
1890CC	91,209	1,971	2,000	2,450	4,850	32,500	—	—
1890S	802,750	1,821	1,846	1,860	2,006	6,350	30,000	—
1891	1,442	8,500	15,000	22,500	75,000	125,000	—	108,000
1891CC	5,000	4,950	9,000	11,000	24,500	71,500	—	—
1891S	1,288,125	1,821	1,846	1,860	2,006	3,000	—	—
1892	4,523	2,000	3,650	6,250	13,500	35,000	—	90,000
1892CC	27,265	1,971	2,100	2,850	7,500	36,500	—	—
1892S	930,150	1,821	1,846	1,919	1,996	2,950	24,500	—
1893	344,339	1,821	1,866	1,925	2,036	2,100	—	95,000
1893CC	18,402	2,068	2,100	2,850	7,000	29,500	—	—
1893S	996,175	1,781	1,801	1,810	1,841	2,850	28,500	—
1894	1,368,990	1,781	1,801	1,810	1,841	1,800	26,500	85,000
1894S	1,048,550	1,781	1,801	1,810	1,841	2,450	27,500	—
1895	1,114,656	1,781	1,801	1,810	1,841	1,650	17,500	82,500
1895S	1,143,500	1,781	1,801	1,810	1,841	2,200	15,500	—
1896	792,663	1,781	1,801	1,810	1,841	1,850	19,500	200,000
1896S	1,403,925	1,781	1,801	1,810	1,841	1,975	23,500	—
1897	1,383,261	1,781	1,801	1,810	1,841	2,250	18,500	200,000
1897S	1,470,250	1,781	1,801	1,810	1,841	1,450	21,500	—
1898	170,470	1,786	1,831	1,910	2,141	4,500	—	200,000
1898S	2,575,175	1,786	1,801	1,810	1,841	1,650	7,950	—
1899	1,669,384	1,781	1,801	1,810	1,841	1,625	12,500	200,000
1899S	2,010,300	1,781	1,801	1,810	1,841	1,750	21,500	—
1900	1,874,584	1,781	1,801	1,810	1,841	2,185	5,900	200,000
1900S	2,459,500	1,781	1,801	1,810	1,841	2,100	23,000	—
1901	111,526	1,781	1,801	1,810	1,841	2,185	5,850	200,000
1901S	1,596,000	1,781	1,801	1,810	1,841	3,850	21,500	—
1902	31,254	1,781	1,996	2,070	2,251	11,750	37,500	200,000
1902S	1,753,625	1,781	1,801	1,810	1,841	2,900	23,500	—
1903	287,428	1,781	1,801	1,810	1,841	2,185	5,500	200,000
1903S	954,000	1,781	1,801	1,810	1,841	2,215	13,500	—
1904	6,256,797	1,781	1,801	1,810	1,841	2,150	4,200	200,000
1904S	5,134,175	1,781	1,801	1,810	1,841	2,150	5,400	—
1905	59,011	1,786	1,821	1,845	2,141	14,500	—	200,000
1905S	1,813,000	1,781	1,801	1,810	1,841	3,250	20,500	—
1906	69,690	1,786	1,806	1,865	2,021	6,850	26,500	200,000
1906D	620,250	1,781	1,801	1,810	1,841	3,450	22,500	—
1906S	2,065,750	1,781	1,801	1,810	1,841	2,350	19,500	—
1907	1,451,864	1,781	1,801	1,810	1,841	2,150	8,200	200,000
1907D	842,250	1,781	1,801	1,810	1,841	2,650	7,350	—
1907S	2,165,800	1,781	1,801	1,810	1,841	2,650	27,000	—

Saint-Gaudens.

Roman numerals in date. No motto below eagle.

KM# 126 Designer: Augustus Saint-Gaudens. **Diameter:** 34 **Weight:** 33.4360 g. **Composition:** 0.9000 Gold, 0.9675 oz. AGW.

Date	Mintage	VF-20	XF-40	AU-50	MS-60	MS-63	MS-65	Prf-65
MCMVII (1907) high relief, unique, AU-55, $150,000	—	—	—	—	—	—	—	—
MCMVII (1907) high relief, wire rim	11,250	7,650	8,750	10,350	14,000	24,500	45,000	—
MCMVII (1907) high relief, flat rim	Inc. above	7,900	9,250	11,350	15,250	26,000	46,500	—

Saint-Gaudens.

Arabic numerals in date. No motto below eagle.

KM# 127 Designer: Augustus Saint-Gaudens. **Diameter:** 34 **Weight:** 33.4360 g. **Composition:** 0.9000 Gold, 0.9675 oz. AGW.

Date	Mintage	VF-20	XF-40	AU-50	MS-60	MS-63	MS-65	Prf-65
1907 large letters on edge, unique	—	—	—	—	—	—	—	—
1907 small letters on edge	361,667	1,796	1,829	1,839	1,865	2,185	4,600	—
1908	4,271,551	1,786	1,819	1,819	1,825	1,975	2,450	—
1908D	663,750	1,796	1,829	1,929	1,850	2,085	11,800	—

Saint-Gaudens.

Roman numerals in date. No motto below eagle.

KM# Pn1874 Designer: Augustus Saint-Gaudens. **Diameter:** 34 **Weight:** 33.4360 g. **Composition:** 0.9000 Gold, 0.9675 oz. AGW. **Notes:** The "Roman numerals" varieties for 1907 use Roman numerals for the date instead of Arabic numerals. The lettered-edge varieties have "E Pluribus Unum" on the edge, with stars between the words.

Date	Mintage	VF-20	XF-40	AU-50	MS-60	MS-63	MS-65	Prf-65
1907 extremely high relief, unique	—	—	—	—	—	—	—	—
1907 extremely high relief, lettered edge	—	—	—	—	—	—	—	—

Note: 1907 extremely high relief, lettered edge, Prf-68, private sale, 1990, $1,500,000.

Saint-Gaudens.

IN GOD WE TRUST below eagle.

KM# 131 Designer: Augustus Saint-Gaudens. **Diameter:** 34 **Weight:** 33.4360 g. **Composition:** 0.9000 Gold, 0.9675 oz. AGW.

Date	Mintage	VF-20	XF-40	AU-50	MS-60	MS-63	MS-65	Prf-65
1908	156,359	1,791	1,824	1,829	1,875	2,300	28,000	76,500
1908 Roman finish; Prf64 Rare	—	—	—	—	—	—	—	—
Note: Rare								
1908D	349,500	1,796	1,829	1,839	1,865	2,105	7,000	—
1908S	22,000	2,450	3,150	4,850	10,650	24,500	52,500	—
1909/8	161,282	1,796	1,829	1,879	1,850	6,250	52,000	—
1909	Inc. above	1,806	1,849	1,849	1,925	3,150	46,000	92,500
1909D	52,500	1,836	1,869	1,974	3,100	8,950	57,500	—
1909S	2,774,925	1,796	1,829	1,839	1,845	2,060	7,000	—
1910	482,167	1,791	1,824	1,829	1,875	2,075	9,000	84,500
1910D	429,000	1,791	1,824	1,829	1,850	2,045	3,450	—
1910S	2,128,250	1,796	1,829	1,844	1,855	2,110	11,350	—
1911	197,350	1,796	1,829	1,849	1,865	2,900	23,500	76,500
1911D	846,500	1,791	1,824	1,829	1,850	2,045	2,950	—
1911S	775,750	1,791	1,824	1,829	1,855	2,045	6,850	—
1912	149,824	1,796	1,829	1,844	1,890	2,050	31,000	76,500
1913	168,838	1,796	1,829	1,844	1,895	3,250	53,500	82,500
1913D	393,500	1,791	1,824	1,829	1,850	2,125	7,850	—
1913S	34,000	1,846	1,879	1,879	2,000	4,350	36,500	—
1914	95,320	1,806	1,839	1,879	1,275	3,900	25,000	81,500
1914D	453,000	1,791	1,824	1,829	1,850	2,055	3,450	—
1914S	1,498,000	1,791	1,824	1,829	1,850	2,045	3,150	—
1915	152,050	1,796	1,829	1,839	1,855	2,650	28,000	125,000
1915S	567,500	1,791	1,824	1,829	1,850	2,045	3,000	—
1916S	796,000	1,796	1,829	1,839	1,890	2,075	3,250	—
1920	228,250	1,786	1,819	1,849	1,850	2,450	118,000	—
1920S	558,000	14,500	18,500	28,500	53,000	105,000	355,000	—
1921	528,500	35,000	43,500	56,500	125,000	300,000	975,000	—
1922	1,375,500	1,786	1,819	1,819	1,825	1,995	6,850	—
1922S	2,658,000	1,906	1,150	1,300	2,450	5,650	63,500	—
1923	566,000	1,786	1,819	1,819	1,830	1,995	8,000	—
1923D	1,702,250	1,796	1,829	1,829	1,835	1,995	2,560	—
1924	4,323,500	1,786	1,819	1,819	1,825	1,975	2,450	—
1924D	3,049,500	2,009	2,042	2,100	3,950	11,200	115,000	—
1924S	2,927,500	1,665	1,750	2,200	3,800	12,250	180,000	—
1925	2,831,750	1,786	1,819	1,819	1,830	1,975	2,450	—
1925D	2,938,500	1,951	2,100	2,375	4,450	11,500	148,000	—
1925S	3,776,500	1,900	2,850	4,850	9,850	23,500	210,000	—
1926	816,750	1,786	1,819	1,819	1,830	1,975	2,450	—
1926D	481,000	10,000	15,500	19,350	27,500	35,000	235,000	—
1926S	2,041,500	1,989	1,550	1,725	3,050	5,650	37,500	—
1927	2,946,750	1,786	1,819	1,819	1,830	1,975	2,450	—
1927D	180,000	155,000	200,000	245,000	325,000	1,500,000	1,950,000	—
1927S	3,107,000	6,850	8,850	13,250	26,750	54,000	160,000	—
1928	8,816,000	1,786	1,819	1,819	1,830	1,975	2,450	—
1929	1,779,750	10,000	13,500	15,500	19,300	38,500	112,000	—
1930S	74,000	35,000	41,000	49,500	72,500	105,000	235,000	—
1931	2,938,250	10,500	13,500	20,500	31,500	63,500	120,000	—
1931D	106,500	8,850	11,500	21,500	42,500	83,500	140,000	—
1932	1,101,750	12,500	14,500	17,850	26,500	73,500	110,000	—
1933	445,500	—	—	—	—	—	9,000,000	—

Note: Sotheby/Stack's Sale, July 2002. Thirteen known, only one currently available.

$20 GOLD

COMMEMORATIVE COINAGE 1892-1954

All commemorative half dollars of 1892-1954 have the following specifications: diameter — 30.6 millimeters; weight — 12.5000 grams; composition — 0.9000 silver, 0.3617 ounces actual silver weight. Values for PDS sets contain one example each from the Philadelphia, Denver and San Francisco mints. Type coin prices are the most inexpensive single coin available from the date and mint mark combinations listed.

QUARTER

Columbian Exposition.

KM# 115 Obverse: Queen Isabella bust left
Reverse: Female kneeling with distaff adn spindle
Diameter: 24.3 **Weight:** 6.2500 g. **Composition:** 0.9000 Silver, 0.1808 oz. ASW.

Date	Mintage	AU-50	MS-60	MS-63	MS-64	MS-65
1893	24,214	450	525	650	950	2,750

HALF DOLLAR

Columbian Exposition.

KM# 117 Obv. Designer: Charles E. Barber
Rev. Designer: George T. Morgan **Obverse:** Christopher Columbus bust right **Reverse:** Santa Maria sailing left, two globes below

Date	Mintage	AU-50	MS-60	MS-63	MS-64	MS-65
1892	950,000	18.50	28.00	80.00	135	525
1893	1,550,405	17.00	28.00	75.00	145	465

Panama-Pacific Exposition.

KM# 135 Designer: Charles E. Barber.
Obverse: Columbia standing, sunset in background
Reverse: Eagle standing on shield

Date	Mintage	AU-50	MS-60	MS-63	MS-64	MS-65
1915S	27,134	465	535	825	1,250	2,650

Illinois Centennial-Lincoln.

KM# 143 Obv. Designer: George T. Morgan
Rev. Designer: John R. Sinnock **Obverse:** Abraham Lincon bust right **Reverse:** Eagle standing left

Date	Mintage	AU-50	MS-60	MS-63	MS-64	MS-65
1918	100,058	135	150	165	200	565

Maine Centennial.

KM# 146 Designer: Anthony de Francisci.
Obverse: Arms of the State of Maine
Reverse: Legend within wreath

Date	Mintage	AU-50	MS-60	MS-63	MS-64	MS-65
1920	50,028	130	165	185	250	500

Pilgrim Tercentenary.

KM# 147.1 Designer: Cyrus E. Dallin.
Obverse: William bradford half-length left
Reverse: Mayflower sailing left

Date	Mintage	AU-50	MS-60	MS-63	MS-64	MS-65
1920	152,112	80.00	100.00	110	120	375

Pilgrim Tercentenary.

KM# 147.2 Designer: Cyrus E. Dallin.
Obverse: William Bradford half-length left, 1921 added at left **Reverse:** Mayflower sailing left

Date	Mintage	AU-50	MS-60	MS-63	MS-64	MS-65
1921	20,053	170	200	220	235	515

Alabama Centennial.

KM# 148.1 Designer: Laura G. Fraser.
Obverse: William W. Bibb and T.E. Kilby conjoint busts left. "2x2" at right above stars **Reverse:** Ealge left on shield **Notes:** "Fake 2x2" counterstamps exist.

Date	Mintage	AU-50	MS-60	MS-63	MS-64	MS-65
1921	6,006	315	330	525	675	1,600

Alabama Centennial.

KM# 148.2 Obv. Designer: Laura G. Fraser
Obverse: William W. Bibb and T.E. Kilby conjoint busts left **Reverse:** Eagle standing left on shield

Date	Mintage	AU-50	MS-60	MS-63	MS-64	MS-65
1921	59,038	190	215	525	685	1,800

Missouri Centennial.

KM# 149.1 Designer: Robert Aitken.
Obverse: Frontiersman in coonskin cap left **Reverse:** Frontiersman and Native American standing left

Date	Mintage	AU-50	MS-60	MS-63	MS-64	MS-65
1921	15,428	400	600	885	1,275	3,650

Missouri Centennial.

KM# 149.2 Designer: Robert Aitken.
Obverse: Frontiersman in coonskin cap left, 2(star)4 in field at left **Reverse:** Frontiersman and Native American standing left **Notes:** "Fake "2*4" counterstamps exist.

Date	Mintage	AU-50	MS-60	MS-63	MS-64	MS-65
1921	5,000	620	720	1,050	1,500	3,450

Grant Memorial.

KM# 151.1 Designer: Laura G. Fraser.
Obverse: Grant bust right **Reverse:** Birthplace in Point Pleasant, Ohio

Date	Mintage	AU-50	MS-60	MS-63	MS-64	MS-65
1922	67,405	120	125	155	250	700

Grant Memorial.

KM# 151.2 Designer: Laura G. Fraser.

Obverse: Grant bust left, star above the word GRANT **Reverse:** Birthplace in Point Pleasant, Ohio **Notes:** "Fake star" counterstamps exist.

Date	Mintage	AU-50	MS-60	MS-63	MS-64	MS-65
1922	4,256	925	1,275	1,750	3,450	7,850

Monroe Doctrine Centennial.

KM# 153 Designer: Chester Beach. **Obverse:** James Monroe and John Quincy Adams conjoint busts left **Reverse:** Western Hemisphere portraied by two female figures

Date	Mintage	AU-50	MS-60	MS-63	MS-64	MS-65
1923S	274,077	56.00	72.50	125	250	1,950

Huguenot-Walloon Tercentenary.

KM# 154 Designer: George T. Morgan. **Obverse:** Huguenot leader Gaspard de Coligny and William I of Orange conjoint busts right **Reverse:** Nieuw Nederland sailing left

Date	Mintage	AU-50	MS-60	MS-63	MS-64	MS-65
1924	142,080	135	145	150	215	385

California Diamond Jubilee.

KM# 155 Designer: Jo Mora. **Obverse:** Fourty-Niner kneeling panning for gold **Reverse:** Grizzly bear walking left

Date	Mintage	AU-50	MS-60	MS-63	MS-64	MS-65
1925S	86,594	195	225	270	485	900

Fort Vancouver Centennial.

KM# 158 Designer: Laura G. Fraser. **Obverse:** John McLoughlin bust left **Reverse** Frontiersmen standing with musket, Ft. Vancouver in background

Date	Mintage	AU-50	MS-60	MS-63	MS-64	MS-65
1925	14,994	320	360	420	475	1,250

Lexington-Concord Sesquicentennial.

KM# 156 Designer: Chester Beach. **Obverse:** Concord's Minute Man statue **Reverse:** Old Belfry at Lexington

Date	Mintage	AU-50	MS-60	MS-63	MS-64	MS-65
1925	162,013	95.00	105	110	145	615

Stone Mountain Memorial.

KM# 157 Designer: Gutzon Borglum. **Obverse:** Generals Robert E. Lee and Thomas "Stonewall" Jackson mounted left. **Reverse:** Eagle on rock at right

Date	Mintage	AU-50	MS-60	MS-63	MS-64	MS-65
1925	1,314,709	62.00	67.50	80.00	190	315

Oregon Trail Memorial.

KM# 159 Designer: James E. and Laura G. Fraser. **Obverse:** Native American standing in full headdress and holding bow, US Map in background

Reverse: Conestoga wagon pulled by oxen left towards sunset

Date	Mintage	AU-50	MS-60	MS-63	MS-64	MS-65
1926	47,955	135	165	175	195	315
1926S	83,055	135	165	180	195	320
1928	6,028	220	245	275	285	375
1933D	5,008	365	380	385	390	465
1934D	7,006	195	205	215	220	365
1936	10,006	165	190	205	220	340
1936S	5,006	175	190	210	235	350
1937D	12,008	175	200	210	225	325
1938	6,006	155	170	205	210	335
1938D	6,005	155	170	205	220	335
1938S	6,006	155	170	205	215	335
1939	3,004	510	585	600	620	675
1939D	3,004	510	585	610	620	675
1939S	3,005	510	585	590	600	665

U.S. Sesquicentennial.

KM# 160 Designer: John R. Sinnock.
Obverse: George Washington and Calvin Coolidge conjoint busts right **Reverse:** Liberty Bell

Date	Mintage	AU-50	MS-60	MS-63	MS-64	MS-65
1926	141,120	85.00	110	118	465	4,800

Vermont Sesquicentennial.

KM# 162 Obv. Designer: Charles Keck
Obverse: Ira Allen bust right **Reverse:** Catamount advancing left

Date	Mintage	AU-50	MS-60	MS-63	MS-64	MS-65
1927	28,142	250	275	290	335	880

Hawaiian Sesquicentennial.

KM# 163 Designer: Juliette May Fraser and Chester Beach. **Obverse:** Captain James Cook bust left **Reverse:** Native Hawaiian standing over view of Diamond Head **Notes:** Counterfeits exist.

Date	Mintage	AU-50	MS-60	MS-63	MS-64	MS-65
1928	10,008	1,785	2,650	3,350	3,775	6,200

Arkansas Centennial.

KM# 168 Designer: Edward E. Burr.
Obverse: Liberty and Indian Chief's conjoint heads left **Reverse:** Eagle with outstreatched wings and Flag of Arkansas in background

Date	Mintage	AU-50	MS-60	MS-63	MS-64	MS-65
1935	13,012	90.00	100.00	110	120	215
1935D	5,505	105	110	120	130	250
1935S	5,506	105	110	120	130	250
1936	9,660	90.00	100.00	110	120	225
1936D	9,660	105	110	120	130	255
1936S	9,662	105	110	120	130	255
1937	5,505	105	115	120	135	275
1937D	5,505	105	115	120	130	265
1937S	5,506	105	115	120	135	290
1938	3,156	155	180	190	200	590
1938D	3,155	160	180	190	200	580
1938S	3,156	160	180	190	200	640
1939	2,104	320	375	380	400	940
1939D	2,104	320	375	380	400	910
1939S	2,105	320	375	380	400	925

Daniel Boone Bicentennial.

KM# 165.2 Designer: Augustus Lukeman.
Obverse: Daniel Boone bust left **Reverse:** Daniel Boone and Native American standing, "1934" added above the word "PIONEER."

Date	Mintage	AU-50	MS-60	MS-63	MS-64	MS-65
1935	10,008	125	135	140	145	260
1935D	2,003	360	390	425	450	835
1935S	2,004	360	390	425	450	815
1936	12,012	120	125	135	140	250
1936D	5,005	130	135	145	155	295
1936S	5,006	130	135	145	155	285
1937	9,810	135	135	138	145	260
1937D	2,506	320	375	385	400	515
1937S	2,506	320	375	385	400	540
1938	2,100	340	380	390	400	535
1938D	2,100	340	380	390	410	525
1938S	2,100	340	380	390	400	565

Daniel Boone Bicentennial.

KM# 165.1 Designer: Augustus Lukeman. **Obverse:** Daniel Boone bust left **Reverse:** Daniel Boone and Native American standing

Date	Mintage	AU-50	MS-60	MS-63	MS-64	MS-65
1934	10,007	120	125	135	140	250
1935	10,010	120	125	135	140	250
1935D	5,005	130	135	145	155	295
1935S	5,005	130	135	145	155	285

Maryland Tercentenary.

KM# 166 Designer: Hans Schuler. **Obverse:** Lord Baltimore, Cecil Calvert bust right **Reverse:** Maryland state arms

Date	Mintage	AU-50	MS-60	MS-63	MS-64	MS-65
1934	25,015	150	175	185	200	375

Texas Centennial.

KM# 167 Designer: Pompeo Coppini. **Obverse:** Eagle standing left, large star in background **Reverse:** Winged Victory kneeling beside Alamo Mission, small busts of Sam Houston and Stephen Austin at sides

Date	Mintage	AU-50	MS-60	MS-63	MS-64	MS-65
1934	61,463	135	140	150	165	300
1935	9,994	140	145	155	160	300
1935D	10,007	140	145	155	160	300
1935S	10,008	140	145	155	160	300
1936	8,911	140	145	155	160	310
1936D	9,039	140	145	155	160	310
1936S	9,055	140	145	155	160	325
1937	6,571	140	145	155	160	310
1937D	6,605	140	145	155	160	300
1937S	6,637	140	145	155	160	300
1938	3,780	235	250	260	305	425
1938D	3,775	240	255	265	305	415
1938S	3,814	235	250	260	305	415

Connecticut Tercentenary.

KM# 169 Designer: Henry Kreiss. **Obverse:** Eagle standing left **Reverse:** Charter oak tree

Date	Mintage	AU-50	MS-60	MS-63	MS-64	MS-65
1935	25,018	240	265	275	325	500

Hudson, N.Y., Sesquicentennial.

KM# 170 Designer: Chester Beach. **Obverse:** Hudson's ship, the Half Moon sailing right **Reverse:** Seal of the City of Hudson

Date	Mintage	AU-50	MS-60	MS-63	MS-64	MS-65
1935	10,008	750	875	1,050	1,550	2,100

Old Spanish Trail.

KM# 172 Designer: L.W. Hoffecker. **Obverse:** Long-horn cow's head facing **Reverse:** The 1535 route of Cabeza de Vaca's expedition and a yucca tree **Notes:** Counterfeits exist.

Date	Mintage	AU-50	MS-60	MS-63	MS-64	MS-65
1935	10,008	1,250	1,375	1,650	1,750	2,000

San Diego-Pacific International Exposition.

KM# 171 Designer: Robert Aitken. **Obverse:** Seated female with bear at her side **Reverse:** State of California exposition building

Date	Mintage	AU-50	MS-60	MS-63	MS-64	MS-65
1935S	70,132	95.00	98.00	105	110	240
1936D	30,092	100.00	120	125	135	275

Albany, N.Y., Charter Anniversary.
KM# 173 Designer: Gertrude K. Lathrop. **Obverse:** Beaver knawing on maple branch **Reverse:** Standing figures of Thomas Dongan, Peter Schyuyler and Robert Livingston

Date	Mintage	AU-50	MS-60	MS-63	MS-64	MS-65
1936	17,671	300	310	330	350	440

Arkansas Centennial.
KM# 187 Obv. Designer: Henry Kreiss
Rev. Designer: Edward E. Burr **Obverse:** Eagle with wings outstreatched, Arkansas flag in backgorund
Reverse: Sen. Joseph T. Robinson bust right

Date	Mintage	AU-50	MS-60	MS-63	MS-64	MS-65
1936	25,265	140	175	210	220	385

Battle of Gettysburg 75th Anniversary. **KM# 181 Designer:** Frank Vittor. **Obverse:** Union and Confederate veteran conjoint busts right **Reverse:** Double blased fasces seperating two shields

Date	Mintage	AU-50	MS-60	MS-63	MS-64	MS-65
1936	26,928	435	460	485	565	925

Bridgeport, Conn., Centennial.
KM# 175 Designer: Henry Kreiss. **Obverse:** P.T. Barnum bust left **Reverse:** Eagle standing right

Date	Mintage	AU-50	MS-60	MS-63	MS-64	MS-65
1936	25,015	130	140	150	175	320

Cincinnati Music Center.
KM# 176 Designer: Constance Ortmayer.
Obverse: Stephen Foster bust right
Reverse: Kneeling female with lyre

Date	Mintage	AU-50	MS-60	MS-63	MS-64	MS-65
1936	5,005	295	310	335	410	725
1936D	5,005	295	310	335	410	750
1936S	5,006	295	310	335	410	750

Cleveland-Great Lakes Exposition.
KM# 177 Designer: Brenda Putnam. **Obverse:** Moses Cleaveland bust left **Reverse:** Dividers and map of the Great Lakes

Date	Mintage	AU-50	MS-60	MS-63	MS-64	MS-65
1936	50,030	110	115	120	160	215

Columbia, S.C., Sesquicentennial.
KM# 178 Designer: A. Wolfe Davidson.
Obverse: Figure of Justice between capitols of 1786 and 1936 **Reverse:** Palmetto tree

Date	Mintage	AU-50	MS-60	MS-63	MS-64	MS-65
1936	9,007	250	265	270	275	310
1936D	8,009	260	270	280	285	340
1936S	8,007	260	270	280	285	340

Delaware Tercentenary.

KM# 179 Designer: Carl L. Schmitz. **Obverse:** Old Swedes Church in Wilmington **Reverse:** Kalmar Nyckel sailing left

Date	Mintage	AU-50	MS-60	MS-63	MS-64	MS-65
1936	20,993	255	265	275	290	465

Elgin, Ill., Centennial.

KM# 180 Designer: Trygve Rovelstad. **Obverse:** Pioneer head left **Reverse:** Statue group

Date	Mintage	AU-50	MS-60	MS-63	MS-64	MS-65
1936	20,015	195	205	215	225	355

Long Island Tercentenary.

KM# 182 Designer: Howard K. Weinman. **Obverse:** Dutch settler and Native American conjoint head right **Reverse:** Dutch sailing vessel

Date	Mintage	AU-50	MS-60	MS-63	MS-64	MS-65
1936	81,826	85.00	92.00	98.00	105	325

Lynchburg, Va., Sesquicentennial.

KM# 183 Designer: Charles Keck. **Obverse:** Sen. Carter Glass bust left **Reverse:** Liberty standing, old Lynchburg courthouse at right

Date	Mintage	AU-50	MS-60	MS-63	MS-64	MS-65
1936	20,013	220	230	265	275	365

Norfolk, Va., Bicentennial.

KM# 184 Designer: William M. and Marjorie E. Simpson. **Obverse:** Seal of the City of Norfolk **Reverse:** Royal Mace of Norfolk

Date	Mintage	AU-50	MS-60	MS-63	MS-64	MS-65
1936	16,936	425	435	445	460	575

Rhode Island Tercentenary.

KM# 185 Designer: Arthur G. Carey and John H. Benson. **Obverse:** Roger Williams in canoe hailing Native American **Reverse:** Shield with anchor

Date	Mintage	AU-50	MS-60	MS-63	MS-64	MS-65
1936	20,013	98.00	105	110	120	290
1936D	15,010	100.00	110	120	125	305
1936S	15,011	100.00	110	120	130	320

Roanoke Island, N.C..

KM# 186 Designer: William M. Simpson. **Obverse:** Sir Walter Raleigh bust left **Reverse:** Ellinor Dare holding baby Virginia, two small ships flanking

Date	Mintage	AU-50	MS-60	MS-63	MS-64	MS-65
1937	29,030	220	225	235	245	315

San Francisco-Oakland Bay Bridge.

KM# 174 Designer: Jacques Schnier. **Obverse:** Grizzly bear facing **Reverse:** Oakland Bay Bridge

Date	Mintage	AU-50	MS-60	MS-63	MS-64	MS-65
1936	71,424	155	160	165	185	365

Wisconsin Territorial Centennial.

KM# 188 Designer: David Parsons.
Obverse: Badger from the Territorial seal
Reverse: Pick axe and mound of lead ore

Date	Mintage	AU-50	MS-60	MS-63	MS-64	MS-65
1936	25,015	215	240	255	265	365

York County, Maine, Tercentenary.

KM# 189 Designer: Walter H. Rich.
Obverse: Stockade **Reverse:** York County seal

Date	Mintage	AU-50	MS-60	MS-63	MS-64	MS-65
1936	25,015	210	215	225	235	340

Battle of Antietam 75th Anniversary.

KM# 190 Designer: William M. Simpson.
Obverse: Generals Robert E. Lee and George McClellan conjoint busts left **Reverse:** Burnside Bridge

Date	Mintage	AU-50	MS-60	MS-63	MS-64	MS-65
1937	18,028	695	735	750	775	950

New Rochelle, N.Y..

KM# 191 Designer: Gertrude K. Lathrop.
Obverse: John Pell and a calf **Reverse:** Fleur-de-lis from the seal of the city

Date	Mintage	AU-50	MS-60	MS-63	MS-64	MS-65
1938	15,266	375	385	425	440	600

Booker T. Washington.

KM# 198 Designer: Isaac S. Hathaway.
Obverse: Booker T. Washington bust right
Reverse: Cabin and NYU's Hall of Fame
Notes: Actual mintages are higher, but unsold issues were melted to produce Washington Carver issues.

Date	Mintage	AU-50	MS-60	MS-63	MS-64	MS-65
1946	1,000,546	14.00	18.00	21.00	23.00	64.00
1946D	200,113	16.50	20.00	32.00	37.00	72.00
1946S	500,729	15.00	18.50	23.00	27.00	66.00
1947	100,017	30.00	36.00	56.00	65.00	80.00
1947D	100,017	32.00	38.00	62.00	70.00	100.00
1947S	100,017	32.00	38.00	59.00	65.00	76.00
1948	8,005	46.00	64.00	77.00	80.00	84.00
1948D	8,005	46.00	62.00	77.00	80.00	84.00
1948S	8,005	46.00	65.00	78.00	82.00	88.00
1949	6,004	67.00	82.00	85.00	96.00	115
1949D	6,004	67.00	82.00	85.00	96.00	115
1949S	6,004	67.00	82.00	85.00	102	105
1950	6,004	46.00	68.00	78.00	82.00	90.00
1950D	6,004	46.00	68.00	75.00	82.00	88.00
1950S	512,091	18.00	20.00	24.00	26.00	65.00
1951	51,082	17.00	22.00	24.00	26.00	65.00
1951D	7,004	47.00	68.00	80.00	85.00	90.00
1951S	7,004	47.00	68.00	80.00	84.00	88.00

Iowa Statehood Centennial.

KM# 197 Designer: Adam Pietz. **Obverse:** First Capitol building at Iowa City **Reverse:** Iowa state seal

Date	Mintage	AU-50	MS-60	MS-63	MS-64	MS-65
1946	100,057	100.00	105	108	112	160

Booker T. Washington and George Washington Carver.

KM# 200 Designer: Isaac S. Hathaway. **Obverse:** Booker T. Washington and George Washington Carver conjoint busts right **Reverse:** Map of the United States

Date	Mintage	AU-50	MS-60	MS-63	MS-64	MS-65
1951	110,018	18.00	20.00	25.00	44.00	290
1951D	10,004	42.00	50.00	80.00	82.00	140
1951S	10,004	42.00	50.00	80.00	86.00	90.00
1952	2,006,292	17.00	18.00	24.00	42.00	83.00
1952D	8,006	40.00	50.00	80.00	85.00	190
1952S	8,006	40.00	50.00	80.00	84.00	185
1953	8,003	40.00	50.00	80.00	85.00	260
1953D	8,003	40.00	50.00	80.00	85.00	175
1953S	108,020	17.00	18.00	24.00	42.00	120
1954	12,006	39.00	48.00	70.00	75.00	200
1954D	12,006	39.00	48.00	70.00	80.00	83.00
1954S	122,024	17.00	18.00	24.00	42.00	83.00

DOLLAR

La Fayette.

KM# 118 Designer: Charles E. Barber. **Obverse:** George Washington and Marquis de La Fayette conjoint busts right **Reverse:** La Fayette on horseback left **Diameter:** 38.1 **Weight:** 26.7300 g. **Composition:** 0.9000 Silver, 0.7734 oz. ASW.

Date	Mintage	AU-50	MS-60	MS-63	MS-64	MS-65
1900	36,026	550	950	1,875	3,250	11,500

Louisiana Purchase Exposition - McKinley.

KM# 120 Obv. Designer: Charles E. Barber **Obverse:** William McKinley bust left **Reverse:** Legend and laurel branch **Diameter:** 15 **Weight:** 1.6720 g. **Composition:** 0.9000 Gold, 0.0484 oz. AGW.

Date	Mintage	AU-50	MS-60	MS-63	MS-64	MS-65
1903	17,500	590	650	800	1,400	2,100

Louisiana Purchase Exposition - Jefferson.

KM# 119 Designer: Charles E. Barber. **Obverse:** Jefferson bust left **Reverse:** Legend and laurel branch **Diameter:** 15 **Weight:** 1.6720 g. **Composition:** 0.9000 Gold, 0.0484 oz. AGW.

Date	Mintage	AU-50	MS-60	MS-63	MS-64	MS-65
1903	17,500	600	660	925	1,450	2,150

Lewis and Clark Exposition.

KM# 121 Obv. Designer: Charles E. Barber **Obverse:** Lewis bust left **Reverse:** Clark bust left **Diameter:** 15 **Weight:** 1.6720 g. **Composition:** 0.9000 Gold, 0.0484 oz. AGW.

Date	Mintage	AU-50	MS-60	MS-63	MS-64	MS-65
1904	10,025	950	1,100	1,850	3,650	7,900
1905	10,041	975	1,450	2,250	3,950	15,000

Panama-Pacific Exposition.

KM# 136 Obv. Designer: Charles Keck **Obverse:** Canal laborer bust left **Reverse:** Value within two dolphins **Diameter:** 15 **Weight:** 1.6720 g. **Composition:** 0.9000 Gold, 0.0484 oz. AGW.

Date	Mintage	AU-50	MS-60	MS-63	MS-64	MS-65
1915S	15,000	565	625	775	1,100	1,700

McKinley Memorial.

KM# 144 Obv. Designer: Charles E. Barber **Rev. Designer:** George T. Morgan **Obverse:** William McKinley head left **Reverse:** Memorial building at Niles, Ohio **Diameter:** 15 **Weight:** 1.6720 g. **Composition:** 0.9000 Gold, 0.0484 oz. AGW.

Date	Mintage	AU-50	MS-60	MS-63	MS-64	MS-65
1916	9,977	520	600	685	1,000	1,750
1917	10,000	575	700	900	1,475	2,250

Grant Memorial.

KM# 152.1 Obv. Designer: Laura G. Fraser **Obverse:** U.S. Grant bust right **Reverse:** Birthplace **Diameter:** 15 **Weight:** 1.6720 g. **Composition:** 0.9000 Gold, 0.0484 oz. AGW. **Notes:** Without an incuse "star" above the word GRANT on the obverse.

Date	Mintage	AU-50	MS-60	MS-63	MS-64	MS-65
1922	5,000	1,875	1,900	2,350	3,650	4,900

Grant Memorial.

KM# 152.2 Obv. Designer: Laura G. Fraser **Obverse:** U.S. Grant bust right **Reverse:** Birthplace **Diameter:** 15 **Weight:** 1.6720 g. **Composition:** 0.9000 Gold, 0.0484 oz. AGW. **Notes:** Variety with an incuse "star" above the word GRANT on the obverse.

Date	Mintage	AU-50	MS-60	MS-63	MS-64	MS-65
1922	5,016	1,650	1,775	2,100	2,150	3,100

$2.50 (QUARTER EAGLE)

Panama-Pacific Exposition.

KM# 137 Obv. Designer: Charles E. Barber **Rev. Designer:** George T. Morgan **Obverse:** Columbia holding cadueus while seated on a hippocamp **Reverse:** Eagle standing left **Diameter:** 18 **Weight:** 4.1800 g. **Composition:** 0.9000 Gold, 0.1209 oz. AGW.

Date	Mintage	AU-50	MS-60	MS-63	MS-64	MS-65
1915S	6,749	1,550	1,950	4,100	5,650	6,750

U.S. Sesquicentennial.

KM# 161 Obv. Designer: John R. Sinnock **Obverse:** Liberty standing holding torch and scroll **Reverse:** Independence Hall **Diameter:** 18 **Weight:** 4.1800 g. **Composition:** 0.9000 Gold, 0.1209 oz. AGW.

Date	Mintage	AU-50	MS-60	MS-63	MS-64	MS-65
1926	46,019	425	500	800	1,375	3,450

$50

Panama-Pacific Exposition Octagonal.

KM# 139 Obv. Designer: Robert Aitken **Obverse:** Minerva bust helmeted left **Reverse:** Owl pearched on California pine branch **Diameter:** 44 **Weight:** 83.5900 g. **Composition:** 0.9000 Gold, 2.4186 oz. AGW.

Date	Mintage	AU-50	MS-60	MS-63	MS-64	MS-65
1915S	645	50,000	52,500	84,500	98,000	146,000

Panama-Pacific Exposition Round.

KM# 138 Obv. Designer: Robert Aitken **Obverse:** Minerva bust helmeted left **Reverse:** Owl pearched on California pin branch **Diameter:** 44 **Weight:** 83.5900 g. **Composition:** 0.9000 Gold, 2.4186 oz. AGW.

Date	Mintage	AU-50	MS-60	MS-63	MS-64	MS-65
1915S	483	46,500	57,500	90,000	105,000	160,000

COMMEMORATIVE COINAGE 1982-PRESENT

All commemorative silver dollar coins of 1982-present have the following specifications: diameter — 38.1 millimeters; weight — 26.7300 grams; composition — 0.9000 silver, 0.7736 ounces actual silver weight. All commemorative $5 coins of 1982-present have the following specificiations: diameter — 21.6 millimeters; weight — 8.3590 grams; composition: 0.9000 gold, 0.242 ounces actual gold weight.

Note: In 1982, after a hiatus of nearly 20 years, coinage of commemorative half dollars resumed. Those designated with a 'W' were struck at the West Point Mint. Some issues were struck in copper-nickel. Those struck in silver have the same size, weight and composition as the prior commemorative half-dollar series.

HALF DOLLAR

George Washington, 250th Birth Anniversary.

KM# 208 Obv. Designer: Elizabeth Jones **Rev. Designer:** Matthew Peloso **Obverse:** George Washington on horseback facing **Reverse:** Mount Vernon **Diameter:** 30.6 **Weight:** 12.5000 g. **Composition:** 0.9000 Silver, 0.3617 oz. ASW.

Date	Mintage	MS-65	Prf-65
1982D	2,210,458	13.70	—
1982S	4,894,044	—	13.70

Statue of Liberty Centennial.

KM# 212 Obv. Designer: Edgar Z. Steever **Rev. Designer:** Sherl Joseph Winter **Obverse:** State of Liberty and sunrise **Reverse:** Emigrant family looking toward mainland **Weight:** 11.3400 g. **Composition:** Copper-Nickel Clad Copper

Date	Mintage	MS-65	Prf-65
1986D	928,008	3.25	—
1986S	6,925,627	—	3.50

Congress Bicentennial.

KM# 224 Obv. Designer: Patricia L. Verani **Rev. Designer:** William Woodward and Edgar Z. Steever **Obverse:** Statue of Freedom head **Reverse:** Capitol building **Weight:** 11.3400 g. **Composition:** Copper-Nickel Clad Copper

Date	Mintage	MS-65	Prf-65
1989D	163,753	7.50	—
1989S	762,198	—	7.50

Mount Rushmore 50th Anniversary.

KM# 228 Obv. Designer: Marcel Jovine **Rev. Designer:** T. James Ferrell **Reverse:** Mount Rushmore portraits **Weight:** 11.3400 g. **Composition:** Copper-Nickel Clad Copper

Date	Mintage	MS-65	Prf-65
1991D	172,754	17.50	—
1991S	753,257	—	16.00

1992 Olympics.

KM# 233 Obv. Designer: William Cousins **Rev. Designer:** Steven M. Bieda **Obverse:** Torch and laurel **Reverse:** Female gymnast and large flag **Weight:** 11.3400 g. **Composition:** Copper-Nickel Clad Copper

Date	Mintage	MS-65	Prf-65
1992P	161,607	8.50	—
1992S	519,645	—	8.50

Columbus Voyage - 500th Anniversary.

KM# 237 Obv. Designer: T. James Ferrell **Rev. Designer:** Thomas D. Rogers, Sr. **Obverse:** Columbus standing on shore **Reverse:** Nina, Pinta and Santa Maria sailing right **Weight:** 11.3400 g. **Composition:** Copper-Nickel Clad Copper

Date	Mintage	MS-65	Prf-65
1992D	135,702	11.50	—
1992S	390,154	—	8.75

James Madison - Bill of Rights.

KM# 240 Obv. Designer: T. James Ferrell **Rev. Designer:** Dean McMullen **Obverse:** James Madison writing, Montpelier in background **Reverse:** Statue of Liberty torch **Weight:** 12.5000 g. **Composition:** 0.9000 Silver, 0.3617 oz. ASW.

Date	Mintage	MS-65	Prf-65
1993W	193,346	19.00	—
1993S	586,315	—	19.00

World War II 50th Anniversary.

KM# 243 Obv. Designer: George Klauba and T. James Ferrell **Rev. Designer:** William J. Leftwich and T. James Ferrell **Obverse:** Three portraits, plane above, large V in backgound **Reverse:** Pacific island battle scene **Weight:** 11.3400 g. **Composition:** Copper-Nickel Clad Copper

Date	Mintage	MS-65	Prf-65
(1993)P	197,072	17.00	—
(1993)P	317,396	—	16.50

1994 World Cup Soccer.

KM# 246 Obv. Designer: Richard T. LaRoche **Rev. Designer:** Dean McMullen **Obverse:** Soccer player with ball **Reverse:** World Cup 94 logo **Weight:** 11.3400 g. **Composition:** Copper-Nickel Clad Copper

Date	Mintage	MS-65	Prf-65
1994D	168,208	8.25	—
1994P	609,354	—	8.00

1996 Atlanta Olympics - Baseball.

KM# 262 Obv. Designer: Edgar Z. Steever **Rev. Designer:** T. James Ferrell **Obverse:** Baseball batter at plate, catcher and umpire **Reverse:** Hemisphere and Atlanta Olympics logo **Weight:** 11.3400 g. **Composition:** Copper-Nickel Clad Copper

Date	Mintage	MS-65	Prf-65
1995S	164,605	19.50	—
1995S	118,087	—	17.50

1996 Atlanta Olympics - Basketball.

KM# 257 Obv. Designer: Clint Hansen and Al Maletsky **Rev. Designer:** T. James Ferrell **Obverse:** Three players, one jumping for a shot **Reverse:** Hemisphere and Atlanta Olympics logo **Weight:** 11.3400 g. **Composition:** Copper-Nickel Clad Copper

Date	Mintage	MS-65	Prf-65
1995S	171,001	17.00	—
1995S	169,655	—	18.00

Civil War Battlefield Preservation.
KM# 254 Obv. Designer: Don Troiani **Rev. Designer:** T. James Ferrell **Obverse:** Drummer and fenceline **Reverse:** Canon overlooking battlefield **Weight:** 11.3400 g. **Composition:** Copper-Nickel Clad Copper

Date	Mintage	MS-65	Prf-65
1995S	119,510	36.50	—
1995S	330,099	—	33.50

1996 Atlanta Olympics - Soccer.
KM# 271 Obverse: Two female soccer players **Reverse:** Atlanta Olympics logo **Weight:** 11.3400 g. **Composition:** Copper-Nickel Clad Copper

Date	Mintage	MS-65	Prf-65
1996S	52,836	130	—
1996S	122,412	—	88.00

1996 Atlanta Olympics - Swimming.
KM# 267 Obv. Designer: William J. Krawczewicz and Edgar Z. Steever **Rev. Designer:** Malcolm Farley and Thomas D. Rogers, Sr. **Obverse:** Swimmer right in butterfly stroke **Reverse:** Atlanta Olympics logo **Weight:** 11.3400 g. **Composition:** Copper-Nickel Clad Copper

Date	Mintage	MS-65	Prf-65
1996S	49,533	140	—
1996S	114,315	—	31.00

U. S. Capitol Visitor Center.
KM# 323 Obv. Designer: Dean McMullen **Rev. Designer:** Alex Shagin and Marcel Jovine **Obverse:** Capitol sillouete, 1800 structure in detail **Reverse:** Legend within circle of stars **Weight:** 11.3400 g. **Composition:** Copper-Nickel Clad Copper

Date	Mintage	MS-65	Prf-65
2001P	99,157	14.50	—
2001P	77,962	—	15.50

First Flight Centennial.
KM# 348 Obv. Designer: John Mercanti **Rev. Designer:** Donna Weaver **Obverse:** Wright Monument at Kitty Hawk **Reverse:** Wright Flyer in flight **Weight:** 11.3400 g. **Composition:** Copper-Nickel Clad Copper

Date	Mintage	MS-65	Prf-65
2003P	57,726	15.00	—
2003P	111,569	—	17.00

American Bald Eagle.
KM# 438 Obv. Designer: Susan Gamble and Joseph Menna **Rev. Designer:** Donna Weaver and Charles Vickers **Obverse:** Two eaglets in nest with egg **Reverse:** Eagle Challenger facing right, American Flag in background **Diameter:** 30.6 **Weight:** 11.3400 g. **Composition:** Copper-Nickel Clad Copper

Date	Mintage	MS-65	Prf-65
2008S	120,180	12.50	—
2008S	222,577	—	14.00

U.S. Army.

KM# 506 Obv. Designer: Donna Weaver and Charles L. Vickers **Rev. Designer:** Thomas Cleveland and Joseph Menna **Obverse:** Army contributions during peacetime, surveying, building a flood wall and space exploration **Reverse:** Continental soldier with musket **Diameter:** 30.6 **Weight:** 11.3400 g. **Composition:** Copper-Nickel Clad Copper

Date	Mintage	MS-65	Prf-65
2011D	39,461	69.00	—
2011	68,349	—	35.00

DOLLAR

1984 Los Angeles Olympics - Discus.

KM# 209 Obv. Designer: Elizabeth Jones **Obverse:** Trippled discus thrower and five star logo **Reverse:** Eagle bust left

Date	Mintage	MS-65	Prf-65
1983P	294,543	34.80	—
1983D	174,014	34.70	—
1983S	174,014	34.80	—
1983S	1,577,025	—	36.80

1984 Los Angeles Olympics - Stadium Statues.

KM# 210 Obv. Designer: Robert Graham **Obverse:** Statues at exterior of Los Angeles Memorial Coliseum **Reverse:** Eagle standing on rock

Date	Mintage	MS-65	Prf-65
1984P	217,954	34.80	—
1984D	116,675	35.30	—
1984S	116,675	35.30	—
1984S	1,801,210	—	36.80

Statue of Liberty Centennial.

KM# 214 Obv. Designer: John Mercanti **Rev. Designer:** John Mercanti and Matthew Peloso **Obverse:** Statue of Liberty and Ellis Island great hall **Reverse:** Statue of Liberty torch

Date	Mintage	MS-65	Prf-65
1986P	723,635	34.80	—
1986S	6,414,638	—	36.80

Constitution Bicentennial.

KM# 220 Obv. Designer: Patricia L. Verani **Obverse:** Feather pen and document **Reverse:** Group of people

Date	Mintage	MS-65	Prf-65
1987P	451,629	34.80	—
1987S	2,747,116	—	36.80

Congress Bicentennial.

KM# 225 Designer: William Woodward and Chester Y. Martin. **Obverse:** Statue of Freedom in clouds and sunburst **Reverse:** Mace from the House of Represenatives

Date	Proof Mintage	MS-65	Prf-65
1989D	135,203	34.80	—
1989S	762,198	—	36.80

1988 Olympics.

KM# 222 Obv. Designer: Patricia L. Verani **Rev. Designer:** Sherl Joseph Winter **Obverse:** Olympic torch and Statue of Liberty torch within laurel wreath **Reverse:** Olympic rights within olive wreath

Date	Mintage	MS-65	Prf-65
1988D	191,368	34.80	—
1988S	1,359,366	—	36.80

Eisenhower Centennial.

KM# 227 Obv. Designer: John Mercanti **Rev. Designer:** Marcel Jovine and John Mercanti **Obverse:** Two Eisenhower profiles, as general, left, as President, right **Reverse:** Eisenhower home at Gettysburg

Date	Mintage	MS-65	Prf-65
1990W	241,669	34.80	—
1990P	1,144,461	—	36.80

Mount Rushmore 50th Anniversary.

KM# 229 Obv. Designer: Marika Somogyi and Chester Martin **Rev. Designer:** Frank Gasparro **Obverse:** Mount Rushmore portraits, wreath below **Reverse:** Great seal in rays, United States map in background

Date	Mintage	MS-65	Prf-65
1991P	133,139	39.80	—
1991S	738,419	—	42.80

Korean War - 38th Anniversary.

KM# 231 Obv. Designer: John Mercanti **Rev. Designer:** T. James Ferrell **Obverse:** Solder advancing right up a hill; planes above, ships below **Reverse:** Map of Korean pensiluar, eagle's head

Date	Mintage	MS-65	Prf-65
1991D	213,049	37.80	—
1991P	618,488	—	36.80

USO 50th Anniversary.

KM# 232 Obv. Designer: Robert Lamb **Rev. Designer:** John Mercanti **Obverse:** USO banner **Reverse:** Eagle pearched right atop globe

Date	Mintage	MS-65	Prf-65
1991D	124,958	37.80	—
1991S	321,275	—	38.80

1992 Olympics - Baseball.

KM# 234 Obv. Designer: John R. Deecken and Chester Y. Martin **Rev. Designer:** Marcel Jovine **Obverse:** Baseball pitcher, Nolan Ryan as depicted on card **Reverse:** Shield flanked by stylized wreath, olympic rings above

Date	Mintage	MS-65	Prf-65
1992D	187,552	37.80	—
1992S	504,505	—	38.80

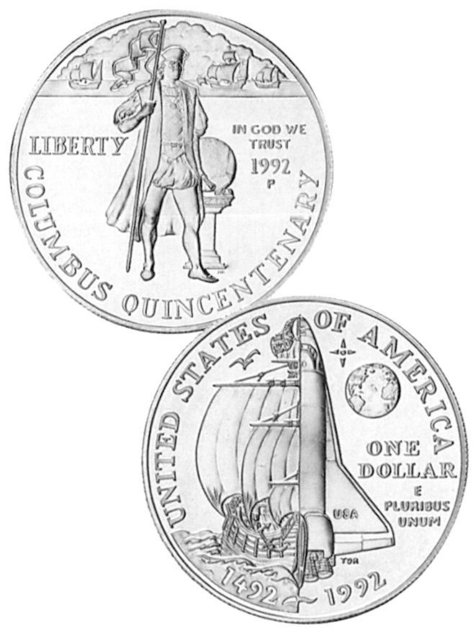

Columbus Discovery - 500th Anniversary.

KM# 238 Obv. Designer: John Mercanti **Rev. Designer:** Thomas D. Rogers, Sr. **Obverse:** Columbus standing with banner, three ships in background **Reverse:** Half view of Santa Maria on left, Space Shuttle Discovery on right

Date	Mintage	MS-65	Prf-65
1992D	106,949	40.80	—
1992P	385,241	—	37.80

1994 World Cup Soccer.

KM# 247 Obv. Designer: Dean McMullen and T. James Ferrell **Rev. Designer:** Dean McMullen **Obverse:** Two players with ball **Reverse:** World Cup 94 logo

Date	Mintage	MS-65	Prf-65
1994D	81,698	38.80	—
1994S	576,978	—	36.80

White House Bicentennial.

KM# 236 Obv. Designer: Edgar Z. Steever **Rev. Designer:** Chester Y. Martin **Obverse:** White House's north portico **Reverse:** John Hoban bust left, main entrance doorway

Date	Mintage	MS-65	Prf-65
1992D	123,803	37.80	—
1992W	375,851	—	38.80

James Madison - Bill of Rights.

KM# 241 Obv. Designer: William Krawczewicz and Thomas D. Rogers, Sr. **Rev. Designer:** Dean McMullen and Thomas D. Rogers, Sr. **Obverse:** James Madison bust right, at left **Reverse:** Montpelier home

Date	Mintage	MS-65	Prf-65
1993D	98,383	37.80	—
1993S	534,001	—	38.80

Thomas Jefferson 250th Birth Anniversary.

KM# 249 Designer: T. James Ferrell. **Obverse:** Jefferson's head left **Reverse:** Monticello home

Date	Mintage	MS-65	Prf-65
1993P	266,927	36.80	—
1993S	332,891	—	40.80

National Prisoner of War Museum.

KM# 251 Obv. Designer: Thomas Nielson and Alfred Maletsky **Rev. Designer:** Edgar Z. Steever **Obverse:** Eagle in flight left within circle of barbed wire **Reverse:** National Prisioner of War Museum

Date	Mintage	MS-65	Prf-65
1994W	54,790	84.00	—
1994P	220,100	—	39.80

World War II 50th Anniversary.

KM# 244 Designer: Thomas D. Rogers, Sr.. **Obverse:** Soldier on Normandy beach **Reverse:** Insignia of the Supreme Headquarters of the AEF above Eisenhower quote

Date	Mintage	MS-65	Prf-65
1993D	94,708	36.80	—
1993W	342,041	—	40.80

U.S. Capitol Bicentennial.

KM# 253 Obv. Designer: William C. Cousins **Rev. Designer:** John Mercanti **Obverse:** Capitol dome, Statue fo Freedom surrounded by stars **Reverse:** Eagle on shield, flags flanking

Date	Mintage	MS-65	Prf-65
1994D	68,352	38.80	—
1994S	279,416	—	40.80

Vietnam Veterans Memorial.

KM# 250 Obv. Designer: John Mercanti
Rev. Designer: Thomas D. Rogers, Sr.
Obverse: Outstretched hand touching names on the Wall, Washington Monument in background
Reverse: Service Medals

Date	Mintage	MS-65	Prf-65
1994W	57,317	79.00	—
1994P	226,262	—	63.00

1996 Atlanta Olympics - Cycling.

KM# 263 Obv. Designer: John Mercanti
Rev. Designer: William J. Krawczewicz and T. James Ferrell **Obverse:** Three cyclists approaching
Reverse: Two clasped hands, Atlanta Olympic logo above

Date	Mintage	MS-65	Prf-65
1995D	19,662	135	—
1995P	118,795	—	45.00

Women in Military Service Memorial.

KM# 252 Obv. Designer: T. James Ferrell
Rev. Designer: Thomas D. Rogers, Sr. **Obverse:** Five uniformed women left **Reverse:** Memorial at Arlington National Cemetery

Date	Mintage	MS-65	Prf-65
1994W	53,054	38.80	—
1994P	213,201	—	38.80

1996 Atlanta Olympics - Gymnastics.

KM# 260 Obv. Designer: James C. Sharpe and Thomas D. Rogers, Sr. **Rev. Designer:** William J. Krawczewicz and T. James Ferrell **Obverse:** Two gymnasts, female on floor exercise and male on rings
Reverse: Two clasped hands, Atlanta Olympic logo above

Date	Mintage	MS-65	Prf-65
1995D	42,497	55.00	—
1995P	182,676	—	36.80

1996 Atlanta Olympics - Track and field. **KM# 264** **Obv. Designer:** John Mercanti **Rev. Designer:** William J. Krawczewicz and T. James Ferrell **Obverse:** Two runners on a track, one crossing finish line **Reverse:** Two clasped hands, Atlanta Olympic logo above

Date	Mintage	MS-65	Prf-65
1995D	24,796	88.00	—
1995P	136,935	—	38.80

Civil War.
KM# 255 **Obv. Designer:** Don Troiani and Edgar Z. Steever **Rev. Designer:** John Mercanti **Obverse:** Soldier giving water to wounded soldier **Reverse:** Chamberlain quote and battlefield monument

Date	Mintage	MS-65	Prf-65
1995P	45,866	65.00	—
1995S	437,114	—	54.00

1996 Atlanta Paralympics - Blind runner. **KM# 259** **Obv. Designer:** Jim C. Sharpe and Thomas D. Rogers, Sr. **Rev. Designer:** William J. Krawczewicz and T. James Ferrell **Obverse:** Blind runner **Reverse:** Two clasped hands, Atlanta Olympic logo above

Date	Mintage	MS-65	Prf-65
1995D	28,649	67.00	—
1995P	138,337	—	45.00

Special Olympics World Games.
KM# 266 **Obv. Designer:** Jamie Wyeth and T. James Ferrell **Rev. Designer:** Thomas D. Rogers, Sr. **Obverse:** Eunice Schriver head left; founder of the Special Olympics **Reverse:** Special Olympics Logo on an award medal, rose, quote from Schriver

Date	Mintage	MS-65	Prf-65
1995W	89,301	40.80	—
1995P	351,764	—	41.80

1996 Atlanta Olympics - High Jump.

KM# A272 Obv. Designer: T. James Ferrell **Rev. Designer:** Thomas D. Rogers, Sr. **Obverse:** High jumper

Date	Mintage	MS-65	Prf-65
1996D	15,697	310	—
1996P	124,502	—	43.00

1996 Atlanta Olympics - Tennis.

KM# 269 Obv. Designer: James C. Sharpe and T. James Ferrell **Rev. Designer:** Thomas D. Rogers, Sr. **Obverse:** Female tennis player **Reverse:** Atlanta Olympics logo

Date	Mintage	MS-65	Prf-65
1996D	15,983	245	—
1996P	92,016	—	83.00

1996 Atlanta Olympics - Rowing.

KM# 272 Obv. Designer: Bart Forbes and T. James Ferrell **Rev. Designer:** Thomas D. Rogers, Sr. **Obverse:** Four man crew rowing left **Reverse:** Atlanta Olympic logo

Date	Mintage	MS-65	Prf-65
1996D	16,258	290	—
1996P	151,890	—	62.00

1996 Atlanta Paralympics - Wheelchair racer.

KM# 268 Obv. Designer: James C. Sharpe and Alfred F. Maletsky **Rev. Designer:** Thomas D. Rogers, Sr. **Obverse:** Wheelchair racer approaching with uplifted arms **Reverse:** Atlanta Olympics logo

Date	Mintage	MS-65	Prf-65
1996D	14,497	305	—
1996P	84,280	—	71.00

National Community Service.

KM# 275 Obv. Designer: Thomas D. Rogers, Sr. **Rev. Designer:** William C. Cousins **Obverse:** Female standing with lamp and shield **Reverse:** Legend within wreath

Date	Mintage	MS-65	Prf-65
1996S	23,500	170	—
1996S	101,543	—	51.00

Smithsonian Institution 150th Anniversary.

KM# 276 Obv. Designer: Thomas D. Rogers, Sr. **Rev. Designer:** John Mercanti **Obverse:** Original Smithsonian building, the "Castle" designed by James Renwick **Reverse:** Female seated with torch and scroll on globe

Date	Mintage	MS-65	Prf-65
1996D	31,230	122	—
1996P	129,152	—	49.00

Jackie Robinson.

KM# 279 Obv. Designer: Alfred Maletsky **Rev. Designer:** T. James Ferrell **Obverse:** Jackie Robinson sliding into base **Reverse:** Anniversary logo

Date	Mintage	MS-65	Prf-65
1997S	30,007	72.00	—
1997S	110,495	—	90.00

National Law Enforcement Officers Memorial.

KM# 281 Designer: Alfred F. Maletsky. **Obverse:** Male and female officer admiring name on monument **Reverse:** Rose on a plain shield

Date	Mintage	MS-65	Prf-65
1997P	28,575	135	—
1997P	110,428	—	78.00

U.S. Botanic Gardens 175th Anniversary.

KM# 278 Obv. Designer: Edgar Z. Steever **Rev. Designer:** William C. Cousins **Obverse:** National Botanic Gardens Conservatory building **Reverse:** Rose

Date	Mintage	MS-65	Prf-65
1997P	57,272	42.00	—
1997P	264,528	—	42.00

Robert F. Kennedy.

KM# 287 Obv. Designer: Thomas D. Rogers, Sr. **Rev. Designer:** James M. Peed and Thomas D. Rogers, Sr. **Obverse:** Kennedy bust facing **Reverse:** Eagle on sheild, Senate Seal

Date	Mintage	MS-65	Prf-65
1998S	106,422	47.50	—
1998S	99,020	—	47.50

Black Revolutionary War Patriots.

KM# 288 Obv. Designer: John Mercanti **Rev. Designer:** Edward Dwight and Thomas D. Rogers, Sr. **Obverse:** Crispus Attucks bust right **Reverse:** Family standing

Date	Proof Mintage	MS-65	Prf-65
1998S	37,210	145	—
1998S	75,070	—	89.00

Dolley Madison.

KM# 298 Obv. Designer: Tiffany & Co. and T. James Ferrell **Rev. Designer:** Tiffany & Co. and Thomas D. Rogers, Sr. **Obverse:** Madison bust right, at left **Reverse:** Montpelier home

Date	Mintage	MS-65	Prf-65
1999P	22,948	38.30	—
1999P	158,247	—	38.30

Yellowstone.

KM# 299 Obv. Designer: Edgar Z. Steever **Rev. Designer:** William C. Cousins **Obverse:** Old Faithful gyser erupting **Reverse:** Bison and vista as on National Parks shield

Date	Proof Mintage	MS-65	Prf-65
1999P	23,614	44.00	—
1999P	128,646	—	40.30

Library of Congress Bicentennial.

KM# 311 Obv. Designer: Thomas D. Rogers, Sr. **Rev. Designer:** John Mercanti **Obverse:** Open and closed book, torch in background **Reverse:** Skylight dome above the main reading room

Date	Proof Mintage	MS-65	Prf-65
2000P	52,771	40.80	—
2000P	196,900	—	38.30

Leif Ericson.

KM# 313 Obv. Designer: John Mercanti **Rev. Designer:** T. James Ferrell **Obverse:** Ericson bust helmeted right **Reverse:** Viking ship sailing left

Date	Mintage	MS-65	Prf-65
2000P	28,150	69.00	—
2000 Iceland	15,947	—	26.80
2000P	58,612	—	62.50

Capitol Visitor Center.

KM# 324 Obv. Designer: Marika Somogyi **Rev. Designer:** John Mercanti **Obverse:** Original and current Capital facades **Reverse:** Eagle with sheild and ribbon

Date	Mintage	MS-65	Prf-65
2001P	66,636	40.80	—
2001P	143,793	—	40.80

Native American - Bison.

KM# 325 Designer: James E. Fraser.
Obverse: Native American bust right **Reverse:** Bison standing left

Date	Mintage	MS-65	Prf-65
2001D	197,131	165	—
2001P	272,869	—	169

2002 Winter Olympics - Salt Lake City.

KM# 336 Obv. Designer: John Mercanti
Rev. Designer: Donna Weaver **Obverse:** Salt Lake City Olympic logo **Reverse:** Stylized skyline with mountains in background

Date	Mintage	MS-65	Prf-65
2002P	35,388	40.80	—
2002P	142,873	—	38.30

U.S. Military Academy at West Point - Bicentennial.

KM# 338 Obv. Designer: T. James Ferrell
Rev. Designer: John Mercanti **Obverse:** Cadet Review flagbearers, Academy buildings in background **Reverse:** Academy emblems - Corinthian helmet and sword

Date	Mintage	MS-65	Prf-65
2002W	103,201	38.30	—
2002W	288,293	—	39.80

First Flight Centennial.

KM# 349 Obv. Designer: T. James Ferrell
Rev. Designer: Norman E. Nemeth **Obverse:** Orville and Wilbur Wright busts left **Reverse:** Wright Flyer over dunes

Date	Mintage	MS-65	Prf-65
2003P	53,761	40.80	—
2003P	193,086	—	46.80

Lewis and Clark Corps of Discovery Bicentennial. **KM# 363** **Designer:** Donna Weaver. **Obverse:** Lewis and Clark standing **Reverse:** Jefferson era clasped hands peace medal

Date	Mintage	MS-65	Prf-65
2004P	90,323	40.80	—
2004P	288,492	—	46.80

John Marshall, 250th Birth Anniversary. **KM# 375** **Obv. Designer:** John Mercanti **Rev. Designer:** Donna Weaver **Obverse:** Marshall bust left **Reverse:** Marshall era Supreme Court Chamber

Date	Mintage	MS-65	Prf-65
2005P	48,953	37.30	—
2005P	141,993	—	35.80

Thomas A. Edison - Electric Light 125th Anniversary. **KM# 362** **Obv. Designer:** Donna Weaver **Rev. Designer:** John Mercanti **Obverse:** Edison half-length figure facing holding light bulb **Reverse:** Light bulb and rays

Date	Mintage	MS-65	Prf-65
2004P	68,031	40.80	—
2004P	213,409	—	41.80

U.S. Marine Corps, 230th Anniversary. **KM# 376** **Obv. Designer:** Norman E. Nemeth **Rev. Designer:** Charles Vickers **Obverse:** Flag Raising at Mt. Suribachi on Iwo Jima **Reverse:** Marine Corps emblem

Date	Proof Mintage	MS-65	Prf-65
2005P	130,000	48.00	—
2005P	370,000	—	52.50

Benjamin Franklin, 300th Birth Anniversary.

KM# 387 Obv. Designer: Norman E. Nemeth **Rev. Designer:** Charles Vickers **Obverse:** Youthful Franklin flying kite **Reverse:** Revolutionary era "JOIN, or DIE" snake cartoon illustration

Date	Proof Mintage	MS-65	Prf-65
2006P	58,000	40.80	—
2006P	142,000	—	45.00

San Francisco Mint Museum.

KM# 394 Obv. Designer: Sherl J. Winter **Rev. Designer:** George T. Morgan **Obverse:** 3/4 view of building **Reverse:** Reverse of 1880s Morgan silver dollar

Date	Mintage	MS-65	Prf-65
2006S	65,609	40.80	—
2006S	255,700	—	40.80

Benjamin Franklin, 300th Birth Anniversary.

KM# 388 Obv. Designer: Don Everhart II **Rev. Designer:** Donna Weaver **Obverse:** Bust 3/4 right, signature in oval below **Reverse:** Continental Dollar of 1776 in center

Date	Mintage	MS-65	Prf-65
2006P	58,000	40.80	—
2006P	142,000	—	51.00

Central High School Desegregation.

KM# 418 Obv. Designer: Richard Masters and Charles Vickers **Rev. Designer:** Don Everhart II **Obverse:** Children's feet walking left with adult feet in military boots **Reverse:** Little Rock's Central High School

Date	Mintage	MS-65	Prf-65
2007P	66,093	40.80	—
2007P	124,618	—	43.00

Jamestown - 400th Anniversary.

KM# 405 Obv. Designer: Donna Weaver and Don Everhart II **Rev. Designer:** Susan Gamble and Charles Vickers **Obverse:** Two settlers and Native American **Reverse:** Three ships

Date	Mintage	MS-65	Prf-65
2007P	79,801	40.80	—
2007P	258,802	—	38.30

Lincoln Bicentennial.

KM# 454 Obv. Designer: Justin Kunz and Don Everhart II **Rev. Designer:** Phebe Hemphill **Obverse:** 3/4 portrait facing right **Reverse:** Part of Gettysburg Address within wreath

Date	Mintage	MS-65	Prf-65
2009P	125,000	55.00	—
2009P	375,000	—	55.00

American Bald Eagle.

KM# 439 Obv. Designer: Joel Iskowitz and Don Everhart II **Rev. Designer:** James Licaretz **Obverse:** Eagle with flight, mountain in background at right **Reverse:** Great Seal of the United States

Date	Mintage	MS-65	Prf-65
2008P	110,073	44.00	—
2008P	243,558	—	38.30

Louis Braille Birth Bicentennial.

KM# 455 Obv. Designer: Joel Iskowitz and Phebe Hemphill **Rev. Designer:** Susan Gamble and Joseph Menna **Obverse:** Louis Braille bust facing **Reverse:** School child reading book in Braille, BRL in Braille code above

Date	Mintage	MS-65	Prf-65
2009P	82,639	38.50	—
2009P	135,235	—	38.30

Medal of Honor.

KM# 504 Obv. Designer: James Licaretz **Rev. Designer:** Richard Masters and Phebe Hemphill **Obverse:** Medal of Honor designs for Army, Navy and Air Force awards **Reverse:** Army infantry doldier carrying another to safety

Date	Mintage	MS-65	Prf-65
2011S	44,769	46.50	—
2011S	112,850	—	43.50

American Veterans Disabled for Life.

KM# 479 Obv. Designer: Don Everhart II **Rev. Designer:** Thomas Cleveland and Joseph Menna **Obverse:** Soldier's feet, crutches **Reverse:** Legend within wreath

Date	Mintage	MS-65	Prf-65
2010W	77,859	40.80	—
2010W	189,881	—	42.30

U.S. Army.

KM# 507 Obv. Designer: Richard Masters and Michael Gaudioso **Rev. Designer:** Susan Gamble and Don Everhart, II **Obverse:** Male and femlae soldier heads looking outward **Reverse:** Seven core values of the Army, Eagle from the great seal

Date	Mintage	MS-65	Prf-65
2011S	—	45.00	—
2011S	—	—	43.50

Boy Scouts of America, 100th Anniversary.

KM# 480 Obv. Designer: Donna Weaver **Rev. Designer:** Jim Licaretz **Obverse:** Cub Scout, Boy Scout and Venturer saluting **Reverse:** Boy Scouts of America logo

Date	Mintage	MS-65	Prf-65
2010P	—	38.50	—
2010P	—	—	42.00

National Infantry Museum and Soldier Center.

KM# 529

Date	Mintage	MS-65	Prf-65
2012	—	—	—
2012	—	—	—

Star-Spangled Banner.

KM# 530

Date	Mintage	MS-65	Prf-65
2012	—	—	—
2012	—	—	—

$5 (HALF EAGLE)

Statue of Liberty Centennial.

KM# 215 Designer: Elizabeth Jones. **Obverse:** Statue of Liberty head right **Reverse:** Eagle in flight left

Date	Mintage	MS-65	Prf-65
1986W	95,248	442	—
1986W	404,013	—	442

Constitution Bicentennial.

KM# 221 Designer: Marcel Jovine. **Obverse:** Eagle left with quill pen in talon **Reverse:** Upright quill pen

Date	Mintage	MS-65	Prf-65
1987W	214,225	442	—
1987W	651,659	—	442

1988 Olympics.

KM# 223 Obv. Designer: Elizabeth Jones **Rev. Designer:** Marcel Jovine **Obverse:** Nike head wearing olive wreath **Reverse:** Stylized olympic couldron

Date	Mintage	MS-65	Prf-65
1988W	62,913	442	—
1988W	281,456	—	442

Congress Bicentennial.

KM# 226 Designer: John Mercanti. **Obverse:** Capitol dome **Reverse:** Eagle atop of the canopy from the Old Senate Chamber

Date	Mintage	MS-65	Prf-65
1989W	46,899	442	—
1989W	164,690	—	442

Mount Rushmore 50th Anniversary.

KM# 230 Obv. Designer: John Mercanti **Rev. Designer:** Robert Lamb and William C. Cousins **Obverse:** Eagle in flight towards Mount Rushmore **Reverse:** Legend at center

Date	Mintage	MS-65	Prf-65
1991W	31,959	442	—
1991W	111,991	—	442

1992 Olympics.

KM# 235 Obv. Designer: James C. Sharpe and T. James Ferrell **Rev. Designer:** James M. Peed **Obverse:** Sprinter, U.S. Flag in background **Reverse:** Heraldic eagle, olympic rings above

Date	Mintage	MS-65	Prf-65
1992W	27,732	442	—
1992W	77,313	—	442

Columbus Quincentenary.

KM# 239 Obv. Designer: T. James Ferrell **Rev. Designer:** Thomas D. Rogers, Sr. **Obverse:** Columbus' profile left, at right, map of Western Hemisphere at left **Reverse:** Arms of Spain, and parchment map

Date	Mintage	MS-65	Prf-65
1992W	79,730	—	442
1992W	24,329	442	—

James Madison - Bill of Rights.

KM# 242 Obv. Designer: Scott R. Blazek **Rev. Designer:** Joseph D. Peña **Obverse:** Madison at left holding document **Reverse:** Eagle above legend, torch and laurel at sides

Date	Mintage	MS-65	Prf-65
1993W	78,651	—	442
1993W	22,266	442	—

World War II 50th Anniversary.

KM# 245 Obv. Designer: Charles J. Madsen and T. James Ferrell **Rev. Designer:** Edward S. Fisher and T. James Ferrell **Obverse:** Soldier with expression of victory **Reverse:** Morse code dot-dot-dot-dash for V, large in background; V for Victory

Date	Mintage	MS-65	Prf-65
1993W	65,461	—	442
1993W	23,089	442	—

1994 World Cup Soccer.

KM# 248 Obv. Designer: William J. Krawczewicz **Rev. Designer:** Dean McMullen **Obverse:** World Cup trophy **Reverse:** World Cup 94 logo

Date	Mintage	MS-65	Prf-65
1994W	22,464	442	—
1994W	89,619	—	442

1996 Olympics - Stadium.

KM# 265 Obv. Designer: Marvel Jovine and William C. Cousins **Rev. Designer:** Frank Gasparro **Obverse:** Atlanta Stadium and logo **Reverse:** Eagle advancing right

Date	Mintage	MS-65	Prf-65
1995W	43,124	—	442
1995W	10,579	2,500	—

1996 Olympics - Torch runner.

KM# 261 Designer: Frank Gasparro. **Obverse:** Torch runner, Atlanta skyline and logo in background **Reverse:** Eagle advancing right

Date	Mintage	MS-65	Prf-65
1995W	57,442	—	442
1995W	14,675	885	—

Civil War.

KM# 256 Designer: Don Troiani and Alfred F. Maletsky. **Obverse:** Bugler on horseback right **Reverse:** Eagle on shield

Date	Mintage	MS-65	Prf-65
1995W	12,735	950	—
1995W	55,246	—	442

1996 Olympics - Cauldron.

KM# 270 Obv. Designer: Frank Gasparro and T. James Ferrell **Rev. Designer:** William J. Krawczewicz and Thomas D. Rogers, Sr. **Obverse:** Torch bearer lighting cauldron **Reverse:** Atlanta Olympics logo flanked by laurel

Date	Mintage	MS-65	Prf-65
1996W	38,555	—	442
1996W	9,210	2,600	—

1996 Olympics - Flag bearer.

KM# 274 Obv. Designer: Patricia Verani and John Mercanti **Rev. Designer:** William J. Krawczewicz and Thomas D. Rogers, Sr. **Obverse:** Flag bearer advancing **Reverse:** Atlanta Olympic logo flanked by laurel

Date	Mintage	MS-65	Prf-65
1996W	32,886	—	442
1996W	9,174	2,600	—

Smithsonian Institution 150th Anniversary.

KM# 277 Obv. Designer: Alfred Maletsky **Rev. Designer:** T. James Ferrell **Obverse:** Smithson bust left **Reverse:** Sunburst museum logo

Date	Mintage	MS-65	Prf-65
1996W	9,068	850	—
1996W	29,474	—	442

Franklin Delano Roosevelt.

KM# 282 Obv. Designer: T. James Ferrell **Rev. Designer:** James M. Peed and Thomas D. Rogers, Sr. **Obverse:** Roosevelt bust right **Reverse:** Eagle shield

Date	Mintage	MS-65	Prf-65
1997W	11,894	1,275	—
1997W	29,474	—	442

Jackie Robinson.

KM# 280 Obv. Designer: William C. Cousins **Rev. Designer:** James M. Peed **Obverse:** Robinson head right **Reverse:** Legend on baseball

Date	Mintage	MS-65	Prf-65
1997W	5,202	2,900	—
1997W	24,072	—	590

George Washington Death Bicentennial.

KM# 300 Designer: Laura G. Fraser. **Obverse:** Washington's head right **Reverse:** Eagle with wings outstretched

Date	Mintage	MS-65	Prf-65
1999W	22,511	452	—
1999W	41,693	—	447

Capitol Visitor Center.

KM# 326 Designer: Elizabeth Jones. **Obverse:** Column at right **Reverse:** First Capital building

Date	Mintage	MS-65	Prf-65
2001W	6,761	1,750	—
2001W	27,652	—	442

2002 Winter Olympics.

KM# 337 Designer: Donna Weaver. **Obverse:** Salt Lake City Olympics logo **Reverse:** Stylized cauldron

Date	Mintage	MS-65	Prf-65
2002W	10,585	452	—
2002W	32,877	—	442

San Francisco Mint Museum.

KM# 395 Obv. Designer: Charles Vickers and Joseph Menna **Rev. Designer:** Christian Gobrecht **Obverse:** Front entrance façade **Reverse:** Eagle as on 1860's $5. Gold

Date	Mintage	MS-65	Prf-65
2006S	16,230	442	—
2006S	41,517	—	442

Jamestown - 400th Anniversary.

KM# 406 Obv. Designer: John Mercanti **Rev. Designer:** Susan Gamble and Norman Nemeth **Obverse:** Settler and Native American **Reverse:** Jamestown Memorial Church ruins

Date	Mintage	MS-65	Prf-65
2007W	18,843	442	—
2007W	47,050	—	442

American Bald Eagle.

KM# 440 Obv. Designer: Susan Gamble adn Phebe Hemphill **Rev. Designer:** Don Everhart II **Obverse:** Two eagles on branch **Reverse:** Eagle with shield

Date	Mintage	MS-65	Prf-65
2008W	13,467	457	—
2008W	59,269	—	442

Medal of Honor.

KM# 505 Obv. Designer: Joseph Menna **Rev. Designer:** Joel Iskowitz and Michael Gaudioso **Obverse:** 1861 Medal of Honor design for the Navy **Reverse:** Minerva standing with shield and Union flag, field artillery canon flanking

Date	Mintage	MS-65	Prf-65
2011S	8,251	585	—
2011S	18,012	—	500

U.S. Army.

KM# 508 Obv. Designer: Joel Iskowitz and Phebe Hemphill **Rev. Designer:** Joseph Menna **Obverse:** Five Soldiers of different eras **Reverse:** Elements from the Army's emblem

Date	Mintage	MS-65	Prf-65
2011P	8,062	585	—
2011P	17,173	—	495

Star-Spangled Banner.

KM# 531

Date	Mintage	MS-65	Prf-65
2012	—	—	—
2012	—	—	—

$10 (EAGLE)

1984 Olympics.

KM# 211 Obv. Designer: James M. Peed and John Mercanti **Rev. Designer:** John Mercanti **Obverse:** Male and female runner with torch **Reverse:** Heraldic eagle **Diameter:** 27 **Weight:** 16.7180 g. **Composition:** 0.9000 Gold, 0.4837 oz. AGW.

Date	Mintage	MS-65	Prf-65
1984W	75,886	883	—
1984P	33,309	—	893
1984D	34,533	—	893
1984S	48,551	—	893
1984W	381,085	—	893

Library of Congress.

KM# 312 Obv. Designer: John Mercanti **Rev. Designer:** Thomas D. Rogers, Sr. **Obverse:** Torch and partial facade **Reverse:** Stylized eagle within laurel wreath **Weight:** 16.2590 g. **Composition:** Bi-Metallic

Date	Mintage	MS-65	Prf-65
2000W	6,683	4,500	—
2000W	27,167	—	1,300

First Flight Centennial.

KM# 350 Obv. Designer: Donna Weaver **Rev. Designer:** Norman Nemeth **Obverse:** Orvile and Wilbur Wright busts facing **Reverse:** Wright flyer and eagle **Weight:** 16.7180 g. **Composition:** 0.9000 Gold, 0.4837 oz. AGW.

Date	Mintage	MS-65	Prf-65
2003P	10,129	1,050	—
2003P	21,846	—	893

$20 (DOUBLE EAGLE)

KM# 464 Designer: Augustus Saint-Gaudens. **Obverse:** Ultra high relief Liberty holding torch, walking forward **Reverse:** Eagle in flight left, sunrise in background **Diameter:** 27 **Composition:** 0.9990 Gold AGW.

Date	Mintage	MS-65	Prf-65
2009	115,178	—	2,650

AMERICA THE BEAUTIFUL SILVER BULLION

SILVER QUARTER

KM# 489 HOT SPRINGS, ARK.
Rev. Desc. Park Headquarters and fountain
Rev. Designer: Don Everhart II and Joseph Menna. **Weight:** 155.5500 g. **Composition:** 0.9990 Silver, 4.9958 oz. ASW.

Date	Mintage	MS65	PF65
2010	33,000	290	—
2010P Vapor Blast finish	27,000	250	—

KM# 490 YELLOWSTONE NATIONAL PARK
Rev. Desc. Old Faithful geyser and bison
Rev. Designer: Don Everhart II. **Weight:** 155.5500 g. **Composition:** 0.9990 Silver, 4.9958 oz. ASW.

Date	Mintage	MS65	PF65
2010	33,000	275	—
2010P Vapor Blast finish	27,000	240	—

KM# 491 YOSEMITE NATIONAL PARK
Rev. Desc. El Capitan, largest monolith of granite in the world **Rev. Designer:** Joseph Menna and Phebe Hemphill. **Weight:** 155.5500 g. **Composition:** 0.9990 Silver, 4.9958 oz. ASW.

Date	Mintage	MS65	PF65
2010	33,000	275	—
2010P Vapor blast finish	27,000	225	—

KM# 492 GRAND CANYON NATIONAL PARK **Rev. Desc.** Grabarues above the Nankoweap Delta in Marble Canyon near the Colorado River **Rev. Designer:** Phebe Hemphill. **Weight:** 155.5500 g. **Composition:** 0.9990 Silver, 4.9958 oz. ASW.

Date	Mintage	MS65	PF65
2010	33,000	250	—
2010P Vapor blast finish	26,019	225	—

KM# 493 MOUNT HOOD NATIONAL PARK
Rev. Desc. Mt. Hood with Lost Lake in the foreground **Rev. Designer:** Phebe Hemphill. **Weight:** 155.5500 g. **Composition:** 0.9990 Silver, 4.9958 oz. ASW.

Date	Mintage	MS65	PF65
2010	33,000	275	—
2010P Vapor blast finish	25,318	200	—

KM# 513 GETTYSBURG NATIONAL MILITARY PARK **Rev. Desc.** 72nd Pennsylvania Infantry Monumnet on the battle line of the Union Army at Cemetery Ridge **Rev. Designer:** Joel Iskowitz and Phebe Hemphill. **Weight:** 155.5500 g. **Composition:** 0.9990 Silver, 4.9958 oz. ASW.

Date	Mintage	MS65	PF65
2011	126,700	200	—
2011P Vapor blast finish	15,243	190	—

KM# 514 GLACIER NATIONAL PARK
Rev. Desc. Northeast slope of Mount Reynolds
Rev. Designer: Barbara Fox and Charles L. Vickers. **Weight:** 155.5500 g. **Composition:** 0.9990 Silver, 4.9958 oz. ASW.

Date	Mintage	MS65	PF65
2011	126,700	200	—
2011P Vapor blast finish	12,209	190	—

KM# 515 OLYMPIC NATIONAL PARK
Rev. Desc. Roosevelt elk on a gravel river bar along the Hoh River, Mount Olympus in the background
Rev. Designer: Susan Gambel and Michael Gaudioso. **Weight:** 155.5500 g. **Composition:** 0.9990 Silver, 4.9958 oz. ASW.

Date	Mintage	MS65	PF65
2011	—	200	—
2011P Vapor blast finish	—	190	—

KM# 516 VICKSBURG NATIONAL MILITARY PARK **Rev. Desc.** U.S.S. Cairo on the Yazoo River
Rev. Designer: Thomas Cleveland and Joseph menna. **Weight:** 155.5500 g. **Composition:** 0.9990 Silver, 4.9958 oz. ASW.

Date	Mintage	MS65	PF65
2011	—	200	—
2011P Vapor blast finish	—	190	—

KM# 517 CHICKASAW NATIONAL RECREATION AREA **Rev. Desc.** Limestone Lincoln Bridge **Rev. Designer:** Donna Weaver and James Licaretz. **Weight:** 155.5500 g. **Composition:** 0.9990 Silver, 4.9958 oz. ASW.

Date	Mintage	MS65	PF65
2011	—	200	—
2011P Vapor blast finish	—	190	—

KM# 536 EL YUNGUE NATIONAL FOREST
Weight: 155.5500 g. **Composition:** 0.9990 Silver, 4.9958 oz. ASW.

Date	Mintage	MS65	PF65
2012	—	200	—
2012P Vapor blast finish	—	190	—

KM# 537 CHACO CULTURE NATIONAL HISTORIC PARK **Weight:** 155.5200 g. **Composition:** 0.9990 Silver, 4.9949 oz. ASW.

Date	Mintage	MS65	PF65
2012	—	200	—
2012P Vapor blast finish	—	190	—

KM# 538 ACADIA NATIONAL PARK
Weight: 155.5200 g. **Composition:** 0.9990 Silver, 4.9949 oz. ASW.

Date	Mintage	MS65	PF65
2012	—	200	—
2012P Vapor blast finish	—	190	—

KM# 539 HAWAII VOLCANOES NATIONAL PARK **Weight:** 155.5200 g. **Composition:** 0.9990 Silver, 4.9949 oz. ASW.

Date	Mintage	MS65	PF65
2012	—	200	—
2012P Vapor blast finish	—	190	—

KM# 540 DENALI NATIONAL PARK
Weight: 155.5520 g. **Composition:** 0.9990 Silver, 4.9959 oz. ASW.

Date	Mintage	MS65	PF65
2012	—	200	—
2012P Vapor blast finish	—	190	—

BULLION COINAGE

AMERICAN EAGLE BULLION COINS

GOLD $5

KM# 216 Obv. Designer: Augustus Saint-Gaudens. **Rev. Designer:** Miley Busiek. **Diameter:** 16.5 **Weight:** 3.3930 g. **Composition:** 0.9167 Gold, 0.1000 oz. AGW.

Date	Mintage	MS65	PF65
MCMLXXXVI (1986)	912,609	199	—
MCMLXXXVII (1987)	580,266	199	—
MCMLXXXVIII (1988)	159,500	199	—
MCMLXXXVIII (1988)P	143,881	—	198
MCMLXXXIX (1989)	264,790	255	—
MCMLXXXIX (1989)P	84,647	—	198
MCMXC (1990)	210,210	199	—
MCMXC (1990)P	99,349	—	198
MCMXCI (1991)	165,200	245	—
MCMXCI (1991)P	70,334	—	198
1992	209,300	199	—
1992P	64,874	—	198
1993	210,709	199	—
1993P	45,960	—	198
1994	206,380	199	—
1994W	62,849	—	198
1995	223,025	199	—
1995W	62,667	—	198
1996	401,964	199	—
1996W	57,047	—	198
1997	528,515	220	—
1997W	34,977	—	198
1998	1,344,520	220	—
1998W	39,395	—	198
1999	2,750,338	199	—
1999W	48,428	—	198
1999W Unfinished Proof die	—	800	—
Note: The 1999 W issues are standard matte finished gold that were struck with unfinished proof dies.			
2000	569,153	199	—
2000W	49,971	—	198
2001	269,147	199	—
2001W	37,530	—	198
2002	230,027	245	—
2002W	40,864	—	198
2003	245,029	199	—
2003W	40,027	—	198
2004	250,016	199	—
2004W	35,131	—	225
2005	300,043	199	—
2005W	49,265	—	225
2006	285,006	199	—
2006W Burnished Unc.	20,643	215	—
2006W	47,277	—	198
2007	190,010	199	—
2007W Burnished Unc.	22,501	175	—
2007W	58,553	—	198
2008	305,000	199	—
2008W Burnished Unc.	12,657	325	—
2008W	—	—	198
2009	27,000	199	—
2010	—	199	—
2010W	—	—	198
2011	—	199	—
2011W	5,000	—	198
2012	—		—

GOLD $10

KM# 217 Obv. Designer: Augustus Saint-Gaudens. **Rev. Designer:** Miley Busiek. **Diameter:** 22 **Weight:** 8.4830 g. **Composition:** 0.9167 Gold, 0.2500 oz. AGW.

Date	Mintage	MS65	PF65
MCMLXXXVI (1986)	726,031	550	—
MCMLXXXVII (1987)	269,255	550	—
MCMLXXXVIII (1988)	49,000	550	—
MCMLXXXVIII (1988)P	98,028	—	471
MCMLXXXIX (1989)	81,789	565	—
MCMLXXXIX (1989)P	54,170	—	471
MCMXC (1990)	41,000	550	—
MCMXC (1990)P	62,674	—	471
MCMXCI (1991)	36,100	550	—
MCMXCI (1991)P	50,839	—	471
1992	59,546	472	—
1992P	46,269	—	471
1993	71,864	472	—
1993P	33,775	—	471
1994	72,650	472	—
1994W	47,172	—	471
1995	83,752	472	—
1995W	47,526	—	471
1996	60,318	472	—
1996W	38,219	—	471
1997	108,805	472	—
1997W	29,805	—	471
1998	309,829	472	—
1998W	29,503	—	471
1999	564,232	472	—
1999W	34,417	—	471
1999W Unfinished Proof die	—	1,350	—
Note: The 1999 W issues are standard matte finished gold that were struck with unfinished proof dies.			
2000	128,964	472	—
2000W	36,036	—	471
2001	71,280	472	—
2001W	25,613	—	471
2002	62,027	472	—
2002W	29,242	—	471
2003	74,029	472	—
2003W	30,292	—	471
2004	72,014	472	—
2004W	28,839	—	471
2005	72,015	472	—
2005W	37,207	—	471
2006	60,004	472	—
2006W Burnished Unc.	15,188	785	—
2006W	36,127	—	471
2007	34,004	472	—
2007W Burnished Unc.	12,786	990	—
2007W	46,189	—	471
2008	—	472	—
2008W Burnished Unc.	8,883	1,750	—
2008W	28,000	—	471
2009	27,500	472	—
2010	—	472	—
2010W	—	—	471
2011	—	472	—
2011W	4,000	—	471
2012	—	472	—

GOLD $25

KM# 218 **Obv. Designer:** Augustus Saint-Gaudens. **Rev. Designer:** Miley Busiek. **Diameter:** 27 **Weight:** 16.9660 g. **Composition:** 0.9167 Gold, 0.5000 oz. AGW.

Date	Mintage	MS65	PF65
MCMLXXXVI (1986)	599,566	995	—
MCMLXXXVII (1987)	131,255	945	—
MCMLXXXVII (1987)P	143,398	—	953
MCMLXXXVIII (1988)	45,000	1,395	—
MCMLXXXVIII (1988)P	76,528	—	953
MCMLXXXIX (1989)	44,829	1,425	—
MCMLXXXIX (1989)P	44,798	—	953
MCMXC (1990)	31,000	1,600	—
MCMXC (1990)P	51,636	—	953
MCMXCI (1991)	24,100	2,350	—
MCMXCI (1991)P	53,125	—	960
1992	54,404	1,100	—
1992P	40,976	—	953
1993	73,324	995	—
1993P	31,130	—	953
1994	62,400	995	—
1994W	44,584	—	953
1995	53,474	1,150	—
1995W	45,388	—	953
1996	39,287	1,200	—
1996W	35,058	—	953
1997	79,605	995	—
1997W	26,344	—	953
1998	169,029	945	—
1998W	25,374	—	953
1999	263,013	945	—
1999W	30,427	—	953
2000	79,287	995	—
2000W	32,028	—	953
2001	48,047	1,100	—
2001W	23,240	—	953
2002	70,027	995	—
2002W	26,646	—	953
2003	79,029	945	—
2003W	28,270	—	953
2004	98,040	945	—
2004W	27,330	—	953
2005	80,023	945	—
2005W	34,311	—	953
2006	66,004	948	—
2006W Burnished Unc.	15,164	1,650	—
2006W	34,322	—	953
2007	47,002	1,100	—
2007W Burnished Unc.	11,458	1,900	—
2007W	44,025	—	953
2008	61,000	948	—
2008W Burnished Unc.	15,683	1,650	—
2008W	27,800	—	953
2009	55,000	948	—
2010	—	945	—
2010W	—	—	953
2011	—	945	—
2011W	2,000	—	953
2012	—	945	—

GOLD $50

KM# 219 **Obv. Designer:** Augustus Saint-Gaudens. **Rev. Designer:** Miley Busiek. **Diameter:** 32.7 **Weight:** 33.9310 g. **Composition:** 0.9167 Gold, 100000 oz. AGW.

Date	Mintage	MS65	PF65
MCMLXXXVI (1986)	1,362,650	1,805	—
MCMLXXXVI (1986)W	446,290	—	1,835
MCMLXXXVII (1987)	1,045,500	1,805	—
MCMLXXXVII (1987)W	147,498	—	1,835
MCMLXXXVIII (1988)	465,000	1,805	—
MCMLXXXVIII (1988)W	87,133	—	1,835
MCMLXXXIX (1989)	415,790	1,805	—
MCMLXXXIX (1989)W	54,570	—	1,835
MCMXC (1990)	373,219	1,805	—
MCMXC (1990)W	62,401	—	1,835
MCMXCI (1991)	243,100	1,805	—
MCMXCI (1991)W	50,411	—	1,835
1992	275,000	1,805	—
1992W	44,826	—	1,800
1993	480,192	1,805	—
1993W	34,369	—	1,800
1994	221,663	1,805	—
1994W	46,674	—	1,800
1995	200,636	1,805	—
1995W	46,368	—	1,800
1995W 10th Anniversary	—	—	—
1996	189,148	1,805	—
1996W	36,153	—	1,800
1997	664,508	1,805	—
1997W	28,034	—	1,800
1998	1,468,530	1,805	—
1998W	25,886	—	1,800
1999	1,505,026	1,805	—
1999W	31,427	—	1,800
1999W Die error	—	3,300	—
Note: The 1999 W issues are standard matte finished gold that were struck with unfinished proof dies.			
2000	433,319	1,805	—
2000W	33,007	—	1,800
2001	143,605	1,805	—
2001W	24,555	—	1,800
2002	222,029	1,805	—
2002W	27,499	—	1,800
2003	416,032	1,805	—
2003W	28,344	—	1,800
2004	417,149	1,805	—
2004W	28,215	—	1,800
2005	356,555	1,805	—
2005W	35,246	—	1,800
2006	237,510	1,805	—
2006W Burnished Unc.	45,912	1,885	—
2006W	47,000	—	1,800
2006W Reverse Proof	10,000	—	2,550
2007	140,016	1,822	—

Date	Mintage	MS65	PF65
2007W Burnished Unc.	18,609	1,980	—
2007W	51,810	—	1,800
2008W	710,000	1,805	—
2008W Burnished Unc.	11,908	—	2,100
2008W Reverse of '07	—	—	—
2008W Proof	29,000	—	1,800
2009	122,000	1,805	—
2010	—	1,805	—
2010W	—	—	1,800
2011	—	1,805	—
2011W	—	—	1,800
2011 Burnished Unc.	—	2,350	—
2012	—	1,805	—

SILVER DOLLAR

KM# 273 **Obv. Desc.** Liberty walking left **Rev. Desc.** Eagle with shield **Obv. Designer:** Adolph A. Weinman. **Rev. Designer:** John Mercanti. **Diameter:** 40.6 **Weight:** 31.1050 g. **Composition:** 0.9993 Silver, 0.9993 oz. ASW.

Date	Mintage	MS65	PF65
1986	5,393,005	44.60	—
1986S	1,446,778	—	70.00
1987	11,442,335	40.90	—
1987S	904,732	—	70.00
1988	5,004,646	38.90	—
1988S	557,370	—	70.00
1989	5,203,327	38.10	—
1989S	617,694	—	70.00
1990	5,840,110	41.40	—
1990S	695,510	—	70.00
1991	7,191,066	37.90	—
1991S	511,924	—	70.00
1992	5,540,068	39.90	—
1992S	498,543	—	66.00
1993	6,763,762	38.90	—
1993P	405,913	—	88.00
1994	4,227,319	40.90	—
1994P	372,168	—	95.00
1995	4,672,051	41.40	—
1995P	407,822	—	82.00
1995W 10th Anniversary	30,102	—	3,600
1996	3,603,386	62.00	—
1996P	498,293	—	72.00
1997	4,295,004	41.90	—
1997P	440,315	—	70.00
1998	4,847,547	40.90	—
1998P	450,728	—	65.40
1999	7,408,640	39.90	—
1999P	549,330	—	63.00
2000	9,239,132	38.90	—
2000P	600,743	—	63.00
2001	9,001,711	36.10	—
2001W	746,398	—	63.00
2002	10,539,026	36.10	—
2002W	647,342	—	67.00
2003	8,495,008	36.10	—
2003W	747,831	—	67.00
2004	8,882,754	36.70	—
2004W	801,602	—	75.00
2005	8,891,025	36.10	—
2005W	816,663	—	63.00
2006	10,676,522	37.40	—
2006W Burnished Unc.	468,000	85.00	—
2006W	1,093,600	—	63.00
2006P Reverse Proof	—	—	265
2006 20th Aniv. 3 pc. set	—	—	385
2007	9,028,036	36.40	—
2007W Burnished Unc.	690,891	40.10	—
2007W	821,759	—	63.00
2008	20,583,000	36.10	—
2008W Burnished Unc.	—	65.00	—
2008W Reverse of '07, U in United with rounded bottom.	—	475	—
2008	713,353	—	63.00
2009	30,459,000	36.10	—
2010	34,764,500	36.10	—
2010	—	—	63.00
2011	—	39.10	—
2011P Reverse Proof	100,000	—	275
2011S Unc.	100,000	285	—
2011W Burnished Unc.	100,000	50.00	—
2011W Proof	100,000	—	63.00
2012	—	36.10	—
2012 Reverse Proof	—	—	125
2012P Proof	—	—	90.00

PLATINUM $10

KM# 283 **Rev. Desc.** Eagle flying right over sunrise **Obv. Designer:** John Mercanti. **Rev. Designer:** Thomas D. Rogers Sr. **Diameter:** 17 **Weight:** 3.1100 g. **Composition:** 0.9995 Platinum, 0.0999 oz.

Date	Mintage	MS65	PF65
1997	70,250	185	—
1997W	36,996	—	235
1998	39,525	185	—
1999	55,955	185	—
2000	34,027	185	—
2001	52,017	185	—
2002	23,005	185	—
2003	22,007	185	—
2004	15,010	185	—
2005	14,013	185	—
2006	11,001	185	—
2006W Burnished Unc.	—	425	—
2007	13,003	285	—
2007W Burnished Unc.	—	265	—
2008	17,000	180	—
2008 Burnished Unc.	—	290	—

BULLION COINAGE

KM# 289 **Rev. Desc.** Eagle in flight over New England costal lighthouse **Obv. Designer:** John Mercanti. **Weight:** 3.1100 g. **Composition:** 0.9995 Platinum, 0.0999 oz.

Date	Mintage	MS65	PF65
1998W	19,847	—	230

KM# 301 **Rev. Desc.** Eagle in flight over Southeastern Wetlands **Obv. Designer:** John Mercanti. **Weight:** 3.1100 g. **Composition:** 0.9995 Platinum, 0.0999 oz.

Date	Mintage	MS65	PF65
1999W	19,133	—	230

KM# 314 **Rev. Desc.** Eagle in flight over Heartland **Obv. Designer:** John Mercanti. **Weight:** 3.1100 g. **Composition:** 0.9995 Platinum, 0.0999 oz.

Date	Mintage	MS65	PF65
2000W	15,651	—	230

KM# 327 **Rev. Desc.** Eagle in flight over Southwestern cactus desert **Obv. Designer:** John Mercanti. **Diameter:** 17 **Weight:** 3.1100 g. **Composition:** 0.9995 Platinum, 0.0999 oz.

Date	Mintage	MS65	PF65
2001W	12,174	—	230

KM# 339 **Rev. Desc.** Eagle fishing in America's Northwest **Obv. Designer:** John Mercanti. **Diameter:** 17 **Weight:** 3.1100 g. **Composition:** 0.9995 Platinum, 0.0999 oz.

Date	Mintage	MS65	PF65
2002W	12,365	—	230

KM# 351 **Rev. Desc.** Eagle pearched on a Rocky Mountain Pine branch against a flag backdrop **Obv. Designer:** John Mercanti. **Rev. Designer:** Al Maletsky. **Diameter:** 17 **Weight:** 3.1100 g. **Composition:** 0.9995 Platinum, 0.0999 oz.

Date	Mintage	MS65	PF65
2003W	9,534	—	250

KM# 364 **Rev. Desc.** Chester French, 1907. The sculpture is outside the N.Y. Customs House, now part of the Smithsonian's Museum of the American Indian **Obv. Designer:** John Mercanti. **Diameter:** 17 **Weight:** 3.1100 g. **Composition:** 0.9995 Platinum, 0.0999 oz.

Date	Mintage	MS65	PF65
2004W	7,161	—	455

KM# 377 **Rev. Desc.** Eagle with cornucopiae **Obv. Designer:** John Mercanti. **Rev. Designer:** Donna Weaver. **Diameter:** 17 **Weight:** 3.1100 g. **Composition:** 0.9995 Platinum, 0.0999 oz.

Date	Mintage	MS65	PF65
2005W	8,104	—	265

KM# 389 **LEGISLATIVE** **Rev. Desc.** Liberty seated writing between two columns **Obv. Designer:** John Mercanti. **Diameter:** 17 **Weight:** 3.1100 g. **Composition:** 0.9995 Platinum, 0.0999 oz.

Date	Mintage	MS65	PF65
2006W	10,205	—	230

KM# 414 **EXECUTIVE BRANCH** **Rev. Desc.** Eagle with shield **Obv. Designer:** John Mercanti. **Diameter:** 17 **Weight:** 3.1100 g. **Composition:** 0.9995 Platinum, 0.0999 oz.

Date	Mintage	MS65	PF65
2007W	8,176	—	230

KM# 434 **Rev. Desc.** Justice standing before eagle **Obv. Designer:** John Mercanti. **Diameter:** 17 **Weight:** 3.1100 g. **Composition:** 0.9995 Platinum, 0.0999 oz.

Date	Mintage	MS65	PF65
2008W	8,176	—	495

KM# 460 **JUDICIAL** **Obv. Designer:** John Mercanti. **Diameter:** 17 **Weight:** 3.1100 g. **Composition:** 0.9995 Platinum, 0.0999 oz.

Date	Mintage	MS65	PF65
2009W	5,600	—	—

PLATINUM $25

KM# 284 **Rev. Desc.** Eagle in flight over sunrise **Obv. Designer:** John Mercanti. **Rev. Designer:** Thomas D. Rogers Sr. **Diameter:** 22 **Weight:** 7.7857 g. **Composition:** 0.9995 Platinum, 0.2502 oz.

Date	Mintage	MS65	PF65
1997	27,100	458	—
1997W	18,628	—	454
1998	38,887	458	—
1999	39,734	458	—
2000	20,054	458	—
2001	21,815	458	—
2002	27,405	458	—
2003	25,207	458	—
2004	18,010	458	—
2005	12,013	458	—
2006	12,001	458	—
2006W Burnished Unc.	—	590	—
2007	8,402	458	—
2007W Burnished Unc.	—	590	—
2008	22,800	458	—
2008 Burnished Unc.	—	665	—

KM# 290 **Rev. Desc.** Eagle in flight over New England costal lighthouse **Obv. Designer:** John Mercanti. **Weight:** 7.7857 g. **Composition:** 0.9995 Platinum, 0.2502 oz.

Date	Mintage	MS65	PF65
1998W	14,873	—	454

KM# 302 **Rev. Desc.** Eagle in flight over Southeastern Wetlands **Obv. Designer:** John Mercanti. **Weight:** 7.7857 g. **Composition:** 0.9995 Platinum, 0.2502 oz.

Date	Mintage	MS65	PF65
1999W	13,507	—	454

KM# 315 **Rev. Desc.** Eagle in flight over Heartland **Obv. Designer:** John Mercanti. **Weight:** 7.7857 g. **Composition:** 0.9995 Platinum, 0.2502 oz.

Date	Mintage	MS65	PF65
2000W	11,995	—	454

KM# 328 **Rev. Desc.** Eagle in flight over Southwestern cactus desert **Obv. Designer:** John Mercanti. **Diameter:** 22 **Weight:** 7.7857 g. **Composition:** 0.9995 Platinum, 0.2502 oz.

Date	Mintage	MS65	PF65
2001W	8,847	—	454

KM# 340 **Rev. Desc.** Eagle fishing in America's Northwest **Obv. Designer:** John Mercanti. **Diameter:** 22 **Weight:** 7.7857 g. **Composition:** 0.9995 Platinum, 0.2502 oz.

Date	Mintage	MS65	PF65
2002W	9,282	—	454

KM# 352 **Rev. Desc.** Eagle pearched on a Rocky Mountain Pine branch against a flag backdrop. **Obv. Designer:** John Mercanti. **Rev. Designer:** Al Maletsky. **Diameter:** 22 **Weight:** 7.7857 g. **Composition:** 0.9995 Platinum, 0.2502 oz.

Date	Mintage	MS65	PF65
2003W	7,044	—	454

KM# 365 **Rev. Desc.** Chester French, 1907. The sculpture is outside the N.Y. Customs House, now part of the Smithsonian's Museum of the American Indian **Obv. Designer:** John Mercanti. **Diameter:** 22 **Weight:** 7.7857 g. **Composition:** 0.9995 Platinum, 0.2502 oz.

Date	Mintage	MS65	PF65
2004W	5,193	—	1,000

KM# 378 **Rev. Desc.** Eagle with cornucopiae **Obv. Designer:** John Mercanti. **Rev. Designer:** Donna Weaver. **Diameter:** 22 **Weight:** 7.7857 g. **Composition:** 0.9995 Platinum, 0.2502 oz.

Date	Mintage	MS65	PF65
2005W	6,592	—	610

KM# 390 LEGISLATIVE Rev. Desc. Liberty seated writing between two columns **Obv. Designer:** John Mercanti. **Diameter:** 22 **Weight:** 7.7857 g. **Composition:** 0.9995 Platinum, 0.2502 oz.

Date	Mintage	MS65	PF65
2006W	7,813	—	458

KM# 415 EXECUTIVE Rev. Desc. Eagle with shield **Obv. Designer:** John Mercanti. **Diameter:** 22 **Weight:** 7.7857 g. **Composition:** 0.9995 Platinum, 0.2502 oz.

Date	Mintage	MS65	PF65
2007W	6,017	—	458

KM# 435 Rev. Desc. Justice standing before eagle **Obv. Designer:** John Mercanti. **Diameter:** 22 **Weight:** 7.7857 g. **Composition:** 0.9995 Platinum, 0.2502 oz.

Date	Mintage	MS65	PF65
2008W	6,017	—	985

KM# 461 JUDICIAL Obv. Designer: John Mercanti. **Diameter:** 22 **Weight:** 7.7857 g. **Composition:** 0.9995 Platinum, 0.2502 oz.

Date	Mintage	MS65	PF65
2009W	3,800	—	—

PLATINUM $50

KM# 285 Rev. Desc. Eagle flying right over sunrise **Obv. Designer:** John Mercanti. **Rev. Designer:** Thomas D. Rogers Sr. **Diameter:** 27 **Weight:** 15.5520 g. **Composition:** 0.9995 Platinum, 0.4997 oz.

Date	Mintage	MS65	PF65
1997	20,500	884	—
1997W	15,432	—	915
1998	32,419	884	—
1999	32,309	884	—
2000	18,892	884	—
2001	12,815	884	—
2002	24,005	884	—
2003	17,409	884	—
2004	13,236	884	—
2005	9,013	884	—
2006	9,602	884	—
2006W Burnished Unc.	—	979	—
2007	7,001	915	—
2007W Burnished Unc.	—	947	—
2008	14,000	884	—
2008W Burnished Unc.	—	1,200	—
2009	—	—	—

KM# 291 Rev. Desc. Eagle in flight over New England costal lighthouse **Obv. Designer:** John Mercanti. **Weight:** 15.5520 g. **Composition:** 0.9995 Platinum, 0.4997 oz.

Date	Mintage	MS65	PF65
1998W	13,836	—	907

KM# 303 Rev. Desc. Eagle in flight over Southeastern Wetlands **Obv. Designer:** John Mercanti. **Weight:** 15.5520 g. **Composition:** 0.9995 Platinum, 0.4997 oz.

Date	Mintage	MS65	PF65
1999W	11,103	—	907

KM# 316 Rev. Desc. Eagle in flight over Heartland **Obv. Designer:** John Mercanti. **Weight:** 15.5520 g. **Composition:** 0.9995 Platinum, 0.4997 oz.

Date	Mintage	MS65	PF65
2000W	11,049	—	907

KM# 329 Rev. Desc. Eagle in flight over Southwestern cactus desert **Obv. Designer:** John Mercanti. **Diameter:** 27 **Weight:** 15.5520 g. **Composition:** 0.9995 Platinum, 0.4997 oz.

Date	Mintage	MS65	PF65
2001W	8,254	—	907

KM# 341 Rev. Desc. Eagle fishing in America's Northwest **Obv. Designer:** John Mercanti. **Diameter:** 27 **Weight:** 15.5520 g. **Composition:** 0.9995 Platinum, 0.4997 oz.

Date	Mintage	MS65	PF65
2002W	8,772	—	907

KM# 353 Rev. Desc. Eagle pearched on a Rocky Mountain Pine branch against a flag backdrop. **Obv. Designer:** John Mercanti. **Rev. Designer:** Al Maletsky. **Diameter:** 27 **Weight:** 15.5520 g. **Composition:** 0.9995 Platinum, 0.4997 oz.

Date	Mintage	MS65	PF65
2003W	7,131	—	907

KM# 366 Rev. Desc. Chester French, 1907. The sculpture is outside the N.Y. Customs House, now part of the Smithsonian's Museum of the American Indian **Obv. Designer:** John Mercanti. **Diameter:** 27 **Weight:** 15.5520 g. **Composition:** 0.9995 Platinum, 0.4997 oz.

Date	Mintage	MS65	PF65
2004W	5,063	—	1,550

KM# 379 Rev. Desc. Eagle with cornucopiae **Obv. Designer:** John Mercanti. **Rev. Designer:** Donna Weaver. **Diameter:** 27 **Weight:** 15.5520 g. **Composition:** 0.9995 Platinum, 0.4997 oz.

Date	Mintage	MS65	PF65
2005W	5,942	—	1,175

KM# 391 LEGISLATIVE Rev. Desc. Liberty seated writing between two columns **Obv. Designer:** John Mercanti. **Diameter:** 27 **Weight:** 15.5520 g. **Composition:** 0.9995 Platinum, 0.4997 oz.

Date	Mintage	MS65	PF65
2006W	7,649	—	907

KM# 416 EXECUTIVE Rev. Desc. Eagle with shield **Obv. Designer:** John Mercanti. **Diameter:** 27 **Weight:** 15.5520 g. **Composition:** 0.9995 Platinum, 0.4997 oz.

Date	Mintage	MS65	PF65
2007W	22,873	—	907
2007W Reverse Proof	16,937	—	907

KM# 436 Rev. Desc. Justice standing before eagle **Obv. Designer:** John Mercanti. **Diameter:** 27 **Weight:** 15.5520 g. **Composition:** 0.9995 Platinum, 0.4997 oz.

Date	Mintage	MS65	PF65
2008W	22,873	—	1,400

KM# 462 JUDICIAL Obv. Designer: John Mercanti. **Diameter:** 27 **Weight:** 15.5520 g. **Composition:** 0.9995 Platinum, 0.4997 oz.

Date	Mintage	MS65	PF65
2009	3,600	—	—

PLATINUM $100

KM# 286 Rev. Desc. Eagle in flight over sun rise **Obv. Designer:** John Mercanti. **Rev. Designer:** Thomas D. Rogers Sr. **Diameter:** 33 **Weight:** 31.1050 g. **Composition:** 0.9995 Platinum, 0.9995 oz.

Date	Mintage	MS65	PF65
1997	56,000	1,768	—
1997W	15,885	—	1,831
1998	133,002	1,768	—
1999	56,707	1,768	—
2000	10,003	1,768	—
2001	14,070	1,768	—
2002	11,502	1,768	—
2003	8,007	1,768	—
2004	7,009	1,768	—
2005	6,310	1,768	—
2006	6,000	1,768	—
2006W Burnished Unc.	—	2,200	—
2007	7,202	1,816	—
2007W Burnished Unc.	—	2,100	—
2008	21,800	1,768	—
2008W Burnished Unc.	—	2,250	—
2009	—	—	—
2011	10,299	1,950	—

KM# 292 Rev. Desc. Eagle in flight over New England costal lighthouse **Obv. Designer:** John Mercanti. **Weight:** 31.1050 g. **Composition:** 0.9995 Platinum, 0.9995 oz.

Date	Mintage	MS65	PF65
1998W	14,912	—	1,814

KM# 304 **Rev. Desc.** Eagle in flight over Southeastern Wetlands **Obv. Designer:** John Mercanti. **Weight:** 31.1050 g. **Composition:** 0.9995 Platinum, 0.9995 oz.

Date	Mintage	MS65	PF65
1999W	12,363	—	1,814

KM# 317 **Rev. Desc.** Eagle in flight over Heartland **Obv. Designer:** John Mercanti. **Weight:** 31.1050 g. **Composition:** 0.9995 Platinum, 0.9995 oz.

Date	Mintage	MS65	PF65
2000W	12,453	—	1,814

KM# 330 **Rev. Desc.** Eagle in flight over Southwestern cactus desert **Obv. Designer:** John Mercanti. **Diameter:** 33 **Weight:** 31.1050 g. **Composition:** 0.9995 Platinum, 0.9995 oz.

Date	Mintage	MS65	PF65
2001W	8,969	—	1,814

KM# 342 **Rev. Desc.** Eagle fishing in America's Northwest **Obv. Designer:** John Mercanti. **Diameter:** 33 **Weight:** 31.1050 g. **Composition:** 0.9995 Platinum, 0.9995 oz.

Date	Mintage	MS65	PF65
2002W	9,834	—	1,814

KM# 354 **Rev. Desc.** Eagle pearched on a Rocky Mountain Pine branch against a flag backdrop **Obv. Designer:** John Mercanti. **Rev. Designer:** Al Maletsky. **Diameter:** 33 **Weight:** 31.1050 g. **Composition:** 0.9995 Platinum, 0.9995 oz.

Date	Mintage	MS65	PF65
2003W	8,246	—	1,831

KM# 367 **Rev. Desc.** Inspired by the sculpture "America" by Daniel Chester French, 1907. The sculpture is outside the N.Y. Customs House, now part of the Smithsonian's Museum of the American Indian **Obv. Designer:** John Mercanti. **Rev. Designer:** Donna Weaver. **Diameter:** 33 **Weight:** 31.1050 g. **Composition:** 0.9995 Platinum, 0.9995 oz.

Date	Mintage	MS65	PF65
2004W	6,007	—	2,184

KM# 380 Rev. Desc. Eagle with cornucopiae **Obv. Designer:** John Mercanti. **Rev. Designer:** Donna Weaver. **Diameter:** 33 **Weight:** 31.1050 g. **Composition:** 0.9995 Platinum, 0.9995 oz.

Date	Mintage	MS65	PF65
2005W	6,602	—	2,400

KM# 392 LEGISLAIVE Rev. Desc. Liberty seated writing between two columns **Obv. Designer:** John Mercanti. **Diameter:** 33 **Weight:** 31.1050 g. **Composition:** 0.9995 Platinum, 0.9995 oz.

Date	Mintage	MS65	PF65
2006W	9,152	—	1,814

KM# 417 EXECUTIVE BRANCH Rev. Desc. Eagle with shield **Obv. Designer:** John Mercanti. **Diameter:** 33 **Weight:** 31.1050 g. **Composition:** 0.9995 Platinum, 0.9995 oz.

Date	Mintage	MS65	PF65
2007W	8,363	—	1,814

KM# 437 Rev. Desc. Justice standing before eagle **Obv. Designer:** John Mercanti. **Diameter:** 33 **Weight:** 31.1050 g. **Composition:** 0.9995 Platinum, 0.9995 oz.

Date	Mintage	MS65	PF65
2008W	8,363	—	3,000

KM# 463 A MORE PERFECT UNION Rev. Desc. Four portraits **Obv. Designer:** John Mercanti. **Diameter:** 33 **Weight:** 31.1020 g. **Composition:** 0.9995 Platinum, 0.9994 oz.

Date	Mintage	MS65	PF65
2009W Proof	4,900	—	2,250

KM# 488 Rev. Desc. Statue of Justice holding scales **Obv. Designer:** John Mercanti. **Diameter:** 33 **Weight:** 31.1050 g. **Composition:** 0.9990 Platinum, 0.9990 oz.

Date	Mintage	MS65	PF65
2010W	—	—	2,200

KM# 518 TO INSURE DOMESTIC TRANQUILITY Diameter: 33 **Weight:** 31.1050 g. **Composition:** 0.9995 Platinum, 0.9995 oz.

Date	Mintage	MS65	PF65
2011W	—	—	1,658

KM# 541 TO PROVIDE FOR THE COMMON JUSTICE Weight: 31.1050 g. **Composition:** 0.9995 Platinum, 0.9995 oz.

Date	Mintage	MS65	PF65
2012	—	—	1,692

BISON BULLION COINAGE

GOLD $5

KM# 411 Obv. Desc. Indian Head right **Rev. Desc.** Bison **Weight:** 3.1100 g. **Composition:** 0.9999 Gold, 0.1000 oz. AGW.

Date	Mintage	MS65	PF65
2008W	19,000	575	—
2008W	19,300	—	660

GOLD $10

KM# 412 Obv. Desc. Indian Head right **Rev. Desc.** Bison **Weight:** 7.7857 g. **Composition:** 0.9999 Gold, 0.2503 oz. AGW.

Date	Mintage	MS65	PF65
2008W	10,500	1,375	—
2008W	13,900	—	1,550

GOLD $25

KM# 413 Obv. Desc. Indian Head right **Rev. Desc.** Bison **Weight:** 15.5520 g. **Composition:** 0.9990 Gold, 0.4995 oz. AGW.

Date	Mintage	MS65	PF65
2008W	17,000	1,350	—
2008W	12,500	—	1,775

GOLD $50

KM# 393 Obv. Desc. Indian head right **Rev. Desc.** Bison standing left on mound **Designer:** James E. Fraser. **Diameter:** 32 **Weight:** 31.1050 g. **Composition:** 0.9999 Gold, 0.9999 oz. AGW.

Date	Mintage	MS65	PF65
2006W	337,012	1,805	—
2006W	246,267	—	1,932
2007W	136,503	1,805	—
2007W	58,998	—	1,932
2008W	189,500	1,805	—
2008W	19,500	—	3,200
2008W Moy Family Chop	—	3,950	—
2009W	—	1,805	—
2009W	—	—	1,902
2010	—	1,805	—
2010W	49,374	—	1,932
2011	—	1,805	—
2011W	—	—	1,932
2012	—	1,805	—
2012W	—	—	1,932

FIRST SPOUSE GOLD COINAGE

GOLD $10

KM# 407 MARTHA WASHINGTON
Obv. Desc. Bust 3/4 facing **Rev. Desc.** Martha Washington seated sewing **Obv. Designer:** Joseph Menna. **Rev. Designer:** Susan Gamble and Don Everhart. **Diameter:** 23.5 **Weight:** 15.5520 g. **Composition:** 0.9999 Gold, 0.4999 oz. AGW.

Date	Mintage	MS65	PF65
2007W	20,000	928	—
2007W	20,000	—	928

KM# 408 ABIGAIL ADAMS
Obv. Desc. Bust 3/4 facing **Rev. Desc.** Abigail Adams seated at desk writing to John during the Revolutionary War **Obv. Designer:** Joseph Menna. **Rev. Designer:** Thomas Cleveland and Phebe Hemphill. **Diameter:** 26.5 **Weight:** 15.5520 g. **Composition:** 0.9999 Gold, 0.4999 oz. AGW.

Date	Mintage	MS65	PF65
2007W	20,000	928	—
2007W	20,000	—	928

KM# 409 JEFFERSON - BUST COINAGE DESIGN **Obv. Desc.** Bust design from coinage **Rev. Desc.** Jefferson's tombstone **Obv. Designer:** Robert Scot and Phebe Hemphill. **Rev. Designer:** Charles Vickers. **Diameter:** 26.5 **Weight:** 15.5520 g. **Composition:** 0.9999 Gold, 0.4999 oz. AGW.

Date	Mintage	MS65	PF65
2007W	20,000	928	—
2007W	20,000	—	928

KM# 410 DOLLEY MADISON **Obv. Desc.** Bust 3/4 facing **Rev. Desc.** Dolley standing before painting of Washington, which she saved from the White House **Obv. Designer:** Don Everhart. **Rev. Designer:** Joel Iskowitz and Don Everhart. **Diameter:** 26.5 **Weight:** 15.5520 g. **Composition:** 0.9999 Gold, 0.4999 oz. AGW.

Date	Mintage	MS65	PF65
2007W	12,500	928	—
2007W	18,300	—	928

KM# 430 ELIZABETH MONROE **Obv. Desc.** Bust 3/4 facing right **Rev. Desc.** Elizabeth standing before mirror **Obv. Designer:** Joel Iskowitz and Don Everhart. **Rev. Designer:** Donna Weaver and Charles Vickers. **Diameter:** 26.5 **Weight:** 15.5520 g. **Composition:** 0.9990 Gold, 0.4995 oz. AGW.

Date	Mintage	MS65	PF65
2008W	4,500	975	—
2008W	7,900	—	950

KM# 431 LOUSIA ADAMS **Obv. Desc.** Bust 3/4 facing right **Rev. Desc.** Lousia and son Charles before entrance **Obv. Designer:** Susan Gamble and Phebe Hemphill. **Rev. Designer:** Joseph Menna. **Diameter:** 26.5 **Weight:** 15.5520 g. **Composition:** 0.9990 Gold, 0.4995 oz. AGW.

Date	Mintage	MS65	PF65
2008W	4,200	1,175	—
2008W	7,400	—	1,125

BULLION COINAGE

KM# 432 JACKSON'S LIBERTY
Obv. Desc. Capped and draped bust left
Rev. Desc. Andrew Jackson on horseback right **Obv. Designer:** John Reich. **Rev. Designer:** Justin Kunz and Don Everhart. **Diameter:** 26.5 **Weight:** 15.5520 g. **Composition:** 0.9990 Gold, 0.4995 oz. AGW.

Date	Mintage	MS65	PF65
2008W	4,800	1,575	—
2008W	7,800	—	1,325

KM# 433 VAN BUREN'S LIBERTY
Obv. Desc. Seated Liberty with shiled
Rev. Desc. Youthful van Buren seated under tree, family tavern in distance **Obv. Designer:** Christian Gobrecht. **Rev. Designer:** Thomas Cleveland and James Licaretz. **Diameter:** 26.5 **Weight:** 15.5520 g. **Composition:** 0.9990 Gold, 0.4995 oz. AGW.

Date	Mintage	MS65	PF65
2008W	15,000	1,500	—
2008W	Inc. above	—	1,525

KM# 456 ANNA HARRISON
Obv. Desc. Bust 3/4 left **Rev. Desc.** Anna reading to her three children **Obv. Designer:** Donna Weaver and Joseph Menna. **Rev. Designer:** Thomas Cleveland and Charles Vickers. **Weight:** 15.5520 g. **Composition:** 0.9990 Gold, 0.4995 oz. AGW.

Date	Mintage	MS65	PF65
2009W	15,000	1,225	—
2009W	Inc. above	—	1,150

KM# 457 LETTIA TYLER
Obv. Desc. Bust facing **Rev. Desc.** Letitia and two children playing outside of Cedar Grove Plantation **Obv. Designer:** Phebe Hemphill. **Rev. Designer:** Susan Gamble and Norm Nemeth. **Weight:** 15.5520 g. **Composition:** 0.9990 Gold, 0.4995 oz. AGW.

Date	Mintage	MS65	PF65
2009W	15,000	1,525	—
2009W	Inc. above	—	1,325

KM# 458 JULIA TYLER
Obv. Desc. Bust facing **Rev. Desc.** Julia and John Tyler dancing **Designer:** Joel Iskowitz and Don Everhart. **Weight:** 15.5520 g. **Composition:** 0.9990 Gold, 0.4995 oz. AGW.

Date	Mintage	MS65	PF65
2009W	15,000	1,650	—
2009W	Inc. above	—	1,800

KM# 459 SARAH POLK
Obv. Desc. Bust 3/4 right **Rev. Desc.** Sarah seated at desk as personal secretary to James Polk **Designer:** Phebe Hemphill. **Weight:** 15.5520 g. **Composition:** 0.9990 Gold, 0.4995 oz. AGW.

Date	Mintage	MS65	PF65
2009W	3,501	1,300	—
2009W	5,157	—	1,100

KM# 465 MARGARET TAYLOR
Obv. Desc. Bust 3/4 left **Rev. Desc.** Margaret Taylor nurses wounded soldier during the Seminole War **Obv. Designer:** Phebe Hemphill and Charles Vickers. **Rev. Designer:** Mary Beth Zeitz and James Licaretz. **Weight:** 15.5520 g. **Composition:** 0.9990 Gold, 0.4995 oz. AGW.

Date	Mintage	MS65	PF65
2009W	3,430	1,050	—
2009W	4,787	—	1,225

KM# 481 ABIGAIL FILMORE
Rev. Desc. Abigail Filmore placing books on library shelf **Obv. Designer:** Phebe Hemphill.

Rev. Designer: Susan Gamble and Joseph Menna. **Weight:** 15.5200 g. **Composition:** 0.9990 Gold, 0.4985 oz. AGW.

Date	Mintage	MS65	PF65
2010W	15,000	1,300	—
2010W	Inc. above	—	1,025

KM# 482 JANE PIERCE
Rev. Desc. Jane Pierce seated on porch
Obv. Designer: Donna Weaver and Don Everhart.
Rev. Designer: Donna Weaver and Charles Vickers.
Weight: 15.5200 g. **Composition:** 0.9990 Gold, 0.4985 oz. AGW.

Date	Mintage	MS65	PF65
2010W	3,333	1,000	—
2010W	4,843	—	1,225

KM# 483 BUCHANAN'S LIBERTY
Rev. Desc. Buchanan as clerk **Obv. Designer:** Christian Gobrecht. **Rev. Designer:** Joseph Menna. **Diameter:** 26.5 **Weight:** 15.5200 g. **Composition:** 0.9990 Gold, 0.4985 oz. AGW.

Date	Mintage	MS65	PF65
2010W	5,348	1,000	—
2010W	7,304	—	1,075

KM# 484 MARY TODD LINCOLN
Rev. Desc. Mary Lincoln visiting soldiers at hospital **Obv. Designer:** Phebe Hemphill.
Rev. Designer: Joel Iskowitz and Pheve Hemphill.
Weight: 15.5200 g. **Composition:** 0.9990 Gold, 0.4985 oz. AGW.

Date	Mintage	MS65	PF65
2010W	3,760	1,000	—
2010W	6,904	—	975

KM# 509 ELIZA JOHNSON
Obv. Desc. Bust of Eliza Johnson **Weight:** 15.5500 g. **Composition:** 0.9990 Gold, 0.4994 oz. AGW.

Date	Mintage	MS65	PF65
2011W	15,000	1,075	—
2011W	Inc. above	—	1,075

KM# 510 JULIA GRANT
Obv. Desc. Bust of Julia Grant**Diameter:** 26.5 **Weight:** 15.5520 g. **Composition:** 0.9990 Gold, 0.4995 oz. AGW.

Date	Mintage	MS65	PF65
2011W	15,000	1,075	—
2011W	Inc. above	—	1,075

KM# 511 LUCY HAYES
Obv. Desc. Bust of Lucy Hayes **Weight:** 15.5520 g. **Composition:** 0.9990 Gold, 0.4995 oz. AGW.

Date	Mintage	MS65	PF65
2011W	15,000	1,325	—
2011W	Inc. above	—	1,075

KM# 512 LUCRETIA GARFIELD
Obv. Desc. Bust of Lucretia Garfield
Weight: 15.5520 g. **Composition:** 0.9990 Gold, 0.4995 oz. AGW.

Date	Mintage	MS65	PF65
2011W	15,000	1,325	—
2011W	Inc. above	—	1,075

KM# 532 Obv. Desc. Alice Paul, suffragist **Weight:** 15.5520 g. **Composition:** 0.9990 Gold, 0.4995 oz. AGW.

Date	Mintage	MS65	PF65
2012W	—	1,050	—
2012W	—	—	1,075

KM# 533 Obv. Desc. Francis Cleveland (first term) **Weight:** 15.5520 g. **Composition:** 0.9990 Gold, 0.4995 oz. AGW.

Date	Mintage	MS65	PF65
2012W	—	1,050	—
2012W	—	—	1,075

KM# 534 Obv. Desc. Caroline Harrison **Weight:** 15.5520 g. **Composition:** 0.9990 Gold, 0.4995 oz. AGW.

Date	Mintage	MS65	PF65
2012W	—	1,050	—
2012W	—	—	1,075

KM# 535 Obv. Desc. Francis Cleveland (second term) **Weight:** 15.5520 g. **Composition:** 0.9990 Gold, 0.4995 oz. AGW.

Date	Mintage	MS65	PF65
2012	—	1,050	—
2012	—	—	1,075

MINT SETS

Mint, or uncirculated, sets contain one uncirculated coin of each denomination from each mint produced for circulation that year. Values listed here are only for those sets sold by the U.S. Mint. Sets were not offered in years not listed. In years when the Mint did not offer the sets, some private companies compiled and marketed uncirculated sets. Mint sets from 1947 through 1958 contained two examples of each coin mounted in cardboard holders, which caused the coins to tarnish. Beginning in 1959, the sets have been packaged in sealed Pliofilm packets and include only one specimen of each coin struck for that year (both P & D mints). Listings for 1965, 1966 and 1967 are for "special mint sets," which were of higher quality than regular mint sets and were prooflike. They were packaged in plastic cases. The 1970 large-date and small-date varieties are distinguished by the size of the date on the coin. The 1976 three-piece set contains the quarter, half dollar and dollar with the Bicentennial design. The 1971 and 1972 sets do not include a dollar coin; the 1979 set does not include an S-mint-marked dollar. Mint sets issued prior to 1959 were double sets (containing two of each coin) packaged in cardboard with a paper overlay. Origional sets will always be toned and can bring large premiums if nicely preserved with good color.

Date	Sets Sold	Issue Price	Value
1947 Est. 5,000	—	4.87	1,325
1948 Est. 6,000	—	4.92	750
1949 Est. 5,200	—	5.45	935
1950 None issued	—	—	—
1951	8,654	6.75	900
1952	11,499	6.14	825
1953	15,538	6.14	565
1954	25,599	6.19	265
1955 flat pack	49,656	3.57	168
1956	45,475	3.34	165
1957	32,324	24.50	275
1958	50,314	4.43	150
1959	187,000	2.40	58.00
1960 large date	260,485	2.40	53.50
1961	223,704	2.40	56.50
1962	385,285	2.40	49.50
1963	606,612	2.40	48.00
1964	1,008,108	2.40	48.00
1965 Special Mint Set	2,360,000	4.00	9.25
1966 Special Mint Set	2,261,583	4.00	8.50
1967 Special Mint Set	1,863,344	4.00	9.35
1968	2,105,128	2.50	7.25
1969	1,817,392	2.50	7.75
1970 large date	2,038,134	2.50	18.25
1970 small date	Inc. above	2.50	62.50
1971	2,193,396	3.50	3.30
1972	2,750,000	3.50	3.00
1973	1,767,691	8.00	8.60
1974	1,975,981	6.75	6.90
1975	1,921,488	6.00	5.50
1976 3 coins	4,908,319	9.00	20.00
1976	1,892,513	6.00	5.50
1977	2,006,869	7.00	7.15
1978	2,162,609	7.00	5.00
1979 Type I	2,526,000	8.00	5.00
1979 Susan B Anthony PDS Souvenir Set	—	—	6.50
1980 Susan B. Anthony PDS Souvenir Set	—	—	6.50

Date	Sets Sold	Issue Price	Value
1980	2,815,066	9.00	5.75
1981 Type I	2,908,145	11.00	8.00
1981 Susan B. Anthony PDS Souvenir Set	—	—	22.00
1982 Souvenir set	—	—	59.00
1982 & 1983 None issued	—	—	—
1983 Souvenir set	—	—	65.00
1984	1,832,857	7.00	3.65
1985	1,710,571	7.00	3.30
1986	1,153,536	7.50	8.00
1987	2,890,758	7.00	3.85
1988	1,646,204	7.00	5.25
1989	1,987,915	7.00	3.10
1990	1,809,184	7.00	3.30
1991	1,352,101	7.00	4.40
1992	1,500,143	7.00	3.10
1993	1,297,094	8.00	6.00
1994	1,234,813	8.00	3.85
1995	1,038,787	8.00	5.00
1996	1,457,949	8.00	15.00
1997	950,473	8.00	7.20
1998	1,187,325	8.00	3.60
1999 9 piece	1,421,625	14.95	8.00
2000	1,490,160	14.95	7.70
2001	1,066,900	14.95	9.50
2002	1,139,388	14.95	10.25
2003	1,002,555	14.95	7.75
2004	844,484	16.95	13.00
2005	—	16.95	8.50
2006	—	16.95	12.25
2007	—	—	17.60
2008	—	—	59.50
2009 18 piece clad set	—	—	24.50
2010 28 piece clad set	—	—	29.70
2010 14 piece clad	—	—	24.50
2011 14 piece clad set	—	—	35.00
2012 14 piece clad set	—	—	—

MODERN COMMEMORATIVE COIN SETS

Olympic, 1983-1984

Date	Price
1983 & 1984 3 coin set: 1983 and one 1984 uncirculated dollar and 1984W uncirculatod gold $10; KM209, 210, 211.	952
1983S & 1984S 3 coin set: proof 1983 and 1984 dollar and 1984W gold $10; KM209, 210, 211.	956
1983 & 1984 6 coin set in a cherrywood box: 1983S and 1984S uncirculated and proof dollars, 1984W uncirculated and proof gold $10; KM209, 210, 211.	1,909
1983S & 1984S 2 coin set: proof dollars.	74.00
1983 collectors 3 coin set: 1983 PDS uncirculated dollars; KM209.	104
1984 collectors 3 coin set: 1984 PDS uncirculated dollars; KM210.	105

Statue of Liberty

Date	Price
1986 2 coin set: uncirculated silver dollar and clad half dollar; KM212, 214.	38.00
1986 2 coin set: proof silver dollar and clad half dollar; KM212, 214.	40.00
1986 3 coin set: uncirculated silver dollar, clad half dollar and gold $5; KM212, 214, 215.	480
1986 3 coin set: proof silver dollar, clad half dollar and gold $5; KM212, 214, 215.	483
1986 6 coin set: 1 each of the proof and uncirculated issues; KM212, 214, 215.	963

Constitution

Date	Price
1987 2 coin set: uncirculated silver dollar and gold $5; KM220, 221.	477
1987 2 coin set: proof silver dollar and gold $5; KM220, 221.	479
1987 4 coin set: silver dollar and $5 gold proof and uncirculated issues; KM220, 221.	958

Olympic, 1988

Date	Price
1988 2 coin set: uncirculated silver dollar and gold $5; KM222, 223.	477
1988 2 coin set: proof silver dollar and gold $5; KM222, 223.	479
1988 4 coin set: silver dollar and $5 gold proof and uncirculated issues; KM222, 223.	958

Congress

Date	Price
1989 2 coin set: uncirculated silver dollar and clad half dollar; KM224, 225.	42.00
1989 2 coin set: proof silver dollar and clad half dollar; KM224, 225.	44.00
1989 3 coin set: uncirculated silver dollar, clad half and gold $5; KM224, 225, 226.	485
1989 3 coin set: proof silver dollar, clad half and gold $5; KM224, 225, 226.	487
1989 6 coin set: 1 each of the proof and uncirculated issues; KM224, 225, 226.	973

Mt. Rushmore

Date	Price
1991 2 coin set: uncirculated half dollar and silver dollar; KM228, 229.	57.00
1991 2 coin set: proof half dollar and silver dollar; KM228, 229.	60.00
1991 3 coin set: uncirculated half dollar, silver dollar and gold $5; KM228, 229, 230.	500
1991 3 coin set: proof half dollar, silver dollar and gold $5; KM228, 229, 230.	502
1991 6 coin set: 1 each of proof and uncirculated issues; KM228, 229, 230.	1,004

Olympic, 1992

Date	Price
1992 2 coin set: uncirculated half dollar and silver dollar; KM233, 234.	46.00
1992 2 coin set: proof half dollar and silver dollar; KM233, 234.	47.00
1992 3 coin set: uncirculated half dollar, silver dollar and gold $5; KM233, 234, 235.	489
1992 3 coin set: proof half dollar, silver dollar and gold $5; KM233, 234, 235.	490
1992 6 coin set: 1 each of proof and uncirculated issues; KM233, 234, 235.	978

Columbus Quincentenary

Date	Price
1992 2 coin set: uncirculated half dollar and silver dollar; KM237, 238.	52.00
1992 2 coin set: proof half dollar and silver dollar; KM237, 238.	47.00
1992 3 coin set: uncirculated half dollar, silver dollar and gold $5; KM237, 238, 239.	495
1992 3 coin set: proof half dollar, silver dollar and gold $5; KM237, 238, 239.	489
1992 6 coin set: 1 each of proof and uncirculated issues; KM237, 238, 239.	985

Jefferson

Date	Price
1993 Jefferson: dollar, 1994 matte proof nickel and $2 note; KM249, 192.	109

Madison / Bill of Rights

Date	Price
1993 2 coin set: uncirculated half dollar and silver dollar; KM240, 241.	57.00
1993 2 coin set: proof half dollar and silver dollar; KM240, 241.	58.00
1993 3 coin set: uncirculated half dollar, silver dollar and gold $5; KM240, 241, 242.	499
1993 3 coin set: proof half dollar, silver dollar and gold $5; KM240, 241, 242.	500
1993 6 coin set: 1 each of proof and uncirculated issues; KM240, 241, 242.	999
Coin and stamp set; KM#240 and 20c stamp	21.00

World War II

Date	Price
1993 2 coin set: uncirculated half dollar and silver dollar; KM243, 244.	54.00
1993 2 coin set: proof half dollar and silver dollar; KM243, 244.	57.00
1993 3 coin set: uncirculated half dollar, silver dollar and gold $5; KM243, 244, 245.	496
1993 3 coin set: proof half dollar, silver dollar and gold $5; KM243, 244, 245.	500
1993 6 coin set: 1 each of proof and uncirculated issues; KM243, 244, 245.	1,000

U.S. Veterans

Date	Price
1994 3 coin set: uncirculated POW, Vietnam, Women dollars; KM250, 251, 252.	202
1994 3 coin set: proof POW, Vietnam, Women dollars; KM250, 251, 252.	142

World Cup

Date	Price
1994 2 coin set: uncirculated half dollar and silver dollar; KM246, 247.	48.00
1994 2 coin set: proof half dollar and silver dollar; KM246, 247.	45.00
1994 3 coin set: uncirculated half dollar, silver dollar and gold $5; KM246, 247, 248.	490
1994 3 coin set: proof half dollar, silver dollar and gold $5; KM246, 247, 248.	487
1994 6 coin set: 1 each of proof and uncirculated issues; KM246, 247, 248.	983

Olympic, 1995-96

Date	Price
1995 4 coin set: uncirculated basketball half, $1 gymnast & blind runner, $5 torch runner; KM257, 259, 260, 261.	1,024

Date	Price
1995 4 coin set: proof basketball half, $1 gymnast & blind runner, $5 torch runner; KM257, 259, 260, 261.	533
1995P 2 coin set: proof $1 gymnast & blind runner; KM259, 260.	82.00
1995P 2 coin set: proof $1 track & field, cycling; KM263, 264.	84.00
1995-96 4 coin set: proof halves, basketball, baseball, swimming, soccer; KM257, 262, 267, 271.	75.00
1995 & 96 8 coins in cherry wood case: proof silver dollars: blind runner, gymnast, cycling, track & field, wheelchair, tennis, rowing, high jump; KM259, 260, 263, 264, 268, 269, 272, 272A.	425
1995 & 96 16 coins in cherry wood case: bu and proof silver dollars: blind runner, gymnast, cycling, track & field, wheelchair, tennis, rowing, high jump; KM259, 260, 263, 264, 268, 269, 272, 272A.	10,400
1995 & 96 16 coins in cherry wood case: proof half dollars: basketball, baseball, swimming, soccer, KM257, 262, 267, 271. Proof silver dollars: blind runner, gymnast, cycling, track & field, wheelchair, tennis, rowing, high jump, KM259, 260, 263, 264, 268, 269, 272, 272A. Proof $5 gold: torch runner, stadium, cauldron, flag bearer, KM 261, 265, 270, 274.	2,370
1995 & 96 32 coins in cherry wood case: bu & proof half dollars: basketball, baseball, swimming, soccer, KM257, 262, 267, 271. BU & proof silver dollars: blind runner, gymnast, cycling, track & field, wheelchair, tennis, rowing, high jump, KM259, 260, 263, 264, 268, 269, 272, 272A. BU & proof $5 gold: torch runner, stadium, cauldron, flag bearer, KM261, 265, 270, 274.	12,800
Young collector 4 coin set; Half dollars: KM#257, 262, 267, 271	205
1996P 2 coin set: proof $1 wheelchair & tennis; KM268, 269.	154
1996P 2 coin set: proof $1 rowing & high jump; KM272, 272A.	105

Civil War

Date	Price
1995 2 coin set: uncirculated half and dollar; KM254, 255.	102
1995 2 coin set: proof half and dollar; KM254, 255.	88.00
1995 3 coin set: uncirculated half, dollar and gold $5; KM254, 255, 256.	1,055
1995 3 coin set: proof half, dollar and gold $5; KM254, 255, 256.	530
1995 6 coin set: 1 each of proof and uncirculated issues; KM254, 255, 256.	1,585
Civil War Young Collectors set KM#245	37.50

Smithsonian

Date	Price
1996 2 coin set: proof dollar and $5 gold; KM276, 277.	495
1996 4 coin set: proof and B.U. ; KM276, 277.	1,465

Franklin Delano Roosevelt

Date	Price
1997W 2 coin set: uncirculated and proof; KM282.	3,500

Jackie Robinson

Date	Price
1997 2 coin set: proof dollar & $5 gold; KM279, 280.	680
1997 4 coin set: proof & BU; KM279, 280.	3,660
1997 legacy set.	650

Botanic Garden

Date	Price
1997 2 coin set: dollar, Jefferson nickel and $1 note; KM278, 192.	220

Black Patriots

Date	Price
1998S 2 coin set: uncirculated and proof; KM288.	220

Kennedy

Date	Price
1998 2 coin set: proof; KM287.	88.00
1998 2 coin collectors set: Robert Kennedy dollar and John Kennedy half dollar; KM287, 202b. Matte finished.	225

Dolley Madison

Date	Price
1999 2 coin set: proof and uncirculated silver dollars; KM298.	76.00

Yellowstone National Park

Date	Price
1999 2 coin set: proof and uncirculated silver dollars; KM299.	84.00

George Washington

Date	Price
1999 2 coin set: proof and uncirculated gold $5; KM300.	900

Millennium Coin & Currency

Date	Price
2000 2 coin set: uncirculated Sacagewea $1, silver Eagle & $1 note.	67.50

Leif Ericson

Date	Price
2000 2 coin set: proof and uncirculated silver dollars; KM313.	85.00

American Buffalo

Date	Price
2001 2 coin set: 90% silver unc. & proof $1.; KM325.	330
2001 coin & currency set 90% unc. dollar & replicas of 1899 $5 silver cert.; KM325.	180

Capitol Visitor Center

Date	Price
2001 3 coin set: proof half, silver dollar, gold $5; KM323, 324, 326.	495

Winter Olympics - Salt Lake City

Date	Price
2002 2 coin set: proof 90% silver dollar KM336 & $5.00 Gold KM337.	465
2002 4 coin set: 90% silver unc. & proof $1, KM336 & unc. & proof gold $5, KM337.	925

Thomas Alva Edison

Date	Price
2004 Uncirculated silver dollar and light bulb.	55.00

Lewis and Clark Bicentennial

Date	Price
2004 Coin and pouch set.	65.00
2004 coin and currency set: Uncirculated silver dollar, two 2005 nickels, replica 1901 $10 Bison note, silver plated peace medal, three stamps & two booklets.	58.00
2004 Westward Journey Nickel series coin and medal set: Proof Sacagawea dollar, two 2005 proof nickels and silver plated peace medal.	40.00

Chief Justice John Marshall

Date	Price
2005 Coin and Chronicles set: Uncirculated silver dollar, booklet and BEP intaglio portrait.	57.00

U.S. Marine Corps

Date	Price
2005 Uncirculated silver dollar and stamp set.	63.00

Benjamin Franklin Tercentennary

Date	Price
2006 Coin and Chronicles set: Uncirculated "Scientist" silver dollar, four stamps, Poor Richards Almanac and intaglio print.	49.00

Central High School Desegregation

Date	Price
2007 Little Rock Dollar and medal set, KM#418	47.80

American Bald Eagle

Date	Price
2008 Proof half dollar, dollar and $5 gold, KM438, KM439, KM440	490
2008 Bald Eagle young collector's set; Half Dollar, KM#438	23.00

Louis Braille

Date	Price
Braille Education set, KM#455	43.50

PROOF SETS

Proof coins are produced through a special process involving specially selected, highly polished planchets and dies. They usually receive two strikings from the coin press at increased pressure. The result is a coin with mirrorlike surfaces and, in recent years, a cameo effect on its raised design surfaces. Proof sets have been sold off and on by the U.S. Mint since 1858. Listings here are for sets from what is commonly called the modern era, since 1936. Values for earlier proofs are included in regular date listings. Sets were not offered in years not listed. Since 1968, proof coins have been produced at the San Francisco Mint; before that they were produced at the Philadelphia Mint. In 1942 the five-cent coin was struck in two compositions. Some proof sets for that year contain only one type (five-coin set); others contain both types. Two types of packaging were used in 1955 -- a box and a flat, plastic holder. The 1960 large-date and small-date sets are distinguished by the size of the date on the cent. Some 1968 sets are missing the mint mark on the dime, the result of an error in the preparation of an obverse die. The 1970 large-date and small-date sets are distinguished by the size of the date on the cent. Some 1970 sets are missing the mint mark on the dime, the result of an error in the preparation of an obverse die. Some 1971 sets are missing the mint mark on the five-cent piece, the result of an error in the preparation of an obverse die. The 1976 three-piece set contains the quarter, half dollar and dollar with the Bicentennial designs. The 1979 and 1981 Type II sets have clearer mint marks than the Type I sets for those years. Some 1983 sets are missing the mint mark on the dime, the result of an error in the preparation of an obverse die. Prestige sets contain the five regular-issue coins plus a commemorative silver dollar from that year. Sets issued prior to 1956 came in transparent envelopes stapled together in a small square box. In mid 1955 sets were changed to a flat clear cellophane envelope. In 1968 sets were changed to a clear hard plastic case as they still are currently issued.

Date	Sets Sold	Issue Price	Value
1795 (2006) XPn1-XPn3	—	—	—
1836 (2006) XPn4, 10-11	—	—	—
1863 (2006) XPn12-14	—	—	—
1871 (2006) XPn15-17	—	—	—
1879 (2006) XPn18-20	—	—	—
1879 (2006) XPn21-23	—	—	—
1936	3,837	1.89	7,500
1937	5,542	1.89	4,350
1938	8,045	1.89	1,900
1939	8,795	—	1,800
1940	11,246	—	1,385
1941	15,287	—	1,450
1942 6 coins	21,120	1.89	1,475
1942 5 coins	Inc. above	1.89	1,250
1950	51,386	2.10	540
1951	57,500	2.10	565
1952	81,980	2.10	225
1953	128,800	2.10	210
1954	233,300	2.10	107
1955 box	378,200	2.10	90.00
1955 flat pack	Inc. above	2.10	115
1956	669,384	2.10	53.00
1957	1,247,952	2.10	30.00
1958	875,652	2.10	35.00
1959	1,149,291	2.10	29.50
1960 large date	1,691,602	2.10	29.00
1960 small date	Inc. above	2.10	33.50
1961	3,028,244	2.10	28.50
1962	3,218,019	2.10	28.50
1963	3,075,645	2.10	28.50
1964	3,950,762	2.10	28.50
1965 Special Mint Set	—	—	—
1966 Special Mint Set	—	—	—
1967 Special mint set	—	—	—
1968S	3,041,509	5.00	7.75
1968S no mint mark dime	Inc. above	5.00	16,500
1969S	2,934,631	5.00	7.25
1970S large date	2,632,810	5.00	9.35
1970S small date	Inc. above	5.00	72.00
1970S no mint mark dime	Inc. above	5.00	820
1971S	3,224,138	5.00	4.50

Date	Sets Sold	Issue Price	Value
1971S no mint mark nickel Est. 1,655	1,655	5.00	1,350
1972S	3,267,667	5.00	5.50
1973S	2,769,624	7.00	9.00
1974S	2,617,350	7.00	10.75
1975S	2,909,369	7.00	8.40
1975S no mint mark dime	Inc. above	7.00	275,000
1976S 3 coins	3,998,621	13.00	29.50
1976S	4,149,730	7.00	7.15
1977S	3,251,152	9.00	7.75
1978S	3,127,788	9.00	6.60
1979S Type I	3,677,175	9.00	7.50
1979S Type II	Inc. above	9.00	73.00
1980S	3,547,030	10.00	5.25
1981S Type I	4,063,083	11.00	5.50
1981S Type II	Inc. above	11.00	285
1982S	3,857,479	11.00	3.60
1983S	3,138,765	11.00	3.60
1983S Prestige Set	140,361	59.00	45.50
1983S no mint mark dime	Inc. above	11.00	600
1984S	2,748,430	11.00	4.65
1984S Prestige Set	316,680	59.00	38.50
1985S	3,362,821	11.00	3.85
1986S	2,411,180	11.00	5.75
1986S Prestige Set	599,317	48.50	36.50
1987S	3,972,233	11.00	4.40
1987S Prestige Set	435,495	45.00	36.50
1988S	3,031,287	11.00	6.10
1988S Prestige Set	231,661	45.00	37.50
1989S	3,009,107	11.00	4.10
1989S Prestige Set	211,087	45.00	45.50
1990S	2,793,433	11.00	5.00
1990S no S 1¢	3,555	11.00	5,100
1990S Prestige Set	506,126	45.00	34.00
1990S Prestige Set, no S 1¢	Inc. above	45.00	5,100
1991S	2,610,833	11.00	5.25
1991S Prestige Set	256,954	59.00	44.50
1992S	2,675,618	12.00	5.00
1992S Prestige Set	183,285	59.00	46.50
1992S Silver	1,009,585	21.00	24.00
1992S Silver premier	308,055	37.00	24.50
1993S	2,337,819	12.50	4.60

Date	Sets Sold	Issue Price	Value
1993S Prestige Set	224,045	57.00	55.00
1993S Silver	570,213	21.00	32.50
1993S Silver premier	191,140	37.00	34.00
1994S	2,308,701	13.00	4.95
1994S Prestige Set	175,893	57.00	51.00
1994S Silver	636,009	21.00	25.50
1994S Silver premier	149,320	37.50	28.50
1995S	2,010,384	12.50	10.50
1995S Prestige Set	107,112	57.00	83.00
1995S Silver	549,878	21.00	43.50
1995S Silver premier	130,107	37.50	59.00
1996S	2,085,191	16.00	7.50
1996S Prestige Set	55,000	57.00	270
1996S Silver	623,655	21.00	26.50
1996S Silver premier	151,366	37.50	33.50
1997S	1,975,000	12.50	11.25
1997S Prestige Set	80,000	57.00	72.00
1997S Silver	605,473	21.00	32.50
1997S Silver premier	136,205	37.50	39.50
1998S	2,078,494	12.50	9.35
1998S Silver	638,134	21.00	28.50
1998S Silver premier	240,658	37.50	31.00
1999S 9 piece	2,557,899	19.95	10.00
1999S 5 quarter set	1,169,958	13.95	6.15
1999S Silver	804,565	31.95	120
2000S 10 piece	3,097,442	19.95	6.35
2000S 5 quarter set	995,803	13.95	3.60
2000S Silver	965,421	31.95	53.00
2001S 10 piece	2,249,498	19.95	12.75
2001S 5 quarter set	774,800	13.95	7.50
2001S Silver	849,600	31.95	53.00
2002S 10 piece	2,319,766	19.95	7.75
2002S 5 quarter set	764,419	13.95	4.50
2002S Silver	892,229	31.95	53.00
2003 X#207, 208, 209.2	—	44.00	28.75
2003S 10 piece	2,175,684	16.75	8.00
2003S 5 quarter set	1,225,507	13.95	3.60
2003S Silver	1,142,858	31.95	52.40
2004S 11 piece	1,804,396	22.95	9.10
2004S 5 quarter set	987,960	23.95	30.10
2004S Silver 11 piece	1,187,673	37.95	52.40
2004S Silver 5 quarter set	594,137	—	34.70
2005S American Legacy	—	—	77.00
2005S 11 piece	—	22.95	6.00
2005S 5 quarter set	—	15.95	35.00
2005S Silver 11 piece	—	37.95	53.40
2005S Silver 5 quarter set	—	23.95	34.70
2005S American Legacy	—	—	77.00
2006S 10 piece clad	—	22.95	10.75
2006S 5 quarter set	—	15.95	4.50
2006S Silver 10 piece	—	37.95	53.40
2006S Silver 5 quarter set	—	23.95	34.70
2006S American Legacy	—	—	71.50
2007S 5 quarter set	—	13.95	4.50
2007S Silver 5 quarter set	—	22.95	34.70
2007S 14 piece clad	—	—	14.50
2007S Silver 14 piece	—	—	58.40
2007S Presidental $ set	—	—	6.00
2007S American Legacy	—	—	116
2008 14 piece clad set	—	—	78.00
2008S 14 piece silver set	734,045	—	61.00
2008S Presidental $ set	—	—	10.50
2008S American Legacy	—	—	116
2008S 5 quarter clad set	—	22.95	34.75
2008S 5 quarter silver set	—	—	34.70
2009S 18 piece clad set	1,477,967	—	22.50
2009S 18 piece silver set	694,406	—	63.00
2009S Presidential $ set	627,925	—	8.25
2009S Lincoln Chronicle	—	—	135
2009S Lincoln 4 piece	—	—	15.50
2009S 6 quarter clad set	—	—	10.50
2009S 6 quarter silver set	—	—	42.10
2010S 14 piece clad set	1,103,950	—	64.00
2010S 14 piece silver set	583,912	—	53.40
2010S Presidential $ set	535,463	—	14.50
2010S 5 quarter clad set	276,335	—	—
2010S 5 quarter silver set	274,003	—	34.70
2011S 5 quarter silver set	—	—	29.20
2011S 14 piece silver set	—	—	70.00
2011S 5 quarter clad set	—	—	14.50
2011S Presidential $ set	—	—	20.00
2012S 5 quarter silver set	—	—	30.10
2012S 14 piece silver set	—	—	70.00
2012S 5 quarter clad set	—	—	15.00
2012S 14 piece clad set	—	—	35.00
2012S Presidential $ set	—	—	—

SETS & ROLLS

UNCIRCULATED ROLLS

Listings are for rolls containing uncirculated coins. Large date and small date varieties for 1960 and 1970 apply to the one cent coins.

Date	Cents	Nickels	Dimes	Quarters	Halves
1934	585	3,500	2,350	1,650	2,350
1934D	2,650	4,350	2,950	9,000	—
1934S	—	—	—	—	—
1935	885	1,700	1,450	1,725	1,250
1935D	750	3,150	2,950	8,850	4,000
1935S	2,500	1,725	1,950	4,650	6,500
1936	285	1,450	885	1,300	1,750
1936D	400	1,450	1,700	—	2,750
1936S	885	1,800	1,675	6,250	3,500
1937	250	1,100	710	1,250	1,150
1937D	250	1,200	1,550	3,450	5,000
1937S	335	1,285	1,650	4,850	3,450
1938	665	535	1,100	3,100	1,850
1938D	710	485	1,000	—	—
1938S	440	355	1,350	3,250	—
1938D Buffalo	—	1,065	—	—	—
1939	180	160	630	1,040	1,250
1939D	535	3,850	610	1,875	1,975
1939S	265	2,750	1,900	3,200	2,350
1940	225	145	535	1,850	975
1940D	265	120	780	5,350	—
1940S	300	265	675	1,275	1,200

Date	Cents	Nickels	Dimes	Quarters	Halves
1941	170	215	430	475	750
1941D	335	330	710	2,750	1,200
1941S	360	295	535	2,450	3,000
1942	140	315	465	450	690
1942P	—	600	—	—	—
1942D	140	2,550	740	1,060	1,350
1942S	585	525	1,050	5,350	1,475
1943	60.00	275	470	365	725
1943D	170	210	610	2,000	1,775
1943S	310	325	650	2,100	1,365
1944	30.00	720	460	280	715
1944D	38.00	680	635	725	1,250
1944S	120	565	660	950	1,300
1945	125	375	410	325	730
1945D	110	315	500	1,000	1,000
1945S	80.00	270	525	575	950
1946	39.00	80.00	140	365	1,025
1946D	36.50	75.00	140	380	900
1946S	185	50.00	140	275	900
1947	220	58.00	215	735	1,000
1947D	46.50	72.00	275	385	1,000
1947S	39.00	72.00	210	415	—
1948	72.50	55.00	188	270	450
1948D	175	155	325	645	425
1948S	165	80.00	255	475	—
1949	180	330	1,200	2,350	1,300
1949D	125	215	550	1,285	1,475
1949S	140	138	2,350	—	2,250
1950	115	120	525	395	750
1950D	42.00	385	200	440	875
1950S	78.00	—	1,550	850	—
1951	165	230	140	435	390
1951D	26.50	285	140	325	800
1951S	60.00	265	690	1,350	750
1952	165	145	140	535	385
1952D	26.50	260	140	300	230
1952S	300	42.00	290	1,000	1,585
1953	42.00	24.50	140	635	490
1953D	22.50	17.00	140	280	280
1953S	35.00	39.00	140	280	850
1954	39.00	57.50	140	280	280
1954D	22.50	24.00	140	280	280
1954S	22.50	39.50	140	280	400
1955	24.50	19.00	140	280	300
1955D	19.00	7.00	170	280	—
1955S	27.50	—	140	—	—
1956	10.50	7.50	140	280	280
1956D	12.50	9.25	140	280	—
1957	10.00	12.50	140	280	280
1957D	9.50	4.75	140	280	280
1958	10.50	6.50	140	280	280
1958D	9.75	5.50	140	280	280
1959	2.50	5.00	140	280	280
1959D	2.10	5.25	140	280	280
1960 large date	1.60	4.40	140	280	280
1960 small date	220	—	—	—	—
1960D large date	1.60	5.00	140	280	280
1960D small date	2.85	—	—	—	—
1961	1.60	4.25	140	280	280
1961D	1.90	4.50	140	280	280
1962	1.65	5.25	140	280	280
1962D	1.65	5.50	140	280	280
1963	1.50	4.25	140	280	280
1963D	1.65	4.75	140	280	280
1964	1.50	3.50	140	280	280
1964D	1.60	3.50	140	280	280
1965	2.25	8.75	8.00	25.00	120
1966	3.75	6.00	10.00	53.00	120
1967	4.50	9.75	8.50	25.00	120
1968	1.75	—	8.50	25.00	—
1968D	1.70	6.00	9.50	33.00	120
1968S	1.90	6.25	—	—	—
1969	7.75	—	44.00	100.00	—
1969D	2.00	6.25	21.50	82.00	120
1969S	3.75	6.75	—	—	—
1970	2.10	—	8.00	26.00	—
1970D	2.10	4.00	7.75	16.00	235
1970S	3.00	4.50	—	—	—
1970S small date	2,650	—	—	—	—

Date	Cents	Nickels	Dimes	Quarters	Halves
1971	17.00	26.50	16.00	50.00	26.00
1971D	3.00	7.50	9.50	19.50	15.50
1971S	4.00	—	—	—	—
1972	2.00	6.50	11.00	23.00	32.00
1972D	6.00	5.75	10.00	21.50	23.00
1972S	4.75	—	—	—	—
1973	1.75	6.25	10.50	22.00	25.50
1973D	1.75	6.25	9.00	23.00	18.00
1973S	3.00	—	—	—	—
1974	1.75	4.50	7.50	18.50	15.00
1974D	1.75	5.75	7.75	17.50	21.00
1974S	3.50	—	—	—	—
1975	3.75	12.50	8.75	—	—
1975D	1.75	5.25	15.50	—	—
1976	1.75	13.50	21.00	17.50	18.00
1976D	2.50	11.00	18.00	17.50	15.50
1977	1.75	6.25	9.75	16.50	21.50
1977D	2.85	5.75	8.50	17.50	24.00
1978	3.00	4.50	7.25	16.00	32.00
1978D	10.00	5.00	8.00	16.50	46.50
1979	1.75	4.75	8.75	17.00	22.50
1979D	3.00	5.75	8.00	22.50	22.50
1980	1.75	4.25	8.00	16.50	20.50
1980D	2.50	4.50	7.50	16.50	20.50
1981	1.75	4.25	7.50	16.50	16.50
1981D	1.85	4.25	8.00	16.50	19.00
1982 Small date	25.00	325	270	250	98.00
1982D Large date	4.00	54.00	66.00	165	80.00
1982 Large date	2.50	—	—	—	—
1982 Copper plated Zinc	8.00	—	—	—	—
1982 Small date, copper plated zinc	3.00	—	—	—	—
1982D Large date, copper plated zinc	35.00	—	—	—	—
1982D Small date, copper plated zinc	2.50	—	—	—	—
1983	7.50	90.00	235	945	80.00
1983D	17.50	39.00	39.00	410	120
1984	5.50	22.00	8.50	17.00	26.00
1984D	14.50	6.50	21.00	29.00	37.00
1985	4.25	10.00	9.75	31.00	76.00
1985D	9.75	8.00	9.25	22.00	44.00
1986	20.00	8.75	25.00	85.00	75.00
1986D	31.50	24.50	22.50	210	90.00
1987	6.50	6.00	7.75	15.50	52.00
1987D	13.50	4.50	8.75	15.50	52.00
1988	6.25	5.50	9.75	39.00	75.00
1988D	12.50	9.00	9.25	22.50	45.00
1989	3.25	5.50	12.00	19.50	42.00
1989D	3.50	8.75	12.50	17.00	25.00
1990	4.00	11.50	14.50	20.00	39.00
1990D	5.85	13.75	10.00	25.00	52.00
1991	2.60	12.00	10.00	29.00	37.50
1991D	11.50	12.00	11.00	31.00	33.00
1992	3.00	46.00	8.00	42.00	21.00
1992D	5.00	9.00	8.00	27.50	50.00
1993	3.25	13.50	9.50	39.00	64.00
1993D	7.50	17.50	13.00	36.00	17.00
1994	2.00	7.75	12.00	42.00	15.00
1994D	2.00	8.00	12.00	47.50	20.00
1995	1.85	10.50	16.50	45.00	17.00
1995D	2.00	20.00	19.50	53.00	40.00
1996	2.25	8.75	11.00	19.00	17.00
1996D	2.85	8.25	11.50	27.50	19.00
1997	2.75	14.50	29.00	22.50	20.00
1997D	3.35	60.00	11.00	39.00	16.50
1998	2.00	13.75	9.75	17.00	20.00
1998D	1.85	14.00	12.00	18.00	16.50
1999P	2.35	5.50	8.50	—	20.00
1999D	2.25	6.25	8.50	—	19.00
2000P	2.50	6.25	7.75	—	15.00
2000D	1.75	4.75	7.00	—	17.00
2001P	3.75	4.75	7.75	—	16.50
2001D	2.00	6.50	7.25	—	16.00
2002P	2.00	4.00	7.25	—	20.00
2002D	3.25	4.10	7.25	—	20.00
2003P	3.35	7.50	7.00	—	22.50
2003D	2.00	3.50	7.00	—	19.50
2004P Peace Medal Nickel	1.75	6.75	7.00	—	30.00
2004D Peace Medal Nickel	2.50	7.00	7.00	—	30.00
2004P Keelboat Nickel	—	4.00	—	—	—
2004D Keelboat Nickel	—	3.50	—	—	—

SETS & ROLLS

Date	Cents	Nickels	Dimes	Quarters	Halves
2005P Bison Nickel	1.75	3.25	7.00	—	21.00
2005D Bison Nickel	2.75	3.25	7.00	—	21.00
2005P Ocean in view Nickel	—	3.25	—	—	—
2005D Ocean in view Nickel	—	3.25	—	—	—
2006P	2.75	3.25	8.50	—	29.00
2006D	1.75	3.25	8.50	—	29.00
2007P	1.75	3.50	8.00	—	21.00
2007D	1.75	3.50	7.75	—	21.00
2008P	1.75	3.75	8.00	—	24.50
2008D	1.75	3.75	7.50	—	25.50
2009P Log Cabin	2.00	23.00	13.50	—	18.50
2009D Log Cabin	2.15	13.50	13.50	—	18.50
2009P Log Splitter	1.75	—	—	—	—
2009D Log Splitter	1.75	—	—	—	—
2009P Professional	1.75	—	—	—	—
2009D Professional	1.75	—	—	—	—
2009P President	2.00	—	—	—	—
2009D President	2.00	—	—	—	—

50 STATE QUARTERS

Listings are for rolls containing uncirculated coins.

State	Philadelphia	Denver
1999 Delaware	15.00	15.50
1999 Pennsylvania	16.00	16.50
1999 New Jersey	16.00	15.50
1999 Georgia	28.00	30.00
1999 Connecticut	26.00	27.00
2000 Massachusetts	14.00	15.00
2000 Maryland	14.00	15.50
2000 South Carolina	15.50	15.50
2000 New Hampshire	13.50	14.50
2000 Virginia	14.50	14.50
2001 New York	14.00	14.00
2001 North Carolina	14.50	15.00
2001 Rhode Island	14.00	15.50
2001 Vermont	14.50	14.50
2001 Kentucky	16.50	18.50
2002 Mississippi	16.50	16.50
2002 Tennessee	30.00	39.50
2002 Ohio	21.50	21.50
2002 Louisiana	14.00	14.00
2002 Indiana	14.50	15.50
2003 Illinois	39.00	45.00
2003 Alabama	17.00	18.50
2003 Maine	14.50	15.50
2003 Missouri	14.50	14.75
2003 Arkansas	14.50	15.50
2004 Michigan	13.75	14.50
2004 Florida	13.75	14.50
2004 Texas	14.00	15.00
2004 Iowa	14.00	14.50
2004 Wisconsin	15.50	16.50
2005 California	21.00	22.50
2005 Minnesota	17.50	17.50
2005 Oregon	13.75	13.75
2005 Kansas	13.75	14.50
2005 West Virginia	13.50	13.75
2006 Nevada	13.75	13.75
2006 Nebraska	13.75	14.00
2006 Colorado	13.75	14.00
2006 North Dakota	13.75	14.50
2006 South Dakota	13.75	13.75
2007 Montana	14.00	17.00
2007 Washington	18.00	18.75
2007 Idaho	15.50	15.50
2007 Wyoming	14.75	15.00
2007 Utah	15.00	14.50
2008 Oklahoma	13.75	13.75
2008 New Mexico	14.00	15.50
2008 Arizona	15.50	13.75
2008 Alaska	13.50	13.75
2008 Hawaii	13.50	13.50
2009 Washington D.C.	18.00	15.50
2009 Puerto Rico	15.00	15.50
2009 Guam	15.00	16.50
2009 American Samoa	15.00	15.00

COLONIAL COINAGE

North America was initially explored by the Vikings, but it was not until the age of Discovery, that active and expansive colonization began. The French, Spanish, Dutch, English and Portuguese were all involved in colonizing North, Central and South America.

The Spanish were strongest in Central and South America, taking that whole continent except for Brazil, which went to Portugal. Their expansion also spread into what became modern day Florida, Texas, and California.

The French settled in the Mississippi River Delta, from New Orleans northward to St. Louis, then east to the Ohio River basin, and west to the Rockies; they also progressed to the north, in the St. Lawrence River area in Canada; Quebec and Montreal being their principal cities.

The Dutch had a presence from the 1620's through 1664, mainly in the New York region, but lost that territory to the English, and never again gained a stronghold on the mainland during this period.

The English settled on the East Coast of the United States, from Georgia north to what later became Maine, and east of the Allegheny and Appalachian Mountains. To the north in Canada, they worked their way into Nova Scotia, Newfoundland, and north of the French in Quebec, Ontario, and with the explorers of the Hudson Bay Company, westward on the plains to the Pacific North West.

On the basis of the voyage of John Cabot to the North American mainland in 1497, England initially claimed the entire continent. The first permanent English settlement was established at Jamestown, Va., in 1607. France and Spain had also claimed extensive territory in North America, but at the end of the French and Indian Wars in 1763, England acquired all of the territory east of the Mississippi River, including east and west Florida. From 1776 to 1781, the States were governed by the Continental Congress. From 1781 to 1789, they were organized under the Articles of Confederation, during which period the individual States, formed from the former 13 British- American colonies; New York, New Jersey, New Hampshire, Massachusetts, Rhode Island, Connecticut, Pennsylvania, Delaware, Maryland, Virginia, North Carolina, South Carolina and Georgia, had the right to issue money.

While British and Spanish silver coins circulated freely in the American Colonies, several of the Colonies and later States did issue copper or silver coins. In addition, both merchant and political tokens, mainly in copper, were issued in several locations. The most popularly circulated, and now collected, of these Colonial and State issues are listed here.

The population of the colonies during this political phase of America's history (1781-1789) was about 3 million, most of whom lived on self-sufficient family farms. Fishing, lumbering and the production of grains for export were major economic endeavors. Rapid strides were also being made in industry and manufacturing by 1775, when the North American colonies were accounting for one-seventh of the world's production of raw iron.

Independence from Great Britain was attained with the American Revolution in 1776. The Constitution organized and governs the present United States. It was ratified on Nov. 21, 1788.

MONETARY SYSTEM
12 Pence = 1 Shilling
5 Shillings = 1 Crown
21 Shillings = 1 Guinea

MARYLAND

LORD BALTIMORE

PENNY (DENARIUM)

KM#1 Composition: Copper. **Obverse Legend:** CAECILIVS Dns TERRAE MARIAE.

Date	VG	Fine	VF	XF	Unc
(1659) 9 known	—	65,000	120,000	200,000	—

Note: Stack's Auction 5-04, Proof realized $241,500

4 PENCE (GROAT)

KM#2 Composition: Silver. **Obverse:** Large bust. **Obverse Legend:** CAECILIVS Dns TERRAE MARIAE. **Reverse:** Large shield.

Date	AG	Good	VG	Fine	VF	XF
(1659)	1,250	1,950	3,500	6,250	13,500	22,000

KM#3 Composition: Silver. **Obverse:** Small bust. **Obverse Legend:** CAECILIVS Dns TERRAE MARIAE. **Reverse:** Small shield.

Date	AG	Good	VG	Fine	VF	XF
(1659) unique	—	—	—	—	—	—

Note: Norweb $26,400

6 PENCE

KM#4 **Composition:** Silver. **Obverse:** Small bust. **Obverse Legend:** CAECILIVS Dns TERRAE MARIAE. **Note:** Known in two other rare small-bust varieties and two rare large-bust varieties.

Date	AG	Good	VG	Fine	VF	XF
(1659)	850	1,400	2,400	5,000	9,500	15,000

SHILLING

KM#6 **Composition:** Silver. **Obverse Legend:** CAECILIVS Dns TERRAE MARIAE. **Note:** Varieties exist; one is very rare.

Date	AG	Good	VG	Fine	VF	XF
(1659)	1,100	1,850	3,250	6,000	13,500	20,000

MASSACHUSETTS

NEW ENGLAND

3 PENCE

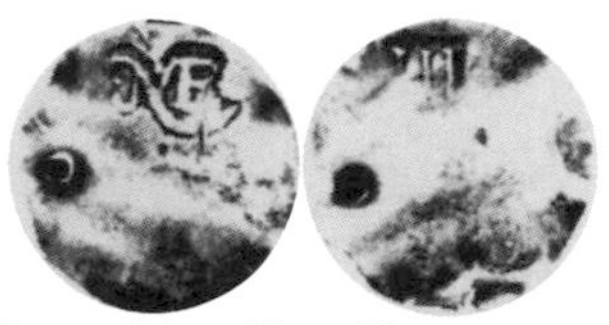

KM#1 **Composition:** Silver. **Obverse:** NE. **Reverse:** III.

Date	AG	Good	VG	Fine	VF	XF
(1652) Unique	—	—	—	—	—	—

Note: Massachusetts Historical Society specimen

6 PENCE

KM#2 **Composition:** Silver. **Obverse:** NE. **Reverse:** VI.

Date	AG	Good	VG	Fine	VF
(1652) 8 known	—	28,000	60,000	115,000	225,000

Note: Garrett $75,000

SHILLING

KM#3 **Composition:** Silver. **Obverse:** NE. **Reverse:** XII.

Date	AG	Good	VG	Fine	VF	XF
(1652)	—	37,500	75,000	150,000	250,000	—

OAK TREE

2 PENCE

KM#7 **Composition:** Silver. **Note:** Small 2 and large 2 varieites exist

Date	AG	Good	VG	Fine	VF	XF	Unc
1662	—	500	900	2,000	3,850	6,500	15,000

3 PENCE

KM#8 **Composition:** Silver. **Note:** Two types of legends.

Date	AG	Good	VG	Fine	VF	XF
1652	350	650	1,250	3,000	6,500	12,000

6 PENCE

KM#9 **Composition:** Silver. **Note:** Three types of legends.

Date	AG	Good	VG	Fine	VF	XF	Unc
1652	400	900	1,350	3,500	8,000	17,500	35,000

SHILLING

KM#10 **Composition:** Silver. **Note:** Two types of legends.

Date	AG	Good	VG	Fine	VF	XF	Unc
1652	375	750	1,250	3,000	6,000	11,500	27,500

PINE TREE

3 PENCE

KM#11 **Composition:** Silver. **Obverse:** Tree without berries.

Date	AG	Good	VG	Fine	VF	XF	Unc
1652	250	500	750	1,650	3,250	6,500	18,500

KM#12 **Composition:** Silver. **Obverse:** Tree with berries.

Date	AG	Good	VG	Fine	VF	XF	Unc
1652	250	500	750	1,650	3,500	6,750	19,500

6 PENCE

KM#13 **Composition:** Silver. **Obverse:** Tree without berries; "spiney tree".

Date	AG	Good	VG	Fine	VF	XF	Unc
1652	400	700	1,400	2,000	4,000	7,000	22,000

KM#14 **Composition:** Silver. **Obverse:** Tree with berries.

Date	AG	Good	VG	Fine	VF	XF	Unc
1652	300	600	1,000	1,850	3,750	6,500	20,000

SHILLING

KM#15 **Composition:** Silver. **Note:** Large planchet. Many varieties exist; some are very rare.

Date	AG	Good	VG	Fine	VF	XF	Unc
1652	375	700	1,100	2,200	4,500	7,750	22,500

KM#16 **Composition:** Silver. **Note:** Small planchet; large dies. All examples are thought to be contemporary fabrications.

Date	AG	Good	VG	Fine	VF	XF	Unc
1652	—	—	—	—	—	—	—

KM#17 **Composition:** Silver. **Note:** Small planchet; small dies. Many varieties exist; some are very rare.

Date	AG	Good	VG	Fine	VF	XF	Unc
1652	285	550	850	1,750	3,750	7,250	25,000

WILLOW TREE

3 PENCE

KM#4 **Composition:** Silver.

Date	AG	Good	VG	Fine	VF	XF
1652 3 known	—	—	—	—	—	—

6 PENCE

KM#5 **Composition:** Silver.

Date	AG	Good	VG	Fine	VF	XF
1652 14 known	9,500	18,500	30,000	60,000	135,000	225,000

SHILLING

KM#6 Composition: Silver.

Date	AG	Good	VG	Fine	VF	XF
1652	10,000	20,000	35,000	85,000	165,000	250,000

NEW JERSEY

ST. PATRICK OR MARK NEWBY

FARTHING

KM#1 Composition: Copper. **Obverse Legend:** FLOREAT REX. **Reverse Legend:** QUIESCAT PLEBS.

Date	AG	Good	VG	Fine	VF	XF	Unc
(1682)	70.00	125	285	775	2,750	6,500	—

Note: One very rare variety is known with reverse legend: QUIESAT PLEBS

KM#1a Composition: Silver. **Obverse Legend:** FLOREAT REX. **Reverse Legend:** QUIESCAT PLEBS.

Date	AG	Good	VG	Fine	VF	XF	Unc
(1682)	800	1,750	2,750	5,500	9,500	17,500	—

HALFPENNY

KM#2 Composition: Copper. **Obverse Legend:** FLOREAT REX. **Reverse Legend:** ECCE GREX.

Date	AG	Good	VG	Fine	VF	XF	Unc
(1682)	180	365	850	1,650	4,000	12,500	—

EARLY AMERICAN TOKENS

AMERICAN PLANTATIONS

1/24 REAL

KM#Tn5.1 Composition: Tin. **Obverse Legend:** ET HIB REX.

Date	AG	Good	VG	Fine	VF	XF	Unc
(1688)	125	200	300	450	850	2,000	—

KM#Tn5.3 Composition: Tin. **Reverse:** Horizontal 4.

Date	AG	Good	VG	Fine	VF	XF	Unc
(1688)	275	400	900	1,750	4,250	6,750	—

KM#Tn5.4 Composition: Tin. **Obverse Legend:** ET HB REX.

Date	AG	Good	VG	Fine	VF	XF	Unc
(1688)	—	250	450	850	1,900	3,250	11,500

KM#Tn6 Composition: Tin. **Reverse:** Arms of Scotland left, Ireland right.

Date	AG	Good	VG	Fine	VF	XF	Unc
(1688)	450	750	1,250	2,150	5,000	7,750	—

KM#Tn5.2 Composition: Tin. **Obverse:** Rider's head left of "B" in legend. **Note:** Restrikes made in 1828 from two obverse dies.

Date	AG	Good	VG	Fine	VF	XF	Unc
(1828)	75.00	110	175	275	500	1,000	—

ELEPHANT

KM#Tn1.1 Weight: 15.5500 g. **Composition:** Copper. **Note:** Thick planchet.

Date	AG	Good	VG	Fine	VF	XF	Unc
(1664)	125	200	300	550	1,000	1,750	4,500

KM#Tn1.2 Composition: Copper. **Note:** Thin planchet.

Date	AG	Good	VG	Fine	VF	XF	Unc
(1664)	175	300	500	900	3,000	5,500	12,500

KM#Tn2 Composition: Copper. **Reverse:** Diagonals tie shield.

Date	AG	Good	VG	Fine	VF	XF	Unc
(1664)	250	450	650	2,250	7,000	11,500	35,000

KM#Tn3 Composition: Copper. **Reverse:** Sword right side of shield.

Date	AG	Good	VG	Fine	VF	XF
(1664) 3 known	—	—	—	—	25,000	—

Note: Norweb $1,320

KM#Tn4 Composition: Copper. **Reverse Legend:** LON DON.

Date	AG	Good	VG	Fine	VF	XF	Unc
(1684)	340	650	1,000	2,250	4,250	8,000	20,000

KM#Tn7 Composition: Copper. **Reverse Legend:** NEW ENGLAND.

Date	AG	Good	VG	Fine	VF	XF
(1694) 2 known	—	—	55,000	85,000	110,000	160,000

Note: Norweb $25,300

KM#Tn8.1 Composition: Copper. **Reverse Legend:** CAROLINA (PROPRIETORS).

Date	AG	Good	VG	Fine	VF	XF
(1694) 5 known	—	—	4,750	7,500	15,000	25,000

Note: Norweb $35,200

KM#Tn8.2 Composition: Copper. **Reverse Legend:** CAROLINA (PROPRIETORS, O over E).

Date	AG	Good	VG	Fine	VF	XF
1694	1,300	2,500	4,500	7,000	12,500	20,000

Note: Norweb $17,600

GLOUCESTER

KM#Tn15 Composition: Copper. **Obverse Legend:** GLOVCESTER COVRTHOVSE VIRGINIA. **Reverse Legend:** RIGHAVLT DAWSON.ANNO.DOM.1714..

Date	AG	Good	VG	Fine	VF	XF
(1714) 2 known	—	—	—	—	—	—

Note: Garrett $36,000

COLONIAL COINAGE

HIBERNIA-VOCE POPULI

FARTHING

KM#Tn21.1 Composition: Copper. **Note:** Large letters

Date	AG	Good	VG	Fine	VF	XF	Unc
1760	145	250	375	750	1,850	3,500	11,500

KM#Tn21.2 Composition: Copper. **Note:** Small letters

Date	AG	Good	VG	Fine	VF	XF	Unc
1760	—	—	3,250	6,500	25,000	60,000	—

Note: Norweb $5,940.

HALFPENNY

KM#Tn22 Composition: Copper.

Date	AG	Good	VG	Fine	VF	XF	Unc
1700 Extremely rare	—	—	—	—	—	—	—
Note: Date is in error; ex-Roper $575. Norweb $577.50. Stack's Americana, VF, $2,900							
1760	40.00	75.00	145	185	365	675	2,500
1760	50.00	80.00	135	195	425	775	3,500
Note: legend VOOE POPULI							
1760 P below bust	65.00	120	200	375	750	1,750	8,250
1760 P in front of bust	55.00	110	180	325	650	1,450	6,500

HIGLEY OR GRANBY

KM#Tn16 Composition: Copper. **Obverse Legend:** CONNECTICVT. **Reverse Legend:** THE VALVE OF THREE PENCE.

Date	AG	Good	VG	Fine	VF	XF	Unc
1737	—	10,000	18,500	40,000	85,000	—	—

Note: Garrett $16,000

KM#Tn17 Composition: Copper. **Obverse Legend:** THE VALVE OF THREE PENCE. **Reverse Legend:** I AM GOOD COPPER.

Date	AG	Good	VG	Fine	VF	XF
1737 2 known	—	11,000	20,000	42,500	87,500	—

Note: ex-Norweb $6,875

KM#Tn18.1 Composition: Copper. **Obverse Legend:** VALUE ME AS YOU PLEASE. **Reverse Legend:** I AM GOOD COPPER.

Date	AG	Good	VG	Fine	VF	XF	Unc
1737	6,500	10,000	18,500	42,000	87,500	—	—

KM#Tn18.2 Composition: Copper. **Obverse Legend:** VALVE.ME.AS.YOU.PLEASE.. **Reverse Legend:** I AM GOOD COPPER..

Date	AG	Good	VG	Fine	VF	XF
1737 3 known	—	—	—	—	—	275,000

KM#Tn19 Composition: Copper. **Reverse:** Broad axe.

Date	AG	Good	VG	Fine	VF	XF
(1737)	—	10,000	20,000	45,000	125,000	—
Note: Garrett $45,000						
1739 5 known	—	—	—	—	—	—

Note: Eliasberg $12,650. Oechsner $9,900. Steinberg (holed) $4,400.

KM#Tn20 Composition: Copper. **Obverse Legend:** THE WHEELE GOES ROUND. **Reverse:** J CUT MY WAY THROUGH.

Date	AG	Good	VG	Fine	VF	XF
(1737) unique	—	—	—	150,000	—	—

Note: Roper $60,500

NEW YORKE

KM#Tn9 Composition: Brass. **Obverse Legend:** NEW.YORK.IN.AMERICA.

Date	AG	Good	VG	Fine	VF	XF	Unc
1700	1,800	3,750	7,250	17,500	28,000	60,000	—

KM#Tn9a Composition: White Metal. **Obverse Legend:** NEW.YORK.IN.AMERICA.

Date	AG	Good	VG	Fine	VF	XF
1700 4 known	—	—	7,750	22,500	32,500	75,000

PITT

FARTHING

KM#Tn23 Composition: Copper.

Date	AG	Good	VG	Fine	VF	XF	Unc
1766	—	3,750	7,000	11,500	28,500	42,500	—

HALFPENNY

KM#Tn24 Composition: Copper.

Date	AG	Good	VG	Fine	VF	XF	Unc
1766	145	275	450	750	1,650	3,000	9,500

KM#Tn24a Composition: Silver Plated Copper.

Date	AG	Good	VG	Fine	VF	XF	Unc
1766	—	—	—	—	2,250	5,000	12,500

ROYAL PATENT COINAGE

HIBERNIA

FARTHING

KM#20 Composition: Copper. **Note:** Pattern.

Date	AG	Good	VG	Fine	VF	XF	Unc
1722	135	250	400	600	1,250	3,250	11,500

KM#24 Composition: Copper. **Obverse:** 1722 obverse. **Obverse Legend:** ...D:G:REX..

Date	AG	Good	VG	Fine	VF	XF	Unc
1723	20.00	75.00	120	170	300	550	1,250

KM#25 Composition: Copper. **Obverse Legend:** DEI • GRATIA • REX •.

Date	AG	Good	VG	Fine	VF	XF	Unc
1723	25.00	45.00	60.00	180	300	550	950
1724	—	90.00	125	225	700	1,750	4,250

KM#25a Composition: Silver. ASW.

Date	AG	Good	VG	Fine	VF	XF	Unc
1723	—	—	1,600	2,250	4,200	6,500	12,000

HALFPENNY

KM#21 Composition: Copper. **Obverse:** Bust right. **Obverse Legend:** GEORGIUS • DEI • GRATIA • REX •. **Reverse:** Harp left, head left. **Reverse Legend:** • HIBERNIA • 1722 •.

Date	AG	Good	VG	Fine	VF	XF	Unc
1722	50.00	90.00	110	160	325	700	1,750

KM#22 Composition: Copper. **Obverse:** Bust right. **Obverse Legend:** GEORGIVS D: G: REX. **Reverse:** Harp left, head right. **Reverse Legend:** • HIBERNIÆ •. **Note:** "Rocks Reverse" pattern.

Date	AG	Good	VG	Fine	VF	XF	Unc
1722	—	—	—	5,000	7,500	12,500	—

KM#23.1 Composition: Copper. **Reverse:** Harp right.

Date	AG	Good	VG	Fine	VF	XF	Unc
1722	35.00	60.00	80.00	120	285	600	1,750
Note: 850							
1723	20.00	35.00	45.00	75.00	190	285	850
1723/22	35.00	60.00	80.00	150	400	850	2,500
1724	25.00	50.00	90.00	160	400	850	2,500

KM#23.2 Composition: Copper. **Obverse:** DEII error in legend.

Date	AG	Good	VG	Fine	VF	XF	Unc
1722	75.00	125	160	325	750	1,500	3,000

KM#26 Composition: Copper. **Reverse:** Large head. **Note:** Rare. Generally mint state only. Probably a pattern.

Date	AG	Good	VG	Fine	VF	XF	Unc
1723	—	—	—	—	—	—	—

KM#27 Composition: Copper. **Reverse:** Continuous legend over head.

Date	AG	Good	VG	Fine	VF	XF	Unc
1724	45.00	80.00	150	300	900	1,850	4,500

ROSA AMERICANA

HALFPENNY

KM#1 Composition: Copper. **Obverse Legend:** D • G • REX •.

Date	AG	Good	VG	Fine	VF	XF	Unc
1722	20.00	50.00	140	250	525	1,050	4,000

KM#2 Composition: Copper. **Obverse:** Uncrowned rose. **Obverse Legend:** ... • DEI • GRATIA • REX •. **Note:** Several varieties exist.

Date	AG	Good	VG	Fine	VF	XF	Unc
1722	50.00	90.00	135	250	450	975	3,500
1723	385	700	850	1,750	3,600	—	—

KM#3 Composition: Copper. **Reverse Legend:** VTILE DVLCI.

Date	AG	Good	VG	Fine	VF	XF	Unc
1722	250	450	850	2,200	3,800	7,500	—

KM#9 Composition: Copper. **Reverse:** Crowned rose.

Date	AG	Good	VG	Fine	VF	XF	Unc
1723	45.00	85.00	110	165	425	1,100	4,500

PENNY

KM#4 Composition: Copper. **Reverse Legend:** UTILE DULCI. **Note:** Several varieties exist.

Date	AG	Good	VG	Fine	VF	XF	Unc
1722	60.00	100.00	135	240	450	950	3,750

KM#5 Composition: Copper. **Note:** Several varieties exist. Also known in two rare pattern types with long hair ribbons, one with V's for U's on the obverse.

Date	AG	Good	VG	Fine	VF	XF	Unc
1722	18.00	35.00	150	275	750	1,450	6,000

KM#10 Composition: Copper. **Note:** Several varieties exist.

Date	AG	Good	VG	Fine	VF	XF	Unc
1723	40.00	75.00	110	175	425	900	3,600

KM#12 Composition: Copper. **Note:** Pattern.

Date	AG	Good	VG	Fine	VF	XF
1724 2 known	—	—	—	—	—	—

KM#13 Composition: Copper. **Reverse Legend:** ROSA: SINE: SPINA •.

Date	AG	Good	VG	Fine	VF	XF
(1724) 5 known	—	—	—	—	—	—

Note: Stack's Bowers 5-05, VF ralized $21,850; Norweb $2,035

KM#14 Composition: Copper. **Obverse:** George II. **Note:** Pattern.

Date	AG	Good	VG	Fine	VF	XF
1727 2 known	—	—	—	—	—	—

2 PENCE

KM#6 Composition: Copper. **Reverse:** Motto with scroll.

Date	AG	Good	VG	Fine	VF	XF	Unc
(1722)	80.00	150	200	425	750	1,650	7,000

KM#7 Composition: Copper.**Reverse:** Motto without scroll.

Date	AG	Good	VG	Fine	VF	XF
(1722) 3 known	—	—	—	—	—	—

KM#8.1 Composition: Copper. **Obverse Legend:** ...REX •. **Reverse:** Dated.

Date	AG	Good	VG	Fine	VF	XF	Unc
1722	70.00	125	175	275	750	1,500	5,500

KM#8.2 Composition: Copper. **Obverse Legend:** ...REX.

Date	AG	Good	VG	Fine	VF	XF	Unc
1722	70.00	125	175	275	775	1,600	6,000

KM#11 Composition: Copper. **Obverse:** No stop after REX. **Reverse:** Stop after 1723. **Note:** Several varieties exist.

Date	AG	Good	VG	Fine	VF	XF	Unc
1723	65.00	125	175	300	550	1,200	3,500

KM#15 Composition: Copper. **Note:** Pattern. Two varieties exist; both extremely rare.

Date	AG	Good	VG	Fine	VF	XF	Unc
1724	—	—	—	—	—	—	—

Note: Stack's Bowers 5-05 choice AU realized $25,300. Ex-Garrett $5,775. Stack's Americana, XF, $10,925

KM#16 **Composition:** Copper. **Obverse:** Bust left. **Reverse:** Crowned rose. **Note:** Pattern.

Date	AG	Good	VG	Fine	VF	XF
1733 4 known	—	—	—	—	—	—

Note: Stacks-Bowers 5-05, Gem Proof realized $63,250; Norweb $19,800

VIRGINIA HALFPENNY

KM#Tn25.1 **Composition:** Copper. **Reverse:** Small 7s in date.. **Note:** Struck on Irish halfpenny planchets.

Date	Good	VG	Fine	VF	XF	Unc	Proof
1773	—	—	—	—	—	—	22,000

KM#Tn25.2 **Composition:** Copper. **Obverse Legend:** GEORGIVS •.... **Reverse:** Varieties with 7 or 8 strings in harp.

Date	AG	Good	VG	Fine	VF	XF	Unc
1773	30.00	50.00	70.00	110	235	425	1,000

KM#Tn25.3 **Composition:** Copper. **Obverse Legend:** GEORGIVS.... **Reverse:** Varieties with 6, 7 or 8 strings in harp.

Date	AG	Good	VG	Fine	VF	XF	Unc
1773	35.00	60.00	75.00	135	275	525	1,350

KM#Tn25.4 **Composition:** Copper. **Obverse Legend:** GEORGIVS.... **Reverse:** 8 harp strings, dot on cross.

Date	AG	Good	VG	Fine	VF	XF	Unc
1773	—	—	—	—	—	—	—

Note: ex-Steinberg $2,600

KM#Tn26 **Composition:** Silver. **Note:** So-called "shilling" silver proofs.

Date	AG	Good	VG	Fine	VF	XF
1774 6 known	—	—	—	—	—	—

Note: Garrett $23,000

REVOLUTIONARY COINAGE

CONTINENTAL "DOLLAR"

KM#EA1 **Composition:** Pewter **Obverse Legend:** CURRENCY.

Date	Good	VG	Fine	VF	XF	Unc
1776	7,500	9,350	12,000	21,000	32,500	70,000

KM#EA2 **Composition:** Pewter **Obverse Legend:** CURRENCY, EG FECIT.

Date	Good	VG	Fine	VF	XF	Unc
1776	8,000	10,500	13,500	25,000	37,500	80,000

KM#EA2a **Composition:** Silver **Obverse Legend:** CURRENCY, EG FECIT.

Date	Good	VG	Fine	VF	XF	Unc
1776 2 known	—	—	300,000	450,000	—	—

KM#EA3 **Composition:** Pewter **Obverse Legend:** CURRENCEY

Date	Good	VG	Fine	VF	XF
1776 extremely rare	—	—	—	—	150,000

KM#EA4 **Composition:** Pewter **Obverse Legend:** CURRENCY. **Reverse:** Floral cross.

Date	AG	Good	VG	Fine	VF	XF
1776 3 recorded	—	—	—	—	—	400,000

Note: Norweb $50,600. Johnson $25,300

COLONIAL COINAGE

KM#EA5 **Composition:** Pewter **Obverse Legend:** CURENCY.

Date	Good	VG	Fine	VF	XF	Unc
1776	7,500	9,500	12,000	22,500	33,500	75,000

KM#EA5a **Composition:** Brass **Obverse Legend:** CURENCY. **Note:** Two varieties exist.

Date	AG	Good	VG	Fine	VF	XF
1776	—	22,500	28,500	40,000	75,000	135,000

KM#EA5b **Composition:** Silver **Obverse Legend:** CURENCY.

Date	Good	VG	Fine	VF	XF
1776 2 known	—	—	285,000	425,000	—

Note: Stacks-Bowers 5-05, VF realized $345,000; Romano $99,000

STATE COINAGE

CONNECTICUT

KM# 1 **Composition:** Copper **Obverse:** Bust facing right.

Date	AG	Good	VG	Fine	VF	XF	Unc
1785	35.00	55.00	90.00	200	650	1,750	—

KM# 2 **Composition:** Copper **Obverse:** "African head."

Date	AG	Good	VG	Fine	VF	XF	Unc
1785	55.00	85.00	150	600	1,500	3,800	—

KM# 3.1 **Composition:** Copper **Obverse:** Mailed bust facing left.

Date	AG	Good	VG	Fine	VF	XF	Unc
1785	125	220	375	750	1,800	3,850	—
1786	30.00	50.00	90.00	175	500	1,400	—
1787	30.00	50.00	85.00	160	450	1,350	—
1788	30.00	50.00	80.00	160	435	1,150	—

KM# 3.3 **Composition:** Copper **Obverse:** Perfect date. **Reverse Legend:** IN DE ET.

Date	AG	Good	VG	Fine	VF	XF	Unc
1787	50.00	80.00	125	350	750	1,850	—

KM# 3.4 **Composition:** Copper **Obverse Legend:** CONNLC.

Date	AG	Good	VG	Fine	VF	XF	Unc
1788	44.00	65.00	130	265	700	2,150	—

COLONIAL COINAGE

KM# 4 **Composition:** Copper **Obverse:** Small mailed bust facing left. **Reverse Legend:** ETLIB INDE.

Date	AG	Good	VG	Fine	VF	XF	Unc
1786	45.00	90.00	175	400	1,100	2,750	—

KM# 5 **Composition:** Copper **Obverse:** Small mailed bust facing right. **Reverse Legend:** INDE ET LIB.

Date	AG	Good	VG	Fine	VF	XF	Unc
1786	60.00	100.00	175	450	2,000	4,250	—

KM# 6 **Composition:** Copper **Obverse:** Large mailed bust facing right.

Date	AG	Good	VG	Fine	VF	XF	Unc
1786	55.00	90.00	160	400	1,750	3,750	—

KM# 7 **Composition:** Copper **Obverse:** "Hercules head."

Date	AG	Good	VG	Fine	VF	XF	Unc
1786	60.00	110	220	600	2,500	5,800	—

KM# 8.1 **Composition:** Copper **Obverse:** Draped bust.

Date	AG	Good	VG	Fine	VF	XF	Unc
1786	50.00	100.00	200	500	1,250	2,850	—

KM# 8.2 **Composition:** Copper **Obverse:** Draped bust. **Note:** Many varieties.

Date	AG	Good	VG	Fine	VF	XF	Unc
1787	28.00	42.00	70.00	115	325	775	—

KM# 8.3 **Composition:** Copper **Obverse Legend:** AUCIORI.

Date	AG	Good	VG	Fine	VF	XF	Unc
1787	30.00	55.00	90.00	175	450	1,100	—

KM# 8.4 **Composition:** Copper **Obverse Legend:** AUCTOPI.

Date	AG	Good	VG	Fine	VF	XF	Unc
1787	35.00	65.00	110	200	650	1,650	—

KM# 8.5 **Composition:** Copper **Obverse Legend:** AUCTOBI.

Date	AG	Good	VG	Fine	VF	XF	Unc
1787	35.00	65.00	110	200	625	1,550	—

KM# 8.6 **Composition:** Copper **Obverse Legend:** CONNFC.

Date	AG	Good	VG	Fine	VF	XF	Unc
1787	32.00	60.00	95.00	185	525	1,100	—

KM# 8.7 **Composition:** Copper **Obverse Legend:** CONNLC.

Date	AG	Good	VG	Fine	VF	XF	Unc
1787	60.00	90.00	180	375	950	3,000	—

KM# 8.8 **Composition:** Copper **Reverse Legend:** FNDE.

Date	AG	Good	VG	Fine	VF	XF	Unc
1787	35.00	55.00	85.00	175	525	1,650	—

KM# 8.9 **Composition:** Copper **Reverse Legend:** ETLIR.

Date	AG	Good	VG	Fine	VF	XF	Unc
1787	32.00	50.00	75.00	160	475	1,275	—

KM# 8.10 **Composition:** Copper **Reverse Legend:** ETIIB.

Date	AG	Good	VG	Fine	VF	XF	Unc
1787	35.00	50.00	75.00	160	485	1,300	—

KM# 9 **Composition:** Copper **Obverse:** Small head. **Reverse Legend:** ETLIB INDE.

Date	AG	Good	VG	Fine	VF	XF	Unc
1787	65.00	110	180	425	1,750	4,300	—

KM# 10 **Composition:** Copper **Obverse:** Small head. **Reverse Legend:** INDE ET LIB.

Date	AG	Good	VG	Fine	VF	XF	Unc
1787	75.00	135	200	525	2,300	4,600	—

KM# 11 **Composition:** Copper **Obverse:** Medium bust. **Note:** Two reverse legend types exist.

Date	AG	Good	VG	Fine	VF	XF	Unc
1787	60.00	90.00	150	400	1,750	3,450	—

KM# 12 **Composition:** Copper **Obverse:** "Muttonhead" variety. **Note:** Extremely rare with legend INDE ET LIB.

Date	AG	Good	VG	Fine	VF	XF	Unc
1787	60.00	90.00	175	575	2,550	5,200	—

KM# 13 **Composition:** Copper **Obverse:** "Laughing head"

Date	AG	Good	VG	Fine	VF	XF	Unc
1787	35.00	60.00	120	240	650	1,800	—

KM# 14 **Composition:** Copper **Obverse:** "Horned head"

Date	AG	Good	VG	Fine	VF	XF	Unc
1787	30.00	50.00	80.00	165	450	1,200	—

KM# 15 **Composition:** Copper **Reverse Legend:** IND ET LIB

Date	AG	Good	VG	Fine	VF	XF
1787/8	100.00	150	250	750	2,000	5,000
1787/1887	85.00	150	225	600	1,750	4,750

KM# 16 **Composition:** Copper **Obverse Legend:** CONNECT. **Reverse Legend:** INDE ET LIB. **Note:** Two additional scarce reverse legend types exist.

Date	AG	Good	VG	Fine	VF	XF	Unc
1787	35.00	50.00	120	240	675	1,750	—

KM# 22.1 **Composition:** Copper **Obverse:** Draped bust facing left. **Reverse Legend:** INDE ET LIB.

Date	AG	Good	VG	Fine	VF	XF	Unc
1788	49.50	75.00	140	325	750	1,800	—

KM# 22.2 **Composition:** Copper **Reverse Legend:** INDLET LIB.

Date	AG	Good	VG	Fine	VF	XF	Unc
1788	60.00	90.00	195	425	875	1,950	—

KM# 22.3 **Composition:** Copper **Obverse Legend:** CONNEC. **Reverse Legend:** INDE ET LIB.

Date	AG	Good	VG	Fine	VF	XF	Unc
1788	58.00	85.00	190	400	875	1,850	—

KM# 22.4 **Composition:** Copper **Obverse Legend:** CONNEC. **Reverse Legend:** INDL ET LIB.

Date	AG	Good	VG	Fine	VF	XF	Unc
1788	58.00	85.00	190	400	925	2,250	—

KM# 20 **Composition:** Copper **Obverse:** Mailed bust facing right.

Date	AG	Good	VG	Fine	VF	XF	Unc
1788	28.00	45.00	90.00	200	650	1,650	—

KM# 21 **Composition:** Copper **Obverse:** Small mailed bust facing right.

Date	AG	Good	VG	Fine	VF	XF	Unc
1788	850	1,650	3,750	5,500	12,500	22,500	—

MASSACHUSETTS

HALFPENNY

KM# 17 **Composition:** Copper

Date	AG	Good	VG	Fine	VF	XF
1776 unique	—	—	—	200,000	—	—

Note: Garrett $40,000

PENNY

KM# 18 **Composition:** Copper

Date	AG	Good	VG	Fine	VF	XF
1776 unique	—	—	—	—	—	—

HALF CENT

KM# 19 **Composition:** Copper **Note:** Varieties exist; some are rare.

Date	AG	Good	VG	Fine	VF	XF	Unc
1787	60.00	90.00	140	225	575	1,000	3,250
1788	70.00	115	175	275	600	1,100	3,500

CENT

KM# 20.1 **Composition:** Copper **Reverse:** Arrows in right talon

Date	Good	VG	Fine	VF	XF	Unc
1787 7 known	9,000	22,500	45,000	—	—	350,000

Note: Ex-Bushnell-Brand $8,800. Garrett $5,500

KM# 20.2 **Composition:** Copper **Reverse:** Arrows in left talon

Date	AG	Good	VG	Fine	VF	XF	Unc
1787	60.00	90.00	165	240	650	1,350	6,800

KM# 20.3 **Composition:** Copper **Reverse:** "Horned eagle" die break

Date	AG	Good	VG	Fine	VF	XF	Unc
1787	70.00	110	190	275	775	1,550	7,750

KM# 20.4 **Composition:** Copper **Reverse:** Without period after Massachusetts

Date	AG	Good	VG	Fine	VF	XF	Unc
1788	70.00	105	190	260	675	1,600	6,250

KM# 20.5 **Composition:** Copper **Reverse:** Period after Massachusetts, normal S's

Date	AG	Good	VG	Fine	VF	XF	Unc
1788	60.00	90.00	170	235	600	1,350	5,750

KM#20.6 **Composition:** Copper **Reverse:** Period after Massachusetts, S's like 8's

Date	AG	Good	VG	Fine	VF	XF	Unc
1788	50.00	75.00	135	200	575	1,250	5,400

NEW HAMPSHIRE

KM#1 **Composition:** Copper

Date	AG	Good	VG	Fine	VF	XF
1776 extremely rare	—	—	—	—	—	—

Note: Garrett $13,000

NEW JERSEY

KM#8 **Composition:** Copper **Obverse:** Date below draw bar.

Date	Good	VG	Fine	VF	XF
1786 extremely rare	—	—	75,000	135,000	—

Note: Garrett $52,000

KM#9 **Composition:** Copper **Obverse:** Large horse head, date below plow, no coulter on plow.

Date	AG	Good	VG	Fine	VF	XF	Unc
1786	450	850	1,500	3,000	8,500	22,500	—

KM#10 **Composition:** Copper **Reverse:** Narrow shield, straight beam.

Date	AG	Good	VG	Fine	VF	XF	Unc
1786	38.00	60.00	140	210	550	1,350	—

KM#11.1 **Composition:** Copper **Reverse:** Wide shield, curved beam. **Note:** Varieties exist.

Date	AG	Good	VG	Fine	VF	XF	Unc
1786	45.00	75.00	150	225	600	2,000	—

KM#11.2 **Composition:** Copper **Obverse:** Bridle variety (die break). **Note:** Reverse varieties exist.

Date	AG	Good	VG	Fine	VF	XF	Unc
1786	45.00	70.00	145	235	650	2,400	—

KM# 12.1 **Composition:** Copper **Reverse:** Plain shield. **Note:** Small planchet. Varieties exist.

Date	AG	Good	VG	Fine	VF	XF	Unc
1787	35.00	55.00	110	200	500	950	—

KM# 12.2 **Composition:** Copper **Reverse:** Shield heavily outlined. **Note:** Small planchet.

Date	AG	Good	VG	Fine	VF	XF	Unc
1787	38.00	60.00	120	215	550	1,150	—

KM# 13 **Composition:** Copper **Obverse:** "Serpent head."

Date	AG	Good	VG	Fine	VF	XF	Unc
1787	55.00	85.00	200	375	1,650	4,200	—

KM# 14 **Composition:** Copper **Reverse:** Plain shield. **Note:** Large planchet. Varieties exist.

Date	AG	Good	VG	Fine	VF	XF	Unc
1787	45.00	60.00	135	240	750	1,650	—

KM# 15 **Composition:** Copper **Reverse Legend:** PLURIBS.

Date	AG	Good	VG	Fine	VF	XF	Unc
1787	85.00	150	275	500	1,500	3,250	—

KM# 16 **Composition:** Copper **Obverse:** Horse's head facing right. **Note:** Varieties exist.

Date	AG	Good	VG	Fine	VF	XF	Unc
1788	42.00	60.00	115	190	700	1,275	—

KM# 17 **Composition:** Copper **Reverse:** Fox before legend. **Note:** Varieties exist.

Date	AG	Good	VG	Fine	VF	XF	Unc
1788	75.00	145	295	575	2,150	4,750	—

KM# 18 **Composition:** Copper **Obverse:** Horse's head facing left. **Note:** Varieties exist.

Date	AG	Good	VG	Fine	VF	XF	Unc
1788	235	425	900	1,650	4,800	13,000	—

NEW YORK

KM# 1 **Composition:** Copper **Obverse:** Bust right **Obverse Legend:** NON VI VIRTUTE VICI. **Reverse Legend:** NEO-EBORACENSIS

Date	AG	Good	VG	Fine	VF	XF	Unc
1786	3,250	5,000	7,500	15,000	35,000	—	—

KM# 2 **Composition:** Copper **Obverse:** Eagle on

globe facing right. **Obverse Legend:** EXCELSIOR **Reverse Legend:** E. PLURIBUS UNUM

Date	AG	Good	VG	Fine	VF	XF	Unc
1787	1,400	2,250	3,850	7,000	17,500	33,500	—

KM#3 Composition: Copper **Obverse:** Eagle on globe facing left. **Obverse Legend:** EXCELSIOR **Reverse Legend:** E. PLURIBUS UNUM

Date	AG	Good	VG	Fine	VF	XF	Unc
1787	1,250	2,000	3,500	6,500	16,500	32,000	—

KM#4 Composition: Copper **Obverse Legend:** EXCELSIOR **Reverse:** Large eagle, arrows in right talon. **Reverse Legend:** E. PLURIBUS UNUM

Date	AG	Good	VG	Fine	VF	XF	Unc
1787	—	4,500	9,000	16,500	35,000	55,000	—

Note: Norweb $18,700

KM#5 Composition: Copper **Obverse:** George Clinton. **Reverse Legend:** EXCELSIOR

Date	AG	Good	VG	Fine	VF	XF	Unc
1787	5,000	9,000	15,500	35,000	75,000	185,000	—

KM#6 Composition: Copper **Obverse:** Indian. **Obverse Legend:** LIBERNATUS LIBERTATEM DEFENDO **Reverse:** New York arms. **Reverse Legend:** EXCELSIOR

Date	AG	Good	VG	Fine	VF	XF	Unc
1787	4,500	7,500	12,500	30,000	65,000	160,000	—

KM#7 Composition: Copper **Obverse:** Indian. **Obverse Legend:** LIBERNATUS LIBERTATEM DEFENDO **Reverse:** Eagle on globe. **Reverse Legend:** NEO EBORACUS EXCELSIOR

Date	AG	Good	VG	Fine	VF	XF	Unc
1787	6,500	11,500	17,500	37,500	75,000	145,000	—

KM#8 Composition: Copper **Obverse:** Indian. **Reverse:** George III.

Date	AG	Good	VG	Fine	VF	XF
1787 3 Known	—	—	75,000	—	—	—

MACHIN'S MILL

KM#9 Composition: Copper **Obverse:** Bust right **Obverse Legend:** NOVA EBORAC. **Reverse:** Figure seated right. **Reverse Legend:** VIRT.ET.LIB.

Date	AG	Good	VG	Fine	VF	XF	Unc
1787	75.00	115	220	360	1,150	2,700	—

KM#10 Composition: Copper **Obverse:** Bust right **Obverse Legend:** NOVA EBORAC **Reverse:** Figure seated left. **Reverse Legend:** VIRT.ET.LIB.

Date	AG	Good	VG	Fine	VF	XF	Unc
1787	60.00	100.00	200	325	825	1,750	—

NOVA EBORACS

KM#11 Composition: Copper **Obverse:** Small head,

COLONIAL COINAGE

star above. **Obverse Legend:** NOVA EBORAC. **Reverse:** Figure seated left **Reverse Legend:** VIRT.ET.LIB.

Date	AG	Good	VG	Fine	VF	XF	Unc
1787	2,450	3,750	5,500	9,500	22,500	—	—

KM# 12 **Composition:** Copper **Obverse:** Large head, two quatrefoils left. **Obverse Legend:** NOVA EBORAC. **Reverse:** Figure seated left **Reverse Legend:** VIRT.ET.LIB.

Date	AG	Good	VG	Fine	VF	XF	Unc
1787	350	600	1,250	2,500	7,750	15,000	—

KM# 13 **Composition:** Copper **Note:** Crude, lightweight imitations of the British Halfpenny were struck at Machin's Mill in large quantities bearing the obverse legends: GEORGIVS II REX, GEORGIVS III REX, and GEORGIUS III REX, with the BRITANNIA reverse. There are many different mulings. Plain crosses in the shield of Britannia are noticeable on high grade pieces, unlike common British made imitations, which usually have outlined crosses in the shield. Some Machin's Mill varieties are very rare.

Date	AG	Good	VG	Fine	VF	XF
(1747-1788)	40.00	75.00	145	325	800	2,250

Note: Prices are for most common within date ranges. Examples are dated: 1747, 1771, 1772, 1774, 1775, 1776, 1777, 1778, 1784, 1785, 1786, 1787 and 1788. Other dates may exist

VERMONT

KM# 1 **Composition:** Copper **Reverse Legend:** IMMUNE COLUMBIA

Date	AG	Good	VG	Fine	VF	XF	Unc
(1785)	4,000	6,000	9,500	13,750	35,000	—	—

KM# 2 **Composition:** Copper **Obverse:** Sun rising over field with plow **Obverse Legend:** VERMONTIS. RES. PUBLICA. **Reverse:** Eye, with rays and stars **Reverse Legend:** QUARTA. DECIMA. STELLA.

Date	AG	Good	VG	Fine	VF	XF	Unc
1785	140	300	750	1,650	5,250	12,500	—

KM# 3 **Composition:** Copper **Obverse:** Sun rising over field with plow **Obverse Legend:** VERMONTS. RES. PUBLICA. **Reverse:** Eye, with rays and stars **Reverse Legend:** QUARTA. DECIMA. STELLA.

Date	AG	Good	VG	Fine	VF	XF	Unc
1785	150	285	600	1,250	3,150	7,500	—

KM# 4 **Composition:** Copper **Obverse:** Sun rising over field with plow **Obverse Legend:** VERMONTENSIUM.RES.PUBLICA **Reverse:** Eye, with pointed rays and stars **Reverse Legend:** QUARTA. DECIMA. STELLA.

Date	AG	Good	VG	Fine	VF	XF	Unc
1786	140	235	425	775	2,000	4,400	—

KM# 5 **Composition:** Copper **Obverse:** "Baby head." **Obverse Legend:** AUCTORI: VERMON: **Reverse:** Seated figure left **Reverse Legend:** ET:LIB: INDE

Date	AG	Good	VG	Fine	VF	XF	Unc
1786	200	350	650	1,750	4,800	12,500	—

COLONIAL COINAGE

KM#6 **Composition:** Copper **Obverse:** Bust facing left. **Obverse Legend:** VERMON: AUCTORI: **Reverse:** Seated figure left **Reverse Legend:** INDE ETLIB

Date	AG	Good	VG	Fine	VF	XF
1786	115	175	350	825	2,850	5,000
1787 extremely rare	—	4,500	10,000	22,500	42,500	—

KM#7 **Composition:** Copper **Obverse:** Bust facing right. **Obverse Legend:** VERMON. AUCTORI. **Reverse:** Seated figure left **Reverse Legend:** INDE ETLIB **Note:** Varieties exist.

Date	AG	Good	VG	Fine	VF	XF	Unc
1787	70.00	150	260	575	1,450	3,000	—

KM#8 **Composition:** Copper **Obverse:** Bust right **Obverse Legend:** VERMON AUCTORI **Reverse:** Seated figure left **Note:** Britannia mule.

Date	AG	Good	VG	Fine	VF	XF	Unc
1787	65.00	120	170	300	700	1,650	—

KM#9.2 **Composition:** Copper **Obverse:** Bust right. "C" backward in AUCTORI. **Reverse:** Seated figure left

Date	AG	Good	VG	Fine	VF	XF
1788 extremely rare	—	4,200	7,000	17,500	38,000	—

Note: Stack's Americana, Fine, $9,775

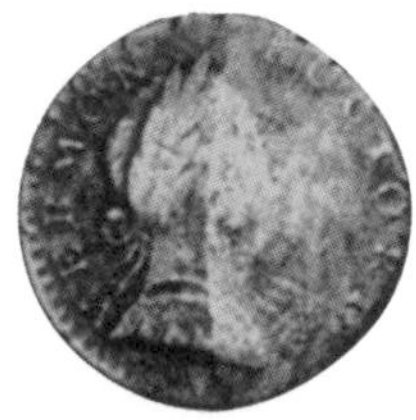

KM#10 **Composition:** Copper **Obverse:** Bust right **Reverse:** Seated figure left **Reverse Legend:** .ET LIB. .INDE.

Date	AG	Good	VG	Fine	VF	XF	Unc
1788	200	325	675	1,450	4,750	13,500	—

KM#11 **Composition:** Copper **Obverse:** Bust right **Reverse:** Seated figure left **Note:** George III Rex mule.

Date	AG	Good	VG	Fine	VF	XF	Unc
1788	325	575	950	5,000	12,500	12,000	—

KM#9.1 **Composition:** Copper **Obverse:** Bust right **Obverse Legend:** VERMON. AUCTORI. **Reverse:** Seated figure left **Reverse Legend:** INDE . ET LIB. **Note:** Varieties exist.

Date	AG	Good	VG	Fine	VF	XF	Unc
1788	65.00	125	200	450	950	2,250	—

EARLY AMERICAN TOKENS

ALBANY CHURCH "PENNY"

KM#Tn54.1 **Composition:** Copper **Obverse:** Without "D" above church. **Note:** Uniface.

Date	AG	Good	VG	Fine	VF	XF	Unc
5 known	—	—	10,000	25,000	45,000	75,000	—

COLONIAL COINAGE

KM# Tn54.2 **Composition:** Copper **Obverse:** With "D" above church. **Note:** Uniface.

Date	AG	Good	VG	Fine	VF	XF	Unc
rare	—	—	9,000	22,500	42,500	67,500	—

AUCTORI PLEBIS

KM# Tn50 **Composition:** Copper **Obverse:** Bust left **Obverse Legend:** AUCTORI: PLEBIS: **Reverse:** Seated figure left **Reverse Legend:** INDEP: ET. LIBER

Date	AG	Good	VG	Fine	VF	XF	Unc
1787	—	100.00	165	340	700	1,650	15,000

BAR "CENT"

KM# Tn49 **Composition:** Copper **Obverse:** USA monogram **Reverse:** Horizontal bars

Date	AG	Good	VG	Fine	VF	XF	Unc
(1785)	—	1,400	1,750	3,100	6,250	9,500	27,500

CASTORLAND "HALF DOLLAR"

KM# Tn87.1 **Composition:** Silver **Obverse Legend:** FRANCO.AMERICANA COLONIA **Edge:** Reeded.

Date	AG	Good	VG	Fine	VF	XF	Unc
1796	—	—	—	—	—	4,500	13,500

KM# Tn87.1a **Composition:** Copper **Obverse Legend:** FRANCO.AMERICANA COLONIA **Edge:** Reeded.

Date	AG	Good	VG	Fine	VF	XF
1796 3 known	—	—	—	—	—	3,500

KM# Tn87.1b **Composition:** Brass **Obverse Legend:** FRANCO.AMERICANA COLONIA **Edge:** Reeded.

Date	AG	Good	VG	Fine	VF	XF	Unc
1796	—	—	—	—	—	225	650

KM# Tn87.2 **Composition:** Copper **Obverse Legend:** FRANCO.AMERICANA COLONIA **Edge:** Plain. **Note:** Thin planchet.

Date	AG	Good	VG	Fine	VF	XF
1796 unique	—	—	—	—	—	—

KM# Tn87.3 **Composition:** Silver **Obverse Legend:** FRANCO.AMERICANA COLONIA **Edge:** Reeded. **Note:** Thin planchet. Restrike.

Date	Good	VG	Fine	VF	XF	Unc	Proof
1796	—	—	—	—	—	1,250	—

KM# Tn87.4 **Composition:** Silver **Obverse Legend:** FRANCO.AMERICANA COLONIA **Edge:** Lettered. **Edge Lettering:** ARGENT. **Note:** Thin planchet. Restrike.

Date	Good	VG	Fine	VF	XF	Unc	Proof
1796	—	—	—	—	—	150	—

KM# Tn87.3a **Composition:** Copper **Obverse Legend:** FRANCO.AMERICANA COLONIA **Edge:** Reeded. **Note:** Thin planchet. Restrike.

Date	Good	VG	Fine	VF	XF	Unc	Proof
1796	—	—	—	—	—	350	—

KM# Tn87.5 **Composition:** Copper **Obverse Legend:** FRANCO.AMERICANA COLONIA **Edge:** Lettered. **Edge Lettering:** CUIVRE. **Note:** Thin planchet. Restrike.

Date	Good	VG	Fine	VF	XF	Unc	Proof
1796	—	—	—	—	—	100.00	—

CHALMERS

3 PENCE

KM# Tn45 **Composition:** Silver

Date	AG	Good	VG	Fine	VF	XF	Unc
1783	650	1,150	2,200	4,250	9,500	17,500	—

6 PENCE

KM# Tn46.1 **Composition:** Silver **Reverse:** Small date

Date	AG	Good	VG	Fine	VF	XF	Unc
1783	900	1,650	2,750	6,750	16,500	28,500	—

KM#Tn46.2 **Composition:** Silver **Reverse:** Large date

Date	AG	Good	VG	Fine	VF	XF	Unc
1783	775	1,450	2,250	6,000	14,500	27,500	—

SHILLING

KM#Tn47.1 **Composition:** Silver **Reverse:** Birds with long worm

Date	AG	Good	VG	Fine	VF	XF	Unc
1783	450	775	1,350	2,750	6,000	11,500	—

KM#Tn47.2 **Composition:** Silver **Reverse:** Birds with short worm

Date	AG	Good	VG	Fine	VF	XF	Unc
1783	450	750	1,250	2,350	5,500	11,000	—

KM#Tn48 **Composition:** Silver **Reverse:** Rings and stars

Date	AG	Good	VG	Fine	VF	XF
1783 4 known	—	—	—	—	200,000	—

Note: Garrett $75,000

COPPER COMPANY OF UPPER CANADA

HALFPENNY

KM#Tn86 **Composition:** Copper **Obverse Legend:** BRITISH SETTLEMENT KENTUCKY

Date	Good	VG	Fine	VF	XF	Unc	Proof
1796	—	—	—	—	—	—	10,000

FRANKLIN PRESS

KM#Tn73 **Composition:** Copper **Obverse:** Printing press **Obverse Legend:** SIC ORITUR DOCTRINA SURGETQUE LIBERTAS **Edge:** Plain.

Date	AG	Good	VG	Fine	VF	XF	Unc
1794	30.00	75.00	110	150	285	450	1,350

KENTUCKY TOKEN

KM#Tn70.1 **Composition:** Copper **Obverse Legend:** UNANIMITY IS THE STRENGTH OF SOCIETY **Reverse Legend:** E. PLURIBUS UNUM **Edge:** Plain. **Note:** 1793 date is circa.

Date	AG	Good	VG	Fine	VF	XF	Unc
(1793)	12.00	25.00	40.00	150	200	375	1,210

KM#Tn70.2 **Composition:** Copper **Obverse Legend:** UNANIMITY IS THE STRENGTH OF SOCIETY **Reverse Legend:** E. PLURIBUS UNUM **Edge:** Engrailed.

Date	AG	Good	VG	Fine	VF	XF	Unc
(1793)	35.00	75.00	125	200	500	950	3,400

KM#Tn70.3 **Composition:** Copper **Obverse Legend:** UNANIMITY IS THE STRENGTH OF SOCIETY **Reverse Legend:** E. PLURIBUS UNUM **Edge:** Lettered. **Edge Lettering:** PAYABLE AT BEDWORTH.

Date	AG	Good	VG	Fine	VF	XF
(1793) unique	—	—	—	—	—	1,980

KM#Tn70.4 **Composition:** Copper **Obverse Legend:** UNANIMITY IS THE STRENGTH OF SOCIETY **Reverse Legend:** E. PLURIBUS UNUM **Edge:** Lettered. **Edge Lettering:** PAYABLE AT LANCASTER.

Date	AG	Good	VG	Fine	VF	XF	Unc
(1793)	14.00	28.00	45.00	65.00	225	400	1,250

KM#Tn70.5 **Composition:** Copper **Obverse Legend:** UNANIMITY IS THE STRENGTH OF SOCIETY **Reverse Legend:** E. PLURIBUS UNUM **Edge:** Lettered. **Edge Lettering:** PAYABLE AT I.FIELDING.

Date	AG	Good	VG	Fine	VF	XF
(1793) unique	—	—	—	—	—	—

COLONIAL COINAGE

KM# Tn70.6 Composition: Copper **Obverse Legend:** UNANIMITY IS THE STRENGTH OF SOCIETY **Reverse Legend:** E. PLURIBUS UNUM **Edge:** Lettered. **Edge Lettering:** PAYABLE AT W. PARKERS.

Date	AG	Good	VG	Fine	VF	XF
(1793) unique	—	—	—	—	20,000	—

KM# Tn70.7 Composition: Copper **Obverse Legend:** UNANIMITY IS THE STRENGTH OF SOCIETY **Reverse Legend:** E. PLURIBUS UNUM **Edge:** Ornamented branch with two leaves.

Date	AG	Good	VG	Fine	VF	XF
(1793) unique	—	—	—	—	—	—

MOTT TOKEN

KM# Tn52.1 Composition: Copper **Obverse:** Clock **Reverse:** Eagle with shield **Note:** Thin planchet.

Date	AG	Good	VG	Fine	VF	XF	Unc
1789	50.00	80.00	150	300	550	1,200	1,750

KM# Tn52.2 Composition: Copper **Obverse:** Clock **Reverse:** Eagle with shield **Note:** Thick planchet. Weight generally about 170 grams.

Date	AG	Good	VG	Fine	VF	XF	Unc
1789	60.00	95.00	175	325	525	100.00	—

KM# Tn52.3 Composition: Copper **Obverse:** Clock **Reverse:** Eagle with shield **Edge:** Fully engrailed. **Note:** Specimens struck with perfect dies are scarcer and generally command higher prices.

Date	AG	Good	VG	Fine	VF	XF	Unc
1789	90.00	160	325	450	700	1,750	4,800

MYDDELTON TOKEN

KM# Tn85 Composition: Copper **Obverse Legend:** BRITISH SETTLEMENT KENTUCKY **Reverse Legend:** PAYABLE BY P.P.P.MYDDELTON.

Date	Good	VG	Fine	VF	XF	Unc	Proof
1796	—	—	—	—	—	—	37,500

KM# Tn85a Composition: Silver ASW.

Date	Good	VG	Fine	VF	XF	Unc	Proof
1796	—	—	—	—	—	—	28,000

NEW YORK THEATRE

KM# Tn90 Composition: Copper **Obverse:** Theater building **Obverse Legend:** THE.THEATRE.AT.NEW. YORK. AMERICA **Reverse:** Ships at sea, viewed from dock **Reverse Legend:** MAY.COMMERCE.FLOURISH **Note:** 1796 date is circa.

Date	AG	Good	VG	Fine	VF	XF	Unc
1796	—	—	—	—	7,500	10,000	26,500

NORTH AMERICAN

HALFPENNY

KM# Tn30 Composition: Copper **Obverse:** Seated figure left, with harp **Obverse Legend:** NORTH AMERICAN TOKEN **Reverse:** Ship **Reverse Legend:** COMMERCE

Date	AG	Good	VG	Fine	VF	XF	Unc
1781	32.00	50.00	70.00	140	300	750	3,250

RHODE ISLAND SHIP

KM#Tn27a Composition: Brass **Obverse:** Without wreath below ship.

Date	AG	Good	VG	Fine	VF	XF	Unc
1779	—	—	325	550	1,000	2,000	7,500

KM#Tn27b Composition: Pewter **Obverse:** Without wreath below ship.

Date	AG	Good	VG	Fine	VF	XF	Unc
1779	—	—	—	—	5,000	8,500	18,500

KM#Tn28a Composition: Brass **Obverse:** Wreath below ship.

Date	AG	Good	VG	Fine	VF	XF	Unc
1779	—	—	—	675	1,100	2,100	7,750

KM#Tn28b Composition: Pewter **Obverse:** Wreath below ship.

Date	AG	Good	VG	Fine	VF	XF	Unc
1779	—	—	—	—	5,500	9,000	20,000

KM#Tn29 Composition: Brass **Obverse:** VLUGTENDE below ship

Date	AG	Good	VG	Fine	VF	XF
1779 unique	—	—	—	—	—	35,000

Note: Garrett $16,000

STANDISH BARRY

3 PENCE

KM#Tn55 Composition: Silver **Obverse:** Bust left **Obverse Legend:** BALTIMORE • TOWN • JULY • 4 • 90 • **Reverse:** Denomination **Reverse Legend:** STANDISH BARRY •

Date	AG	Good	VG	Fine	VF	XF	Unc
1790	—	—	15,000	23,500	55,000	—	—

TALBOT, ALLUM & LEE

CENT

KM#Tn71.1 Composition: Copper **Reverse:** NEW YORK above ship **Edge:** Lettered. **Edge Lettering:** PAYABLE AT THE STORE OF

Date	AG	Good	VG	Fine	VF	XF	Unc
1794	32.00	50.00	85.00	165	275	550	2,000

KM#Tn71.2 Composition: Copper **Reverse:** NEW YORK above ship **Edge:** Plain. **Note:** Size of ampersand varies on obverse and reverse dies.

Date	AG	Good	VG	Fine	VF	XF
1794 4 known	—	—	—	—	10,000	24,000

KM#Tn72.1 Composition: Copper **Reverse:** Without NEW YORK above ship **Edge:** Lettered. **Edge Lettering:** PAYABLE AT THE STORE OF

Date	AG	Good	VG	Fine	VF	XF	Unc
1794	200	375	600	1,250	3,750	7,500	22,000

COLONIAL COINAGE

KM# Tn72.2 **Composition:** Copper **Edge:** Lettered. **Edge Lettering:** WE PROMISE TO PAY THE BEARER ONE CENT.

Date	AG	Good	VG	Fine	VF	XF	Unc
1795	30.00	50.00	75.00	135	250	400	1,200

KM# Tn72.3 **Composition:** Copper **Edge:** Lettered. **Edge Lettering:** CURRENT EVERYWHERE.

Date	AG	Good	VG	Fine	VF	XF
1795 unique	—	—	—	—	—	—

KM# Tn72.4 **Composition:** Copper **Edge:** Olive leaf.

Date	AG	Good	VG	Fine	VF	XF
1795 unique	—	—	—	—	—	15,000

Note: Norweb $4,400

KM# Tn72.5 **Composition:** Copper **Edge:** Plain.

Date	AG	Good	VG	Fine	VF	XF
1795 plain edge, 2 known	—	—	—	—	—	—
1795 Lettered edge; unique	—	—	—	—	—	15,000

Note: Edge: Cambridge Bedford Huntington.X.X.; Norweb, $3,960

WASHINGTON PIECES

KM# Tn35 **Composition:** Copper **Obverse Legend:** GEORGIVS TRIUMPHO.

Date	AG	Good	VG	Fine	VF	XF	Unc
1783	—	95.00	135	285	650	1,150	—

KM# Tn36 **Composition:** Copper **Obverse:** Large military bust. **Note:** Varieties exist.

Date	AG	Good	VG	Fine	VF	XF	Unc
1783	—	—	50.00	90.00	185	450	2,600

KM# Tn37.1 **Composition:** Copper **Obverse:** Small military bust. **Edge:** Plain.

Date	AG	Good	VG	Fine	VF	XF	Unc
1783	—	—	70.00	95.00	220	525	3,800

Note: One proof example is known. Value: $25,000

KM# Tn37.2 **Composition:** Copper **Obverse:** Small military bust. **Edge:** Engrailed.

Date	AG	Good	VG	Fine	VF	XF	Unc
1783	—	75.00	110	150	300	750	4,250

KM# Tn38.1 **Composition:** Copper **Obverse:** Draped bust, no button on drapery, small letter.

Date	AG	Good	VG	Fine	VF	XF	Unc
1783	—	40.00	60.00	95.00	185	400	2,250

KM# Tn38.2 **Composition:** Copper **Obverse:** Draped bust, button on drapery, large letter.

Date	AG	Good	VG	Fine	VF	XF	Unc
1783	—	85.00	110	150	325	625	4,500

KM#Tn38.4 **Composition:** Copper **Edge:** Engrailed. **Note:** Restrike.

Date	Good	VG	Fine	VF	XF	Unc	Proof
1783	—	—	—	—	—	—	800

KM#Tn38.4a **Composition:** Copper **Note:** Bronzed. Restrike.

Date	Good	VG	Fine	VF	XF	Unc	Proof
1783	—	—	—	—	—	—	—

KM#Tn83.3 **Composition:** Copper **Obverse:** Large modern lettering. **Edge:** Plain. **Note:** Restrike.

Date	Good	VG	Fine	VF	XF	Unc	Proof
1783	—	—	—	—	—	—	950

KM#Tn83.4b **Composition:** Silver **Note:** Restrike.

Date	Good	VG	Fine	VF	XF	Unc	Proof
1783	—	—	—	—	—	—	1,750

KM#Tn83.4c **Composition:** Gold **Note:** Restrike.

Date	AG	Good	VG	Fine	VF	XF
1783 2 known	—	—	—	—	—	—

KM#Tn60.1 **Composition:** Copper **Obverse Legend:** WASHINGTON PRESIDENT. **Edge:** Plain.

Date	AG	Good	VG	Fine	VF	XF	Unc
1792	850	1,450	3,000	7,500	18,500	—	—

Note: Steinberg $12,650. Garrett $15,500

KM#Tn60.2 **Composition:** Copper **Obverse Legend:** WASHINGTON PRESIDENT. **Edge:** Lettered. **Edge Lettering:** UNITED STATES OF AMERICA.

Date	AG	Good	VG	Fine	VF	XF	Unc
1792	—	—	—	—	—	—	—

KM#Tn61.1 **Composition:** Copper **Obverse Legend:** BORN VIRGINIA. **Note:** Varieties exist.

Date	AG	Good	VG	Fine	VF	XF	Unc
(1792)	500	1,000	2,000	4,000	7,500	12,000	—

KM#Tn61.2 **Composition:** Silver **Edge:** Lettered. **Edge Lettering:** UNITED STATES OF AMERICA.

Date	AG	Good	VG	Fine	VF	XF
(1792) 2 known	—	—	—	—	—	—

KM#Tn61.1a **Composition:** Silver **Edge:** Plain.

Date	AG	Good	VG	Fine	VF	XF
(1792) 4 known	—	—	—	—	—	200,000

Note: Roper $16,500

KM#Tn62 **Composition:** Silver **Reverse:** Heraldic eagle. 1792 half dollar. **Note:** Mule.

Date	AG	Good	VG	Fine	VF	XF
(1792) 3 known	—	—	—	—	50,000	75,000

KM#Tn77.1 **Composition:** Copper **Obverse Legend:** LIBERTY AND SECURITY. **Edge:** Lettered. **Note:** "Penny."

Date	AG	Good	VG	Fine	VF	XF	Unc
(1795)	70.00	110	165	300	500	850	3,500

KM# Tn77.2 **Composition:** Copper **Edge:** Plain. **Note:** "Penny."

Date	AG	Good	VG	Fine	VF	XF
(1795) extremely rare	—	—	—	—	—	—

KM# Tn77.3 **Composition:** Copper **Note:** "Penny." Engine-turned borders.

Date	Good	VG	Fine	VF	XF	Unc
(1795) 12 known	275	450	650	1,250	2,400	7,500

KM# Tn78 **Composition:** Copper **Note:** Similar to "Halfpenny" with date on reverse.

Date	AG	Good	VG	Fine	VF	XF
1795 very rare	—	—	—	—	—	—

Note: Roper $6,600

HALFPENNY

KM# Tn56 **Composition:** Copper **Obverse Legend:** LIVERPOOL HALFPENNY

Date	AG	Good	VG	Fine	VF	XF	Unc
1791	40.00	70.00	1,000	125	300	550	3,250

KM# Tn66.1 **Composition:** Copper **Reverse:** Ship **Edge:** Lettered.

Date	AG	Good	VG	Fine	VF	XF	Unc
1793	25.00	45.00	85.00	225	450	825	3,500

KM# Tn66.2 **Composition:** Copper **Reverse:** Ship **Edge:** Plain.

Date	AG	Good	VG	Fine	VF	XF
1793 5 known	—	—	—	—	15,000	—

KM# Tn75.1 **Composition:** Copper **Obverse:** Large coat buttons **Reverse:** Grate **Edge:** Reeded.

Date	AG	Good	VG	Fine	VF	XF	Unc
1795	—	—	70.00	110	200	400	900

KM# Tn75.2 **Composition:** Copper **Reverse:** Grate **Edge:** Lettered.

Date	AG	Good	VG	Fine	VF	XF	Unc
1795	90.00	140	210	275	400	800	2,800

KM# Tn75.3 **Composition:** Copper **Obverse:** Small coat buttons **Reverse:** Grate **Edge:** Reeded.

Date	AG	Good	VG	Fine	VF	XF	Unc
1795	50.00	75.00	120	190	275	585	2,650

KM# Tn76.1 **Composition:** Copper **Obverse Legend:** LIBERTY AND SECURITY. **Edge:** Plain.

Date	AG	Good	VG	Fine	VF	XF	Unc
1795	18.00	35.00	60.00	160	350	700	3,250

KM# Tn76.2 **Composition:** Copper **Edge:** Lettered. **Edge Lettering:** PAYABLE AT LONDON ...

Date	AG	Good	VG	Fine	VF	XF	Unc
1795	40.00	65.00	90.00	140	300	650	3,000

KM# Tn76.3 **Composition:** Copper **Edge:** Lettered. **Edge Lettering:** BIRMINGHAM ...

Date	AG	Good	VG	Fine	VF	XF	Unc
1795	55.00	85.00	125	175	350	800	3,600

KM# Tn76.4 **Composition:** Copper **Edge:** Lettered. **Edge Lettering:** AN ASYLUM ...

Date	AG	Good	VG	Fine	VF	XF	Unc
1795	18.00	35.00	60.00	275	600	1,600	6,500

KM# Tn76.5 **Composition:** Copper **Edge:** Lettered. **Edge Lettering:** PAYABLE AT LIVERPOOL ...

Date	AG	Good	VG	Fine	VF	XF
1795 unique	—	—	—	—	—	—

KM#Tn76.6 **Composition:** Copper **Edge:** Lettered. **Edge Lettering:** PAYABLE AT LONDON-LIVERPOOL.

Date	AG	Good	VG	Fine	VF	XF
1795 unique	—	—	—	—	—	—

KM#Tn81.1 **Composition:** Copper **Reverse Legend:** NORTH WALES **Edge:** Plain.

Date	AG	Good	VG	Fine	VF	XF
(ca.1795)	60.00	110	175	265	625	1,750

KM#Tn82 **Composition:** Copper **Reverse:** Four stars at bottom **Reverse Legend:** NORTH WALES

Date	AG	Good	VG	Fine	VF	XF	Unc
(1795)	1,250	2,250	4,750	7,750	21,500	—	—

KM#Tn81.2 **Composition:** Copper **Reverse Legend:** NORTH WALES **Edge:** Lettered.

Date	AG	Good	VG	Fine	VF	XF	Unc
(1795)	350	550	1,150	1,750	5,500	9,500	—

CENT

KM#Tn39 **Composition:** Copper **Obverse:** Draped Bust left **Obverse Legend:** WASHINGTON & INDEPENDENCE **Reverse:** Denomination in wreath **Reverse Legend:** UNITY STATES OF AMERICA

Date	AG	Good	VG	Fine	VF	XF	Unc
1783	30.00	50.00	70.00	10.00	265	550	2,250

KM#Tn40 **Composition:** Copper **Note:** Double head.

Date	AG	Good	VG	Fine	VF	XF	Unc
(1783)	25.00	45.00	60.00	95.00	250	500	2,750

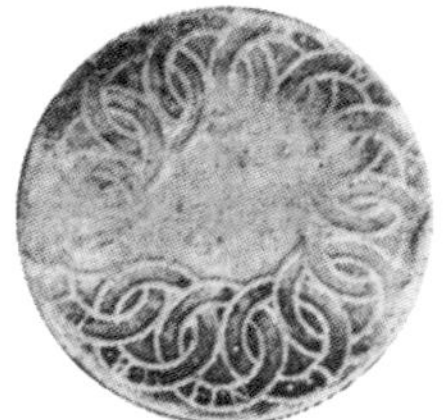

KM#Tn41 **Composition:** Copper **Obverse:** "Ugly head." **Note:** 3 known in copper, 1 in white metal.

Date	AG	Good	VG	Fine	VF	XF	Unc
1784	—	120,000	—	—	—	—	—

Note: Roper $14,850

KM#Tn57 **Composition:** Copper **Obverse:** Military bust left **Obverse Legend:** WASHINGTON PRESIDENT. **Reverse:** Small eagle

Date	AG	Good	VG	Fine	VF	XF	Unc
1791	—	—	350	500	725	1,000	4,250

KM#Tn58 **Composition:** Copper **Obverse:** Military bust left **Obverse Legend:** WASHINGTON PRESIDENT **Reverse:** Large eagle

Date	AG	Good	VG	Fine	VF	XF	Unc
1791	—	200	325	485	650	900	3,200

KM#Tn65 **Composition:** Copper **Obverse:** "Roman" head **Obverse Legend:** WASHINGTON PRESIDENT.

Date	AG	Good	VG	Fine	VF	XF	Unc
1792	—	—	—	—	—	—	—

HALF DOLLAR

KM#Tn59.1 **Composition:** Copper **Edge:** Lettered. **Edge Lettering:** UNITED STATES OF AMERICA

Date	AG	Good	VG	Fine	VF	XF
1792 2 known	—	—	—	—	—	75,000

Note: Roper $2,860. Benson, EF, $48,300

KM#Tn59.2 **Composition:** Copper **Edge:** Plain.

Date	AG	Good	VG	Fine	VF	XF
1792 3 known	—	—	—	—	125,000	200,000

KM#Tn59.1a **Composition:** Silver **Edge:** Lettered. **Edge Lettering:** UNITED STATES OF AMERICA

Date	AG	Good	VG	Fine	VF	XF
1792 rare	—	—	—	—	40,000	65,000

Note: Roper $35,200

KM#Tn59.2a **Composition:** Silver **Edge:** Plain.

Date	AG	Good	VG	Fine	VF	XF
1792 rare	—	—	—	—	—	—

KM#Tn59.1b **Composition:** Gold **Edge:** Lettered. **Edge Lettering:** UNITED STATES OF AMERICA

Date	AG	Good	VG	Fine	VF	XF
1792 unique	—	—	—	—	—	—

KM#Tn63.1 **Composition:** Silver **Reverse:** Small eagle **Edge:** Plain.

Date	AG	Good	VG	Fine	VF	XF	Unc
1792	—	—	—	—	200,000	300,000	—

KM#Tn63.2 **Composition:** Silver **Edge:** Ornamented, circles and squares.

Date	Good	VG	Fine	VF	XF	Unc
1792 5 known	—	—	—	100,000	175,000	400,000

KM#Tn63.1a **Composition:** Copper **Edge:** Plain.

Date	AG	Good	VG	Fine	VF	XF	Unc
1792	—	4,000	6,500	12,500	32,000	65,000	—

Note: Garrett $32,000

KM#Tn63.3 **Composition:** Silver **Edge:** Two olive leaves.

Date	AG	Good	VG	Fine	VF	XF
1792 unique	—	—	—	—	—	—

KM#Tn64 **Composition:** Silver **Reverse:** Large heraldic eagle

Date	AG	Good	VG	Fine	VF	XF
1792 unique	—	—	—	—	100,000	—

Note: Garrett $16,500

EARLY AMERICAN PATTERNS

CONFEDERATIO

KM# EA22 **Composition:** Copper **Obverse:** Standing figure with bow & arrow **Obverse Legend:** INIMICA TYRANNIS • AMERICANA • **Reverse:** Small circle of stars **Reverse Legend:** • CONFEDERATIO •

Date	AG	Good	VG	Fine	VF	XF	Unc
1785	—	—	—	—	50,000	95,000	—

KM# EA23 **Composition:** Copper **Obverse:** Standing figure with bow & arrow **Obverse Legend:** INIMICA TYRANNIS • AMERICANA • **Reverse:** Large circle of stars **Reverse Legend:** • CONFEDERATIO • **Note:** The Confederatio dies were struck in combination with 13 other dies of the period. All surviving examples of these combinations are extremely rare.

Date	AG	Good	VG	Fine	VF	XF
extremely rare	—	—	—	—	50,000	100,000

IMMUNE COLUMBIA

KM# EA20 **Composition:** Copper **Obverse:** George III **Obverse Legend:** GEORGIVS III • REX • **Reverse Legend:** IMMUNE COLUMBIA •

Date	AG	Good	VG	Fine	VF	XF	Unc
1785	3,500	5,250	7,750	11,500	22,500	—	—

KM# EA21 **Composition:** Copper **Obverse:** Head right **Obverse Legend:** VERMON AUCTORI **Reverse Legend:** IMMUNE COLUMBIA •

Date	AG	Good	VG	Fine	VF	XF	Unc
1785	—	6,000	9,500	12,500	35,000	—	—

KM# EA17a **Composition:** Silver **Obverse Legend:** IMMUNE COLUMBIA • **Reverse:** Eye, with pointed rays & stars **Reverse Legend:** NOVA CONSTELLATIO

Date	AG	Good	VG	Fine	VF	XF	Unc
1785	—	—	—	—	45,000	75,000	—

KM# EA19a **Composition:** Gold **Obverse Legend:** IMMUNE COLUMBIA • **Reverse:** Blunt rays **Reverse Legend:** NOVA CONSTELATIO •

Date	AG	Good	VG	Fine	VF	XF
1785 unique	—	—	—	—	—	—

Note: In the Smithsonian Collection

KM# EA17 **Composition:** Copper **Obverse Legend:** IMMUNE COLUMBIA. **Reverse:** Eye, with pointed rays & stars **Reverse Legend:** NOVA • CONSTELLATIO

Date	AG	Good	VG	Fine	VF	XF	Unc
1785	—	—	—	—	25,000	45,000	—

KM# EA18 **Composition:** Copper **Obverse Legend:** IMMUNE COLUMBIA • **Reverse:** Eye, with pointed rays & stars. Extra star in reverse legend **Reverse Legend:** NOVA • CONSTELLATIO *

Date	AG	Good	VG	Fine	VF	XF	Unc
1785	—	—	—	—	25,000	45,000	—

Note: Caldwell $4,675

KM# EA19 **Composition:** Copper **Obverse Legend:** IMMUNE COLUMBIA • **Reverse:** Blunt rays **Reverse Legend:** NOVA CONSTELATIO

Date	AG	Good	VG	Fine	VF	XF
1785 2 known	—	—	—	—	—	120,000

Note: Norweb $22,000

KM# EA28 **Composition:** Copper **Obverse Legend:**

IMMUNIS COLUMBIA **Reverse:** Eagle **Reverse Legend:** * E * PLURIBUS * UNUM *

Date	AG	Good	VG	Fine	VF	XF
1786 3 known	—	—	—	—	50,000	90,000

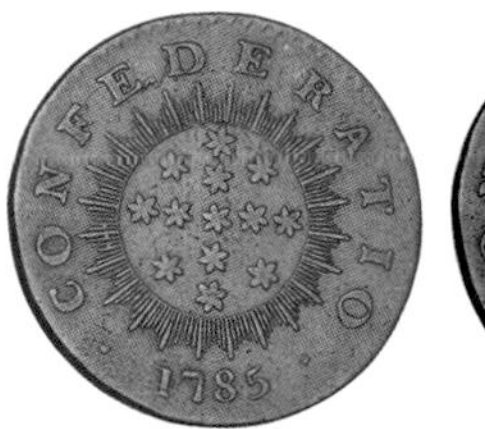

KM# EA24 Composition: Copper **Obverse:** Washington **Reverse:** Stars in rayed circle **Reverse Legend:** • CONFEDERATIO •

Date	AG	Good	VG	Fine	VF	XF
1786 3 known	—	—	—	—	60,000	—

Note: Garrett $50,000. Steinberg $12,650

KM# EA25 Composition: Copper **Obverse:** Eagle, raw shield **Obverse Legend:** * E • PLURIBUS UNUM • **Reverse:** Shield **Reverse Legend:** * E * PLURIBUS * UNUM *

Date	AG	Good	VG	Fine	VF	XF
1786 unique	—	—	—	—	—	—

Note: Garrett $37,500

KM# EA26 Composition: Copper **Obverse:** Washington **Obverse Legend:** GEN • WASHINGTON • **Reverse:** Eagle

Date	AG	Good	VG	Fine	VF	XF
1786 2 known	—	—	—	—	—	—

KM# EA27 Composition: Copper **Obverse Legend:** IMMUNIS COLUMBIA • **Reverse:** Shield **Reverse Legend:** * E * PLURIBUS * UNUM *

Date	Good	VG	Fine	VF	XF
1786 extremely rare	—	—	—	40,000	60,000

Note: Rescigno, AU, $33,000. Steinberg, VF, $11,000

NOVA CONSTELLATIO

KM# EA6.1 Composition: Copper **Obverse:** Pointed rays **Obverse Legend:** NOVA • CONSTELLATIO • **Reverse:** Small "U•S"

Date	AG	Good	VG	Fine	VF	XF	Unc
1783	50.00	70.00	100.00	225	440	950	3,750

KM# EA6.2 Composition: Copper **Obverse:** Pointed rays **Obverse Legend:** NOVA • CONSTELLATIO • **Reverse:** Large "US"

Date	AG	Good	VG	Fine	VF	XF	Unc
1783	55.00	75.00	110	250	600	1,400	7,000

KM# EA7 Composition: Copper **Obverse:** Blunt rays **Obverse Legend:** NOVA • CONSTELATIO •

Date	AG	Good	VG	Fine	VF	XF	Unc
1783	50.00	75.00	110	250	575	1,350	5,000

KM# EA8 Composition: Copper **Obverse:** Blunt rays **Obverse Legend:** NOVA • CONSTELATIO •

Date	AG	Good	VG	Fine	VF	XF	Unc
1785	50.00	75.00	110	260	650	1,550	6,500

KM# EA9 **Composition:** Copper **Obverse:** Pointed rays **Obverse Legend:** NOVA • CONSTELLATIO •

Date	AG	Good	VG	Fine	VF	XF	Unc
1785	—	—	100.00	225	450	1,000	3,600

KM# EA10 **Composition:** Copper **Note:** Contemporary circulating counterfeit. Similar to previously listed coin.

Date	AG	Good	VG	Fine	VF	XF
1786 extremely rare	—	—	—	—	—	—

5 UNITS

KM# EA12 **Composition:** Copper **Obverse:** Eye, with pointed rays & stars **Obverse Legend:** NOVA CONSTELLATIO **Reverse Legend:** • LIBERTAS • JUSTITIA •

Date	AG	Good	VG	Fine	VF	XF
1783 unique	—	—	—	—	—	—

100 (BIT)

KM# EA13.1 **Composition:** Silver **Obverse:** Eye, with pointed rays & stars **Obverse Legend:** NOVA CONSTELLATIO **Reverse Legend:** • LIBERTAS • JUSTITIA • **Edge:** Leaf.

Date	AG	Good	VG	Fine	VF	XF
1783 2 known	—	—	—	—	—	—

Note: Garrett $97,500. Stack's auction, May 1991, $72,500

KM# EA13.2 **Composition:** Silver **Obverse:** Eye, with pointed rays & stars **Obverse Legend:** NOVA CONSTELLATIO **Reverse Legend:** • LIBERTAS • JUSTITIA • **Edge:** Plain

Date	AG	Good	VG	Fine	VF	XF
1783 unique	—	—	—	—	—	—

500 (QUINT)

KM# EA14 **Composition:** Silver **Obverse:** Eye with pointed rays & stars **Obverse Legend:** NOVA CONSTELLATIO **Reverse Legend:** • LIBERTAS • JUSTITIA •

Date	AG	Good	VG	Fine	VF	XF
1783 unique	—	—	—	—	—	250,000

Note: Garrett $165,000

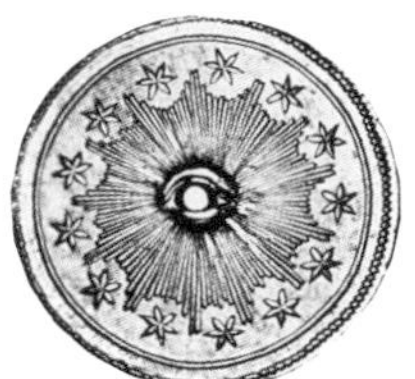

KM# EA15 **Composition:** Silver **Obverse:** Eye, with rays & stars, no legend **Reverse Legend:** • LIBERTAS • JUSTITIA •

Date	AG	Good	VG	Fine	VF	XF
1783 unique	—	—	—	—	75,000	—

Note: Garrett $55,000

1000 (MARK)

KM# EA16 **Composition:** Silver **Obverse:** Eye, with pointed rays & stars **Obverse Legend:** NOVA CONSTELLATIO **Reverse Legend:** • LIBERTAS • JUSTITIA •

Date	AG	Good	VG	Fine	VF	XF
1783 unique	—	—	—	—	—	350,000

Note: Garrett $190,000

EARLY FEDERAL COINAGE

BRASHER

KM# Tn51.1 Composition: Gold **Obverse:** Sunrise over mountains. **Reverse:** Displayed eagle with shield on breast, EB counterstamp on wing.

Date	AG	Good	VG	Fine	VF	XF
1787 6 known	—	—	—	—	—	—

Note: Heritage FUN Sale, January 2005, AU-55, $2.415 million.

KM# Tn51.2 Composition: Gold **Obverse:** Sun rise over mountains **Reverse:** Displayed eagle with sheild on breast. EB counterstamp on breast.

Date	AG	Good	VG	Fine	VF	XF
1787 unique	—	—	—	—	—	—

Note: Heritage FUN Sale, January 2005, XF-45, $2.99 million. Foreign gold coins with the EB counterstamp exist. These are valued at over $5,000, with many much higher.

FUGIO "CENT"

KM# EA30.1 Composition: Copper **Obverse:** Club rays, round ends.

Date	AG	Good	VG	Fine	VF	XF	Unc
1787	225	325	450	950	2,000	3,850	—

KM# EA30.2 Composition: Copper **Obverse:** Club rays, concave ends.

Date	AG	Good	VG	Fine	VF	XF	Unc
1787	1,500	2,500	4,500	900	27,500	—	—

KM# EA30.3 Composition: Copper **Obverse Legend:** FUCIO.

Date	AG	Good	VG	Fine	VF	XF	Unc
1787	—	2,000	3,000	7,000	25,000	35,000	—

KM# EA31.1 Composition: Copper **Obverse:** Pointed rays. **Reverse:** UNITED above, STATES below.

Date	AG	Good	VG	Fine	VF	XF	Unc
1787	600	950	1,500	3,250	80,000	11,500	—

KM# EA31.2 Composition: Copper **Reverse:** UNITED STATES at sides of ring.

Date	AG	Good	VG	Fine	VF	XF	Unc
1787	110	175	275	550	900	1,800	3,500

KM# EA31.3 Composition: Copper **Reverse:** STATES UNITED at sides of ring.

Date	AG	Good	VG	Fine	VF	XF	Unc
1787	110	190	275	550	850	1,650	3,500

KM# EA31.4 Composition: Copper **Reverse:** Eight-pointed stars on ring.

Date	AG	Good	VG	Fine	VF	XF	Unc
1787	150	285	475	700	1,250	2,750	9,000

KM# EA31.5 Composition: Copper **Reverse:** Raised rims on ring, large lettering in center.

Date	AG	Good	VG	Fine	VF	XF	Unc
1787	185	325	550	950	2,750	6,000	18,500

KM# EA32.1 Composition: Copper **Obverse:** No cinquefoils, cross after date. **Obverse Legend:** UNITED STATES.

Date	AG	Good	VG	Fine	VF	XF	Unc
1787	300	485	750	1,450	3,850	6,700	—

KM# EA32.2 Composition: Copper **Obverse:** No cinquefoils, cross after date. **Obverse Legend:** STATES UNITED.

Date	AG	Good	VG	Fine	VF	XF	Unc
1787	175	350	750	1,500	4,000	7,200	—

KM#EA32.3 Composition: Copper **Obverse:** No cinquefoils, cross after date. **Reverse:** Raised rims on ring.

Date	AG	Good	VG	Fine	VF	XF	Unc
1787	—	—	—	—	27,500	—	—

KM#EA33 Composition: Copper **Obverse:** No cinquefoils, cross after date. **Reverse:** With rays. **Reverse Legend:** AMERICAN CONGRESS.

Date	AG	Good	VG	Fine	VF	XF
1787 extremely rare	—	—	—	—	225,000	300,000

Note: Norweb $63,800

KM#EA34 Composition: Brass **Note:** New Haven restrike.

Date	AG	Good	VG	Fine	VF	XF	Unc
1787	—	—	—	—	—	450	1,000

KM#EA34a Composition: Copper **Note:** New Haven restrike.

Date	AG	Good	VG	Fine	VF	XF	Unc
1787	—	—	—	—	450	750	1,000

KM#EA34b Composition: Silver **Note:** New Haven restrike.

Date	Good	VG	Fine	VF	XF	Unc
1787(ca.1858)	—	—	—	—	2,750	4,000

KM#EA34c Composition: Gold **Note:** New Haven restrike.

Date	AG	Good	VG	Fine	VF	XF
1787(ca.1858) 2 known	—	—	—	—	—	—

Note: Norweb (holed) $1,430

ISSUES OF 1792

CENT

KM#PnE1 Composition: Bi-Metallic. **Weight:** Silver center in Copper ring

Date	AG	Good	VG	Fine	VF	XF
1792 14 known	—	—	—	185,000	325,000	475,000

Note: Norweb, MS-60, $143,000; Heritage 4-12; MS61 $1.15 million

KM#PnF1 Composition: Copper **Note:** No silver center.

Date	AG	Good	VG	Fine	VF	XF
1792 9 known	—	—	—	250,000	500,000	750,000

Note: Norweb, EF-40, $35,200; Benson, VG-10, $57,500

KM#PnG1 Composition: Copper **Edge:** Plain **Note:** Commonly called "Birch cent."

Date	AG	Good	VG	Fine	VF	XF
1792 unique	—	—	—	—	—	650,000

KM#PnH1 Composition: Copper **Obverse:** One star in edge legend **Note:** Commonly called "Birch cent."

Date	AG	Good	VG	Fine	VF	XF
1792 2 known	—	—	—	—	—	600,000

Note: Norweb, EF-40, $59,400

KM#PnI1 Composition: Copper **Obverse:** Two stars in edge legend **Note:** Commonly called "Birch cent."

Date	AG	Good	VG	Fine	VF	XF
1792 8 known	—	—	—	200,000	400,000	550,000

Note: Hawn, strong VF, $57,750

KM# PnJ1 **Composition:** White Metal **Reverse:** "G.W.Pt." below wreath tie **Note:** Commonly called "Birch cent."

Date	AG	Good	VG	Fine	VF	XF
1792 unique	—	—	—	—	—	—

Note: Garrett, $90,000

HALF DISME

KM# 5 **Composition:** Silver

Date	AG	VG	Fine	VF	XF	Unc
1792	25,000	35,000	55,000	90,000	125,000	450,000

KM# PnA1 **Composition:** Copper

Date	AG	Good	VG	Fine	VF	XF	Unc
1792 unique	—	—	—	—	—	—	—

Note: Heritage Auction, 4-06, 5p-67 realized $1,322,500

DISME

KM# PnB1 **Composition:** Silver

Date	AG	Good	VG	Fine	VF	XF
1792 3 known	—	—	—	—	700,000	1,000,000

Note: Norweb, EF-40, $28,600

KM# PnC1 **Composition:** Copper **Edge:** Reeded

Date	Good	VG	Fine	VF	XF	Unc
1792 14 known	—	—	—	150,000	250,000	500,000

Note: Hawn, VF, $30,800; Benson, EF-45, $109,250

KM# PnD1 **Composition:** Copper **Edge:** Plain

Date	AG	Good	VG	Fine	VF	XF
1792 2 known	—	—	—	—	450,000	750,000

Note: Garrett, $45,000

QUARTER

KM# PnK1 **Composition:** Copper **Edge:** Reeded **Note:** Commonly called "Wright quarter."

Date	AG	Good	VG	Fine	VF	XF
1792 2 known	—	—	—	—	—	—

KM# PnL1 **Composition:** White Metal **Edge:** Plain **Note:** Commonly called "Wright quarter."

Date	AG	Good	VG	Fine	VF	XF
1792 4 known	—	—	—	—	175,000	—

Note: Norweb, VF-30 to EF-40, $28,600

KM# PnM1 **Composition:** White Metal **Note:** Commonly called "Wright quarter."

Date	AG	Good	VG	Fine	VF	XF
1792 die trial	—	—	—	—	—	—

Note: Garrett, $12,000

US TERRITORIAL GOLD

Territorial gold pieces (also referred to as "Private" and "Pioneer" gold) are those struck outside the U.S. Mint and not recognized as official issues by the federal government. The pieces so identified are of various shapes, denominations, and degrees of intrinsic value, and were locally required because of the remoteness of the early gold fields from a federal mint and/or an insufficient quantity of official coinage in frontier areas.

The legality of these privately issued pieces derives from the fact that federal law prior to 1864 prohibited a state from coining money, but did not specifically deny that right to an individual, providing that the privately issued coins did not closely resemble those of the United States.

In addition to coin-like gold pieces, the private minters of the gold rush days also issued gold in ingot and bar form. Ingots were intended for circulation and were cast in regular values and generally in large denominations. Bars represent a miner's deposit after it had been assayed, refined, cast into convenient form (generally rectangular), and stamped with the appropriate weight, fineness, and value. Although occasionally cast in even values for the convenience of banks, bars were more often of odd denomination, and when circulated were rounded off to the nearest figure. Ingots and bars are omitted from this listing.

CALIFORNIA

Fractional and Small Size Gold Coinage

During the California gold rush a wide variety of U.S. and foreign coins were used for small change, but only limited quantities of these coins were available. Gold dust was in common use, although this offered the miner a relatively low value for his gold.

By 1852 California jewelers had begun to manufacture 25¢, 50¢ and $1 gold pieces in round and octagonal shapes. Makers included M. Deriberpe, Antoine Louis Nouizillet, Isadore Routhier, Robert B. Gray, Pierre Frontier, Eugene Deviercy, Herman J. Brand, and Herman and Jacob Levison. Reuben N. Hershfield and Noah Mitchell made their coins in Leavenworth, Kansas and most of their production was seized in August 1871. Herman Kroll made California gold coins in New York City in the 1890s. Only two or three of these companies were in production at any one time. Many varieties bear the makers initials. Frontier and his partners made most of the large Liberty Head, Eagle reverse, and Washington Head design types. Most of the small Liberty Head types were made first by Nouizillet and later by Gray and then the Levison brothers and lastly by the California Jewelry Co. Coins initialed "G.G." are apparently patterns made by Frontier and Deviercy for the New York based firm of Gaime, Guillemot & Co.

Most of the earlier coins were struck from gold alloys and had an intrinsic value of about 50-60 percent of face value. They were generally struck from partially hubbed dies and with reeded collars. A few issues were struck with a plain collar or a collar with reeding on only 7 of the 8 sides. Many issues are too poorly struck or too thin to have a clear and complete image of the collar. The later coins and some of the earlier coins were struck from laminated or plated gold planchets, or from gold plated silver planchets. Most of the last dates of issue are extremely thin and contain only token amounts of gold.

Circumstantial evidence exists that the coins issued through 1856 circulated as small change. The San Francisco mint was established in 1854, and by 1856 it had ramped up its production enough to satisfy the local need for small change. However, some evidence exists that these small gold coins may have continued to circulate on occasion through to 1871. After 1871, the gold content of the coins dramatically decreases and it is very unlikely that any of these last issues circulated.

Although the Private Coinages Act of 1864 outlawed all private coinage, this law was not enforced in California and production of small denominated gold continued through 1882. In the spring of 1883, Col. Henry Finnegass of the U.S. Secret Service halted production of the denominated private gold pieces. Non-denominated tokens (lacking DOLLARS, CENTS or the equivalent) were also made during this latter period, sometimes by the same manufacturing jeweler using the same obverse die and the same planchets as the small denomination gold coins. Production of these tokens continues to this day, with most issues made after the 1906 earthquake and fire being backdated to 1847-1865 and struck from brass or gold plated brass planchets.

Approximately 25,000 pieces of California small denomination gold coins are estimated to exist, in a total of over 500 varieties. A few varieties are undated, mostly gold rush era pieces; and a few of the issues are backdated, mostly those from the 1880's. This listing groups varieties together in easily identified categories. The prices quoted are for the most common variety in each group. UNC prices reflect the median auction prices realized of MS60 to MS62 graded coins. BU prices reflect the median auction prices realized of MS63 to MS64 graded coins. Pre-1871 true MS-65 coins are rare and sell for substantial premiums over the prices on this list. Post-1871 coins are rarely found with wear and often have a cameo proof appearance. Auction prices realized are highly volatile and it is not uncommon to find recent records of sales at twice or half of the values shown here. Many of the rarity estimates published in the 1980s and earlier have proven to be too high, so caution is advised when paying a premium for a rare variety. In addition, many varieties that have a refined appearance command higher prices than equivalent grade but scarcer varieties that have a more crude appearance.

Several counterfeits of California Fractional Gold coins exist. Beware of 1854 and 1858 dated round 1/2 dollars, and 1871 dated round dollars that have designs that do not match any of the published varieties. Beware of reeded edge Kroll coins being sold as originals (see the listings below).

For further information consult "California Pioneer Fractional Gold" by W. Breen and R.J. Gillio and "The Brasher Bulletin" the official newsletter of The Society of Private and Pioneer Numismatists.

CALIFORNIA

1/4 DOLLAR (OCTAGONAL)

KM# 1.1 Obverse: Large Liberty head, left **Reverse:** Value and date within beaded circle

Date	Fine	VF	XF	Unc	BU
1853	—	—	—	250	350
1854	—	—	—	300	400
1855	—	—	—	300	400
1856	—	—	—	310	425

KM# 1.10 Obverse: "Oriental" Liberty head, left, above date **Reverse:** 1/4 CALDOLL withn wreath

Date	Fine	VF	XF	Unc	BU
1881	—	—	—	1,000	3,000

KM# 1.11 Obverse: Large Liberty head, left, above 1872 **Reverse:** Value and 1871 within wreath

Date	Fine	VF	XF	Unc	BU
1872-71	—	—	—	1,000	3,000

KM# 1.2 Obverse: Liberty head, left **Reverse:** Value and date within wreath

Date	Fine	VF	XF	Unc	BU
1859	—	—	—	200	450
1864	—	—	—	250	400
1866	—	—	—	250	400
1867	—	—	—	250	400
1868	—	—	—	200	350
1869	—	—	—	200	350
1870	—	—	—	200	350
1871	—	—	—	200	350

KM# 1.3 Obverse: Large Liberty head, left, above date **Reverse:** 1/4 DOLLAR and CAL within wreath

Date	Fine	VF	XF	Unc	BU
1872	—	—	—	250	400
1873	—	—	—	175	300

KM# 1.4 Obverse: Small Liberty head, left **Reverse:** Value and date within beaded circle

Date	Fine	VF	XF	Unc	BU
1853	—	—	200	325	475

KM# 1.5 Obverse: Small Liberty head, left, above date **Reverse:** Value within wreath

Date	Fine	VF	XF	Unc	BU
1854	—	—	—	300	400

KM# 1.6 Obverse: Small Liberty head, left **Reverse:** Value and date within wreath

Date	Fine	VF	XF	Unc	BU
1855	—	—	—	300	400
1856	—	—	—	275	350
1857 Plain edge	—	—	—	100	150
Note: Kroll type date					
1857 Reeded edge	—	—	—	75.00	110
Note: Kroll type date					
1860 Rare	—	—	—	—	—
1860	—	—	—	200	300
1870	—	—	—	250	350

KM# 1.7 Obverse: Liberty head, left **Reverse:** 1/4 in shield, DOLLAR and date below, all within wreath

Date	Fine	VF	XF	Unc	BU
1863	—	—	—	500	—
1864	—	—	—	240	350
1865	—	—	—	250	550
1866	—	—	—	250	400
1867	—	—	—	200	400
1868	—	—	—	200	—
1869	—	—	—	190	300
1870	—	—	—	200	350

 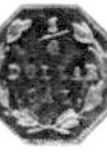

KM# 1.8 Obverse: Small Liberty head, left, above date **Reverse:** 1/4 DOLLAR and CAL, all within wreath

Date	Fine	VF	XF	Unc	BU
1870	—	—	—	225	300
1871	—	—	—	200	250
1871	—	—	—	200	250
1873	—	—	—	400	—
1874	—	—	—	200	275
1875/3	—	—	—	1,000	—
1876	—	—	—	225	300

KM# 1.9 Obverse: "Goofy" Liberty head, left **Reverse:** Value and date within wreath

Date	Fine	VF	XF	Unc	BU
1870	—	—	—	200	300

KM# 2.1 Obverse: Large Indian head, left, above date **Reverse:** Value within wreath

Date	Fine	VF	XF	Unc	BU
1852	—	—	—	340	500

Note: Back dated issue

Date	Fine	VF	XF	Unc	BU
1868	—	—	—	340	500
Note: Back dated issue					
1874	—	—	—	320	450
Note: Back dated issue					
1876	—	—	—	320	450
1878/6	—	—	—	450	650
1880	—	—	—	300	400
1881	—	—	—	320	450

KM# 2.2 Obverse: Large Indian head, left, above date **Reverse:** Value and CAL within wreath

Date	Fine	VF	XF	Unc	BU
1872	—	—	100	260	350
1873/2	—	—	200	600	850
1873	—	—	120	300	400
1874	—	—	100	260	350
1875	—	—	120	300	400
1876	—	—	120	300	400

KM# 2.3 Obverse: Small Indian head, left, above date **Reverse:** 1/4 DOLLAR and CAL, all within wreath

Date	Fine	VF	XF	Unc	BU
1875	—	—	—	250	350
1876	—	—	—	250	500
1881	—	—	—	500	1,100

KM# 2.4 Obverse: "Aztec" Indian head, left, above date **Reverse:** Value and CAL within wreath

Date	Fine	VF	XF	Unc	BU
1880	—	—	—	210	300

KM# 2.6 Obverse: "Dumb" Indian head, left, date below **Reverse:** Value and CAL within wreath

Date	Fine	VF	XF	Unc	BU
1881	—	—	—	650	—

KM# 2.7 Obverse: "Young" Indian head, left, above date **Reverse:** Value within wreath

Date	Fine	VF	XF	Unc	BU
1881	—	—	—	750	—

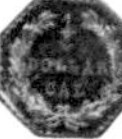

KM# 2.8 Obverse: Indian head, left, above date **Reverse:** 1/4 DOLLAR and CAL, all within wreath

Date	Fine	VF	XF	Unc	BU
1882	—	—	—	500	750

KM# 3 Obverse: Washington head, left, above date **Reverse:** Value and CAL within wreath

Date	Fine	VF	XF	Unc	BU
1872	—	—	—	1,250	2,000

1/4 DOLLAR (ROUND)

KM# 4 Obverse: Defiant eagle above date **Reverse:** 25 CENTS within wreath

Date	Fine	VF	XF	Unc	BU
1854	—	—	11,000	33,000	44,000

KM# 5.1 Obverse: Large Liberty head, left **Reverse:** Value and date within wreath

Date	Fine	VF	XF	Unc	BU
1853	—	—	400	1,000	1,500
1853	—	—	600	1,500	2,250
1853	—	—	600	1,500	2,250
1854	—	—	175	425	625
1858					
Rare	—	—	—	—	—
1859	—	—	95.00	250	300
1865	—	—	115	275	375
1866	—	—	—	250	350
1867	—	—	—	250	350
1868	—	—	—	250	350
1870	—	—	—	250	350
1871	—	—	—	250	350

KM# 5.2 Obverse: Large Liberty head, left, above date **Reverse:** Value and CAL within wreath

Date	Fine	VF	XF	Unc	BU
1871	—	—	—	250	325
1872	—	—	—	300	375
1873	—	—	—	230	300

KM# 5.3 Obverse: Small Liberty head, left **Reverse:** 25 CENTS within wreath

Date	Fine	VF	XF	Unc	BU
	—	—	1,000	2,450	3,500

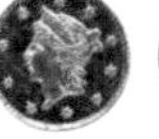

KM# 5.4 Obverse: Small Liberty head, left **Reverse:** "1/4 DOLL." or "DOLLAR" and date in wreath

Date	Fine	VF	XF	Unc	BU
1853	—	—	500	1,200	2,500
	—	—	115	225	375
Note: Rare counterfeit exists					
1855 10 stars	—	—	145	300	400
1855 11 stars	—	—	—	50.00	100
Note: Kroll type					
1856	—	—	125	275	375
1860	—	—	90.00	200	300
1864	—	—	100	225	325
1865	—	—	115	250	375
1866	—	—	150	625	375
1867	—	—	90.00	200	375
1869	—	—	90.00	200	325
1870	—	—	150	275	475

KM# 5.5 Obverse: Small Liberty head, left **Reverse:** Value in shield and date within wreath

Date	Fine	VF	XF	Unc	BU
1863/1860 Rare	—	—	—	—	—
Note: Struck over 1/4 Dollar KM#5.4					
1863	—	—	80.00	200	—
1870 Rare	—	—	—	—	—

KM# 5.6 Obverse: Small Liberty head, left, above date **Reverse:** 1/4 DOLLAR CAL within wreath

Date	Fine	VF	XF	Unc	BU
1870	—	—	100	200	250
1871	—	—	100	200	250
1871	—	—	—	210	350
1873	—	—	—	300	500
1874	—	—	—	300	500
1875	—	—	—	250	475
1876	—	—	—	225	400

KM# 5.7 Obverse: "Goofy" Liberty head, left **Reverse:** Value and date within wreath

Date	Fine	VF	XF	Unc	BU
1870	—	—	110	220	275

KM# 5.8 Obverse: Liberty head left, H and date below **Reverse:** 1/4 DOLLAR CAL within wreath

Date	Fine	VF	XF	Unc	BU
1871	—	—	180	225	375

KM# 6.1 Obverse: Large Indian head left, date below **Reverse:** Value within wreath

Date	Fine	VF	XF	Unc	BU
1852	—	—	—	350	450
Note: Back dated issue					
1868	—	—	—	400	525
Note: Back dated issue					
1874	—	—	—	350	425
Note: Back dated issue					
1876	—	—	—	350	475
1878/6	—	—	—	350	450
1880	—	—	—	250	375
1881	—	—	—	250	375

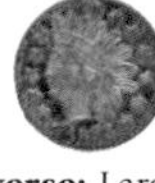

KM# 6.2 Obverse: Large Indian head left, date below **Reverse:** 1/4 DOLLAR CAL within wreath

Date	Fine	VF	XF	Unc	BU
1872/1	—	—	—	250	350
1873	—	—	—	325	425
1874	—	—	—	230	325
1875	—	—	—	250	350
1876	—	—	—	250	350

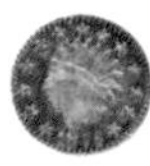

KM# 6.3 Obverse: Small Indian head left, date below **Reverse:** Value within wreath

Date	Fine	VF	XF	Unc	BU
1875	—	—	125	300	450
1876	—	—	115	250	400
1881 Rare	—	—	—	—	—

KM# 6.4 Obverse: "Young" Indian head left, date below **Reverse:** 1/4 DOLLAR CAL within wreath

Date	Fine	VF	XF	Unc	BU
1882	—	—	400	1,225	1,750

KM# 7 Obverse: Washington head left, date below **Reverse:** 1/4 DOLLAR CAL within wreath

Date	Fine	VF	XF	Unc	BU
1872	—	—	—	1,100	1,450

1/2 DOLLAR (OCTAGONAL)

KM# 8.1 Obverse: Liberty head left, date below **Reverse:** 1/2 DOLLAR in beaded circle, CALIFORNIA GOLD around

Date	Fine	VF	XF	Unc	BU
1853	—	—	165	350	450
1854	—	—	110	285	350
Note: Rare counterfeit exists					
1854	—	—	165	350	450
1856	—	—	165	365	450

KM# 8.10 Obverse: "Goofy" Liberty head, left **Reverse:** Value and date within wreath

Date	Fine	VF	XF	Unc	BU
1870	—	—	75.00	200	300

KM# 8.11 Obverse: "Oriental" Liberty head left, date below **Reverse:** 1/2 CALDOLL within wreath

Date	Fine	VF	XF	Unc	BU
1881	—	—	250	750	1,150

KM# 8.2 Obverse: Liberty head, left **Reverse:** Small eagle with rays ("peacock")

Date	Fine	VF	XF	Unc	BU
1853	—	—	800	2,000	3,000

KM# 8.3 Obverse: Large Liberty head, left **Reverse:** Large eagle with date

Date	Fine	VF	XF	Unc	BU
1853	—	—	5,000	10,000	—

KM# 8.4 **Obverse:** Liberty head, left **Reverse:** Value and date within wreath

Date	Fine	VF	XF	Unc	BU
1859	—	—	—	225	300
1866	—	—	—	325	425
1867	—	—	—	250	325
1868	—	—	—	250	325
1869	—	—	—	275	375
1870	—	—	—	275	375
1871	—	—	—	250	325

KM# 8.5 **Obverse:** Large Liberty head left, date below **Reverse:** HALF / DOLLAR / CAL within wreath

Date	Fine	VF	XF	Unc	BU
1872	—	—	—	275	375
1873	—	—	—	250	325

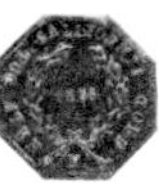

KM# 8.6 **Obverse:** Liberty head, left **Reverse:** HALF DOL. CALIFORNIA GOLD around wreath, date within

Date	Fine	VF	XF	Unc	BU
1854	—	—	100	350	500
1855	—	—	90.00	300	400
1856	—	—	90.00	265	325
1856	—	—	165	1,100	—
Note: Back date issue struck in 1864					
1868	—	—	70.00	185	275
Note: Kroll type					

KM# 8.7 **Obverse:** Small Liberty head left **Reverse:** HALF / DOLLAR /date all within wreath

Date	Fine	VF	XF	Unc	BU
1864	—	—	—	275	350
Note: A rare silver strike of 1864G is known					
1870	—	—	—	275	—

KM# 8.8 **Obverse:** Liberty head left **Reverse:** CAL. GOLD / HALF DOL and date within wreath

Date	Fine	VF	XF	Unc	BU
1869	—	—	—	200	350
1870	—	—	—	200	350

KM# 8.9 **Obverse:** Small Liberty head left, date below **Reverse:** HALF DOLLAR CAL within wreath

Date	Fine	VF	XF	Unc	BU
1870	—	—	75.00	200	300
1871	—	—	75.00	200	250
1871	—	—	75.00	165	250
1873	—	—	95.00	300	600
1874	—	—	95.00	300	600
1875	—	—	250	1,000	—
1876	—	—	75.00	200	250

KM# 9.1 **Obverse:** Large Indian head left, date below **Reverse:** Value within wreath

Date	Fine	VF	XF	Unc	BU
1852	—	—	—	700	1,100
Note: Back dated issue					
1868	—	—	—	850	1,200
Note: Back dated issue					
1874	—	—	—	700	1,100
Note: Back dated issue					
1876	—	—	—	350	450
1880	—	—	—	350	450
1881	—	—	—	350	450

KM# 9.2 **Obverse:** Large Indian head left, date below **Reverse:** 1/2 DOLLAR CAL within wreath

Date	Fine	VF	XF	Unc	BU
1852	—	—	—	500	750
Note: Back dated issue					
1868	—	—	—	300	600
Note: Back dated issue					
1872	—	—	—	250	350
1873/2	—	—	—	250	450
1873	—	—	—	250	350
1874/3	—	—	—	300	400
1874	—	—	—	250	475
1875	—	—	—	300	350
1876	—	—	—	300	450
1878/6	—	—	—	300	450
1880	—	—	—	550	1,050
1881	—	—	—	300	450

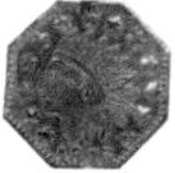

KM# 9.3 **Obverse:** Small Indian head left, date below **Reverse:** Value and CAL within wreath

Date	Fine	VF	XF	Unc	BU
1875	—	—	—	350	525
1876	—	—	—	350	525

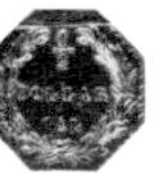

KM# 9.4 **Obverse:** "Young" Indian head left, date below **Reverse:** 1/2 DOLLAR CAL within wreath

Date	Fine	VF	XF	Unc	BU
1881	—	—	—	550	850
1882 Rare	—	—	—	—	—

1/2 DOLLAR (ROUND)

KM# 10 **Obverse:** Arms of California and date **Reverse:** Eagle and legends

Date	Fine	VF	XF	Unc	BU
1853	—	—	—	—	—

KM# 11.1 Obverse: Liberty head, left **Reverse:** Large eagle and legends

Date	Fine	VF	XF	Unc	BU
1854	—	—	1,000	6,000	—

Note: Similar obverse paired with reverse of KM#12.2, or an eagle with no denomination are modern counterfeits

KM# 11.11 Obverse: "Goofy" Liberty head, left **Reverse:** Value and date within wreath

Date	Fine	VF	XF	Unc	BU
1870	—	—	150	400	700

KM# 11.12 Obverse: Liberty head left, H and date below **Reverse:** Value and CAL within wreath

Date	Fine	VF	XF	Unc	BU
1871	—	—	210	500	575

KM# 11.2 Obverse: Liberty head left, date below **Reverse:** HALF DOL. CALIFORNIA GOLD around wreath

Date	Fine	VF	XF	Unc	BU
1854	—	—	200	450	600

KM# 11.3 Obverse: Liberty head left **Reverse:** Date in wreath, value and CALIFORNIA GOLD around wreath

Date	Fine	VF	XF	Unc	BU
1852	—	—	195	375	500
1852	—	—	195	375	500
1853	—	—	195	375	500
1853	—	—	215	400	525
1853	—	—	215	400	525
1854	—	—	300	750	1,000
1854 Large head, small stars	—	—	750	1,500	3,000
1854 Small head, small stars	—	—	—	200	300
Note: Kroll type.					
1854 Large stars	—	—	—	—	—
Note: Common counterfeit					
1855	—	—	225	425	650
1856	—	—	150	325	425
1860/56	—	—	175	350	500

KM# 11.4 Obverse: Liberty head, left **Reverse:** Small eagle and legends

Date	Fine	VF	XF	Unc	BU
1853 Rare	—	—	—	—	—
1853	—	—	5,000	10,000	15,000

KM# 11.5 Obverse: Liberty head left **Reverse:** Value in wreath; CALIFORNIA GOLD and date around wreath

Date	Fine	VF	XF	Unc	BU
1853	—	—	150	750	1,500

KM# 11.6 Obverse: Liberty head left **Reverse:** Value and date within wreath

Date	Fine	VF	XF	Unc	BU
Rare	—	—	—	—	—
1854 13 stars	—	—	850	3,000	—
1854 12 stars	—	—	—	—	—
Note: Rare counterfeit without "FD" beneath truncation					
1855	—	—	180	450	600
1859	—	—	275	750	1,000
1859	—	—	—	275	425
1865	—	—	—	250	375
1866	—	—	—	275	425
1867	—	—	—	250	375
1868	—	—	—	275	425
1869	—	—	—	275	425
1870	—	—	—	250	375
1871	—	—	—	225	325
1873	—	—	—	275	475

Note: A rare counterfeit exists for this date

KM# 11.7 Obverse: Liberty head left, date below **Reverse:** Value and CAL within wreath

Date	Fine	VF	XF	Unc	BU
1870	—	—	—	300	450
1871	—	—	—	300	450
Note: Common, yet deceptive, counterfeits exist					
1871	—	—	—	450	—
1872	—	—	—	300	450
1873	—	—	—	450	1,000
1874	—	—	—	300	750
1875	—	—	—	350	800
1876	—	—	—	300	—

KM# 11.8 Obverse: Liberty head left **Reverse:** Value and date within wreath, CALIFORNIA GOLD around

Date	Fine	VF	XF	Unc	BU
1863	—	—	275	675	950

Note: This issue is a rare Kroll type. All 1858 dates of this type are counterfeits

KM# 11.9 Obverse: Liberty head left **Reverse:** HALF DOLLAR and date within wreath

Date	Fine	VF	XF	Unc	BU
1864	—	—	150	300	400
Note: A rare silver strike is known					
1866	—	—	330	800	1,000
1867	—	—	150	300	375

Date	Fine	VF	XF	Unc	BU
1868	—	—	150	300	375
1869	—	—	175	350	—
1870	—	—	—	400	—

KM# 12.1 Obverse: Large Indian head left, date below **Reverse:** Value within wreath **Note:** 1852, 1868 and 1874 are backdated issues

Date	Fine	VF	XF	Unc	BU
1852	—	—	—	375	675
1868	—	—	—	325	600
1874	—	—	—	325	600

Note: Similar obverse paired with reverse of KM#11.2 or an eagle with no denomination are modern counterfeits

Date	Fine	VF	XF	Unc	BU
1876	—	—	—	225	275
1878/6	—	—	—	325	475
1880	—	—	—	275	425
1881	—	—	—	275	425

KM# 12.2 Obverse: Large Indian head left, date below **Reverse:** Value and CAL within wreath

Date	Fine	VF	XF	Unc	BU
1872	—	—	—	250	350
1873/2	—	—	—	400	700
1873	—	—	—	250	350
1874/3	—	—	—	350	500
1874	—	—	—	250	350
1875/3	—	—	—	250	350
1875	—	—	—	350	550
1876/5	—	—	—	250	350
1876	—	—	—	400	650

KM# 12.3 Obverse: Small Indian head left, date below **Reverse:** Value and CAL within wreath

Date	Fine	VF	XF	Unc	BU
1875	—	—	100	300	500
1876	—	—	75.00	250	350

KM# 12.4 Obverse: "Young" Indian head left, date above **Reverse:** Value and CAL within wreath

Date	Fine	VF	XF	Unc	BU
1882	—	—	—	850	—

DOLLAR (OCTAGONAL)

KM# 13.1 Obverse: Liberty head left **Reverse:** Large eagle and legends

Date	Fine	VF	XF	Unc	BU
	—	—	1,000	2,200	4,000
1853	—	—	5,000	7,500	—
1854	—	—	1,500	3,200	5,000

KM# 13.2 Obverse: Liberty head left **Reverse:** Value and date in beaded circle; CALIFORNIA GOLD and initials around

Date	Fine	VF	XF	Unc	BU
1853	—	—	275	750	1,100
1853	—	—	450	1,100	—
1853	—	—	300	900	—
1853	—	—	325	900	1,450
1854	—	—	550	1,300	—
1854	—	—	350	1,100	1,900
1855	—	—	425	1,100	—
1856	—	—	2,100	5,000	—
1863 Reeded edge, restrike	—	—	—	175	275
1863 Plain edge	—	—	—	150	250

Note: Plain edge 1863 dates are original Kroll types, while reeded edge examples are Kroll restrikes

KM# 13.3 Obverse: Liberty head left **Reverse:** Value and date inside wreath; legends outside

Date	Fine	VF	XF	Unc	BU
1854 Rare	—	—	—	—	—

Note: Bowers and Marena sale 5-99, XF $9,775

Date	Fine	VF	XF	Unc	BU
1854	—	—	325	900	1,300
1855	—	—	325	900	1,300
1858	—	—	180	425	725

Note: 1858 dates are Kroll types

Date	Fine	VF	XF	Unc	BU
1859	—	—	1,900	—	—
1860	—	—	—	900	1,200
1868	—	—	—	900	1,300
1869	—	—	—	800	1,100
1870	—	—	—	725	1,100
1871	—	—	—	475	1,000

KM# 13.4 Obverse: "Goofy" Liberty head, left **Reverse:** Value and date within wreath

Date	Fine	VF	XF	Unc	BU
1870	—	—	—	1,200	1,800

Note: Deceptive counterfeits exist

KM# 13.5 Obverse: Liberty head left, date below **Reverse:** Value and date within wreath; CALIFORNIA GOLD around

Date	Fine	VF	XF	Unc	BU
1871	—	—	—	725	1,100
1874	—	—	—	—	—
1875	—	—	—	—	—
1876	—	—	—	—	—

KM# 14.1 Obverse: Large Indian head left, date below **Reverse:** 1 DOLLAR within wreath; CALIFORNIA GOLD around

Date	Fine	VF	XF	Unc	BU
1872	—	—	—	900	1,350
1873/2	—	—	—	1,050	1,650
1873	—	—	—	1,150	—
1874	—	—	—	1,300	1,950

Date	Fine	VF	XF	Unc	BU
1875	—	—	—	900	1,500
1876/5	—	—	—	1,500	1,950

KM# 14.2 **Obverse:** Small Indian head left, date below **Reverse:** 1 DOLLAR CAL within wreath

Date	Fine	VF	XF	Unc	BU
1875	—	—	1,050	1,800	—
1876	—	—	—	2,100	—

KM# 14.3 **Obverse:** Indian head left, date below **Reverse:** 1 DOLLAR within wreath; CALIFORNIA GOLD around

Date	Fine	VF	XF	Unc	BU
1876	—	—	—	1,150	—

DOLLAR (ROUND)

KM# 15.1 **Obverse:** Liberty head left **Reverse:** Large eagle and legends

Date	Fine	VF	XF	Unc	BU
1853 Rare	—	—	—	—	—

Note: Superior sale Sept. 1987 MS-63 $35,200

KM# 15.2 **Obverse:** Liberty head left **Reverse:** Value and date within wreath; CALIFORNIA GOLD around

Date	Fine	VF	XF	Unc	BU
1854	—	—	3,000	—	—
1854	—	—	5,000	—	—
1854 Rare	—	—	—	—	—
Note: Superior sale Sept. 1988 Fine $13,200					
1857 4 known	—	—	—	—	—
1870	—	—	750	3,000	—
1871	—	—	1,300	3,750	—

Note: Counterfeit exists

KM# 15.3 **Obverse:** Liberty head left, date below **Reverse:** Value within wreath; CALIFORNIA GOLD around

Date	Fine	VF	XF	Unc	BU
1870	—	—	750	2,100	3,000
1871	—	—	750	2,100	3,000

KM# 15.4 **Obverse:** "Goofy" Liberty head left **Reverse:** Value and date within wreath; CALIFORNIA GOLD around

Date	Fine	VF	XF	Unc	BU
1870	—	—	600	2,250	—

KM# 16 **Obverse:** Large Indian head left, date below **Reverse:** Value within wreath; CALIFORNIA GOLD outside

Date	Fine	VF	XF	Unc	BU
1872	—	—	975	2,700	3,600

U.S. Territorial Gold Coinage

Private Assay Office Issues

CALIFORNIA

Norris, Grieg & Norris produced the first territorial gold coin struck in California, a $5 piece struck in 1849 at Benicia City, though it bears the imprint of San Francisco. The coining facility was owned by Thomas H. Norris, Charles Greig, and Hiram A. Norris, members of a New York engineering firm. A unique 1850 variety of this coin has the name STOCKTON beneath the date, instead of SAN FRANCISCO.

Early in 1849, John Little Moffat, a New York assayer, established an assay office at San Francisco in association with Joseph R. Curtis, Philo H. Perry, and Samuel Ward. The first issues of the **Moffat & Co.** assay office consisted of rectangular $16 ingots and assay bars of various and irregular denominations. In early August, the firm began striking $5 and $10 gold coins which resemble those of the U.S. Mint in design, but carry the legend S.M.V. (Standard Mint Value) CALIFORNIA GOLD on the reverse. Five-dollar pieces of the same design were also issued in 1850.

On Sept. 30, 1850, Congress directed the Secretary of the Treasury to establish an official Assay Office in California. Moffat & Co. obtained a contract to perform the duties of the U.S. Assay Office. **Augustus Humbert**, a New York watchcase maker, was appointed U.S. Assayer of Gold in California. Humbert stamped the first octagonal coin-ingots of the Provisional Government Mint on Jan. 31, 1851. The $50 pieces were accepted at par with standard U.S. gold coins, but were not officially recognized as coins. Officially, they were designated as "ingots." Colloquially, they were known as slugs, quintuple eagles, or 5-eagle pieces.

The $50 ingots failed to alleviate the need of California for gold coins. The banks regarded them as disadvantageous to their interests and utilized them only when compelled to do so by public need or convenience. Being of sound value, the ingots drove the overvalued $5, $10, and $20 territorial gold coins from circulation, bringing about a return to the use of gold dust for everyday transactions. Eventually, the slugs became so great a nuisance that they were discounted 3 percent when accepted. This unexpected turn of events forced Moffat & Co. to resume the issuing of $10 and $20 gold coins in 1852. The $10 piece was first issued with the Moffat & Co. imprint on Liberty's coronet, and later with the official imprint of Augustus Humbert on reverse. The $20 piece was issued with the Humbert imprint.

On Feb. 14, 1852, John L. Moffat withdrew from Moffat & Co. to enter the diving bell business, and Moffat & Co. was reorganized as the **United States Assay Office of Gold**, composed of Joseph R. Curtis, Philo H. Perry, and Samuel Ward. The U.S. Assay Office of Gold issued gold coins in denominations of $50 and $10 in 1852, and $20 and $10 in 1853. With the exception of the $50 slugs, they carry the imprint of the Assay Office on reverse. The .900 fine issues of this facility reflect an attempt to bring the issues of the U.S. Assay Office into conformity with the U.S. Mint standard.

The last territorial gold coins to bear the imprint of Moffat & Co. are $20 pieces issued in 1853, after the retirement of John L. Moffat. These coins do not carry a mark of fineness, and generally assay below the U.S. Mint standard.

Templeton Reid, previously mentioned in connection with the private gold issues of Georgia, moved his coining equipment to California when gold was discovered there, and in 1849 issued $10 and $25 gold pieces. No specimens are available to present-day collectors. The only known $10 piece is in the Smithsonian Collection. The only known specimen of the $25 piece was stolen from the U.S. Mint Cabinet Collection in 1858 and was never recovered.

Little is known of the origin and location of the **Cincinnati Mining & Trading Co.** It is believed that the firm was organized in the East and was forced to abandon most of its equipment while enroute to California. A few $5 and $10 gold coins were struck in 1849. Base metal counterfeits exist.

The **Massachusetts & California Co.** was organized in Northampton, Mass., in May 1849 by Josiah Hayden, S. S. Wells, Miles G. Moies, and others. Coining equipment was taken to San Francisco where $5 gold pieces were struck in 1849. The few pieces extant are heavily alloyed with copper.

Wright & Co., a brokerage firm located in Portsmouth Square, San Francisco, issued an undated $10 gold piece in the autumn of 1849 under the name of **Miners' Bank**. Unlike most territorial gold pieces, the Miners' Bank eagle was alloyed with copper. The coinage proved to be unpopular because of its copper-induced color and low intrinsic value. The firm was dissolved on Jan. 14, 1850.

In 1849, Dr. **J. S. Ormsby** and Major William M. Ormsby struck gold coins of $5 and $10 denominations at Sacramento under the name of Ormsby & Co. The coinage, which is identified by the initials J. S. O., is undated. Ormsby & Co. coinage was greatly over-valued, the eagle assaying at as little as $9.37.

The **Pacific Co.** of San Francisco issued $5 and $10 gold coins in 1849. The clouded story of this coinage is based on conjecture. It is believed that the well-struck pattern coins of this type were struck in the East by the Pacific Co. that organized in Boston and set sail for California on Feb. 20, 1849, and that the crudely hand-struck pieces were made by the jewelry firm of Broderick and Kohler after the dies passed into their possession. In any event, the intrinsic value of the initial coinage exceeded face value, but by the end of 1849, when they passed out of favor, the coins had been debased so flagrantly that the eagles assayed for as little as $7.86.

Dubosq & Co., a Philadelphia jewelry firm owned by Theodore Dubosq Sr. and Jr. and Henry Dubosq, took melting and coining equipment to San Francisco in 1849, and in 1850 issued $5 and $10 gold coins struck with dies allegedly made by U.S. Mint Engraver James B. Longacre. Dubosq & Co. coinage was immensely popular with the forty-niners because its intrinsic worth was in excess of face value.

The minting equipment of David C. Broderick and Frederick D. Kohler (see Pacific Co.) was acquired in May 1850 by San Francisco jewelers George C. Baldwin and Thomas S. Holman, who organized a private minting venture under the name of **Baldwin & Co**. The firm produced a $5 piece of Liberty Head design and a $10 piece with Horseman device in 1850. Liberty Head $10 and $20 pieces were coined in 1851. Baldwin & Co. produced the first $20 piece issued in California.

Schultz & Co. of San Francisco, a brass foundry located in the rear of the Baldwin & Co. establishment, and operated by Judge G. W. Schultz and William T. Garratt, issued $5 gold coins from early 1851 until April of that year. The inscription "SHULTS & CO." is a misspelling of SCHULTZ & CO.

Dunbar & Co. of San Francisco issued a $5 gold piece in 1851, after Edward E. Dunbar, owner of the California Bank in San Francisco, purchased the coining equipment of the defunct Baldwin & Co.

The San Francisco-based firm of **Wass, Molitor & Co.** was owned by 2 Hungarian exiles, Count S. C. Wass and A. P. Molitor, who initially founded the firm as a gold smelting and assaying plant. In response to a plea from the commercial community for small gold coins, Wass, Molitor & Co. issued $5 and $10 gold coins in 1852. The $5 piece was coined with small head and large head varieties, and the $10 piece with small head, large head, and small close-date varieties. The firm produced a second issue of gold coins in 1855, in denominations of $10, $20, and $50.

The U.S. Assay Office in California closed its doors on Dec. 14, 1853, to make way for the newly established San Francisco Branch Mint. The Mint, however, was unable to start immediate quantity production due to the lack of refining acids. During the interim, John G. Kellogg, a former employee of Moffat & Co., and John Glover Richter, a former assayer in the U.S. Assay Office, formed **Kellogg & Co.** for the purpose of supplying businessmen with urgently needed coinage. The firm produced $20 coins dated 1854 and 1855, after which Augustus Humbert replaced Richter and the enterprise reorganized as Kellogg & Humbert Melters, Assayers & Coiners. Kellogg & Humbert endured until 1860, but issued coins, $20 pieces, only in 1855.

BALDWIN & COMPANY

5 DOLLARS

KM# 17 Obverse: Liberty head left, date below **Reverse:** Eagle

Date	Fine	VF	XF	Unc	BU
1850	7,500	12,000	22,500	47,500	—

10 DOLLARS

KM# 18 Obverse: Figure on horseback right, swinging rope, date and value below **Reverse:** Eagle **Obverse Legend:** CALIFORNIA GOLD. **Reverse Legend:** BALDWIN & C.o

Date	Fine	VF	XF	Unc	BU
1850	32,500	65,000	97,500	200,000	—

Note: Bass Sale May 2000, MS-64 $149,500

KM# 19 Obverse: Coronet head left within circle of stars, date below **Reverse:** Eagle **Reverse Legend:** S.M.V. CALIFORNIA GOLD

Date	Fine	VF	XF	Unc	BU
1851	10,000	22,000	37,500	125,000	—

20 DOLLARS

KM# 20 Obverse: Coronet head, left, within circle of stars, date below **Reverse:** Eagle **Reverse Legend:** S.M.V. CALIFORNIA GOLD

Date	Fine	VF	XF	Unc	BU
1851 Rare	—	—	—	—	—

Note: Stack's Superior Sale Dec. 1988, XF-40 $52,800; Beware of copies cast in base metals

BLAKE & COMPANY

20 DOLLARS

KM# 21 Obverse: Value within small center circle, legend around **Reverse:** Coining screw press at centre, date and value below **Obverse Legend:** BLAKE & CO. ASSAYERS **Reverse Legend:** ...CALIFORNIA GOLD

Date	Fine	VF	XF	Unc	BU
1855	—	—	—	—	—

Note: No original specimens are known. Most experts believe this to be a counterfeit circa 1950. Many modern copies exist

J. H. BOWIE

5 DOLLARS

KM# 22 Obverse: Value at center, Company name above **Reverse:** Pine tree **Reverse Legend:** CAL. GOLD 1849

Date	Fine	VF	XF	Unc	BU
1849 Rare	—	—	—	—	—

Note: Americana Sale Jan. 2001, AU-58 $253,000

CINCINNATI MINING AND TRADING COMPANY

5 DOLLARS

KM# 23 Obverse: Draped bust with headress left **Reverse:** Eagle with shield left, date below **Obverse Legend:** CINCINNATI MINING & TRADING COMPANY.

Date	Fine	VF	XF	Unc	BU
1849 Unique	—	—	—	—	—

10 DOLLARS

KM# 24 Obverse: Draped bust with headdress left **Reverse:** Eagle with shield left, date below **Obverse Legend:** CINCINNATI MINING & TRADING COMPANY.

Date	Fine	VF	XF	Unc	BU
1849 Rare	—	—	—	—	—

Note: Stack's-Bowers sale 2004, XF realized $431,250; Brand Sale 1984, XF $104,500

DUBOSQ & COMPANY

5 DOLLARS

KM# 26

Date	Fine	VF	XF	Unc	BU
1850	120,000	225,000	—	—	—

10 DOLLARS

KM# 27 Obverse: Coronet head left, within circle of stars, date below **Reverse:** Eagle **Reverse Legend:** S.M.V. CALIFORNIA GOLD

Date	Fine	VF	XF	Unc	BU
1850	120,000	200,000	300,000	—	—

DUNBAR & COMPANY

5 DOLLARS

KM# 28 Obverse: Coronet head left, within circle of stars, date below **Reverse:** Eagle **Reverse Legend:** S.M.V. CALIFORNIA GOLD.

Date	Fine	VF	XF	Unc	BU
1851	125,000	200,000	350,000	—	—

Note: Spink & Son Sale 1988, AU $62,000

AUGUSTUS HUMBERT / UNITED STATES ASSAYER

10 DOLLARS

KM# 29.1 Obverse: Eagle with ribbon, value below **Reverse:** Inscription and date **Obverse Legend:** UNITED STATES OF AMERICA. **Note:** "AUGUSTUS HUMBERT" imprint.

Date	Fine	VF	XF	Unc	BU
1852/1	3,000	5,300	8,500	30,000	—
1852	2,750	4,000	7,250	23,500	—

KM# 29.2 Obverse: Eagle with ribbon, value below **Reverse:** Inscription and date **Note:** Error: IINITED in obverse legend

Date	Fine	VF	XF	Unc	BU
1852/1 Rare	—	—	—	—	—
1852 Rare	—	—	—	—	—

20 DOLLARS

KM# 30 Obverse: Eagle with ribbon and shield **Reverse:** Inscription and date **Obverse Legend:** UNITED STATES OF AMERICA, 884 THOUS on ribbon

Date	Fine	VF	XF	Unc	BU
1852/1	6,500	10,000	22,500	—	—

Note: Mory Sale June 2000, AU-53 $13,800; Garrett Sale March 1980, Humbert's Proof $325,000; Private Sale May 1989, Humbert's Proof (PCGS Pr-65) $1,350,000; California Sale Oct. 2000, Humbert's Proof (PCGS Pr-65) $552,000

50 DOLLARS

KM# 31.1 Obverse: Eagle with ribbon and shield **Reverse:** Target, 50 stamped incuse in center **Obverse Legend:** UNITED STATES OF AMERICA, 880 THOUS on ribbon

Date	Fine	VF	XF	Unc	BU
1851	22,500	40,000	65,000	—	—

KM# 31.1a **Obverse:** 887 THOUS **Reverse:** 50 in center **Obverse Legend:** UNITED STATES OF AMERICA

Date	Fine	VF	XF	Unc	BU
1851	20,000	32,500	55,000	150,000	—

KM# 31.2 **Obverse:** Eagle with ribbon and shield **Reverse:** Target design, without value **Obverse Legend:** UNITED STATES OF AMERICA, 880 THOUS on ribbon

Date	Fine	VF	XF	Unc	BU
1851	17,500	28,500	50,000	130,000	—

KM# 31.2a **Obverse:** Eagle with ribbon and shield **Reverse:** Target design without value **Obverse Legend:** UNITED STATES OF AMERICA, 887 THOUS on ribbon

Date	Fine	VF	XF	Unc	BU
1851	—	45,000	70,000	—	—

KM# 31.3 **Obverse:** Eagle with ribbon and shield **Reverse:** Target design, without value **Obverse Legend:** UNITED STATES OF AMERICA **Note:** ASSAYER inverted on edge.

Date	Fine	VF	XF	Unc	BU
1851 Unique	—	—	—	—	—

KM# 31.4 **Obverse:** Eagle with ribbon and shield **Reverse:** Target design, rays from center, without value **Obverse Legend:** UNITED STATES OF AMERICA, 880 THOUS on ribbon

Date	Fine	VF	XF	Unc	BU
1851 Unique	—	—	—	—	—

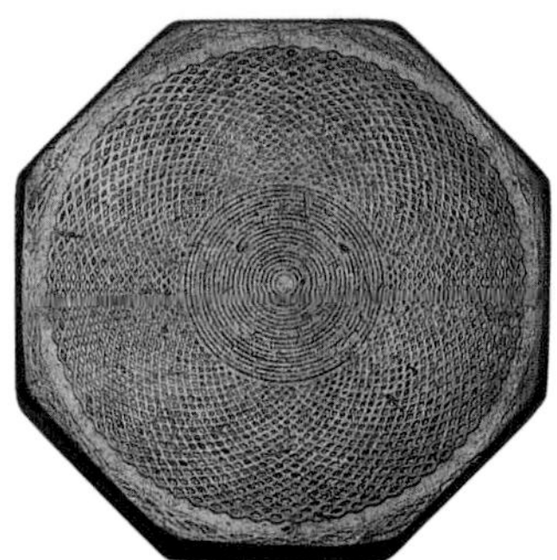

KM# 32.1 **Obverse:** Eagle with ribbon and shield **Reverse:** Target with circular center **Obverse Legend:** UNITED STATES OF AMERICA, 880 THOUS on ribbon

Date	Fine	VF	XF	Unc	BU
1851	12,000	20,000	30,000	75,000	—

Note: Garrett Sale March 1980, Humberts Proof $500,000

KM# 32.2 **Obverse:** Eagle with ribbon and shield **Reverse:** Target, small design **Obverse Legend:** UNITED STASTES OF AMERICA

Date	Fine	VF	XF	Unc	BU
1851	10,000	17,500	35,000	—	—
1852	9,500	16,500	32,000	80,000	—

Note: Bloomfield Sale December 1996, BU $159,500

KELLOGG & COMPANY

20 DOLLARS

KM# 33.1 **Obverse:** Coronet head left, thick date **Reverse:** Eagle with shield, short arrows **Reverse Legend:** SAN FRANCISCO CALIFORNIA

Date	Fine	VF	XF	Unc	BU
1854	2,500	3,500	5,500	19,500	—

KM# 33.2 **Obverse:** Coronet head left, medium date **Reverse:** Eagle with shield

Date	Fine	VF	XF	Unc	BU
1854	2,500	3,500	5,500	19,500	—

KM# 33.3 Obverse: Coronet head left, thin date **Reverse:** Eagle with shield, short arrows **Reverse Legend:** SAN FRANCISCO CALIFORNIA

Date	Fine	VF	XF	Unc	BU
1854	2,500	3,500	5,500	19,500	—

KM# 33.4 Obverse: Coronet head left, thick date **Reverse:** Eagle with shield, large and long arrows **Reverse Legend:** SAN FRANCISCO CALIFORNIA

Date	Fine	VF	XF	Unc	BU
1854	2,500	3,500	5,750	20,000	—
1855	2,650	3,750	6,500	22,000	—

Note: Garrett Sale March 1980 Proof $230,000

KM# 33.5 Obverse: Coronet head left, thick date **Reverse:** Eagle with shield, medium arrows **Reverse Legend:** SAN FRANCISCO CALIFORNIA

Date	Fine	VF	XF	Unc	BU
1855	2,650	3,750	6,500	22,000	—

KM# 33.6 Obverse: Coronet head left **Reverse:** Eagle with shield, short arrows

Date	Fine	VF	XF	Unc	BU
1855	2,650	3,750	6,000	20,000	—

50 DOLLARS

KM# 34 Obverse: Coronet head left, within circle of stars **Reverse:** Banner above eagle, FIFTY DOLLS. in legend **Reverse Legend:** SAN FRANCISCO CALIFORNIA.

Date	Fine	VF	XF	Unc	BU
1855	—	—	—	—	—

Note: Heritage FUN Sale January 2007, Pr64 $747,500. Heritage ANA Sale August 1977, Proof $156,500

MASSACHUSETTS AND CALIFORNIA COMPANY

5 DOLLARS

KM# 35 Obverse: Rearing equestrian figure within shield with bear and dear supporters **Reverse:** Value within wreath, date below **Reverse Legend:** MASSACHUSETTS & CALIFORNIA CO.

Date	Fine	VF	XF	Unc	BU
1849	120,000	170,000	260,000	—	—

US TERRITORIAL GOLD

MINERS BANK

10 DOLLARS

Date	Fine	VF	XF	Unc	BU
(1849)	—	18,500	35,000	90,000	—

Note: Garrett Sale March 1980, MS-65 $135,000

Date	Fine	VF	XF	Unc	BU
(1849)	—	—	—	—	—

Note: Rare, as most specimens have heavy copper alloy

MOFFAT & COMPANY

5 DOLLARS

KM# 37.1 **Obverse:** Coronet head left, within circle of stars, date below **Reverse:** Eagle with shiled **Reverse Legend:** S.M.V. CALIFORNIA GOLD.

Date	Fine	VF	XF	Unc	BU
1849	1,350	2,400	3,750	12,500	—

KM# 37.2 **Obverse:** Coronet head left, within circle of stars, date below **Reverse:** Eagle with shield, die break at DOL

Date	Fine	VF	XF	Unc	BU
1849	1,350	2,400	3,750	12,500	—

KM# 37.3 **Obverse:** Coronet head left, within circle of stars, date below **Reverse:** Eagle with shield, die break on shield

Date	Fine	VF	XF	Unc	BU
1849	1,350	2,400	3,750	12,500	—

KM# 37.4 **Obverse:** Coronet head left, within circle of stars, date below **Reverse:** Eagle with shield, small letters **Reverse Legend:** S.M.V. CALIFORNIA GOLD

Date	Fine	VF	XF	Unc	BU
1850	1,450	2,750	4,500	14,000	—

KM# 37.5 **Obverse:** Coronet head left, within circle of stars, date below **Reverse:** Eagle with shield, large letters

Date	Fine	VF	XF	Unc	BU
1850	1,450	2,750	4,500	14,000	—

Note: Garrett Sale March 1980, MS-60 $21,000

10 DOLLARS

KM# 38.1 **Obverse:** Coronet head left, within circle of stars, date below **Reverse:** Eagle with shield, TEN DOL., middle arrow points below period at end of GOLD **Reverse Legend:** S.M.V. CALIFORNIA GOLD.

Date	Fine	VF	XF	Unc	BU
1849	3,250	6,000	12,000	35,000	—

KM# 38.2 **Obverse:** Coronet head left, within circle of stars, date below **Reverse:** Eagle with shield, middle arrow points above period at end of GOLD.

Date	Fine	VF	XF	Unc	BU
1849	3,250	6,000	12,000	35,000	—

KM# 38.3 **Obverse:** Coronet head, left, within circle of stars, date below **Reverse:** Value: "TEN D.", large letters

Date	Fine	VF	XF	Unc	BU
1849	3,500	6,500	13,500	40,000	—

KM# 38.4 **Obverse:** Coronet head left, within circle of stars, date below **Reverse:** Eagle with shield, small letters

Date	Fine	VF	XF	Unc	BU
1849	3,500	6,500	13,500	40,000	—

KM# 39.1 **Obverse:** Coronet head left, within circle of stars, wide date below **Reverse:** Eagle with ribbon and shield **Reverse Legend:** 264 GRS. CALIFORNIA GOLD **Note:** "MOFFAT & CO." imprint

Date	Fine	VF	XF	Unc	BU
1852	3,750	37,500	12,500	70,000	—

US TERRITORIAL GOLD

KM# 39.2 **Obverse:** Coronet head left, within circle of stars, date below, close date **Reverse:** Eagle with ribbon and shield, 880 THOUS. above **Reverse Legend:** 264 GRS. CALIFORNIA GOLD **Note:** Struck by Augustus Humbert.

Date	Fine	VF	XF	Unc	BU
1852	3,500	6,000	11,500	70,000	—

20 DOLLARS

KM# 40 **Obverse:** Coronet head left, within circle of stars, date below **Reverse:** Eagle and shield, circle of stars and rays above **Reverse Legend:** SAN FRANCISCO CALIFORNIA **Note:** Struck by Curtis, Perry, & Ward.

Date	Fine	VF	XF	Unc	BU
1853	4,250	6,750	10,000	32,500	—

NORRIS, GREIG, & NORRIS

HALF EAGLE

KM# 41.1 **Obverse:** Date in center of circle of stars and legend **Reverse:** Eagle with laurel and arrows, period after ALLOY **Reverse Legend:** CALIFORNIA GOLD ï WITHOUT ALLOY. ï

Date	Fine	VF	XF	Unc	BU
1849	4,250	6,750	13,500	32,500	—

KM# 41.2 **Obverse:** Date in center of circle of stars and legend **Reverse:** Eagle with laurel and arrows, period after ALLOY **Reverse Legend:** CALIFORNIA GOLD ï WITHOUT ALLOY. ï

Date	Fine	VF	XF	Unc	BU
1849	4,250	6,750	13,500	32,500	—

KM# 41.3 **Obverse:** Date in center of circle of stars and legend **Reverse:** Eagle with laurel and arrows, period after ALLOY

Date	Fine	VF	XF	Unc	BU
1849	3,750	6,000	12,500	32,000	—

KM# 41.4 **Obverse:** Date in center of circle of stars and legend **Reverse:** Eagle with laurel and arrows, without period after ALLOY

Date	Fine	VF	XF	Unc	BU
1849	3,750	6,000	12,500	32,000	—

KM# 42 **Obverse:** STOCKTON beneath date **Reverse:** Eagle with laurel and arrows

Date	Fine	VF	XF	Unc	BU
1850 Unique	—	—	—	—	—

J. S. ORMSBY

5 DOLLARS

KM# 43.1 **Obverse:** J.S.O. in center **Reverse:** Value within circle of stars **Obverse Legend:** UNITED STATES OF AMERICA

Date	Fine	VF	XF	Unc	BU
(1849) Unique	—	—	—	—	—

KM# 43.2 **Obverse:** J.S.O. in center **Reverse:** Value within circle of stars

Date	Fine	VF	XF	Unc	BU
(1849) Unique	—	—	—	—	—

Note: Superior Auction 1989, VF $137,500

10 DOLLARS

KM# 44 **Obverse:** J.S.O. in center **Reverse:** Value in center circle of stars **Obverse Legend:** UNITED STATES OF AMERICA

US TERRITORIAL GOLD

Date	Fine	VF	XF	Unc	BU
(1849) Rare	—	—	—	—	—

Note: Garrett Sale March 1980, F-12 $100,000; Ariagno Sale June 1999, AU-50 $145,000

PACIFIC COMPANY

1 DOLLAR

KM# A45 **Obverse:** Liberty cap on pole, stars and rays around, value below **Reverse:** Eagle

Date	Fine	VF	XF	Unc	BU
(1849) Rare	—	—	—	—	—

Note: Stack's Old West Sale August 2006, AU $126,500. Mory Sale June 2000, EF-40 $57,500

5 DOLLARS

KM# 45 **Obverse:** Liberty cap on pole, stars and rays around, value below **Reverse:** Eagle **Reverse Legend:** PACIFIC COMPANY CALIFORNIA

Date	Fine	VF	XF	Unc	BU
1849 Rare	—	—	—	—	—

Note: Garrett Sale March 1980, VF-30 $180,000

10 DOLLARS

KM# 46.1 **Obverse:** Liberty cap on pole, stars and rays around, value below **Reverse:** Eagle, date below **Reverse Legend:** PACIFIC COMPANY CALIFORNIA

Date	Fine	VF	XF	Unc	BU
1849 Rare	—	—	—	—	—

Note: Waldorf Sale 1964, $24,000

KM# 46.2 **Obverse:** Liberty cap on pole, stars and rays around **Reverse:** Eagle

Date	Fine	VF	XF	Unc	BU
1849 Rare	—	—	—	—	—

TEMPLETON REID

10 DOLLARS

KM# 47 **Obverse:** Date in center **Reverse:** Value in center **Obverse Legend:** TEMPLETON... **Reverse Legend:** CALIFORNIA * GOLD *

Date	Fine	VF	XF	Unc	BU
1849 Unique	—	—	—	—	—

20 DOLLARS

KM# 48

Date	Fine	VF	XF	Unc	BU
1849 Unknown	—	—	—	—	—

Note: The only known specimen was stolen from the U.S. Mint in 1858 and has never been recovered. For additional listings of Templeton Reid, see listings under Georgia

SCHULTZ & COMPANY

5 DOLLARS

KM# 49 **Obverse:** Coronet head left, within circle of stars, date below **Reverse:** Eagle, shield on breast, value below **Reverse Legend:** PURE CALIFORNIA GOLD.

Date	Fine	VF	XF	Unc	BU
1851	25,000	55,000	85,000	—	—

UNITED STATES ASSAY OFFICE OF GOLD

10 DOLLARS

KM# 51.1 **Obverse:** Eagle with ribbon and shield **Reverse:** O of OFFICE below I of UNITED **Obverse Legend:** UNITED STATES OF AMERICA TEN DOLS 884 THOUS

Date	Fine	VF	XF	Unc	BU
1852	—	—	—	—	—

Note: Garrett Sale March 1980, MS-60 $18,000

KM# 51.2 **Obverse:** Eagle with ribbon and shield **Reverse:** O below N, strong beads **Obverse Legend:** UNITED STATES OF AMERICA TEN DOLS 884 THOUS

Date	Fine	VF	XF	Unc	BU
1852	1,750	3,000	5,000	17,500	—

KM# 51.3 **Obverse:** Eagle with ribbon and shield **Reverse:** Weak beads **Obverse Legend:** UNITED STATES OF AMERICA TEN DOLS 884 THOUS

Date	Fine	VF	XF	Unc	BU
1852	1,750	3,000	5,000	17,500	—

KM# 52 **Obverse:** Eagle with ribbon and shield **Reverse:** Inscription, date **Obverse Legend:** UNITED STATES OF AMERICA TEN D, 884 THOUS

Date	Fine	VF	XF	Unc	BU
1853	7,500	13,500	25,000	—	—

KM# 52a **Obverse:** Eagle with ribbon and shield **Reverse:** Inscription, date **Obverse Legend:** UNITED STATES OF AMERICA TEN D. 900 THOUS

Date	Fine	VF	XF	Unc	BU
1853	42,000	6,500	10,000	27,500	—

Note: Garrett Sale March 1980, MS-60 $35,000

20 DOLLARS

KM# 53 **Obverse:** Eagle with ribbon and shield **Reverse:** Inscription, date **Obverse Legend:** UNITED STATES OF AMERICA TWENTY D. 884/880 THOUS

Date	Fine	VF	XF	Unc	BU
1853	8,500	12,500	18,500	47,500	—

KM# 53a **Obverse:** Eagle with ribbon and shield **Reverse:** Inscription, date **Obverse Legend:** UNITED STATES OF AMERICA TWENTY D. 900/880 THOUS

Date	Fine	VF	XF	Unc	BU
1853	2,250	3,250	5,000	12,500	—

Note: 1853 Liberty Head listed under Moffat & Company

50 DOLLARS

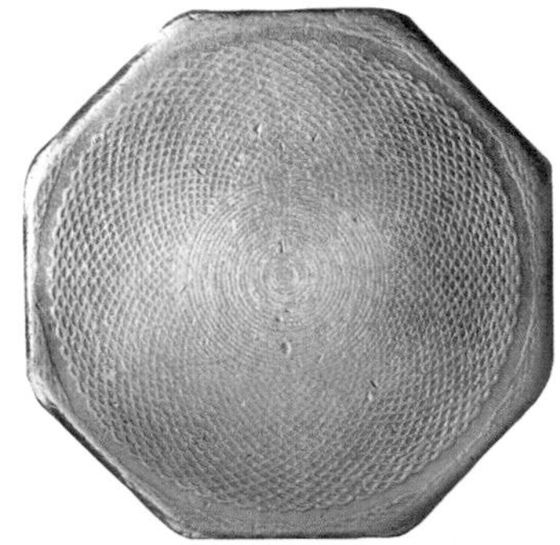

KM# 54 **Obverse:** Eagle with ribbon and shield **Reverse:** Target **Obverse Legend:** UNITED STATES OF AMERICA FIFTY FOLLS. 887 THOUS

Date	Fine	VF	XF	Unc	BU
1852	12,500	20,000	32,000	77,500	—

KM# 54a **Obverse:** Eagle and ribbon with shield **Reverse:** Target **Obverse Legend:** UNITED STATES OF AMERICA FIFTY DOLLS. 900 THOUS

Date	Fine	VF	XF	Unc	BU
1852	12,500	20,000	33,500	82,500	—

WASS, MOLITOR & COMPANY

5 DOLLARS

KM# 55.1 **Obverse:** Small Liberty head, rounded bust **Reverse:** Eagle, shield on breast **Reverse Legend:** ï IN CALIFORNIA GOLD ï FIVE DOLLARS

Date	Fine	VF	XF	Unc	BU
1852	4,500	10,000	20,000	67,500	—

KM# 55.2 **Obverse:** Coronet head, left, within circle of stars **Reverse:** Eagle, shield on breast **Reverse Legend:** ï IN CALIFORNIA GOLD ï FIVE DOLLARS **Note:** Thick planchet.

Date	Fine	VF	XF	Unc	BU
1852 Unique	—	—	—	—	—

KM# 56 **Obverse:** Large Liberty head, pointed bust **Reverse:** Eagle, shield on breast **Reverse Legend:** ï IN CALIFORNIA GOLD ï FIVE DOLLARS

Date	Fine	VF	XF	Unc	BU
1852	4,000	9,000	17,500	60,000	—

10 DOLLARS

KM# 57 **Obverse:** Liberty head with long neck, large date **Reverse:** Eagle, shield on breast **Reverse Legend:** ï S.M.V. CALIFORNIA GOLD ï TEN D.

Date	Fine	VF	XF	Unc	BU
1852	5,500	9,500	18,500	—	—

KM# 58 **Obverse:** Liberty head, short neck, wide date **Reverse:** Eagle, shield on breast **Reverse Legend:** ï S.M.V. CALIFORNIA GOLD ï TEN D.

Date	Fine	VF	XF	Unc	BU
1852	2,800	4,650	7,500	27,500	—

KM# 59.1 **Obverse:** Liberty head, short neck, small date **Reverse:** Eagle, shield on breast **Reverse Legend:** ï S.M.V. CALIFORNIA GOLD ï TEN D.

Date	Fine	VF	XF	Unc	BU
1852	13,500	28,000	50,000	—	—

Note: Eliasberg Sale May 1996, EF-45 $36,300; S.S. Central America Sale December 2000, VF-30 realized $12,650

KM# 59.2 **Obverse:** Plugged date **Reverse:** Eagle, shield on breast **Reverse Legend:** S.M.V.CALIFORNIA GOLD.

Date	Fine	VF	XF	Unc	BU
1855	9,000	14,500	22,000	55,000	—

20 DOLLARS

KM# 60 **Obverse:** Large Liberty head **Reverse:** Eagle, shield on breast, value in banner above **Reverse Legend:** SAN FRANCISCO CALIFORNIA TWENTY DOL. 900 THOUS

Date	Fine	VF	XF	Unc	BU
1855 Rare	—	—	—	—	—

KM# 61 **Obverse:** Small head **Reverse:** Eagle, shield on breast, value in banner above **Reverse Legend:** SAN FRANCISCO CALIFORNIA TWENTY DOL.

Date	Fine	VF	XF	Unc	BU
1855	12,500	25,000	45,000	—	—

Note: Heritage CSNS Sale May 2007, AU55 $43,125

50 DOLLARS

KM# 62 **Obverse:** Coronet head, left, within circle of stars, date below **Reverse:** Value within wreath **Reverse Legend:** SAN FRANCISCO CALIFORNIA WASS MOLITOR & Co 50 DOLLARS

Date	Fine	VF	XF	Unc	BU
1855	22,500	32,500	55,000	165,000	—

Note: Heritage Baltimore Sale July-August 2008, MS-61 $207,000, AU-50 $63,250. Heritage FUN Sale January 2008, MS-60 $161,000. Bloomfield Sale December 1996, BU $170,500

COLORADO

The discovery of gold in Colorado Territory was accompanied by the inevitable need for coined money. Austin M. Clark, Milton E. Clark, and Emanuel H. Gruber, bankers of Leavenworth, Kansas, moved to Denver where they established a bank and issued $2.50, $5, $10, and $20 gold coins in 1860 and 1861. To protect the holder from loss by abrasion, **Clark, Gruber & Co.** made their coins slightly heavier than full value required. The 1860 issues carry the inscription PIKE'S PEAK GOLD on reverse. CLARK, GRUBER & CO. appears on the reverse of the 1861 issues, and PIKE'S PEAK on the coronet of Liberty. The government purchased the plant of Clark, Gruber & Co. in 1863 and operated it as a federal Assay Office until 1906.

In the summer of 1861, **John Parsons**, an assayer whose place of business was located in South Park at the Tarryall Mines, Colorado, issued undated gold coins in the denominations of $2.50 and $5. They, too, carry the inscription PIKE'S PEAK GOLD on reverse.

J. J. Conway & Co., bankers of Georgia Gulch, Colorado operated the Conway Mint for a short period in 1861. Undated gold coins in the denominations of $2.50, $5, and $10 were issued. A variety of the $5 coin does not carry the numeral 5 on reverse. The issues of the Conway Mint were highly regarded for their scrupulously maintained value.Clark, Gruber & Company

2-1/2 DOLLARS

KM# 63 Obverse: Coronet head, left, within circle of stars, date below **Reverse:** Eagle, shield on breast **Reverse Legend:** ï PIKES PEAK GOLD DENVER ï 2 1/2 D.

Date	Fine	VF	XF	Unc	BU
1860	1,500	2,500	3,750	12,500	40,000

Note: Garrett Sale March 1980, MS-65 $12,000

KM# 64.1 Obverse: Coronet head, left, within circle of stars, date below **Reverse:** Eagle, shield on breast **Reverse Legend:** ï CLARK GRUBER & CO DENVER ï 2 1/2 D

Date	Fine	VF	XF	Unc	BU
1861	1,650	2,750	4,000	13,500	—

KM# 64.2 Obverse: Coronet head, left, within circle of stars, date below **Reverse:** Eagle, shield on breast **Reverse Legend:** ï CLARK, GRUBER & CO. DENVER ï 2 1/2 D **Note:** Extra high edge.

Date	Fine	VF	XF	Unc	BU
1861	1,750	3,000	4,500	14,500	—

5 DOLLARS

KM# 65 Obverse: Coronet head, left, within circle of stars, date below **Reverse:** Eagle, shield on breast **Reverse Legend:** ï PIKES PEAK GOLD DENVER ï 2 1/2 D

Date	Fine	VF	XF	Unc	BU
1860	2,000	3,200	4,500	12,500	—

Note: Garrett Sale March 1980, MS-63 $9,000

KM# 66 Obverse: Coronet head, left, within circle of stars, date below **Reverse:** Eagle, shield on breast **Reverse Legend:** ï CLARK GRUBER & CO DENVER ï 2 1/2 D

Date	Fine	VF	XF	Unc	BU
1861	2,500	3,650	6,000	35,000	—

10 DOLLARS

KM# 67 Obverse: Mountain above value **Reverse:** Eagle, shield on breast **Obverse Legend:** PIKES PEAK GOLD / DENVER / TEN D. **Reverse Legend:** CLARK GRUBER & CO.

Date	Fine	VF	XF	Unc	BU
1860	7,250	11,000	17,500	47,500	—

KM# 68 Obverse: Coronet head, left, within circle of stars, date below **Reverse:** Eagle, shield on breast **Reverse Legend:** * CLARK GRUBER & CO DENVER * TEN D.

Date	Fine	VF	XF	Unc	BU
1861	2,500	3,850	6,750	27,500	—

20 DOLLARS

US TERRITORIAL GOLD

KM# 69 Obverse: Mountain above value **Reverse:** Eagle, shield on breast **Obverse Legend:** PIKES PEAK GOLD / DENVER / TWENTY D. **Reverse Legend:** CLARK GRUBER & CO.

Date	Fine	VF	XF	Unc	BU
1860	50,000	100,000	175,000	525,000	—

Note: Heritage FUN Sale January 2006, MS-64 $690,000. Eliasberg Sale May 1996, AU $90,200. Schoonmaker Sale June 1997, VCF $62,700

KM# 70 Obverse: Coronet head, left, within circle of stars, date below **Reverse:** Circle of stars and rays above eagle **Reverse Legend:** CLARK GRUBER & CO DENVER .TWENTY D.

Date	Fine	VF	XF	Unc	BU
1861	14,500	32,500	57,500	—	—

J. J. CONWAY

2-1/2 DOLLARS

KM# 71 Obverse: legend **Reverse:** Value in center **Obverse Legend:** * J.J. CONWAY * / & CO. / BANKERS **Reverse Legend:** * PIKES PEAK * 2 1/2 DOLS

Date	Fine	VF	XF	Unc	BU
(1861)	—	140,000	180,000	—	—

5 DOLLARS

KM# 72.1 Obverse: Legend, ring of stars within **Reverse:** Large 5 in center **Obverse Legend:** * J.J. CONWAY * / & CO. / BANKERS **Reverse Legend:** PIKES PEAK / FIVE DOLLARS

Date	Fine	VF	XF	Unc	BU
(1861) Rare	—	—	—	—	—

Note: Brand Sale June 1984, XF-40 $44,000

KM# 72.2 Obverse: Legend **Reverse:** Legend without large 5 in center **Obverse Legend:** * J.J. CONWAY * / & CO. / BANKERS

Date	Fine	VF	XF	Unc	BU
(1861) Unique	—	—	—	—	—

10 DOLLARS

KM# 73 Obverse: & CO. within circle **Reverse:** Numeral value within circle of stars **Obverse Legend:** * J.J. CONWAY * / & CO. / BANKERS **Reverse Legend:** * PIKES PEAK * TEN DOLLARS

Date	Fine	VF	XF	Unc	BU
(1861) Rare	—	—	—	—	—

JOHN PARSONS

2-1/2 DOLLARS

KM# 74 Obverse: Assay office window and minting machine **Reverse:** Eagle, shield on breast, value below **Obverse Legend:** J PARSON & Co / ORO **Reverse Legend:** PIKES PEAK GOLD / 2 1/2 D

Date	Fine	VF	XF	Unc	BU
(1861) Rare	—	—	—	—	—

Note: Garrett Sale March 1980, VF-20 $85,000

5 DOLLARS

KM# 75 Obverse: Assay office window and minting machine **Reverse:** Eagle, shield on breast, value below **Obverse Legend:** J N. PARSON & Co. / ORO **Reverse Legend:** PIKES PEAK GOLD / TEN D.

Date	Fine	VF	XF	Unc	BU
(1861) Rare	—	—	—	—	—

Note: Garrett Sale March 1980, VF-20 $100,000

GEORGIA

The first territorial gold pieces were struck in 1830 by **Templeton Reid**, a goldsmith and assayer who established a private mint at Gainesville, Georgia, at the time gold was being mined on a relatively large scale in Georgia and North Carolina. Reid's pieces were issued in denominations of $2.50, $5, and $10. Except for an undated variety of the $10 piece, all are dated 1830.Christopher Bechtler

2-1/2 DOLLARS

KM# 76.1 Obverse: 2.50 in center **Reverse:** 64. G. / 22. in center **Obverse Legend:** BECHTLER . RUTHERF : **Reverse Legend:** :GEORGIA GOLD: CARATS

Date	Fine	VF	XF	Unc	BU
	4,200	6,750	12,500	28,500	—

KM# 76.2 Obverse: 2.50 in center **Reverse:** 64. G. / 22. in center, even 22 **Obverse Legend:** BECHLER . RUTHERF : **Reverse Legend:** GEORGIA GOLD : CATATS :

Date	Fine	VF	XF	Unc	BU
	4,500	7,500	13,750	37,500	—

5 DOLLARS

KM# 77 Obverse: Value in center **Reverse:** 128 G / * in center **Obverse Legend:** C. BECHTLER. AT RUTHERF * 5 DOLLARS **Reverse Legend:** GEORGIA GOLD. 22 CARATS.

Date	Fine	VF	XF	Unc	BU
	4,000	7,000	11,000	28,500	—

KM# 78.1 Obverse: Value in center **Reverse:** 128. G. / * in center **Obverse Legend:** C. BECHTLER. AT RUTHERFORD * 5 DOLLARS **Reverse Legend:** GEORGIA GOLD. / 22 CARATS.

Date	Fine	VF	XF	Unc	BU
	4,000	7,500	12,000	32,000	—

KM# 78.2 Obverse: Value in center **Reverse:** 128 G: in center **Obverse Legend:** C. BECHTLER. AT RUTHERFORD / 5 DOLLARS. **Reverse Legend:** GEORGIA GOLD. 22 CARATS.

Date	Fine	VF	XF	Unc	BU
Rare	—	—	—	—	—

Note: Stack's Americana Sale January 2008 AU-58 $115,000. Akers Pittman Sale October 1997, VF-XF $26,400

TEMPLETON REID

2-1/2 DOLLARS

KM# 79 Obverse: Date in center **Reverse:** Value in center **Obverse Legend:** GEORGIA /GOLD. / 1830 **Reverse Legend:** T. REID / ASSAYER.

Date	Fine	VF	XF	Unc	BU
1830	55,000	85,000	165,000	—	—

Note: Stack's Berngard/S.S. New York Sale July 2008 VF35 $103,500. Stack's Norweb Sale November 2006 AU55 $299,000

5 DOLLARS

KM# 80 Obverse: Value in center **Reverse:** Value in center **Obverse Legend:** GEORGIA GOLD. / 1830 / $5 **Reverse Legend:** TEMPLETON REID / ASSAYER. / $5

Date	Fine	VF	XF	Unc	BU
1830 Rare, 7 known	—	—	—	—	—

Note: Garrett Sale November 1979, XF-40 $200,000

10 DOLLARS

KM# 81 **Obverse:** Date at center **Reverse:** Written value at center **Obverse Legend:** GEORGIA / GOLD / 1830 **Reverse Legend:** TEMPLETON REID / ASSAYER / TEN / DOLLARS

Date	Fine	VF	XF	Unc	BU
1830 Rare, 6 known	—	—	—	—	—

KM# 82 **Obverse:** Without date at center **Reverse:** Written value at center **Obverse Legend:** GEORGIA / GOLD **Reverse Legend:** TEMPLETON REID / ASSAYER / TEN / DOLLARS

Date	Fine	VF	XF	Unc	BU
(1830) Rare, 3 known	—	—	—	—	—

Note: Also see listings under California

NORTH CAROLINA

The southern Appalachians were also the scene of a private gold minting operation conducted by Christopher Bechtler Sr., his son August, and nephew Christopher Jr. The Bechtlers, a family of German metallurgists, established a mint at Rutherfordton, North Carolina, which produced territorial gold coins for a longer period than any other private mint in American history. Christopher Bechtler Sr. ran the Bechtler mint from July 1831 until his death in 1842, after which the mint was taken over by his son August who ran it until 1852.

The Bechtler coinage includes but 3 denominations -- $1, $2.50, and $5 - but they were issued in a wide variety of weights and sizes. The coinage is undated, except for 3 varieties of the $5 piece which carry the inscription "Aug. 1, 1834" to indicate that they conform to the new weight standard adopted by the U.S. Treasury for official gold coins. **Christopher Bechtler Sr.** produced $2.50 and $5 gold coins for Georgia, and $1, $2.50, and $5 coins for North Carolina. The dollar coins have the distinction of being the first gold coins of that denomination to be produced in the United States. While under the supervision of **August Bechtler**, the Bechtler mint issued $1 and $5 coins for North Carolina.

AUGUST BECHTLER

DOLLAR

KM# 83.1 **Obverse:** Large 1 in center **Reverse:** 27. G. in center **Obverse Legend:** A. BECHTLER. / 1 / DOL: * **Reverse Legend:** CAROLINA GOLD. / 21C.

Date	Fine	VF	XF	Unc	BU
(1842-52)	900	1,450	2,250	4,750	—

KM# 83.2 **Obverse:** Value in center **Reverse:** 27 G. in center **Obverse Legend:** A. BECHTLER . / 1 /DOL: **Reverse Legend:** CAROLINA GOLD . / 21 C.

Date	Fine	VF	XF	Unc	BU
(1842-52)	900	1,450	2,250	4,750	—

5 DOLLARS

KM# 84 **Obverse:** Value in two lines in center **Reverse:** 134 G. at center **Obverse Legend:** A. BECHTLER. RUTHERFORD * / 5 / DOLLARS **Reverse Legend:** CAROLINA GOLD. / 21/ CARATS.

Date	Fine	VF	XF	Unc	BU
(1842-52)	2,650	5,300	9,000	32,500	—

KM# 85 **Obverse:** Value in two lines in center **Reverse:** 128 G. in center **Obverse Legend:** A. BECHTLER. RUTHERFORD / 5 / DOLLARS **Reverse Legend:** CAROLINA GOLD. / 22 / CARATS

Date	Fine	VF	XF	Unc	BU
(1842-52)	7,000	12,500	18,000	42,500	—

KM# 86 **Obverse:** Value in two lines in center **Reverse:** 141. G: in center **Obverse Legend:** A.

BECHTLER. RUTHERFORD / 5 / DOLLARS. **Reverse Legend:** CAROLINA GOLD. / 20 / CARATS

Date	Fine	VF	XF	Unc	BU
(1842-52)	6,500	11,500	17,000	38,500	—
(1842-52) Proof restrike	—	—	—	—	—

Note: Struck from original dies by Henry Chapman in 1908. Stack's Nerngard/S.S. New York Sale July 2008 Pr63 sold for $34,500. Akers Pittman Sale October 1997 chPr $14,300

CHRISTOPHER BECHTLER

DOLLAR

KM# 87 **Obverse:** 28 G. in center **Reverse:** ONE in center, N reversed **Obverse Legend:** * BECHTLER RUTHERF: / 28. G. **Reverse Legend:** * CAROLINA DOLLAR / ONE

Date	Fine	VF	XF	Unc	BU
(1831-42)	1,250	2,200	3,000	7,500	—

KM# 88.1 **Obverse:** 28. G. centered in center **Reverse:** ONE at center **Obverse Legend:** C: BECHTLER. RUTHERF: **Reverse Legend:** N: CAROLINA GOLD. DOLLAR. / ONE

Date	Fine	VF	XF	Unc	BU
(1831-42)	2,400	4,000	6,000	24,000	—

KM# 88.2 **Obverse:** 28 G high in center **Reverse:** ONE in center **Obverse Legend:** C: BECHTLER RUTHERF: / 28 G. **Reverse Legend:** N. CAROLINA GOLD DOLLAR / ONE

Date	Fine	VF	XF	Unc	BU
(1831-42)	5,000	8,500	12,500	32,500	—

KM# 89 **Obverse:** 30 G. /* in center **Reverse:** ONE at center **Obverse Legend:** C. BECHTLER. RUTHERF: / 30 G. / * **Reverse Legend:** N: CAROLINA GOLD. DOLLAR. / ONE

Date	Fine	VF	XF	Unc	BU
(1831-42)	1,650	2,750	4,250	15,000	—

2-1/2 DOLLARS

KM# 90 **Obverse:** 250 in center **Reverse:** 67 G. 21 CARATS at center **Obverse Legend:** BECHTLER RUTHERF: **Reverse Legend:** CAROLINA GOLD.

Date	Fine	VF	XF	Unc	BU
(1831-42)	2,500	5,500	11,500	27,000	—

Note: Stack's Old Colony Sale December 2005 MS62 $23,000

KM# 91 **Obverse:** 250 in center **Reverse:** 70 G. 20 CARATS at center **Obverse Legend:** BECHTLER. RUTHERF. **Reverse Legend:** CAROLINA GOLD

Date	Fine	VF	XF	Unc	BU
(1831-42)	2,750	5,750	12,000	29,500	—

Note: Stack's Norweb Sale November 2006 MS60 $26,450. Stack's Allison Park Sale August 2004 MS62 $28,750. Bowers and Merena Long Sale May 1995, MS-63 $31,900

KM# 92.1 **Obverse:** RUTHERFORD in a circle, border of large beads **Reverse:** 250 / 20 C. / 75 G. in center **Obverse Legend:** C. BECHTLER, ASSAYER. **Reverse Legend:** NORTH CAROLINA GOLD

Date	Fine	VF	XF	Unc	BU
(1831-42)	12,500	22,500	34,500	75,000	—

KM# 92.2 **Obverse:** RUTHERFORD in circle **Reverse:** 250. / wide 20 C. in center **Obverse Legend:** C. BECHTLER, ASSAYER. **Reverse Legend:** NORTH CAROLINA GOLD

Date	Fine	VF	XF	Unc	BU
(1831-42)	15,000	25,000	35,000	85,000	—

Note: Stack's Norweb Sale November 2006 MS62 $83,375

KM# 93.1 **Obverse:** RUTHERFORD in a circle **Reverse:** 250 / 20 G in center **Obverse Legend:** C. BECHTLER, ASSAYER. **Reverse Legend:** NORTH CAROLINA GOLD.

Date	Fine	VF	XF	Unc	BU
(1831-42) Unique	—	—	—	—	—

KM# 93.2 **Obverse:** * / 75 G in center, border finely serrated **Reverse:** 250. / 20 G. in center **Obverse Legend:** C. BECHLER ASSAYER / 75 G **Reverse Legend:** NORTH CAROLINA GOLD

Date	Fine	VF	XF	Unc	BU
(1831-42) Rare	—	—	—	—	—

5 DOLLARS

KM# 94 Obverse: two-line value in center **Reverse:** 134 G. / * in center **Obverse Legend:** C. BECHTLER. AT RUTHFER. * / 5 / DOLLARS * **Reverse Legend:** CAROLINA GOLD: / 21 CARATS

Date	Fine	VF	XF	Unc	BU
(1831-42)	2,750	5,500	8,500	22,500	—

KM# 95 Obverse: Two-line value in center **Reverse:** 134. G at center, 21 above CARATS, no star **Obverse Legend:** C. BECHTLER. AT RUTHERF / 5 / DOLLARS **Reverse Legend:** CAROLINA GOLD / 21 / CARATS

Date	Fine	VF	XF	Unc	BU
(1831-42) Unique	—	—	—	—	—

KM# 96.1 Obverse: Value in center **Reverse:** 140 G. in center **Obverse Legend:** C. BECHTLER. AT RUTHERFORD. **Reverse Legend:** CAROLINA GOLD. / 20 / CARATS

Date	Fine	VF	XF	Unc	BU
1834	2,500	5,000	8,000	25,000	—

KM# 96.2 Obverse: Value in center **Reverse:** 140. G. in center **Obverse Legend:** C. BECHTLER. AT RUTHERFORD / 5 / DOLLARS **Reverse Legend:** CAROLINA GOLD / 20 / CARATS

Date	Fine	VF	XF	Unc	BU
1834	7,500	14,500	27,500	65,000	—

KM# 97.1 Obverse: Value at center **Reverse:** 140 / G / in center, 20 close to CARATS **Obverse Legend:** C. BECHTLER. AT RUTHERF: **Reverse Legend:** CAROLINA GOLD. / 20 / CARATS

Date	Fine	VF	XF	Unc	BU
1834	4,000	8,500	16,500	47,500	—

KM# 97.2 Obverse: Value in center **Reverse:** 140 / G in center, 20 far away from CARATS **Obverse Legend:** C. BECHTLER. AT RUTHERF: / 5 / DOLLARS **Reverse Legend:** CALIFORNIA GOLD. / 20 / CARATS

Date	Fine	VF	XF	Unc	BU
1834	2,500	6,500	11,500	32,500	—

Note: Stack's Berngard/S.S. New York Sale July 2008 AU58 $29,900

KM# 98 Obverse: Value in center **Reverse:** 141. G: in center **Obverse Legend:** C. BECHTLER. AT RUTHERF: / 5 / DOLLARS. **Reverse Legend:** CAROLINA GOLD. / 20 CARATS

Date	Fine	VF	XF	Unc	BU
(1831-42) Proof restrike	—	—	—	—	—

Note: Struck from original dies by Henry Chapman in 1908. Heritage ANA Sale Auguust 2007 Pr65 $37,375

KM# 99.1 Obverse: Legend in double circle **Reverse:** 5 / DOLLARS / 20 CARATS / 150 G in center **Obverse Legend:** C. BECHTLER, ASSAYER. / RUTHERFORD COUNTY. **Reverse Legend:** NORTH CAROLINA GOLD.

Date	Fine	VF	XF	Unc	BU
(1831-42)	12,000	20,000	35,000	85,000	—

Note: Stack's Berngard/S.S. New York Sale July 2008 AU50 $69,000. Stack's Americana Sale January 2008 AU55 $74,750. Heritage ANA Sale August 2007 MS62 $97,750

KM# 99.2 Obverse: Legend in two circles **Reverse:** 5 / DOLLARS / 20 CARATS. in center **Obverse Legend:** C. BRECHTLER, ASSAYER. / RUTHERFORD COUNTY. **Reverse Legend:** NORTH CAROLINA GOLD.

Date	Fine	VF	XF	Unc	BU
(1831-42) Rare	—	—	—	—	—

OREGON

The Oregon Exchange Co., a private mint located at Oregon City, Oregon Territory, issued $5 and $10 pieces of local gold in 1849. The initials K., M., T., A., W. R. C. (G on the $5 piece), and S. on the obverse represent the eight founders of the **Oregon Exchange Co.**. William Kilborne, Theophilus Magruder, James Taylor, George Abernathy, William Willson, William Rector, John Campbell, and Noyes Smith. Campbell is erroneously represented by a G on the $5 coin. For unknown reasons, the initials A and W are omitted from the $10 piece. O.T. (Oregon Territory) is erroneously presented as T.O. on the $5 coin.

OREGON EXCHANGE COMPANY

5 DOLLARS

KM# 100 **Obverse:** Beaver above date and sprigs **Reverse:** Weight and value in center **Obverse Legend:** R. M. T. A. W. R. C. S. / T. O. / 1849 **Reverse Legend:** OREGON EXCHANGE COMPANY / 130 G. / NATIVE / GOLD. / 5 D.

Date	Fine	VF	XF	Unc	BU
1849	22,500	37,500	70,000	—	—

Note: Heritage Internet Sale February 2009 AU53 $69,000. Heritage FUN Sale January 2009 VF25 $37,375

10 DOLLARS

KM# 101 **Obverse:** Beaver above date and sprigs **Reverse:** Weight and value within wreath **Obverse Legend:** R. M. T. R. C. S. / O. T. / 1849 **Reverse Legend:** OREGON EXCHANGE COMPANY. / 10 D. 20 G. / NATIVE / GOLD / TEN D.

Date	Fine	VF	XF	Unc	BU
1849	65,000	125,000	225,000	—	—

Note: Heritage Long Beach Sale September 2002 XF40 $126,500

UTAH

MORMON ISSUES

2-1/2 DOLLARS

KM# 102 **Obverse:** Hat design above eye **Reverse:** Clasped hands above date **Obverse Legend:** HOLINESS • TO • THE • LORD • **Reverse Legend:** G. S. L. C. P. C. / TWO . AND . HALF . DO.

Date	Fine	VF	XF	Unc	BU
1849	11,500	17,500	28,500	75,000	—

5 DOLLARS

KM# 103 **Obverse:** Hat design above eye **Reverse:** Clasped hands above date **Obverse Legend:** HOLINESS • TO • THE • LORD • **Reverse Legend:** G. S. L. C. P. C. / FIVE.DOLLARS

Date	Fine	VF	XF	Unc	BU
1849	7,750	18,500	24,500	70,000	—

KM# 104 **Obverse:** Hat design above eye and stars **Reverse:** Clasped hands above date **Obverse Legend:** HOLINESS •TO • THE • LORD • **Reverse Legend:** G. S. L. C. P. C. / FIVE DOLLARS

Date	Fine	VF	XF	Unc	BU
1850	9,500	18,500	32,000	80,000	—

Note: Heritage Long Beach Sale February 2009 MS61 $54,625

KM# 105 **Obverse:** Seated lion facing left above date **Reverse:** Beehive design on eagle breast

Date	Fine	VF	XF	Unc	BU
1860	13,500	27,500	45,000	85,000	—

Note: Heritage Los Angeles Sale August 2009 AU55 $63,250. Stack's Bergstrom/Husky Sale June 2008 MS61 $74,750

10 DOLLARS

KM# 106 **Obverse:** Hat design above eye **Reverse:** Clasped hands above date **Obverse Legend:** HOLINESS • TO • THE • LORD **Reverse Legend:** PURE GOLD. / TEN DOLLARS

Date	Fine	VF	XF	Unc	BU
1849	175,000	275,000	385,000	—	—

Note: Heritage ANA Sale July 1988, AU $93,000

20 DOLLARS

KM# 107 **Obverse:** Hat design above eye **Reverse:** Clasped hands above date **Obverse Legend:** HOLINESS • TO • THE • LORD **Reverse Legend:** G. S. L. C. P. C. / TWENTY. DOLLARS

Date	Fine	VF	XF	Unc	BU
1849	75,000	145,000	225,000	—	—

Note: Stack's Old West Sale August 2006 XF45 $207,000

HAWAII

Hawaii, the 50th state, consists of eight main islands and numerous smaller islets of coral and volcanic origin. Situated in the central Pacific Ocean, 2,400 miles from San Francisco, the Hawaiian archipelago has an area of 6,450 square miles. Capital: Honolulu. The principal sources of income are in order: tourism, defense, and agriculture.

The Hawaiian Islands, originally populated by Polynesians from the Society Islands, were rediscovered by British navigator Capt. James Cook in 1778. He named them the Sandwich Islands. King Kamehameha I (the Great) united the islands under one kingdom, which endured until 1893, when Queen Lilioukalani was deposed and a provisional government established. This was followed in 1894 by a republic, which governed Hawaii until 1898, when the islands were ceded to the United States. Hawaii was organized as a territory in 1900 and attained statehood on Aug. 21, 1959.

Official coinage issued under the Kingdom of Hawaii was limited. The 1847 cent or Hapa Haneri coins were ordered by the Minister of Finance through an agent by the name of James Jackson Jarves. Jarves contracted the striking of 100,000 large copper coins from an unknown firm located somewhere in New England. The lack of acceptance by merchants limited the success of the 1847 coppers, which lead to a long gap before the next Hawaiian coinage issue in 1883.

The 1883 Kingdom coinage was contracted through Claus Spreckels, with circulation coins being struck at the San Francisco Mint. Very limited numbers of proof strikes were completed at the Philadelphia Mint, where Charles E. Barber designed these coins. Weights and measures on the 1883 Hawaiian coinage are the same as standard U.S. coins of the time period.

RULERS

Kamehameha I, 1795-1819
Kamehameha II, 1819-1824
Kamehameha III, 1825-1854
Kamehameha IV, 1854-1863
Kamehameha V, 1863-1872
Lunalilo, 1873-1874
Kalakaua, 1874-1891
Liliuokalani, 1891-1893
Provisional Government, 1893-1894
Republic, 1894-1898
Annexed to U.S., 1898-1900
Territory, 1900-1959

MONETARY SYSTEM

100 Hapa Haneri - Akahi Dala
100 Cents - 1 Dollar (Dala)

KM# 1a CENT

Copper **Ruler:** Kamehameha III **Obv:** Uniformed bust, facing **Obv. Legend:** KAMEHAMEHA III.KA.MOI. **Rev:** Value within wreath **Rev. Legend:** AUPUNI HAWAII

Date	Mintage	VG	F	VF	XF	Unc
1847 Plain 4, 13 berries (6 left, 7 right)	100,000	250	375	475	775	1,100

KM# 1b CENT

Copper **Ruler:** Kamehameha III **Obv:** Uniformed bust, facing **Obv. Legend:** KAMEHAMEHA III.KA.MOI. **Rev:** Value within wreath **Rev. Legend:** AUPUNI HAWAII

Date	Mintage	VG	F	VF	XF	Unc
1847	Inc. above	250	375	475	775	1,000

Note: Plain 4, 15 berries (8 left, 7 right)

KM# 1f CENT

Copper **Ruler:** Kamehameha III **Obv:** Uniformed bust, facing **Obv. Legend:** KAMEHAMEHA III.KA.MOI. **Rev:** Value within wreath **Rev. Legend:** AUPUNI HAWAII

Date	Mintage	VG	F	VF	XF	Unc
1847	Inc. above	550	800	1,500	2,000	—

Note: Plain 4, 15 berries (7 left, 8 right)

KM# 1c CENT

Copper **Ruler:** Kamehameha III **Obv:** Uniformed bust, facing **Obv. Legend:** KAMEHAMEHA III.KA.MOI. **Rev:** Value within wreath **Rev. Legend:** AUPUNI HAWAII

Date	Mintage	VG	F	VF	XF	Unc
1847	Inc. above	275	400	500	775	1,300

Note: Plain 4, 17 berries (8 left, 9 right)

KM# 1d CENT

Copper **Ruler:** Kamehameha III **Obv:** Uniformed bust, facing **Obv. Legend:** KAMEHAMEHA III.KA.MOI. **Rev:** Value within wreath **Rev. Legend:** AUPUNI HAWAII

Date	Mintage	VG	F	VF	XF	Unc
1847	Inc. above	250	375	475	750	1,100

Note: Crosslet 4, 15 berries (7 left, 8 right)

KM# 1e CENT
Copper **Ruler:** Kamehameha III **Obv:** Uniformed bust, facing **Obv. Legend:** KAMEHAMEHA III.KA.MOI. **Rev:** Value within wreath **Rev. Legend:** AUPUNI HAWAII

Date	Mintage	VG	F	VF	XF	Unc
1847	Inc. above	300	450	600	900	2,500

Note: Crosslet 4, 18 berries (9 left, 9 right)

KM# 2 5 CENTS (Pattern)
Nickel **Ruler:** Kalakaua I **Obv:** Head left, date below **Obv. Legend:** KALAKAUA KING OF SANDWICH ISLANDS **Rev:** Value within crowned belt

Date	Mintage	VG	F	VF	XF	Unc
1881	200	5,000	6,500	9,500	14,000	19,000

Note: Original examples of this pattern were struck on thin nickel planchets, presumably in Paris and some have "MAILLECHORT" stamped on the edge. In the early 1900's, deceptive replicas of the issue were produced in Canada, on thick and thin nickel and aluminum planchets, and thin copper planchets (thick about 2.7 to 3.1mm; thin about 1.4 to 1.7mm). The original patterns have a small cross atop the crown, the replicas do not have the cross.

KM# 3 10 CENTS (Umi Keneta)
2.5000 g., 0.9000 Silver 0.0723 oz. ASW **Ruler:** Kalakaua I **Obv:** Head right, date below **Obv. Legend:** KALAKAUA I KING OF HAWAII **Rev:** Crown and value within wreath

Date	Mintage	VG	F	VF	XF	Unc
1883	250,000	45.00	65.00	95.00	250	1,000
1883 Proof	26	Value: 7,500				

KM# 4a 1/8 DOLLAR (Hapawalu)
Copper **Ruler:** Kalakaua I **Obv:** Head right **Obv. Legend:** KALAKAUA I KING OF HAWAII **Note:** Pattern issue.

Date	Mintage	VG	F	VF	XF	Unc
1883 Proof	18	Value: 25,000				

KM# 4 1/8 DOLLAR (Hapawalu)
0.9000 Silver **Ruler:** Kalakaua I **Obv:** Head right **Obv. Legend:** KALAKAUA I KING OF HAWAII **Note:** Pattern issue.

Date	Mintage	VG	F	VF	XF	Unc
1883 Proof	20	Value: 50,000				

KM# 5 1/4 DOLLAR (Hapaha)
6.2200 g., 0.9000 Silver 0.1800 oz. ASW **Ruler:** Kalakaua I **Obv:** Head right, date below **Obv. Legend:** KALAKAUA I KING OF HAWAII **Rev:** Crowned arms divides value **Rev. Legend:** UA MAU KE...

Date	Mintage	VG	F	VF	XF	Unc
1883	500,000	40.00	55.00	75.00	125	250
1883/1383	Inc. above	45.00	65.00	95.00	150	300
1883 Proof	26	Value: 10,000				

KM# 5a 1/4 DOLLAR (Hapaha)
Copper **Ruler:** Kalakaua I **Obv:** Head right, date below **Obv. Legend:** KALAKAUA I KING OF HAWAII **Rev:** Crowned arms divides value **Rev. Legend:** UA MAU KE... **Note:** Pattern issue.

Date	Mintage	VG	F	VF	XF	Unc
1883 Proof	18	Value: 10,000				

KM# 6 1/2 DOLLAR (Hapalua)
12.5000 g., 0.9000 Silver 0.3617 oz. ASW **Ruler:** Kalakaua I **Obv:** Head right, date below **Obv. Legend:** KALAKAUA I KING OF HAWAII **Rev:** Crowned arms divides value **Rev. Legend:** UA MAU KE...

Date	Mintage	VG	F	VF	XF	Unc
1883	700,000	100	125	175	300	1,200
1883 Proof	26	Value: 14,000				

KM# 6a 1/2 DOLLAR (Hapalua)
Copper **Ruler:** Kalakaua I **Obv:** Head right, date below **Obv. Legend:** KALAKAUA I KING OF HAWAII **Rev:** Crowned arms divides value **Rev. Legend:** UA MAU KE... **Note:** Pattern issue.

Date	Mintage	VG	F	VF	XF	Unc
1883 Proof	18	Value: 14,000				

KM# 7 DOLLAR (Akahi Dala)

26.7300 g., 0.9000 Silver 0.7734 oz. ASW **Ruler:** Kalakaua I **Obv:** Head right, date below **Obv. Legend:** KALAKAUA I KING OF HAWAII **Rev:** Crowned arms with supporters within crowned mantle **Rev. Legend:** UA MAU KE...

Date	Mintage	VG	F	VF	XF	Unc
1883	500,000	275	375	500	800	4,000
1883 Proof	26	Value: 25,000				

KM# 7a DOLLAR (Akahi Dala)

Copper **Ruler:** Kalakaua I **Obv:** Head right, date below **Obv. Legend:** KALAKAUA I KING OF HAWAII **Rev:** Crowned arms with supporters within crowned mantle **Rev. Legend:** UA MAU KE... **Note:** Pattern issue.

Date	Mintage	VG	F	VF	XF	Unc
1883 Proof	18	Value: 20,000				

Note: Official records indicate the following quantities of the above issues were redeemed and melted: KM#1 - 88,405; KM#3 - 79; KM#5 - 257,400; KM#6 - 612,245; KM#7 - 453,652. That leaves approximate net mintages of: KM#1 - 11,600; KM#3 - 250,000; KM#5 (regular date) - 242,600, (unknown) 40,000; KM#6 - 87,700; KM#7 - 46,300.

PHILIPPINES

UNITED STATES ADMINISTRATION

1899-1946

The Philippines, an archipelago in the western Pacific 500 miles (805 km.) from the southeast coast of Asia, has an area of 115,830 square miles (300,000 sq. km.) and a current population of 64.9 million. Its capital city is Manila. From its acquisition in 1898 until 1992, the U.S. has had a military presence in the Philippines.

Migration to the Philippines began about 30,000 years ago when land bridges connected the islands with Borneo and Sumatra. Ferdinand Magellan claimed the islands for Spain in 1521. Miguel de Legazpi established the first permanent settlement at Cebu in April 1565. Manila was established in 1572. A British expedition captured Manila and occupied the Spanish colony in October 1762, but returned it to Spain by the treaty of Paris, 1763. Spain held the Philippines despite growing Filipino nationalism until 1898 when they were ceded to the United States at the end of the Spanish-American War.

A military government was established on the Islands until a civil administration was put in place in 1901. The Philippines became a self-governing commonwealth under the United States in 1935. In 1942, during the Second World War, the Philippines were occupied by the Japanese. U.S forces and Filipinos both fought during 1944-45 to regain control of the Islands. On July 4, 1946, the Philippines became an independent Republic.

The coins listed here were issued under United States Administration of the Philippines. Coins dated 1903 to 1919 were struck at both the Philadelphia and San Francisco Mints, while coins dated 1920 and after were produced at the Manila Mint in the Philippines. With Japanese forces advancing in 1942, much of the Philippine Treasury's silver coinage was returned to the United States for safekeeping. Coinage that remained at the Mint in Manila was crated and dumped in the bay before the Japanese arrived. During the struggle to regain control of the Philippines near the end of WWII, coins dated 1944 to 1945 were struck by the U.S. Mint at Denver, San Francisco and Philadelphia.

Symbolically the first series of U.S. Philippines coins with its American eagle perched on a stars and stripes shield places emphasis on U.S. dominance of the islands. The second series, struck under Commonwealth authority began the move towards independence by placing a new Commonwealth of the Philippines shield on the reverses of all denominations.

MINT MARKS
D - Denver, 1944-1945
S - San Francisco, 1903-1947
M – Manila, 1920-1941

MONETARY SYSTEM
4 Quartos = 1 Real
8 Reales = 1 Peso
1 Peso = 100 Centavos

KM# 162 1/2 CENTAVO
Bronze **Obv:** Man seated beside hammer and anvil **Rev:** Eagle above stars and striped shield

Date	Mintage	F	VF	XF	Unc	BU
1903	12,084,000	0.50	1.25	2.50	25.00	90.00
1903 Proof	2,558	Value: 100				
1904	5,654,000	1.00	2.25	4.50	30.00	100
1904 Proof	1,355	Value: 100				
1905 Proof	471	Value: 300				
1906 Proof	500	Value: 250				
1908 Proof	500	Value: 250				

KM# 163 CENTAVO
4.7000 g., Bronze **Obv:** Man seated beside hammer and anvil **Rev:** Eagle above stars and striped shield

Date	Mintage	F	VF	XF	Unc	BU
1903	10,790,000	0.50	1.25	2.50	20.00	45.00
1903 Proof	2,558	Value: 100				
1904	17,040,000	0.50	1.25	3.00	30.00	55.00
1904 Proof	1,355	Value: 95.00				
1905	10,000,000	0.75	1.50	3.50	30.00	55.00
1905 Proof	471	Value: 250				
1906 Proof	500	Value: 250				
1908 Proof	500	Value: 225				
1908S	2,187,000	2.50	4.00	7.50	50.00	85.00
1908S/S	—	15.00	25.00	50.00	150	250
1909S	1,738,000	7.00	16.00	25.00	100	175
1910S	2,700,000	2.00	5.00	8.00	60.00	85.00
1911S	4,803,000	1.00	2.50	5.00	27.00	75.00
1912S	3,000,000	3.50	6.50	15.00	85.00	150
1913S	5,000,000	2.00	4.00	7.00	40.00	85.00
1914S	5,000,000	1.75	3.50	6.00	55.00	100
1915S	2,500,000	30.00	40.00	90.00	600	1,500
1916S	4,330,000	6.00	12.50	25.00	100	200
1917/6S	7,070,000	25.00	40.00	50.00	375	550
1917S	Inc. above	2.50	3.50	6.50	55.00	100
1918S	11,660,000	2.50	4.50	7.50	75.00	150
1918S Large S	Inc. above	100	150	250	1,200	1,800
1919S	4,540,000	1.00	2.50	7.00	65.00	150
1920S	2,500,000	4.50	8.00	25.00	125	225
1920	3,552,000	1.00	2.50	5.00	55.00	200
1921	7,283,000	0.75	3.00	6.00	50.00	100
1922	3,519,000	0.50	3.00	7.50	50.00	125
1925M	9,332,000	0.50	2.50	6.00	30.00	60.00
1926M	9,000,000	0.50	2.50	5.50	30.00	70.00
1927M	9,270,000	0.50	2.50	6.00	35.00	55.00
1928M	9,150,000	0.35	2.00	4.00	25.00	45.00
1929M	5,657,000	1.00	3.00	6.00	35.00	80.00
1930M	5,577,000	0.50	2.00	4.50	22.00	60.00
1931M	5,659,000	0.50	2.25	5.00	27.00	50.00
1932M	4,000,000	0.75	3.00	5.00	30.00	70.00
1933M	8,393,000	0.25	1.50	3.00	22.00	45.00
1934M	3,179,000	0.75	3.00	4.50	40.00	65.00
1936M	17,455,000	0.50	2.50	4.00	26.00	50.00

KM# 164 5 CENTAVOS

5.2500 g., Copper-Nickel, 21.3 mm. **Obv:** Man seated beside hammer and anvil **Rev:** Eagle above stars and striped shield

Date	Mintage	F	VF	XF	Unc	BU
1903	8,910,000	0.50	1.25	3.50	22.00	40.00
1903 Proof	2,558	Value: 100				
1904	1,075,000	0.75	2.50	5.00	25.00	40.00
1904 Proof	1,355	Value: 125				
1905 Proof	471	Value: 200				
1906 Proof	500	Value: 200				
1908 Proof	500	Value: 200				
1916S	300,000	40.00	70.00	150	700	1,200
1917S	2,300,000	2.25	4.00	8.00	125	300
1918/7S	—	10.00	20.00	40.00	250	—
1918S	2,780,000	3.00	8.00	14.00	125	250
1919S	1,220,000	3.50	10.00	18.00	150	300
1920	1,421,000	3.00	8.50	25.00	150	250
1921	2,132,000	3.00	8.00	20.00	100	200
1925M	1,000,000	8.00	12.00	20.00	150	250
1926M	1,200,000	4.00	6.00	17.50	125	200
1927M	1,000,000	2.50	6.00	9.00	75.00	125
1928M	1,000,000	3.00	6.00	10.50	75.00	125

KM# 173 5 CENTAVOS

Copper-Nickel **Obv:** Man seated beside hammer and anvil **Rev:** Eagle above stars and striped shield **Note:** Mule.

Date	Mintage	F	VF	XF	Unc	BU
1918S	—	250	550	1,800	5,000	9,500

KM# 175 5 CENTAVOS

4.7500 g., Copper-Nickel, 19 mm. **Obv:** Man seated beside hammer and anvil **Rev:** Eagle above stars and striped shield

Date	Mintage	F	VF	XF	Unc	BU
1930M	2,905,000	1.00	2.50	6.50	40.00	95.00
1931M	3,477,000	1.00	2.50	5.00	65.00	150
1932M	3,956,000	1.00	2.00	4.00	50.00	100
1934M	2,154,000	1.00	3.50	8.00	60.00	125
1935M	2,754,000	1.00	2.00	6.00	80.00	200

KM# 165 10 CENTAVOS

2.6924 g., 0.9000 Silver 0.0779 oz. ASW **Obv:** Female standing beside hammer and anvil **Rev:** Eagle above stars and striped shield

Date	Mintage	F	VF	XF	Unc	BU
1903	5,103,000	2.50	4.00	5.00	35.00	75.00
1903 Proof	2,558	Value: 100				
1903S	1,200,000	11.00	20.00	35.00	300	800
1904	11,000	15.00	20.00	35.00	80.00	125
1904 Proof	1,355	Value: 125				
1904S	5,040,000	2.50	4.00	7.00	50.00	100
1905 Proof	471	Value: 250				
1906 Proof	500	Value: 175				

KM# 169 10 CENTAVOS

2.0000 g., 0.7500 Silver 0.0482 oz. ASW **Obv:** Female standing beside hammer and anvil **Rev:** Eagle above stars and striped shield **Edge:** Reeded

Date	Mintage	F	VF	XF	Unc	BU
1907	1,501,000	1.75	4.50	6.00	50.00	125
1907S	4,930,000	1.75	2.00	3.00	40.00	100
1908 Proof	500	Value: 200				
1908S	3,364,000	*BV*	2.00	3.50	45.00	75.00
1909S	312,000	*BV*	25.00	60.00	450	1,200
1910S	—	—	—	—	—	—

Note: Unknown in any collection. Counterfeits of the 1910S are commonly encountered

Date	Mintage	F	VF	XF	Unc	BU
1911S	1,101,000	2.50	4.50	10.00	150	500
1912S	1,010,000	2.50	4.50	12.00	125	300
1913S	1,361,000	2.00	4.50	12.00	100	300
1914S Short bar on "4"	1,180,000	2.00	7.50	25.00	175	350
1914S Long bar on "4"	—	2.00	7.00	20.00	125	300
1915S	450,000	7.00	14.00	30.00	175	750
1917S	5,991,000	*BV*	2.00	3.00	50.00	125
1918S	8,420,000	—	*BV*	2.25	25.00	55.00
1919S	1,630,000	*BV*	2.50	4.00	40.00	125
1920	520,000	4.50	6.00	15.00	95.00	250
1921	3,863,000	*BV*	2.00	3.00	22.00	50.00
1929M	1,000,000	*BV*	1.75	4.00	25.00	60.00
1935M	1,280,000	*BV*	2.00	3.00	20.00	50.00

KM# 166 20 CENTAVOS

5.3849 g., 0.9000 Silver 0.1558 oz. ASW **Obv:** Female standing beside hammer and anvil **Rev:** Eagle above stars and striped shield **Edge:** Reeded

Date	Mintage	F	VF	XF	Unc	BU
1903	5,353,000	*BV*	5.00	8.50	40.00	100
1903 Proof	2,558	Value: 125				
1903S	150,000	10.00	20.00	60.00	800	1,700
1904	11,000	20.00	30.00	40.00	100	200
1904 Proof	1,355	Value: 150				
1904S	2,060,000	5.00	6.50	11.00	100	200
1905 Proof	471	Value: 250				
1905S	420,000	7.50	16.50	35.00	500	1,150
1906 Proof	500	Value: 160				

KM# 170 20 CENTAVOS
4.0000 g., 0.7500 Silver 0.0964 oz. ASW **Obv:** Female standing beside hammer and anvil **Rev:** Eagle above stars and striped shield **Edge:** Reeded

Date	Mintage	F	VF	XF	Unc	BU
1907	1,251,000	3.00	5.50	13.50	200	350
1907S	3,165,000	*BV*	3.50	6.50	70.00	200
1908 Proof	500	Value: 300				
1908S	1,535,000	*BV*	4.50	10.00	70.00	175
1909S	450,000	11.50	23.00	50.00	400	1,000
1910S	500,000	12.50	25.00	100	400	1,000
1911S	505,000	10.00	20.00	55.00	250	750
1912S	750,000	5.00	14.00	30.00	200	350
1913S/S	949,000	9.00	25.00	50.00	250	400
1913S	Inc. above	4.00	8.50	15.00	175	300
1914S	795,000	3.50	6.00	20.00	200	350
1915S	655,000	14.00	17.00	50.00	550	1,550
1916S	1,435,000	5.00	9.00	16.00	175	550
1917S	3,151,000	*BV*	3.00	5.00	80.00	175
1918S	5,560,000	*BV*	3.00	4.50	45.00	100
1919S	850,000	3.00	5.00	12.50	100	200
1920	1,046,000	3.50	7.00	20.00	125	225
1921	1,843,000	—	*BV*	5.00	75.00	125
1929M	1,970,000	—	*BV*	4.00	25.00	75.00

KM# 174 20 CENTAVOS
4.0000 g., 0.7500 Silver 0.0964 oz. ASW **Obv:** Female standing beside hammer and anvil **Rev:** Eagle above stars and striped shield **Note:** Mule.

Date	Mintage	F	VF	XF	Unc	BU
1928M	100,000	8.00	20.00	90.00	900	1,800

KM# 167 50 CENTAVOS
13.4784 g., 0.9000 Silver 0.3900 oz. ASW **Obv:** Female standing beside hammer and anvil **Rev:** Eagle above stars and striped shield

Date	Mintage	F	VF	XF	Unc	BU
1903	3,102,000	—	*BV*	19.00	70.00	125
1903 Proof	2,558	Value: 175				
1903S 2 Known	—	—	—	22,000	—	—
1904	11,000	25.00	40.00	75.00	150	300
1904 Proof	1,355	Value: 200				
1904S	2,160,000	—	*BV*	19.00	125	225
1905 Proof	471	Value: 350				
1905S	852,000	*BV*	15.50	40.00	700	2,000
1906 Proof	500	Value: 300				

KM# 171 50 CENTAVOS
10.0000 g., 0.7500 Silver 0.2411 oz. ASW **Obv:** Female standing beside hammer and anvil **Rev:** Eagle above stars and striped shield **Edge:** Reeded

Date	Mintage	F	VF	XF	Unc	BU
1907	1,201,000	*BV*	15.00	40.00	150	300
1907S	2,112,000	*BV*	10.00	21.00	125	300
1908 Proof	500	Value: 300				
1908S	1,601,000	*BV*	12.00	25.00	225	1,000
1909S	528,000	10.00	19.00	50.00	300	750
1917S	674,000	*BV*	11.00	20.00	150	350
1918S	2,202,000	—	*BV*	13.00	100	200
1919S	1,200,000	—	*BV*	15.50	125	250
1920	420,000	—	*BV*	12.50	50.00	125
1921	2,317,000	—	*BV*	10.00	35.00	90.00

KM# 168 PESO
26.9568 g., 0.9000 Silver 0.7800 oz. ASW **Obv:** Female standing beside hammer and anvil **Rev:** Eagle above stars and striped shield

Date	Mintage	F	VF	XF	Unc	BU
1903	2,791,000	27.50	30.00	45.00	175	450
1903 Proof	2,558	Value: 250				
1903S	11,361,000	*BV*	27.50	40.00	150	250
1904	11,000	65.00	75.00	125	300	450
1904 Proof	1,355	Value: 350				
1904S	6,600,000	*BV*	27.50	35.00	175	400
1905S curved serif on 1	6,056,000	27.50	35.00	50.00	450	750
1905S straight serif on 1	—	35.00	50.00	75.00	850	2,500
1905 Proof	471	Value: 1,300				
1906 Proof	500	Value: 1,150				
1906S	201,000	1,000	1,600	3,000	17,500	30,000

Note: Counterfeits of the 1906S exist

KM# 172 PESO

20.0000 g., 0.8000 Silver 0.5144 oz. ASW **Obv:** Female standing beside hammer and anvil **Rev:** Eagle above stars and striped shield **Edge:** Reeded

Date	Mintage	F	VF	XF	Unc	BU
1907 Proof, 2 known	—	—	—	—	—	—
1907S	10,276,000	*BV*	18.00	20.00	85.00	225
1908 Proof	500	Value: 850				
1908S	20,955,000	*BV*	18.00	20.00	85.00	225
1909S	7,578,000	*BV*	18.00	25.00	100	350
1910S	3,154,000	*BV*	20.00	25.00	225	550
1911S	463,000	30.00	45.00	90.00	750	3,500
1912S	680,000	46.00	55.00	125	2,000	6,500

UNITED STATES ADMINISTRATION

Commonwealth

DECIMAL COINAGE

KM# 179 CENTAVO

5.3000 g., Bronze, 25 mm. **Obv:** Male seated beside hammer and anvil **Rev:** Eagle above shield

Date	Mintage	F	VF	XF	Unc	BU
1937M	15,790,000	0.25	2.00	3.00	25.00	40.00
1938M	10,000,000	0.25	1.50	2.50	17.50	35.00
1939M	6,500,000	0.25	2.50	4.00	20.00	45.00
1940M	4,000,000	0.25	1.25	2.50	15.00	27.00
1941M	5,000,000	0.25	2.25	3.50	16.50	30.00
1944S	58,000,000	—	0.25	0.50	2.50	9.00

KM# 180 5 CENTAVOS

4.8000 g., Copper-Nickel **Obv:** Male seated beside hammer and anvil **Rev:** Eagle with wings open above shield

Date	Mintage	F	VF	XF	Unc	BU
1937M	2,494,000	1.25	3.00	5.50	45.00	100
1938M	4,000,000	0.50	1.00	2.50	30.00	65.00
1941M	2,750,000	2.00	4.00	8.50	55.00	150

KM# 180a 5 CENTAVOS

4.9200 g., Copper-Nickel-Zinc, 19 mm. **Obv:** Male seated beside hammer and anvil **Rev:** Eagle with wings open above shield

Date	Mintage	F	VF	XF	Unc	BU
1944	21,198,000	—	0.50	1.00	2.25	5.00
1944S	14,040,000	—	0.25	0.50	1.00	2.50
1945S	72,796,000	—	0.50	0.80	1.00	2.25

KM# 181 10 CENTAVOS

2.0000 g., 0.7500 Silver 0.0482 oz. ASW, 16.7 mm. **Obv:** Female standing beside hammer and anvil **Rev:** Eagle with wings open above shield **Edge:** Reeded

Date	Mintage	F	VF	XF	Unc	BU
1937M	3,500,000	1.75	2.25	3.50	19.50	40.00
1938M	3,750,000	1.50	1.75	2.50	10.50	15.50
1941M	2,500,000	1.50	1.75	2.50	10.50	18.00
1944D	31,592,000	—	—	1.75	3.50	5.00
1945D	137,208,000	—	—	1.75	2.50	5.00
Note: 1937, 1938, and 1941 dated strikes have inverted W's for M's						
1945D/D	—	—	8.50	16.00	28.00	50.00

KM# 182 20 CENTAVOS

4.0000 g., 0.7500 Silver 0.0964 oz. ASW, 21 mm. **Obv:** Female standing beside hammer and anvil **Rev:** Eagle with wings open above shield **Edge:** Reeded

Date	Mintage	F	VF	XF	Unc	BU
1937M	2,665,000	3.00	4.00	6.50	23.00	40.00
1938M	3,000,000	—	*BV*	3.50	12.50	27.00
1941M	1,500,000	—	*BV*	3.50	12.50	29.00
1944D	28,596,000	—	—	*BV*	3.50	5.00
1944D/S	—	—	10.00	15.00	45.00	65.00
1945D	82,804,000	—	—	*BV*	3.50	5.00

KM# 176 50 CENTAVOS
10.0000 g., 0.7500 Silver 0.2411 oz. ASW, 27.5 mm. **Subject:** Establishment of the Commonwealth **Obv:** Busts facing each other **Rev:** Eagle above shield **Designer:** Ambrosia Morales

Date	Mintage	F	VF	XF	Unc	BU
1936	20,000	—	35.00	50.00	125	175

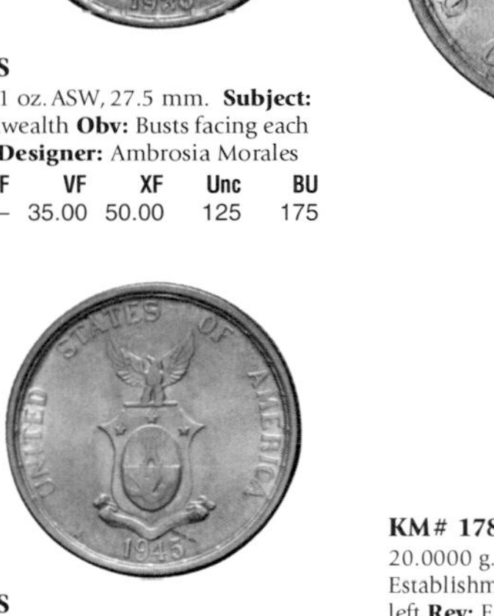

KM# 183 50 CENTAVOS
10.0000 g., 0.7500 Silver 0.2411 oz. ASW, 27.5 mm. **Obv:** Female standing beside hammer and anvil **Rev:** Eagle with wings open above shield **Edge:** Reeded

Date	Mintage	F	VF	XF	Unc	BU
1944S	19,187,000	—	*BV*	8.50	9.50	15.00
1945S	18,120,000	—	*BV*	8.50	9.50	12.00

KM# 177 PESO
20.0000 g., 0.9000 Silver 0.5787 oz. ASW, 35 mm. **Subject:** Establishment of the Commonwealth **Obv:** Conjoined busts left **Rev:** Eagle with wings open above shield **Designer:** Ambrosia Morales

Date	Mintage	F	VF	XF	Unc	BU
1936	10,000	—	50.00	75.00	150	250

KM# 178 PESO
20.0000 g., 0.9000 Silver 0.5787 oz. ASW, 35 mm. **Subject:** Establishment of the Commonwealth **Obv:** Conjoined busts left **Rev:** Eagle with wings open above shield **Designer:** Ambrosia Morales

Date	Mintage	F	VF	XF	Unc	BU
1936	10,000	—	50.00	75.00	150	250

PUERTO RICO

The Commonwealth of Puerto Rico, the eastern-most island of the Greater Antilles in the West Indies, has an area of approximately 3,435 square miles (9,104 sq. km.), with sandy beaches on the costal areas and much mountainous territory inland. Puerto Rico's capital, San Juan, affords the island one of the best natural harbors in the Caribbean and has become an important stop on the Mona Passage shipping route to the Panama Canal.

Columbus discovered Puerto Rico (*Rich Port*) and took possession for Spain on Nov. 19, 1493 - the only time Columbus set foot on the soil of what is now a possession of the United States. The first settlement, Caparra, was established by Ponce de Leon in 1508. The early years of the colony were not promising. Considerable gold was found, but the supply was soon exhausted. Efforts to enslave the Indians caused violent reprisals. Hurricanes destroyed crops and homes. French, Dutch, and English freebooters burned the towns. Puerto Rico remained a Spanish possession until 1898, when it was ceded to the United States following the Spanish-American War.

When the Spanish first colonized Puerto Rico, native populations were operating on a barter system of exchange. Spanish coinage was introduced and eventually accepted for exchange. As mints developed in the Americas, their coins, first cobs and later milled coins, were also circulated in Puerto Rico. This mix of Spanish and Spanish Colonial coins served Puerto Rico for several centuries, though copper and bronze coins were easier to keep in circulation, while silver and gold tended to be taken away by traders. Paper money was also used in Puerto Rico from the mid 18th century on, though counterfeiting lead to the devaluation of many of these banknotes. Economic conditions were in great disarray by the early part of the 19th century. All sorts of currency and coinage were in circulation with counterfeits diluting the money supply. Cob coins, Spanish coins, cut and countermarked coins of the various West Indies, along with several issues of bank notes were all in circulation, leading to confusion and lack of fluid acceptance.

In 1895 the first coinage specifically struck for the Island of Puerto Rico was produced by Spain. Additional denominations were struck in 1896 completing Puerto Rico's only official coinage series. These coins brought some semblance of order to the daily economic transactions on the island and remained in use until Puerto Rico was taken over by the United States in 1898. Redemption of all peso denominated coins took place from July 1900 until March 1901 at the rate of 60 U.S. cents to the peso.

RULER
Spanish, until 1898

ASSAYERS' INITIALS
G - Antonio Garcia Gonzalez
P - Felix Miguel Peiro Rodrigo

MONETARY SYSTEM
100 Centavos = 1 Peso

DECIMAL COINAGE

KM# 20 5 CENTAVOS
1.2500 g., 0.9000 Silver 0.0362 oz. ASW **Ruler:** Alfonso XIII
Obv: Value, date **Rev:** Crowned arms, pillars

Date	Mintage	F	VF	XF	Unc	BU
1896 PGV	600,000	30.00	50.00	90.00	225	300

KM# 21 10 CENTAVOS
2.5000 g., 0.9000 Silver 0.0723 oz. ASW **Ruler:** Alfonso XIII
Obv: Young head left **Rev:** Crowned arms, pillars

Date	Mintage	F	VF	XF	Unc	BU
1896 PGV	700,000	35.00	65.00	175	375	—

KM# 22 20 CENTAVOS
5.0000 g., 0.9000 Silver 0.1447 oz. ASW **Ruler:** Alfonso XIII
Obv: Young head left **Rev:** Crowned arms, pillars

Date	Mintage	F	VF	XF	Unc	BU
1895 PGV	3,350,000	45.00	100	200	425	—

KM# 23 40 CENTAVOS
10.0000 g., 0.9000 Silver 0.2893 oz. ASW **Ruler:** Alfonso XIII
Obv: Young head left **Rev:** Crowned arms, pillars

Date	Mintage	F	VF	XF	Unc	BU
1896 PGV	725,000	250	375	875	2,850	—

KM# 24 PESO
25.0000 g., 0.9000 Silver 0.7234 oz. ASW **Ruler:** Alfonso XIII
Obv: Young head left **Rev:** Crowned arms, pillars

Date	Mintage	F	VF	XF	Unc	BU
1895 PGV	8,500,000	350	550	950	2,500	4,500

Glossary

Adjustment marks: Marks made by use of a file to correct the weight of overweight coinage planchets prior to striking. Adjusting the weight of planchets was a common practice at the first U.S. Mint in Philadelphia and was often carried out by women hired to weigh planchets and do any necessary filing of the metal.

Altered coin: A coin that has been changed after it left the mint. Such changes are often to the date or mintmark of a common coin in an attempt to increase its value by passing to an unsuspecting buyer as a rare date or mint.

Alloy: A metal or mixture of metals added to the primary metal in the coinage composition, often as a means of facilitating hardness during striking. For example, most U.S. silver coins contain an alloy of 10 percent copper.

Anneal: To heat in order to soften. In the minting process planchets are annealed prior to striking.

Authentication: The act of determining whether a coin, medal, token or other related item is a genuine product of the issuing authority.

Bag marks: Scrapes and impairments to a coin's surface obtained after minting by contact with other coins. The term originates from the storage of coins in bags, but such marks can occur as coins leave the presses and enter hoppers. A larger coin is more susceptible to marks, which affect its grade and, therefore, its value.

Base metal: A metal with low intrinsic value.

Beading: A form of design around the edge of a coin. Beading once served a functional purpose of deterring clipping or shaving parts of the metal by those looking to make a profit and then return the debased coin to circulation.

Blank: Often used in reference to the coinage planchet or disc of metal from which the actual coin is struck. Planchets or blanks are punched out of a sheet of metal by what is known as a blanking press.

Business strike: A coin produced for circulation.

Cast copy: A copy of a coin or medal made by a casting process in which molds are used to produce the finished product. Casting imparts a different surface texture to the finished product than striking and often leaves traces of a seam where the molds came together.

Center dot: A raised dot at the center of a coin caused by use of a compass to aid the engraver in the circular positioning of die devices, such as stars, letters, and dates. Center dots are prevalent on early U.S. coinage.

Chop mark: A mark used by Oriental merchants as a means of guaranteeing the silver content of coins paid out. The merchants' chop marks, or stamped insignia, often obliterated the original design of the host coin. U.S. Trade dollars, struck from 1873 through 1878 and intended for use in trade with China, are sometimes found bearing multiple marks.

Clash marks: Marks impressed in the coinage dies when they come together without a planchet between them. Such marks will affect coins struck subsequently by causing portions of the obverse design to appear in raised form on the reverse, and vice versa.

Clipping: The practice of shaving or cutting small pieces of metal from a coin in circulation. Clipping was prevalent in Colonial times as a means of surreptitiously extracting precious metal from a coin before placing it back into circulation. The introduction of beading and a raised border helped to alleviate the problem.

Coin alignment: U.S. coins are normally struck with an alignment by which, when a coin is held by the top and bottom edge and rotated from side-to-side, the reverse will appear upside down.

Collar: A ring-shaped die between which the obverse and reverse coinage dies are held during striking. The collar contains the outward flow during striking and can be used to produce edge reeding.

Commemorative: A coin issued to honor a special event or person. United States commemorative coins have historically been produced for sale to collectors and not placed in circulation, though the 50-states quarters are circulating commemoratives.

Copy: A replica of an original issue. Copies often vary in quality and metallic composition from the original. Since passage of the Hobby Protection

Act (Public Law 93-167) of Nov. 29, 1973, it has been illegal to produce or import copies of coins or other numismatic items that are not clearly and permanently marked with the word "Copy."

Counterfeit: A coin or medal or other numismatic item made fraudulently, either for entry into circulation or sale to collectors.

Denticles: The toothlike pattern found around a coin's obverse or reverse border.

Die: A cylindrical piece of metal containing an incuse image that imparts a raised image when stamped into a planchet.

Die crack: A crack that develops in a coinage die after extensive usage, or if the die is defective or is used to strike harder metals. Die cracks, which often run through border lettering, appear as raised lines on the finished coin.

Device: The principal design element.

Double eagle: Name adopted by the Act of March 3, 1849, for the gold coin valued at 20 units or $20.

Eagle: Name adopted by the Coinage Act of 1792 for a gold coin valued at 10 units or $10. Also a name used to refer to gold, silver, and platinum coins of the American Eagle bullion coinage program begun in 1986.

Edge: The cylindrical surface of a coin between the two sides. The edge can be plain, reeded, ornamented, or lettered.

Electrotype: A copy of a coin, medal, or token made by electroplating.

Exergue: The lower segment of a coin, below the main design, generally separated by a line and often containing the date, designer initials, and mintmark.

Face value: The nominal legal-tender value assigned to a given coin by the governing authority.

Fasces: A Roman symbol of authority consisting of a bound bundle of rods and an axe.

Field: The flat area of a coin's obverse or reverse, devoid of devices or inscriptions.

Galvano: A reproduction of a proposed design from an artist's original model produced in plaster or other substance and then electroplated with metal. The galvano is then used in a reducing lathe to make a die or hub.

Glory: A heraldic term for stars, rays or other devices placed as if in the sky or luminous.

Grading: The largely subjective practice of providing a numerical or adjectival ranking of the condition of a coin, token, or medal. The grade is often a major determinant of value.

Gresham's law: The name for the observation made by Sir Thomas Gresham, 16th century English financier, that when two coins with the same face value but different intrinsic values are in circulation at the same time, the one with the lesser intrinsic value will remain in circulation while the other is hoarded.

Half eagle: Name adopted by the Coinage Act of 1792 for a gold coin valued at five units or $5.

Hub: A piece of die steel showing the coinage devices in relief. The hub is used to produce a die that, in contrast, has the relief details incuse. The die is then used to produce the final coin, which looks much the same as the hub. Hubs may be reused to make new dies.

Legend: A coin' principal lettering, generally shown along its outer perimeter.

Lettered edge: Incuse or raised lettering on a coin's edge.

Matte proof: A proof coin on which the surface is granular or dull. On U.S. coins this type of surface was used on proofs of the early 20th century. The process has since been abandoned.

Magician's coin: A term sometimes used to describe a coin with two heads or two tails. Such a coin is considered impossible in normal production due to physical differences in obverse and reverse die mountings, though as of 2001 two have been certified as genuine by professional coin authenticators. The vast majority are products made outside the Mint as novelty pieces.

Medal: Made to commemorate an event or person. Medals differ from coins in that a medal is not legal tender and, in general, is not produced with the intent of circulating as money.

Medal alignment: Medals are generally struck with the coinage dies facing the same direction during striking. When held by the top and bottom edge and rotated from side-to-side, a piece struck in this manner will show both the obverse and reverse right side up.

Mintage: The total number of coins struck during a given time frame, generally one year.

Mintmark: A letter or other marking on a coin's surface to identify the mint at which the coin was struck.

Mule: The combination of two coinage dies not intended for use together.

Numismatics: The science, study or collecting of coins, tokens, medals, paper money, and related items.

Obverse: The front or "heads" side of a coin, medal, or token.

Overdate: Variety produced when one or more digits of the date are re-engraved over an old date on a die at the Mint, generally to save on dies or correct an error. Portions of the old date can still be seen under the new one.

Overmintmark: Variety created at the Mint when a different mintmark is punched over an already existing mintmark, generally done to make a coinage die already punched for one mint usable at another. Portions of the old mintmark can still be seen under the new one.

Overstrike: A coin, token or medal struck over another coin, token, or medal.

Pattern: A trial strike of a proposed coin design, issued by the Mint or authorized agent of a governing authority. Patterns can be in a variety of metals, thicknesses, and sizes.

Phrygian cap: A close-fitting, egg-shell-shaped hat placed on the head of a freed slave when Rome was in its ascendancy. Hung from a pole, it was a popular symbol of freedom during the French Revolution and in 18th century United States.

Planchet: A disc of metal or other material on which the image of the dies are impressed, resulting in a finished coin. Also sometimes called a blank.

Proof: A coin struck twice or more from specially polished dies and polished planchets. Modern proofs are prepared with a mirror finish. Early 20th century proofs were prepared with a matte surface.

Prooflike: A prooflike coin exhibits some of the characteristics of a proof despite having been struck by regular production processes. Many Morgan dollars are found with prooflike surfaces. The field will have a mirror background similar to that of a proof, and design details are frosted like some proofs.

Quarter eagle: Name adopted by the Coinage Act of 1792 for a gold coin valued at 2.5 units or $2.50.

Reeding: Serrated (toothlike) ornamentation applied to the coin's edge during striking.

Relief: The portion of a design raised above the surface of a coin, medal, or token.

Restrike: A coin, medal or token produced from original dies at a later date, often with the purpose of sale to collectors.

Reverse: The backside or "tails" side of a coin, medal or token, opposite from the principal figure of the design or obverse.

Rim: The raised area bordering the edge and surrounding the field.

Series: The complete group of coins of the same denomination and design and representing all issuing mints.

Token: A privately issued piece, generally in metal, with a represented value in trade or offer of service. Tokens are also produced for advertising purposes.

Type coin: A coin from a given series representing the basic design. A type coin is collected as an example of a particular design rather than for its date and mintmark.

Variety: Any coin noticeably different in dies from another of the same design, date and mint. Overdate and overmintmarks are examples of varieties.

Wire edge: Created when coinage metal flows between the coinage die and collar, producing a thin flange of coin metal at the outside edge or edges of a coin.

Index

A

B

C

D

INDEX

E

F

G

H

I

J

K

L

M

N

O

P

Q

R

S

T

U

W

INDEX